1 MONTH OF
FREE
READING

at

www.ForgottenBooks.com

By purchasing this book you are eligible for one month membership to ForgottenBooks.com, giving you unlimited access to our entire collection of over 1,000,000 titles via our web site and mobile apps.

To claim your free month visit:

www.forgottenbooks.com/free1007584

ISBN 978-0-332-23328-4
PIBN 11007584

DECISIONS

OF

THE DEPARTMENT OF THE INTERIOR

IN

APPEALED PENSION AND BOUNTY-LAND CLAIMS;

ALSO

A TABLE OF CASES REPORTED, CITED, OVERRULED, AND MODIFIED,

AND OF

STATUTES CITED AND CONSTRUED.

VOLUME IX.

Edited by JOHN W. BIXLER,

MEMBER OF THE BOARD OF PENSION APPEALS.

WASHINGTON:
GOVERNMENT PRINTING OFFICE.
1898.

This publication is held for sale by the Department at cost price, as follows:

Volume 1........................... $1.10
Volume 2........................... 1.10
Volume 3 .... 1.10
Volume 4.... .... 1.10
Volume 5........................... .85
Volume 6........................... .95
Volume 7........................... 1.10
Volume 8........................... 1.05
Volume 9.......... .... 1.05

Digest of Pension and Bounty-Land Decisions 1.15

Correspondence relating to the above publications and all remittances should be addressed to the Secretary of the Interior, Washington, D. C.

OFFICE OF THE ASSISTANT SECRETARY OF THE INTERIOR.

The decisions of the Interior Department in pension and bounty-land cases are prepared in the board of pension appeals, in the office of the Secretary of the Interior, under the supervision of the Assistant Secretary, who signs and promulgates them when approved by him.

————————

WEBSTER DAVIS,
Assistant Secretary of the Interior.

MEMBERS AND ACTING MEMBERS OF THE BOARD OF PENSION APPEALS.

HARRISON L. BRUCE, *Chairman.*
JOHN W. BIXLER, *First Vice-Chairman.*
EDWARD P. HALL, *Second Vice-Chairman.*

JOHN A. LACY.	JOSEPH C. MCALLISTER.
ROBERT F. HILL.	HERBERT I. BRACKETT.
WILLIAM L. CHITTY.	RALPH W. KIRKHAM.
AMBROSE E. ROWELL.	WALTER E. STEVENS.
GEORGE EWING. *	HENRY M. HAYNES.
EMMETT WOMACK.	PHILIP METZGER.

MELBOURNE M. LEWIS, *Clerk of the Board.*

————————

* Resigned August 30, 1898.

TABLE OF CASES REPORTED.

TABLE OF CASES CITED.

XII

TABLE OF CASES OVERRULED.

LAWS CITED AND CONSTRUED.

United States Statutes at Large.

United States Statutes at Large—Continued.

Sections of the Revised Statutes of the United States.

State Statutes.

DECISIONS RELATING TO PENSIONS.

ISABELLA VARCO (WIDOW).

In considering a widow's claim under the act of June 27, 1890, it is her condition, dependent or nondependent, that governs, and it matters not whether the property or income that keeps her from dependence is derived from her husband's estate. It is the widow's pecuniary condition, as a fact, that is the criterion under said act.

Assistant Secretary John M. Reynolds to the Commissioner of Pensions, March 13, 1897.

Appellant filed her widow's claim, under the act of June 27, 1890, on February 20, 1894. Same was rejected September 28, 1895, on the ground that she had means of support other than that of her daily labor. An appeal is filed February 13, 1897, alleging that rejection is contrary to law and evidence.

The facts in evidence are as follows: Claimant has a dower interest in 80 acres of land, and there appears to be no contention but this would take her outside the statute invoked were it not for the reason that the dower is subject to the life estate of her mother-in-law. It is shown, however, that claimant has the free use of the land, her interest in fact being not that of her dower interest, but that of a free tenant by permission of the holder of the life estate. The real question involved is not as to the means the claimant's husband left her, but it is rather, What means of support did this widow actually have when she filed her declaration?

I held in the appeal of Frances Kendall (8 P. D., 197) that—

The right of a widow to a pension under said act (June 27, 1890) must be determined by her condition at the time she seeks to establish her right.

Now, it is immaterial by what right this claimant holds her tenure of the 80 acres of land; as a matter of fact she does hold it and she holds it undisturbed.

In order for attorney's contention to prevail we must read the statute as stating that the widow shall be pensionable, if the husband dies, unless he himself leaves his widow means of support other than that of her daily labor. This would be an unwarranted transposing of the words of the sentence involved. The wording of the statute has frequently caused much discussion as to different phases of the question among those not accustomed to the construing of statutes, but to my mind the intent of Congress is clearly apparent in the act. The intent is to bestow the benefits of the act upon those widows of soldiers who are left (after the soldier's death) without other means of support than their daily labor, the words "leaving a widow" referring simply to the fact that the soldier at his death was in the married status and not referring to the fact that soldier himself did not leave or bestow upon his widow any property.

It certainly will not be seriously contended that if a soldier's widow is, when she seeks the benefit of the act, possessed in her own right, outside of her husband's estate, of a sum of $50,000, that she would be entitled to a pension under the act of June 27, 1890, and yet such must be the conclusion if attorney's argument should prevail. It is the widow's pecuniary condition, as a fact, that must be the criterion, and it matters not whether her money or property comes from her husband or from any other source, or by gift or by operation of law. It is her condition, dependent or nondependent, that governs, and not how she obtains the property or income that keeps her from a state of dependency. I believe the above to be a proper and just interpretation of the law, and to the intent of Congress as expressed in the act of June 27, 1890, and under this construction your rejection of the within claim must be sustained.

The action appealed from is affirmed.

DEPENDENCE—ACT JUNE 27, 1890.

EVALINE DAVIS (WIDOW).

The soldier died December 9, 1892, leaving a widow and seven minor children under 16 years of age. He owned a farm valued at $800, also some personal property.

Held, That when the income, as in this case, is derived mainly from the widow's manual labor, or the labor of her children, it is held that the widow is without other means of support, under the provisions of the act of June 27, 1890, and therefore occupies a pensionable status.

Assistant Secretary John M. Reynolds to the Commissioner of Pensions, March 20, 1897.

The appellant filed a claim for pension under the act of June 27, 1890, on the 29th of December, 1892, as widow of Thomas L. Davis, late Company A, Seventeenth Kentucky Infantry, alleging, among other things, that her late husband died on the 9th day of December, 1892, leaving seven minor children under 16 years of age.

Her claim was rejected December 11, 1893, on the ground that she was not dependent within the meaning of the act of June 27, 1890.

From said action an appeal was entered August 11, 1896, the cause of rejection being assigned as error, contending that she is possessed of a farm consisting of 200 acres of land, but according to the evidence on file, it is so poor that nothing can be cultivated on it; at least one-half of it would not pay to plant it in anything; that she has only a part interest in the farm, and, according to the proof, the income would not exceed $50 per year. That her minor children must be fed and clothed, as they are too young to do very much toward helping themselves.

According to the appellant's statement the soldier left the following-named children under 16 years of age at the time of his death, December 9, 1892, viz: Fanny Hay, born March 8, 1877; Viola and Capitola (twins), born April 5, 1878; Mary Evaline, born July 10, 1880; Ida Belle, born February 27, 1882; Venia Pendleton, born September 14, 1883; Daisy Dean, born February 20, 1886.

The farm of 200 acres consists of hill and bottom land, assessed at $800, which in appellant's opinion is a fair valuation of the land. The personal property at death of the soldier consisted of 2 mules, 1 horse, 1 colt, 5 head of cattle, 6 hogs, some farming implements, also a little wheat and corn and some household and kitchen furniture, all free of debt, excepting $25, the balance due on a mowing machine.

I. N. Dukes and S. J. Carter, the appraisers of the decedent's estate, are of the opinion that $800 is the cash value of the farm and that no greater price could be obtained for the land at a bona fide sale. They state that the bottom land is wet crawfish ground and the hill land in a worn-out condition, the house and outbuildings being only in a tolerably good condition. In their opinion the cash annual income from the land is about $175.

Thomas H. Bean, another witness, values the land at $800 and the cash annual income therefrom at $150.

Now, if the true value of the land is $800, as stated by the witnesses in this case, the annual net income under ordinary circumstances would not exceed 6 per cent of the value of the farm, or $48, and in all probability would not exceed 4 per cent of its value. Two of the witnesses whose testimony has been referred to are of the opinion that the annual income from said farm will average about $175, while the other witness is of the opinion that the income will not exceed $150. However, if the highest estimate be taken as the true amount, it is evident that the annual net income would fall greatly below $100, for the reason that the expense of farming the land, including taxes and the necessary repairs, could not be estimated at a figure less than $100, and in my judgment it would greatly exceed that amount. The appellant states that in 1893 she rented 3 acres of land, for use in the production of tobacco, at the rate of $4 per acre, or $12, and raised on the farm, with her childrens' assistance, about 1,200 pounds of tobacco, valued at $50, and that 200 bushels of corn were produced, the value of which was $80, her share, three-fourths, being worth $60; also 70 bushels of wheat, her share thereof being worth $35. Thus it appears that the gross income of that year, including the value of appellant's own manual labor, did not exceed $150, and after deducting taxes, necessary expenses of running the farm, and repairs, the net income would fall considerably below $100.

The evidence does not indicate definitely whether or not the appellant has an estate in fee simple in the land, but according to her own statement, and the proof showing that the title to the farm was in the soldier at the time of his death, in the absence of any evidence showing that the widow took the land under a will of her deceased husband, it is fair to presume that she has only a life interest in the land, and that her share of the estate would probably be only one-third of the income thereof.

Where the income, as in this case, is mainly derived from the appellant's own manual labor or the labor of her children, it is held that the claimant is without other means of support, under the provisions of the act of June 27, 1890, and therefore occupies a pensionable status.

The rejection is, therefore, reversed, the claim to be readjudicated in accordance with this opinion.

———

CERTIFICATE OF MEDICAL EXAMINATION—RATING, ACT MARCH 2, 1895.

WILLIAM H. FARMER.

In the absence of medical examination describing a disabling cause it can not be presumed, under the act of March 2, 1895, that it was the opinion of the board of examining surgeons that no pensionable disability existed.

*Assistant Secretary John M. Reynolds to the Commissioner of Pensions,
March 29, 1897.*

Appellant, late of Company A, Thirty-sixth Indiana Infantry, on August 1, 1896, filed his claim (certificate No. 383760) for rerating under the general law, alleging that the rating of $6 per month, allowed on October 5, 1892, was not in accordance with the evidence. The same was rejected on January 4, 1897, on the ground that there was no injustice shown in the rating. It is contended on appeal, filed April 23, 1896, that the allowance of $6 in a claim filed October 11, 1892, under the act of June 27, 1890, was error, inasmuch as the same was based upon an invalid medical certificate.

Appellant was pensioned from October 5, 1892, at $6 per month, for disease of testicles, result of mumps. He claims that said rating should be $10, and his contention is based upon the report of examining surgeons. In 1883 he was shown to have atrophy of both testicles, no rating being affixed. In 1887 the same report, virtually, was made, with the additional statement that the testicles were not tender nor were the cords sensitive; four-eighteenths was recommended. The same report was made in 1888. In 1892 the board reported an almost complete atrophy of both testicles, and a tenderness of spermatic cords, with history of effeminency, moroseness, emaciation and debility, and a total incapacity for propagation. A rating was advised at $10 per month.

A careful consideration of the evidence leads me to believe that the rate of $6 per month is fully adequate under the law for all disability due to disease of the testicles.

It is not clear in what respect attorney herein claims that the medical certificate referred to is invalid. The statutes provide that—

The certificate shall contain a full description of the physical condition of the claimant at the time, which shall include all the physical and rational signs and a statement of all structural changes.

An examination of said certificate, dated September 25, 1895, shows that the law has been fulfilled in this respect, and the certificate is signed by each member of the board. The act of March 2, 1895, however, provides that the surgeons—

shall specifically state the rating which in their judgment the appellant is entitled to.

The certificate which is the basis of the rating allowed under the act of June 27, 1890, shows atrophy of both testicles, the left one being very soft, but the board did not affix a rating therefor. I am convinced that the law requires that if a disability be found the examining surgeons must state whether or not, in their opinion, such disability is entitled to a rating. One of the objects to be gained by the act referred to is to give to the Commissioner of Pensions the benefit of the opinion of those who have the applicant before them, as to whether or not a claimant has a pensionable disability, and if so to what degree. In the absence of a rating to a disability found it can not be presumed, under the act, to mean that the disability is not of a pensionable degree. Your action in the claim under the act of June 27, 1890, is not sustained, and the case is reopened for adjudication under a lawful medical certificate.

The action under the general law is affirmed.

The action under the act of June 27, 1890, is reversed.

MARRIAGE AND DIVORCE—CIVIL DEATH.

ELIZABETH W. FOX (WIDOW).

1. Claimant at date of her marriage to soldier had a former husband living from whom she had not been divorced, but who had been convicted of a felony and imprisoned.

Held, The doctrine of civil death is not recognized by the law or courts of the State of Virginia, and imprisonment for felony, while affording just grounds for a divorce, does not per se operate as a divorce.

2. Under the statutes of Indiana, where claimant married the soldier, all marriages where either party thereto has a former wife or husband living, if solemnized in that State, are declared to be absolutely void without any legal proceedings.

Assistant Secretary John M. Reynolds to the Commissioner of Pensions, April 3, 1897.

Claimant, as the widow of William F. Knox, late of Company C, Second Indiana Cavalry, on February 23, 1897, appealed from the action of your Bureau of August 9, 1889, rejecting her old-law widow's claim, No. 395317, filed May 13, 1889, on the ground that her former husband, from whom she was never divorced, is still living, and that she is, therefore, not the legal widow of soldier.

It is contended in brief that the evidence in this case would be accepted in any court as establishing claimant's legal rights as the widow of the deceased soldier.

Claimant, whose maiden name was Elizabeth Weddle, was at the age of 19 years married to one William W. Hutchinson, now a practicing physician residing at Cleveland, Webster County, W. Va., January 8, 1856, who testified before a special examiner August 3, 1889, that she eloped with his cousin William F. Knox, January 10, 1865; that he gave her $100 to go to his brother's in Illinois, so that she left with his knowledge; that he never applied for a divorce from her and had never received notice of her application for divorce.

Claimant testified before the special examiner, and sustained her testimony by the original marriage certificate, that she married said soldier, William F. Knox, at Milford, Mich., December 15, 1865, under the name of Elizabeth W. Hutchinson.

Learning that her second husband, the soldier, had a first wife living, from whom he was not divorced until August 13, 1867, or nearly two years and seven months subsequent to his remarriage to claimant, a second marriage ceremony was performed between claimant and soldier, and she was for the second time married to soldier November 20, 1882. This second marriage took place in Cass County, State of Indiana, in which State soldier died April 16, 1889. The question therefore presented is the legality of claimant's marriage to soldier as tested by the laws of Indiana, in conformity with the provisions of section 2 of the act of August 7, 1882, which provides that marriages, except such as are mentioned in section 4705, R. S., shall be proven in pension cases to be legal marriages according to the law of the place where the parties resided at the time of the marriage, or at the time when the right to pension accrued.

Claimant does not attack the legality of her first marriage to Hutchinson, but relies upon his conviction and sentence to imprisonment in the State prison at Richmond, Va., for a term of years, and prior to her first marriage to soldier, as dissolving the marriage relations between her and Hutchinson. She testified that she was so legally advised and believed, and for this reason she never applied for or obtained a divorce from him.

Assuming that her first husband was convicted of forgery and sentenced, as alleged, such facts did not dissolve their marriage relations, although good grounds for divorce under the laws of Virginia (see chap. 105, par. 6, p. 85 of the Code of Virginia, 1873); nor does the evidence establish a case of void marriage within the provisions of chap. 105, par. 1, p. 850 of the Code of 1873, or chap. 109, par. 1, p. 529 of the Code of 1860.

Nor is the doctrine of civil death recognized by the laws of Virginia. See Minors' Institutes, vol. 1, p. 68, and the case of Branch *v.* Bowman (2 Leigh., 170).

It therefore appears that claimant had a lawful husband living at date of her first and second marriage to soldier.

Section 1024, R. S., Indiana, 1896, in force March 10, 1873, provides that—

All marriages where either party thereto has a former wife or husband living, if solemnized in this State, shall be absolutely void without any legal proceedings.

It follows that claimant's marriages to soldier were both void, and the action appealed from is accordingly affirmed.

The papers in the case are herewith returned.

DECLARATIONS—ACT OF JULY 4, 1864 (SECTION 4714).

MICHAEL TIERNEY.

An unsworn application for pension filed subsequent to July 4, 1864, is fatally defective and does not authorize the commencement of pension subsequently allowed, . on a sufficient declaration subsequently filed, to date from the filing of such defective declaration.

Assistant Secretary John M. Reynolds to the Commissioner of Pensions, April 3, 1897.

Claimant, late of U. S. S. *Huron,* on February 16, 1897, appealed from the action of your Bureau of February 4, 1894, dating the commencement of his pension from July 11, 1894, the date of filing his duly executed declaration.

It is contended that the pension should have commenced April 11, 1865, the date of filing his first application.

The first application consists of a memorial signed by claimant and witnessed by Surgeons Leach and Smith, and is not sworn to.

It appears to have been the practice of your Bureau to adjudicate pensions on such unsworn applications prior to July 4, 1864, at which date Congress enacted section 4714, R. S., which provides that declarations should be made under oath.

It follows, therefore, that an unsworn application for pension filed subsequent to July 4, 1864, is fatally defective and does not authorize the commencement of pension subsequently allowed, on a sufficient declaration subsequently filed, to date from the filing of such defective declaration. Neither your Bureau nor this Department has any authority to date the commencement of pension prior to the filing of a sworn application or declaration, and the action of your Bureau is accordingly affirmed. The papers in the case are herewith returned.

ACCRUED PENSION—ACT OF MARCH 2, 1895—SECTION 4702, R. S.

MINORS OF ANDREW W. HASKETT.

The minors, being over 16 years of age at the death of the widow of soldier who was in receipt of pension, are not entitled to the accrued pension due the widow at date of her death, nor are they entitled to pension under the provisions of section 4702, R. S., as she had received a part of pension named in said section.

Assistant Secretary John M. Reynolds to the Commissioner of Pensions,
April 24, 1897.

Claimant on January 28 and March 29, 1897, appealed from the action of your Bureau of March 10, 1897, rejecting their minor's claim, No. 389186, filed November 18, 1896, on the ground of—

no title, as claimants were over 16 years of age when the widow, who was a pensioner, died.

It is contended that, as the widow drew no part of her pension, the minors are entitled to pension under the provisions of section 4702, R. S., in accordance with the Departmental decision in the case of the minors of Eli Phipps.

It appears, however, that the widow was pensioned April 27, 1886, on her application filed March 18, 1885, alleging death of soldier November 27, 1868. Her pension was made to commence from date of filing her application, in accordance with the law then in force, and the pension certificate No. 221988 was sent to her May 3, 1886.

On June 16, 1888, she filed an application for arrears of pension under the act of June 7, 1888, on behalf of herself and four minor children under 16 years of age at date of soldier's death, and the face brief shows that her said application was approved for allowance October 15, 1888. She died September 30, 1888, without having received any part of said arrears. At the date of her death all of said minors were over 16 years of age, the youngest having attained the age of 16 years June 22, 1884. They are therefore not entitled to the accrued pension under the provisions of the act of March 2, 1895, and this fact is conceded by appellants, who insist that their claim is not one for accrued pension, as they claim no pension, except as minors, from the date of the death of their father until they severally attained the age of 16 years, and that the claim is based solely on section 4702, R. S.

The language of this section limits the title of the minors in their own right to cases where—

there be no widow or in case of her death without payment to her of any part of the pension hereinafter mentioned,

or in case " the widow remarry."

The " pension hereinafter mentioned " in section 4702 is—

the same pension as the husband or father would have been entitled to had he been totally disabled,

i. e., $8 per month, plus $2 per month for each minor child, as provided by the next section, 4703, plus \$4 per month, as increased by the act of March 19, 1886.

It is therefore plain that the widow did draw a "part" of the pension "hereinafter mentioned," and to support claimants' contention the word "any" in said section 4702 would have to be construed to mean the whole, all, or total, instead of some or a portion of, as the word naturally implies.

I am further of the opinion that the pension involved is "accrued pension," and its disposition must be governed by the provisions of the act of March 2, 1895.

See case of Adolph Spraggler (8 P. D., 51).

As the minors were over 16 years of age at the date of the widow's death, they would not be entitled to her accrued pension.

The action appealed from is accordingly affirmed.

The appeal filed March 29, 1897, appears to be from the same action as that appealed from in the appeal filed January 28, 1897, and presents no new question. Said appeal of March 29, 1897, is therefore dismissed. The papers in the case are herewith returned.

HELPLESS MINOR—ACT JUNE 27, 1890—WIDOW'S INCREASE.

FRANCES STETZELL (WIDOW).

Evidence shows that the child claimed for (for whom pension was received till she was 16 years of age), is afflicted with incurable epilepsy, rendering her liable to frequent spasms and spells of unconsciousness, and which has made her weak and of low vitality, so that she can perform only the lightest household duties and no renumerative labor, besides causing her to be the subject of constant watchfulness and of some aid and attendance.

Held, That she is permanently helpless in the contemplation of the law, and the pension on her account should be continued.

Assistant Secretary John M. Reynolds to the Commissioner of Pensions, April 24, 1897.

Frances Stetzel, widow of Joseph Stetzel, late of Company G, One hundred and twenty-eighth Ohio Infantry, is a pensioner under the general law. Her certificate was issued in 1891, and she drew pension on account of four minor children up to the time they became 16 years of age, which, in the case of the youngest, Catherine, was February 24, 1889. She filed July 20, 1892, an application to have the pension of \$2 per month continued on account of said youngest child, under the proviso of the third section of the act of June 27, 1890, alleging that said child was afflicted and permanently helpless. The claim was rejected December 15, 1896, on the ground that said child is not permanently helpelss. From this action appeal was entered March 1, 1897, by Henry Holt, attorney, who contends that the evidence on file is sufficient to justify allowance.

The evidence in support of the claim is as follows:

Dr. Laycock testified, in 1892, that he had known the child, Catherine, for seven months, and had been her medical adviser for four months, treating her almost constantly for that length of time; that her disease is epilepsy, and, taking the length of time she has had it and the results of his treatment, he thinks it will never be cured. She is wholly incapacitated for doing any kind of business or work.

Dr. Orange G. Pfaff testified, in 1895, that he had known said child for seven years. She has been an invalid by reason of frequent and very violent attacks of a nervous character. Treated her for several months during 1889, and her condition seemed to be entirely unmodified by any treatment he could give her. Since that time her condition has grown worse, and she is certainly a confirmed invalid, and is totally unable to do anything toward supporting herself. The history of the case, as given by her mother, indicated that she had been afflicted in the manner related for several years prior to the time affiant first saw her.

Dr. W. B. Fletcher testified, 1894, that he had treated said child for the past five years for epilepsy, which she had in the form of petit mal from the period of 7 years of age until the menstrual period—14 years of age; this disease developed into grand mal. She is unable to pursue any work, except the simplest household duties, under the direction of her mother.

These physicians were seen by special examiners of the Bureau, and all of them corroborated their foregoing statements, Dr. Pfaff adding the following:

I treated said child at irregular intervals for a period of two years, 1889 and 1890. When I first called to see her she was subject to nervous spells, presumably epilepsy, and would frequently become unconscious. The spells came on at very irregular periods. I can not even approximate at this time how often she had them. She was entirely helpless when she had one of the spells. When not suffering from these attacks she was in the usual condition of a very delicate girl. She was weakly—didn't have much vitality. I don't recall that she had any mental peculiarities. She was about like other children in that respect. I knew of her having quite a number of spells while she was under my treatment, but I can't say how many. Saw her have several and heard of her having others. My impression is that her trouble was a form of epilepsy. I know I gave her that kind of treatment. I have no record of the case, and I can not at this time recall all of the particulars or give symptoms. It was my opinion after I had treated her a while that her trouble was incurable. She was allowed to go and come like other children, but a constant watch had to be kept on her. She ought to have had attention all the time, as she would sometimes be attacked with a spasm while on the street.

A medical examination was held April 10, 1895, which shows the condition of the said child as follows:

General nutrition a little below par. Acne form of eruption on face, evidently of long standing, due perhaps to bromides. Muscles flabby, palms lightly calloused (helps a little around house). Tongue somewhat furred, shows indentation of teeth, and on right margin a slight scar. No other scars found. Teeth fairly good; gums spongy. Heart and lungs normal. No abnormalities of abdominal viscera. Alleges extreme irregularity of menstruation, also attacks of sickness of stomach, usually preceding epileptic attack. Ascribes epilepsy to an attack of scarlet fever, with resulting dropsy and convulsions, at age of 7 years. Real epileptic attacks—at first petit mal—began at the age of 14 and have been increasing in severity.

Claimant has the epileptic face and expression, made more characteristic by acne present. No evidence of injury to cranium. No paralysis of cranial or spinal nerves. Speech is fluent and intellect good. Can state her own case very well. Is not idiotic nor insane. Claimant can not earn a livelihood on account of frequent attacks, and requires the care of another person much of the time. Except the scar on tongue there is no evidence of injury during an attack. No œdema. Except as above no disability found to exist. No evidence of vicious habits. Entirely disabled, and probably permanently, for manual labor.

It is plain from this evidence that the child claimed for is not insane or idiotic, and the only question to be determined is whether she is "otherwise permanently helpless" in the sense contemplated by the statute. In the consideration of claims of this character, heretofore decided on appeal, I have held that the conditions referred to in this first proviso to the third section of the act of June 27, 1890, had relation to the ability of the child to earn a support, or to perform some useful labor to that end, and the pension provided therein was intended to supplement such efforts, and secure to the child some part of the support which it failed to secure for itself by reason of its "helpless condition." At the same time it was held that a condition of helplessness must be shown, and that the same should be permanent, and in the decision of the appeal of John M. Laughlin (8 P. D., 52) this language is used:

We may judge of the meaning of the term "permanently helpless" by its conjunction with the words "insane," "idiotic," with which it is relatively synonymous, as shown by the connecting adverb "otherwise," this identity of meaning having special reference to the ability of the beneficiary to earn a support. That is, in the sense that an insane or idiotic person would be incapable of earning a living or attending to his personal comforts, so one suffering from permanent injuries or disease of body, in a degree that would prevent him from performing any labor or from caring for himself, would be helpless and entitled to the benefits conferred by the said proviso.

Considered, then, in the light of these interpretations of the law, how does this case present itself. This child, now a young woman of 22 years of age, has been afflicted since she was 7 years old by a nervous trouble, which has gradually grown worse, developing, at the age of 14 into pronounced epilepsy, and the attacks of this malady have become more and more frequent until she needs constant watching. Just how often she has the spasms is not shown, but she is unconscious while they last, and she has become weak and of low vitality by reason of them. Then, it is stated by the physicians that she can not do any manual labor, except the simplest household duties, as directed by her mother, and can not earn her own support. It is not apparent that her mind has become impaired, and she has ordinary intelligence. Her affliction up to this time has been entirely physical, and her helplessness has not extended to the degree that she needs personal attention in supplying her wants, except when under the immediate influence of an epileptic fit.

The whole matter, then, resolves itself to this: That this child has an incurable physical malady which, judged by its past history, is liable to become more and more severe, and which, besides rendering her weak and unable to do remunerative labor, keeps her also in a constant state of liability to attacks or spasms, requiring aid and attention from others. Thus, while said child can dress and undress herself and attend to her other personal needs, she could not probably obtain employment that would give her a support, by reason of the liability to fits, even if she were physically able to work, which she is not, except in the lightest employment, and guided by her mother.

Taking all the evidence together, and considering the sex of this child as well as her afflicted condition, I am disposed to the opinion that she is permanently helpless in the sense intended by the law, and that the pension on her account should be continued. The action of the Bureau is accordingly overruled and the case is returned for readjudication favorable to the claim.

***

CONTRIBUTORY NEGLIGENCE—DEATH CAUSE.
WINNIFRED J. COOK (WIDOW).

A person disabled by deafness who adopts a railroad track as a highway of travel is required to exercise that care and caution which ordinary prudence would dictate to a person in his condition in order to avoid harm or peril, and a failure to do so is contributory negligence; and where a soldier is killed by a passing train while pursuing such course his widow is not pensionable under the general law.

Assistant Secretary John M. Reynolds to the Commissioner of Pensions May 8, 1897.

The soldier, Benjamin F. Cook, Company I, One hundred and thirty-fourth Pennsylvania Volunteer Infantry, was pensioned December 10, 1892, under the general law (certificate No. 830226), at $10 per month from September 3, 1890, and $22 from August 24, 1892, for naso-pharyngeal catarrh and resulting slight deafness of both ears, resulting in severe deafness of both ears and neuralgia, payable to the widow.

The pensioner died November 18, 1892, from being run over by a railroad train. The widow filed declaration for widow's pension under the general law January 10, 1893, which claim was rejected January 11, 1897, on the ground that the soldier's death in a railroad accident is not shown by the evidence to be due to his military service.

From this action appeal was received March 22, 1897, it being contended on behalf of appellant that by reason of his deafness, for which pensioned, the soldier was unable to hear the approaching train which caused his death, although the trainmen called out to him and gave him such warning as would have been sufficient to save his life had it not been for his inability to hear on account of said deafness.

The proceedings before the coroner of Mahoning County, Ohio, and testimony taken at the inquest held November 22, 1892, at Youngstown, in said county and State, are as follows:

E. F. Wood, conductor, testified that on the evening of November 18, 1892, he was engaged dropping a coach into the coal truck; the cars were being brought from the upper yard as the cars were passing over the Market street crossing; witness was standing on the west end of the coach, nearest the engine, and on the north side of the car; noticed Mr. Cook standing between the rails of the west-bound track; also saw a train approaching on the west-bound track; called to Cook several times, also pointed in the direction of the approaching train; before the engine and coaches were on the crossing the gates were lowered and were not raised until after the accident; Mr. Cook had been standing about on the west line of the sidewalk; the force of the blow from the locomotive knocked the body about 6 or 8 feet to the west and under the last coach on the east-bound track.

S. C. Comstock testified that at the time of the accident he was standing on the east end of the platform of the P. and L. E. car; saw Mr. Cook standing on the inside of the west-bound track; heard the calling at the head of the train; the guard gates were down.

W. R. Graham testified that on the evening of November 18 he was walking on North Market street toward the N. Y., P. and O. Railroad; as witness approached the crossing saw a train composed of an engine and two coaches; the rear car had been cut loose; witness noticed that the guard gates were down; just as witness approached the track heard calling on the other side; stooped to look under cars and saw the last truck of the last coach pass over the body of a man; witness also noticed a freight train going west on the west-bound track.

After hearing the evidence the coroner found that the deceased came to his death by accident and that the railroad company was in no way to blame, as the crossing was fully protected at the time of the accident.

In the case of Thomas S. Bennett (2 P. D., 9) Assistant Secretary Hawkins held, by opinion of date January 20, 1888, as follows:

Where total deafness exists, the claimant, knowing his condition, is required to exercise that care and caution which ordinary prudence would dictate in order to avoid harm or peril, and a failure to do so is equivalent to such contributory negligence as renders the injury thereby incurred nonpensionable, the said injury not being exclusively due to the total deafness that had been contracted by reason of the service.

In the case of Phebe, widow of Clark J. Castalor (2 P. D., 32), Assistant Secretary Hawkins held, by opinion of date January 31, 1888, as follows:

1. To establish a claim for increase of pension by reason of secondary and contributory cause of disability, claimant must clearly prove, by competent and satisfactory evidence, that the accident resulting in the injury relied upon as the basis of the claim was directly occasioned by his previously incurred disability, and was not the result of negligence or carelessness or risk on his part, nor of a lack of that care and caution which should be exercised by one in a disabled condition.

2. Where a person voluntarily places himself in a position of peril or of hazard, he thereby takes upon himself all the risks so incurred, and is alone responsible for any injury that may result therefrom.

The foregoing cited decisions were reaffirmed in the case of Lucy Adams, widow of James S. Adams (8 P. D., 93), by opinion of date March 1, 1894, wherein I held as follows:

A person disabled by deafness, impaired vision, and an injury which interferes with locomotion who adopts a railroad track as a highway is grossly negligent in so doing, and if killed by a passing train while pursuing such course of travel his widow is not pensionable under the general law.

The well-settled principles of law governing contributory negligence were properly and justly applied in the cited decisions relating to pension claims. The established rule is as follows:

That a person blind or deaf who is injured in a public and dangerous place, where sight and hearing are ordinarily required, does not establish contributory negligence as a matter of law, but the blindness or deafness may be considered upon the question of due care and as an evidence of contributory negligence; and if it appears that the defect of sight or hearing, coupled with the exposure to danger, was the cause of an injury which otherwise would not have occurred, it may be held that contributory negligence exists as a matter of law. It is clear that the misfortune of being blind or deaf does not relieve the afflicted person from the duty to exercise ordinary care, but rather imposes upon him the duty of greater precautions to avoid injury. (American and English Encyclopedia of Law, vol. 4, p. 79.)

For effect of blindness or deafness on doctrines of negligence see Harris v. Ubelhoer (75 N. Y., 169); Salem v. Goller (76 Ind., 291); Sluper v. Sandown (52 Vt., 251).

It is contributory negligence for one of defective eyesight or hearing to walk upon a railroad track at a time when a train is known to be due. See Maloy v. Wabash, etc., R. Co. (84 Mo., 270); Davenport v. Ruckman (10 Bosworth, N. Y., 20; 37 N. Y., 568); Shapley v. Wyman (134 Mass., 118); Stewart v. Ripon (38 Wis., 584); Phillips v. Dickerson (85 Ill., 11); O'Mara v. Hudson, etc., R. Co. (38 N. Y., 445); Holmes's Common Law, 109.

Blindness, or deafness does not relieve from duty to exercise ordinary care. See Cleveland, Columbus, etc., R. Co. v. Terry (8 Ohio St., 570); Purl v. St. Louis, etc., R. Co. (72 Mo., 168); Winn v. Lowell (1 Allen, Mass., 177); Simmerman v. H. & St. J. R. Co. (71 Mo., 476); s. c., (2 Am. & Eng. R. R. Cas., 191); Ill. Central R. R. Co. v. Buckner (28 Ill., 299); Gonzales v. N. Y., etc., R. Co. (1 Jones & S., N. Y., 57); Peach v. Utica (10 Hun., N. Y., 477); City of Centralia v. Krouze (64 Ill., 19); Central, etc., R. Co. v. Feller (84 Pa. St., 226); Morris, etc., R. Co. v. Haslan (33 N. J. L., 147); West v. N. J., etc., Trans. Co. (32 N. J. L., 91); Elkins v. Boston, etc., R. Co. (115 Mass., 190).

In the case at bar no evidence is presented other than that given before the coroner, and upon which a verdict was rendered exonerating the railroad company from all blame or responsibility for the accident which resulted in the death of the soldier. No apparent effort is made by claimant to establish by testimony that the soldier exercised due care and diligence and did not contribute in any way to the negligence which caused his death. It is not sufficient to simply aver in the letter of appeal that, by reason of deafness, for which disability the soldier was pensioned, he came to his death by a railroad accident, that such death was due to his military service, and therefore the widow has title to the pension.

Indisputable evidence should have been presented, in order to maintain the widow's claim, showing that the soldier's presence on the tracks of the railroad, where trains were constantly passing and repassing, was nevertheless legitimate and unavoidable, and that he then and there exercised all possible care and prudence and observed the duty of taking more than ordinary care or precaution to avoid injury. Failing in these essentials of proof, the death of the soldier must be held to have been the result of contributory negligence on his part, and not the result of deafness of service origin, for which pensioned, and hence the widow has no title to pension under the general law.

The action of your Bureau rejecting the claim under the general law, for the reasons stated, being in harmony with previous departmental decisions and the law in cognate cases, is hereby affirmed.

SERVICE—UNASSIGNED RECRUIT—ACT JUNE 27, 1890—DROPPING FROM THE ROLLS.

JAMES T. VELEY.

Soldier was enrolled as a substitute November 1, 1864, received at Indiana rendezvous, November 3, 1864, examined by a board of inspectors and rejected by reason of extreme youth on November 7, 1864, and was furloughed to await discharge on the same day. The order for discharge was finally approved by the general commanding the department November 30, 1864, but the certificate for discharge was dated March 9, 1865.

Held, That he was not in the service of the United States exceeding thirty days, and his name was properly dropped from the rolls under the act of June 27, 1890.

Assistant Secretary John M. Reynolds to the Commissioner of Pensions, May 8, 1897.

James T. Veley, late unassigned substitute, Tenth Congressional district of Indiana, was pensioned in May, 1892, under the act of June 27, 1890, at the rate of $12 per month from date of filing his claim, July 18, 1891. Upon a revision of his rating by the Bureau in 1895, his pension was reduced to $6 per month from May 4, 1895. Subsequently another revision of his claim resulted in the dropping of his name from the rolls February 2, 1897, on the ground that allowance was erroneous because of insufficient service to give title under said act. From this action appeal has been made March 20, 1897; by P. J. Lockwood, attorney, upon the contention that soldier had a service of more than four months, as shown by the records of the War Department.

Following is the report, dated October 23, 1891, from the War Department, on which the pension was granted:

James T. Veley, priv. unassg'd Ind. Vols., was enrolled November 1, 1864, and discharged March 9, 1865, on S. C. D.

The surgeon's certificate of disability on which soldier was discharged shows that he was—

incapable of performing the duties of a soldier because of extreme youth. The boy appears to be less than 17 years of age and is very feeble. Said disability existed at time of enlistment.

This certificate is dated "Draft Rend'z., Ind'polis, Ind., November 22, 1864," and is signed "Henry Blamington, Brig. Gen. U. S. V." It is indorsed "Medical Director's Office, Northern Department, Cincinnati. O., November 29, 1864, approved by medical director." Also, "Headquarters Northern Dep't., Cincinnati, O., November 30, 1864. To be discharged. By command of Maj. Gen. Hooker, signed by his A. D. C."

The actual discharge or certificate was dated March 9, 1865. The next report of the War Department is dated January 16, 1896, and states:

The records show that James T. Veley was enrolled November 1, 1864, as a substitute to serve one year, and that he was received at Indiana draft rendezvous on November 3, 1864, where he was examined by a board of inspectors on November 7, 1864, and was rejected by reason of "extreme youth; the boy appears to be less than 17 years of age and is very feeble. Said disability existed at the time of enlistment." The records further show that he was furloughed to await discharge November 7, 1864, and that a discharge certificate based on a surgeon's certificate was prepared for him March 9, 1865.

It has this day been determined by this Department that this man's service terminated November 7, 1864, the date on which he was sent home to await discharge.

It was upon this report that pensioner's name was dropped from the rolls. Since the appeal was filed a similar report has been made, April 16, 1897, as follows:

Upon the decisions of this Department, the within-named James T. Veley is regarded as having been in the military service of the United States from November 1, 1864, the date of his enrollment and acceptance by the board of enrollment, to November 7, 1864, the date on which he was furloughed to await discharge.

The status of this soldier and his title to pension is to be determined by the decision of the Judge-Advocate-General, U. S. A., as embodied in my decision of the claim of Elizabeth H. Poland (8 P. D., 266). According to that decision this soldier's service could not properly be regarded as having continued until the discharge certificate was delivered to him, but terminated at the time he was actually discharged by the commanding officer of the general rendezvous pursuant to the order of the department commander. In the above reports from the War Department it appears that the soldier was furloughed and sent home to await discharge November 7, 1864, but the final order for his discharge was approved November 30, 1864, so that his service might be said to have been for one month, November 1 to 30, 1864, but no longer, although, as seen, the War Department holds the service was ended November 7, 1864. But it is clear that the soldier's actual or technical term of service was less than ninety days and he was not entitled to pension under the act of June 27, 1890.

It may be remarked further that the reports in this case show that this claimant did not in reality render any service whatever and could have no right to pension under the said law, which confers title upon—

all persons who served ninety days or more in the military or naval service of the United States during the war of the rebellion, etc.

It is unnecessary to elaborate this view, as the subject has been fully discussed in the decisions of the following cases by Assistant Secretary Bussey: Albert K. Ransom (5 P. D., 183), Sarah A. Kersey, widow (6 P. D., 1).

The pension was erroneously granted to this claimant in the first instance, and the action of the Bureau in dropping his name from the rolls was entirely proper, and is affirmed.

ADULTEROUS COHABITATION—WIDOW'S INCREASE ON ACCOUNT OF MINORS.

ELVIRA HALL (WIDOW).

As it is accepted that the widow has no title to individual pension under act of June 27, 1890, by reason of open and notorious adulterous cohabitation, she has no title to the $2 per month additional allowed the widow under said act for each minor until arriving at the age of 16 years.

Assistant Secretary John M. Reynolds to the Commissioner of Pensions, May 15, 1897.

Elvira Hall, claiming to be the widow of Peter Hall, Company G, Fifty-second United States Colored Volunteer Infantry, filed declaration October 1, 1890 (No. 467722), for pension under the act of June 27, 1890, claiming for herself and four minors, Nettie, Lewis, Arthur, and Robert. This claim was rejected January 20, 1897, on the ground of claimant's open and notorious adulterous cohabitation with one Ben. Cooper, which began prior to passage of the act of June 27, 1890, and has continued ever since, as is shown by special examination.

From this action appeal was received April 7, 1897, the contention on the part of appellant being that, while she accepts the rejection of her claim on the ground that she was living in adultery with one Ben. Cooper, if the evidence be satisfactory of the forfeiture of claimant's rights as widow under the act of August 7, 1882, yet your Bureau erred in not giving her the benefit as mother, as provided in section 3 of the act of June 27, 1890, of the evidence showing that she was the legal wife of the soldier, the legal mother of his children, and had the care and custody of his minor children, and that adultery does not affect her rights as mother.

Section 3 of the act of June 27, 1890, provides in part as follows:

That if any officer or enlisted man who served ninety days or more in the Army or Navy of the United States during the late war of the rebellion, and who was honorably discharged, has died, or shall hereafter die, leaving a widow without other means of support than her daily labor, or minor children under the age of sixteen years, such widow shall, upon due proof of her husband's death, without proving his death to be the result of his army service, be placed on the pension roll from the date of the application therefor under this act, at the rate of eight dollars per month during her widowhood, and shall also be paid two dollars per month for each child of such officer or enlisted man under sixteen years of age, and in case of the death or remarriage of the widow, leaving a child or children of such officer or enlisted man under the age of sixteen years, such pension shall be paid such child or children until the age of sixteen. * * *

The question presented on appeal in the case at bar is whether the forfeiture by the widow of her title to pension under act of June 27,

1890, by reason of adulterous cohabitation (which forfeiture is accepted by appellant), carries with it forfeiture of the $2 per month provided by said act to be paid the widow for each minor until arriving at the age of 16 years.

It will be observed by the terms of section 3 of the act of June 27, 1890, that the right or title of the widow to receive the additional pension of $2 per month for each minor, until the latter arrives at the age of 16 years, is made wholly dependent or consequent upon the right or title of the widow to receive the pension of $8 per month during her widowhood. The additional pension allowed for the minor or minors therefore can not be paid the widow if she be not entitled to the pension provided for herself, the alternative, however, being that in case of the death or remarriage of the widow, leaving a child or children of the officer or enlisted man under the age of 16 years, the pension shall inure to such child or children until they shall have attained the age of 16.

It must therefore be held that inasmuch as the widow has no title to individual pension at $8 per month under act of June 27, 1890, she has no title to the additional pension of $2 per month provided by said act to be paid her for each minor until arriving at the age of 16 years.

The action of your Bureau rejecting the claim for the reasons stated is therefore affirmed.

SERVICE—DISCHARGE—PRESUMPTION.

MINORS OF DANIEL HALLOWAY.

Where the record of the War Department shows soldier's enlistment in a three months' service in 1861, and said Department reports that it is unable from any evidence before it to determine soldier's final record; and the records of said Department shows a subsequent honorable service and discharge of said soldier from a three years' service, it is

Held, That as no charge of desertion, absence without leave, or other counter presumption is involved, the legal presumption of innocence should prevail, and soldier be presumed to have been discharged from said first service at the expiration of his first term of enlistment.

Assistant Secretary John M. Reynolds to the Commissioner of Pensions, May 15, 1897.

Claimant on April 6, 1897, appealed from the action of your Bureau rejecting the minors' claim, No. 454182, filed October 9, 1890, on the ground that—

the records of the War Department fail to show that the soldier was discharged from his former service in Company I, Thirteenth Ohio Volunteer Infantry.

It appears that said claim was not rejected until April 26, 1897.

The appeal is irregular, as no final action appears to have been taken at the date of said appeal, but in view of the manifest error on the part of your Bureau in the action of April 26, 1897, the irregularity of the appeal will be waived, and the question presented by the appeal will be considered.

Appellant contends that it was error to reject the claim for pension on account of death of soldier from causes originating in a service from which he was honorably discharged on the ground that the soldier was not honorably discharged from a former service.

The records of the War Department show that soldier was enrolled as a private in Company I, Thirteenth Regiment Ohio Volunteer Infantry, April 28, 1861, to serve three months, and that his name appears only on the muster-in rolls, and that the War Department on January 23, 1896, reports that—

the final record of this man or of this organization can not be determined upon any evidence before this Department.

It further appears that soldier enlisted August 19, 1862, to serve three years; that he was wounded at the battle of the Wilderness, May 6, 1864, and was pensioned on account of said wound up to the date of his death, October 8, 1871.

The minors' claim for pension is based upon the alleged facts that soldier died of disease contracted in his second service, from which he was honorably discharged. The record discloses no charge of desertion from his first service, nor is the question of dishonorable discharge or other adverse presumption involved in the case. The War Department is simply unable from the record to determine soldier's final termination of his first three months' service.

I am of the opinion that in such a case the legal presumption of innocence should prevail, and that the soldier should be presumed to have been discharged from the service at the expiration of his term of enlistment.

The action appealed from is accordingly reversed, and the papers in the case are herewith returned.

ATTORNEYSHIP—POWER OF ATTORNEY—FEE.

J. F. VINAL (ATTORNEY).

ELISHUP P. ALLEN, INSANE (CLAIMANT).

1. A power of attorney to prosecute a pension claim executed by a claimant after having been judicially declared insane, or while confined in an asylum for the insane, will not be recognized, and the attorney filing the same should be so notified. (Case of Joel Ames, 8 P. D., 171.)

2. Evidence filed by a duly authorized attorney when not entitled to recognition is actual service, and it inures to his benefit if he becomes entitled to recognition at any time before the claim is prima facie complete, and may entitle him to a fee.

Assistant Secretary John M. Reynolds to the Commissioner of Pensions, May 29, 1897.

J. F. Vinal, of Washington, D. C., May 20, 1897, appealed in the matter of fee on the issue of March 2, 1894, in the claim (certificate No. 310692), under the general laws, of Elishup P. Allen (insane), late of Company D, Twenty-third Massachusetts Volunteers.

James W. Loomis, of Fairhaven, Mass., December 9, 1889, filed an application for additional pension on account of sunstroke and results. Said application contained a power of attorney in favor of Mr. Loomis, and was executed by the claimant in personam.

May 3, 1890, the appellant filed a new declaration containing a power of attorney to him, executed by Eveline A: Allen as guardian of the soldier. He filed material evidence June 9 and 10, 1890, and was called upon for additional evidence December 7, 1891.

Mr. Loomis, January 26, 1892, filed evidence responsive to said call.

The appellant was paid a fee. Upon the protest of Mr. Loomis he was requested to refund, hence this appeal.

If the evidence filed by the appellant prima facie completed the case, there is no doubt that under the rules Mr. Loomis would have been entitled to the fee had he been duly authorized to prosecute the claim; but such is not the case. If entitled to recognition under the power of attorney to him, he became in neglect on the expiration of one year from the date of filing the declaration, or on December 9 1890, as he rendered no material service in the interim, and the evidence filed during that period did not complete the claim. Thereafter the power of attorney to the appellant became operative.

The appellant was requested to refund upon the ground that he had rendered no service at a time when he was entitled to recognition. The rule that an attorney has no title to a fee unless he rendered material service when entitled to recognition is held to be subject to the condition that the power of attorney to him does not become operative before the claim is prima facie complete, or upon the failure of the attorney of record to respond to a call for additional evidence within the time allotted to him by the rules of practice. For, upon the same principle that an attorney's services, rendered at a time when he is not entitled to recognition, inure to the benefit of the attorney of record, all services, by whomsoever rendered, within the allotted time of the former inure to his benefit upon the power of attorney to him becoming operative under the conditions noted; and having actually rendered material service, which eventually inures to his benefit, he may become entitled to the fee. The primary principle is, as stated in the case of Martin J. Craiglow (7 P. D., 517), viz, an attorney must render actual service in order to be entitled to a fee. The appellant appears to have complied with this requirement. I am not informed of any case in which the rule invoked against the appellant has been applied to the conditions here arising. Such are the elements entering into the appellant's title to fee in this case. So, were Mr. Loomis properly authorized to appear in this case, it is held that the appellant is entitled to the fee for the reasons herein set forth.

However, the power of attorney to Mr. Loomis is invalid; it never conferred any rights upon him, although contained in a declaration which has been accepted as the basis of this claim.

The essential features relative to the matter under discussion arising in this case are like those in the case of Joel Ames (8 P. D., 171), upon which the following rules are based:

2. A declaration for pension may be made by a person non compos mentis, but, if it appear that he was at the time of executing the same, or thereafter becomes, incapable of understanding the nature of his claim and incapable of prosecuting the same, the case must thereafter be prosecuted by the next friend, guardian, or committee of such person.

4. A power of attorney to prosecute a pension claim executed by a claimant after having been judicially declared insane, or while confined in an asylum for the insane will not be recognized, and the attorney filing the same should be so notified.

In that case the power of attorney was contained in the declaration; the power was rejected, and the declaration was accepted as the basis of the claim.

At the time the power of attorney to Mr. Loomis was executed the soldier had been adjudged insane by competent authority, so far as it appears; in fact, it appearing that he was insane at the time said power was executed, and was under guardianship.

As bearing on the appellant's authority to represent the claimant and on his title to a fee, it may properly be added that the guardian, by appointing appellant as attorney in this case, thereby repudiated any power the soldier may have executed, viz, the power of attorney to Mr. Loomis; and this she was at liberty to do. (See case of Joel Ames, supra.)

As it appears that the appellant is entitled to the fee paid him, action requiring him to refund was error, and accordingly is overruled.

SERVICE—MILITIA—ACT JUNE 27, 1890.

WILLIAM BICE.

1. Pennsylvania Emergency Militia, while serving in the Army of the United States, under command of United States officers, in response to the call of the President, were a part of that Army while so serving, and are, for that time and as regards the character of the service, brought within the scope of the first subdivision of section 4693, Revised Statutes, and the act of June 27, 1890, for pensionable purposes, other conditions of those laws having been met.

2. The peculiar conditions under which said militia were recognized as a part of the Army, the manner in which received into and released from the service of the United States, obviated the necessity of enlistment and discharge in the usual manner, the records of the State in that respect being taken as a substitute for the records of the War Department, and the period of actual service being counted as if rendered under enlistment by United States officers.

3. Two terms of service, each less than ninety days, may be added together to make the required period under said act of June 27, 1890.

Assistant Secretary John M. Reynolds to the Commissioner of Pensions, May 29, 1897.

This appellant filed an application February 23, 1892, for pension under the act of June 27, 1890, alleging ninety days' service in Company H, One hundred and forty-ninth Pennsylvania Infantry, during the war of the rebellion. This claim was rejected June 31, 1893, upon the ground of insufficient service, the same being less than ninety days, or from March 11 to May 5, 1865, as shown by the records of the War Department.

Subsequently, or on October 1, 1895, appellant filed another application under said act, alleging additional service in Company F, Forty-sixth Pennsylvania Emergency Militia. He was paid for service of one month and twenty days in this organization, as shown by report of the Auditor for the War Department. Without taking formal action on this claim appellant was notified by the Bureau that this latter service was not pensionable under the act of June 27, 1890. An appeal was taken from this conclusion, but in view of the fact that no formal action had been taken, the appeal was dismissed and the case remanded for proper action by the Bureau.

The claim has been briefed and rejected, November 27, 1896, on the ground of no title, claimant not having served ninety days in the United States military service, as required by the act of June 27, 1890, the service in Company F, Forty-sixth Pennsylvania Emergency Militia, not being recognized as pensionable. From this action appeal is taken, January 5, 1897, on the contention that both services should be counted in appellant's favor in calculating the length of his service, and as the two together amount to more than ninety days, pension should be granted him under said act. In support of his contention he cites the fact that pension has been allowed to John C. Shore, whose only service was in the same regiment of Pennsylvania Emergency Militia (Certificate No. 891774).

It has been ascertained by reference to the files of the Bureau that the grant of pension to said John C. Shore was under the general law, for a disability contracted in the line of duty during his service. That grant was in accordance with the decisions of Assistant Secretary Bussey, of March 3, 1892, and May 14, 1892, in the cases of Randolph M. Manley, late of Company I, Forty-seventh Pennsylvania Militia, and B. F. Beazell, late of Company H, Fifty-eighth Pennsylvania Militia (5 P. D., 295 and 384). By those decisions it was held that those and similar organizations when called into the service of the United States by the proclamation of the President, of June 15, 1863, and while serving with the Army of the United States, under command of its officers, were a part of that Army, and the members thereof were pensionable for any disability contracted in the line of duty, while so serving, as provided by section 4693, Revised Statutes, paragraph 1.

These decisions had special reference to claims under the general law. There is no direct allusion therein to the act of June 27, 1890, nor any reason to believe that claims under that act were considered. At the end of a note following the decision in the Manley case, it is stated:

It is perceived that the ruling has no application to claims filed under the act of June 27, 1890.

Previous to the rendition of that decision the practice of the Bureau excluded members of the organization mentioned (the Pennsylvania Emergency Militia) from the benefits of pension under both the general law and act of June 27, 1890, except when they might be entitled under one of the subdivisions, 2, 3, 4, or 5, of section 4693, Revised Statutes, or some special law.

Since that decision they have been barred only under the act of June 27, 1890.

This debarment has been sanctioned by decisions of the Department which have construed said act as intended only for the benefit of soldiers and sailors who enlisted and served in the regularly organized forces of the Army, Navy, and Marine Corps of the United States, and as excluding those who served in any irregular organization, not a part of the Army or Navy or Marine Corps, or in a capacity not recognized as strictly within the military or naval establishment of the United States. Some of these irregular organizations were the militia of various States serving for a time in cooperation with the United States Army, the Mississippi Marine Brigade, and United States Revenue Marine. Some of the positions not recognized as regular were those of provost marshals, contract surgeons, enrolling officers, and the like. As stated, these were provided for in one or another of the four last paragraphs of section 4693, Revised Statutes, and in some special laws of limited scope. The reasons for the construction given as to those organizations may be gathered by a reference to the decisions in the following cases, and others cited therein: Irving C. Rosse (6 P. D., 68); Evelyn S. Tallman (6 P. D., 261, reaffirmed in Letter Book No. 199, 367); Andrew J. Shannon (7 P. D., 64); Henry Cushman (7 P. D., 408); David Oliver (7 P. D., 597).

The decisions on this line have been, for the most part, uniform, and the rulings have been accepted as properly enunciating the law applicable to the granting of pension to these irregular organizations. A careful reading of said decisions will reveal that the chief reason for denying pension to the members of these organizations under the first subdivision of section 4693, Revised Statutes, is that they are not shown by the records of the War and Navy Departments to have been regularly and legally enlisted into the Army or Navy. In other words, being pensionable, if at all, under the general law, only by virtue of some of the other subdivisions of 4693, Revised Statutes, or some special law, they are excluded from the benefits of the first subdivision and likewise of the act of June 27, 1890. Title under said act is made to hinge on title under the first subdivision of section 4693, Revised Statutes, as regards the character of the service.

The correctness of the departmental decisions referred to was recognized by Congress, and it was deemed essential to enact the act of February 15, 1895, extending the provisions of the act of June 27, 1890, to include officers and privates of the Missouri State Militia and the Provisional Missouri Militia who served ninety days during the war of the rebellion.

If, then, the Pennsylvania Emergency Militia (in which this appellant served) were only irregular organizations, which could not be regarded as a part of the Army of the United States and included in the regular military establishment, and the members thereof were not pensionable under the first subdivision of section 4693, Revised Statutes, neither are they pensionable under the act of June 27, 1890. But, as we have seen in the decisions of the Manley and Beazell appeals before cited, these organizations were held to be a part of the Army for such time as they were serving under the command of United States officers, in response to the call of the President, and the members are pensionable for disability contracted while so serving. And being thus pensionable, they are also pensionable under the act of June 27, 1890, if they otherwise met the requirements of that act relative to length of service, honorable discharge, extent of present disability, etc.

This is true, because it has been held in various decisions that the act of June 27, 1890, is a part of the pension code, and is to be construed with existing pension laws in pari materia. (Adolph Bernstein, Sarah H. Ozborn, and Ellen J. Pipes, 7 P. D., 229, 317, and 489.) And, while the decision in the Manley case was made probably with no special reference to the act named, yet, since it has the effect of giving to certain irregular organizations, for a time, the status of the regular volunteer forces of the Army and Navy, and thus makes them pensionable under the first subdivision of section 4693, Revised Statutes, the same organizations can not be denied the benefits of the regular forces under the act of June 27, 1890.

It is not a new ruling to hold that persons pensionable under said first subdivision of section 4693, Revised Statutes, are also pensionable under the act of June 27, 1890.

Various decisions discuss this subject, as in the following cases: Louisa S. Norris (5 P. D., 42); Sarah A. Kersey (6 P. D., 1); Messmer and Morrison (6 P. D., 20); Phillip John (8 P. D., 64); Marcis M. Rhodes (8 P. D., 99).

It will be found by reference to these decisions that the services of the appellants were of an irregular nature, but for certain reasons pointed out were, in most of the cases, brought within the purview of section 4693, paragraph 1, and their services were held to be also pensionable under the act of June 27, 1890. It will be further found that in some of the cases cited a difficulty arose in the granting of pension, not because of the character of the service per se, but by reason of a lack of honorable discharge, or of sufficient length of service, or because the particular service was not such as (from the records of the War Department) could be regarded as a part of the regular military or naval establishment of the United States. It may be remarked here that the decision in the Louisa S. Norris case is cited simply because of the reasoning therein, although it was afterwards found that that reasoning was based on a false state of facts, and the decision was over-ruled because the case was decided upon a theory without facts to sustain it. (Alvin West, 7 P. D., 74.) The same is partly true as to the decision in the Messmer and Morrison case.

More has been said, probably, than was actually essential to show that certain irregular organizations are pensionable under paragraph 1, section 4693, Revised Statutes, and the act of June 27, 1890, and yet the details of the law and facts on which the rulings are justified have not been gone into. These are fully discussed in decisions heretofore made and cited—those of the Manley and Beazell appeals and of the Alvin West appeal (7 P. D., 74) and of the appeals mentioned in the preceding paragraph. These decisions also show why certain other irregular organizatians can not be pensioned under the laws referred to.

Having demonstrated by the foregoing remarks that in so far as the character of this claimant's service is concerned he would be entitled under the act of June 27, 1890, provided the other requirements of that act are fulfilled in his case, it becomes necessary to inquire into the evidence regarding the length of his service and the nature of his discharge. As stated in the beginning, the records show, and the appellant admits, that the service in the Forty-sixth Pennsylvania Emergency Militia covered a period of only fifty-one or two days. This, of course, is not sufficient length of service, and the only question is whether, as contended, this period of service should be added to that of about fifty-five days in the One hundred and forty-ninth Pennsylvania Infantry to make the essential length of service, ninety days or more. There seems to be no good reason why this may not be done. The act provides—

that all persons who served ninety days or more in the military or naval service of the United States during the war of the rebellion and have been honorably discharged therefrom, etc.

shall be pensioned. Nothing is said as to continuous service, and there is no implication that different periods of service may not be added together, provided all the service was during the war of the rebellion. The contention in this regard may be therefore sustained.

And so, touching the discharge necessary to be shown, it seems only requisite that the final discharge, as well as all others, from service during the war of the rebellion, covering the essential period of ninety days, shall be honorable, that the separation from the service shall be complete, with no taint on account of deserting or dismissal. I apprehend that the rulings and decisions on this subject are so familiar that it is unnecessary to elaborate the statement here made, or to cite the said decisions. The only question to be determined in this case is whether the claimant's separation from each service was complete and his discharge honorable.

As to his service in the One hundred and forty-ninth Pennsylvania Infantry there can be no question raised as to the nature of his discharge. The record shows that it was formal and honorable. And this being his last service his discharge therefrom was a final honorable discharge. But this service, as before indicated, covered a period of less than ninety days, and to make up that period, as required by the act, it is necessary to add the service of fifty-one days in the Pennsylvania Emergency Militia.

But (and here lies the gist of the adverse action) it is in effect contended that the records of the War Department do not show an honorable discharge from the latter service, or any discharge at all, and for that reason the claimant is not entitled under the act. In contravention of that position it seems sufficient to point out the fact that this organization was recognized as a part of the Army of the United States for the period above stated, and that the peculiar conditions under which it was received into and released from that Army obviated the necessity of enlistment and discharge in the usual manner. In other words, the fact being shown that it was accepted for service by the United States, as if it had been enlisted by United States officers, and was released and paid for services by such officers, as shown by the records of the Auditor of the Treasury, must be construed as a compliance with the requirements of the law.

In this view, then, I am of the opinion that the service of this claimant in the Forty-sixth Pennsylvania Emergency Militia for the time he was serving under the call of the President should be counted in making up the period of his United States service during the war of the rebellion, and as this service when added to the service in the One hundred and forty-ninth Pennsylvania Infantry covers a period of more than ninety days he would be entitled to pension under the act of June 27, 1890, the other requirements of the act being met.

Your action in rejecting the claim on the ground stated is reversed, and the papers are returned for readjudication in accordance with the views herein expressed.

INSANE OR HELPLESS MINOR—ACT OF JUNE 27, 1890.

HELENA, MINOR OF JOSEPH COX.

A claimant for pension under the first proviso of section 3, act of June 27, 1890, as a helpless minor, who was over the age of 16 years at the date of the soldier's death, has no pensionable status.

Assistant Secretary John M. Reynolds to the Commissioner of Pensions, May 29, 1897.

The above-named soldier, late of Company C, Thirty-sixth Ohio Infantry, was a pensioner at the date of his death, April 3, 1889.

Martha Cox, as his widow, was pensioned under the general law, in her own right, and on behalf of two minor children of the deceased soldier, viz, Mary M. and Rosa K. Cox, from date of his death.

July 20, 1892, Martha Cox, the soldier's widow, and as the natural guardian of Helena Cox, another child of the deceased soldier, filed an application for pension under the act of June 27, 1890, on her behalf, alleging that the said Helena Cox was suffering from hip disease, which rendered her permanently helpless.

This claim was rejected February 20, 1897, on the ground that the alleged helpless minor, Helena Cox, was not on the pension rolls in her own right or in connection with the widow's claim prior to becoming 16 years of age, and was over 16 at date of the soldier's death.

In the appeal filed April 14, 1897, it is contended that rejection of the claim is contrary to the intent of the act of June 27, 1890, which provides a pension for the permanently disabled children, without regard to age.

The third section of the act of June 27, 1890, provides a pension to the surviving widow of the deceased soldier at the rate of $8 per month, and also an additional allowance of $2 per month for each minor child of the deceased soldier under 16 years of age, and in case of the death or remarriage of the widow, leaving a child or children of the soldier under the age of 16 years, such pension shall be paid such child or children until the age of 16.

It is further provided:

That in case a minor child is insane, idiotic, or otherwise permanently helpless, the pension shall continue during the life of said child, or during the period of such disability, and this proviso shall apply to all pensions heretofore granted or hereafter to be granted under this or any former statute, and such pension shall commence from the date of application therefor after the passage of this act.

It is apparent that this claim is based upon the latter clause, or proviso, of said act, as above quoted.

The evidence shows that this claimant as a minor child of the deceased soldier was born May 15, 1868. She therefore became 16 years of age in May, 1884, about five years prior to the soldier's death.

As the widow was, and still is, a pensioner, said minor child could not be pensioned in her own right, and as she was over 16 years of age at the date of the soldier's death, the widow could not be granted an allowance of $2 per month on her behalf. It therefore appears that this claimant, now 29 years of age, has never had a pensionable status in her own right, or in connection with the widow's pension. Nor do the provisions of the third section of the act of June 27, 1890, provide a pensionable status for this claimant, under existing conditions. The widow's pension can not succeed to the claimant, for the reason she is over 16 years of age, and the widow is still living and is a pensioner. The proviso quoted does not create a new pension for a helpless minor child independent of these conditions, but provides only for the continuance of "such pension" heretofore granted to such minor child under 16 years of age, on account of its helpless condition.

In other words, the intent of the act is to continue payment of pension to minors over 16 years of age whose names were on the pension roll at the date of the passage of the act, upon proof of continuance of their helpless condition.

As the claimant never had a pensionable status in her own right, or in connection with the widow's pension, there is no provision of law by which a pension may be continued to her on account of her alleged helplessness. Rejection of the claim was proper and is hereby affirmed.

SERVICE—MEXICAN WAR.

HELEN M. GEIGER (WIDOW).

Soldier enlisted March 20, 1848; was mustered in April 30, 1848, to serve during the war with Mexico; was forwarded May 5, and joined his company near Matamoras, Mexico, May 26, 1848, and he remained with said company until after July 31, 1848, and was mustered out November 7, 1848. It is

Held, That he actually served sixty days in Mexico and en route thereto.

Assistant Secretary John M. Reynolds to the Commissioner of Pensions, May 29, 1897.

Claimant, on October 16, 1896, appealed from the action of your Bureau of September 28, 1896, rejecting her widow's claim, No. 13364, filed May 25, 1896, under the act of January 29, 1887, on the ground that soldier (David M. Geiger, late of Captain Dunlap's Independent Company Illinois Mounted Volunteers) was not in Mexico sixty days, or on the coasts or frontier thereof, or en route thereto during the war with that country.

The soldier was in receipt of a pension under said act at the date of his death, and it is contended by appellant that as he was pensioned by a former Administration as a Mexican survivor his widow should be allowed a pension, on the ground that his military status was duly adjudicated by competent authority.

The case was considered by this Department on appeal and returned to your Bureau for a report from the Treasury Department, Second Auditor, stating the period of time for which soldier was paid for his Mexican war service, and also for a report from the War Department; and on January 29, 1897, these reports having been returned with the papers, they were again returned to your Bureau for a further report, and this being furnished the case will now be considered on its merits.

The records of the War Department show that soldier enlisted March 20, 1848, at Nauvoo, Ill., and was mustered in April 30, 1848, at Jefferson Barracks, Mo., to serve during the war with Mexico, he being a recruit for Captain Dunlap's Company Illinois Mounted Volunteers (Mexican war); that he was forwarded to said company on or after May 5, 1848, and joined his company near Matamoras, Mexico, May 26, 1848, and was mustered out at Alton, Ill., November 7, 1848; that the stations of said company between muster in and muster out were as follows: May 26, 1848, near Matamoras, Mexico; June 30, 1848, same station; July 31, 1848, Camargo, Mexico, and August 31, 1848, at San Antonio, Tex.

The records of the Treasury Department, Second Auditor's Office, show that soldier was paid from date of enlistment, March 20, 1848, to November 7, 1848, and five and one-half days' travel for 110 miles home.

The facts in this case are quite different from the facts upon which the decision in the case of George Ackenback (7 P. D., 169) was based, and the evidence in this case of actual service with his command in Mexico for a period of over three months outweighs the presumptions as to actual termination of service.

As stated in Instructions to the Commissioner of Pensions (7 P. D., 242):

The general principle adverted to in the late case of George Ackenback (7 P. D., 169), that "Congress intended that the service * * * must have had some direct connection with and have formed a part of the military or naval operations in that war," is sound, and is applicable to cases arising under section 4730, Revised Statutes, as under the act of January 29, 1887. That is, in each case, wholly a matter of proof, and is not to be presumed from the mere fact of the existence of the war.

It may reasonably, however, be presumed that after February 2, 1848, no service was rendered "in going to" or "en route" to said war, since, by the express terms of the treaty, hostilities were to cease, and did, in fact, cease on that date. It is extremely improbable that any such service was rendered thereafter, but it is a rebuttable presumption and may be overborne by positive evidence to the contrary.

It is not to be presumed, however, that after that date service was not rendered during the "provisional suspension of hostilities" agreed upon in said treaty. The war still subsisted, and pensionable service may legally have been rendered, both at the seat of war, as specified in said act of January 29, 1887, and, under said section 4730, in returning from the same.

Nor is it to be presumed in cases arising under said section 4730 that no service was rendered after May 30, 1848; though it will be presumed that all belligerent forces were withdrawn and returned from the war within a reasonable time thereafter, in compliance with good faith and the terms of said treaty.

In the case under consideration the rebuttable presumptions give way to positive record evidence. The soldier enlisted as a recruit in a company already serving in the war with Mexico, and he is deemed to be en route to Mexico from date of enlistment to the date of joining his company in Mexico, although for the purposes of this case it would be sufficient to date the commencement of his serving from the date of muster in, or the date he was forwarded from Jefferson Barracks, Mo., to Matamoras, Mexico, as his company is shown to have served in Mexico over sixty days subsequent to May 25, 1848.

So also the date of actual muster in is immaterial in this case, for the act of January 29, 1887, makes no condition which limits the benefits of the act to those who were mustered in. The language of the act grants pension to "surviving officers and enlisted men, etc., who being duly enlisted actually served," etc.

The soldier established his claim under said act and he was pensioned in 1890. He subsequently applied for an increase under the provisions of January 5, 1893, and was, after a special examination, allowed his increased pension from November 23, 1894. He died November 22, 1895, leaving an aged widow, to whom he was married in 1848, and who is shown to be in a destitute condition.

As the evidence in this case shows that soldier was duly enlisted and actually served sixty days in the army of the United States in Mexico, and en route thereto, the action appealed from is reversed, and the papers in the case are herewith returned.

MARRIAGE AND DIVORCE—ACT JUNE 27, 1890.

MARY MUNSELL (WIDOW).

Claimant and soldier were divorced, a viniculo, on claimant's petition, May 6, 1887. The decree of divorce was disregarded by both parties, they continuing to cohabit together the same as if no decree had been granted. They were remarried by ceremony on February 27, 1891.

Held, The relation existing between soldier and claimant, from May 6, 1887, and February 27, 1891, was illicit, and claimant was not the legal wife of soldier on June 27, 1890.

Assistant Secretary John M. Reynolds to the Commissioner of Pensions, May 29, 1897.

Claimant, on January 25, 1894, filed her application under the act of June 27, 1890, as the widow of Henry Munsell, late of Company D, Seventy-fifth Indiana Volunteers, claim being rejected on January 5, 1897, on the ground that claimant had no title, having married soldier subsequent to the passage of the act of June 27, 1890. An appeal is filed in this claim on March 27, 1897, which will be considered as alleging that rejection was contrary to law.

The issue raised in the appeal from your action is wholly one of law. The appeal from this section is also of considerable length, and is filled with arguments upon facts which are not found in the evidence, and even if such facts were in evidence, they would have but little bearing upon the question of law at issue, for they go wholly to what claimant considered to be the relation between the soldier and herself.

The evidence shows claimant and soldier to have been married on January 3, 1871, and that claimant procured a divorce a viniculo on May 6, 1887. It is apparent from claimant's testimony, corroborated in part by that of a brother-in-law of soldier, with whom they lived at date of divorce and after, that the decree of divorce was disregarded by both soldier and claimant, they continuing to live and cohabit together the same as if said decree had never been granted. On February 27, 1891, they were remarried, and a daughter was born to them on the 13th of the succeeding month. There is evidence showing that the brother-in-law considered and told them that their relationship after divorce was meretricious, and about January 1, 1891, insisted that they should either be married or cease to live together, and as a result, the remarriage was brought about.

It ought to need no argument to maintain that a divorce a viniculo breaks the marriage tie in toto, and puts both of the parties back into the same personal status as before marriage.

By absolute dissolution, the party or parties, or the survivor, reenters or reenter the ordinary status of unmarried persons. (Stewart on M. and D., sec. 168.)

The wording of the divorce decree, which is in evidence, bears out this truth, said decree reciting:

And it is therefore considered and adjudged by the court that the bonds of matrimony heretofore existing between the plaintiff and said defendant be dissolved, set aside, and held for naught, as fully and completely as if the same never existed.

The law made soldier and claimant man and wife, and the law, on claimant's petition and proof, sundered their matrimonial tie; their connection from the time the divorce was granted up to the time they remarried was illicit and illegal; the very fact that they again went through a ceremonial marriage tending strongly to show that they understood it so to be.

The question discussed in the appeal as to claimant's chastity, her faithful care of soldier's children, and her devotion to soldier between the dates of divorce and remarriage are not pertinent to the issue; neither is the question of the legitimacy of the child who was born within one month after remarriage necessary to be considered. None of these facts can do away with the effect of the divorce decree, and no act of the parties after the decree was granted can affect the validity of the decree. The cohabitation recited was meretricious, being nothing less than an illicit sexual connection between an unmarried male and an unmarried female, and after the divorce was granted it was not until the date of the remarriage that their cohabitation was lawful.

The actions appealed from are affirmed.

MARRIAGE AND DIVORCE—PRESUMPTIONS.

JENNETTE BURTON (WIDOW).

1. Claimant having established by the record that she was married to the sailor by a ceremony June 23, 1878, and lived with him from that time until he died, April 28, 1895, her title as widow can not be invalidated by a mere presumption of a previous common-law marriage of the sailor to another woman.
2. The burden of proof against the validity of the ceremonial marriage does not rest upon the widow, but upon the parties who attack the validity of such ceremonial marriage, and the presumption of law favors innocence of the latter marriage, until the contrary be proved.

(*Assistant Secretary John M. Reynolds to the Commissioner of Pensions, May 29, 1897.*)

At the time of his death, on April 28, 1895, the sailor, John, alias James Burton, U. S. S. *Galena*, was a pensioner under act of June 27, 1890 (certificate No. 8167), at $8 per month, for partial inability to earn a support by manual labor. On April 7, 1890, he filed a claim for pension under the general law, alleging inflammatory rheumatism and disease of lungs and kidneys, which claim was pending and unadjudicated at the time of his death, and finally rejected, September 26, 1896, because of his death and the inability of the alleged widow. Jennette

Burton, although aided by special examination, to establish her identity as the legal widow of the sailor.

The widow filed declaration May 14, 1895, for pension under the act of June 27, 1890, which claim was rejected on the same date and for the same reasons specified in the claim under the general law.

From this action appeal was received December 30, 1896, it being contended on behalf of appellant that the evidence establishes that claimant was the sailor's legal wife. This appeal was considered by the Department and, by opinion of date January 30, 1897, the rejection of the claim was affirmed, it being then held that the evidence was insufficient to establish that appellant is the lawful widow of the sailor. A motion for reconsideration of the said departmental action was overruled by opinion of date March 29, 1897, the previous ruling as to legal widowhood being practically reaffirmed.

A second motion for reconsideration was received May 1, 1897, accompanied by three affidavits bearing materially upon the question of legal widowhood, and which, it is insisted, are sufficient to establish, in connection with other evidence, that the appellant is the legal widow of the salior. The motion also suggests partiality and prejudice on the part of one of the examiners who took testimony in the case.

The sole issue to be determined in the present status of the case is whether, the law and all the evidence being duly considered, claimant has established that she is the legal widow of the sailor.

It is shown by the record that claimant was united in marriage to the sailor by ceremony on June 23, 1878, and that thenceforward the parties lived and cohabited together as husband and wife continuously to the date of his death, no issue having been born of said marriage.

The case was sent to the field for special examination to determine origin of the sailor's disabilities, and also concerning the legal widowhood of claimant.

George W. John testified that in 1871 sailor was living with a woman on Dearborn street, Chicago, Ill., but sailor said he was not married to her.

Samuel J. Bowles testified that he met sailor in 1872; that they worked together in a restaurant; that sailor was then living with a woman, and continued to live with her for about six months, when he was taken to the hospital, and never lived with her afterwards, and that the woman afterwards got married; that sailor introduced the woman to him one day as Mrs. Burton—they had a little girl about a year old with them. He did not know her name, nor know that they were married, but he has heard that the woman married another man after she lived with the sailor.

Claimant says sailor told her when he married her that he had lived with a woman in Chicago, but was never married to her; that while he was in the hospital the woman married another man; that about two years after her marriage to sailor she first met his daughter, a little girl, who was then living with a white family in Chicago; saw the girl again in 1892, when she was about 18 years old, but don't know what became of the girl; nor did sailor ever tell claimant who was the child's mother or whether she was the daughter of the woman he had lived with.

Dr. Lawther testified that the sailor introduced to him a young woman as his daughter, and spoke about her coming to live with him. He was then living with the claimant as husband and wife. Claimant says the girl never was with them but two nights.

A great number of witnesses, some relatives, testify that they never heard or knew of sailor living with any woman other than claimant, and that the acquaintance and relations were such that they would have known it if he had.

The rejection of the claims seem to have been based upon the theory that the burden of proof to rebut the presumption of a former marriage, or to show that a former marriage has been dissolved by divorce or death prior to remarriage, rests upon the party affirming the validity of the second marriage and claiming its benefits, and that as the evidence submitted is held to fail to satisfactorily rebut the presumption of such former marriage or to show that a former marriage has been dissolved by divorce or death prior to the ceremonial marriage between the sailor and claimant, she has not shown title as the legal widow of the sailor.

Upon careful review of all the testimony submitted, I am of the opinion that nothing is shown to establish or even warrant the presumption that the sailor ever entered upon a common-law marriage prior to his ceremonial marriage with claimant, or that if he maintained relations with any woman prior to said ceremonial marriage, which is suspected rather than proved, that such relations were other than those of mere concubinage.

It is laid down as the established principle of law that marriage at common law is a marriage of common right, and if permanently maintained all considerations of public policy, founded upon the preservation of public morality and decency and the protection of families, inspire the courts to uphold its legal validity wherever the statutes or lex loci do not expressly forbid. But such relation, to be recognized as legal, must be marriage in fact and intention, a relation entered into by mutual consent with matrimonial purposes, and, to be so proved, must be consistently maintained. Cohabitation and repute undoubtedly raise the presumption of such mutual consent and intention, indeed the presumption of actual marriage, and, if such cohabitation be permanent, no impediment existing, the presumption becomes conclusive. But the presumption is rebutted when the cohabitation ceases and the parties definitely separate, and especially so when other marriages with different persons are entered into with due legal ceremony.

The proposition that a ceremonial marriage can be deemed invalid on the mere presumption of a former common-law marriage can not be maintained as a principle of law. Such presumption is repugnant to the settled rule of law, that presumptions can not contradict facts nor overcome facts that have been proved. (See Lawson on Presumptive Evidence, 576; Gilpin v. Page, 18 Wall. 364; Whitaker v. Morrison, 1 Fla., 29; Van Buren v. Cockburn, 14 Barb., N. Y., 122; Neitz v. Carpenter, 21 Cal., 456.)

Legal presumptions must be based on facts, not on presumptions. (See Pennington v. Yell, 11 Ark., 212; Richmond v. Aiken, 25 Vt., 324; Tanner v. Hughes, 53 Pa. 289; McAleer v. McMurray, 58 Pa., 126.)

The proposition that a presumption of prior marriage at common law can invalidate a subsequent ceremonial marriage in due legal form, is also repugnant to the rule that the law always presumes in favor of the validity of marriage unless the contrary is clearly shown. After a marriage is proved every presumption favors its validity. (See Patterson v. Gaines, 6 How., 550; Powell v. Powell, 27 Miss., 783; Fleming v. People, 27 N. Y., 329; Ward v. Dulaney, 23 Miss., 410; Ferrie v. Pub. Adm., 4 Barb., N. Y., 28.)

The proposition that the burden of proof to rebut the presumption of a former marriage, or to establish that a former marriage has been dissolved by divorce or death prior to remarriage, rests upon the party affirming the validity of the second marriage and claiming its benefits, is not in harmony with but is repugnant to the general and accepted rule of law laid down in cognate cases.

Those objecting to the validity of a second marriage, on the ground that the husband has a former wife living, have the burden of proving that there has been no divorce. * * * Evidence that a man had a previous wife living at the time of his second marriage is not sufficient to prove the marriage invalid, since it will be presumed that the previous marriage had been dissolved by divorce. The presumption that a wife from whom her husband has not heard for sometime is still alive yields to the presumption in favor of the innocence of a second marriage by the husband. (Schmisseur v. Beatrice, 117 Ill., 210.)

When the presumption of innocence and morality conflicts with the presumption of life, the presumption of innocence will generally prevail. Innocence and validity of marriage will be presumed in the absence of evidence in rebuttal. (Johnson v. Johnson, 114 Ill., 611.)

After a lapse of time, less than nine years even, the law treats the presumption of the legality of the second marriage as overcoming that of the continuance of life, and requires that direct proof should be made that the former husband or wife was living at the date of the second marriage. (Harris v. Harris, 8 Ill., App., 57.)

The foregoing citations show, under the decisions in the State of Illinois, where the parties lived for more than a quarter of a century, and where the widow now lives, that a marriage is presumed to be legal, and that the burden of proof to the contrary rests upon those who assert its invalidity and not upon those who assert its validity and claim its benefits, and that the mere fact (if it be a fact) that there was a former husband or wife is not sufficient alone to establish such invalidity, but there must be direct proof that the former husband or wife was living and that neither had a divorce, since death or divorce must be presumed in the absence of proof to the contrary. The following additional authorities on the proposition are cited:

Marriage being proved by competent evidence, the law raises a presumption in favor of its legality upon which the party has a right to rely until its illegality is proved. Here proof of an earlier marriage, years before, does not destroy the legal presumption as to the legality of the second marriage, if duly proved, nor does it change the burden of proof. (Erwin *r.* English, 61 Conn., 502.)

The presumption of innocence—that she would not commit the crime of bigamy by marrying the defendant while Phillips was alive—rendered it obligatory on the court, in the absence of testimony to the contrary, to conclusively presume the death of Phillips and the validity of her marriage to the defendant. (Dixon *r.* The People, 18 Mich., 84.)

The second marriage, two years after desertion by first husband, is not to be presumed illegal and void, there being no evidence that the first husband was living at the date of the second marriage. Continuance of life can not be presumed against the presumption of the validity of the second marriage, notwithstanding there has not been seven years' absence. (Greensborough *v.* Underhill, 12 Vt., 604.)

The law presumes in favor of the validity of a marriage, and where one claims that a marriage is illegal, the burden is upon such person to show the illegality, the mere showing that one of the parties to the marriage has been married before not being sufficient to establish such illegality. (Boulden *r.* McIntyre, 119 Ind., 574.)

Where a woman marries for the second time after her husband has been absent for four years, and he is not heard of thereafter, the presumption of lawfulness and innocence applies, and she is presumed to be the second husband's lawful wife. (Kelly *r.* Drew, 94 Mass., 207.)

The burden is upon the libelant to show not only the alleged prior marriage of the respondent, but also that the parties to such marriage were living at the date of the second marriage. (Stymest *r.* Stymest, 4 Dist. Rep., Pa., 305.)

In this case (second marriage after four years' absence) the trial occurred nearly twenty years after Bushnell's disappearance, and on the assumption that he has not since been heard of the law presumes that he is dead, and that his death occurred before the appellant's marriage to Thomas Cooper. (Cooper *r.* Cooper, 86 Ind., 75.)

There was not any evidence that the first husband of Mrs. Kline was living; but if this had been established we think she was entitled to the benefit of the favorable presumption that the first marriage had been dissolved by divorce. (Klein *r.* Landman, 29 Mo., 259.)

Where a husband and wife separate, and the former lives and cohabits for years with a woman whom he claims and who is reputed to be his wife, the law presumes a divorce from the first wife, and the latter may legally marry again. (Blanchard *r.* Lambert, 43 Iowa, 228; Holmes *v.* Holmes, 6 La., 463.)

The State was required to satisfy the jury beyond a reasonable doubt, either by direct evidence or presumptions arising from facts proved, that the first wife was living at the time of the second marriage. There was no direct evidence. The presumption of continuance of life was neutralized by the presumption of the innocence of the parties. (Squire *r.* State, 46 Ind., 459.)

Where a woman married after her husband had been absent one year, and was not known to be living eleven years afterwards, the second marriage is held to be valid, the onus being upon defendants to show the contrary to the presumption of validity, by proving that the first husband was living at or shortly before the second marriage. (Wilkie *r.* Collins, 48 Miss., 496.)

Where the fact of the celebration of the marriage in due form of law is fully proved, there appears to be no difference as to its validity between civil and criminal consequences which may proceed from it. The question in both respects is, whether the parties were competent to contract a legal marriage, and when the presumption of law exists that the husband is dead by reason of his absence for five successive years unheard of, the disability of the other party is removed by the legal presumption, and she is competent to contract a new marriage, which is legal and valid to all intents and purposes until the presumption of death be removed by proof that the husband was alive at the time of its celebration. It only becomes illegal, either as to civil rights or criminal consequences, upon the production of such proof. (Gibson v. State, 38 Miss., 322.)

The fact that the deceased was living in 1844 with a woman believed to be his wife is no evidence that she was living on the 6th of December, 1848 (date of second marriage). This marriage having been solemnized according to the forms of law, every presumption must be indulged in favor of its validity. The statement of Rawles (made after his second marriage) that his first wife was then living in Georgia, while it could have been used as evidence against him in a proper proceeding in which he was directly interested or could be affected, can not be used to the prejudice of the petitioner. By assenting to the marriage he admitted that he could then legally enter into the alliance. The statement may have been true that his first wife was then living, and still it would not necessarily follow that she was in a legal sense his wife, as the parties may have been legally divorced. (Hull v. Rawles, 27 Miss., 471.)

The presumption of life within five years is not sufficient to establish the illegality of a second marriage of such person's wife within that time; for that would be to establish a crime by mere presumption of law; and especially ought the second marriage to be deemed legal when it is attacked after twenty years, and during all that time the party has not been heard from. (Spears v. Burton, 21 Miss., 546.)

Though the law presumes a continuance of life, yet when this presumption necessarily involves a presumption of crime, and comes in conflict with the presumption of innocence, the former, which is the weaker, yields to the latter, and the party affirming that an individual is not dead will be bound to prove it. (Lockhart v. White, 18 Tex., 102.)

When the presumption of law is in favor of the affirmative the opposite party has the burden of proving the contrary. (Am. and Eng. Enc. of Law, vol. 2, p. 654; 1 Hale, P. C., 26; 4 Black. Com., 23; Willett v. Com., 13 Bush. (Ky.), 230; State v. Guild, 5 Halst. (N. Y.), 192; Stage's Case, 5 C. H. R. (N. Y.), 120; Com. v. Mead, 10 Allen (Mass.), 398; Angel v. People, 96 Ill., 209; State v. Bostwick, 4 H. (Del.), 563; Com. v. French, Thatcher (Mass.), 163; Com. v. Green, 2 Pick. (Mass.), 380.)

The fact of marriage being proved, the presumptions of law are all in favor of good faith. To disprove good faith in such case there should be full proof to the contrary, and it must be irrefragable. (Gaines v. New Orleans, 6 Wall., 642.)

When a marriage is proved but alleged to be invalid by reason of a prior marriage the burden of proof is on those who assert its invalidity to establish the validity of the prior marriage. (Patterson v. Gaines, 6 How., 550.)

In the case of Augusta Watkins (6 P. D., 63), in overruling a motion for reconsideration of a previous departmental decision, my immediate predecessor used the following language:

It is only when all the circumstances favor a valid marriage and a mutual consent and desire for matrimonial relations that marriage will be inferred from the fact of cohabitation and repute; but where this cohabitation is interrupted and not continuous, and where the repute is not uniform but varied, the opposite presumption attaches that the cohabitation is meretricious and not matrimonial.

The length of time during which the cohabitation continued is a material circumstance in considering its weight in proof of marriage. (Bishop, sec. 437, Notes.)

The weight of evidence of marriage by cohabitation and repute depends upon the circumstances of the individual case, controlled by matter happening even after the cohabitation ceased, as by the cessation itself, the contracting of another marriage, and the like. (Bishop, sec. 513.)

Cohabitation and declaration of parties are prima facie evidence of marriage, but a long-continued separation after a short cohabitation would rebut such presumption. (Jackson v. Clear, 18 Johns. (N. Y.), 346.)

A marriage will not be presumed from a long period of cohabitation and repute and the birth of children where it is shown that after such period the parties separated and each contracted a formal marriage with another party. (Newton r. Southron. 7 N. Y., 130.)

The presumption of an actual marriage arising from the fact of cohabitation may be rebutted by parol proof of a subsequent permanent separation between the parties, without any apparent cause, and the marriage of one of them soon afterwards. (Weatherford r. Weatherford, 20 Ala., 548.)

The former marriage can not be established by reputation. (5 Ohio, 529.)

If a marriage in fact between A and B during the lifetime of C be proved all mere presumptions of a previous marriage of A with C, founded simply upon habit and repute, is at once overthrown, and it becomes incumbent upon the party alleging such previous marriage to establish it as an actual fact by distinct proof. (Jones r. Jones, 48 Md., 397.)

In the case at bar the evidence shows inferentially rather than positively that the sailor lived for a short period with some woman whose identity is unknown, and concerning whose previous history or subsequent movements nothing is either known or proved except that, by the same character and chain of testimony, she married somebody after deserting the sailor upon his isolation in a hospital.

Accepting, however, as fully proved that the sailor did so cohabit with this mysterious woman, and that there appeared on the scene a girl whom the sailor stated was his child, it is equally conclusively shown that neither this woman nor the child ever claimed the sailor as husband or father; that the woman never asserted that she was the common-law wife of the sailor, or that they occupied any relations toward each other save that of the meretricious one of concubinage. Conceding also that this girl was the offspring of the sailor, not a particle of evidence is adduced showing or tending to show that this mysterious woman was its mother or that the offspring was the result of the relations which briefly existed between her and the sailor. It can not be successfully contended that the presence of this child and the acknowledgment of its paternity by the sailor thereby establishes the validity of a common-law marriage with its mother, whoever that mother may have been, and non constat that this woman, or any other woman known to the history of the case, was its mother.

The premises considered, I am of the opinion that neither the facts nor the law justify the holding that claimant has failed to establish her title as the legal widow of the sailor because of a presumed or suspected common-law marriage arising from cohabitation for a short period with another woman prior to claimant's ceremonial marriage to the sailor. On the contrary, the presumption of law favors the validity of the ceremonial marriage, and the burden of proof does not rest upon claimant to show that the sailor was not previously married or contracted a common-law marriage with the woman with whom he had previously cohabited, or any other person.

It may be here appropriately remarked that there is no contest between alleged widows in the claims for pension by reason of the death of the sailor, but even if there were, the burden would rest upon the woman claiming as widow by common-law marriage to prove its validity, and seeking thereby to reap its benefits, or upon those who attacked the validity of the ceremonial marriage, the presumption of law being in favor of the latter marriage.

For these reasons the motion for reconsideration is granted, the previous departmental decisions recalled, and the action of your Bureau, rejecting the claim under the general law and the widow's claim under the act of June 27, 1890, for the reasons stated, is reversed, and you will please direct that the claim be readjudicated in accordance with this opinion.

––––

ATTORNEYSHIP–POWER OF ATTORNEY.

JAMES M. MULHOLLAN (CLAIMANT).

W. H. MUSSEE (ATTORNEY).

A valid power of attorney filed in the Bureau at a time when no claim is pending in behalf of the person granting the same, and to which it may be applicable, does not entitle an attorney therein named to recognition as against another who subsequently is duly authorized by the same person to prosecute a claim for pension and has filed one in his behalf, to which both powers of attorney are applicable.

Assistant Secretary John M. Reynolds to the Commissioner of Pensions, June 15, 1896.

In your communication of February 29, 1896, in the claim (No. 1115478) of James L. Mulhollan, late of Company C, Two hundred and tenth Pennsylvania Volunteers, the question submitted for the opinion of this Department is in effect as follows: Whether a valid power of attorney filed in the Bureau at a time when no claim is pending in behalf of the person granting the same, and to which it may be applicable, entitles an attorney therein named to recognition as against another who subsequently is duly authorized by the same person to prosecute a claim for pension and has filed one in his behalf, to which both powers of attorney are applicable.

An agent who is authorized to prosecute a claim for pension is not clothed with any greater authority than is an attorney at law who is engaged to commence judicial proceedings, nor has the Bureau any more power to enforce a specific contract between a claimant and his agent for the prosecution of a pension claim than a court has to enforce a contract between a client and his attorney for the prosecution of judicial proceedings in case the first party named in either instance refuse to carry out his contract.

Under the conditions involved in the question to be decided, the first power of attorney was inoperative when filed. Subsequently the claimant refused to carry out the terms of his contract with the first attorney and entered into a new and like agreement with the second attorney, who pursuant thereto filed a valid declaration.

In judicial proceedings a court would, under similar circumstances, recognize the attorney who first entered them. I fail to perceive any reason why a different rule should obtain in the Bureau, nor why the attorney who first filed a valid declaration should not be recognized so long as he observed the rules of practice. The first attorney did not acquire title to recognition by filing a power of attorney, and therefore the rules of practice governing the question of recognition are not applicable. He would not have any more rights in the claim than would an attorney in judicial proceedings in the instance mentioned.

It appears that in the case at bar the facts are as follows: On September 20, 1895, a declaration under the act of June 27, 1890, in behalf of Mr. Mulhollan (the claimant) was filed by W. H. Mussee, which contained a power of attorney in his favor. On January 17, 1896, in behalf of the claimant, Matt Savage filed another declaration for pension under the same law, which contained a power of attorney to him. Assuming that the first declaration filed was invalid, it is held that the power of attorney to Mr. Mussee would not become operative unless Mr. Savage's attorneyship had ceased.

FEE—PRACTICE—MOTIONS FOR RECONSIDERATION.

JAMES F. RUSLING (ATTORNEY).
HENRY C. WILLIAMS (CLAIMANT).

Under rule 9, Rules of Practice before the Secretary of the Interior, a second motion for reconsideration of a decision adverse to a fee or for recognition will not be considered, and the decisions in this case having been adhered to on a former motion to reconsider, this motion is dismissed.

Assistant Secretary Webster Davis to the Commissioner of Pensions June 11, 1897.

James F. Rusling of Trenton, N. J., April 27, 1897, filed a second motion for reconsidering the decision of the Department of November 19, 1896, in his claim for recognition in the case under the act of June 27, 1890, of Henry C. Williams, late of Company H, Fourth New Jersey Infantry (27 P. L. Bk., 259).

A motion for reconsideration was overruled February 27, 1897. In overruling said motion the Department considered at length the merits of the case, and all material matter germane to the issue seems to have received attention.

Rule 9 of the Rules of Practice in Appeals before the Secretary of the Interior provides that—

From and after September 1, 1893, more than one motion for reconsideration of a decision adverse to a claim for a fee *   *   * or for recognition will not be entertained by the Department of the Interior.

Under the foregoing this motion for reconsideration is dismissed.

DECLARATIONS—AMENDMENTS.

MINORS OF LEVI ROBINS.

A declaration containing all of the necessary allegations for minor's pension under the act of June 27, 1890, except it fails to state that it was filed under said act, an amendatory affidavit having been filed in which it is stated that the claim was intended to be filed under said act, is a valid declaration.

Assistant Secretary Webster Davis to the Commissioner of Pensions, June 12, 1897.

Levi Robins, late of Company D, One hundred and fifteenth Ohio Infantry, was a pensioner under the act of June 27, 1890. He died April 17, 1894, leaving no widow, but two minor children survived him. Chester E. Haskell, as guardian of these children, filed an application for pension, April 29, 1895, which was treated by the Bureau as a claim under the general laws, and calls were made for the necessary evidence to establish it, including evidence of the origin in service and continuance of soldier's fatal disease. In response to such calls claimant filed, January 24, 1896, an affidavit in which he stated—

that he never intended to file a claim under the general laws; that his intention was to file under the act of June 27, 1890; that he did not know of any disability that soldier contracted in the Army which led to his death; that he was informed by his attorney, at the time of filing, of the difference between the two laws, and he believed he did file a claim under the act of June 27, 1890.

Claimant was then informed by the Bureau that his application could not be regarded or accepted as a claim under said act of June 27, 1890, as it did not contain the necessary allegations, but it was essentially a claim under the general laws. He filed, thereupon, another application, April 4, 1896, containing the allegation that it was made under the act of June 27, 1890. Final action was taken March 29, 1897, upon both claims, the first being rejected on the ground that soldier's death was not shown to be due to his military service, while the other was admitted, pension being allowed on account of one of the children, he only being 16 years of age when this claim was filed.

From this action an appeal was filed April 17, 1897, by J. R. H. King, attorney, who contends that the first application, filed April 29, 1895, was intended to be under the act of June 27, 1890, that it contained all necessary allegations: that its rejection was on a technicality, and the same should be set aside, and pension allowed from the date of filing that application.

From a careful examination of the papers in this case, in the light of former decisions bearing on the point at issue, I am of the opinion that there is force in the contention of this appeal relating to the sufficiency of the first application, and the date of commencement of the pension. In the decision of June 17, 1896, in the case of James J. Durkee (8 P. D., 152), the essential averments in an invalid claim under the act of June 27, 1890, were set out, and in the decision of September 11, 1896, in the case of Susan M. Minor (8 P. D., 263), were pointed out the allegations necessary to a widow's claim under said act. And while in the Durkee decision it was held that one of the essentials of title was an averment that the claim was made under the act of June 27, 1890, in the other case it was stated that it was not, however, intended by said first paragraph in the Durkee case that it was absolutely necessary to specifically designate the act under which the claim was filed by mentioning the date of the same, but that facts must be stated which bring the case within the statute, as was held in the case of Ellen Lyons (6 P. D., 151).

This decision in the Susan M. Minor case in effect reaffirmed that in the Ellen Lyons case, and in the latter this was the holding:

> A declaration for pension under the act of June 27, 1890, need not specify the law under which the same is filed. If it alleges the fact required by the statute to be proved it is sufficient.

This holding was on the principle that it is not necessary to plead a general law so long as the facts which bring a case within the scope and provisions of that law are set out and made the basis of a claim or action at law.

In the claim under consideration, the first declaration, which is not on a printed form, but is written out, probably by the attorney, all the allegations necessary to a minor's claim under the act of June 27, 1890, are made, except that it is nowhere stated therein that the claim is made under said act. On the other hand, it fails to contain one allegation that usually distinguishes a claim under the general law, viz. that the soldier died of disability contracted in the service and line of duty. It would seem, therefore, that it may as well be urged that this latter omission prevents the declaration being placed in the category of a claim under the general law as that the failure to state the law under which it was filed would debar it from being accepted as a claim under act of June 27, 1890.

In this case, then, the issue resolves itself into a mere matter of uncertainty as to which law the first declaration refers to. With a slight amendment it might very well be made to apply to either the old or new law, and applying the legal maxim, id certum est quod certum reddi potest, there seems to be no good reason why the explanation made by claimant in his affidavit before referred to should not be accepted as an amendment to his declaration and determine the law under which it was his purpose to claim pension. It is a well-settled principle that amendments are allowable when they are germane to the averments originally made and do not change the character of the claim. It is hardly necessary to cite the numerous decisions which sustain this principle. One only, which is peculiarly applicable to the point stated and to this case, is sufficient to be referred to, and is that of the appeal of Oliver P. Pierce (7 P. D., 91).

In the view and for the reasons here stated, it is therefore held that the first declaration of claimant and his amendatory affidavit are sufficient, to constitute a valid claim for pension under the act of June 27, 1890, and the pension allowed should commence from the date of filing that declaration. The action of Bureau in so far as it was in conflict with this holding is reversed, and the papers are returned for readjudication of the claim in accordance with this decision.

DECLARATIONS—ACT JUNE 27, 1890.

JUDITH S. LUCKINGBEAL (WIDOW).

A declaration for widow's pension under the act of June 27, 1890, alleging all the essential elements of title except the date of her husband's discharge (or duration of his service), and that his discharge was honorable, but stating that he was a pensioner, and giving the number of his pension certificate, is a good and sufficient application under said act.

Assistant Secretary Webster Davis to the Commissioner of Pensions June 23, 1897.

It appears that this appellant, on January 22, 1897, filed a declaration stating, among other things, that she desired to obtain the pension provided for widows by the act of Congress approved June 27, 1890; that she was the widow of Nathan Luckingbeal, who enlisted on the 7th day of October, 1862, in Company K, Second Regiment Ohio Cavalry, for service in the war of the rebellion, and also served in Company A, Eleventh Ohio Infantry, and who died on the 2d day of January, 1897; that she was married to him on November 19, 1840; that the said soldier was pensioned at $25 per month under certificate No. 437575; and that she was without other means of support than her daily labor. With this declaration she filed the soldier's pension certificate and some other papers, the contents of which are not stated.

By a communication from your Bureau dated February 6, 1897, she was notified that said declaration would not be accepted to confer any rights upon her, for the reason that it did not contain the following essential allegations, namely: That the soldier served ninety days during the war of the rebellion and was honorably discharged.

From that action an appeal was taken June 10, 1897, the contention being that as the soldier was a pensioner it was not necessary that his widow should allege the duration or period of his service or the character of his discharge, such facts being shown by the evidence on file in his case.

A declaration, being the claimant's formal statement of the grounds on which his or her claim is based, should allege facts which, if proved, would establish title to the pension claimed. It is a general and accepted rule, however, that claimants for pension shall not be held to a strict compliance with the rules of technical pleading so long as the general conditions prescribed by law are fulfilled and there is a substantial compliance with the regulations. Accordingly, it was held by Assistant Secretary Bussey, in the case of Ellen Lyons (6 P. D., 151), that the failure of the applicant to allege that she was without other means of support than her daily labor, or that her claim was made under the act of June 27, 1890, did not invalidate her declaration, the facts alleged being sufficient to give notice that she desired to claim under said act. Also, it was held by Assistant Secretary Reynolds, in the case of Israel Snyder (8 P. D., 265), that the omission of the applicant to state that he served ninety days during the war of the rebellion, he having stated the dates of his enlistment and discharge, was not a fatal defect. And in the case of Maria Blew (8 P. D., —) a declaration under section 3 of the act of June 27, 1890, which failed to state that the soldier's discharge from service was honorable was accepted as valid.

In the case now under consideration, while the applicant did not state the date of her husband's discharge, or that he served ninety days and was honorably discharged, she referred to his claim for invalid pension, in which all necessary information on those points was to be found. Her declaration, therefore, contained every allegation that was essential to enable your Bureau to determine promptly whether she had status as an applicant under the act of June 27, 1890, or not. I can not conceive of any good purpose to be subserved by requiring applicants to state, specifically, facts which have been already established by documentary evidence on file in your Bureau. To throw out a declaration or application for omitting to state such facts is to deprive the applicant of pension upon a mere technicality such as should have no place in the execution of the pension laws.

I do not overlook the holding of the Department in the case of Susan M. Minor (8 P. D., 263), relative to the essentials of a valid declaration for widow's pension under the act of June 27, 1890, or the earlier decision in the case of James J. Durkee (8 P. D., 152), in regard to declarations generally under said act. It will be observed that the holding in those cases was not that the essentials of title should be specifically alleged in every application, but that they should be shown. I am of the opinion that a declaration which shows that the information or data necessary to the consideration of the claim is of record in the Pension Bureau complies, substantially, with such holding. In so far, however, as the views herein expressed may be deemed to conflict with any former ruling or decision of the Department, such ruling or decision will be considered by you as to that extent modified. The appellant's declaration, filed January 22, 1897, should be treated as a valid application for pension under section 3 of the act of June 27, 1890.

SERVICE—MEXICAN WAR.

ELIZABETH YOUNG (WIDOW).

The period of time included in the term "en route thereto" in the act of January 29, 1887, commences at the date of soldier's enlistment, when his service in the war with Mexico conforms in other respects with the requirements of the terms of said act, and where the soldier is not responsible or chargeable with delay in finally reaching Mexico, the coasts or frontier thereof.

Assistant Secretary Webster Davis to the Commissioner of Pensions, June 26, 1897.

Claimant, as the widow of William F. Young, late of Company H, Fourth Illinois Volunteers, Mexican war, on March 15, 1897, appealed from the action of your Bureau of December 8, 1896, rejecting her widow's claim No. 13424, filed June 27, 1896, under the act of January 29, 1887, on the ground that soldier did not render sixty days' service in Mexico, on the coasts or frontier thereof, or en route thereto.

Claimant takes issue with your Bureau as to the correctness of said conclusion and contends that her husband enlisted in said war June 20, 1846, and served till August 31, 1846, when he was honorably discharged; that he was allowed a pension under said act, which pension was subsequently increased under the act of January 5, 1893, from $8 to $12 per month; that he died June 19, 1896, and she was allowed and paid his accrued pension as his widow, and it is urged that after these three decisions in favor of her husband the Government should, in the absence of any new evidence, be estopped to deny the fact that her husband did not serve sixty days as required by said act.

This appeal was considered by Assistant Secretary John M. Reynolds May 1, 1897, and returned to your Bureau for a report stating the grounds upon which the action appealed from was based and the reason for the allowance of the soldier's claim, and also requesting that you quote the evidence upon which your Bureau relied to establish the fact that soldier did not serve sixty days as required by the act of January 29, 1887. On May 25, 1897, your Bureau reported as follows:

The records of the War Department show that the soldier, William F. Young, served from June 2 to August 31, 1846, a period of seventy-three days, a portion of which was rendered en route to and on the frontier of Mexico, and his claim was allowed as was then the practice of the Bureau, based upon the ruling of the Commissioner of Pensions of May 18, 1887, as follows:

"That where troop were en route thereto, or in Mexico or the borders thereof, this fact, in connection with the fact that they were duly enlisted and honorably discharged and were sixty days in the service, or in actual battle, and have reached the stated age (62), shall be sufficient to entitle the survivors or their widows to the benefit of the act."

That ruling was revoked by a decision of the honorable Secretary of the Interior to the effect that to give title under the act the soldier must have served sixty days in Mexico, on the coasts or frontier thereof or en route thereto, and this decision has been affirmed by several subsequent decisions. (See vol. 2, Pension Decisions, p. 180, case of R. W. P. Muse, July 23, 1888; vol. 2, P. D., p. 248, case of Anne Quinn, October 20, 1888; vol. 2, P. D., p. 356, case of B. J. French, February 18, 1889; vol. 7,

P. D., p. 54, case of J. Shattuck, November 22, 1893; vol. 7, P. D., p. 169, case of George Ackenback, July 20, 1893, and decision No. 56 of March 18, 1896 (8 P. D., 106), in case of Julia B. Hollywood).

In the claim of the widow of the soldier, William F. Young, the records show that said soldier left Jefferson Barracks, Mo., July 23, 1846, en route to Mexico, and was discharged at Camp Patterson, Texas, August 31, 1846. It appears, therefore, that the soldier served but forty days from the time he was en route to Mexico, and his widow's claim was rejected under the decisions referred to which govern the present practice of the Bureau.

. I am of the opinion that your Bureau is in error in stating that the ruling of the Commissioner of Pensions of May 18, 1887, as above quoted, has ever been revoked by the Secretary of the Interior, either in terms or by implication. I find nothing in the cases cited by your Bureau to sustain your position; on the contrary, said decision appears to be in perfect harmony with said ruling, assuming that the word "service" in said order referred to the "service" named in the act, viz, sixty days' service "in Mexico, on the coasts or frontier thereof or en route thereto."

In the case of Muse (2 P. D., 180), the claimant was only in the service fifty-one days, allowing for time in going and returning from his rendez- vous near Cincinnati, Ohio, and was discharged because the State's quota was filled. He therefore failed to show sixty days' service.

In the Ackenback case (ibid., 169), in which the former cases were cited and approved, the soldier's alleged en route service consisted in his being ordered from Philadelphia, Pa , to Fort Gibson, Ind. T., and . he was held not to be en route to Mexico or the coasts or frontier thereof.

In the Hollywood case (8 P. D., 106), soldier after his enlistment was forwarded as a recruit to the Sixth United States Infantry, at Fort Gibson, Ind. T., at which post he continued to serve until discharged, and his service was very properly held not to have been in Mexico, or on the coasts or frontier thereof.

In none of these cases is the order of the Commissioner of Pensions, quoted by you in said report, referred to either in terms or inferentially.

Coming now to the case under consideration, there appears to be no dispute as to the facts. Soldier enlisted in an Illinois regiment for the war with Mexico, June 20, 1846. He was mustered in at Jefferson Barracks, Mo., on the same day. He was forwarded to the seat of war, and was discharged at Camp Patterson, near Barita, Tex., on account of disability August 31, 1846. He was paid from June 20, 1846, to August 31, 1846, and the final payment is dated at the Rio Grande Headquarters of the Fourth Illinois Infantry, and signed by William C. McReynolds, lieutenant-colonel. The records show that the regiment left Jefferson Barracks in two detachments July 23, 1846, for Point Isabella, Tex., via New Orleans; arrived at New Orleans on July 29, and embarked for Brazos Santiago on July 31, and arrived at that station with nine companies on August 10, 1846. Marched for Camp Patterson, near Barita, Tex., followed by one company, completing the command, on the 18th of August, 1846. Camp Patterson therefore was but a few miles from the battlefield of Palo Alto, Brownsville, and Matamoras, Mexico. It is an historic fact that the Fourth Illinois Regiment, commanded by Col. E. D. Baker, who was subsequently killed at Balls Bluff, October 21, 1861, in the war of the rebellion, was at Matamoras, Mexico, under command of General Patterson in 1846 (Furber's Twelve Month Volunteers, pp. 238, 239), and that this regiment served in the war with Mexico.

Claimant's husband, the soldier, is shown to have served with his command, and his service therefore comes within the requirements of said act, and he is deemed to have been en route from date of enlistment.

As held in the recent case of widow of David M. Geiger, Captain Dunlap's Independent Company Illinois Mounted Volunteers, Certificate No. 13364, decided by Secretary Reynolds, May 29, 1897—

Soldier enlisted as a recruit in a company already in service in the war with Mexico, and he is deemed to be en route to Mexico from date of enlistment to the date of joining the company in Mexico.

In the Geiger case, as in this, the soldier had established his claim to sixty days' service in and en route to Mexico. He has applied for, and, after a special examination, been allowed an increase under the act of January 5, 1893. After his death his widow had applied for and been allowed and paid his accrued pension, yet, with no new evidence on the subject of his Mexican war service, his widow was denied a pension on the ground that her husband, the soldier, had not served sixty days in Mexico, or on the coasts or frontier thereof or en route thereto. That decision was reached on the ground that he was not en route from date of enlistment, but from date of muster in. In that case, as in this, the soldier's enlistment was in a volunteer service for the war with Mexico and not in the Regular Army. In that case, as in this, the companies in which the men enlisted served in Mexico in the war with that country, and their point of destination at date of enlistment was Mexico. In such cases I am of the opinion that the period of time included in the term "en route thereto" in the act of January 29, 1887, commences at the date of soldier's enlistment, when his service in the war with Mexico conforms in other respects with the requirements of the terms of said act, and where the soldier is not responsible or chargeable with delay in finally reaching Mexico, the coasts or frontier thereof. In the case of Lyon (7 P. D., 215), soldier was delayed by sickness, yet he was held to be en route, and his widow was pensioned.

I am of the opinion that the reason given by your Bureau for rejecting the widow's claim is not sustained, and that the evidence in the case of soldier's claim for pension fairly establishes the fact that he served over sixty days on the coast and frontier of Mexico and en route thereto, in the war with that country, within the meaning of the act of January 29, 1887, and the action appealed from is accordingly reversed.

DISABILITY—EVIDENCE, SUFFICIENCY OF.

CHARLES ENGLEMAN.

When the evidence presented by a claimant is sufficient to satisfy the mind of a candid and impartial person that a pensionable disability from some obscure cause exists, although no physical signs of it can be discovered by the examining surgeons, pension should be allowed at a rate proportionate to the degree of disability proved.

Assistant Secretary Webster Davis to the Commissioner of Pensions, June 29, 1897.

Claimant on March 27, 1897, appealed from the actions of your Bureau of April 26, 1884, June 6, 1887, and August 1, 1889, rejecting his old-law claim (Certificate No. 831540), Original No. 494676, filed September 6, 1883, on the ground of no ratable degree of disability shown from rheumatism since date of filing claim.

The contention is that the testimony of Dr. Louis Busse, Dr. Charles H. Gundlach, Dr. Edward Boemer, Dr. H. E. Ahlbrandt, Dr. P. J. Lungenfelder, and Dr. G. W. Vogt shows clearly that the claimant had been during that period under treatment for alleged rheumatism, and that he was disabled in consequence of the same from September 6, 1883.

It appears from the testimony of these witnesses and others that claimant has, prior to date of filing his claim and since, been a sufferer from rheumatism and received medical treatment therefor; that he suffered from said rheumatism in 1864, and continuously since date of discharge, on account of disability, to date from February 28, 1862. The testimony shows that he was treated for rheumatism in service, and the records of the War Department show treatment from November 28, 1861, to January 4, 1862, for rheumatism and from January 5 to 7, 1862, for tonsilitis and sore throat. He is a school-teacher and a man of good habits.

The case was considered on appeal May 8, 1897, and in view of the foregoing evidence was returned for a further report of the medical referee, who, on June 15, 1897, reported as follows:

The appellant filed a claim for pension under the general law September 6, 1883, alleging disability as a result of rheumatism. Claim was rejected April 26, 1884, June 6, 1887, and August 1, 1889, based on four certificates of medical examination, which failed to show any disability from the alleged cause. From these adverse actions an appeal is filed.

In response to a request from your division as to whether the rejections were proper an opinion was expressed, in a slip from this division April 16, 1897, in effect that inasmuch as the certificates of medical examination had failed to show a ratable degree of disability from rheumatism the action of rejection was proper.

The case is returned by the Honorable Assistant Secretary for a further report of the medical referee and his opinion whether in view of the record evidence of rheumatism in service and the medical evidence of continuance rheumatism in a pensionable degree may not exist without manifesting any objective signs.

While the certificates of examination do not describe any objective signs of rheumatism the medical testimony shows that the claimant has suffered since filing claim from repeated attacks of rheumatism.

In view of the nature of the disease, which does not always manifest itself by organic changes, a medical examination would not reveal its exisence.

In accordance with the opinion expressed by the Department, published in the Douglass case, Digest 1885, page 202, this claim is admissible, if there be no legal objection.

It was held by Secretary Teller in the case of John Douglass (14 P. D. (o. s.), 385; Digest of 1897, 230) that when the evidence presented by a claimant is sufficient to satisfy the mind of a candid and impartial person that a pensionable disability from some obscure cause (such as rheumatism, neuralgia, myalgia, or angina pectoris) exists, although no physical signs of it can be discovered by the examining surgeons, pension should be allowed at a rate proportionate to the degree of disability proved. In harmony with said decision I am of the opinion that the actions appealed from should be reversed, and it is accordingly so ordered, and the papers in the case are herewith returned for further action in accordance with this decision.

REDUCTION—NOTICE—PRACTICE.

JOHN S. HUBLEY.

An unsworn statement by a claimant that he never received notice to appear before a board of surgeons in a reduction case is not sufficient to warrant a reversal of the action of the Commissioner of Pensions reducing the rate of his pension; but good practice demands that a record of such notices be kept in the future, and when a pensioner claims that he was not notified, he should be advised at once to file a sworn statement of the fact, and corroborative proof, when the issue thus raised will be passed upon.

Assistant Secretary Webster Davis to the Commissioner of Pensions, June 21, 1897.

Claimant was pensioned under the act of June 27, 1890, at $12 per month, for injury to both hands and naso-pharyngeal catarrh. He was reduced to $8 per month, said reduction dating from June 4, 1895. He filed an appeal on December 23, 1896, alleging that your action of reduction was error, basing said contention upon the departmental decision in the case of William L. Hulse (8 P. D., 349), in which it was held that action of reduction was error when a medical examination had not been had for more than three years.

The files in the case disclose the following: He was medically examined on May 6, 1891, and was pensioned as recited at $12 per month, commencing August 11, 1890. On February 16, 1894, the medical referee approved the claim for reduction from $12 to $8 per month. An indorsement on the jacket shows the following: "Oct. 12/94, Ex. ord. Bd. Portsmouth, N. H." A slip in the files, which is a memorandum in lead pencil, and bears no date or signature, states: "Med. exam. ordered Oct. 12, 1894. Failed to appear."

On March 7, 1894, he was notified of intention to reduce, and he filed, not later than March 19, 1894, affidavits from three acquaintances, stating, among other things, that claimant was so disabled, and had been for some length of time, that he required aid in putting on and taking off his coat. On July 26, 1895, after having received his reissue certificate, he filed with the Commissioner of Pensions a letter stating that he had never received any notice to be reexamined, and asked to be sent before a board of surgeons, stating also that he would abide by the results of that examination. No attention appears to have been paid to this request, but on January 11, 1897, twelve days after the within appeal was forwarded to you by the Secretary, you ordered a medical examination to be had, which took place on January 27, 1897. There can be no question but that there is a fair presumption in this case that claimant was actually notified to appear, but the presumption is not conclusive by any means. There is no record made that he was so notified, and it seems (allowing his statement that he never received the notification to be true) that he made his complaint to you promptly after knowledge that his rate had been reduced.

The main issue involved is identical with the one in the Hulse appeal, but there is a new question in the within appeal, as to what steps should be taken when the Pension Bureau assumes that a claimant was notified to appear for examination, and the claimant denies receipt of notification, and promptly so advises the Commissioner of Pensions. I am of the opinion that claimant's simple statement that he did not receive notification would not be sufficient to put the question at issue; but I conceive it to have been your duty to at once advise claimant that he should make such contention under oath, and in the absence of any fact or presumption that his affidavit was not true, his request for another medical examination should be allowed. It does not appear to have been your practice to keep a copy of such notification, and I can not concede that the indorsement upon the jacket, hereinbefore referred to, can by any construction be deemed to be a record of the fact that claimant was notified to appear before the board of surgeons.

I can find no indication whatever in the files that claimant was notified to appear, and I deem it against good practice on your part that you did not, in some way, take notice of the fact that he advised you promptly, when actual knowledge reached him, that he had never received such notice; but such fact is not, however, sufficient to warrant a reversal of your action. Issues of this kind can not be raised upon mere statements, not only unsworn to but unaccompanied by corroborative proof, when the nature of the case is such that corroborative proof can be obtained.

I note that no medical evidence was filed by claimant in answer to your notice of intended reduction, but inasmuch as you state that you ordered a medical examination, it is evident that you deemed the evidence filed to be sufficient to warrant a medical examination previous to reduction.

If claimant had sworn to his contention, he would have raised a direct issue, but by reason of the fact that claimant did not swear to his statement, no issue was raised, and your action will be sustained, upon the well-founded rule that officials of the Government are presumed to have done their whole duty, and that such presumption can not be overthrown by a mere allegation on the part of claimant.

Inasmuch, however, as an important principle is involved in this case, it is suggested that a record of such notices be kept; and in like cases and contentions claimants should be at once notified to file sworn statements and corroborative proof, when the nature of the case admits of such proof, and when the direct issue is raised that said issue be decided by you and claimant notified of such decision. Such procedure is considered necessary for the reason that the evidence adduced at medical examinations is an important factor in cases of reduction, and it is evident that the notice to the board of surgeons requiring them to examine a claimant is seldom of avail if claimant is not notified to appear before said board.

The action appealed from is affirmed.

NOTICE—DROPPING FROM THE ROLLS.

SPENCER PAYNE

As the evidence tends to show that claimant failed to receive notice of the proposed dropping from the rolls and to appear for a medical examination, the action dropping his name from the rolls is reversed and the case remanded for further adjudication, that claimant may have an opportunity to file rebutting evidence and to be examined.

Assistant Secretary Webster Davis to the Commissioner of Pensions. June 29, 1897.

December 17, 1889, appellant filed a declaration for pension under the general law, alleging disability from gunshot wound of left side of head, causing severe pains in his head and dizziness when stooping, defective hearing, and impaired vision.

Under said claim he was examined May 21, 1890, the examining board recommending the rate of two-eighteenths for wound of head, ten-thirtieths for impaired hearing, and total for loss of sight of left eye.

There does not appear to have been any evidence filed in support of said claim, and no further action was taken therein.

June 22, 1891, he filed a claim under the act of June 27, 1890, on account of gunshot wound of head, disease of eyes, and general debility.

This claim was allowed in January, 1892, without another medical examination, at the rate of $12 per month.

Claimant's name was dropped from the roll in September, 1895, after due notice, on the ground that he was not ratably disabled under act of June 27, 1890.

September 28, 1895, he applied to your Bureau for a reconsideration of the action taken, stating that as he was away from home, he did not receive the notice for dropping or the order for a medical examination, and knew nothing of said proposed action until September 20, when he was informed his pension had been dropped.

No change of action was deemed warranted by the Bureau. Accordingly, an appeal was filed December 17, 1896, in which he asserted that the notice did not come into his hands, as he was away from home and was not apprised of it in time to take steps in defense of his rights, and that he was not fully aware of the fact that such a notice had been sent until he received notice of the discontinuance of his pension.

The action taken was affirmed on appeal February 20, 1897.

A motion for reconsideration was filed June 7, 1897.

Upon a review of the case, it was found that on June 6, 1895, the usual notice for dropping was sent to claimant; that on July 9, 1895, the registry return receipt was returned to your Bureau, signed Spencer Payne.

It also appears that on December 1, 1894, claimant was ordered to appear before a board of examining surgeons at Salisbury, Mo. He failed to appear for medical examination, and no evidence was filed in rebuttal.

He contends, first, that he did not receive said order for medical examination; that if such order was sent, some other Spencer Payne must have received it, and failed to deliver it to him.

Secondly. He did not sign the receipt for the registered notice, as he was away from home, and said letter or notice was not brought to his notice until September, 1895, as shown by his daughter's affidavit.

Thirdly. He is and always has been ready to go before any board of medical examiners, and that the fact that he is disabled will appear upon such an examination.

Adora Payne, claimant's daughter, swears that in September, 1895, her father was in St. Louis, visiting a sick son; that the postmaster gave her an order for her father to sign for a registered letter; that she sent the order to St. Louis for him to sign, which he signed and returned to her. She took the same to the postmaster and got the registered letter, and in the belief that her father would return soon she placed the letter in a bureau drawer, but after her father returned it could not be found. She also stated positively that she signed the receipt for the registered letter while he was in St. Louis. She also stated there were then three Spencer Paynes living in the town where they resided.

In comparing the signature in the registry return receipt with claimant's signatures, it is very evident it was not signed by him, and the resemblance to his daughter's own signature is so apparent, that it may safely be concluded that she signed her father's name to the receipt as she has stated.

If these statements be true, claimant received no notice of dropping and no order to appear for medical examination, and it naturally follows he filed no evidence in rebuttal.

It will be observed that claimant received no medical examination after his original claim was filed under the act of June 27, 1890.

Apparently the claim was originally allowed under a medical examination previously had pending adjudication of the claim filed December 17, 1889, under the general law, which it was conceded showed a pensionable degree of disability. Upon revision, it was subsequently held he was not ratably disabled, without any additional evidence or a medical examination.

In view of these conditions, which seem to be largely the result of unfortunate circumstances, it is but just to claimant that the action of dropping claimant's name from the pension rolls be reconsidered, and that claimant be directed to appear for a medical examination and be given an opportunity to file evidence in rebuttal showing the degree of disability. Should it be found that he is ratably disabled from the causes on account of which he was pensioned, and that such a degree of disability existed when his name was dropped from the roll, the action of dropping should be rescinded and his name restored to the rolls from said date.

The action taken is therefore reversed, and the case is returned for reconsideration accordingly.

———

LINE OF DUTY—ACCIDENTAL DISCHARGE OF FIREARMS.

GEORGE E. WYKOFF.

Soldier was wounded by the accidental discharge of a gun while hunting for his own pleasure, and was not in the line of duty.

Assistant Secretary Webster Davis to the Commissioner of Pensions. July 3, 1897.

This appellant filed a claim for pension under the general law, on the 3d day of October, 1895, alleging, among other things, that while in service at Fort Grant, Ariz., on or about the 16th day of July, 1895, he lost his right thumb while hunting.

His claim was rejected February 14, 1896, on the ground that claimant was not in line of duty when he received the wound that caused the loss of his right thumb.

An appeal from said action was entered October 26, 1896, and on the 8th of December, 1896, Assistant Secretary Reynolds reversed the action of your Bureau, holding that a special examination should be ordered, with instructions to obtain the testimony of the several officers in command at the time the pass was issued, for the purpose of deter mining whether or not the soldier was hunting for the troop or merely for his own recreation.

A special examination was subsequently ordered by your Bureau, and after further consideration of the evidence thus obtained the claim was again rejected January 23, 1897, on the ground that the claimant was not in the line of duty when he received the wound which caused the loss of his right thumb as shown by his statement to the special examiner.

From said action this appeal was entered April 23, 1897, contending that he was in the line of duty when the gunshot wound of hand was received.

The appellant made the following statement to the special examiner January 16, 1897:

We were stationed at Fort Grant, Ariz., and it was generally known that there was considerable game at the foot of the Graham Mountain, at about 2 miles from the fort * * *. The discharge of the gun that wounded my right thumb was purely accidental and I was alone at the time. * * * I was on an orderly's pass when I was wounded. I came by the pass in this way: So many men, privates (ten men), were appointed each day for squad duty, and the man whose general appearance was the best—such as having his accouterments and clothing in fine trim—was made the commanding officer's orderly, and as soon as returned from the squad that man was given a twenty-four hours' pass as a reward of merit, or whatever you are a mind to term it.

On the day of my receiving the gunshot wound of thumb, I was the man to receive the orderly's pass. In the troop was two shotguns and powder and shot as well, and all furnished by the Government and for the purpose of hunting game, and no soldier could get one of those guns except when on a pass, as in case of myself. Yes; I got the shotgun from the orderly sergeant, Sender, who, knowing I was on pass, let me have the gun.

Q. Did you take the gun and go hunting with the understanding that the game you received was to be used in the troop, or did you simply go hunting for recreation?—A. Well, of course, it would have to go to the troop; no other place to cook it. Of course, I was not ordered to go hunting, but I was given the gun with the understanding that I should turn in what game I killed to the troop mess; in fact, it was a general understanding, as the guns were placed in the troop for that purpose, and for use in hunting by soldiers on passes who liked to hunt. Of course, I went of my own accord, but as I was on a pass, I had a right to do so unless in case of urgent necessity.

The soldier then gave a detailed description of his wound and the manner of its incurrence.

It is evident, from the appellant's own statement, that he was not in the performance of any military duty when the accident occurred, but was hunting for his own recreation, and was therefore not in the line of duty.

Assistant Secretary Reynolds held in James E. Harrison's appeal (7 P. D., 97), that when a soldier received permission to hunt for his own recreation, and while hunting was shot in the hand by an accidental discharge of his gun, he was not in the line of duty.

Therefore, after a careful consideration of the evidence, I have failed to discover error in your aforesaid action.

INCREASE—ACT MARCH 3, 1885—SPECIFIC DISABILITY.

JOHN R. HARLOW.

Increase of pension under the act of March 3, 1885, relating to pension on account of loss of arm at the shoulder joint can not commence prior to that date (Nichols appeal 4 P. D., 213).

Assistant Secretary Webster Davis to the Commissioner of Pensions. July 3, 1897.

This appellant is at present in receipt of a pension of $45 per month under the provisions of the act of August 4, 1886, for amputation of left arm at the shoulder joint. He had been previously pensioned for the same disability at the rate of $37.50 per month, under the provisions of the act of March 3, 1885, from the date of said act.

On February 23, 1897, he filed in your Bureau an application for a rerating of his said pension, contending that under the provisions of the act of March 3, 1885, he was entitled to receive the rating of $37.50 per month from March 3, 1879, the date of the act providing the same rate for the loss of a leg at the hip joint, which was rejected on February 25, 1897, upon the ground that he had been properly rated from the correct date in accordance with the provisions of the law governing the case.

From this action appeal was taken on June 15, 1897.

The identical question presented by this case, and the same arguments urged in this appeal in support of the position contended for by the attorneys of this appellant, were most carefully considered and fully discussed by this Department in deciding the appeal of Charles A. Nichols (4 P. D., 213), on October 2, 1890. In deciding said case, which was identical in all respects with the one now under consideration, Assistant Secretary Bussey said:

This soldier lost his right arm by amputation at the shoulder joint and is now pensioned at $45 per month under the act of August 4, 1886. His pension was increased to $37.50 from March 3, 1885, in compliance with the act of that date. The contention of the appeal is that the increase to $37.50 should have rated back to commence from March 3, 1879. The act of March 3, 1885, is as follows:

"That all soldiers and sailors of the United States who have had an arm taken off at the shoulder joint, caused by injuries received in the service of their country while in the line of duty, and who are now receiving pensions, shall have their pensions increased to the same amount that the law now gives to soldiers and sailors who have lost a leg at the hip joint; and this act shall apply to all who shall be *hereafter* placed on the pension roll."

The appellant insists that, because this act fixed no date for the *increase*, nor in terms any exact rate to which increase should be made, it was the intent of Congress simply to make this act supplemental to the act which had, preceding this date, fixed the rate of pension for amputation or loss of leg at the hip joint, and to make it effective from the date of said act, thereby rendering it *retroactive*. The law fixing the rate for loss of a leg at the hip joint was approved March 3, 1879, and it is from this date that the soldier claims it was intended to increase the rate for loss of arm at shoulder joint. The act of March 3, 1885, says: "All soldiers and sailors * * * shall have their pension increased to the same *amount* that the law *now* gives to soldiers and sailors who have lost a leg at the hip joint; and this act shall apply to all who shall be hereafter placed on the pension roll."

It is contended that, having used the word "amount" instead of *rate*, it was intended to equalize the pension of the two classes of cases from the date of the *increase* of the one class in 1879.

The soldier seems to have assumed that Congress, being impressed that it was injustice to discriminate between the two classes, undertook to redress the wrong by legislation which should have this retroactive effect. But, however perfectly we may agree with this soldier that there was no proper reason for the distinction, as made by the act of March 3, 1879, we are compelled to dissent from the interpretation sought to be placed upon the act of March 3, 1885.

In the absence of an express declaration in the act as to the date when, or from which, its provisions shall operate, the only guide must be the general rule that it shall take effect from and after the date of its *passage and approval*. Had it been the intent of the legislative power to make this law *retroactive*, it is safe to assume that it would have so stated in the act itself, and by analogy we may refer to the law of June 16, 1880, which increased the pensions of soldiers who were totally disabled (as specified in the act of June 18, 1874) to $72 a month, to correspond with the rate which had been given for the loss of both hands or of both feet. In this act of June 16, 1880, it was specifically declared that the rating should go back to the 17th of June, when the increase for the loss of both hands or of both feet had been granted. Therefore, it can not be expected that, in the act of March 3, 1885, Congress intended anything except what was directly declared by the law, that the pension should be increased to the amount then being paid for the loss of leg at hip joint, which was $37.50. In this connection the word "amount" means, clearly, not a sum resulting from the accrual of arrears, but, at the same rate, from the date of the act. The Department is not aware of any rule of interpretation by which any other meaning can be extended to this law than is now expressed, and, therefore, must affirm the action of your Bureau in the rejection of this claim for rerating.

After careful consideration of this question I am unable to discover any good or sufficient reason for disturbing or modifying the foregoing well-settled departmental ruling which has governed the practice of this Department and your Bureau since the date of its rendition and which fully covers this case, and is, in my opinion, sound in reason and correctly states the law.

The action appealed from in this case was clearly in accord with said departmental ruling, and will, therefore, not be disturbed, and is hereby affirmed.

———

GUARDIANS—PAYMENT OF PENSION—JURISDICTION.

EDWARD W. MOORE.

1. The words appearing in the act of August 8, 1882, "But the payment to persons laboring under legal disabilities may be made to the guardians of such persons" are not mandatory, but permissive.

2. The pension system now in force, and the whole thereof, in substance and in form of procedure, is without the plane of State control and exclusively within the jurisdiction of the United States.

3. Payment of pension to the guardian of a pensioner under legal disability is not obligatory, and if the Commissioner of Pensions shall become satisfied that the

pensioner's interests would be better subserved by payment to the pensioner himself he may so direct; but until there is evidence warranting the belief that the pensioner is deprived of his rights under the pension laws, by the guardian, and the appointing court will not administer relief, the Commissioner of Pensions will not be warranted in refusing payment to such guardian.

Assistant Secretary Webster Davis to the Commissioner of Pensions. July 7, 1897.

The papers in the claim of Edward W. Moore, late private, Fourteenth Independent Battery, Ohio Light Artillery, Certificate No. 132169, together with your letter of the 22d ultimo, submitting the same, are before me.

By reference to the papers, it appears that the soldier, a pensioner under the general law on the roll of the Columbus, Ohio, agency at the rate of $30 per month, for chronic diarrhea and resulting disease of rectum and lungs, was on April 8, 1895, by order of the probate court of Warren County, Ohio, placed under the guardianship of M. S. Clapp, of Warren, Ohio, on the ground that the soldier was an imbecile, and payment has since been made to the guardian aforesaid.

In June, 1896, Mr. Charles Freer, of Warren, Ohio, who filed power of attorney from the pensioner, represented to your Bureau that the records of the probate court show the pensioner was placed under guardianship on the ground that he was an habitual drunkard; that such a statement is untrue; that the pensioner is neither an habitual drunkard nor an imbecile, but is entirely capable of attending to his business affairs. He charged that the appointment of the guardian was a result of a conspiracy, offering to prove his assertions by undoubted evidence, and asked that the guardian be either removed or ignored and payment of pension made directly to the pensioner.

Your Bureau denied his request on the ground that you are compelled to recognize the acts of probate courts in the appointment of guardians, and that the pensioner's only remedy, if he has been dealt with unjustly, is in the local courts.

Thereupon appeal was taken on October 15, 1896, to the Secretary of the Interior, in which, among other things, it was contended as follows, viz:

Mentally and morally he is all right, which I am ready and anxious to show. The number of cases of this character is becoming alarmingly frequent—cases where scheming relatives or others, by their acts, through the assistance of inferior courts, are defeating the intentions of a very generous Government. It does seem strange to me that your Department can not protect its own in the full enjoyment of what it gives them.

The appeal considered, it was held by my predecessor in office, Hon. John M. Reynolds (8 P. D., 400), that—

Payment of pension to the guardian of a person under legal disability is not obligatory, and if the Commissioner of Pensions shall become satisfied that the pensioner's interests would be better subserved by payment to the pensioner himself, he may so direct.

Your Bureau was at the same time directed to permit the filing of the evidence tendered—

and if the same shall, prima facie, substantiate his allegations, make an investigation, through a special examiner, to determine whether or not the present arrangement is beneficial to the pensioner. If it is not, then—

said Assistant Secretary Reynolds—

it will be the duty of your Bureau to make or cause to be made such a change as will best secure to him the proper enjoyment of the Government's bounty.

The special examination having been made, you have by your letter of the 22d instant referred the papers back, calling attention to the evidence obtained by the special examiner, which you say tends to show that he may be competent to handle his pension money, but that we are met by a decree of a court of competent jurisdiction declaring him incompetent.

You say that—

from a legal standpoint I do not think or believe any payment can be made to this pensioner direct until the guardian has been properly removed and the pensioner declared a person competent within the eyes of the law.

You ask for my careful consideration of the doctrine as laid down in the departmental decision of January 16, 1897, and say:

Upon this line your attention is called to the legislation of Congress relative to the embezzlement of pension moneys by the curator, committee, or guardian of any pensioner. In passing this legislation Congress certainly recognized these appointments as valid and regular and provided a penal statute to meet such dereliction of duty imposed upon such guardians by the proper courts, and I am seriously inclined to doubt the jurisdiction of this office to ignore the rights of a properly appointed guardian over an incompetent person and make payment directly to the party who has been declared incompetent. I do not think such a payment would be legal or lawful, and I request that due consideration be given this phase of the case.

I have carefully considered both the evidence submitted and the legal proposition involved. The latter raises the question of the jurisdiction of the United States over the payment of pension to all pensioners, necessarily including such as are, or are alleged to be, under legal disability. As this phase of the question is one of paramount importance, it will be considered first in order.

In the case of Edward F. Waite, United States district court in and for the northern district of Iowa, general division, June term, 1897, hearing on writ of habeas corpus, Judge Shiras said:

The Government of the United States has created the pension system now in force, and the whole thereof, in substance and in form of procedure, is without the plane of State control.

He further held that—

in the operations of the Government of the United States, in connection with the pension system, the laws of the United States are not only paramount and supreme, but touching the subject-matter the jurisdiction of the United States is exclusive, and the matter wholly within Federal control.

Attorney-General Brewster, in an opinion dated April 28, 1882 (17 Op., 339), said:

> Section 471 of the Revised Statutes designates the Commissioner of Pensions as the officer provided by law whose special duty it is, under the direction of the Secretary of the Interior, to administer and carry into execution these [pension] laws.

Section 4766, R. S., as amended by the act of Congress approved August 8, 1882, provides that—

> hereafter no pension shall be paid to any person other than the pensioner entitled thereto, nor otherwise than according to the provisions of this title; * * * but the payment to persons laboring under legal disabilities may be made to the guardians of such persons.

I understand from your letter that you regard this statute as mandatory in its provisions, in so far as it relates to payment to guardians on account of persons under legal disability.

I do not so understand it. The words used "may be made" are permissive in character.

On May 10, 1895, Attorney-General Olney, in an opinion (21 Op., 169), said:

> It has been so often decided as to have become an axiom that in public statutes words only directory, permissory, or enabling may have a compulsory force, where the thing to be done is for the public benefit, or in advancement of public justice.
>
> The general rule is that permissive words in a statute are peremptory when used to clothe a public officer with power to do an act which concerns the public interest.

The subject of pensions is a special matter, resting wholly in the gift of the nation, upon its own terms. It is a subject which is confined to certain specified beneficiaries, either as individuals or as a class, and therefore can not be said to concern the public interest.

Under the rule stated, therefore, there is no warrant to make a payment to guardians a mandatory provision of the law cited, nor do I regard the words employed, "may be made," etc., as otherwise than directory, and within the discretion of the Commissioner of Pensions to use or pass by, as he may determine that the interest of the pensioner demands.

The law declares that the pension allowed "shall inure wholly to the benefit of the pensioner." (Section 4747, R. S.) The Commissioner of Pensions, as the officer legally designated to carry into effect the pension laws, is the person who is to see to it that the law shall be carried into effect and that the pension shall inure wholly to the benefit of the pensioner. If there could be any doubt as to the proper construction of the effect of the act of August 8, 1882, that doubt is effectually removed by the language of the act itself, which declares in express terms, after making provision for the permissive payment to guardians referred to, as follows, viz:

> And payments in person shall be made to the pensioner, in cash, by the pension agent, whenever in the discretion of the Commissioner of Pensions such personal payment shall by him be deemed necessary or proper to secure to the pensioner his ·hts.

The mere fact that a guardian or committee has been appointed under a proceeding in a State court does not of itself confer any authority upon such guardian to receive payment of the pension of his ward.

It was said by Secretary Vilas (2 P. D., 94):

The decree of the court establishing the legal disability of the pensioner and appointing a conservator of his person and property in no manner assumes to direct the disposal of his pension nor to seize to his own deprivation. No State court possesses the power. It is by virtue of the statute of the United States only that when the condition of legal disability is established and a guardian appointed by the State court the pension may be paid to such guardian. The statute affords warrant, and, unless in a particular case there be sufficient reason for other action, imposes the general duty to make avail of the benevolent guardianship of the State courts over all pensioners under legal disabilities to secure to their best use the provision of the Government for their benefit.

In Hall's Case (98 U. S., 343) the Supreme Court of the United States said:

The word "guardian," as used in the acts of Congress, is merely the designation of the person to whom the money granted may be paid for the use and benefit of the pensioner.

He receives the pension payment not by virtue of any authority conferred by the State court to do so, but solely by virtue of the Federal law, which permits the Commissioner of Pensions to authorize payment over to him of the funds of a pensioner under legal disability, if thereby the use and benefit be better secured to the pensioner; and if the Commissioner of Pensions should determine in the exercise of his powers that the pension did not inure to the benefit of the pensioner when paid through a guardian appointed under the authority of the State law it would be his right and, in my opinion, his duty to refuse payment to such guardian, and even to direct a personal payment to the pensioner himself whenever he deemed it necessary or proper "to secure to the pensioner his rights."

You refer to the Federal statutes relative to embezzlement of pension money by fiduciaries, and say that—

Congress certainly recognized these appointments as valid and regular, and provided a penal statute to meet any dereliction of duty imposed upon such guardians by the proper courts.

You add that you are—

seriously inclined to doubt the jurisdiction of this office to ignore the rights of a properly appointed guardian over an incompetent person.

By this I understand you to mean that when a probate court or other appropriate tribunal has passed upon the question of the legal disability of a citizen of the State, by virtue of whose law such court acts, and has appointed a guardian for such citizen, the Government of the United States is bound thereby, and must make payment to such fiduciary.

But the State can only exercise authority over persons and things falling within its own jurisdiction. The subject of pensions is exclusively one of Federal jurisdiction, nor can any State pass laws or authorize courts to regulate any proceeding having reference to the allowance or payment of pensions; for, being without authority itself in the premises, it is powerless to bestow upon its fiduciary or agent any power not possessed by itself.

In Hall's Case, supra, the Supreme Court said:

> The United States, as the donors of the pensions, may, through the legislative department of the Government, annex such conditions to the donation as they see fit, to insure its transmission unimpaired to the beneficiary. The guardian, no more than the agent or attorney of the pensioner, is obliged by the laws of Congress to receive the fund; but if he does, he must accept it subject to the annexed conditions.

The punishment for embezzlement of pension is not by virtue of a State law, for the State can exercise no jurisdiction over the subject-matter but by virtue of a Federal law. It punishes him, not because he has violated the trust of the court which appointed him, but because he has embezzled pension money placed in his hands for the use and benefit of a pensioner. Practically the same question was raised in Hall's Case (supra), which was also an Ohio case. In that case the circuit court judges for the southern district of Ohio certified the questions in issue to the Supreme Court of the United States, viz, whether the circuit court has jurisdiction over the offense (embezzlement) or any power to punish the defendant for an appropriation of the money after its legal payment to him as guardian (it appearing that the defendant is the legal guardian of his ward under the laws of the State, etc.), and whether the defendant, if he did embezzle the money, is liable to indictment for the offense under the act of Congress or only under the State law.

The Supreme Court held that the elements of the offense defined by the act of Congress consist of the wrongful acts of the individual named in the indictment, wholly irrespective of the duties devolved upon him by the State law, and that the jurisdiction is in the courts of the United States to try and to punish the offense.

It was said in Waite's Case, supra, that the point is—

> whether the Government of the United States has not the right to assert that its operations within the jurisdiction conferred by the Constitution, and wherein it is supreme and paramount, can not be interfered with under the laws of a State. * * *
>
> The legislation of the State may be unfriendly. It may deny the authority conferred by the laws of the National Government. The State court may administer not only the laws of the State but equally Federal laws in such a manner as to paralyze the operations of the Government. * * * While it (United States) is limited in the number of its powers, so far as its sovereignty extends it is supreme. No State government can exclude it from the exercise of any authority conferred upon it by the Constitution, * * * or withhold from it for a moment the cognizance of any subject which that instrument has committed to it.

Referring inter alia to the subject of pensions, the court added:

> These matters are outside the plane of State control and jurisdiction, and therefore the general statutes of the State can not by judicial interpretation be made applicable thereto.

As the United States are the donors of the pensions, the Federal Government alone has jurisdiction over the subject-matter; and since it has enacted certain laws making up a pension system and regulating and controlling all matters incident to the subject-matter, its jurisdiction is absolute and exclusive.

These laws provide that the pension shall inure wholly to the benefit of the pensioner. They permit the payment of pension on account of persons under legal disability to the guardians of such pensioners; but they do not, in my opinion, require it. Rather, these laws require their administrator, the Commissioner of Pensions, to enforce them so that they shall inure to the pensioner's benefit, and authorize him, in his discretion, to direct a personal payment to the pensioner whenever it is deemed necessary and proper to secure to the pensioner his rights. And this is a wise provision; because, but for it, if the Government were compelled to make the pension payable to the pensioner through his guardian, it would be possible, through the machinery of the State courts, to secure the appointments of agents in whose hands the rights of the pensioner could be made to suffer diminution or absolute loss.

A dishonest or unsuitable person could not be ignored by the United States if the appointing power should refuse to remove him, and thus would the Federal laws respecting pensions be paralyzed and utterly defeated. It is well to punish the person who embezzles the pension money; but if this were all the power possessed by the Federal Government, Congress might in vain enact laws to cause the pension to inure to the benefit of the pensioner.

I am, therefore, of opinion that the only thing to be considered in such a case is the benefit of the pensioner. Further, that the Government may make avail of a guardian appointed by a State court to convey to a pensioner under legal disabilities the use and benefit of the pension allowed in his behalf, and to refuse the aid of such guardian when he ceases to transmit unimpaired to the pensioner the benefits conferred upon him by the pension laws, even directing personal payment to such pensioner, when it is necessary so to do, to secure to him his rights.

Coming down to the facts in this case, it appears by the evidence obtained by the special examiner that the pensioner is qualified to receive and disburse his funds and manage his estate without the aid or assistance of a guardian. That, however, is a question within the jurisdictional power of the Trumbull County, Ohio, probate court to consider.

I see no reason to doubt that, if the evidence now in the possession of the Pension Bureau were made available for the use of the next friend of the pensioner, or other person authorized to ask for his release from guardianship, the present probate judge for that county would make such an order.

It is not sufficiently clear from the evidence presented, nor is it charged, that the guardian deprives the pensioner of the full use and benefit of his pension. In such case, I am of opinion that, until there is evidence to warrant you in believing the pensioner is deprived of his rights under the pension laws, no sufficient reason is shown to justify you in refusing payment to the guardian, through whom, so far as appears by the evidence before me, the pensioner appears to be receiving the pecuniary benefit of the pension laws in his behalf.

It is for the pensioner and his friends to move for a release from guardianship; and, while it would be proper to furnish the evidence in the case in aid of such a proceeding, if requested so to do by the party in interest, it is not for the Government, in the present state of the case, to take the initiative in such a proceeding.

When it shall be known that the pensioner's right to have the pension inure wholly to his benefit is being abridged or forfeited by the malfeasance of the guardian, and that the appointing court will not administer relief, then, in my judgment, you would be legally authorized to refuse payment to the guardian and, if need be, to pay the pensioner himself.

ADULTEROUS COHABITATION—FORFEITURE.

ANN FAGIN (WIDOW).

The adulterous cohabitation of a widow subsequent to the passage of the act of August 7, 1882, works a forfeiture of her pension, or right to a pension under the act of June 27, 1890.

Assistant Secretary Webster Davis to the Commissioner of Pensions, July 7, 1897.

Claimant, as the widow of Christopher Fagin, Company C, Seventh Ohio Cavalry, on May 5, 1897, appealed from the action of your Bureau of March 31, 1897, dropping her name from the rolls as a pensioner under the act of July 27, 1890, Certificate No. 278068, on the ground that she is shown to have forfeited her pension under the act of June 27, 1890, by open and notorious adulterous cohabitation since the death of her husband, with one Thomas McCue, since August 7, 1882.

The contention of claimant is, in brief, that to justify the action appealed from she must be shown to be guilty of adulterous cohabitation since June 27, 1890, in order to defeat her pension under the act of that date; that if any violation of the act of August 7, 1882, occurred it must have been between that date and March 17, 1884, as that was the date of the death of the person with whom she was charged with cohabiting; that all the facts were before the Bureau when she was pensioned under the act of June 27, 1890, and to reverse the decision of a predecessor is contrary to the well settled practice of the Bureau; that the law of August 7, 1882, has no application to the act of June 27, 1890; that "open and notorious adulterous cohabitation" was not shown prior to June 27, 1890, within the meaning of the act of June 27, 1890, and that the act of August 7, 1882, only applies to a widow who is a pensioner, and, lastly, that under a liberal administration of the pension laws soldiers' widows should not be the victims of discriminating rulings.

In support of the contention that in order to bring the case within the letter of the act of August 7, 1882, the widow must have been a pensioner claimant cites the cases of Susan Larimer (3 P. D., 235), Sarah E. West (Ibid., 115), Louisa H. Pratt (5 P. D., 93), and Matilda Payne (Ibid., 161).

It was held, however, in the case of Sarah J. Grooms (7 P. D., 207):

1. The open, notorious, and adulterous cohabitation of a widow who is a pensioner, or an applicant for a pension on account of the service and death of her husband, will work a forfeiture of her pension or her right to a pension; and such cohabitation may be proved by her conduct in habitually, openly, and notoriously consorting with one or more persons of the opposite sex, under circumstances which would lead the guarded discretion of a reasonable and just man to infer from such relation, as a necessary conclusion, that it was illicit.

2. The decisions in the cases of Sarah E. West (3 P. D., 115), Caroline Knappenberger (3 P. D., 263), Sophia Lingers (4 P. D., 287), Cynthia Evans (5 P. D., 188), and all other decisions, modified and overruled, in so far as they are in conflict with the above holding.

So also in the case of Ellen J. Pipes (7 P. D., 489) it was held:

The act of August 7, 1882, operates as a bar to pension from the commencement of adulterous cohabitation. If, therefore, said condition existed after the passage of said act, and even prior to the date of filing the declaration, it is obvious the right to pension does not exist. It matters not that said adulterous cohabitation had ceased at the date of filing the declaration; the fact that it existed after August 7, 1882, as in this case, is a forfeiture of all pensionable rights.

The law makes no provision for restoring the pensionable right when such unlawful relations cease, and the inhibition contained in said act applies with equal force to applicants and pensioners, whether under the act of June 27, 1890, or under prior laws. (Citing the case of Sarah Jane Houser, 6 P., 281.)

As to the doctrine of res adjudicata and stare decisis implied in the contention that the decisions of a predecessor can not be reversed, it was held in the case of Mary E. Eastridge (8 P. D., 5) that—

Neither the doctrine of res adjudicata nor stare decisis is strictly applicable to pension cases, and when adopted by the Department simply becomes a rule which each administration prescribes for itself as a matter of policy or convenience, and may be waived, suspended, or ignored, as justice, policy, or convenience requires.

So in the case of Jackson Martin (7 P. D., 265), the Department held that cases long since adjudicated by former administrations should not be reopened, reconsidered, or readjudicated except * * *

when on presentation of new and material evidence it is indubitably shown that through mistake the pension was in whole or in part illegally reduced or granted.

In the case under consideration a special examination held in December, 1886, disclosed the fact that after soldier's death, August 2, 1880, one Thomas McCue, a policeman, who had recently lost his wife, boarded with claimant until a short time before sent to hospital, where he died, as testified by claimant in March, 1883, but as now alleged on appeal the date of his death is fixed as March 17, 1884; that many of claimant's witnesses and neighbors testified that their relations were reputed to be adulterous.

The city police surgeon of Cincinnati, Ohio, testified that while acting as such surgeon one Tom McHugh kept reporting himself as sick, and that he investigated the case by going to where he was stopping with a woman, and said to be living in adultery with her. He found from her statements and others that the sole cause of his sickness was alcoholism, and he (witness) so reported to the chief of police and mayor, and McHugh was discharged in the summer of 1881. He further testified that the woman, whose name he believed was Ann Fagin, informed him of her improper relations with said policeman.

Claimant, who on this examination denied before the special examiner any improper relations with said policeman, testified before a special examiner January 5, 1897, as follows:

I admit that occasionally I was on terms of carnal intimacy with Thomas McHugh (sic), but with no other person since the death of Fagin. McHugh died many years ago in Betts Street Hospital.

While the evidence is not clear when claimant's illicit relations with McCue or McHugh ceased, it is shown to have existed from shortly after soldier's death, and to have continued until 1882 or 1883. There is nothing to justify the inference that it ceased prior to August 7, 1882. On the contrary, a state of illicit relations having been shown to exist they are presumed to continue, and the burden of proof is upon the guilty party to show that they terminated at any particular time prior to the death of one of the parties. It is shown by the evidence that claimant has not been guilty of a violation of the act of August 7, 1882, subsequent to the passage of the act of June 27, 1890, but this fact does not give her a pensionable status, which was lost by violation of the act of August 7, 1882.

The action appealed from is accordingly affirmed, and the papers in the case are herewith returned.

PRACTICE—READJUDICATION—APPEAL.

LEROY F. WOOD.

Under departmental decision in the case of James Quigg (8 P. D., 248), claimant should first make application to the Pension Bureau for readjudication in accordance with the provisions of the act of March 6, 1896. As such application has not been made, the motion for reconsideration is overruled.

Assistant Secretary Webster Davis to the Commissioner of Pensions July 7, 1890.

The soldier, Leroy F. Wood, Company A, Ninety-first Illinois Volunteer Infantry, was originally pensioned (certificate No. 136831)

November 23, 1873, under the general law at \$2 per month from July 24, 1875, for gunshot wound of left leg.

He filed declaration August 7, 1890, for pension under act of June 27, 1890, alleging gunshot wound of left leg, rupture, and partial deafness of left ear. This claim was not adjudicated when, on January 31, 1893, he filed an affidavit alleging piles as an additional disability.

On November 19, 1894, the claim was medically approved for gunshot wound of left leg and disease of rectum from January 31, 1893, at \$6, no other disability shown and not ratable prior to January 31, 1893. Accordingly claimant was pensioned November 26, 1894, under act of June 27, 1890, at \$6 from January 31, 1893, for partial inability to earn a support by manual labor.

Claimant appealed January 6, 1896, from the action dating commencement of the \$6 pension from January 31, 1893, claiming that commencement should be from August 7, 1890, date of filing the original declaration. This appeal was duly considered by the Department and, by opinion of date January 25, 1896, the action of your Bureau was affirmed, it being held that appellant was not disabled in a degree ratable under the act of June 27, 1890, at the time of filing his first declaration thereunder, and that his pension was properly made to commence from the date of filing his second declaration.

Claimant entered a motion May 8, 1897, for reconsideration of the departmental decision affirming the said action of your Bureau, alleging that he was ratably disabled at least to \$6 per month, upon the evidence introduced in his claim, from August 7, 1890. Claimant cites the act of March 6, 1896, in support of his contention.

The act of March 6, 1896, provides, inter alia, as follows:

That whenever a claim for pension under the act of June 27, 1890, has been or shall hereafter be rejected, suspended, or dismissed, and a new application shall have been or shall hereafter be filed, and a pension has been or shall hereafter be allowed in such claim, such pension shall date from the time of filing the first application, provided the evidence in the case shall show a pensionable disability to have existed or to exist at the time of filing such first application, anything in any law or ruling of the Department to the contrary notwithstanding.

In the case of James Quigg (8 P. D., 248), in a communication addressed to the Commissioner of Pensions, of date August 29, 1896, my immediate predecessor, Assistant Secretary Reynolds, held as follows:

Where claimant relies upon an act of Congress passed subsequent to the action of your Bureau, and the decision of this Department approving said action, to secure a reversal of said action, he should first make an application to your Bureau, and a second appeal in absence of such application can not be entertained.

While the case at bar is a motion for reconsideration and not a second appeal, I am of opinion that the same rule of practice should apply, and that in lieu of petitioning the Department for reconsideration of its previous action because of an act of Congress passed subsequent to the action of your Bureau and the decision of the Department approving the same, the claimant should first make application to your Bureau for readjudication in accordance with the provisions of the said act of Congress approved March 6, 1896, passed subsequent to the action of your Bureau and the decision of this Department approving the same.

By this practice your Bureau will be afforded the opportunity of passing upon a question of law not previously arising or considered in the case, and the right of claimant to appeal to the Department from whatever action may be taken thereon by your Bureau is meantime preserved.

Inasmuch as such application to your Bureau has not been made by claimant, the motion for reconsideration must be and is accordingly overruled. You will please direct that the claimant be duly advised of the reasons for overruling his motion.

RERATING—SCHEDULE OF RATES.

HENRY CRITTENDEN.

The fact that the pensioner did not receive as high a rate of pension for slight deafness of both ears as others have received for the same disability during the same period (the schedule of rates for partial deafness having been modified prior to the adjudication of his claim) is not good ground for rerating, the inequality complained of resulting, not from any violation of law, but from a difference of judgment between two administrative officers, each of whom acted within the scope of his legal authority.

Assistant Secretary Webster Davis to the Commissioner of Pensions, July 7, 1897.

The motion filed June 5, 1897, by Smith and Talley, attorneys, for reconsideration of the decision rendered December 14, 1896, by Assistant Secretary Reynolds, affirming the action of your Bureau in the case of Henry Crittenden, pensioner under certificate No. 574087, is hereby overruled.

A certificate was issued to said pensioner November 1, 1895, for pension under the general law on account of slight deafness of both ears, at the rate of $6 per month, commencing March 26, 1890, and ending July 15, 1890, from which date he had been previously pensioned at $12 per month, under the act of June 27, 1890. The contention of the attorneys is that as $15 per month was the established rate for slight deafness of both ears prior to December 4, 1891, it was error to allow this pensioner only $6 per month during the period covered by his certificate. They claim that in affirming that action the late Assistant Secretary "overlooked the law."

The only law now in force governing the matter of rates for deafness is the act of August 27, 1888, which fixed the rate for total deafness at $30 per month, and authorized the allowance of—

such proportion thereof in cases of partial deafness as the Secretary of the Interior may deem equitable, the amount paid to be determined by the degree of disability existing in each case.

Under the provisions of that act a schedule of rates was arranged for the various degrees of partial deafness, in which the rate for slight deafness of both ears was fixed at $15 per month. That schedule continued in force until December 4, 1891, and was followed in all cases of partial deafness adjudicated prior to that date. It being then considered that the rates affixed to certain degrees of partial deafness were excessive, inequitable, and not in accordance with the actual degree of disability, a revision of the schedule was made, with the approval of the then Secretary of the Interior, under which the rate for slight deafness of both ears was reduced to $6 per month.

By ruling 257 (quoted in the decision of December 14, 1896), promulgated by the Commissioner of Pensions February 28, 1894, it was ordered that from and after that date all new and pending claims on account of deafness should be rated from August 27, 1888, in accordance with the schedule of December 4, 1891.

It is inferred that in claims adjudicated prior to February 28, 1894, the rating for the period between August 27, 1888, and December 4, 1891, had been made under the old schedule. As this man's claim was pending on February 28, 1894, and was not allowed until November 1, 1895, the rating (in accordance with ruling 257) followed the schedule of December 4, 1891, giving him $6 per month. If his claim had been allowed prior to February 28, 1894, he would have been given $15 per month for the same period. The attorneys contend that "the Department is estopped from discriminating against pensioners in the matter of rating" in this manner.

The law provides that—

the rate at which arrears of invalid pensions shall be allowed and computed * * * shall be graded according to the degree of the pensioner's disability from time to time, and the provisions of the pension laws in force over the period for which the arrears shall be computed. (Act March 3, 1879.)

It is to be observed that the act of August 27, 1888, did not fix the rate for any degree of impaired hearing except total deafness. The rates named for minor degrees of deafness, in the schedule adopted soon after the passage of said act, were not rates established by law, but existed only by order of the Secretary of the Interior. The law required him to allow such rates as he might deem equitable and proportionate to the degree of disability. But, obviously, rates which might be deemed equitable and proportionate to the degree of disability by one Secretary might be considered inequitable and disproportionate by another. There is no law which makes the judgment of one Secretary, in a matter of that kind, binding upon his successors, and, while it is the general practice not to disturb the rulings of a previous administration for light or trivial reasons, yet, whenever a Secretary is convinced that a former ruling is not in accord with the spirit and intent of the law, it is his right to abolish or amend it. And he may make the new or amended rule apply to all cases thereafter adjudicated.

I find, therefore, that ruling 257, requiring that all cases of partial deafness adjudicated after February 28, 1894, should be rated, as to any period after August 27, 1888, in accordance with the schedule of December 4, 1891, was not in violation of any law but was clearly within the discretionary power of those at that time in authority. The rating in the case of this pensioner for the period in question therefore can not be disturbed.

It is not to be denied that the effect of said ruling was to give some applicants lower rates of pension than others had received during the same period for the same degree of disability, but that is not a sufficient reason for annulling the action. If a pensioner can show that the pension allowed him was not in accordance with the law he will be entitled to relief, but when the inequality complained of resulted simply from a difference of judgment between two administrative officers, each of whom acted clearly within the scope of the authority vested in him by law, there is no ground for interference.

DISABILITY—RATE—ACT JUNE 27, 1890.

FRANCIS FRANK.

A claimant who has attained the age of 65 years shall be deemed entitled to at least the minimum rate of pension unless the evidence discloses an unusual vigor and ability for the performance of manual labor in one of that age.

Assistant Secretary Webster Davis to the Commissioner of Pensions, July 7, 1897.

November 2, 1895, the appellant filed a new declaration, under the act of June 27, 1890, in which he alleged disability due to rheumatism, defective sight, enlarged prostate gland, pain in back, kidney disease, and senility. In a subsequent declaration filed March 14, 1896, he alleged additional causes as follows: Chronic bronchitis, emphysema of lungs, affection of heart, liver, bladder, and neurasthenia.

January 23, 1897, the claim was rejected upon the ground that a pensionable degree of disability was not shown. From this action appeal was entered April 1, 1897.

The claimant was examined by a board of surgeons at New York City, September 9, 1896. The surgeons report that the claimant is well nourished and looks healthy; pulse rate, 80; respiration, 28; temperature, 98½; height, 5 feet 8 inches; weight, 182 pounds; age, 66 years. No disability found due to disease of lungs, kidneys, neurasthenia. Heart sounds, area of dullness, and apex beat, normal; affection of the bladder, frequent urinations; specific gravity, 1.018; reaction, acid; examination shows no albumen, urates, nor sugar; slight cloud of phosphates; mild chronic cystitis; rating, six-eighteenths. Enlarged prostate; some enlargement exists to which cystitis is due; rating, four-eighteenths. Rheumatism, pain on pressure and on motion in both lower extremities from knee down; all joints normal as to size and motion; no limitation of motion; no atrophy of muscles; no contraction of tendons; rated, two-eighteenths. Defective eyesight, right eye reads Snellen 100 at 15 feet; left eye reads 50 at 15 feet; rating, four-eighteenths. Pain in back. Pain on pressure and on motion in lumbar muscles; both sides; does not hold spine erect when he stoops; some lumbago present; rating, two-eighteenths. Senility; arcus senilis present in both eyes.

Claimant was also medically examined July 10, 1895. No additional objective conditions were found, except as follows: Right knee limited in motion one-sixth; crepitation in same; left knee tender and stiff; rating for each, three-eighteenths. Rating for defective eyesight, each eye, three-eighteenths. Vision of right eye, twelve two-hundredths; left eye, twelve two-hundredths. Prostate gland enlarged to twice its normal size; due to senility; no rating.

Dr. William Hasslock, in affidavit dated February 15, 1896, states that he found the condition of the soldier's lungs is that of chronic bronchitis and beginning emphysema; objective conditions of disease of heart; limitation of motion of knees, one-fourth; that soldier suffers from lumbago and impaired eyesight and neurasthenia. In his opinion, the claimant is impaired for the performance of manual labor about one-half.

I am not unaware that age as a factor in the consideration of these claims under the act of June 27, 1890, is somewhat uncertain as a means of determining title. But it must be remembered that all pension statutes, wherein age is taken into consideration, deal liberally, and with justice, I think, with this disabling cause. In retirements from the Army the age of 62 is fixed as, of itself, sufficient reason for considering the advance to this age as a warrant for cessation of the active duties of an officer. Again, the act of January 29, 1887, fixed the same age (62) as entitling a soldier or sailor of the Mexican war to the rate of pension therein provided, independent of any disability.

In the claim of Jacob Rinkel, decided by this Department, July 6, 1895 (8 P. D., 30), it was held that a declaration which alleged no disabling cause whatever save that the applicant was 75 years of age or over would be held to be a sufficient allegation of disability, and further that where disabling causes have been alleged which indicate senility as the pathological factor, such a declaration would be held good without allegation or statement as to age.

By order No. 241 your Bureau declared that in cases in which the pensioner has reached the age of 75, his rate shall not be disturbed if he is receiving the maximum ($12), and if he is not a pensioner he shall receive the maximum for senility alone if there are no special pensionable disabilities shown.

On the 6th of September, 1893, carrying out the directions of this

Department in the claim of Rinkle, above cited, and extending your order No. 241, your Bureau issued order No. 242, holding that it shall be presumed, in claims for increase under the act of June 27, 1890, that claimants who have attained the age of 75 years are wholly disabled for manual labor within the meaning of this law entitling them to the maximum rate of $12 per month.

Now, if age alone may be settled upon as entitling a claimant to the maximum rate, age as a factor in connection with disabilities, or alone, may justly be considered as entitling claimant to the minimum or intermediate rates.

As hereinbefore stated age alone is a more or less uncertain basis for determining title; some men are senile at 50 while others are comparatively vigorous at a later age. But it is my desire to at least approximate a just and equitable rule.

I therefore hold that unless the evidence and medical examinations disclose an unusual vigor and activity for the performance of manual labor (the bases of title under the statute) a claimant for pension under the act of June 27, 1890, who has attained the age of 65 years shall be deemed entitled to at least the minimum rate of pension provided by that act.

In the case under consideration the claimant is 66 years of age. He was found to be suffering, at least in a mild degree, from chronic cystitis, enlarged prostate, rheumatism, defective eyesight (arcus senilis, due alone to effect of age), and lumbago.

These disabilities in connection with claimant's age clearly entitle him to a rating, and I therefore reverse your action denying him title, and return the papers for adjudication in conformity with the findings herein set forth.

AMPUTATION ACT OF AUGUST 4, 1886.

SAMUEL SCOTT.

The nearness of an amputation to the shoulder joint or hip joint is the only condition to be considered in determining the right to the increase of pension to $45 per month provided by the act of August 4, 1886. It is held that if more than one-half of the humerus or femur is left the stump is of sufficient length to permit the use of an artificial limb.

Assistant Secretary Webster Davis to the Commissioner of Pensions, July 9, 1897.

The appellant, Samuel Scott, is in receipt of a pension of $36 per month under the act of August 4, 1886 (certificate No. 75453), on account of disability from the loss of his left arm above the elbow. On the 3d of September, 1896, he filed an application in which he claimed the pension provided by the act of August 4, 1886, for those who have lost an arm at the shoulder joint or so near the joint as to be unable to wear an artificial arm. His claim was rejected, February 26, 1897, on the ground that the case was one merely of the loss of an arm above the elbow, for which the pension of $36 per month is provided by the act of August 4, 1886. From this action an appeal was taken, April 19, 1897.

The purport of the evidence bearing upon the question involved in the appeal is as follows:

The examining surgeon at Lafayette, Ind., in his certificate of August 11, 1863, stated that—

The amputation was performed just above the elbow.

The Board at Frankfort, Ind., by whom pensioner was examined on the 28th of September, 1892, stated—

The left arm is amputated 9½ inches below the point of the acromion process.

The board further stated that—

In our opinion, from the poorly cushioned condition of the stump and atrophied condition of the muscles of the arm, he could not wear an artificial arm. The length of the right humerus is 13½ inches. The length of the left is 9½ inches.

It was held by this Department in the decision of May 9, 1896, in the pension claim of William A. Till (8 P. D., 159), that under the act of August 4, 1886, the rate of $45 per month is allowed only for the loss of either an arm at the shoulder joint or a leg at the hip joint, or so near the joint as to prevent the use of an artificial limb; that no other condition of the stump should be considered in determining title under said act except the nearness of the amputation to the joint

It is held that an amputation which has left more than half the femur or the humerus is not so near the joint as to prevent the use of an artificial limb. (Case of John W. Curran, 5 P. D., 1.)

The views set forth in the decisions cited are adhered to and the decision of the Pension Office in this case is accordingly affirmed.

——

PRACTICE—ACT JUNE 27, 1890—MEDICAL EXAMINATION.

CHARLES A. ARMSTRONG.

A medical examination should not be held to show the extent of alleged disabilities under a declaration filed under the act of June 27, 1890, until claimant has shown at least a prima facie title under said act.

Assistant Secretary Webster Davis to the Commissioner of Pensions, July 9, 1897.

On October 7, 1896, claimant filed his declaration (No. 984155) under the act of June 27, 1890, said declaration reciting that he was enrolled October 11, 1862, in Company B, First Battalion, Southern Border Brigade, which organization was disbanded March 16, 1864. Claim was rejected on October 22, 1896, on the ground that no service was shown in the military or naval service of the United States, and an appeal is filed on May 12, 1897, alleging error in law, in that claimant was not given a medical examination by which his alleged disabilities might be shown.

, Section 2 of the act of June 27, 1890, makes as a first condition pre-cedent to title under said section of said act that the claimant must have "served ninety days or more in the military or naval service of the United States."

Claimant's name is not found on the records of the War Department, and the proof filed by him shows him as mustered into an organization for State service (Iowa), and that said organization was disbanded by act of legislature of the State of Iowa, dated March 6, 1864.

It has been the universal holding of the Department since the passage of the act of June 27, 1890, and such holding is made necessary by the express terms of the act, that one whose military service was rendered in a State organization which was never a part of the Federal Army, and whose sole service was under the authority of a State, said organization or person never having acted under orders of an officer of the United States, was not pensionable. (Assistant Secretary Reynolds in Hick's appeal, 8 P. D., 518.)

Claimant not having shown, prima facie, a title under the act of June 27, 1890, it is manifest that a medical examination would not only be useless and of no benefit to claimant, but it would also be an unwarranted expenditure of public money and time which could subserve no good purpose.

I therefore hold that under a declaration filed under the act of June 27, 1890, claimant must show at least a prima facie title under said act before a medical examination should be had to show the extent of alleged disabilities.

The action appealed from is affirmed.

PRACTICE—REOPENING.

LUTHER CASE.

As a matter of practice a claimant is entitled to file at any time new evidence and request action thereon by the Commissioner of Pensions. If said new evidence, either considered separately or in connection with previously filed evidence, establishes a prima facie case, the Commissioner of Pensions will order a new medical examination as a matter of course, and after the report of said examination has been received will take action on all of the evidence. If a request is made to the Commissioner of Pensions for a new medical examination without the filing of new evidence, such rejection goes to the sound discretion of that official, who will, nevertheless, take action upon such request. In such cases an appeal will lie to the Secretary only from the action taken by the Commissioner of Pensions.

Assistant Secretary Webster Davis to the Commissioner of Pensions July 10, 1897.

Claimant, late of Company A, Fourth United States Infantry, filed his declaration under the act of June 27, 1890, on June 28, 1892 (No.

1129385), basing claim on rheumatism and fever and ague. It was rejected January 15, 1894, on the ground of no ratable disability, and an appeal was filed April 21, 1897. Said appeal requests that claimant be allowed to file further evidence in his claim, and that an order for another medical examination be issued.

The attorney herein who prepared this appeal has had a long practice before the Department, and ought to know that the requests set out in the appeal are not matters for me to primarily pass on. The universal practice of the Pension Bureau has always been to allow new evidence to be filed at any time, and to consider and pass upon said new evidence. If a prima facie case is made, then another medical examination will be ordered by the Commissioner of Pensions as a matter of course.

If a new medical examination is desired without the filing of new evidence, then such a request should be made primarily to the Commissioner of Pensions, and it goes to the sound discretion of that official upon his reviewing the evidence already produced.

In view of the fact that many appeals to the Secretary have been, and are being made upon practically the same conditions and circumstances as are shown in the within case, and in order that the adjudication of such claims may be facilitated, it may be here stated:

As a matter of practice a claimant is entitled at any time to file new evidence in a claim and to request action thereon by the Commissioner of Pensions. If said new evidence, either considered separately or in connection with previous evidence, establishes a prima facie case, then the Commissioner of Pensions will order a new medical examination as a matter of course, and an appeal will lie to the Secretary only when the Commissioner of Pensions has taken action after considering all the evidence. If a request is made to the Commissioner of Pensions for a new medical examination without the filing of new evidence, then an appeal will lie to the Secretary, after action has been taken by the Commissioner of Pensions upon such request.

By reason of the foregoing the appeal herein will not lie.

The within appeal is hereby dismissed.

EVIDENCE—SPECIALIST.

WILLIAM HARRIS.

The evidence of a specialist, he being an agent of the Government and being required by law (section 4744, R. S.) to make his examination thorough and searching, will, when such evidence is made the basis of a holding by the medical referee, be ordinarily accepted as against the evidence of claimant's physicians.

Assistant Secretary Webster Davis to the Commissioner of Pensions, July 10, 1897.

On October 28, 1891, appellant's claim for increase was rejected under a declaration filed on May 1, 1888, alleging deafness. Since said rejection additional testimony has been filed, and you adhere to the former rejection. An appeal was filed on May 15, 1897, which alleges that the evidence lately filed shows a pensionable disability by reason of deafness.

Two physicians file their affidavits regarding deafness, Dr. Scott stating that claimant is unable to hear a watch tick when pressed against his left ear, while Dr. Wilson states that there is a paralytic condition of the auditory nerves. By reason of said testimony a test examination was ordered, and said examination was conducted by a specialist, Dr. Wheelock, of Fort Wayne, Ind.

Said specialist reports that claimant can hear with his right ear a low whisper at 6 inches and a moderate voice at 6 feet. He hears a loud whisper with left ear at 6 inches and a moderate voice at 6 feet. He finds no evidence whatever of any pathological change or of catarrhal inflammation.

The physicians whose testimony is produced by claimant are not claimed to be aurists, and, as has been the universal practice in such cases, the evidence of a specialist, who is an agent of the Government, and is bound by law to make his examinations thorough and searching, and to include in his report all physical and rational signs, and to give a statement as to all structural changes (section 4744, R. S.), will be ordinarily accepted when made the basis of a holding by the medical referee as against such evidence as is furnished by claimant. It may be further stated that the medical referee, on reviewing the evidence, holds in accordance with the testimony of Dr. Wheelock.

The action appealed from is affirmed.

LINE OF DUTY.

HENRY MILLER.

Claimant, after being relieved from guard duty, assisted a teamster in watering mules. He was not disobeying orders, his act was not in violation of army regulations, but was aiding a comrade in caring for and protecting Government property, and was doing something which he not only had a right to do, but said act was commendable, and resulted, if his allegations are true, in his being tired upon by the enemy and injured, and he was in line of duty.

Assistant Secretary Webster Davis to the Commissioner of Pensions, July 10, 1897.

Claimant, late of Company K, One hundred and first Ohio Infantry, on July 31, 1889, filed his declaration under the general law (No. 720064), alleging injury to testicles. Claim was rejected on February 12, 1894, the following words of rejection being used:

Approved for rejection for alleged injury to privates, upon claimant's own statement that the same was incurred while in pursuit of pleasure, and not in line of duty, as shown by recent special examination.

An appeal is filed on May 6, 1897, which alleges that claimant did not state to the special examiner that his injury was received while in pursuit of pleasure, but that he told the special examiner his injury was incurred by reason of something done "wholly as an act of which he considered a duty." The appeal is sworn to, and an affidavit to the same effect is on file in the case.

The evidence discloses that claimant had just been relieved from guard duty, when a teamster of the command, an intimate friend, asked claimant to go with him and help to water some mules; claimant at first declined on the ground that he had never ridden a mule, but finally mounted one of them, and the teamster another. They drove them into the water, when they were fired upon by the enemy, and claimant's mule wheeled and ran, entangling claimant in the harness and injuring his testicles. Claimant states that it was not his particular duty to water the mules, but that he was not disobeying orders in going with the teamster.

I do not find in the evidence any admission by claimant that he did go for pleasure, and such statement should not be made in any way a basis for rejection; but the real issue now before me is wholly as to whether or not claimant was in line of duty when he received the alleged injury.

I find, upon carefully reviewing the evidence, that the command to which claimant was attached was in a section of the country that they had not previously occupied; that claimant came from guard duty to camp in the night, and met the teamster of his company in charge of six mules in search of water for the mules, and that it required considerable search in a new locality to find water; that the teamster requested claimant's aid, who, against his own personal wishes, went with and assisted him; that in so doing he was not in pursuit of his own pleasure, but was actuated by a commendable motive toward his comrade, as well as humanity in caring for the mules, and in the care and preservation of Government property.

His act was in no way in violation of any army regulations and he was not disobeying orders. He was off duty, inside the lines, and while so situated, in pursuit of a lawful and commendable purpose, he alleges he was hurt; if, as a matter of fact, he was actually hurt as alleged (which must be hereafter decided), his injury was a direct result of the enemy firing upon him. Such a condition of facts is vastly different from those cases in which injury is incurred while on leave, away from camp, or in pursuit of pleasure, during which time one is wholly outside of and away from his post of duty.

I do not conceive the circumstances surrounding the case at bar to be practically different than if soldier had been hurt by reason of the enemy firing upon him while he was off duty in his tent in pursuance of any employment at which he had a right to be employed, saving that claimant's case has an additional advantage, in that it shows him as aiding a comrade in caring for and protecting the property of the Government.

I therefore hold that claimant was in line of duty at the time at which he alleges he was hurt. Whether or not he did actually receive the injury alleged, under the circumstances alleged, is a question to be decided by the Commissioner of Pensions, and to that end the action appealed from is reversed, and case reopened for adjudication upon the evidence now in the case, or upon further evidence to be produced, if such is deemed necessary to arrive at a just conclusion.

The action appealed from is reversed.

DEPENDENCE—ACT OF JUNE 27, 1890.

EMMA T. WANGELIN (WIDOW).

When it is proved that a widow, by reason of age, or permanent and physical or mental infirmities, is incapable of exerting a reasonable effort to add to the income of which she is possessed, or the property of which she is possessed, reduced to an income, is not sufficient to provide her with the necessaries of life, such widow is dependent within the terms of the act of June 27, 1890.

Assistant Secretary Webster Davis to the Commissioner of Pensions, July 10, 1897.

On July 17, 1895, claimant filed her widow's application under the act of June 27, 1890; evidence was filed showing her physical and financial condition, and her claim was rejected on January 24, 1897, on the ground that she was not dependent within the meaning of the statute. An appeal was filed on May 29, 1897, the contention being that, under such circumstances shown in this case, it is proper to take into consideration, in passing upon the question of dependency, the physical condition of claimant, the question raised going to the intent of the words in section 3 of the act of June 27, 1890, which refer to a "widow without other means of support than her daily labor."

The facts in the present case are as follows:

Claimant was 48 years of age in 1895. Her entire estate is repre-sented by $2,000, which yields her an annual income of $120. Testi-mony of two physicians shows claimant to have been, for at least three years, subject to severe attacks, which attacks are induced by organic disease of the heart. Both physicians state that, by reason of her per-manent disability, she is unable to do any manual or other labor.

The intent of the act of June 27, 1890, as relating to alleged depend-ent widow's claims, was discussed by Assistant Secretary Bussey in the case of Jennie D. Lewis (6 P. D., 294). He states, in considering said appeal, that there were two extreme limits of meaning possible to the use of the words which I have quoted, viz:

That if a widow has any other means of support whatever than the proceeds of her daily labor, she is not entitled; the other is, that unless she has adequate means for her comfortable support, aside from the proceeds of her daily labor, she is entitled.

He reached the conclusion that "the true interpretation is to be found between these extremes." This conclusion was adopted, inferentially, by Assistant Secretary Reynolds in the appeal of Katherine Klein (7 P. D., 278). I believe such holding to be a correct one, and fully concur in such doctrine.

But the real question now at issue is, at what point between those two extremes shall the line be drawn, beyond which we can not go in admitting a widow's dependency? After mature and careful consideration, I am convinced that no inflexible rule can be laid down, but that each case must be governed by the peculiar surrounding circumstances and conditions, and that the proceeds which might be derived from reasonable effort on the part of claimant must be taken into consideration, and such appears to have been the conclusion arrived at in both of the cases cited.

Assistant Secretary Bussey passed directly upon the issue raised in the case at bar, in the Lewis appeal supra, in the following words:

Age, physical and mental infirmity, location (as affecting living expenses), and social condition, must all be taken into account in such cases.

The question of locality and social condition in no wise enters into the case under discussion, and I forbear to express any opinion as to those terms; but I do concur in the holding as to age and physical and mental infirmity.

If we attempt to construe the terms of this statute strictly, its evident intent would be frustrated, but it is not necessary to either construe it strictly, or to construe it so broadly as to defeat its purpose. Confining this decision, however, to direct issue involved in the case at bar, I believe the following principle may be laid down for this and similar cases: When it is proved by the evidence that a widow, by reason of her age or permanent physical or mental infirmities, is incapable of exerting a reasonable effort to add to her income by labor, and the income of which she is possessed, or the property of which she is possessed reduced to an income, is not sufficient to provide her with the necessaries of life which are essential by reason of her age or physical or mental infirmities, then, in such a case, the widow is dependent within the meaning of the act of June 27, 1890.

Now, applying the principles to the within case, I find there is some evidence tending to show her physical infirmities to be so permanent and of such a degree as to prevent her, by a reasonable effort on her part, to add to the income of $120 per year; her age (48 years) is not per se a factor in the case. The testimony of the two physicians lack detail, and I am unable to conclude whether or not claimant actually is permanently unable to make a reasonable effort toward adding to her income.

I believe it to be necessary that such an actual physical condition be shown, whereby it can be reasonably assumed and believed that the conclusions of the physicians are warranted and based upon facts; to that end, therefore, I return the papers to you with the request that the medical referee advise as to whether or not, in his opinion, the testimony in this case is sufficient to warrant a reasonable conclusion that claimant is unable to perform manual labor in such a degree as to prevent her from adding by her daily labor to her income.

Upon a return of the case to me with the opinion herein requested the appeal will be duly considered.

_____

MARRIAGE—LEGITIMACY.

THERESIA SCHREVE (NOW SCHMIDT).

There being evidence in the case showing that soldier had a wife living in Germany, whom he deserted prior to his marriage to claimant, it is incumbent upon her to show the death of said first wife, or that the parties were divorced, before she can be regarded the legal widow of said soldier; and in the absence of such proof the minor child of soldier by said claimant can not be regarded as legitimate.

Assistant Secretary Webster Davis to the Commissioner of Pensions, July 9, 1897.

Theodore Schreve, of Company F, First Benton Hussars, was enrolled October 14, 1861, and was mustered out October 18, 1864, with Company K, Fourth Missouri Cavalry, to which he had been transferred. He did not apply for pension. He died on the 9th of November, 1883. On the 25th of July, 1890, Theresia Schmidt filed an application for pension as widow of Theodore Schreve, alleging that she was married to him on the 26th of May, 1875, at St. Louis, Mo., under the name of Theresia Becker; that said Theodore Schreve died on the 9th of October, 1883, of rheumatism contracted in the service. She further states that she was married on the 8th of October, 1887, to Julius Schmidt; that she had been married prior to her marriage to Schreve, but was divorced from her former husband. Her claim was rejected August 19, 1896, on the ground that she was unable, although aided by a special examination, to prove the legality of her marriage to Theodore Schreve. From this action an appeal was taken September 19, 1896.

A claim on behalf of Martha Schreve as minor child of said Theodore Schreve, under the general law, was filed on the 21st of November, 1890. A claim under the act of June 27, 1890, was filed at the same time. These claims were rejected August 19, 1896, on the ground that claimants were unable to prove that the marriage of Theodore Schreve and the person claiming as his widow, who is the mother of the person claiming as minor child, was legal. From this action appeal was taken, September 19, 1896.

The facts of the case are as follows:

The records of the city of St. Louis set forth that Theodore Schreve and Theresia Becker were married on the 26th of May, 1875, in said city, by Louis A. Raum, a justice of the peace. There is one child, the offspring of this marriage, Martha Schreve, who was born on the 6th of November, 1876, in the city of St. Louis, Mo. It is shown that the claimant, Theresia Schreve, had been married twice before her marriage to Schreve, but from both marriages had been divorced. She is not now living with her present husband.

The ground upon which her claim was rejected is that it is not shown that the marriage of claimant to Schreve was legal, for the reason that it does not appear that he was free to marry, there being some evidence showing that he had a wife living at the time of her marriage to him. The evidence on this point is as follows:

Frederick W. Lohman testified, July 29, 1896, before a special examiner, that he was adjutant of the Fourth Missouri Cavalry; that he enlisted in the Fifth Missouri Cavalry, which by consolidation became the Fourth Missouri Cavalry. Affiant became acquainted with Theodore Schreve at enlistment in 1861. He had not been in the country long, and could not speak a word of English. * * * Schreve was discharged in 1864, and came to St. Louis. When affiant came home in 1865 Schreve was engaged as a porter in a grocery store, and affiant was engaged as a bookkeeper by the same employer, and they were thrown together again for quite a number of years. Affiant learned something about Schreve's past history from talks with him. Affiant also learned about Schreve's past life from the proprietor of "The Rhine Wein Halle," a favorite resort for officers during the war, and a popular place in St. Louis for years. The proprietor of said establishment was from the same place in Germany as Schreve; that is, Münster, Westphalia. Schreve went to his place a good deal. What affiant learned was that Schreve was of good family in the old country, might have done well, but went wrong. He deserted a wife and children in Münster, and came to this country. Affiant understood that his wife in Germany was living when he was married to the claimant. There is no doubt about the correctness of this statement, but affiant can not refer to anyone to substantiate it.

Claimant in an affidavit made July 31, 1896, before a special examiner, stated that she understood from her husband that he came from Westphalia in 1859, and that he learned brewing and baking in the city of Münster. He never told affiant that he had been married in the old country. After her marriage to him affiant heard a good deal of talk about such a marriage, but does not know anything about it. When he was unkind to affiant others threw that in his face. They lived for years in a six-family tenement on Wyoming avenue, St. Louis. When Theodore would act mean, the tenants would twit him of a family in Germany. Affiant never found out whether it was so.

The contention of the attorney that the validity of the marriage should be presumed can not be conceded in the face of the evidence that the husband was not free to contract a marriage. His contention that the party charged with a matrimonial offense must be presumed to be innocent until proved guilty, has no application to this case, as the inquiry in this claim is not as to the criminality of the applicant, but as to her right to a pension, which under the law it is incumbent upon her to prove. It is not presumed that she has been guilty of any offense. There are not two parties having dissimilar interests with respect to this case or to any pension claim. The interests of all concerned are presumed to be identical. The efforts of all having anything to do with the pension claim are presumed to be directed to ascertaining whether the claimant is entitled to the pension provided by law. There is not a party for and a party against the case, as in a suit at law. The burden of proof of all facts necessary to establish a pension claim rests upon the claimant.

The claim of the widow is not established. It will be necessary for her, in order to establish the same, to show that at the time when she went through the ceremony of marriage to the soldier there was no impediment on either side to their lawful marriage. Whatever presumptions might ordinarily arise in favor of the legality of her marriage to the soldier are overcome by the uncontroverted facts in this case that the soldier, at the time of his alleged marriage to Theresia Becker, had a living wife in Münster, Westphalia, and between the date of the alleged marriage in 1875 and the date of the soldier's death in 1883 there is no evidence that there was ever any point of time during which Theresia Becker could be regarded as his lawful wife, by reason of the removal of the impediment and the formation of a new contract between Theresia and the soldier.

The question then turns upon the validity of the title of Martha Schreve to pension as the minor child of the soldier, and this question must turn upon the legitimacy of the child.

Congress has, from time to time, provided pension for the widow and child or children under 16 years of age of the soldier. It has been uniformly held that the "children" referred to are the legitimate children of the soldier. These children are plainly indicated in the statutes as the fruits of a marriage or marriages of the soldier. (See secs. 4702, 4703, and 4706, R. S.)

Section 4702 confers pension on the soldier's widow and, conditionally, upon his children (all his children) under 16 years of age.

Section 4703, R. S., provides the conditions of payment of additional pension granted to the widow on account of the child or children of the husband by a former wife.

Section 4706, R. S., provives for the payment, under certain conditions, of pension when the soldier leaves a widow entitled to pension by reason of his death and a child or children under 16 years of age by such widow.

In every instance it is plain that the children intended are the legitimate offspring of some marriage which is recognized as sufficient in law to confer pensionable title on a surviving widow. It is true that in a few instances it has been held that the lex loci fixing legitimacy of children shall prevail to establish the pensionable rights of such as claim as children of the soldier. Case of widow and minors of Griswold (3 P. D. (o. s.), 492); minors of Henry M. Wilkerson (2 P. D., 251). These cases are based expressly upon the statutes of Ohio, New Hampshire, and Kentucky, respectively, the rule in Ohio and Kentucky providing that the issue of an illegal or void marriage shall be legitimate. In New Hampshire, however, the rule is almost identical with the provisions of section 4704, R. S., and provides that where parents of children born before marriage afterwards

intermarry, and recognize such children as their own, such children shall inherit equally with the children under the statute of distribution, and shall be deemed legitimate.

Otherwise the holdings of the Department have been uniformly to the effect that minor children born out of lawful wedlock, and not subsequently legitimated by the contraction of lawful marriage, are excluded from the benefit of the pension laws. J. F. Kinney (4 P. D., 132); Elizabeth Felber (4 P. D., 329); George and Albert Koler (5 P. D., 99); John Pendleton (5 P. D., 217); Emma Gierhart (6 P. D., 155); Ida M. Downard (7 P. D., 290), and Hartwell Trickey (8 P. D., 84).

In the last-named case it was held that, legitimacy being a prerequisite to the legal title to pension of minor children, the fact that the parents of the children were never lawfully married bars them from receiving any pension, except by special act of Congress for their benefit.

Title to pension is made to depend not upon the local enactments of States touching domestic relations, but upon the statutes of the United States as the sovereign power. The Congress as the original donor of the pension has the power to affix whatever conditions it sees fit to the gift. It alone has the power to define the bounty and to describe the beneficiaries, and no enactment of any State could avail to confer a title to pension, because the State had no jurisdiction over the subject-matter. (United States v. Hall, 98 U. S., 343.)

The general statutes declare that under certain conditions the widows of soldiers shall be pensioned. The beneficiaries being described the next thing is to determine who are such widows. To be such widows the parties must have been the lawful wives of the soldiers through whom title is traced. The Federal statute is silent as to how this shall be proved. It only presupposes lawful marriage, whether by ceremony or by the course of the common law. For purposes of convenience in making the necessary proof Congress has provided that marriages, except such as are mentioned in section 4705, R. S., shall be proven in pension cases to be legal marriages according to the law of the place where the parties resided at the time of the marriage or at the time when the right to pension accrued. (Act of August 7, 1882.) The beneficiaries who are thus identified are pensioned not by virtue of the lex loci, but by virtue of the statute of the United States, which is permissive in its character as to the use of the lex loci as a vehicle of proof, and in this the United States has simply adopted the rule of the civilized world as a safeguard of society and the conservator of public policy. Different States have different laws regulating proof of marriage, which of itself is a thing of common right. (Meister *v.* Moore. 96 U. S., 76.) But all require proof, of whatever kind, that a lawful marriage subsisted between the parties.

In like manner title to minor children descends not by reason of any State enactments, but by reason of the pension laws themselves, originally enacted by the United States through the Congress. The construction and frame of the Federal statutes plainly point to the fact that the children must be legitimate. But, in the absence of any statute permitting resort to the State codes for a definition of legitimacy, it is obvious that such definition must be sought in the Federal statutes conferring the rights. An examination of these leads me to the belief that, in order to confer title on minors, there must at some time have been a lawful mother for the minors whose antecedent rights would be recognized by the pension laws. There must have been, at some time, a relation between the mother of the soldier's children and the soldier which was sufficient to confer title on her as his widow in case he had died while that relation remained unchanged. The relation necessary is that she shall have been his lawful wife, and the children who are pensionable are only such as may be legally accepted as legitimate offspring of the soldier by such lawful wife; for marriage is the vehicle, both of nature and of law, to distinguish between filius nullius and that legitimate offspring which affixes legal responsibility to the parental relation. But we are not without assistance from the courts of the United States in determining this point. In the case of United States *v.* Skam (5 Cr., C. C., 367) we find an interesting study of the question. This was an indictment for perjury. The perjury was assigned in a joint affidavit made by the defendant and one Jane Berkemer, who, in order to obtain from the United States a pension for one Mary Ann Thomas, as the child of Orral T. Thomas (a marine who died in the service of the United States), made oath before a justice of the peace in Washington, D. C., that they are well acquainted with Mary Ann Thomas and know her to be the legitimate heir and only child left by the said Thomas, whereas the defendant then and there knew and believed that the said Mary Ann Thomas was not the child of the said Orral T. Thomas.

By the Maryland law of 1786, chapter 45, section 7—

if any man shall have one or more children by any woman whom he shall afterwards marry, such child or children, if acknowledged by the man, shall, in virtue of such marriage and acknowledgment, be hereby legitimated and capable in law to inherit and transmit inheritance as if born in wedlock.

Evidence was procured by the defendant that the said Orral T. Thomas married the mother about a year after the birth of the child, and called her his child, and suffered her to call him father and to be called by his name, Mary Ann Thomas. The court upon the trial instructed the jury that the facts that the said Orral T. Thomas married the mother of the said Mary Ann after the birth of the latter, and received and maintained the child as his own, and called her his child and suffered her to call him father and to be called by his name, if believed by the jury, were evidences from which, if not contradicted by other evidence, the jury may infer that she was begotten by the said Orral T. Thomas, and such child becomes legitimated by the law of Maryland and is entitled to a pension, etc.

Reference is made to this case, because in it, as in the New Hampshire case cited herein, the child was declared to be legitimate by virtue of the State law, and because the condition on which legitimacy was founded was in virtue of an actual legal subsequent marriage between the parties and acknowlegment of the offspring as his own.

Section 4704, R. S., is legislative adoption by the Federal Congress of a rule of law adopted in some of the States, in which, as well as in it, legitimacy is made to depend after all upon legal marriage of the parents of the child. The States may adopt such rules as public policy may dictate to prevent escheat of estates, or for such political reasons as may exist, but if such enactments contravene the spirit or the letter of the pension laws they are of no effect whatever to change the operation of the latter.

In my opinion the soldier's children referred to in the pension laws who may be pensioned are the legitimate children of the soldier; by which I understand is meant the soldier's children by a lawful marriage, by virtue of which the mother of the children might, if living at the time of the soldier's death, first be pensioned as his widow. It is true that section 4475, R. S. of Missouri, the State in which the minor resides, provides that—

the issue of all marriages decreed null in law, or dissolved by divorce, shall be deemed legitimate.

But we are to try the pensionable rights of this minor not by the law of Missouri but by the pension laws of the United States.

In the case at bar it is not shown that the child's mother was ever the legal wife of the soldier. On the contrary, it appears that there was an effective bar to their legal union, and until that fact can be overturned by proof I must hold that the child in question, not being the offspring of a legal marriage, does not come within the beneficial operation of the pension laws granting pensions to minor children.

Your action rejecting the claims is hereby affirmed.

REDUCTION—RERATING.

GOTTLIEB SPITZER, ALIAS GOTTFRIED BRUNNER.

Where the allowance of a certain rate of pension was directed by a decision of the Department, and subsequently the Commissioner of Pensions ordered a medical examination of the pensioner by a specialist and upon the report of such examination proceeded to reduce the rate of pension, it is

Held, That such action was not ultra vires, but was within the scope of the authority given him by the proviso to section 3, act of June 21, 1879.

The rate allowed under departmental decision of June 13, 1894, not being manifestly erroneous, but the question as to its correctness being one of judgment merely, it will not be disturbed. (Citing decision of Secretary Teller in case of James S. Coleman, Digest of 1885, p. 422.)

Assistant Secretary Webster Davis to the Commissioner of Pensions, July 10, 1897.

This soldier was originally pensioned at the rate of $4 per month from June 6, 1865, for disease of eyes. The pension was increased to $50 per month from April 22, 1884, and to $72 per month from March 4, 1890. It was reduced to $30 per month from June 4, 1891, upon evidence obtained through a special examination. Upon appeal the action reducing the pension to $30 per month was approved by the Department August 27, 1891. On a motion for reconsideration further special examination was ordered, and upon a review of the evidence, after such special examination, the motion was granted, and the Pension Bureau was directed to restore the $72 rate from the date of reduction, June 4, 1891.

The case was opened up by the Pension Bureau in July, 1893, and was referred to the medical referee for an opinion as to the extent of the pensioner's disability. A medical examination by a specialist in diseases of the eye was had, and upon the report of such examination the medical referee recommended the reduction of the rate to $30 per month. After notice to the pensioner the rate was reduced in accordance with that recommendation, to take effect from September 4, 1893. An appeal from that action was taken January 22, 1894.

In a decision rendered June 13, 1894, the Department held that the pensioner was not entitled to $72 per month, but was entitled to $50 per month under the act of July 14, 1892. Under this decision a certificate was issued allowing the $50 rate from September 4, 1893.

On May 26, 1897, the claimant filed a motion for reconsideration of the decision of June 13, 1894, contending that he is entitled to a restoration of the $72 rate and that in accepting the $50 rate under the aforesaid decision of Assistant Secretary Reynolds he did not waive his right to subsequently appeal for restoration of the $72 rate.

In the appeal of January 22, 1894, it was contended that it was not within the authority of the Commissioner of Pensions to reduce the rate to $30 per month after the Department had, upon practically the same state of facts, held that the pensioner was entitled to $72. This contention was discussed by Assistant Secretary Reynolds in his decision of June 13, 1894, but as the question is one of considerable importance, as affecting the practice of your Bureau, and is of vital importance in this case (since, if the action of the Commissioner was illegal, restoration of the $72 rate must follow as a matter of course), I deem it proper to touch upon it again, although it is not distinctly raised in the pending motion.

It may be stated as a general proposition that the Commissioner of Pensions has no authority to change the action of the Department in a given case, by reduction or increase of rate, upon the same evidence. Any other or different rule would be subversive of all proper order.

But in the case now under consideration the reduction in the rate of pension was based, ostensibly at least, upon new evidence, to wit, the report of a medical examination. The right of the Commissioner to order such examination is, I think, unquestionable. The act of June 21, 1879, declares that he shall have power—

* * * to order special examinations whenever, in his judgment, the same may be necessary, and to increase or reduce the pension according to right and justice.

There is no limitation in the act upon his power based upon any former holding of the head of the Department. Aside from the fact that the doctrine of res adjudicata or stare decisis is plainly inapplicable to pension cases, and that title is always contingent upon the existence of facts that beget it and keep it alive, the very object of the bestowal of power upon the Commissioner to inquire and increase or reduce is that he may be enabled to so carry into effect the pension laws as at the same time to do justice to the pensioner and to protect the interests of the United States. It is as much his duty to see that the bounties of the Government are not squandered or improperly disbursed as it is to see that the beneficiaries receive their just share under the law. If the Commissioner may not, in a case where the rate has been fixed by a departmental decision, order a medical or special examination and, upon the evidence thus obtained, reduce the pension, it would logically follow that he is prohibited from taking similar action looking to an increase of pension. The effect of such a rule would be to compel applicants for increase in all such cases to apply to the appellate power rather than to the Bureau of original jurisdiction which is charged with first considering and passing upon pension claims. I am convinced that such a rule, besides being contrary to ordinary methods of procedure, would not operate beneficially either to claimants or to the Government. It is better that the duty of initiating action should rest with the Commissioner of Pensions, leaving to the claimant or pensioner his right of appeal to the Secretary of the Interior for correction of any injustice.

I find, moreover, that the right of the Commissioner to investigate and reduce pension in such a case as this, where the rating of the pensioner had been directed by a decision of the Department, was distinctly affirmed by Assistant Secretary Hawkins in the case of Wallace G. Bone (2 P. D., 310) and subsequently, in connection with the same case, by Assistant Secretary Reynolds, whose letter on the subject I quote:

COMMISSIONER OF PENSIONS.

SIR: The attention of the Department has been again called, by your communication of May 19, 1893, to the invalid pension claim, certificate No. 24155, of Wallace G. Bone, late corporal, Company D, Seventh Illinois Cavalry.

You transmit the papers in said claim, with a brief of the evidence, and submit to the Department the question whether suspension of payment under this certificate should be directed by you pending further action touching the proper rate of pension to be allowed in this case.

You state that the claim is submitted by you directly to the Department for decision of this question for the reason that the present rating of the pensioner was directed by a decision of this Department rendered in 1885, and therefore any action taken or contemplated would possibly necessitate a review of said decision.

This identical question was submitted to the Department, in this claim, by your predecessor in office on March 23, 1888, and on December 29, 1888, the Department rendered a decision thereon which fully and exhaustively discussed the subject. This decision will be found attached to the "brief face" in this claim, and is also reported in volume 2, Pension Decisions, at page 310. The position taken by the Department in said decision is believed to be sound, and the law governing the case is therein fully, clearly, and correctly stated. Said decision has never been changed, modified, or overruled by the Department, and it is not considered necessary to add anything thereto at the present time, the views therein expressed fully covering the case and completely answering the question submitted by you.

As was stated in said opinion, you have a clear and unquestionable right, within the jurisdiction given you expressly by law, to adjust the rate of pension to be received by this pensioner in accordance with his actual pensionable disability as shown to exist at the present time, and the former departmental decision of 1885, to which you refer, does not operate to prevent such action as you may, in your discretion, see fit to take at the present time.

You are accordingly directed to proceed with the adjustment of this pensioner's rate as may be deemed by you just and proper under the evidence in the case, and in accordance with the law and the views of the Department as set forth in said decision of December 29, 1888.

Very respectfully,   JNO. M. REYNOLDS, *Assistant Secretary.*

The above letter was an instruction which, though elicited in a particular case, was general in its character. It was given anterior to the action in this case, and fully advised the Commissioner of his right under the law and under the sanction of the Department to do the very thing he did do, and that, too, notwithstanding a former departmental holding in the case. The rule therein stated is hereby reaffirmed and will govern in all similar cases.

It is hardly necessary to say that the authority vested in the Commissioner extends only to adjustment of rates for future payment. He has no right to change rates fixed by the Department for any past period.

I may add that so far as this case is concerned, even if it be conceded that the action of the Commissioner in reducing the pension was unauthorized, the fact that the Department subsequently took cognizance of the case on appeal and, after weighing the whole case on its merits, decided that the Commissioner had properly proceeded to reduce the rate and had erred only in the amount of the reduction, must be held to have cured any defect that may have attended the action.

The only question remaining to be considered is whether, on the evidence in the case, the appellant is entitled to receive $72 per month, in lieu of $50, from September 4, 1893.

It is admitted that he was not, at the date named, totally blind. He is entitled to the $72 rate, if at all, only on the ground that he was, at said date—

so permanently and totally disabled as to require the regular personal aid and attendance of another person.

The rate he is now receiving is that provided by law for those soldiers and sailors who are shown to be—

totally incapacitated for performing manual labor by reason of injuries received or disease contracted in the service of the United States and in line of duty, and who are thereby disabled to such a degree as to require frequent and periodical, though not regular and constant, personal aid and attendance of another person.

There has always been some doubt as to whether the degree of disability shown in his case quite reached the standard prescribed by law for the allowance of the $72 rate. Secretary Bussey concluded, however, that it was more in accord with justice to give him the benefit of that doubt than to cut him down to the $30 rate, which was conceded to be greatly disproportionate to the degree of his disability. At that time there was no intermediate rate between $30 and $72. In June, 1894, Assistant Secretary Reynolds, after careful consideration of all the evidence, was of the opinion that his disability most nearly approaches that for which the rate of $50 per month is prescribed by law.

It is a well-settled rule that rates allowed by former administrations will not be disturbed where it is merely a question of judgment as to whether the rate was or was not fully proportionate to the degree of disability. Rerating will be made only where manifest error, either of law or fact, is shown. (See decision of Secretary Teller in case of James S. Coleman, Digest of 1885, p. 422.) It can not be said that the allowance of $50 per month, in this case, from September 4, 1893, was a manifest error or mistake. The making of a change in the rate, to take effect from that date, would be but the substitution of one opinion for another, and would inaugurate a practice in contravention of long-existing rules and decisions on that subject. If the applicant believes that he is now entitled to the rate of $72 per month his remedy consists in filing an application for increase of pension, under which, if the evidence should justify such action, the rate can be increased. The pending motion is overruled.

SERVICE–JURISDICTION–RECORD.

DAVID H. DYER.

The amended record of the War Department shows claimant accepted into service on December 20, 1864; paid as private up to and discharged on April 13, 1865. He was furloughed on January 14, 1865; availed himself of said furlough on February 2, 1865; held himself under military orders, and obeyed the order of the military authorities requiring him to report at Indianapolis. His discharge was delivered on May 29, 1865. He had no knowledge, neither did he receive any intimation of any kind, previous to April 13, 1865, that he had been or was to be discharged.

Held, 1. On the record, corroborated by reliable evidence, soldier was in the service of the United States during the war of the rebellion for more than ninety days. (Poland's Appeal, 8 P. D., 266, followed.)

2. This Department is bound to accept as true the unimpeached record of the War Department, but it alone has power to determine what effect such record shall have on a claimant's pensionable rights.

Assistant Secretary Webster Davis to the Commissioner of Pensions, July 10, 1897.

This case came before the Secretary on a motion for reconsideration on February 20, 1897, and it was referred back in order that further information might be obtained from the War Department. (See case of David H. Dyer, 8 P. D., 491). That information having been received, the motion was duly considered and granted, and as the decision granting the motion recited certain facts and principles which pertain vitally to the question now before me, it is incorporated herein, and is hereby made part of this opinion. That decision is as follows:

In the within claim, declaration under the act of June 27, 1890, was filed on January 31, 1896. Rejection was had June 16, 1896, and the same was affirmed by me, on appeal, August 29, 1896, on the ground that the War Department reported claimant's military service as commencing December 20, 1864, and ending February 2, 1865. On December 9, 1896, a motion for reconsideration was filed, and I found, upon a careful review, the following facts: Claimant was drafted December 12, 1864; examined and held to service December 20, 1864; received at draft rendezvous December 30, 1864; admitted to post hospital, Camp Carrington, Indiana, January 8, 1865; rejected by board of inspectors January 10, 1865; papers sent to department headquarters January 20, 1865; ordered to be discharged by Major-General Hooker, said order being dated January 27, 1865; said order received on January 30, 1865; discharged on April 13, 1865, by Alvin P. Hovey, brevet major-general, commanding draft rendezvous; paid, by the record in the Treasury Department, from December 12, 1864, to April 13, 1865. The foregoing was the record, and it was apparent that the conclusion of the War Department was totally at variance with such record. I held, therefore, on February 20, 1897, on the motion for reconsideration, that it was error to reject a claim upon a conclusion based upon evidence not in the case, which alleged evidence was contrary to the record on file. I further requested you to obtain from the War Department a summary of claimant's service de novo, and more especially a copy of the record whereon was based the holding of the War Department, viz, "that he was furloughed to await discharge on or about February 2, 1865; that he was discharged from service February 2, 1865, on surgeon's certificate of disability." The amended record of the War Department is now before me, and the following facts are shown:

Drafted December 12, 1864; examined and held to service December 20, 1864; received at general draft rendezvous December 30, 1864; admitted to post hospital January 8, 1865, with erysipelas; rejected by board of inspectors January 10, 1865, on account of general feebleness of constitution existing at time of enlistment; furloughed home to White Hall, Owen County, Ind., January 14, 1865; papers recommending discharge sent to headquarters January 20, 1865; papers indorsed for discharge January 27, 1865; papers received back January 27, 1865; soldier returned to duty February 2, 1865; notified to report for discharge May 19, 1865; discharge delivered May 29, 1865. The War Department also states that no record has been found of his presence at the general rendezvous after February 2, 1865, and that the conclusion is that on February 2, 1865, the date at which he was returned from hospital to duty, he availed himself of the furlough granted on January 14, 1865, and that it is believed "that he received proper notice of his discharge at the time he was released from control of the military authorities, February 2, 1865."

The gist of the issue lies in the last quotation, which is a conclusion based upon a record recited. I stated in my former holding, in substance, that this Department is bound by the record of the War Department until that record is successfully impeached, but that it is not bound by the conclusion of the War Department when such conclusion is contrary to facts set out in the record, which record is furnished by the War Department.

The fallacy of the War Department's conclusion is plainly apparent in view of the following: It concludes that on February 2, 1865, Dyer was furloughed to await discharge; the record shows that he was furloughed on January 14, 1865, and the War Department admits that on that date he was in the hospital, and concludes that "February 2, 1865, is the date he availed himself of the furlough granted him January 14, 1865." There is no record, and no contention made by the War Department, that the furlough of January 14, 1865, was superseded or modified on February 2, 1865, and it needs no argument to prove that the aforesaid conclusion of the War Department is squarely against its amended record. There is nothing whatever in the record to show that Dyer was ever at any date "furloughed to await discharge." And again: The War Department states, as heretofore recited, that it believes "that he received proper notice of his discharge at the time he was released from control of the military authorities, February 2, 1865." Was he released from the control of the military authorities on that date? The record not only shows that he was on a furlough at that date, but it also shows that he was on May 19, 1865, ordered to report for discharge, which discharge was completed, by manual delivery, on May 29, 1865; and still further, the War Department concludes that "he was discharged from the service February 2, 1865, on surgeon's certificate of disability, and that so much of the record (surgeon's certificate of disability) as shows him discharged on April 13, 1865, is erroneous." This conclusion is somewhat startling, in view of the fact that there is no record in evidence of any surgeon's certificate of disability for discharge, but that there is on file with the papers his original discharge certificate, which states that he "is hereby discharged from the service of the United States this 13th day of April, 1865, at Indianapolis. * * * Given at Indianapolis, Ind., this 13th day of April, 1865. (Signed) Alvin P. Hovey, brevet major-general, United States Volunteers, commanding draft rendezvous, Indiana." It is manifest that this discharge certificate can not be summarily thrown out of the evidence upon a conclusion of the War Department based upon facts not in evidence. It is worthy of note that this certificate is not a "surgeon's certificate of disability;" it is the actual discharge certificate, signed by the general commanding the rendezvous, and whose authority for such procedure is evidenced by an indorsement upon the back of the document, viz: "To be discharged by command of Maj. Genl. Hooker. P. von Radowitz, A. A. A. G."

I held in my previous consideration of this motion, which holding is based upon the decision of the Judge-Advocate-General of the Army in the Poland appeal, that the fact of payment up to a certain date, or the date of discharge, as shown by his discharge certificate, was not conclusive evidence that a soldier remained in the service up to those dates, for a soldier is held to be discharged when "he is released from his contract to serve and the control of his officers, and is a civilian, and at liberty to act accordingly." (Poland Appeal, 8 P. D., 266.) And it is upon this principle that the War Department holds that claimant was "discharged" on February 2, 1865. Unfortunately, however, for the argument, the record (and that is all that we are bound by, as far as the War Department holding in this particular case is concerned) absolutely negatives the War Department's conclusion, and I again repeat, that there is nothing in the record, as originally filed, or as amended by the War Department, that warrants any such conclusion.

I am not, however, satisfied but that claimant was notified earlier than the record shows that he was released from his contract to service, and was relegated by the proper authorities into a civilian's status. It is apparent that the record can furnish nothing further as to this point, and this being true, verbal testimony may be resorted to to fix, if possible, the date on which he was "released from his contract to serve and the control of his officers, and is (was) a civilian, and at liberty to act accordingly."

The question then is, Was soldier informed, upon his release from the hospital. that he had been ordered by the proper authorities to be discharged, and did he go to his home with the knowledge that he was released from the service, although his discharge papers were not at that time made out? A vital principle is involved in this case, and a special examination is ordered, to determine with great thoroughness and care, and the date that the knowledge of release from service was actually received by claimant should be actually or approximately fixed.

The action appealed from is reversed and special examination ordered.

The examination ordered by my immediate predecessor has been held and the case is again before the Secretary. Technically speaking. the proper practice would be for you to take action upon the new evidence, leaving claimant, if said action was against him, to appeal if he so desired; but inasmuch as such procedure would tend to delay any rights that claimant might have, and for the further and good reason that in your return of the files to me you request a ruling upon the important point involved, it is deemed that justice will be better conserved by an immediate review of the case.

As stated in the above quoted opinion, the only question now involved is as to the date, actual or approximate, that knowledge was brought home to this soldier that he was released from his contract to serve. and the control of his officers, and was a civilian and at liberty to act as such. (See Judge-Advocate-General's ruling embodied in the Poland appeal, 8 P. D., 266.)

Claimant testifies that while he was in the hospital at Camp Carrington, Indiana, with a severe case of erysipelas, the surgeon at said hospital, sometime during February, 1865, told him that he could go home if he so desired and stay until he was ordered back, because he could have better care at his home than at the hospital. He believes that he had some kind of a written leave of absence, but is positive that said writing, if he ever had one, was of the nature of a "sick furlough." He states that he did not receive, at or about that time, any intimation that he had been, or was about to be, discharged, but that he went home with the clear conviction that he was under military orders, and was only on sick leave. He has been subjected to a close cross-examination, and he tells his story in a straightforward way, and clearly and unequivocally narrates all of the circumstances, steadfastly denying that he was ever informed, or had any reason to believe, that he was furloughed to await discharge, or that he was to be discharged, until he reached Indianapolis in pursuance to an order of the military authorities to report at that city. The special examiner who took his testimony states that his reputation for veracity is good, and that he gave his testimony with an openness that impressed him with the soldier's honesty of purpose and truthfulness.

His brother testifies that while soldier was sick in hospital, he, affiant, received word that his brother was dangerously ill. He went to see him and returned home without making any arrangements for soldier's return. He saw soldier the day after soldier reached home and states that he, affiant, thought he was discharged. Upon being questioned he states that his reason for such belief was that "there was no call for him after that." This affiant further states that he did not know that soldier ever returned to Indianapolis, when the record shows that he did. Affiant says his memory is not of the best, and has no knowledge or reason for his belief that soldier was discharged, except as above stated.

William H. Medaris, a neighbor, remembers the drafting of soldier, but does not recall his return in February, and does not remember that he was sick. Isaac Blown (aged 39 years in 1897) thinks soldier did not come home until the war ended, but on reflection thinks he was home on a sick furlongh, but is not positive. If affiant's age is correctly stated he probably remembers but little about it. Henry H. McHurley, a neighbor, recalls the visit of soldier's brother to Indianapolis, and thinks soldier returned home with him. He further states that he did not see soldier at the time, and did not go to his house until sometime "inside of a month and a half" or "inside of two months" after his return. He thinks soldier was discharged, but has no reason for this belief, save that he thinks he heard so; he, however, recalls no such fact as having been told him by soldier, but has the impression that he was told so by "neighbors in passing." All of the above affiants are rated as men of veracity and are entitled to full credit. S. T. Isom, evidently a neighbor, reported as unreliable generally, but as perhaps worthy of belief in this case, testifies that he was at soldier's home when he returned sick; that affiant understood soldier was at home on "a discharge furlough," but that afterwards this discharge furlough was revoked; that soldier did not understand the letter which called him back to Indianapolis, but that when soldier returned again from that city he told affiant that he was "released." On being questioned as to what soldier "thought" about the nature of his furlough, he says first one thing and then another, but finally states he does not think soldier made any arrangement to "put in a crop" until he was finally discharged. The testimony of affiant Isom is the only testimony that militates against claimant's testimony, and it is very evident that Isom's evidence, in material particulars, is based upon a very vague and misty recollection. He does not pretend to testify as to anything that soldier told him, his statements going to what he supposed soldier "thought." Such evidence, from such a source, can have but little weight, and can not be received as sufficient to explain any material fact, much less to overthrow the record or claimant's own positive statements as to facts and his own belief.

I have carefully considered the issues involved herein, and, after mature deliberation, I believe the principle laid down by my immediate predecessor in the decision quoted herein is sound and just, and is founded upon both law and equity. It is of the greatest importance that one Department of the Government shall not usurp the functions, rights, and powers of another Department of the Government. The War Department is, by law, the proper repository of the military archives of the Government, and therein, of the records showing the personal military history of its soldiers. A transcript of the record in any given case, properly attested by the legal custodian of the military records aforesaid, is competent and sufficient proof, if unrebutted, of the facts therein recited.

This Department is likewise charged by law with a special function, as the court of last resort in such cases, to wit, to determine whether, upon all the proofs adduced, a given claimant has made out such title as gives him an acknowledged right to the benefits contained within the pension laws. Among the kinds of evidence adduced for the trial of this issue is the record in possession of the Government showing the military history of the soldier in question. This Department, in the final adjudication of the question in issue, is bound by the record. But the record can only be conclusive of the facts which it contains, and is to be weighed, in so far as its effects on the pensionable rights of a claimant is concerned, precisely like any and all other evidence admitted in the hearing. This Department is bound to accept as true the unimpeached record which the War Department shall supply in any given case, but this Department alone has the power under the law, in the absence of any statutory direction or restriction, to determine what effect such record shall have upon the pensionable rights sued for.

The record in this case shows the Government to have accepted claimant into the United States service, and to have held him to such service, on December 20, 1864; he was sent to the post hospital on January 8, 1865; furloughed home January 14, 1865; he was returned to duty, and availed himself of his furlough home, on February 2, 1865; discharged on April 13, 1865; notified to report for discharge on May 19, 1865; and discharge certificate delivered May 29, 1865; he was paid by the United States Government to include the period between the date he was drafted, viz, December 12, 1864, and the date of his discharge, viz, April 13, 1865, and there being no evidence of any kind to show that this soldier, previous to April 13, 1865, was ever advised, or received any intimation from any one, that he "was relieved from his contract to serve, and the control of his officers, and was a civilian and at liberty to act accordingly," I hold that for pensionable purposes it is shown that claimant served more than ninety days in the military service of the United States during the late war of the rebellion.

You will therefore reopen this case and readjudicate it under the above holding.

DECLARATIONS UNDER ACT OF JUNE 27, 1890.

INSTRUCTIONS.

1. Every application for pension under the second section of the act of June 27, 1890, should state that the same is made under said act, the dates of enlistment and discharge, the name or nature of the diseases, wounds, or injuries by which the claimant is disabled, and that they are not due to vicious habits: *Provided, however*, That the omission of any of these averments shall not invalidate the application (the intent to claim pension being manifest and the declaration being executed in accordance with law), but such application shall be subject to amendment by means of a supplemental affidavit, in the particulars wherein it is defective; said supplemental affidavit or affidavits to be read in connection with and as a part of the application itself: *And provided further*, That a declaration *in the terms of the act* shall be sufficient.

2. Should the paper filed fail to show upon its face, with certainty, that it is intended as a claim for the benefits of the act of June 27, 1890, the claimant may make it certain, by means of a supplemental affidavit, which shall be read in connection with and as a part of the original application.

3. Should the medical examination disclose the existence of any disease, wound, or injury not alleged in the original or amendatory application, which is a factor in the applicant's inability to earn a support by manual labor, the claimant shall be called upon to state, under oath, the time, place, and circumstance, when, where, and under which such wound or injury was received or disease contracted, and whether it was in any manner caused by vicious habits.

4. Should the wound, injury, or disease not specified in the original or amendatory declaration, but discovered on medical examination, be shown to have existed at the time when the original declaration was filed, and it is found not to be due to vicious habits, it shall be taken into account, the same as if formally specified in the original application, in estimating the degree of the permanent mental or physical disability to which it contributes.

Should it be found, however, not to have existed at the time when the original application was filed, but from a subsequent date prior to medical examination, the degrees of the disability of the applicant being below the maximum rating, pension may be increased accordingly from the date when such wound or injury was incurred or disease contracted, provided the degree of disability from all contributory causes is thereby enhanced to a sufficient extent to justify a higher rating.

Should it be found impossible to fix the exact date when such wound or injury was received or disease contracted, the higher rating shall commence from the date of the certificate of medical examination showing its existence.

5. *Vicious habits.*—A liberal and reasonable rule in regard to the proof as to "vicious habits" was laid down by the Department in the case of John Martin (7 P. D., 578), and the same is hereby affirmed: *Provided, however*, That where the nature of the disease, wound, or injury is such as to show that it is not due to vicious habits, the Commissioner of Pensions may, in his discretion, accept the sworn statement of the applicant as sufficient.

6. Original pension having been allowed, any subsequent *increase* of pension must be based on the fact that there is increased incapacitation for earning a support by manual labor, and must be adjudicated, so far as commencement of the increased rate is concerned, under section 4698½, Revised Statutes of the United States.

7. All former rules and decisions in conflict herewith are hereby set aside.

Assistant Secretary Webster Davis to the Commissioner of Pensions, July 28, 1897.

I have considered your suggestions relative to a modification of the rules governing the adjudication of claims arising under the second section of the act of June 27, 1890. It is represented to me that the present rules, by reason of technicalities, necessitate an uneconomical distribution of the clerical force at your command, and in other ways render the administration of the law difficult and embarrassing.

After a careful examination of the various enactments of law that go to make up the pension system, I can not think it was the intention of Congress to hedge their administration with the difficulties and pitfalls of any system of special pleading, the technicalties and refinements of which may tend to a practical defeat of the benevolent aid intended to be extended to the soldiers of the Republic.

The pension law is essentially a law sui generis; and while a proceeding had thereunder, when not expressly regulated by statute, may draw to itself the aid of certain canons of law and rules of evidence, yet the very nature of cases arising under this law forbids that strictness and technicality that attend upon regular court proceedings.

Here, the will of the legislature being ascertained, the attendant proceedings should be as simple as possible. A multitude of rules tends to confusion; and the way of the claimant should not be hedged about with any difficulty that can be avoided.

The act of June 27, 1890, provides that pension thereunder—

shall commence from the date of the filing of the application in the Pension Office after the passage of this act, upon proof that the disability then existed.

So that application must be made in order to receive a pension under this act.

In its terms this law declares that—

all persons who served ninety days or more in the military or naval service of the United States during the late war of the rebellion, and who have been honorably discharged therefrom, and who are now, or who may hereafter be, suffering from a mental or physical disability of a permanent character, not the result of their own vicious habits, which incapacitates them for the performance of manual labor in such a degree as to render them unable to earn a support, shall, upon making due proof of the fact, according to such rules and regulations as the Secretary of the Interior may provide, be placed upon the list of invalid pensioners, etc.

Although the statute has clearly indicated the conditions precedent to title under this law, yet it is silent as to the form of application. It has, however, conferred upon the Secretary of the Interior the power to make rules by which "due proof" shall be made of the facts required to be established, in order to draw to the applicant the benefits of the statute, and this power, I take it, includes authority to prescribe what shall constitute an "application" within the meaning and intent of the law.

After a careful consideration of the whole matter, I have concluded that a faithful compliance with the following "rules" will obviate the difficulties complained of and furnish a safe, speedy, and uniform system of adjudicating claims that arise under the second section of the act of June 27, 1890, viz:

1. Every application for pension under the second section of the act

of June 27, 1890, should state that the same is made under said act, the dates of enlistment and discharge, the name or nature of the diseases, wounds, or injuries by which the claimant is disabled, and that they are not due to vicious habits: *Provided, however*, That the omission of any of these averments shall not invalidate the application (the intent to claim pension being manifest and the declaration being executed in accordance with law), but such application shall be subject to amendment by means of a supplemental affidavit in the particulars wherein it is defective; said supplemental affidavit or affidavits to be read in connection with and as a part of the application itself: *And provided further*, That a declaration *in the terms of the act* shall be sufficient.

2. Should the paper filed fail to show upon its face with certainty that it is intended as a claim for the benefits of the act of June 27, 1890, the claimant may make it certain by means of a supplemental affidavit, which shall be read in connection with and as a part of the original application.

3. Should the medical examination disclose the existence of any disease, wound, or injury not alleged in the original or amendatory application, which is a factor in the applicant's inability to earn a support by manual labor, the claimant shall be called upon to state, under oath, the time, place, and circumstance, when, where, and under which such wound or injury was received or disease contracted, and whether it was in any manner caused by vicious habits.

4. Should the wound, injury, or disease not specified in the original or amendatory declaration, but discovered on medical examination, be shown to have existed at the time when the original declaration was filed, and it is found not to be due to vicious habits, it shall be taken into account the same as if formally specified in the original application in estimating the degree of the permanent mental or physical disability to which it contributes.

Should it be found, however, not to have existed at the time when the original application was filed, but from a subsequent date prior to medical examination, the degrees of the disability of the applicant being below the maximum rating; pension may be increased accordingly from the date when such wound or injury was incurred or disease contracted, provided the degree of disability from all contributory causes is thereby enhanced to a sufficient extent to justify a higher rating.

Should it be found impossible to fix the exact date when such wound or injury was received or disease contracted, the higher rating shall commence from the date of the certificate of medical examination showing its existence.

5. *Vicious habits.*—A liberal and reasonable rule in regard to the proof as to "vicious habits" was laid down by the Department in the case of John Martin (7 P. D., 578), and the same is hereby affirmed: *Provided, however*, That where the nature of the disease, wound, or injury is such as to show that it is not due to vicious habits, the Com-

missioner of Pensions may, in his discretion, accept the sworn statement of the applicant as sufficient.

6. Original pension having been allowed, any subsequent *increase* of pension must be based on the fact that there is increased incapacitation for earning a support by manual labor, and must be adjudicated, so far as commencement of the increased rate is concerned, under section 4698½ Revised Statutes of the United States.

7. All former rules and decisions in conflict herewith are hereby set aside.

SERVICE—REVENUE CUTTER—MEXICAN WAR.

WILLIAM F. ROGERS.

Under the act of March 2, 1799 (section 2757, Revised Statutes), the revenue-cutter *Forward* was embraced within and constituted a part of the naval establishment of the United States for more than sixty days in the war with Mexico, and claimant, being an officer on said revenue cutter and serving with the Navy of the United States in Mexico or on the coasts thereof during the war with that nation for more than sixty days and having engaged in battle in said war, he has title to pension under act of January 29, 1887.

Assistant Secretary Webster Davis to the Commissioner of Pensions, August 2, 1897.

I have the honor to state that I am in receipt of the following communication, addressed by you to the Hon. Thomas Ryan, First Assistant Secretary of the Interior, of date July 16, 1897, in reply to a letter of inquiry made by him of date July 15, 1897, concerning dropping from the rolls the name of Capt. W. F. Rogers, a pensioner under act of January 29, 1887 (Mexican war), certificate No. 6641, which communication has been referred to me for consideration and appropriate action:

Sir: In reply to the inclosed letter, I have the honor to state that William F. Rogers was pensioned June 27, 1887, for service as lieutenant on the United States revenue-cutter *Forward* from June 30, 1846, to April 30, 1847, the said vessel having been in active cooperation with the Navy, by order of the President of the United States, in prosecuting the war with Mexico. The claim was allowed, under the practice then existing in this Bureau, that all persons who rendered the necessary service on board of revenue cutters while cooperating with the Navy in the war with Mexico had title under the act of January 29, 1887. His name was dropped from the pension roll on the ground that he was not legally enlisted into the military or naval service of the United States.

In a decision, dated June 22, 1895, by the Hon. John M. Reynolds, Assistant Secretary of the Interior, in the case of David Oliver, Navy certificate 15069, act of June 27, 1890, he held "that those who served in the revenue marine on vessels which cooperated, by direction of the President, with the Navy, as provided in section 2757, R. S., were not in the Navy or the naval establishment of the United States, and are not pensionable under said act, nor their widows or minor children."

It is true that the decision referred to was made in a claim under the act of June 27, 1890, for service which was alleged to have been rendered during the war of the rebellion. That decision held, however, that the revenue marine is not a part of or included in the regular naval service. It is a civil branch only of service which is, in a popular and general sense, naval because on the water, but is wholly separate and distinct from the organized governmental military and naval forces, and is so recognized by the law, which provides that "the revenue cutters shall, when the President so directs, cooperate with the Navy."

It was further held that those persons in the revenue-marine service were in the civil employment, and not in either the military or naval branches of the Government, and that their status as civilian employees was not changed by reason of the fact that the vessels on which they served cooperated with the Navy by order of the President, as provided by law.

The conditions as to the nature of service in the act of January 29, 1887, being identical with those in the act of June 27, 1890, viz, "in military or naval service of the United States."

It is believed that this decision is adverse to the rights of this pensioner and all other persons who have been pensioned for service while attached to revenue cutters, and who were not regularly enlisted in the military or naval service of the United States.

Very respectfully,

H. CLAY EVANS.

Hon. THOMAS RYAN,
First Assistant Secretary of the Interior.

The naval history of Lieutenant Rogers, as certified by the honorable Secretary of the Treasury of date March 19, 1897, shows that he was appointed third lieutenant in the revenue-cutter service June 30, 1846, was promoted successively to the grades of second and first lieutenant, and tendered his resignation March 2, 1861. Upon his appointment in 1846 he was assigned to duty on the revenue-cutter *Forward*, then in active cooperation, by order of the President, with the Navy, in the prosecution of the war with Mexico, and served thereon until subsequent to April 30, 1847, the date of her withdrawal from said cooperation.

The record shows that on February 4, 1887, this officer filed declaration for Mexican-war pension under act of January 29, 1887, and on June 27, 1889, he was pensioned under said act at $8 per month from January 29, 1887.

On April 21, 1897, steps were taken by your Bureau by notice to drop the pensioner's name from the roll, and on June 4, 1897, the dropping was approved by your Bureau on the ground—

that pensioner had no title to pension under act of January 29, 1887, as he was not an officer or enlisted man in the United States Army or Navy as required by said act, but served on a United States revenue cutter, which service does not confer title to pension except for disabilities incurred or contracted while cooperating with the Navy. Evidence filed in rebuttal is not deemed sufficient to warrant change of action.

Accordingly, on June 16, 1897, the United States pension agent was notified to drop pensioner's name from the rolls.

It appears that this officer's claim was allowed under the practice then existing in your Bureau, that all persons who rendered the necessary service on board of revenue cutters while cooperating with the Navy, in the war with Mexico, had title thereto under the act of January 29, 1887.

It also appears that pensioner's name was dropped from the rolls, consequent upon the decision of Assistant Secretary Reynolds, in the case of David Oliver (7 P. D., 597), of date June 22, 1895, a claim under act of June 27, 1890, wherein it was held as follows:

1. Those only are pensionable under section 2 of the act of June 27, or their widows and minor children under section 3, thereof, who were regularly enlisted men or officers in the military or naval establishment of the United States.

2. Those who served in the revenue marine on vessels which cooperated, by direction of the President, with the Navy, as provided in section 2757 R. S., were not in the Navy or the naval establishment of the United States, and are not pensionable under said act, nor their widows or minor children. Case of Louis Schaffer (6 P. D., 137), overruled in part.

In the case of Louis Schaffer (6 P. D., 137), thus overruled in part, Assistant Secretary Bussey, by opinion of date December 6, 1892, held as follows:

1. Actual cooperation with the Navy by revenue cutters during the war of the rebellion must be shown to entitle those serving thereon to pension under section 4741 R. S.

2. Persons serving on revenue cutters under like conditions would also be entitled to pension under the second paragraph of section 4693 R. S.

3. Ninety days of actual cooperation with the Navy must be shown to entitle officers and seamen of the revenue-marine service to pension under section 2, act of June 27, 1890.

4. The widows, minors or dependent relatives of such officers and seamen, would not be entitled to pension under section 4741 R. S.

5. They would be entitled under the second paragraph of section 4693 and sections 4702 and 4707 R. S.

6. The widows and minors of such officers and seamen would be entitled to pension under the provisions of section 3 of the act of June 27, 1890.

Section 4741 of the Revised Statutes provides as follows:

The officers and seamen of the revenue cutters of the United States, who have been or may be wounded or disabled in the discharge of their duty while cooperating with the Navy by order of the President, shall be entitled to be placed on the Navy pension list at the same rate of pension and under the same regulations and restrictions as are provided by law for the officers and seamen of the Navy.

The second paragraph of section 4693 of the Revised Statutes confers title to pension under the general law to the following-described persons:

Any master serving on a gunboat, or any pilot, engineer, sailor, or other person not regularly mustered serving upon any gunboat or war vessel of the United States, disabled by any wound or injury received or otherwise incapacitated, while in the line of duty, for procuring his subsistence by manual labor.

It will be observed that the foregoing citations from the Revised Statutes expressly confer title to a disability pension to the beneficiaries named therein.

The act of January 29, 1887, granting pensions to the soldiers and sailors of the Mexican war, provides, inter alia, as follows:

That the Secretary of the Interior be, and he is hereby, authorized and directed to place on the pension roll the names of the surviving officers and enlisted men, including marines, militia, and volunteers, of the military and naval services of the

United States who, being duly enlisted, actually served sixty days with the Army or Navy of the United States in Mexico, or on the coasts or frontier thereof, or en route thereto, in the war with that nation, or were actually engaged in a battle in said war, and were honorably discharged, and to such other officers and soldiers and sailors as may have been personally named in any resolution of Congress for any specific service in said war, and the surviving widows of such officers and enlisted men: *Provided,* That such widows have not remarried: *Provided,* That every such officer, enlisted man, or widow who is or may become sixty-two years of age, or who is or may become subject to any disability or dependency equivalent to some cause prescribed or recognized by the pension laws of the United States as a sufficient reason for the allowance of a pension, shall be entitled to the benefits of this act; but it shall not be held to include any person not within the rule of age or disability or dependence herein defined, or who incurred such disability while in any manner voluntarily engaged in or aiding or abetting the late rebellion against the authority of the United States. * * *

That the pension laws now in force which are not inconsistent or in conflict with this act are hereby made a part of this act, so far as they may be applicable thereto

The dropping of pensioner's name from the roll appears to have been actuated or directed by the conclusion of your Bureau that, as the act of June 27, 1890, as construed by Assistant Secretary Reynolds in the case of David Oliver, herein cited, is identical in conditions touching the nature of service specified in the act of January 29, 1887, for survivors of the Mexican war, namely, "in the military or naval service of the United States," and hence the pensioner had no title to the pension granted him. Therefore, as you suggest in your communication—

it is believed by your Bureau that this decision is adverse to the rights of this pensioner and all other persons who have been pensioned for service while attached to revenue cutters, and who were not regularly enlisted in the military or naval service of the United States.

The legal question, therefore, is whether the rulings of the Department as laid down in the case of David Oliver (7 P. D., 597), in construing the provisions of the act of June 27, 1890, touching title to pension under said act of those who served during the late rebellion in the Revenue-Marine Service, cooperating with the Navy by direction of the President, and overruling in part the adverse previous decision of the Department in the case of Louis Schaffer (6 P. D., 137), operate to deny title to pension, under the Mexican war survivors act of January 29, 1887, to those who served during said war on revenue cutters and were engaged sixty days or more, under order of the President, in active cooperation with the Navy in the prosecution of the war in Mexico.

The acts of January 29, 1887, and June 27, 1890, both provide a service pension, but are essentially at variance in respect to the terms and conditions by which title thereto is created and conferred. These acts are of similar import in that the beneficiaries are relieved from the operation of the general law which requires the disability to have been incurred, either directly or by result, in the service and line of duty.

The act of January 29, 1887, confers title to pension upon the surviving officers and enlisted men, including marines, militia, and volunteers, of the military and naval service of the United States who, being duly enlisted, actually served sixty days with the Army or Navy of the United States in Mexico, or on the coasts or frontier thereof, or en route thereto in the war with that nation, etc., with the proviso only that every such officer or enlisted man or widow who is or may become 62 years of age or who is or may become subject to any disability or dependency equiv- alent to some cause prescribed by the pension laws of the United States as a sufficient reason for the allowance of a pension, etc., shall be entitled to the benefit of the act.

The act of June 27, 1890, requires as condition precedent to pension service of ninety days or more in the military or naval service of the United States during the war of the rebellion; honorable discharge therefrom, and the existence of permanent mental or physical disability, not the result of vicious habits, to a degree which incapacitates for earning a support by the performance of manual labor.

The cases of Schaffer and Oliver were both claims under the act of June 27, 1890. The case at bar is a claim under the act of January 29, 1887.

In the Schaffer case Assistant Secretary Bussey held, as claimant had not proved that during the time he served on the revenue cutter *Miami*, from April 14 to July 25, 1865, said vessel was engaged in "cooperation with the Navy by order of the President," in arresting rebel depredations on American commerce and transportation, etc., but on the contrary that said cutter was not employed in any such duty during the period of claimant's service on board, he had no title to pen- sion under either section 4741 of the Revised Statutes or the second paragraph of section 4693 of the Revised Statutes, and consequently no title under act of June 27, 1890.

In the case of Oliver, Assistant Secretary Reynolds held that even though the revenue marine vessel on which claimant served was "coop- erating, by order of the President," with the Navy in the war of the rebellion, yet he was not in the Navy or naval establishment of the United States and hence not pensionable under act of June 27, 1890.

It will be observed that these contrary decisions were not made upon any claim under the act of January 29, 1887.

Section 2757 of the Revised Statutes (act of March 2, 1799) provides as follows:

The revenue cutters shall, whenever the President so directs, cooperate with the Navy, during which time they shall be under direction of the Secretary of the Navy, and the expense thereof shall be defrayed by the Navy Department.

Section 2, paragraph 1, of Article II of the Constitution of the United States, provides, inter alia, as follows:

The President shall be commander in chief of the Army and Navy of the United States and of the militia of the several States when called into the actual service of the United States.

The record shows that the revenue cutter on which this officer served was, by order of the President, the constitutional commander in chief of the Army and Navy of the United States, and under the power specially conferred upon him by the act of March 2, 1799 (section 2757, R. S.), in active cooperation with the Navy of the United States in the prosecution of the war with Mexico from June 30, 1846, to April 30, 1847, the date of withdrawal of said revenue cutter from said cooperation. The record also shows that the officers and enlisted men of this cutter, including the pensioner, were repeatedly in action with the enemy under the immediate direction and orders of officers of the Navy and performed gallant and important service. The following is extracted from the report of Commodore M. C. Perry to Commodore Conner, United States Navy:

It seems to be just and proper, and it is certainly a gratifying task, to make known to you, for the information of the Department, the excellent conduct of the officers and men who served under my command in the late expedition to Tobasco. The enterprise and spirit displayed by them on every occasion gave sufficient evidence that in scenes more sanguinary they would do full honor to the corps. * * * I am gratified to bear witness also to the valuable services of the revenue schooner *Forward*, in command of Captain Nones, and to the skill and gallantry of her officers and men.

It is beyond dispute that from June 30, 1846, to April 30, 1847, the revenue cutter *Forward*, not in contemplation of law, but under actual provision and mandate of law, and by virtue of the order of the President, became part and parcel of the naval establishment of the United States, under direction of the Secretary of the Navy, and hence during that period ceased to be part and parcel of the Treasury establishment, the jurisdiction of the Secretary of the Treasury over that vessel and her officers and men having been temporarily ousted by operation of the act of March 2, 1799.

The officers and enlisted men of that cutter thereby became, by merger, subject, and were subjected, to the orders of the commodore commanding the navy on that station and amenable to the Rules and Articles of War in the practice then in operation.

If, then, the revenue cutter *Forward* became part of the naval establishment of the United States from June 30, 1846, to April 30, 1847, it necessarily follows that the pensioner had title to pension under the act of January 29, 1887, having actually served more than sixty days with the Navy of the United States in Mexico, he not being barred by the proviso to that act.

To hold otherwise, by the severe and technical construction that under no circumstances nor operation of law can a revenue marine vessel, temporarily or otherwise, be transferred to the naval establishment so as to confer title to pension thereunder, would operate to wrest from this officer in his old age and advancing infirmities that measure of honor, credit, and recognition provided by the lawmaking power for those who imperil life in the war service of the country.

The Acting Secretary of the Treasury, in a communication on this subject addressed to the Secretary of the Interior of date February 11, 1891, states as follows:

> The revenue cutters were, at the opening of hostilities, armed, manned, and equipped in the same manner as naval vessels of like size and were maintained upon that footing throughout the war, and from the nature of their regular duties were always in readiness for any duty or emergency, even to the extent of active cooperation with the Navy. They were regarded as a part of the naval force of the Government.

I can not, with my view of official duty, give countenance to any action which would, by implication, impair or deny to a claimant the just and liberal interpretation of the pension laws.

The premises considered, I am of opinion that this officer had title to the pension granted him under the act of January 29, 1887, and that the action of your Bureau, dropping his name from the rolls for the reasons stated, was erroneous and is disapproved. Therefore you will please direct that the pensioner's name be restored to the rolls and that he be paid the accrued pension.

———

COMMENCEMENT RATE—REDUCTION—ACT JUNE 27, 1890.

GALEN PETERS.

The evidence in this case fairly shows that a pensionable degree of disability entitling claimant to $12 per month under the act of June 27, 1890, and on account of which he was pensioned at such rate from September 23, 1896, existed at the time of filing his first application July 9, 1890, and his pension should have dated from said first application, deducting payments made.

Assistant Secretary Webster Davis to the Commissioner of Pensions, August 3, 1897.

Claimant on April 5, 1897, appealed from the action of your Bureau of March 9, 1897, dating the commencement of pension (certificate No. 550169) at $12 from September 23, 1896.

The contention is that claimant should have been paid $12 per month from December 4, 1895, to September 23, 1896, instead of $8.

Claimant on July 9, 1890, filed his declaration under the act of June 27, 1890, in which he alleged as causes of total disability to obtain his subsistence by manual labor—

> loss of three fingers and thumb on left hand and compound fracture of left leg, resulting in rheumatism and general debility.

He was medically examined January 14, 1891, and pensioned March 14, 1892, at $12 from July 9, 1890, date of application, for loss of three fingers and distal phalanx of thumb of left hand.

On March 9, 1894, the medical referee approved action for reducing his rate to $8 per month, and on May 28, 1894, claimant filed a claim for additional pension on account of pensioned causes, and also fracture of left leg received in a railroad accident in 1879, and stating that he had received notice of proposed reduction, and instead of contesting the matter he files the above application; and thereupon your Bureau appears to have delayed action on the proposed reduction, and claimant was again medically examined September 4, 1895, whereupon your Bureau on November 14, 1895, reduced his rate for loss of three fingers and distal phalanx of left thumb to $8 per month from December 4, 1895, and certificate in conformity with said action was issued in lieu of certificate dated March 26, 1891. This action appears to have been based on the medical examination of September 4, 1895. This certificate, however, failed to make any mention of the injury to the right forearm, or to the injury of the right foot, although the evidence shows that both said injuries existed at the date of said medical examination and long prior thereto. This certificate will be further considered later on.

On July 11, 1896, claimant filed a declaration for increase in which he alleged that he was—

crippled in the left leg by a compound fracture of both bones caused by an injury received by having three freight cars run over it at Fort Wayne, Ind., September 11, 1878. At same time and place he received an injury to the left knee by a large piece of iron running through and dislocating the knee. At the same time and place the right foot was broken in two places and never was set, causing it to be weak, stiff, and painful when he walks on it a good deal. That his right arm was broken at Massillon, Ohio, in October, 1870, by a coupling link run through the arm between the bones, making the arm weak and painful.

Then follows the formal application for rerating on the ground that the former rate was too low. This was in violation of Order No. 143, of August 15, 1889, which required rerating claims to be separately made, and when joined in a claim for increase the claim will be adjudicated as a claim for increase only. His claim filed July 14, 1896, was, therefore, properly adjudicated as a claim for increase, and was allowed, as hereinbefore stated, at $12 per month for "loss of three fingers and distal phalanx of left thumb and injury of left leg and right foot."

The evidence unquestionably establishes the fact that all of the causes of disability contributing to claimant's incapacity to earn a support by manual labor existed prior to the date of filing his first declaration in 1890. It also established the further fact that said injuries or disabling causes were of a permanent character.

The ex parte testimony, both lay and medical, filed by claimant tends strongly to show that said injuries totally incapacitated claimant for the performance of manual labor.

The board of surgeons who first medically examined claimant January 14, 1891, reported his physical condition as follows:

Pulse rate, 70; respiration, 16; temperature, 98¼; height, 5 feet 3½ inches; weight, 124 pounds; age, 42 years.

Has lost left little finger with the whole of the metacarpal bone of same. Has lost the ring finger of left hand with half the metacarpal bone of same. Has lost the distal phalanx of the thumb on left hand and most of the distal phalanx of index finger, same hand. Large finger of left hand is in good condition though it has some scars and turns to the left a good deal. Left leg has been broken at its lower third, both bones being fractured. The result of treatment was not satisfactory. At point of injury limb is bent outward markedly, apposition being imperfect. The old scar at point of fracture he says breaks open occasionally. The appearance of scar would indicate that his statement is true, though it is not open to-day. Left leg is 1½ inches shorter than right one. Over inner tuberosity of left tibia is a scar 2 by 1 inches. Right foot has been fractured through the metatarsal bones, two of these being broken. Foot is tender at the instep, and the two toes adjoining the great one are stiffened some. Over anterior aspect and middle third of right arm is a scar 2¼ by 1 inches. On back of same arm is a scar 5 by 1 inches running from the upper part of the ulna obliquely down toward the lower end of the radius. Both of these scars are largely adherent, indurated, and contracted and sensitive. They are the result of a railroad injury

Muscles not sore. Tendons not contracted. Joints not enlarged or stiffened from rheumatism. No calcareous deposits. Area of heart's dullness normal. Heart's rate action and sounds normal. Is physically frail. Not otherwise debilitated.

Dr. Fisher is out of the city to-day, and for this reason his name is not signed to this certificate.

He is, in our opinion, entitled to a twelve-eighteenths rating for the disability caused by injury to left hand; six-eighteenths for that caused by fracture of left leg, and nothing for that caused by rheumatism.

The board of surgeons who examined claimant September 4, 1895, report as follows:

Pulse rate, 72; respiration, 18; temperature, 98.4; height, 5 feet 2 inches; weight, 118 pounds; age, 46 years.

We find upon examination entire loss of fourth and fifth fingers of left hand at carpo-metacarpal articulation. Also loss of thumb of left hand at first distal joint. Rating, six-eighteenths.

We also find evidence of an old compound fracture of left tibia and fibula 4 inches above ankle joint. Union complete, but bones not in perfect apposition. Left leg 1½ inches shorter than right leg. Movements of knee and ankle joints perfect. Skin about seat of fracture adherent and dragging. Rating, six-eighteenths. No other disability is found to exist. Claimant is a laborer Muscles fairly well developed. Palms hard. Nutrition fair and general physical appearance healthy.

Claimant was last medically examined September 23, 1896, when the board reported as follows:

Pulse rate, 72; respiration, 18; temperature, 98.6; height, 5 feet 3½ inches; weight, 120 pounds; age, 49 years.

Claimant has lost the two outer fingers of left hand and a large part of the meta-carpal bone of these fingers; also the distal extremity of left thumb and part of the distal extremity of left forefinger, which is also stiffened and wanting in function and power. Rate, $12.

Claimant has also suffered a compound fracture of the left leg, both bones, lower third, with 1½ inches shortening and some deformity. There are two eschars, one on inner and one on outer side of left knee (said to be from an iron splinter passing through this region of the limb), which add to the crippling of this leg, which is deformed, weak, and wanting in function and power. He can not walk well nor stand long on the limb. Rate, twelve-eighteenths. There has been an injury to right tarsal bones. The instep is raised up and deformed. The injury interferes with proper use of the foot in standing or walking. Rate, four-eighteenths.

There has been an injury of right forearm, middle third, an eschar on outer side of arm 3 inches long and one on inner side 1½ inches long. Eschars are attached and interfere with the strength and usefulness of the arm. Rate, two-eighteenths. Claimant has no rheumatism; joints, muscles, and tendons are normal. No rate.

He has no general debility. Nutrition and muscular condition fair, but muscles and hand are soft and show no signs of labor. No rate.

Claimant is, by reason of his injuries and resulting permanently crippled condition, totally incapacitated for the performance of any manual labor and is entitled to a second-grade rating, $30. There is no other disability and habits are good.

On April 27, 1897, the acting chief of the board of review referred the case to the medical referee with the request that—

He decide whether the action of reduction to $8 should not be reconsidered. Notice was served of reduction in April, 1894, and instead of filing evidence in rebuttal pensioner forwarded a formal declaration for increase, realleging the fracture of left leg which had already been claimed in his original declaration. He was examined in September, 1895, and the fracture was described and rated, but in December, 1895, the reduction took effect.

On the claim filed July 11, 1896, increase was allowed from September 23, 1896, date of the examination thereunder, at $12, the disabilities being those for which originally pensioned, the injury (fracture) of left leg, and an injury of right foot, alleged for the first time in declaration of July 11, 1896.

It seems that this injury of right foot was the determining factor in the medical action, for the condition of the fractured left leg could not have changed materially from 1895 to 1896, nearly ten years after it was broken, this conclusion being reached from the fact that the reduction was effected after the injury to leg had been alleged and shown and before the injury to the foot had been shown, while the increase was granted for both.

The last examination does not seem to show a serious disability in the foot, while the leg was rated $12.

If my supposition that the condition of the leg did not vary materially in 1896 from what it was in 1895 has a basis in fact, and if it be further true that the injury of foot was and is comparatively unimportant, would it not be proper to restore the $12 rate from December 4, 1895, for the injuries of hand and leg?

If not, no action of this board can afford relief, as the declaration of July 11, 1896, is not a claim for restoration, but for simple increase, with an informal and inoperative clause relating to a rerating added.

To this slip the acting medical referee, on May 22, 1897, expressed the following opinion from a medical standpoint:

I do not think the action of reduction should be reconsidered. The reduction was due to the change of practice in adjudicating June claims which was inaugurated by the "Bennett" decision. At the time the revision was made it was distinctly stated on the brief face that the injury to the left leg was considered in connection with the pensioned cause in estimating the disability existing for the performance of manual labor under the act. No manifest injustice appears to have been done in the revision, and an examination of the two medical certificates, that of September 4, 1895, and that of September 23, 1896, indicates that the disability due to the injury to the leg has actually increased since September 4, 1895, and the injury to the right foot does add to the claimant's general inability to do labor.

It is to be noted, however, that the disability due to the injury of right foot is but slight, the first board giving him no rating, although describing more fully the injury and results than the last board, who rate him but four-eighteenths therefor.

It is true that claimant did not in terms allege the injury to his right foot and ankle in the first or second declarations.

I am of the opinion that the evidence in this case fairly shows that a pensionable degree of disability entitling claimant to $12 per month under the act of June 27, 1890, and on account of which he was pensioned at $12 per month from September 23, 1896, existed at the time of filing his first application, July 9, 1890, and his pension should have dated from said first application, deducting payments made.

The action appealed from is accordingly reversed and the papers in the case are herewith returned.

The former departmental decision of July 3, 1897, in this case is recalled and this decision is substituted in lieu thereof.

DISABILITY—ACT OF JUNE 27, 1890.

WILLIAM FEATHERLY.

The claimant is by trade a stone mason. The condition of his hand being such as to prevent his working at his trade, and being too old to learn another, it is held that he has a pensionable status under the act of June 27, 1890. Reaffirming departmental decision in the case of Charles Stone (8 P. D., 477).

Assistant Secretary Webster Davis to the Commissioner of Pensions, August 11, 1897.

The appellant filed a claim in your Bureau under the act of June 27, 1890, on June 25, 1891, alleging loss of first three fingers of right hand and broken thumb of same hand, loss of sense of smell, and heart trouble. The claim was rejected July 14, 1893, on the ground that no ratable disability is shown under the act of June 27, 1890.

From this action he appealed January 15, 1894, contending that he is entitled to a rating under ruling of Commissioner of Pensions of July 12, 1893.

Under date of August 18, 1894, the action of your Bureau was affirmed, the Department holding that while the claimant is shown to be disabled in his right hand, yet the evidence in the case fails to show that he is thereby incapacitated for earning a support in whole or in part by manual labor.

The claimant filed this appeal April 1, 1897, which is, however, in fact a motion for reconsideration of the departmental decision of August 18, 1894, though it purports also to be an appeal from rejection of a claim filed under the general law on account of an injury to right hand, claimed to be of service origin, consisting of a disabled thumb and the loss of the first three fingers at first joint.

So far as the appeal relates to said claim under the general law it must be dismissed, as it is found, on inspection of the papers, that that claim is still pending and unadjudicated.

That part of the appeal which relates to the claim under the act of June 27, 1890, is evidently based upon erroneous action on the part of your Bureau. I find the appeal of January 15, 1894 (which was filed in the Pension Bureau January 8, 1894), has, since the decision on said appeal, been taken out of its appeal jacket and filed or bound in the brief of action taken July 14, 1893 (from which that appeal was taken), as though it were a part of the evidence, or of the claim, then finally adjudicated upon. This, of itself, was erroneous; but in addition thereto a second error, and one inconsistent with the former, was made, viz: On May 17, 1895, the claimant was notified that his claim under said act should not be reopened unless a new declaration should be filed, and that the affidavit filed under date of January 8, 1894, can not be accepted as a valid declaration under the act. From this action, evidenced by your communication to the claimant, filed with the appeal, the present appeal is filed.

It is clear the claimant has been misled by this erroneous action of your Bureau into filing this appeal; as, in fact, said "affidavit," from your action on which this appeal was filed, is the original appeal which was finally acted on by the Department on August 18, 1894. That "affidavit" or appeal, as it should properly be called, should have been retained within its appeal jacket, and thus the present misconceived appeal would have been avoided.

That part of the appeal, however, which asks a reconsideration of the departmental decision of August 18, 1894, will be entertained, the question being whether, in the light of more recent decisions, entertaining broader views as to the intent of the act of June 27, 1890, the Department should adhere thereto.

In the case of Charles Stone (8 P. D., 477), Assistant Secretary Reynolds states:

Where it is shown that a claimant for invalid pension under the act of June 27, 1890, is prevented from following his trade * * * and because of his advanced age it is not probable that he could earn a support by any other occupation the provisions of said act may properly be held to apply. The reasonable and just interpretation of said act is not whether by chance or charity the soldier can find some means of supplying the necessities of life, but whether he is disabled in a degree preventing him from following his trade or some kindred occupation which might yield him a support.

The appellant is a stone mason by trade, and from the condition of his hand it is evident that he can not grasp the tools of his trade, and hence can not support himself by working at it. In view of the fact that he is about 60 years old, it is not probable that he could learn some other trade by which he could earn a support at his time of life.

Such being the case, under a just and reasonable interpretation of the act of June 27, 1890, the claimant is entitled to a rating under that act.

The departmental action of August 18, 1894, is reconsidered, and the action of your Bureau rejecting the claim for the reasons stated is reversed.

The papers are herewith returned for readjudication and allowance of the claim under said act, on account of said injury to right hand, reaffirming departmental decision in the case of Charles Stone (8 P. D., 477).

SERVICE—MEXICAN WAR—GILPIN'S BATTALION.

MARTINEAU WINTERS (WIDOW).

1. Under report of the War Department, of date August 11, 1897, the organization known as Gilpin's Battalion Missouri Volunteers has service title to pension under act of January 29, 1887, and therefore the widow's title follows.
2. Departmental decision of August 29, 1896, in the case of Anton Brunz (8 P. D., 344). having been rendered under misapprehension of facts, is recalled and annulled.

Assistant Secretary Webster Davis to the Commissioner of Pensions,
August 18, 1897.

The soldier, William McK. Winters, Company A, Gilpin's battalion Missouri Volunteers, was pensioned March 22, 1889, at $8 per month, under the Mexican war survivors' act of January 29, 1887, granting pensions to the soldiers and sailors of the Mexican war. This pension he enjoyed until his death, September 20, 1896, and the accrued pension was paid his widow.

The widow, Martineau Winters, filed declaration, December 26, 1896, for widow's pension under said act of January 29, 1887, which claim was rejected April 20, 1897—

on the ground that service in Gilpin's battalion Missouri Volunteers is not a pensionable service under act of January 29, 1887. See decision of August 29, 1896.

Appeal from this action of rejection was received July 23, 1897, it being contended in effect that as the soldier's title to pension under act of January 29, 1887, for service in Gilpin's battalion Missouri Volunteers had been adjudicated favorably and pension granted, therefore the widow had title under said act, and if such title is now denied by reason of a departmental decision rendered August 29, 1896, as stated, said decision should be reviewed.

This rejection by your Bureau was based upon a decision rendered August 29, 1896, by Assistant Secretary Reynolds (8 P. D., 344) in the case of Anton Brunz, in which it was held as follows:

Claimant's regiment (Company C, Gilpin's battalion Missouri Infantry) was called into the service during the war with Mexico for the purpose of protecting the United States trains on the Santa Fe route and to punish the Indians who had attacked those trains, and claimant's service in said command was all rendered at Fort Leavenworth, Independence, Mo., on the Santa Fe road near Bent's Fort, Fort Mann on the Arkansas River, Walnut Creek, and Council Grove, and not in Mexico, on the coasts or frontier thereof, nor en route thereto, and he is not, therefore, pensionable as a survivor of the Mexican war under the act of January 29, 1887.

This opinion referred to departmental decision in Brockman's case (1 P. D., 453). Powell's battalion Missouri Mounted Volunteers, its reaffirmance on motion for reconsideration, 2 P. D., 239; also to decisions bearing on the same subject, 2 P. D., 265, 6 P. D., 149, and 7 P. D., 260. The cited case of Brunz, however, is the only decision specifically affecting the pensionable status of Gilpin's battalion of Missouri Infantry Volunteers.

The military history of the soldier, as certified by the War Department of date January 20, 1897, simply states that the soldier, of Company A, Gilpin's battalion of Missouri Infantry, Mexican war, was enrolled September 1, 1847, mustered in September 3, 1847, at Fort Leavenworth, and mustered out as private with company September 28, 1848, at Independence, Mo.; that the stations of the company between muster in and the last-named date were as follows: April 30, 1848, Fort Mann, middle Arkansas, in the country of the Comanche Indians. Company started for seat of war September, 1847.

In view of the fact that this history failed to state the stations of the company between date of starting for the seat of war in September, 1847, and the date of station at Fort Mann, April 30, 1848, middle Arkansas, in the country of the Comanches, and with the view of definitely ascertaining the character of military service rendered by this organization, and whether it did actually serve for sixty days or more with the Army of the United States in Mexico or on the coast or frontier thereof or en route thereto in the war with that nation, or were actually engaged in battle in said war, and to the further essential and end that the Department should have reliable and thorough information before definitely pronouncing upon widows' claims rejected after pensions had been granted their husbands for such Mexican war service, the following communication was addressed to the honorable the Secretary of War:

DEPARTMENT OF THE INTERIOR,
Washington, July 26, 1897.

The Honorable the SECRETARY OF WAR.

SIR: I have the honor to request that you will cause this Department to be advised touching Gilpin's battalion Missouri Infantry (Mexican war service), in respect to the following issues which have direct bearing upon the claim for pension preferred by Mrs. Martineau Winters, widow of William K. Winters, private Company A, Gilpin's battalion Missouri Volunteers, No. 13701, now before this Department on appeal from the action of the Pension Bureau rejecting said claim:

1. Was this battalion organized and called into the service of the United States during the war with Mexico for the specific purpose of protecting the United States' trains on the Santa Fe route, and to punish the hostile Indians who had attacked those trains?

2. Was this military service duly performed by said battalion; and if so, at what stations or posts, and whether in the Indian country en route to Mexico?

3. Did such service have direct connection with and form part of the military operations in that war, with the Army as part of its establishment on the frontier in belligerent attitude, other than that of performing mere garrison duty?

4. In what military status is the said Gilpin's battalion of Missouri Infantry held and esteemed by your Department in connection with the United States forces serving in the war with Mexico?

5. Was the duty of guarding or protecting the supply trains from attack of hostile Indians, and punishing them, a necessary service had in direct connection with the military operations of the Army of the United States in the war with Mexico?

I would be gratified to have these questions answered by the authorities of your Department at as early a day as possible.

Very respectfully, WEBSTER DAVIS,
Assistant Secretary.

The Department is in receipt of the following reply, of date August 11, 1897, forwarded by the honorable Acting Secretary of War.

RECORD AND PENSION OFFICE, WAR DEPARTMENT,
Washington, August 11, 1897.

Respectfully returned to the honorable the Secretary of War.

An important part of the military operations of the Mexican war was the invasion and subsequent occupation by armed forces of the United States of portions of the territory which is now comprised within the limits of northern Mexico, New Mexico, Arizona, and California, but all of which was owned or claimed by Mexico at the time of the war. The Santa Fe route was that by which land communication with the troops occupying this territory was principally maintained, and over which trains carrying supplies and munitions of war were frequently sent. Keeping this route open by an armed force, against the attacks of hostile Indians, was a necessary and extremely important military operation of the war.

The battalion of Missouri Infantry Volunteers, commanded by Lieut. Col. W. Gilpin, was called into the service of the United States by the President under the act of Congress approved May 13, 1846, which authorized the President to accept the services of not exceeding 50,000 volunteers for the purpose of prosecuting the war with Mexico. The muster-in rolls do not show that the battalion was mustered in with any limitation or restriction as to the place or character of its service, but other records show that it was the understanding at the time that the battalion should be used "to protect the United States trains on the Santa Fe route, and to punish the Indians who recently attacked those trains." * * *

A detailed account of the movements of this command and the actions in which it was engaged with hostile Indians is to be found in the reports of Lieutenant-Colonel Gilpin and his subordinate officers, which were printed with the report of the Secretary of War for 1848. These reports show that the battalion took an active part in the necessary and important military operations of keeping open the Santa Fe route, and in protecting the Government trains thereon.

Lieutenant-Colonel Gilpin's report also shows that he crossed over into New Mexico with a portion of his command and marched down the Canadian River for a long distance, thus actually entering and marching through territory which was claimed by Mexico at the time, and to which neither Texas nor the United States acquired an undisputed title until the conclusion of the war.

The military status of this battalion differed in no wise from that of any other volunteer organization that was in active service during the Mexican war, except, perhaps, that it was mustered in with the understanding that its service should be limited to that which it afterwards actually rendered. The duty upon which it was engaged was that of keeping open a line of communication with the Army of the United States in Mexican territory, and this duty had a direct and important connection with the military operations of that Army.

Following is a copy of a letter which shows the views of this Department, in 1847, as to the status of troops serving on the Indian frontier, as regards their right to bounty land:

"WAR DEPARTMENT,
"*Washington, December 22, 1847.*

"JAMES L. EDWARDS, Esq.,
    "*Commissioner of Pensions.*

"SIR: The question has been presented whether such volunteers called out under the act of Congress of the 13th of May, 1846, authorizing the President to accept 50,000 volunteers, as have been mustered into service and stationed on the Indian frontier, etc., are entitled to bounty land? My construction of that law is that the volunteers who were mustered into service under that act and who went to the place where their services were required by the Government, whether it was in Mexico or on the Indian frontier or in Florida, are entitled to bounty lands, in the same manner and under the same conditions as if the company to which they belonged had been ordered to service in Mexico.

"I am, with great respect, your obedient servant,

"W. L. MARCY,
"*Secretary of War.*"

F. C. AINSWORTH, *Colonel, United States Army, Chief of Office.*

WAR DEPARTMENT,
Washington, August 11, 1897.

Respectfully returned to the Secretary of the Interior, inviting attention to the preceding indorsement of the chief of the Record and Pension Office of this Department.

G. D. MEIKLEJOHN,
Acting Secretary of War.

It is apparent from this exhaustive and intelligent report that the Department has not been hitherto correctly or fully advised touching the nature of service rendered by Gilpin's battalion of Missouri Volunteers in the war with Mexico, nor yet concerning the proper status of that organization as recognized by the military authorities of the Government at that time and likewise at the present date. Hence, it is equally evident that the Department has been laboring under grave misapprehension of the facts in considering and denying the pensionable status of those officers and enlisted men who served in said battalion.

I am therefore impelled to hold, in view of the present report, that the officers and enlisted men of Gilpin's battalion of Missouri Volunteers, who are shown by the record to have served with that organization for sixty days or more, and were honorably discharged, actually served with the Army of the United States in Mexico, on the frontier thereof, and also en route thereto, in the war with that nation, and, as inferentially shown in said report, were engaged in battle, and not being obnoxious to the other provisions and limitations of the act of January 29, 1887, they have title to pension under said act.

It therefore follows that claimant in the case at bar has title to widow's pension under said act, and the action of your Bureau, rejecting the widow's claim for the reasons stated, is reversed. You will please direct that the same be admitted at an early date and certificate issue.

The Departmental decision of August 29, 1896, in the case of Anton Brunz (8 P. D., 344), having been rendered under misapprehension of facts, is hereby recalled and annulled.

———

FEE—MATERIAL—SERVICE.

J. B. CRALLE & CO. (ATTORNEYS).

JOHN L. STAFFORD (CLAIMANT).

Where a claim for original pension stands rejected and a duplicate declaration is filed resulting in the reopening of the claim the filing thereof is deemed material service.

Assistant Secretary Webster Davis to the Commissioner of Pensions, August 18, 1897.

J. B. Cralle & Co., of Washington, D. C., June 10, 1897, appealed in the matter of fee on the issue of February 11, 1897, in the claim, under the general laws, of John L. Stafford.

The claimant was pensioned under the general law for gunshot wound of right hip, when on March 16, 1889, J. B. Cralle, of Washington, D. C., filed an application for additional pension in which gunshot wound of head was alleged. He filed fee agreements for $25. In accordance with the practice, a fee was denied the appellants upon the ground that they performed no material service in securing the pension allowed. The question involved is submitted by your Bureau for the opinion of the Department.

Pension was claimed for disability due to gunshot wound of head in the original declaration, filed April 27, 1876.

The records of the War Department showed the incurrence of gunshot wound of the head in the service. The original claim was allowed June 11, 1878, at $4 per month for gunshot wound of right hip. The brief face shows action as follows:

Wound of head established but not rated.

As pension for wound of head was not allowed and final action was had, the logical conclusion from the record is that so much of the claim as was based on said wound was rejected.

The appellants filed no evidence. The declaration filed by them does not constitute the basis of the claim on account of said wound, for it is duplicative to that extent of the original declaration.

But in my opinion the filing of the said declaration by the appellants must be deemed material service, in view of the fact that the claim for gunshot wound stood rejected when the appellants appeared in the case, for the rules of practice before the Commissioner of Pensions (Rule 13) provide for and specify the steps to be taken in the prosecution of a case when it stands rejected in the Bureau. It can not be consistently maintained that an attorney has not rendered material service when he has taken the steps provided and specified by the rules of practice for the further prosecution of a case.

The declaration filed by Mr. Cralle was treated as a motion for reconsideration. The filing of such a motion is one of the steps provided by rules in that stage of the proceedings met with in this case. Further steps were not required, for the evidence already on file was deemed sufficient to allow the claim.

In the report of the Bureau it is suggested that—

there is no doubt their (appellants') coming into the case, filing a declaration and pressing the claim, was what caused the Bureau to take favorable action, and was therefore of benefit to the claimant. * * *

As I have manifested, I concur in the foregoing and am of the opinion that the appellant should be allowed a fee. But in addition I would add that the cases coming within the rule here laid down should be carefully distinguished from those cases in which a duplicate declaration is filed that do not stand rejected, but on the contrary are awaiting action.

So where a claim for original pension or additional pension stands rejected and a duplicate declaration is filed resulting in the reopening of the claim the filing thereof will be deemed material service.

You will please decide the appellants' title to fee in accordance herewith. In case a fee is allowed you will please so report to this Department, that the appeal may be dismissed.

DEATH CAUSE.

NAPOLEON B. TRASK.

The rule laid down in decision in the case of Mary A. Cox (3 P. D., 313), that "where the evidence, lay and medical, goes to show that the cause for which pension was granted to soldier was complicated with a disease which was the immediate cause of his death, the Department will sustain the widow's claim," has not been amended, qualified, recalled, or annulled, and the same is reaffirmed.

Assistant Secretary Webster Davis to the Commissioner of Pensions, August 21, 1897.

In the matter of the appeal of the minors of Napoleon B. Trask, Company E, Thirty-second Missouri Volunteer Infantry, No. 347354, the action of your Bureau rejecting the claim was affirmed by the Department by opinion of date October 5, 1894, by which it was held that the evidence was insufficient to show that the soldier's death was due to his military service.

By communication of July 10, 1897, it was represented to the Department that your office entertained the opinion that this claim should be reopened for further adjudication upon additional information adduced in support thereof since date of affirmance by the Department on the action of rejection, and the papers were transmitted for consideration and approval of your recommendation for reopening under Rule 8.

By departmental communication of July 17, 1897, the papers were returned with advice that your recommendation of July 10, 1897, that the claim be reopened for further adjudication was approved, it appearing that new and material evidence had been filed since the rejection of said claim was affirmed by opinion of date October 5, 1894.

It appears, however, that the papers now contain a communication from the medical referee, addressed to the chief of the board of review, of date August 16, 1897, of which the following is a copy:

No. 347344.

Minors of Napoleon B. Trask, E, 32 Mo. Inf.

MEDICAL DIVISION, *August 16, 1897.*

Respectfully returned to the chief of the board of review.

By reference to the slip of medical referee, dated July 7, 1897, it will be seen that the obstacle to favorable action was the fact that a strictly pathological relation did not exist between the fatal disease and disabilities of service origin; but the aforesaid opinion presents other and apparently sufficient grounds for admission of the claim, provided the Department would approve the action proposed.

It does not appear that the honorable Secretary has authorized the change suggested, or passed upon the question at issue. It is, therefore, requested that his decision be had.

The chief of the board of review, by communication of date August 17, 1897, returned the communication of the medical referee with the following remarks:

Respectfully returned to the medical referee for action on the brief face. I do not feel justified in sending this case to the honorable Assistant Secretary on the question suggested in your slip of July 7, 1897.

This complication having been brought to the attention of the Department, and it appearing that a very important issue had been raised by the medical referee which had not received the attention of the Department in considering your recommendation for reopening the claim for further adjudication, the papers were recalled with the view to further inquiry and consideration of the question in conformity with the suggestion of the medical referee.

The record shows that, on June 10, 1897, the assistant chief of the southern division forwarded the papers to the medical referee under the following communication:

Respectfully referred to the medical referee, inviting attention to the testimony herewith, and requesting that he state whether the same, in connection with that in the case, will justify submission to the honorable Secretary with reference to reopening the case for further consideration. Please see special examiner's report at pages 16, 17, 19, and 29, passages checked in the margin, which appear to contain all the evidence tending to show the heredity of consumption.

On July 7, 1897, the medical referee replied as follows to the inquiry of the chief of the southern division:

Respectfully returned to the chief of the southern division. All the testimony furnished in this case has been carefully considered in connection with the papers heretofore filed, including evidence obtained by special examination.

The soldier was pensioned for rheumatism and resulting disease of heart. It appears that death was due to suppurative disease of lungs, and that disease of heart was also present.

It is not medically established that there was a pathological connection between the lung lesion and the heart affection, although it may be admitted that both were factors in the death cause, yet the former, disease of lungs, was the most prominent.

It is a well-established theory that the existence of disease of heart seriously complicates any lung lesion, and if we can be authorized to admit this class of cases it is believed that justice will be done to many claimants, whose cases would be rejected if we adhere to the requirement of a strictly pathological connection between the fatal disease and the disability of service origin.

The record further shows that on July 10, 1897, the papers in the case were forwarded by the acting chief of the Southern Division to the chief of the board of review by communication as follows:

Respectfully referred to the chief of the board of review for transmission to the honorable Secretary of the Interior.

This case, with the new evidence, has been submitted to the medical referee, who returns an opinion that would seem to justify and require a reconsideration of the case.

Independently of that opinion, the affidavit of the Hon. B. F. Russell seems to be a very complete rebuttal of the testimony upon which was based a theory of hereditary tendency to lung disease, and it also has an important bearing upon the question as to intemperance being a factor of the causes which led to death of the soldier. This and other testimony so changes the aspect of the case as to indicate the justice of a reconsideration. For these reasons, therefore, reopening is recommended.

In the case of Mary A. Cox (3 P. D., 313), Assistant Secretary Bussey held as follows:

Where the evidence, lay and medical, goes to show that the cause for which pension was granted to a soldier was complicated with a disease which was the immediate cause of his death, the Department will sustain the widow's claim for pension on account of the soldier's death from said complication of causes, holding the same, for pensionable purposes, to be due to the line of duty in the service.

This decision, in my opinion, fully meets the issue presented by the medical referee and lays down a proper rule for the guidance of your Bureau in the adjudication of kindred cases.

In the case of widow of Ernest Bierbaum (4 P. D., 172), Assistant Secretary Bussey held as follows:

The true rule would seem to be that the case should hinge upon the predominating cause of death, provided the question as to what was the predominating cause is susceptible of proof; but if several causes combine to produce death, only a part of which are due to service and none to fault of the soldier, and from the obscure character and effect of the diseases, the extent to which each contributed toward producing death can not be determined, the question should be, Would the disability not due to the service have probably produced death independently of the disability of army origin? If not, the claimant should be given the benefit of the doubt.

In the case of Alma Niedhammer (8 P. D., 276), Assistant Secretary Reynolds held as follows:

Soldier, during his fatal illness, suffered from disease of heart, for which he was pensioned, and also from disease of lungs, which is not conclusively shown to be due to the service, though the evidence strongly tends to establish the same. Both disease of lungs and disease of heart were factors in causing death, but it can not be determined with any degree of certainty which of the two diseases was the predominating cause or contributed most toward producing death; and it is held that, from the evidence, it is more reasonable to assume that death was due to soldier's military service than to assume that it was not, and the doubts in the case will be resolved in favor of the claimant.

Careful analysis of the departmental decisions in the cited cases of Bierbaum and Niedhammer and the underlying principles of the same does not disclose any material conflict with the decision in the cited case of Cox or its underlying principles. The conclusions attending these cases all depend upon and are characterized by different state of facts, and it does not appear that the decision in the cited case of Mary A. Cox has been in any wise amended, qualified, questioned, recalled, or annulled by other or contrary decisions.

I am of the opinion that the rule laid down by Assistant Secretary Bussey in the case of Mary A. Cox is based upon reason and good judgment and is in accord with that long and unvaried holding of the Department that—

the pension laws should be construed in the liberal and generous spirit which prompted their enactment, and where doubts can not be resolved by evidence presumption should incline toward claimant.

If it be necessary, therefore, to reaffirm the departmental decision in the cited case of Mary A. Cox (3 P. D., 313) and the rule laid down therein by Assistant Secretary Bussey, the same is hereby reaffirmed, and the action of your Bureau should be governed accordingly in cognate cases.

ADULTEROUS COHABITATION.

MATILDA BAKER (WIDOW).

The open and notorious adulterous cohabitation of a widow bars her right to pension under the act of June 27, 1890, on account of her husband's death.

Assistant Secretary Webster Davis to the Commissioner of Pensions, August 28, 1897.

The appellant filed a claim for pension under the act of June 27, 1890, on the 9th day of February, 1893, as widow of Esau Baker, late of U. S. S. *St. Lawrence*, alleging, among other things, that her said husband died in September, 1889, and that she is without other means of support than her daily labor.

Her claim was rejected October 19, 1893, on the ground that she has been living in open and notorious adulterous cohabitation with one Armstead Johnson.

From said action this appeal was entered May 19, 1897, the appellant, by her attorney, contending that the evidence filed since the rejection is sufficient to rebut the evidence obtained on special examination, and that the action of rejection was error.

Peter Ames testified as follows before the special examiner September 20, 1890:

I do know that she (appellant) lived with one Armstead Johnson as his wife after Esau Baker died, but I can't give the dates when they began to cohabit together. She told me that they were married by Rev. M. King in Norfolk. The way I came to know of this is as follows:

She and I were members of the same lodge of Good Samaritans, and when she took up with Armstead Johnson, not being married to him, we tried her and expelled her from the lodge. Then she and the said Johnson came to Norfolk to live, and she again returned to Bayside and made application to be reinstated, saying that she and Armstead Johnson had been regularly married in Norfolk by Rev. King, and on the strength of that we took her back into the lodge.

After she came to Norfolk to live she severed her connection with our lodge at Bayside, so that I do not know whether she is a member of that order.

William Joyner made the following statement:

Claimant has not remarried since Esau Baker's death, but she has lived and cohabited with one Armstead Johnson. They commenced to live together in about a year after Esau Baker died, and they lived together as husband and wife until about two years ago, when they separated.

Eliza Joyner, a sister of the appellant, says:

My sister, the claimant, has not remarried since her said husband's death, but she began to live and cohabit with one Armstead Johnson in about a year after Esau

Baker died, and they sustained the relation of husband and wife up to within the past two years.

Henry Nimmer, Samuel Whitehurst, and Reuben White have testified that to their knowledge the appellant lived and cohabited with Armstead Johnson.

Americus Petty made the following statement May 12, 1890:

Yes, sir; she took up and lived with Armstead Johnson as his wife for about two years, to my knowledge. During that period they lived within about a half mile of me. I have frequently seen them together in the same one-room cabin, and have seen them eat together at the same table in their house, and they looked upon each other as husband and wife, although it was generally understood that they were not married. He provided for her and her children the same as a husband generally does.

This cohabiting commenced in a little less than four years after Esau Baker died. They moved from my neighborhood together, and came here to Norfolk, since when I have not visited them. Some time ago I asked her where the man was that she had with her, and she told me that he had left her.

The testimony in the case clearly establishes the fact that the appellant has been living in open notorious adulterous cohabitation with Armstead Johnson, and that they claimed each other at times as husband and wife.

The testimony filed in rebuttal is merely negative in character, and is wholly insufficient to contradict the testimony obtained on special examination.

Therefore, after a careful review of the evidence on file in the case, I am clearly of the opinion that your action in the premises was correct.

Rejection affirmed.

FEE—ONE CLAIM ONE FEE—INCREASE.

ELIZABETH M. WILLIAMS (WIDOW).

Where a declaration filed in a widow's original claim for pension sets forth that the claimant is entitled to increase on account of helpless condition of a minor child of the soldier, the attorney who is authorized to prosecute said claims by a power of attorney contained in said declaration is not entitled to an additional fee for securing such increase upon the child attaining its sixteenth year.

Assistant Secretary Webster Davis to the Commissioner of Pensions, September 9, 1897.

C. E. Foote, of Kalamazoo, Mich., July 10, 1897, appealed in the matter of fee on the supplemental issue of June 21, 1897, in the claim under the act of June 27, 1890, of Eliza M. Williams, as widow of Andrew H. Williams, late of Company F, First Battalion, Sixteenth United States Infantry.

The declaration in the widow's claim was filed by the appellant April 23, 1894. It was substantially alleged therein that she was entitled to pension on account of the soldier's minor child, Earl V. Williams, imbecile, born November 28, 1879. Said declaration contained a power of attorney in favor of the appellant, authorizing him to prosecute the claim, and stipulated for a fee of $10. The appellant filed medical and lay evidence tending to establish the helplessness of said minor.

August 11, 1894, certificate issued to allow the claimant pension at the rate of $8 per month, and the additional sum of $2 on account of said minor, the latter sum to terminate upon the minor attaining his sixteenth year, November 28, 1895.

The appellant, October 10, 1895, on behalf of the widow, filed a claim for continuance of pension for said child, on the ground of his helplessness. In the declaration filed herein, the power of attorney to the appellant was renewed.

June 21, 1897, there was a supplemental issue to allow increase on account of said helpless minor, but an additional fee was refused the appellant upon the ground that he was obligated by the terms of his contract to prosecute the claim for increase on account of said helpless minor, as well as the original claim, and all for one fee.

The action of the Bureau in denying the appellant a fee upon said issue, and under the foregoing conditions, is based upon the ruling of the Department in the case Elizabeth Lohr, widow, certificate No. 304,175 (13 Fee P. L. Bk., 144).

In that case, as in this, claim for pension on account of the helplessness of the minor was made in the widow's original declaration.

The power of attorney contained in the original declaration, which also set up the widow's future contingent right to pension on account of the helplessness of a minor, may properly be construed as relating to said contingent claim and as applicable thereto. Furthermore, said power would become operative when proper proceedings were instituted, and at the proper time, to secure pension in behalf of the widow on account of the permanent helplessness of a soldier's child. Such is the purport of the decision of the Department in the case of Sarah Miznerr (7 P. D., 62). The facts in that case and those in the case under consideration are analogous, and are substantially set forth, together with the rule there laid down, in the syllabus of the case cited, as follows:

Where an attorney commences and prosecutes a claim for widow's pension to a successful issue, he is not bound to prosecute a subsequent claim for additional pension for a posthumous child born after making the contract for the prosecution of the widow's claim; such claim is a new claim, and the attorney prosecuting is entitled to a fee of $10 under the act of June 27, 1890.

The following is from the text of said decision (7 P. D., 63).

At the time that claim (the original claim) was filed the child was not born, and consequently the widow had and could have no title to pension on its account. If, in anticipation of the birth of a posthumous child, she and her attorney had executed a contract in which the latter undertook, among other things, to prosecute a claim for increase to which she would become entitled immediately upon such birth, though a new declaration claiming for said child would have been necessary, said attorney should have prosecuted the new claim, and without additional compensation, for in so doing he would but have executed an essential part of said contract.

It appears that in the case under consideration the appellant and the claimant, in anticipation of the continued helplessness of the minor child, executed a contract (the declaration) whereby the appellant agreed to prosecute her claim for increase on account of said helpless minor, to which she would become entitled upon the child attaining its sixteenth year; and although the filing of a new application became necessary, the attorney, in prosecuting said claim, simply carried out an essential part of his original contract.

It follows, therefore, that, as the appellant received the full fee to which he was entitled under his original contract, he is not entitled to any additional fee on the supplemental issue to allow increase on account of said helpless minor.

For the foregoing reasons the action of the Bureau from which this appeal is entered is affirmed.

SERVICE—WAR OF THE REBELLION—ACT JUNE 27, 1890.

CHARLES E. SHINGUIN.

1. Pensioner's service, extending from December 5, 1865, to December 5, 1868, is not shown to have had any connection with the war of the rebellion, and he can not, therefore, be held to have served in or during said war, and is not pensionable under the second section of said act. The dropping of his name from the rolls was proper.
2. This holding is in accordance with the decisions in the cases of Barleyoung and Edward Farrell et al. (7 P. D., 453 and 532), which are indorsed as being sustained by the law.

Assistant Secretary Webster Davis to the Commissioner of Pensions, September 9, 1897.

This appellant, Charles E. Shinguin, late of Company E, Fifteenth United States Infantry, was pensioned in 1892 at $12 per month, under section 2, act of June 27, 1890. His service was from December 5, 1865, to December 5, 1868.

Assistant Secretary Reynolds rendered a decision December 8, 1894, in the case of John Barleyoung (7 P. D., 453), in which, among other things, it was held that—

1. The technical legal termination of the war of the rebellion was August 20, 1866.
2. Under section 2 of the act of June 27, 1890, service must have been rendered both during and in some necessary connection with the war of the rebellion, as a part of its belligerent operations.
3. Service rendered after July, 1865, will be presumed to have not been in said war; and the burden of proof will be upon claimants to show, by positive and satisfactory evidence, that such service was in some actual connection with the war as existing at the time the service was rendered.

In pursuance of these rulings, notice was sent, March 6, 1895, to the pensioner to show that his service had some necessary connection with the war of the rebellion; otherwise his name would be dropped from the pension rolls. In the meantime a report was received from the

WILLIAM HULSE.

Pensioner's rating having been reduced from $12 to $8 per month under the act of June 27, 1890, after due notice in accordance with the provisions of the act of December 21, 1893, he appealed, and such action was set aside for the purpose of according him another medical examination, it having been three years since his last examination. Such examination having been made, and it appearing therefrom that such reduction was justly and properly made, pensioner is not entitled to a new notice to reduce nor additional payment at a higher rate for the period from date of original reduction and the date of the action had on the last medical examination.

Assistant Secretary Webster Davis to the Commissioner of Pensions, September 9, 1897.

In a decision rendered August 22, 1896, by my predecessor, Assistant Secretary Reynolds, upon the appeal of William L. Hulse, late of the Fifth Battery, Indiana Light Artillery, it was held that the reduction of his rate of pension under the act of June 27, 1890, from $12 to $8 per month, without a medical examination having been held for more than three years, was error, and the case was ordered reopened in order that such an examination might be held. The decision referred to sets forth the history of the case in full.

A new medical examination being held October 21, 1896, in pursuance of said decision, the medical referee rendered the following opinion, dated February 4, 1897:

The certificate of medical examination made October 21, 1896, under decision of the honorable Assistant Secretary, on appeal, does not show, under present practice of this Bureau, a pensionable degree of disability under act of June 27, 1890; but in view of the evidence filed in the case July 9, 1895, the action of reduction to $8 is deemed proper, and is adhered to.

Thereupon, the pensioner's attorney, N. C. Miller, was informed April 6, 1897, that the reduction of the rate of pension to $8 per month was proper, as the disabilities for which pension was allowed did not incapacitate the pensioner for earning his support by manual labor in such a degree as to warrant the continuance of the rate of $12 per month. Also, that the certificate of medical examination, held after the rendition of the decision upon pensioner's appeal, did not show him entitled to the higher rating, but the rate of $8 per month appeared proportionate to the degree of disability described and shown. From this action another appeal has been filed, April 17, 1897, by said attorney, in which it is insisted that in view of the decision rendered August 22, 1896, the claim should have been reopened to the extent of having a new notice of proposed reduction served upon pensioner, thus requiring payment of his original rate in full until reduction was ordered in pursuance of the last medical examination; and then no reduction at all should be made, because the evidence justifies continuance of the maximum rate.

The last of these contentions will be disposed of first. In the former decision it was shown that a portion of the basis of the pension as first allowed was deafness, which under later rulings was not considered a cause of incapacity for manual labor, so that, if the deafness and rheumatism were still the only disabilities existing, and in the same degree, the reduction from $12 to $8 per month would not have been erroneous. But, as that decision points out, other disabilities had been alleged, and pensioner's exact condition had not been ascertained for three years. In such case therefore it was held that he was entitled to have his condition made manifest at the time of the proposed reduction. The medical examination held October 21, 1896, shows his condition as follows:

Poorly nourished; muscles flabby; skin healthy, tongue coated heavily; disability from general debility two-eighteenths. Crepitation in right shoulder; complains of pain in left hip; no joint, tendon, or muscle changes. Disability from rheumatism one-eighteenth. Says used to have neuralgia over lower part of right chest; not troubling him now; no disability. Apex beat of heart diffused but not strong; apex 2 inches within and 3 inches below nipple. Sounds and size normal. No cyanosis or œdema; no disability from heart disease. Rectum normal now, but has scar of old (1878) operation for fistula; no disability. Can't hear ordinary tones with right ear. Hears ordinary tones with left ear at 6 inches; no physical changes in ears. Disability from deafness twenty-thirtieths. Considerable cough; auscultation and percussion of lungs show nothing. Naso-pharynx normal. Disability from bronchitis one-eighteenth. No bad habits. No venereal disease. No other diseases.

From this showing it will be seen that the opinion of the medical referee, already quoted, is sustained, no ratable disability under the act being here described, and the only real basis for continuance of any rating is the testimony of Drs. Heaton and McCullough, referred to in the former decision. Thus, as a matter of fact, the rating of $8 per month is all that is justified by the evidence.

But, as to the first ground of contention, that even if a reduction is warranted by the evidence as now on file, such reduction should commence from a date subsequent to the last examination, and after another notice to pensioner, as required by the act of December 21, 1893. There is little force in this contention. It is not claimed that the former notice of reduction was not ample and regular in all respects or that pensioner did not have the opportunity to furnish all rebutting testimony he desired. As already seen, he did furnish such testimony, and this, with all other evidence before and since, shows that he is not entitled to more than the $8 per month, and has not been since the notice was sent him. To pay him now the higher rate of $12 per month for all the period since August, 1895, when reduction was made, simply on the plea of technical failure to comply with the law, or rather because all necessary evidence was not obtained before action was taken, would be to give pensioner an amount to which he is not entitled.

Proper notice was sent and received, there was no suspension of payment, and payment at the maximum rate was made to the date of the actual decision to reduce.

In the decision of Assistant Secretary Reynolds, May 9, 1895, in the case of Mary J. Rice (7 P. D., 569), it was held—

The act of December 21, 1893, relieves the Commissioner of Pensions of the power theretofore exercised of suspending the payment of a pension pending the proceeding to annul or reduce it, leaving the pension to accrue during that period, and to the pensioner the right to demand and receive payment at the times fixed for payments under the law. But when the decision of the Commissioner of Pensions is rendered the effect thereof under the act of December 21, 1893, is to authorize a withdrawal of payment, not only as to such illegal part which, but for the decision, might thereafter have accrued, but as to all unpaid pension adjudged illegal under that decision.

This ruling is in accordance with law, and as applied to the present case no payment can be made to pensioner as contended for, he having received all he is entitled to under the evidence on file. The action appealed from is therefore correct, and the same is affirmed.

———

HONORABLE DISCHARGE—ACT JUNE 27, 1890.

DENNIS MURPHY.

Soldier was dishonorably discharged from the Regular Army March 19, 1861, having been in arrest for more than a year prior to that date. He enlisted March 22, 1862, and served in the Fourth California Volunteers until March 31, 1866, when he was mustered out. It is held that he was honorably discharged within the meaning and intent of the act of June 27, 1890.

Assistant Secretary Webster Davis to the Commissioner of Pensions, September 9, 1897.

The appellant, Dennis Murphy, was enrolled on the 22d of March, 1862, and was a private in Company G, Fourth California Infantry, until the 31st of March, 1866, when he was mustered out with his company.

On the 3d of July, 1890, Mr. Murphy filed an application for pension under the act of June 27, 1890. A certificate was issued on the 23d of May, 1891, to allow pension under said act at the rate of $8 per month.

After this certificate was issued it was found that Mr. Murphy had served in the Regular Army before the enlistment under which he served in the Fourth California Volunteers and was dishonorably discharged from the Regular Army March 19, 1861. The War Department reported, under date of May 18, 1896, that Dennis Murphy enlisted on the 23d of February, 1857, and was assigned to Company D, Ninth Regiment of United States Infantry. He deserted September 15, 1858, and was apprehended February 2, 1859. He again deserted July 3, 1859. The muster rolls from March and April, 1860, to January and February, 1861, show him absent in confinement at Benicia Barracks, Cal., since March 9, 1860. Date of apprehension not stated. He was tried for repeated desertions, found guilty, and duly sentenced. Muster roll for March and April, 1861, reports him dishonorably discharged at Benicia Barracks, Cal., by sentence of general court-martial, Special

Orders, No. 28, Headquarters Department of California, March 19, 1861.

Upon this evidence the name of the pensioner was, after legal notice to him, dropped from the pension roll by an order, dated September 26, 1896, on the view that he was not honorably discharged from the whole period of his service during the war of the rebellion.

From this action an appeal was taken, June 3, 1897, the contention being that soldier was discharged from the Ninth United States Infantry before the war of the rebellion commenced and at a place 3,000 miles distant from what was afterwards the seat of war; that his service in said organization had no connection whatever with the war of the rebellion; that he was honorably discharged from the organization in which he served for four years during the war of the rebellion.

It is held that it was the intention of Congress in the act of July 14, 1862, to designate the 4th of March, 1861, as the commencement of the war of the rebellion. (Case of Ellen Pearson, 5 P. D., 258.)

It is also held that to entitle to pension under the act of June 27, 1890, the soldier must have been discharged from all service contracted to be rendered by him in the war of the rebellion, whether under one enlistment or more than one, and whether it continued for but ninety days or the whole period of the war.

The question to be determined in this case is, therefore, whether applicant was honorably discharged from the whole period of his service in the war of the rebellion.

The honorable discharge required by the act of June 27, 1890, is an honorable discharge from the organization or organizations in which service was rendered during the war of the rebellion. The applicant in this case can not be regarded as having served during the war of the rebellion in the Ninth United States Infantry. He was absent in confinement during the period from March 9, 1860, until his discharge by sentence of a general court-martials March 19, 1861.

It has been held that the period during which a soldier was in confinement at hard labor under the sentence of a general court-martial, with loss of all pay and allowances, due and to become due, could not be taken into calculation in determining the period of his service under the act of June 27, 1890. (Claim of George W. Fleck, 7 P. D., 343.)

The soldier in the case under consideration was in confinement from March 4, 1861, to March 19, 1861. He was in circumstances during said period under which he was not required to render any military service. It can not be held that as a member of Company D, Ninth United States Infantry, he "served" during the war of the rebellion.

If he had been dishonorably discharged from the Regular Army on or before March 3, 1861, no question in regard to his right to pension under the act of June 27, 1890, would have arisen. He had, however, as little connection, under his enlistment in the Regular Army, with the war of the rebellion as if he had been discharged before the 4th of March, 1861.

The soldier served more than four years in the Fourth Regiment of California Infantry, and was honorably discharged after the close of active hostilities. He was honorably discharged from the organization in which he rendered all the service rendered by him during the war of the rebellion. The conditions giving title to pension under the act of June 27, 1890, were fulfilled in his case. The action rejecting his claim for pension under said act is, therefore, set aside.

You will please adjudicate his claim upon the views herein set forth.

RATING—GRADE RATES, ACT MARCH 3, 1888—INSTRUCTIONS.

GEORGE W. BAKER.

1. The act of March 3, 1883, increased the amount of pension for third-grade rating from $18 to $24 per month, and since that date there has been no $18 rate, and any allowance of $18 as a third-grade rating or otherwise is erroneous.
2. The basis of rating above $17 per month (aside from total of rank) is that the disability shall produce inability to perform manual labor equivalent to the loss of a hand or a foot.

Assistant Secretary Webster Davis to the Commissioner of Pensions, October 2, 1897.

I return herewith your letter of the 1st instant, together with Departmental call of the 9th ultimo, for an advisory opinion of the medical referee of your Bureau, in the case of George W. Baker, Company G, Eighteenth Michigan Volunteers, certificate No. 388,725.

Replying to the inquiry contained in your letter I have to state as follows, viz:

The act of Congress approved June 6, 1866, in its first section provided a rate of $15 per month for such disability (incurred in the service of the United States and in line of duty) as is "equivalent to the loss of a hand or a foot," and this rate was designated as a third-grade rating. The act of March 3, 1873, by its fourth section increased this rate to $18 from and after June 4, 1872, and provided, in section 5, that the rate of $18 per month may be proportionately divided for any degree of disability established, for which the second section of the act (now section 4695, Revised Statutes) makes no provision.

Section 4695, Revised Statutes, declares the pecuniary value of a pension for total disability according to rank.

The act of March 3, 1883, increased the rate for the same disability to $24 per month from and after the passage of the act.

Up to March 3, 1883, by virtue of the proviso contained in the fifth section of the act of March 3, 1873, it was legally both possible and proper to divide a disability producing inability to perform manual labor "equivalent to the loss of a hand or foot" into eighteenths, and to say, by way of describing extent of disability, seventeen-eighteenths of third grade for anything that came short of "total third grade."

But the act of March 3, 1883, substituted the rate of $24 for disability "equivalent to the loss of a hand or foot," and retained $18 only for the purpose of dividing proportionately for any degree of disability more than total ($8) and less than the loss of a hand or a foot, or for a disability equivalent thereto. (Smith's case, 3 P. D., 172.)

There is no $18 rate provided by law nor has there been since the passage of the act of March 3, 1883. (Williams's case, 3 P. D., 401.)

An allowance subsequent to March 3, 1883, of $18 as a third-grade rating is erroneous. (Martin's case, 4 P. D., 378.)

The basis of any rating above $17, aside from total for rank, in excess of that amount, is, inter alia, that the disability shall produce inability to perform manual labor equivalent to the loss of a hand or foot.

The true rule of progression, therefore, in such a case is not to determine whether the disability of a pensioner rated at $17 has increased one-eighteenth or two eighteenths, but whether the disability has increased to such an extent as to produce inability to perform manual labor equivalent to the loss of a hand or foot. For, since it is this "equivalent" disability that is the basis of the specified rate of $18, now $24, it necessarily follows that unless the disability of a pensioner drawing $17 has increased to an extent that would be the equivalent of loss of a hand or foot, for which $24 is now allowed, there is no intervening rate that can be given to such pensioner.

If any other doctrine has been announced in a decision of this Department, it has been by inadvertence or error, and will be promptly corrected on notice.

***

SERVICE—WAR OF THE REBELLION.

IDA E. FILLER (WIDOW).

Soldier's service for ninety days or more in the Regular Army subsequent to November 23, 1865, under an enlistment on that date, is not service for ninety days in the war of the rebellion as contemplated in the act of June 27, 1890. (Cases of Barleyoung and Farrell, 7 P. D., 453 and 532, cited.)

Assistant Secretary Webster Davis to the Commissioner of Pensions, October 2, 1897.

On the 23d day of December, 1895, appellant filed a claim (No. 625484) for pension under the act of June 27, 1890, as widow of Eli Filler, deceased, late of Company F, Eighteenth United States Infantry, alleging among other things that her husband died November 25, 1895.

Her claim was rejected January 22, 1896, on the ground that the service of the soldier was rendered after the close of the war of the rebellion.

An appeal from said action was entered December 7, 1896, and on the 9th of January, 1897, Assistant Secretary Reynolds affirmed said action, under the decisions in Barleyoung's appeal (7 P. D., 453), and Farrell's appeal (7 P. D., 532). This motion for reconsideration was entered August 2, 1897, appellant contending that the war of the rebellion ended on the 21st day of August, 1866, and that soldier's service from date of enlistment, November 23, 1865, was more than ninety days in said war.

The question was carefully considered in Assistant Secretary Reynolds's opinion, January 9, 1897, and his holding is correct under the decisions therein cited. There is no evidence showing soldier's active war service in aiding the suppression of the armed force of the Confederate States subsequent to the date of his enlistment; therefore, under the facts of this case, the appellant's claim under the third section of the act of June 27, 1890, has not been established.

The reasons for affirming your action, January 22, 1896, were fully set forth in the opinion to which I have referred, and I do not deem it necessary to restate them.

Motion overruled.

MARRIAGE IN MISSISSIPPI—IMPEDIMENT OF BLOOD.

ANN CAHAL (ALLEGED WIDOW).

Evidence secured by special examination shows that soldier was a white man and claimant is a negro. The intermarriage of the races being prohibited by the laws of Mississippi, in which State the parties resided, their cohabitation could not be regarded as a legal marriage, but was mere concubinage, and claimant is not the lawful widow of the soldier, nor entitled to pension as such.

Assistant Secretary Webster Davis to the Commissioner of Pensions, October 2, 1897.

Appellant filed this appeal June 26, 1897, from the rejection on June 9, 1897, of her claim (No. 545309) for pension as widow of William Cahal, Company B, First Mississippi Mounted Rifles, under the act of June 27, 1890. The cause of rejection is stated as follows:

Claimant is a colored woman, of negro blood, and soldier was a white man, of the Caucasian race. The laws of Mississippi, where claimant and soldier lived, and where the alleged marriage occurred, prohibited such marriage, and said alleged marriage was void on the ground of said impediment of blood.

The appeal contends that soldier was a colored man and not a white man, that this is shown by the fact that he conducted himself as a colored man, associated with colored people, enlisted in a colored regiment, and was borne on the records of the War Department as colored.

The claim was previously rejected, in October, 1896, and a similar appeal was filed. The decision of that appeal set aside the adverse action on the basis of insufficient evidence upon which to determine the point in issue. Since then further special examination has been held and the claim again rejected and appealed, as stated.

The former decision sets forth the principal facts touching the matter in question, as far as shown by the evidence then in the case. That decision is hereto attached.

From the evidence secured by the later investigation the following facts may be summarized: The claimant, as she herself states, was the daughter of a colored woman, her father being a white man. She was freeborn, and therefore not under the same legal disabilities as to marriage and other matters as colored people who were slaves in the same State. The soldier was a white man, his mother and father both being white people. This is distinctly stated by two or three witnesses, old men, who knew him from infancy. He was a bastard, but it was generally known that he was white. His mother had come to the county from Missouri. She was disreputable in character, and was what was known in the South as "poor white trash." The soldier was her oldest son. She had two other children, one by a white man and the other by a negro. Naturally she was looked down upon by respectable white people, and soon came to be the associate of such colored people as would recognize her. The soldier, with this example and his inherited instincts as well, probably, as from force of circumstances, also associated with negroes, and took the claimant as wife or paramour.

The claimant states that she was married to soldier about 1847 by a magistrate, but there is no proof of this, the only evidence of marriage being that they lived together in the relation of husband and wife. There is evidence to the effect that, after leaving Wilkinson County, the claimant and soldier went to Natchez, Miss., and, while he continued to live with her, he showed that he recognized the difference in race, because it is stated that on one occasion he negotiated to sell her as a slave, but was prevented by a man who knew her well.

Beside the foregoing facts, as they appear in the evidence, and which are undoubtedly sufficient to determine the racial status of the claimant and soldier, it may be stated that there was a rule invariably observed in the South during the existence of slavery, and doubtless still in force, by which the race to which a child belonged was fixed. That rule was that the race of the mother should control that of the child in any case of mixed blood. If the mother was Caucasian, the child was regarded as of the white race. If the mother was a negro or mulatto, the child was denominated a negro. Thus, in this case, the claimant is a negro, and the soldier was a white man.

It only remains to be stated, then, that under the laws of Mississippi, which prohibited the intermarriage of whites and negroes, the claimant could not have been the legal wife of the soldier, and is not his lawful widow. It is unnecessary to elaborate the statement as to the illegality of such marriages. The claimant has recognized this fact as far as the State of her residence is concerned, her only contention having been that soldier was not a white man, and therefore these laws did not apply. As shown, however, there can be no doubt on the question of the race of each, and the relationship was mere concubinage. This being true, claimant has no title to pension as widow, and the rejection of her claim was proper. That action is affirmed.

DEATH CAUSE.

ANGELINE EMMONS (WIDOW).

Soldier was pensioned for disease of heart and died of abscess of bowels, as shown by the records of death of the city of Lowell, Mass., and claimant's declaration filed about a week after soldier's death.

The affidavit of one physician stating that disease of bowels would not have terminated fatally had it not been for the disease of heart amounts to no more than mere conjecture, and is not accepted as showing that death resulted from the pensioned cause.

Assistant Secretary Webster Davis to the Commissioner of Pensions, October 2, 1897.

I have considered the motion, filed August 4, 1897, for a reconsideration of the decision rendered by Assistant Secretary Reynolds, on April 3, 1897, affirming the rejection of the claim (No. 834549) of Angeline Emmons, widow of Benjamin Emmons, late of Company B, Second Massachusetts Infantry, for a pension under the general law. It is contended, in support of the motion for reconsideration, that the testimony of Dr. Patterson, who treated the soldier during the last four years of his life, shows that disease of the heart, for which he was pensioned, was one of the factors, and, in fact, the main factor, in the death cause.

There seems to be no reason to doubt that at the time of the soldier's death abscess of the bowels was recognized as the immediate and efficient cause of death. The public record of deaths kept in the city of Lowell, Mass., gives "abscess of bowels" as the cause of death, and the claimant, in her declaration filed about a week after his death, alleged the same cause.

The theory upon which the claim is based is that the disease of bowels would not have terminated fatally had it not been for the disease of heart. Dr. Patterson gives this theory the support of his opinion, but, from the very nature of the case, such an opinion amounts to little more than a conjecture or guess. The soldier was of feeble constitution, independent of the heart trouble. He was 73 years old. Dr. Patterson states in one affidavit that within the five years preceding his death he treated him for "five different illnesses;" that his general health was poor; and that he was subject to chronic constipation.

To say that abscess of the bowels would not have caused the death of a man of that age and in that condition of general health, if his heart had not been diseased, is manifestly to abandon the field within which evidence can operate and to enter the realm of pure speculation.

The claimant is pensioned under the act of June 27, 1890. I see no good reason for modifying the decision affirming the rejection of the claim under the old law.

The motion is, therefore, overruled.

LINE OF DUTY—ACCIDENTAL INJURY.

HENRY A. HELMER.

Soldier while riding over the battlefield of Pea Ridge, Ark., after that battle, for his own amusement, on a horse he had borrowed from his captain, was thrown and sustained an injury upon which he based a claim for pension. It is held that said injury was not incurred in line of duty. (Reaffirming action in same case, 2 P. D., 385, and 3 P. D., 111.)

Assistant Secretary Webster Davis to the Commissioner of Pensions, October 2, 1897.

In July 16, 1897, was filed a motion for reconsideration of departmental decision of October 30, 1894, in the case of Henry A. Helmer, in which it was ruled as follows:

Henry A. Helmer can not be considered as having been in line of duty at the time he received the disability for which he is pensioned. He was engaged in a private matter for his own pleasure or gratification, and was not engaged in the performance of that which the law required of him as a military duty. The decision of July 2, 1889, is, therefore, overruled, and you are directed to take the necessary steps to drop the claimant from the rolls. (7 P. D., 376.)

The issue presented by the motion for review arises in this way: Soldier had borrowed the horse of his captain for the purpose of riding over and reviewing the battlefield of Pea Ridge, in Arkansas, shortly after the occurrence of said battle, and while so doing was thrown by the horse against a tree, thereby sustaining a compound fracture of the left ankle.

On account of said injury he was discharged from the service, and afterwards applied for pension based upon the facts above stated.

The issue to be determined is, Was the injury sustained incurred while in line of duty in legal contemplation?

The claim was rejected by your office on March 2, 1885, on the ground that the disabilities were not incurred in line of duty, which decision was subsequently, on March 1, 1889, affirmed by the Department.

On July 2, 1889, the case was again brought before the Department on motion for review, on which occasion the above-mentioned decision of March 1, 1889, was overruled, and directions given that claimant's name be placed upon the pension roll. (3 P. D., 111.)

Subsequent to this, on July 14, 1894, the Commissioner of Pensions transmitted the papers in the case to the Department, accompanied by the following letter:

I have the honor herewith to submit the papers in the above designated case for your consideration, with a view to having a decision rendered therein that will serve as a precedent in similar cases.

The case has been before the Department twice before this, the question at issue being "the line of duty."

On March 1, 1889, the honorable Assistant Secretary Hawkins decided that claimant was not in line of duty when he received the injury for which pension was claimed. (See vol. 2, Pension Decisions, p. 385.)

The case was again before the Department and on July 2, 1889, the honorable Assistant Secretary Bussey overruled the former decision and ordered the appellant's name placed on the pension rolls, which was accordingly done, at $10 per month from October 23, 1882, for fracture of left ankle. Since that time he has been increased to $14 from June 11, 1890. He now has a claim for increase pending.

Upon considering the case in accordance with the suggestion contained in the above quoted letter of the Commissioner of Pensions, the Department, on October 30, 1894, rendered the opinion now under review, the holding in which, has been hereinbefore mentioned.

The issue presented in the motion for reconsideration is embodied in the statement that the disability of soldier was incurred while in the line of duty.

In order that the relevancy of the contention may clearly appear, it is necessary to make a more specific statement of the facts which are disclosed in the testimony of claimant made before a special examiner on November 12, 1884, as follows:

On or about the second day after the battle of Pea Ridge I was taking care of my captain's horse. I asked him for the loan of the horse to go over the battlefield just to look at it. Second Lieut. John Kahoe also went with me on horseback. When I asked the captain for the horse he said: "Henry, I rather you would not take him. He may throw you and kill you. You know he has thrown you once or twice." He throwed me at Osage River over his head, but did me no injury. As we were riding my horse got frightened, I think at a dead horse, and commenced buck jumping, and the first thing I knew I was thrown against a tree. When I went to get up I found I was badly hurt; my ankle just flopped over. The lieutenant went to camp for help. * * * They carried me to my tent, and went and got one of the surgeons of the regiment, who set my ankle, which was broke—the outside bone of the left ankle—and put the splints on it.

Under the above statement of facts, which seems to have been accepted as true, the question arises, Was the soldier in legal contemplation in line of duty when he sustained the injury upon which he bases his claim for pension?

In support of this contention, claimant submits the view that to hold that he was not in line of duty because he was not at the time carrying a musket or executing some order would be to pervert the spirit of the pension system. He points out that he was doing an act which was customary and natural, with the consent of his commanding officer, and that there was nothing in his conduct in conflict with any regulations.

It may be truly said [says claimant] that that which a soldier's superior officer recognizes as right for the soldier to do is right enough to keep him in the line of duty for pensionable purposes.

Attorney-General Cushing, on May 17, 1855, gave an opinion defining the relation of line of duty to pensions, in which, among other things, he said:

Every person who enters the military service of the country—officer, soldier, sailor, or marine—takes upon himself certain moral or legal engagements of duty, which constitute his official or professional obligations. While in the performance of those things which the law requires of him as military duty he is in the line of his duty. But at the same time, though a soldier or sailor, he is not the less a man and a citizen, with private rights to exercise and duties to perform, and while attending to these things he is not in the line of his public duty. In addition to this, a soldier or sailor, like any other man, has the physical faculty of doing many things which are in violation of duties, either general or special, and in doing these things he is not acting in the line of his duty. Around all those acts of the soldier or sailor which are official in their nature the pension law draws a legislative line, and then they say to the soldier or sailor: "If, while performing these acts which are within that line, you thereby incur disability or death, you or your widow or children, as the case may be, shall receive a pension or other allowance, but not if the disability arise from acts performed outside of that line—that is, absolutely disconnected from and wholly independent of the performance of duty. Was the cause of disability or of death a cause within the line of duty or outside of it? Was that cause appertaining to, dependent upon, or otherwise necessarily and essentially connected with duty within the line, or was it unappurtenant, independent, and not of necessary and essential connection?"

The above rule is adhered to by the Department as a true test criterion of such cases as that at bar, measured by which, in my judgment, the claimant is not entitled to a pension under the facts presented in the evidence.

The contention of claimant to the effect that such acts of a soldier as are recognized by his superior officer as being right the law will also recognize as being within the line of duty for pensionable purposes is untenable. It is perfectly legitimate and proper for a soldier to do many things that are not within the line of duty in the sense contemplated by the law relating to pensions.

After carefully considering the issue presented in the motion in the light of the law bearing upon the same, I am of the opinion that there is no error in the departmental decision under review.

The motion is therefore denied.

APPEAL—ATTORNEYSHIP—PRACTICE.

JAMES E. ORAM.

More than ninety days having elapsed since the attorney who filed this appeal was notified that he was not entitled to recognition, and he has filed no appeal in his own behalf, the appeal will be dismissed under rule 1, Rules of Practice, upon the ground that said attorney has not filed a power of attorney authorizing him to enter the appeal.

Assistant Secretary Webster Davis to the Commissioner of Pensions, October 2, 1897.

H. S. Kellogg, of Sandusky, Ohio, May 10, 1897, entered an appeal in behalf of the claimant in the above-entitled case.

On June 15, 1897, the Bureau notified Mr. Kellogg that he was not entitled to recognition in the case, and therefore the appeal would be dismissed.

The appeal has been returned to this Department for further proceedings.

Now, as a reasonable time—more than ninety days—has expired since said attorney has been notified and no appeal in his behalf has been entered from the action of the Bureau denying him recognition in this case, the appeal entered by him is dismissed under rule 1 of the Rules of Practice in appeals before the Commissioner of Pensions, upon the ground that he has not filed a duly executed power of attorney for the purpose of entering an appeal from the claimant, nor is he entitled to recognition under the rules of practice.

————

DISABILITY—ORIGIN—AGGRAVATION AND RECURRENCE OF OLD DISABILITY.

ANDREW J. FLEENER.

Certificate of disability for discharge, corroborated by oral testimony, shows that the alleged disability—bronchitis—existed prior to enlistment. It is not shown that claimant had recovered therefrom, and the recurrence of the same after an attack of measles in service is not such aggravation as would make the disability pensionable.

Assistant Secretary Webster Davis to the Commissioner of Pensions, July 9, 1897.

Andrew J. Fleener, late of Company D, Eighty-second Indiana Infantry, is a pensioner under the act of June 27, 1890, certificate No. 512,950, at the rate of $12 per month, on account of disability arising from bronchitis, rheumatism, and resulting disease of the heart, injury to right foot, and disease of eyes. Before the allowance of that pension, he had filed, June 5, 1880, a claim under the general law, alleging that on September 5, 1862, at Gallatin, Tenn., he contracted measles, which resulted in chronic bronchitis. This was rejected December 11, 1882, "on the ground of no disability since discharge from alleged bronchitis, result of measles." Additional evidence being filed, which shows that claimant was emaciated and had a cough when he returned home after discharge, and has probably suffered from a mild form of bronchitis since, the claim was reopened, but it was again rejected June 21, 1887, on the ground that the records of the War Department show that the alleged disability existed prior to enlistment. Subsequently the claim was again reopened upon the filing of additional evidence, and claimant also filed another declaration June 7, 1890, alleging rheumatism and resulting disease of heart, and injury of right foot, also contracted at Gallatin, Tenn., in the fall of 1862. In an affidavit filed June 24, 1891, he alleged disease of eyes as a result of measles. A special examination of the claim was held in 1892, after which it was rejected July 22, 1892, as follows:

Former action rejecting disease of respiratory organs on grounds of existence prior to enlistment is adhered to, as the adverse record is confirmed by testimony obtained on special examination. Reject rheumatism, disease of eyes, and injury to right foot;

no record, no medical evidence of treatment in service or at discharge: the present condition of foot is not shown as due to service, and from all the evidence in special report it is plain that rheumatism and disease of eyes did not originate in the service, but have developed—been contracted since discharge.

An appeal has been filed, June 21, 1897, by George Bancroft & Co., attorneys, from the action in regard to the claim for bronchitis upon the contention that the evidence is sufficient to establish the prior soundness of claimant, and it is not likely he would have been accepted into the service if he had not been sound. And, even if he was predisposed to lung trouble, yet the disease was brought out or aggravated by the measles, which is a common cause of such troubles. No exception is taken in the appeal to the action relative to the other disabilities named. Such action seems to be acquiesced in, and an examination of the papers indicates that the same was well founded and entirely proper.

Regarding the disability which is the subject of this appeal, the following history may be stated: The claimant was enlisted August 15, 1862. He was sick with measles in November, 1862, as shown by the testimony of comrades, but there is no record of such disability. He was presumably in regimental hospital while being treated for measles. There is a record showing he was in a general hospital from December 8, 1862, to June 26, 1863, with debility. He was discharged to date January 5, 1863, on surgeon's certificate of disability, "because of tuberculosis, with cavity of the right lung, extreme emaciation, night-sweats, and severe cough. Disease contracted prior to enlistment." There is no particular evidence to show that measles was the cause of the lung trouble referred to in this certificate, and while claimant denies the correctness of the statement that the disability was contracted before enlistment, he is unable to furnish such evidence as will sustain his denial, and show that the certificate is erroneous.

The only evidence bearing on this subject is that which shows that he returned home after discharge in a weak, emaciated condition, with some cough, and claimed that this was due to the measles. Claimant also offers, as an explanation of the statement in the certificate, his own and the testimony of one or two witnesses, to the effect that his father went to the hospital to see him while sick; that after being there a time he remarked that he was going to procure a discharge for him, and went off to see the surgeons. Very soon after this the discharge was granted, and he thinks it was procured upon some statement made by his father, although he does not know this. It seems intended that the inference from this testimony shall be that the father stated to the surgeons that soldier was sick with lung trouble before enlistment, and thus the adverse record was made. The claimant also appears to imply that if his father did make such statement it was untrue, but other testimony in the case indicates that said statement was well founded. The claimant's brother and brother-in-law have deposed before the special examiner that claimant, as a child, was subject to frequent attacks of what is called phthisic—sore throat and a cough—and that these spells continued through several years as he grew older, recurring almost every winter. They declare however, that they do not know but he was a sound man at enlistment.

Other evidence of prior soundness is of the same negative character. Witnesses state that they do not remember that claimant was suffering from any disability at the time of enlistment and just before enlistment, and, as far as they are able to judge, he was a sound young man. There is no positive statement that he had no affection of the throat, and had fully recovered from the effects of the frequent attacks of phthisic he had suffered from in his youth. The most that is shown is that witnesses did not know of such disability, and it was not apparent when claimant entered the service. And yet within four months, and upon the commencement of cold weather, the old disability was developed.

It may be true, and doubtless is, that measles is a precursor, if not the efficient cause, of various disabilities when a patient is exposed before completely recovering from the attack. And if it could be shown that soldier had not been subject to disease of the respiratory organs before this attack of measles, and was necessarily exposed afterwards, so that the alleged bronchitis followed, it might be readily admitted that the military service was responsible for said disability. Or, the same would be true if it were positively shown that complainant had completely recovered from his throat trouble previous to enlistment. But neither of these things is established. Claimant declares that he was subjected to exposure and took cold before he had fully recovered from the effects of the measles. Just when or how he was exposed is not shown. It was about three weeks after the attack of measles before he entered the general hospital, where he was treated for debility, and it was four weeks more before the record was made in which he was discharged.

The rule which has prevailed in such cases as this is stated in the following headnotes of decisions heretofore rendered:

Title to pension does not exist where the proof shows that the disability was, no doubt, accelerated by exposure while in service, but did not originate therein. (Jacob Prince, Schurz, 7 P. D., o. s., 121.)

Where it appears that prior to enlistment claimant had a disease which may have created a predisposition to the recurrence of the same, rendering his system more liable than otherwise to a second attack from exposure or unusual hardship, and yet where it appears that there had been, prior to enlistment, a complete recovery from the first attack, and the circumstances necessary to produce the disease, or a recurrence of the same, are due to the performance of claimant's duty as a soldier, and were legitimately incidental to the service, it is held that the recurring disability is pensionable under the law. (Joseph M. Potter, 3 P. D., 82.)

It has been uniformly held by the Department that the mere aggravation in the service of a disease existing prior to enlistment is not pensionable, whether any part of the disability in this case (from deafness) is due to the service being not susceptible of proof. Distinguishing this case from Joseph M. Potter (3 P. D., 82), in that a complete recovery prior to enlistment was shown in that case, while in this the disease was progressive from its inception. (George H. Stakes, 4 P. D., 158.)

The evidence on file fails to bring this claimant's case within the rule here laid down, and it may be further stated that there is nothing in the evidence of continuance to indicate that the disability since discharge has been anything more than a periodical recurrence of the weakness of the bronchi, originating in claimant's childhood. Origin in service and line of duty of the disability claimed and the basis of this appeal is not considered established, and the action of the Bureau in rejecting it for that reason was proper. That action is affirmed.

FEE—RULE TO SHOW CAUSE—ACT JUNE 27, 1890.

COMMISSIONER OF PENSIONS.

A fee, not greater than $10, may be allowed to an attorney for services rendered in preparing and filing evidence under a rule to show cause why pensioner's name should not be dropped from the roll, in cases under the act of June 27, 1890, but the attorney may not collect the same directly from the claimant or pensioner.

Assistant Secretary Webster Davis to the Commissioner of Pensions, October 14, 1897.

In your communication of June 26, 1897, is submitted the question whether an attorney has the right to collect a fee for services rendered in preparing and filing evidence under a rule to show cause why a pensioner's name should not be dropped from the roll, in cases under the act of June 27, 1890.

Your question really embraces two propositions, viz:

First. May a fee be allowed to an attorney for such service; and, second, may an attorney collect the same directly from the claimant or pensioner.

In reply to the first proposition I answer yes. To the second proposition I answer no.

The reasons for such holding were well expressed by Assistant Secretary Reynolds in the case of George D. Hilton (8 P. D., 182), and are hereby reaffirmed.

However, charges for services of the nature referred to by you in claims arising under the act of June 27, 1890, are restricted by the fourth section of that act to a sum not greater than $10, and can not, therefore, be provided for as among those "cases of difficulty and trouble" in which fee agreements may be recognized by the Commissioner of Pensions to sustain a larger payment than $10.

Such service may properly be included within the terms of the statute relative to the preparation, presentation, or prosecution of claims under the provisions of the act.

It is rendered in proceedings which require that pensioners show cause why their names should not be dropped from the roll.

The fact that such proceedings are instituted by and on account of the Government should not, and does not in my judgment, operate adversely against the right to payment for the service of an attorney in behalf of the pensioner's interest. The term "prosecuting a claim" is not limited in designation to initiatory proceedings; nor does it preclude proceedings purely defensive on the part of the pensioner. It includes proceedings looking to the continuation of a pension as well as obtaining one; the securing of an increase of rate and, as well, the prevention of a reduction thereof. And this term, "prosecuting a claim for pension," is found both in section 4785, Revised Statutes, as reenacted and amended by the act of July 4, 1884, and in section 4 of the act of June 27, 1890.

Clearly, to my mind, the service rendered in such a case is of a nature for which a fee may be paid. But it can only be paid upon the order of the Commissioner of Pensions after the filing of a duly executed power of attorney or fee agreements, and in claims under the act of June 27, 1890, is limited in amount to $10 as the maximum that can be allowed.

My communication to you of August 7, 1897, relative to this subject is hereby superseded and canceled, and you will be governed instead by the terms of this letter.

ATTORNEYSHIP—MATERIAL SERVICE—NEGLECT.

JAMES K. POLK (ATTORNEY).
DANIEL B. FORD (CLAIMANT).

1. As the appellant acquired the attorneyship, rendered material service, and was not in neglect when the claim was allowed, he is entitled to a fee.
2. The filing of a declaration in response to a call therefor by the Bureau, if filed at a time when deemed necessary and material, though subsequently deemed immaterial, is such service as may entitle an attorney to a fee.

Assistant Secretary Webster Davis to the Commissioner of Pensions, October 15, 1897.

James K. Polk, of Washington, D. C., July 26, 1897, appealed in the matter of fee on the issue of December 21, 1896, in the claim under the act of June 27, 1890 (Certificate No. 921906), of Daniel B. Ford, late of Company B, First Provisional Enrolled Missouri Militia.

The claimant, March 12, 1896, filed a declaration under the new law, and on July 10 and August 17 and 18, 1896, filed, through a Member of Congress, the evidence necessary to complete the claim. He was medically examined June 10, 1896.

On November 17, 1896, he was called upon for a declaration covering disease of heart, a cause of disability disclosed by the medical examination, and not alleged in the declaration then on file.

November 24, 1896, the appellant filed a declaration, which contained an allegation of disease of heart as a disabling cause, and a power of attorney in his favor. He rendered no other service. He was denied a fee upon the ground that he rendered no material service in the claim.

There was no bar to appellant's recognition. Pension was allowed December 21, 1896, at $12 per month, disease of heart and injury to right side being the approved causes of disability, to commence March 13, 1896, not the date of filing of the amended, but the original declaration. In the original declaration rheumatism was alleged as a disabling cause, and in slip dated November 10, 1896, the medical referee stated that disease of heart is not shown to be a result of rheumatism. Thereupon the claimant was called upon to file a new declaration, and said call was complied with by appellant. The inference from the record in the particular of the date fixed for the commencement of pension would indicate that the filing of a new declaration (under the practice which then obtained) was wholly unnecessary, and, therefore, the filing thereof immaterial, but this conclusion could not be reached if recourse could be had to the proceedings from which the record was made. As the facts appearing from the record are conclusive, the filing of a new declaration was unnecessary, so far as it affected the claimant's title to pension allowed.

In the case Darwin C. Simpson (8 P. D., 311), the Department held that—

The Bureau judges as to the sufficiency of evidence filed for establishing any fact, not the attorney. So, in every instance where an attorney fails for one year to respond to a call for evidence upon the ground that the evidence called for is unnecessary, said failure is neglect.

The import of the rule is that failure to file evidence under the conditions therein set forth would constitute neglect. A like rule would obtain, and of similar import, were an attorney called upon to file a declaration, and he should neglect or refuse to file the same because it was unnecessary. So the converse of the rule and of its corollary should apply; that is, where an attorney is called upon to file evidence or declarations, and file the same, such service should be deemed material, not as bearing upon the merits of claimant's right to pension, but as a compliance with those requirements of the practice deemed essential by the Bureau in the further prosecution of a case, and performing such service as would give title to a fee. In this sense the filing of the declaration by the appellant is deemed material.

The only ground upon which this case might be distinguished is that the call was made at a time when the appellant was not the attorney of record, and therefore the call was not a recognition of his attorneyship nor for any services or efforts upon his part. I would be inclined to deny the appellant a fee upon this ground, and thus create an exception to the rule, were it not a fact appearing from the record that the Bureau did not deem the filing of a new declaration unnecessary until after said new declaration was filed; so the inference would be that the filing of the same was deemed necessary when it was filed.

Therefore it would be an after consideration that would operate to defeat the appellant's title to a fee; that is, the opinion of to-day would overturn the opinion of yesterday. I do not approve of the idea of basing title to fee upon such contingencies.

As it appears that appellant acquired title to the attorneyship, rendered material service, and was not in neglect when the claim was allowed, he should be paid a fee. Action reversed.

MARRIAGE—IMPEDIMENT TO MARRIAGE.

MARGARET L. THOMAS (WIDOW).

Claimant was married to the soldier by a ceremony in 1875, and lived with him in Michigan until his death in 1895; at the time of said marriage soldier had a wife living who procured a divorce from him in 1877, all of which facts were unknown to claimant during the lifetime of the soldier.

Held, That as claimant was the innocent party, and was kept in ignorance of the fact that a legal impediment to her marriage to soldier existed at the time of such marriage, and that during all the time from the removal of the impediment in 1877 to soldier's death in 1895 the parties cohabited together as husband and wife, uniting in conveyances, and joining in church membership, and deporting themselves generally in accordance with good morals, and being universally recognized by their neighbors, friends, and acquaintances as husband and wife, a valid marriage subsequent to the removal of the impediment will be presumed, distinguishing this case from that of Ellen, widow of William A. Palmer (7 P. D., 363).

Assistant Secretary Webster Davis to the Commissioner of Pensions, August 30, 1897.

I have the honor to acknowledge receipt of your communication of date August 4, 1897, submitting for consideration and opinion of the Department the question of title to pension of Margaret L. Thomas as the legal widow of William B. Thomas, Company A, Sixteenth New York Volunteer Heavy Artillery, on a pending claim under the act of June 27, 1890. The facts of the case, as shown by the evidence, are as follows:

The claimant married the soldier by ceremony in Iowa October 4, 1875. They removed to Michigan about a week thereafter, and lived together as husband and wife in that State continuously from that time until the soldier died, May 31, 1895. It supervened after his death that, at the time of his marriage to claimant, he had a former wife living from whom he was not then divorced, but that on March 29, 1877, this former wife obtained a divorce from the said soldier by decree of the court of common pleas of Lake County, State of Ohio.

Claimant deposes before the special examiner that she did not know at the time she married the soldier that he had an undivorced wife. She knew that the soldier had been married, and that the wife was living, but believed or supposed that the said wife had been divorced. She did not, however, discover the true state of facts until after the soldier's death, when she found certain papers which disclosed all about the divorce.

It appears, further, that prior and subsequent to the removal of the legal impediment by the decree of divorce of March 29, 1877, the soldier and claimant cohabited continuously as husband and wife, affiliated with the Baptist Church at Berlin, Mich., and, upon their removal to Ashland, Mich., some twelve or fifteen years since, united with the Baptist Church at Ashland Center. The soldier was a minister of the gospel, and sometimes preached at the Ashland Baptist church. The parties also joined in the execution of a deed and mortgage, and were recognized as man and wife in all relations of coverture by the community among which they held domicile.

Attention of the Department is invited to a decision rendered by Assistant Secretary Reynolds, October 30, 1894, in the case of the widow of William A. Palmer, Company B, Fourth Michigan Volunteer Infantry, No. 575730, wherein it was held as follows:

Where one of the parties to a marriage is ignorant of the fact that the other party had at the time of such marriage a legal husband or wife living from whom he or she had not been divorced, and dies in ignorance of such fact, it becomes a legal impossibility for the surviving party to such second marriage, who alone had knowledge of the legal impediment, to prove a legal marriage, as in such cases no consent can be proved after the removal of the legal impediment.

It is suggested in your communication that the decision in the cited case of the widow of William A. Palmer (7 P. D., 363).

* * * was directed against the person who had what might be called the guilty knowledge; that the deceased soldier was the one who had been kept in ignorance, and the claimant was endeavoring to take advantage of her own wrong, and this, the Department held, she could not do.

The question, therefore, is propounded

* * * to what extent this principle shall be applied to an innocent party? In the case submitted the facts show that the widow claimant was innocent, and that she was kept in ignorance of the fact that a legal impediment existed at the time of her marriage to the soldier.

Attention of the Department in this connection is also invited to a decision recently rendered by the supreme court of Michigan in the case of Mary J. Williams v. Newel Kilburn (88 Mich., 279), wherein it was held as follows:

Pending a suit by a wife for divorce, she remarried and, after securing a decree, lived and cohabited with the second husband as his wife under the belief that another marriage ceremony was not necessary, induced by his statement that he had been so advised by good counsel, and his agreement, which was kept, to make a will in her favor and deliver it to her for safe-keeping. And it is held that the formal marriage ceremony may be treated as evidence, with what subsequently occurred, of the nature of the relation which the parties assumed and occupied, and that the facts establish a valid marriage; citing Hutchins v. Kimmell (31 Mich., 126); Peet v. Peet (52 id., 464).

In this case it appeared that the woman, plaintiff, originally married one Williams, who became a drunkard and abandoned her. The defendant, Kilburn, induced the plaintiff to institute a suit in divorce against Williams, and, pending the divorce, to marry him under agreement that they should not live or cohabit together until after she had obtained her divorce. After the divorce had been granted the defendant urged her to consummate the marriage by cohabiting with him. She doubted the propriety of this proceeding, and insisted upon another marriage ceremony, but he insisted that this was not necessary, stating that he had taken good counsel on the subject, and, to convince her of his good faith, he prepared and signed a will in her favor, calling her his beloved wife in the will, and handed her the document for safe-keeping. Thereupon she yielded and assumed marital relations with him. Three years after coverture the defendant abandoned the plaintiff without notice or warning, and went to live with his son, giving the son all his money and property, thus rendering the will of no value. During these three years the defendant lived in plaintiff's house, using her furniture, where she did weaving to support them.

The plaintiff brought suit against the defendant for damages for breach of promise to marry. The defendant demurred to the declaration, and, the demurrer being sustained, the writ of capias was quashed. The plaintiff appealed, and the supreme court of Michigan held that there was no error in sustaining the demurrer and quashing the writ, because the facts established a valid marriage; that plaintiff's rights grew out of that relation, and her remedy was that of a married woman against a deserting husband.

In the case of Hutchins v. Kimmell (31 Mich., 126) the learned jurist, Mr. Justice Cooley, delivered the opinion of the court. He held, *inter alia*, as follows:

Where parties agree presently to take each other for husband and wife, whatever the form of ceremony, or if all ceremony be dispensed with, and from that time live together professedly in that relation, this, under the laws of this State, constitutes a valid marriage; and such is the settled doctrine of the American courts.

Marriage between parties capable of contracting it is of common right and valid by a common law prevailing throughout Christendom; regulations restrictive of it or imposing conditions upon it are exceptional; they depend on local statutes, and, as in other cases of exceptions, if one claims that a case falls within them the burden of proof is upon him to show the fact; *prima facie* a good marriage is shown by proof of a present agreement, followed by cohabitation; and it will not be presumed, in the absence of proof, that there are regulations anywhere restrictive of this common right.

In the case of Peet v. Peet (52 Mich., 464) it was held as follows:

1. Continued cohabitation as husband and wife establishes the relation without any actual marriage ceremony, if the parties are competent to marry and consent to take each other as husband and wife.

2. Reputation is important as evidence to establish the fact of a marriage, but it can not disprove an actual marriage. And when there is doubt, the presumption should favor a lawful marriage rather than notorious immorality.

The cited departmental decision in the case of Ellen A., widow of William A. Palmer, laid down a rule in nowise in conflict with the principles underlying the numerous uniform decisions concerning marriage and divorce, and is not in conflict with the rule laid down in the cited case of Williams *v.* Kilburn (88 Mich., 279).

The import of the departmental decision referred to is to declare that claimant, in seeking to establish title to pension as the widow of the soldier, may not and will not be permitted to take advantage of her own wrong. Attention is invited to the following extract from the body of the decision which expounds this view:

> The question of a common-law marriage, therefore, does not arise in this case, as the claimant had notice of the legal impediment to a legal marriage, but concealed that fact from her second husband and entered into a bigamous marriage. The relations resulting therefrom were void and illegal in their inception, and must remain so unless changed by some specific act which amounts to consent, after the legal impediment, and as no such act is shown claimant has no title to recognition as the legal widow of her second husband.

It was, therefore, properly held that—

> Where one of the parties to a marriage is ignorant of the fact that the other party had, at the time of such marriage, a legal husband or wife living from whom he or she had not been divorced, and dies in ignorance of such fact, it becomes a legal impossibility for the surviving party to such second marriage, who alone had knowledge of the legal impediment, to prove a legal marriage, as in such cases no consent can be proved after the removal of the legal impediment.

In the submitted case the situation appears to be entirely different. It was the non-surviving party, the soldier, who alone had knowledge of the legal impediment, the surviving party, the claimant, being wholly innocent in the premises, and consent is proved by the cohabitation of the parties and acknowledgment by the soldier of the coverture between himself and claimant continuously for many years after the impediment of a former marriage had been removed by divorce.

The Department held in the cases of McCollum and Schmidlin (6 P. D., 93 and 200, respectively), that where such issues are presented some change in the relation must be shown—some act showing the intent to change the former relation to one matrimonial and recognizable by law.

I am of the opinion that, where it is shown by the evidence that both parties fully intended and consented to the maintenance of *bona fide* marital relations at and subsequent to the time when they were competent to sustain such status by removal of a preexisting impediment, and did consent to the maintenance of such marital relations by consent and continuous cohabitation, acknowledging each other as husband and wife and being universally recognized as such by the community in which they lived, joining in church membership, uniting in deeds and conveyances as husband and wife, and deporting themselves generally in accordance with good morals, a valid marriage is essentially established, not only under the *lex loci* of the State of Michigan, but, as pronounced by Judge Cooley, "such is the settled doctrine of the American courts."

SERVICE—INDIAN WARS—ACT JULY 27, 1892.

WILHELMINA ROTH (WIDOW).

The Florida war closed August 14, 1842. Soldier's service at Newport, Ky., from November 9, 1839, to October 31, 1842, when forwarded to his regiment, which he joined November 29, 1842, was not service "for thirty days in the Black Hawk war, the Creek war, the Cherokee disturbances, or the Florida war with the Seminole Indians, embracing a period from 1832 to 1842, inclusive," and his widow is not pensionable under the act of July 27, 1892.

Assistant Secretary Webster Davis to the Commissioner of Pensions,
November 15, 1897.

Claimant filed a claim, May 29, 1893, for pension under the act of July 27, 1892, as the widow of John Roth, late of Company F, Third United States Infantry, which claim was rejected October 2, 1893, on the ground that—

Soldier did not serve thirty days in any Indian war. Was not forwarded to his regiment until subsequent to August 14, 1842, the date of the close of the Florida war.

From this action an appeal was filed November 9, 1893, and on May 26, 1894, the rejection of the claim was affirmed by the Department.

August 4, 1897, a motion to reconsider and set aside said decision was filed.

A report on soldier's service from the War Department shows that the soldier on account of whose service pension is claimed enlisted November 9, 1839, at Newport, Ky., and was assigned to Company F, Third Regiment of United States Infantry; that from date of enlistment to October 31, 1842, he was at Newport Barracks, and that he joined his company November 29, 1842, and was discharged November 9, 1844.

The act of July 27, 1892, provides pensions for—

the surviving officers and enlisted men, including marines, militia, and volunteers, of the military and naval service of the United States who served for thirty days in the Black Hawk war, the Creek war, the Cherokee disturbances, or the Florida war with the Seminole Indians, embracing a period from eighteen hundred and thirty-two to eighteen hundred and forty-two, inclusive, and were honorably discharged, and such other officers, soldiers, and sailors as may have been personally named in any resolution of Congress, for any specific service in said Indian wars, although their terms of service may have been less than thirty days, and the surviving widows of such officers and enlisted men: *Provided,* That such widows have not remarried.

The Florida or Seminole Indian war in Florida, Georgia, and Alabama commenced December 28, 1835, and ended August 14, 1842; the Cherokee Indian disturbance and removal commenced in 1836 and ended in 1838, and the Black Hawk Indian war, in Illinois and Wisconsin, commenced April 26, 1832, and ended September 30, 1832. (Digest of 1885, p. 480.)

It was held by this Department in the case of James Toal (7 P. D., 35) that—

Service, to give pensionable status under the act of July 27, 1892, must have been actual service in the wars named in said act. Service in the United States Army at a military post remote from the seat of war gives no title.

At no time during the existence of the wars mentioned in the act under which pension is claimed did soldier serve at the seat of any of said wars, all of his service during the period of such wars being at Newport Barracks, Newport, Ky., and it can not, therefore, be said that he served thirty days in any of said wars.

It is manifest from the foregoing that claimant has no title to pension under said act as the widow of said soldier, and the former departmental decision of May 24, 1894, is adhered to. The motion is accordingly overruled.

DISCHARGE—SERVICE—ACT JUNE 27, 1890.

SARAH BUSH (WIDOW).

The soldier having been dishonorably discharged from his first term of enlistment during the war of the rebellion, and having subsequently reenlisted and served for more than ninety days during said war and received an honorable discharge, his widow is not entitled to pension under section 3 of the act of June 27, 1890, said act requiring an honorable discharge from all service contracted to be performed during the war. (Citing Stephen H. Carey, 6 P. D., 42; James Cullen, 6 P. D., 72; Franklin S. Cowen, 7 P. D., 374, and George Vansickle, 8 P. D., 336.)

Assistant Secretary Webster Davis to the Commissioner of Pensions, November 15, 1897.

The claimant's husband at the time of his death (December 29, 1895) was in receipt of a pension of $12 per month under the act of June 27, 1890. Her claim (No. 626464) for a widow's pension under the same act was rejected in May, 1896, on the ground that the soldier was not honorably discharged from all service contracted to be performed during the war of the rebellion. From that action the appeal was taken August 6, 1897.

The records show that the soldier first enlisted as a private in Company K, Ninth Regiment of Pennsylvania Reserves, July 27, 1861, and that he deserted and was subsequently brought to trial and dishonorably discharged March 1, 1862, by general court-martial and sentenced to hard labor for one year in the penitentiary. He again enlisted as a private in Company M, First Regiment of Pennsylvania Provisional Cavalry, February 21, 1865, and was mustered out with his company July 13, 1865. It is contended in the appeal that the soldier having been honorably discharged from a term of service of more than ninety days during the war of the rebellion the requirements of the act of June 27, 1890, as to service and discharge were fully complied with, and it is immaterial whether he was honorably discharged from his prior enlistment or not.

The soldier's claim for pension was allowed in March, 1892. On September 8, 1892, Assistant Secretary Bussey, in deciding the appeal in the case of Stephen H. Carey (6 P. D., 42), used the following language:

The language of the statute (act of June 27, 1890) plainly and unequivocally requires that the discharge from any and all service rendered during the late war of the rebellion, whether such service consisted of one term or of many, must have been honorable, to entitle the soldier to the benefits of said act.

Again, in the case of James Cullen (6 P. D., 72), he said:

It is very strenuously contended by the appellant in his appeal that as his first term of service in the Twenty-fourth Michigan Volunteer Infantry was of more than ninety days' duration, and he was honorably discharged from said term, he thereby fulfilled and complied with the requirements and conditions of the second section of the act of June 27, 1890, relative to service and discharge necessary to give him a pensionable status thereunder, and that his dishonorable dismissal from his subsequent service as captain of Company A, First Michigan Cavalry, should not be permitted to prejudice his case, or be held to render him ineligible for pension under the provisions of said section.

The position contended for by the appellant is wholly untenable under the law.

Both his terms of military service were rendered during the war of the rebellion.

The language of the second section of the act of June 27, 1890, relative to the service and discharge therefrom required as a condition precedent to the grant of a pension thereunder, is as follows:

"That all persons who served ninety days or more in the military or naval service of the United States during the late war of the rebellion, and who have been honorably discharged therefrom, and who are now," etc.

This language unquestionably covers and includes all military or naval service rendered by a claimant for pension under said act "during the late war of the rebellion."

The requirement is not that there should have been merely ninety days' service and an honorable discharge therefrom during said war, but a service of ninety days "or more," ninety days being fixed simply and solely as the minimum length of service required by the act to give a pensionable status thereunder. The plain and obvious meaning of the statute is that a military or naval service "during the late war of the rebellion" of not less than ninety days' duration, and an honorable discharge therefrom, are required as conditions precedent to the grant of pension thereunder, and the "honorable discharge" required is clearly not an honorable discharge from any special or particular part or term of such service only, but from all military or naval service rendered "during the late war of the rebellion."

This view of the law was followed and reaffirmed by Assistant Secretary Reynolds. (Franklin S. Cowen, 7 P. D., 374, and George Vansickle, 8 P. D., 336.)

In all of these decisions the law was construed as if it read:

All persons who rendered service during the war of the rebellion and were honorably discharged therefrom, the duration of such service being not less than ninety days, ` * * shall be entitled to receive pension, etc.

It can not be denied that the language of the act admits of this construction. Nor is it an unreasonable construction. As Assistant Secretary Bussey said in the case of Susan Colgin (5 P. D., 127):

Whether a soldier went into the Army at the beginning of the war, or near the close, each original and subsequent enlistment was for the purpose and with a view to the consummation of one act, to wit, the suppression of the rebellion; and, so long as the war continued, the enrollment of soldiers was practically for this one service to the country.

It may be well argued that in affixing the condition of an honorable discharge to the grant of pension made by the act of June 27, 1890, Congress intended to limit the benefits of said act to those who rendered faithfully all service contracted to be performed in the suppression of the rebellion, and that it did not intend to confer such benefits upon soldiers whose service was faithful only a part of the time.

After careful consideration of the whole matter I do not feel justified in setting aside the construction put upon the statute by my predecessors, and the same will be adhered to. Under that construction the soldier was pensioned improperly, and the denial of pension to his widow must be affirmed.

———

DISLOYALTY—SECTION 4716, REVISED STATUTES.

MILES F. FULLBRIGHT.

It appearing from the official military record in the War Department that this appellant had served in the Confederate army during the war of the rebellion, and there being no evidence to rebut the presumption that said Confederate service was voluntary, it not even being claimed or asserted by appellant that it was involuntary, payment of pension to him under the provisions of section 2, act of June 27, 1890, is expressly prohibited by the provisions of section 4716, Revised Statutes. See White's appeal (7 P. D., 312), Ozborn's appeal (Ibid., 317), and Longee's appeal (Ibid., 586).

Assistant Secretary Webster Davis to the Commissioner of Pensions, November 15, 1897.

This appellant filed in your Bureau on June 23, 1894, an application for pension under the provisions of section 2, act of June 27, 1890, which was rejected on February 5, 1895, upon the ground that he had voluntarily served in the Confederate army during the war of the rebellion.

From this action appeal was taken on June 3, 1897.

The official military record in the War Department of this appellant's army service during the war of the rebellion shows that he first enlisted on February 21, 1862, as a private in Company E, Twenty-ninth North Carolina Infantry, Confederate States army, and served therein until November 30, 1863, upon which date he was captured by the Union forces, and afterwards confined as a Confederate prisoner of war at Rock Island, Ill., until October 31, 1864, when he enlisted in Company I, Third United States Volunteer Infantry (Rebs), and served in this latter organization until November 29, 1865, when he was mustered out of service with said company and honorably discharged.

The foregoing official record clearly indicates on its face that the appellant's service in the Confederate army was voluntary on his part. There is nothing therein to indicate that the appellant was drafted, or conscripted, or in any way compelled or forced to enter the Confederate service against his will, but, on the contrary, it shows that he enlisted therein in February, 1862, before the passage by the Confederate Congress of the first Confederate conscription act of April, 1862, and at a time when the Confederate armies were recruited wholly by voluntary enlistments. Furthermore, this appellant admits his Confederate service, and has never claimed, asserted, or intimated in any way, manner, or form that it was not wholly voluntary on his part, nor is there a scintilla of evidence in this case tending to show that it was not.

It is clear, therefore, that the rejection of this claim by your Bureau, on the ground stated, was in strict accord with the well-settled holding of this Department that the provisions of section 4716, Revised Statutes, prohibiting the payment of money on account of pension to any person, or to the widow, children, or heirs of any deceased person, who in any manner voluntarily engaged in, or aided or abetted, the late rebellion against the authority of the United States, were applicable to pensions granted under the provisions of section 2, act of June 27, 1890, and was not error, and said action is affirmed accordingly. White's appeal (7 P. D., 312); Ozborn's appeal (Ibid., 317), and Longee's appeal (Ibid., 586).

———

FEE—RESTORATION AND INCREASE.

H. S. BERLIN (ATTORNEY).
JACOB YOUNG (CLAIMANT).

Where a pensioner's name has been dropped from the roll solely because he has been allowed and has accepted pension under some other law, and upon application for restoration and increase of pension under the law under which he was pensioned when his name was dropped, his name is restored to the roll under said law at an increased rate, the sole object in filing such claims being to secure a higher rate of pension, and not involving question of title, the attorney prosecuting the same is entitled to a fee of $2 only, the claim being in no sense a claim for restoration, but for increase.

Assistant Secretary Webster Davis to the Commissioner of Pensions, November 20, 1897.

H. S. Berlin, of Washington, D. C., September 27, 1897, appealed in the matter of fee on the issue of July 14, 1897, in the claim under the general law (Certificate No. 487535), of Jacob Young, late of Troop B, Tenth United States Colored Cavalry.

The claimant was pensioned under the general law at the rate of $8 per month, when, on July 14, 1890, he applied for pension under the act of June 27, 1890. Certificate issued March 3, 1892, to allow pension under said act at the rate of $12 per month from date of application, and claimant's name was dropped from the rolls under the general law.

The appellant, in claimant's behalf, September 16, 1896, filed a claim for restoration and increase under the general law. Certificate issued

July 14, 1897, to restore the claimant's name to the rolls under the general law and to allow straight increase at the rate of $14 per month from February 10, 1897, the date of the certificate of medical examination made in the claim showing increase. On this issue Mr. Berlin was certified a fee of $2. Upon appeal he contends that he should be allowed a fee of $10, as, in addition to securing an increase of the former rate of pension allowed under the general law, the claimant's name was restored to the rolls under that law.

Had the claimant's title to pension under the general law been involved in the proceedings and a subject of inquiry arising upon the application made to restore his name to the rolls, as is always the case when a pensioner's name is dropped for the reason that he has no title to pension, there would be some ground for the appellant's contention that he is entitled to a fee as in claims for restoration made under the conditions indicated. But it is manifest that this appellant did not establish in claimant's behalf a right to pension under the general law; on the contrary, the proceedings instituted by the appellant were based upon that right. The object of the proceedings was to secure a higher rate of pension than that formerly allowed, and the appellant is entitled to the fee provided by law for such services and that only.

The question is not a new one. In the case, John S. Green, certificate No. 241630, decided November 22, 1893 (16 Fee, P. L. Bk., 349), the same question was presented. The Department assigned the following reasons in denying the appellants in that case a fee in excess of $2.

So far as the claim filed by appellant related to the restoration of pension under the old law it was but a claim for renewal of certificate, and its successful prosecution gave no title to fee. The claim was in no sense a claim for restoration, as that term is used in the pension practice. The appellant was entitled to $2 for his services in securing straight increase under the general law, and to no more.

The holding in Green's case has been followed in every case coming before the Department involving the question there determined.

Where a pensioner's name has been dropped from the roll solely because he has been allowed and has accepted pension under some other law, and upon application for restoration and increase of pension under the law under which he was pensioned when his name was dropped his name is restored to the roll under said law at an increased rate, the sole object in filing such claims being to secure a higher rate of pension and not involving question of title, the attorney prosecuting the same is entitled to a fee of $2 only, the claim being in no sense a claim for restoration, but for increase.

As the appellant was denied a fee for the reasons indicated, the action of the Bureau is affirmed.

FRAUD AND MISTAKE—REIMBURSEMENT.

ANNIE DEMPSEY (WIDOW).

The soldier was pensioned for rheumatism and resulting disease of the heart. The widow stated in her application that he died of disease contracted in the service and filed a copy of a public record giving the cause of death as "paralysis of the heart," whereupon her claim was allowed. It was subsequently ascertained that the cause of death was inquired into by a coroner's jury and found to be the intemperate use of intoxicants and drugs, and her pension was, therefore, terminated.

Held: That the concealment by claimant of the fact that a coroner's inquest was had amounted to fraud and justified recovery of the amount paid under the old law from the pension subsequently allowed under the act of June 27, 1890.

Assistant Secretary Webster Davis to the Commissioner of Pensions, November 20, 1897.

The soldier, James Dempsey, late of Company C, Fourteenth Michigan Infantry, died on the 26th of April, 1890. He was at the time of his death a pensioner on account of rheumatism and resulting disease of the heart (certificate No. 275900). His widow filed an application for pension on May 7, 1890, alleging that he "died of disease contracted in the United States service." In support of this statement she filed a certified copy of the certificate of death on file in the health office of the city of Detroit, Mich., in which the cause of death was given as "paralysis of the heart." Upon this evidence the widow's claim was allowed, the paralysis of the heart being accepted as a result of the disease for which the soldier was pensioned.

Subsequently a special examiner while looking for Dempsey, with a view to obtaining his testimony in the claim of one of his comrades, received information in regard to the cause of his death which led to a special examination. In the course of such examination it was ascertained that a coroner's inquest was held in regard to the soldier's death, and that the verdict was that the paralysis of the heart of which he died was superinduced by the intemperate use of spirituous liquors and the employment of drugs, taken for the purpose of allaying the excitement of intoxication, as well as for rheumatism.

Thereupon the widow's pension was terminated September 3, 1891.

Subsequently, on December 5, 1891, she applied for a pension under the act of June 27, 1890, which, in August, 1893, was allowed. It was provided, however, that the pension paid under the old law should be deducted from the amount paid under the act of June 27, 1890. From that action an appeal was taken June 21, 1897, the contention being that the payment under the old law was not the result of fraud or mistake of fact, and, therefore, can not, under the rulings of the Department, be recovered.

The question is whether the allowance of the original claim was procured by fraud or was due to erroneous judgment upon the evidence.

Fraud may consist not only in the statement of what is false, but also in the concealment of what is true.

Concealment will amount to fraud where the concealment is of material facts which one party is under some legal or equitable duty to communicate to the other and which the latter has a right, juris et de jure, to know. (8 Am. and Eng. Enc. of Law, 644.)

When one pays money in ignorance of circumstances with which the receiver is acquainted, but does not disclose, and which, if disclosed, would have avoided the payment, the receiver acts fraudulently, and the money may be recovered back. (George v. Taylor, 55 Tex., 97.)

The fact that an inquiry into the cause of the soldier's death had been made by a coroner's jury, and that the jury, from the evidence adduced, found that his fatal disease was due to the use of intoxicants and drugs, was known to this claimant when she applied for pension and was a material fact which it was her duty to have disclosed.

The Pension Bureau had no means of knowing that fact. It relied upon the good faith of the applicant. The case differs from those cited in the appeal (Christian May, 8 P. D., 72; Norman Davis, ib., 288, and Mary Chryst, ib., 242) in this, that in the latter cases the Bureau was in possession of sufficient facts to put it upon notice, so that its failure to ascertain the whole truth was due to its own oversight or careless-ness rather than to any fraudulent concealment on the part of the applicants.

Under the circumstances, I am constrained to hold that the sup-pression, by claimant, of the fact that a coroner's inquest had been held constituted fraud, and, under the rulings of the Department, justified the action of your Bureau in recouping the pension paid under the old law from that granted her under the act of June 27, 1890. The action is affirmed.

EVIDENCE—PRACTICE—DISLOYALTY.

JOHN N. McCOLLUM.

This claim, having been adjudicated and rejected upon insufficient evidence, is remanded for reopening and readjudication under instructions.

Assistant Secretary Webster Davis to the Commissioner of Pensions, November 20, 1897.

This appellant filed in your Bureau on March 2, 1897, an application (No. 1187532) for pension under the provisions of section 2, act of June 27, 1890, which was rejected on May 1, 1897, upon the ground that he rendered voluntary service in the Confederate army during the war of the rebellion.

From said action appeal was taken on July 6, 1897.

There are no papers in this case whatever, other than the appellant's application for pension, and a report from the War Department of his service from December 27, 1863, to June 30, 1865, in the United States

Army. The only evidence on file tending to show a Confederate service consists of the following statement, which appears in his application for pension: "That he has * * * been employed in the military or naval service, otherwise than as stated above, except a short time in rebel army."

It does not appear that the War Department has ever been called upon in this case for the record of the appellant's Confederate service, or that he has been afforded an opportunity to explain the statement relative to his rebel service made in his application, or called upon to furnish evidence to rebut the adverse presumption arising therefrom, which unquestionably should have been done before his case was finally rejected by your Bureau.

I am clearly of the opinion that this case has been passed upon prematurely and adjudicated upon insufficient evidence, and, therefore, the rejection of the same is hereby reversed and set aside, and you are requested to cause the same to be reopened and readjudicated, after calling upon the War Department for information, and give the appellant an opportunity to be heard and to file evidence as above indicated.

MINOR'S PENSION. ACT OF JUNE 27, 1890.

MINORS OF JOHN DAVIS.

The rule promulgated in the case of the minors of Lafayette Howard (8 P. D., 230), that "the minor children of a deceased soldier have no title to pension in their own right under the act of June 27, 1890, while the widow of such soldier is living and not remarried, unless such widow has forfeited her right to pension under the act of August 7, 1882, or section 4706, Revised Statutes, notwithstanding such widow married such soldier subsequent to the passage of said act," is approved and adhered to.

Assistant Secretary Webster Davis to the Commissioner of Pensions,
December 10, 1897.

This is a motion, filed June 24, 1897, requesting reconsideration of decision of this Department of November 7, 1896, affirming on appeal the rejection by your Bureau of the above-entitled claim for minor's pension under the provisions of section 3 of the act of June 27, 1890, upon the ground that the deceased soldier had left a widow surviving him, to whom he had been married subsequent to the passage of said act.

The material facts in this case are sufficiently set forth in the departmental decision rendered on the appeal, which is hereto attached, and a copy of which was furnished the claimant at the time it was rendered.

This motion is merely a repetition of the contention of the appeal that the rejection of the claim upon the grounds stated and the decision affirming the same ignored the evident intention of the act of June 27, 1890, and was "not good law."

The former decision herein followed and was based upon the ruling of the Department on the appeal in the claim of the minor child of Lafayette G. Howard (8 P. D., 230), decided June 30, 1896, wherein it was held that the minor children of a deceased soldier have no title to pension in their own right under the provisions of the third section of the act of June 27, 1890, while the widow of such soldier is living and not remarried and has not forfeited her pensionable rights under the provisions of the general law, notwithstanding such widow married the soldier subsequent to the passage of said act.

I have again reviewed the foregoing ruling of the Department in the Howard case (supra), and after very careful consideration I am convinced that the rule therein announced is in conformity not only with the letter of the law, but also with the spirit and intent of the act of June 27, 1890, and the only safe and sound one that can be followed in the adjudication of claims of this character. A departure therefrom would lead to much uncertainty, confusion, and the unsettlement of many adjudicated cases and well-settled rights, and result, in many instances, in great apparent hardship and injustice, and such a step should not be taken without it were clearly apparent that said ruling was contrary to and not warranted by the law or that some gross wrong or injustice could be remedied by changing or abrogating it.

I have been unable to find in this, or in any similar case, any such potent or controlling reasons to justify or warrant a modification of said departmental ruling; and since it is directly applicable to the facts of the present claim, the former decision herein of November 7, 1896, and the action of your Bureau affirmed thereby will be adhered to, and this motion is overruled.

LIMITATION—PENDING CLAIM—APPEAL.

WILLIAM H. HUGHES (DECEASED).

The power conferred upon the Secretary of the Interior to establish rules and regulations for the examination and adjudication of claims for pension does not authorize the enactment of a rule or statute of limitations, and the decisions in the cases of Jacob Wolhart (8 P. D., 226), Henry Groppe (id., 293), and Briggs Soper (id., 394), in so far as they limit the time of filing an appeal by a widow from the rejection of her husband's pension claim, are overruled and set aside.

Assistant Secretary Webster Davis to the Commissioner of Pensions,
December 15, 1897.

July 16, 1892, William H. Hughes, late sergeant Company D, Sixteenth Ohio Volunteer Infantry, filed a claim for pension under the act of June 27, 1890, alleging chronic bowel trouble and other diseases which "board of examiners may name," and in a formal affidavit filed March 8, 1894, he alleged chronic bowel trouble and pains in back and chest.

His claim was rejected July 31, 1894, on the ground that he was not disabled in a degree ratable under the act of June 27, 1890.

Claimant, it is alleged, died June 13, 1896, without having appealed from the action rejecting his claim, and without taking steps to have his claim reopened.

His widow filed an appeal from the action rejecting her husband's claim May 10, 1897.

Under the decision in the case of Briggs Soper (8 P. D., 394), decided December 22, 1896, this widow has no right to file an appeal from the action taken in her husband's claim prior to his death, on the ground that it was not a pending claim at the date of his death, as nearly two years elapsed from the rejection of his claim to his death, and he did not take steps to have such action changed.

In the case mentioned it was held that—

Where soldier's claim was rejected and notification of the rejection sent to him seven months before his death, and he took no steps toward having the same reopened, and filed no appeal, and no mental disqualification for taking such action is shown: *Held*, That he had reasonable time within which to manifest an intent to prosecute the claim further, and, having failed to do so, he must be held to have abandoned it, and it was therefore not a "pending" claim at the time of his death within the meaning of section 4718, Revised Statutes, and the act of March 2, 1895.

In the act of March 2, 1895, relating to accrued pension, this language is used:

The accrued pension to the date of the death of any pensioner, or of any person entitled to a pension having an application therefor pending, and whether a certificate therefor shall issue prior or subsequent to the death of such person, shall, in the case of a person pensioned or applying for pension, on account of his disabilities or service, be paid, first, to his widow; etc.

This act was a substitute for section 4718, Revised Statutes, which used these words:

If any pensioner has died or shall hereafter die, or if any person entitled to a pension, having an application therefor pending, has died or shall hereafter die, his widow, or if there is no widow, the child or children of such person under the age of sixteen years shall be entitled to receive the accrued pension to the date of the death of such person.

The right of the widow of a soldier, who had made a proper application for a pension, to complete his claim has never been questioned, but she has uniformly been denied the right to set up a new claim in her deceased husband's case after his death. In a soldier's claim in process of adjudication in your Bureau, when the claimant died the widow has been accorded the right to do anything in the claim that her deceased husband could have done had he been living. In other words, under section 4718, Revised Statutes, and the act of March 2, 1895, she succeeded to his rights, not only to receive the pension when granted, but to prosecute the claim to a final adjudication. One of these rights is the right to appeal to the Secretary of the Interior from the rejection of the claim or from the rate allowed, etc.

The right of the widow to appeal from the rejection of her late husband's claim, though the claim was rejected during the soldier's lifetime, is conceded in the cases of Jacob Wolhart (8 P. D., 226), Henry Groppe (8 P. D., 293), and the case of Briggs Soper, heretofore mentioned, but said decisions limit the time of filing such appeal.

The soldier, if living, would have the right to appeal from the rejection of his claim at any time. In other words, there is no limitation as to the time of filing an appeal by an applicant for an invalid pension. By what authority, then, can the Department fix a limitation as to the time of filing an appeal by a widow, her right to appeal being conceded?

The law provides that if a soldier is entitled to a pension, and has an application therefor pending, on his death the widow shall receive the pension he would have received, had he lived, to the date of his death. The question whether soldier was entitled to a pension is not settled by the adverse decision by the Bureau, but the Secretary of the Interior has a right to pass upon the question. Her right to prosecute this case to a final adjudication and to appeal from the adverse action of the Commissioner of Pensions is conceded; then the question arises, Has the Secretary of the Interior power to fix a limitation to the time in which such appeal may be filed?

Secretary Stuart, in the case of Thomas Murray (2 L. B. P., 88), held that in no instance should a case be reviewed after five years, unless upon discovery of new evidence not accessible by the party, by due diligence, at an earlier day, and this case was followed by Acting Secretary Otto, in the case of Charlotte M. Dickenson (6 L. B. P., 318), and by Secretary Delano, in the case of Elizabeth McCluney (1 P. D., o. s., 84); but said doctrine has long since been abandoned, and now in original claims no limitation as to time of filing an appeal is recognized; nor has the Secretary of the Interior, in my judgment, under the power conferred upon him to establish rules and regulations for the adjudication of pension claims, authority to promulgate a rule of limitation.

The question "whether the rule of the Pension Office that an application for a pension can not be entertained after a lapse of twenty-five years from the time when the disability was incurred is authorized by the act of the 26th of March, 1804, empowering the commissioners of the Navy pension fund to make such regulations as might to them appear expedient for the admission of persons on the roll of Navy pensioners," having been submitted to the Attorney-General by the Secretary of the Navy, Mr. Mason, Attorney-General Toucey, under date of February 16, 1849, submitted the following opinion:

This is a power to establish rules and regulations to be observed in the examination and adjudication of the legal claims of a class of persons to be admitted on the roll of Navy pensioners, and does not extend to the enactment of a statute of limitations or of any rule which would preclude any examination, and, of course, any adjudication. Such a rule would be in derogation of the act of Congress, not in execution of it. This being clearly the character of the rule of the Pension Office referred to, I am of the opinion that it is invalid.

This opinion, in my judgment, should control the action of the Department, especially in view of the fact that a pension claim has always been considered pending until finally allowed. If the Department has the authority to fix a limitation within which an appeal may be filed, it has the right to limit it to one day or to one hundred years. Rejected claims are uniformly reopened and readjudicated upon application and additional proofs submitted. Appeals by the original claimant are entertained ten and twenty years after rejection of the claim, and no just reason appears for limiting the time of filing such appeal by the person who succeeds to the rights of such original claimant.

I am therefore of the opinion that the decisions in the cases of Jacob Wolhart, Henry Groppe, and Briggs Soper, before referred to, in so far as they fix or enact a rule of limitation in filing appeals, exceeded the jurisdiction of the Secretary and they are to that extent overruled.

As to the merits of the claim, two of a board of examining surgeons in September, 1892, certified that soldier was, in their opinion, entitled to a rating of four-eighteenths for diarrhea and six-eighteenths for rheumatism.

The papers are returned for the personal consideration of and an opinion by the medical referee as to the degree of disability shown by the certificate of the examination had and for that purpose your action is reversed and the claim reopened for further consideration in your bureau.

DESERTION—ACT JUNE 27, 1890.

BESSIE C. WHEELER (WIDOW).

As this soldier deserted from his first contract of enlistment during the war of the rebellion, which charge of desertion the War Department declines to remove, this claimant has no pensionable status.

Assistant Secretary Webster Davis to the Commissioner of Pensions, December 15, 1897.

This widow's claim for pension under the act of June 27, 1890, was rejected January 5, 1897, on the ground that the records of the War Department show that her husband, the soldier, deserted from his first service and was never honorably discharged therefrom.

It is shown that this soldier enlisted May 20, 1861, in the Second Michigan Infantry and deserted June 30, 1862. He reenlisted under an alias February 23, 1864, in the Twenty-first Connecticut Infantry and was discharged August 25, 1865.

It is contended on appeal that the second service was valid and met the substantial requirements of the law, and in support of this contention a report of the War Department, dated October 12, 1895, is cited, viz:

It is held by this Department that enlistment contracts entered into in violation of the twenty-second (now fiftieth) Article of War were not void, but merely voidable * * *

The act of June 27, 1890, relates only to service rendered during the late war of the rebellion. That service may have been rendered under one or more enlistment contracts, but it all pertains to the war of the rebellion. The record of such service is found solely with the War Department. This Department has no authority to amend or change in any respect the record of this or any other soldier.

It is reported by the War Department that this soldier deserted from his first enlistment June 30, 1862, and that the application for removal of charge of desertion and for an honorable discharge has been denied.

His first enlistment contract was broken and unfulfilled. His discharge from his second service did not relieve him from the obligations of his first enlistment; he is still a deserter therefrom. In effect it legally terminated his service under his second enlistment, a particular part of his service rendered during the war of the rebellion.

The status of this class of claimants is fully considered and made known in the following cases: James Cullen (6 P. D., 72); Joseph C. Williams (7 P. D., 218); Isaac Babb alias John Dunlap (8 P. D., 59); George Vansickle (8 P. D., 336), and George Lessor (8 P. D., 114).

It is substantially held in the foregoing decisions that a claimant against whom there stands a charge of desertion under an enlistment for service during the war of the rebellion, which charge the War Department declines to remove, has no title to pension under the act of June 27, 1890. This has also been confirmed by more recent decisions, and still is adhered to.

As a widow's claim is based upon the military or naval service of her husband, it follows that this claimant is not entitled to pension under the provisions of said act.

Rejection of her claim is therefore affirmed.

———

DISABILITY—ACT JUNE 27, 1890—RATE.

CHARLES C. WHEATON.

It was not intended by the act of June 27, 1890, to grant pensions for such degrees of disability as do not materially impair the ability to earn a support by manual labor; and total deafness of one ear and slight in the other is not such a disability as impairs claimant's ability to earn such support.

Assistant Secretary Webster Davis to the Commissioner of Pensions, December 29, 1897.

Charles C. Wheaton was enlisted and mustered into the service August 30, 1864, at Philadelphia, Pa., for one year. He was rejected September 6, 1864, but was assigned to hospital duty at Haddington General Hospital, Philadelphia, Pa., under the provisions of Special Order No. 19, paragraph 20, War Department, Adjutant-General's Office, January 12, 1865, and performed such duty until June 6, 1865, when he was mustered out of service. He is regarded by the War Department as having been in the military service of the United States.

Mr. Wheaton has made three applications (No. 1,056,057) for pension under the act of June 27, 1890. The first was filed on the 9th of September, 1891, the second on the 31st of May, 1895, the third on the 3d of December, 1896. In all these applications he alleged that he was unable to earn a support by manual labor because of severe deafness of left ear and slight deafness of right ear and piles. These applications were rejected on the following dates, respectively: June 2, 1893, March 31, 1896, and April 30, 1897, on the ground that he was not ratably disabled under the act of June 27, 1890. From the action rejecting his claim an appeal was taken July 6, 1897, the contention being that his deafness is so severe that men would not employ him, notwithstanding he might have the physical ability to do labor.

The board of surgeons at Philadelphia, Pa., by whom applicant was examined on the 12th of December, 1891, reported that they did not find that he had any other cause of disability than slight deafness of both ears. They gave his age as 43 years.

He was examined on the 16th of January, 1897, by the board of surgeons at Philadelphia, Pa., who reported his condition as follows:

Occupation, a file maker. Palms calloused and toil worn. General appearance healthy. Muscles well developed and firm. Movements free, easy, and decided, and, taken all in all, applicant appears to be equal to any kind of manual labor.

Severe deafness of left ear and slight of right. We find, after a close examination, that applicant can not hear the loudest distinct conversation at any distance, not even with the mouth close to the ear on the left. The membrana tympani on this side is not ruptured, but concave. The eustachian tube seems to be occluded. On the right he hears loud, distinct conversation at 4 feet, but not beyond. The membrana tympani is somewhat concave. No scars or rupture. Eustachian tube seems to be pervious, but not freely so. There is no other evidence of disease of the auditory apparatus of either ear—twenty-thirtieths. Piles. There is no evidence of piles at the anus or in the rectum. He states that he has spells of the piles. Has no diarrhea or constipation. No disease of stomach, liver, or intestines.

The medical referee, under date of August 6, 1897, states that the certificates of medical examination on file in the case do not show a pensionable degree of disability under the act of June 27, 1890.

The second section of the act of June 27, 1890, provides that pensions thereunder shall not exceed $12 per month or be less than $6 per month, and shall be proportioned to the degree of inability to earn a support by manual labor. The fact that the law directs that no rate less than one-half of that given for total disability shall be allowed, and the fact that it directs that the pension shall be proportionate to the inability to earn a support by manual labor, indicate that it was not the intention of the law to grant pensions for such degrees of disability as do not materially impair the ability to earn a support by manual labor. The evidence in the case under consideration does not show that applicant's ability to earn a support by manual labor is seriously impaired. The action rejecting the claim for pension is therefore affirmed.

SERVICE—DRAFTED MAN AND SUBSTITUTE.

WRIGHT SIMS.

Claimant, a drafted man who had furnished a substitute who was examined and accepted into the service by a board of enrollment October 29, 1864, was injured in a railroad accident October 31, 1864, and contends that at the time of his injury he was acting under military orders to proceed from his home, where he had been permitted to go, to Lafayette, Ind., and was therefore in the line of duty in the service.

Held: That as he had furnished a substitute who had been accepted into the service in his stead two days prior to said accident claimant was no longer in the service of the United States, but when injured was a civilian.

Assistant Secretary Webster Davis to the Commissioner of Pensions, December 29, 1897.

This is a motion, filed July 9, 1897, requesting reconsideration of decision of this Department of December 11, 1891, affirming on appeal the rejection by your Bureau of the above-entitled claim for original invalid pension under the provisions of the general law upon the ground that the claimant was not in the military service of the United States at the time his alleged disability was incurred.

The facts in this case, as shown by the record and the evidence on file, were very fully set forth in the decision on the appeal, but, inasmuch as it is contended in this motion that said decision was based upon a misapprehension of the facts in evidence in the claim, it was deemed best, before finally passing thereon, to again call upon the War Department for a full and complete report of the military history of this claimant and that of his substitute, George T. Robbins, as shown by the official military records, and as to the military status of the claimant at the date of his alleged injury. This was done on August 7, 1897, and on September 29, 1897, the War Department replied as follows:

The official records show that Wright Sims was drafted from Worth Township, Boone County, Eighth Congressional district of Indiana, and that on October 11, 1864, he was served with notice of his draft and ordered to report on October 21, 1864. He was examined and accepted by the board of enrollment on October 22, 1864, at Lafayette, Ind., but was not held to service under the draft, because he furnished a substitute who was accepted and held to service in his stead.

The records show that George T. Robbins enlisted October 29, 1864, as a substitute for Wright Sims, a drafted man from Worth Township, Boone County, Eighth Congressional district of Indiana. He was examined and accepted by the board of enrollment on the day of his enlistment—October 29, 1864. He was sent from Lafayette, Ind., to the draft rendezvous at Indianapolis, Ind., where he remained until November 23, 1864, when he was assigned and sent to the Thirty-first Indiana Infantry Volunteers at Nashville, Tenn.

Nothing has been found of record to show or to indicate that a furlough was granted to Wright Sims at any time after October 22, 1864, when he was examined by the board of enrollment. On the contrary, the records show that on October 29, 1864, George T. Robbins was accepted as a substitute for Wright Sims, thus releasing Sims from liability to be held to service under the draft. After the last-named date it was neither necessary nor proper for the military authorities to furlough Sims, or to do anything to him beyond releasing him from all military restraint, because on that date Robbins was substituted for him and assumed all the obligations that had devolved upon Sims under the operation of the draft.

The records show that the railway accident referred to within occurred on the Indianapolis and Lafayette Railroad on October 31, 1864. If Sims was injured, as he claims, his injury was not incurred while he was in the military service of the United States, because two days prior to the accident another man had been substituted for him under the draft and had been accepted by the military authorities.

As it does not appear that any furlough was granted to Sims, there seems to be no necessity for considering the question raised within relative to furloughs granted to drafted men.

There is on file with the papers in Sims's pension claim a "certificate of exemption on account of his having furnished a substitute." This certificate is dated at Lafayette, Ind., November 15, 1864, and appears to be genuine. Such certificates were merely furnished as a protection from arrest, etc., and the dates of their issue do not in any way determine the dates when the persons in whose names they were issued were released from liability to be held to service under the draft. In the case now under consideration the official records show that Sims was released from such liability by the acceptance of his substitute some time prior to the date on which his certificate of exemption was issued to him. It is evident that this certificate was not issued until some time after Sims had been released and permitted to leave Lafayette, and that the date of the certificate has no bearing upon the question of his status at the time of the accident of October 31, 1864. At that time he was a civilian, and had no nearer or other relation to the military service than if he had never been drafted at all.

It has been most earnestly contended by this claimant that as his substitute was not formally mustered into the service until October 31, 1864, the day he was injured, he was still held to military service under the draft at the time said injury was incurred, and was in the act of obeying orders to report to the provost-marshal at Lafayette, Ind.; but it will be perceived from the foregoing official report that his substitute had enlisted and been accepted by the military authorities two days prior to that date—on October 29, 1864—and that at the time the accident occurred in which the claimant was injured he was released from all military obligations and was not in the military service of the United States and not then subject to orders from the military authorities. As to whether or not this claimant was in the military service of the United States at any given time must appear from the official records of the War Department, which are conclusive upon all such questions, this Department having no authority or jurisdiction to put any man into the military service by implication or construction.

The statements of this claimant himself very clearly indicate that he was returning to Lafayette, Ind., at the time he was injured, not to be mustered into the service, but out of abundant caution, to see that his arrangement and contract with his substitute were fully carried out and completed by the formal muster of the substitute into the military service.

It is furthermore contended in this motion that one Daniel Kinnaman had been drafted at the same time with the claimant and accepted, and was also returning to Lafayette, Ind., in company with him, on the same train, and for the same purpose, and that said Kinnaman was injured by the same accident and under precisely the same circumstances as the claimant, but that Kinnaman applied for and was granted an invalid pension for the injuries so incurred, which he has been and is now receiving. An examination of the papers in the claim of Kinnaman shows that, except for the coincidence that they were both drafted at the same time and both injured by the same railroad accident while passengers on the same train en route to Lafayette, Ind., the two cases are widely dissimilar, and that the grant of a pension to Kinnaman has no bearing whatever upon the case of the claimant.

Kinnaman was shown to have been a drafted recruit who had been accepted and enrolled, and who was in the act of obeying orders to report and be mustered into the service at Lafayette, Ind., at the time he was injured.

The claimant, on the other hand, had furnished a substitute who had been accepted and enrolled, and he was thereby relieved and released from all obligations and liability to service under the draft, and was on his way in his capacity as a civilian to see that his private arrangement and contract with his substitute were duly carried out and completed.

In other words, Kinnaman was in the military service and the claimant was not at the time they were both injured by the same accident, consequently the former occupied a pensionable status under the law and the latter did not.

In view of the foregoing, I am clearly of the opinion that no error was committed and no injustice done the claimant by the decision on the appeal of this claim, or by the action of your Bureau thereby affirmed, and the same will therefore be adhered to and this motion is overruled.

LIMITATION—ORPHAN BROTHERS AND SISTERS.

LUCY HUNT.

The limitation as to the date of commencement of pension because of the date of filing the claim therefor, contained in the second section of the act of March 3, 1879, applies to claims in behalf of orphan brothers and sisters.

Assistant Secretary Webster Davis to the Commissioner of Pensions, December 29, 1897.

Samuel Hunt was enrolled on the 30th of November, 1863, and was discharged on the 25th of January, 1866, on a surgeon's certificate of disability, which sets forth that he was

incapable of performing the duties of a soldier because of phthisis pulmonalis developed since enlistment.

He died in May, 1866. On the 14th of April, 1890, Lucy Hunt filed an application for pension, in which she alleged that said Samuel Hunt was her brother; that she was dependent upon him for support. That his mother died about 1872 or 1873. It is alleged that this claimant was born on the 25th of December, 1855. The claim was rejected on the 4th of December, 1896, on the ground that claimant was over 16 years of age at the date of filing the claim. From this action an appeal was taken August 7, 1897, the contention being that the limitation as to the date of filing a claim for pension should not be held to run against a minor.

The question involved in the appeal was fully considered by this Department in the decision of April 10, 1896, in the pension claim of the minor sisters of Alexander Sutton (8 P. D., 137), in which it was held that the claims of orphan brothers and sisters, under section 4707 of the Revised Statutes, do not come within the exception to the limitation as to commencement of pension in the proviso to the second section of the act of March 3, 1879, applicable to claims by and in behalf of insane persons and children under 16 years of age; that in claims of orphan brothers and sisters under the age of 16 years, filed under section 4707 of the Revised Statutes, subsequent to June 30, 1880, pensions can not commence prior to the filing of the declaration, and such claims are barred when so filed after claimants arrive at the age of 16 years, there being no pensionable periods in such cases.

It was stated in said decision that—

The grant in section 4707, upon which this claim rests, is made to orphan brothers and sisters under 16 years of age, subject to the other conditions therein. In a general sense these brothers and sisters are children, but they are not granted pension in that relation. They derive pension through the soldier not as "children" of anyone, but as his "orphan brothers and sisters," and it is in the latter relation only that the law gives them right to pension. None but the children of the soldier himself are pensioned as "children." In every instance where the clause "children under 16 years of age" is used in the pension laws the reference is uniformly (save in the act of March 2, 1895) to the children of the soldier, and to no others.

It would seem that the claims of a soldier's orphan brothers and sisters are within the reason of the law which except those filed by or in behalf of a soldier's own children from the limitation of the second section of the act of March 3, 1879, but likewise it may be urged, are the claims of children and insane persons under the act of June 27, 1890, as to the limitation therein concerning the commencement of pension? But Congress has not seen fit to act upon this reason and remove the limitations in any claims except those specified in said second section. This Department can only execute the law as it is, and according to its intent as gathered from the language of the law itself. The claims of orphan brothers and sisters are not believed to be included within the exception above indicated.

For the reasons stated in the decision cited, the action of the Pension Office, from which the appeal in the case under consideration is taken, is affirmed.

NANCY RATHTON (WIDOW).

Soldier enlisted October 15, 1864, was accepted by the board of enrollment of the Eighth Congressional district of Indiana on the same day as a substitute. He was examined by a board of inspectors November 7, 1864, and rejected. He was furloughed to await discharge and was discharged April 1, 1865, on a surgeon's certificate because of "deficient amplitude and expansive mobility of chest: said disqualification existed at date of enlistment." He was never assigned to any military organization, nor ordered on detached service, nor is it shown that he ever performed any active military service.

Held: That soldier did not serve ninety days in the war of the rebellion, or in the Army of the United States, within the meaning of sections 2 and 3 of the act of June 27, 1890. (See case of Albert K. Ransom, 5 P. D., 183.)

Assistant Secretary Webster Davis to the Commissioner of Pensions, December 29, 1897.

Claimant on March 9, 1897, appealed from the action of your Bureau of December 4, 1896, rejecting her widow's claim, No. 630,205, filed September 29, 1892, under section 3 of the act of June 27, 1890, on the ground of—

No title, the soldier not having rendered naval or military service for ninety days during the war of the rebellion, and his original pension under the act of June 27, 1890, having been erroneously allowed.

She also appeals from the action of the same date rejecting her application for accrued pension on the same grounds as above stated.

Soldier enlisted October 15, 1864, was accepted by the board of enrollment of the Eighth Congressional district of Indiana on the same day as a substitute. He was examined by a board of inspectors November 7, 1864, and rejected. He was furloughed to await discharge, and was discharged April 1, 1865, on a surgeon's certificate of disability because of

Deficient amplitude and expansive mobility of chest; said disqualification existed at date of enlistment.

He was never assigned to any military organization nor ordered on detached service, nor is it shown that he ever performed any active military service.

As was said in the case of Albert K. Ransom (5 P. D., 184):

Ordinarily a man is said to be "in the service" from the time he takes upon himself the obligation to render service until he is relieved from that obligation, or, in other words, from the time of his enrollment until his discharge. The phrase has thus acquired a kind of technical sense, signifying under an engagement or contract to serve. It is noteworthy, in this connection, that the act of June 27, 1890, under which this claim is made, does not confer pensionable rights upon those who were "in the service" ninety days, but upon those who served ninety days, so that it may be conceded that the claimant was in the service for nine months in the technical sense above indicated, without conceding his right to pension.

The language of the law is, "All persons who served ninety days or more in the military or naval service of the United States during the late war of the rebellion," etc.

In the act of January 29, 1887, granting pension for service in the war with Mexico, the language is, "the surviving officers and enlisted men * ' * who, being duly enlisted *actually served* sixty days with the Army or Navy of the United States in Mexico," etc. The employment of the adverb was unnecessary, inasmuch as no distinction can be made between those who "served" and those who "actually served." Whether or not the claimant served ninety days is, therefore, a question of fact entirely distinct from the question whether he *engaged* to serve for that length of time, if called upon.

In the case of George W. Fleck (7 P. D., 343) it was held that where the soldier's only service was compulsory, in compliance with a sentence of a court-martial, and consists of confinement at hard labor with forfeiture of pay and allowances due or to become due, the term of his military service being postponed by the terms of the sentence, he could not be regarded as having "served in the military or naval service of the United States during the war of the rebellion" within the meaning of the act of June 27, 1890. Webster defines the word "serve" to mean, "to work for; to labor in behalf of; to exert one's self continuously or statedly for the benefit of;" and the word is used in said act to indicate the performance of active military or naval duties on the part of the soldier or sailor.

It appears to have been conceded in the case of Elizabeth H. Poland (8 P. D., 266) that because the War Department held that the soldier in that case was in the service of the United States from September 26, 1864 to January 20, 1865, that he served in or during the war of the rebellion ninety days, notwithstanding the fact that the surgeon's certificate of disability showed that his disability existed at date of enlistment, and as a matter of fact he performed no active duty while waiting for his discharge.

I am of the opinion that it is a strained and forced construction of the act of June 27, 1890, to hold that such a man "served ninety days or more in the military or naval service of the United States during the late war of the rebellion," as provided in section 2 of the act of June 27, 1890, or in section 3 of said act.

Congress in this act provided for those who served, and the man who is sent home to await discharge on account of disabilities which disabled him from serving as a soldier, and which disabilities had existed at the time he enlisted as a substitute for a drafted man, who was presumably able to perform service, did not, in my opinion, serve within the plain meaning of that word as used in said act.

Without, therefore, in any manner conflicting with the rule announced in the Poland decision, regarding the weight given the records of the War Department, and conceding that said soldier in that case was in the military service of the United States during the war of the rebellion for more than ninety days, it would not necessarily or legally follow that he served ninety days or that his widow was entitled to a pension.

So much of said decision, therefore, in the case of Elizabeth H. Poland (8 P. D., 266) as implied that claimant was entitled to a pension under section 3 of the act of June 27, 1890, on account of her husband's said alleged service, is overruled.

I am of the opinion that soldier did not serve ninety days in the war of the rebellion, or in the Army of the United States, within the meaning of sections 2 and 3 of the act of June 27, 1890, and the action appealed from is accordingly affirmed.

APPEAL—PRACTICE—FINAL ACTION.

MINORS OF WILLIAM HOCKEY.

A letter from the Commissioner of Pensions, in response to a communication, reciting former action of the Bureau from which claimant had previously appealed, and which action had been affirmed on appeal, and reaffirmed on motion for reconsideration, is not such final action of the Pension Bureau as will furnish a basis for another appeal.

Assistant Secretary Webster Davis to the Commissioner of Pensions, December 29, 1897.

Claimant on July 14, 1897, appealed from an alleged action by your Bureau of July 6, 1897.

The alleged action consists of the following communication, under date of July 6, 1897:

In response to your communication in the above-cited claim, you are informed that this Bureau advised you February 2, 1893, that the soldier's minor children could not be pensioned in their own right under the special act of Congress which granted pension to the widow, for the reason that said act did not provide that widow's title thereunder should, after her death, descend to the minors.

Said action of the Bureau was affirmed on appeal February 24, 1894, by the Assistant Secretary of the Interior, and your motion for reconsideration was overruled by said officer on June 27, 1895.

The minors have no title to pension under act of July 14, 1862, for the reason that soldier's death was not in any manner due to his military service, as shown by evidence on file in the widow's claim; therefore, the allowance under act of June 27, 1890, is all the pension to which the minors are entitled.

Nothing pending in the case.

Very respectfully,

H. CLAY EVANS, *Commissioner.*

Claimant invites attention to the concluding phrase, "Nothing pending in the case."

This letter merely recites the former action, and fully justifies the concluding statement. (See s. c., 7 P. D., 212.)

I am of the opinion that a letter from the Commissioner of Pensions, in response to a communication, reciting former action of the Bureau from which claimant had previously appealed, and which action had been affirmed on appeal, and reaffirmed on motion for reconsideration, is not such final action of the Pension Bureau as will furnish a basis for another appeal, and the appeal is accordingly dismissed.

NOTICE, ACT DECEMBER 21, 1893—RATES.

ALVA H. HALL.

1. Where the question involved on appeal is whether claimant had due notice of the proposed action as required by section 3 of the act of June 21, 1879, or the act of December 21, 1893, the report from the Commissioner of Pensions in response to the appeal should fully and clearly state whether notice was served on the claimant, and if so, the form of the notice or its substance, and the date and manner of service should be stated

2. The notice specified in the act of June 21, 1879, and the thirty days' notice specified in the act of December 21, 1893, are essential prerequisites without which the reduction or suspension of a pension is not authorized. Due statutory notice is necessary to confer jurisdiction to reduce or suspend pensions once issued.

3. Where the record shows that the statutory notice was duly issued and mailed to claimant's address, and is not returned to your Bureau, the presumption is that the notice was duly received by claimant, and this presumption is not outweighed by the affidavit of claimant first made in his appeal, but in such a case the Department will, on its own motion, examine into the merits of the claim to ascertain if any injustice has been done claimant in the action complained of.

4. The evidence in this case shows that claimant was improperly pensioned at the rate of $12 per month under the act of June 27, 1890, and that his disability did not entitle him to a rate in excess of the minimum rate under said act.

5. Combination of ratings to establish a pensionable degree of disability is not authorized under the act of June 27, 1890.

Assistant Secretary Webster Davis to the Commissioner of Pensions,
October 15, 1897.

Claimant on June 28, 1894, appealed from the action of your Bureau of February 7, 1894, reducing his rate of pension in his claim (certificate No. 514454) under section 2 of the act of June 27, 1890, from $12 to $6 per month.

Claimant contends that he never received the thirty days' notice under the act of December 21, 1893, and that as his pension certificate reducing his rate from $12 to $6 per month was dated February 10, 1894, he had no opportunity to furnish proof that he was entitled to the rate he was then drawing; that his reduction was therefore unlawful. He also complained of the failure of your Bureau to adjudicate his old law claim.

This case was considered on appeal August 18, 1894, and the papers returned to your Bureau for adjudication of the old law claim and a further report as to the evidence of notice. In the communication to your Bureau of that date accompanying the papers it was said, on the subject of notice, that—

Where the question involved on appeal is whether claimant had due notice of the proposed action as required by section 3 of the act of June 21, 1879, or the act of December 21, 1893, the report from the Commissioner of Pensions in response to the appeal should fully and clearly state whether notice was served on the claimant, and if so, the form of the notice or its substance, and the date and manner of service should be stated.

On February 16, 1895, Commissioner Lochren reported as follows:

Pension was originally granted in this case under the act approved June 27, 1890, at $12 per month from July 14, 1890, the certificate having been issued December 20, 1890.

August 4, 1893, the pension agent at Des Moines, Iowa, was notified to suspend payment of said allowance pending a medical examination ordered August 1, 1893, and on the same day the Third Auditor was advised of such action.

On the 28th of September, 1893, the pension agent was instructed to resume payment in the premises, and the Third Auditor duly advised thereof. At the same time the soldier was informed that the rate of his pension would be reduced unless he furnished satisfactory testimony within sixty days showing that he was totally disqualified for earning a support.

February 10, 1894, a new certificate was issued in the case reducing the pension to $6 from January 4, 1894.

In light of the fact that final action of reduction was not taken by this office until February, 1894, I have the honor to retransmit all papers on file, recommending that the appeal entered June 28, 1894, be dismissed.

This report not being deemed responsive to the instructions and request of August 18, 1894, in this case, the papers were again returned for a further report in accordance with the requirements of said communication, viz, the adjudication of the old-law claim and a report as to the substance of the notice to claimant of the proposed action of reduction and the date and manner of service.

On July 16, 1897, you returned the papers with the report that the old-law claim had been allowed under a new certificate issued June 12, 1896.

In reference to the substance of notice and manner and time of serving the same, your Bureau, under date of May 11, 1895, reported as follows:

That on September 28, 1893, a notice was served on this pensioner advising him in substance as follows: That it appears from medical evidence on file in this Bureau that you were not disabled from the effects of rheumatism, disease of heart, and piles in such a degree as to render you unable to earn a support by manual labor as contemplated by the act of June 27, 1890. Said rate, therefore, will be reduced to $6 per month unless satisfactory evidence shall be furnished to show that such action is not warranted. If you believe that you are still disabled in such degree as to entitle you to $12 per month, you may, within sixty days from this date, file in this Bureau competent proof (medical, if possible) that your disability continues in the same degree. Your case will thereupon be reconsidered, and if the testimony filed warrants such action, your present rate will be allowed to remain unchanged. If, however, such evidence shall not be satisfactory or shall not have been furnished, said reduction will be made without further notice at the expiration of said sixty days. This letter should be returned with your reply, and the envelope inclosing the same should be addressed to the Commissioner of Pensions and marked in the lower left-hand corner "Finance Division."

This notice was mailed in the usual way, and the practice was based on the presumption of law that when a communication is mailed and not returned within a reasonable time it was delivered. Further than this there is no evidence of its delivery on file.

The notice specified in the act of June 21, 1879, and the thirty days' notice specified in the act of December 21, 1893, are essential prerequisites, without which the reduction or suspension of a pensioner is not authorized.

The only evidence in this case to controvert the presumption that your Bureau acted regularly and in accordance with law, and that due and proper notice was given claimant of the proposed reduction, consists of the affidavit of claimant in his appeal from the action of reduction, in which he denied that he received the thirty days' notice.

It appears, however, prima facie, that claimant did receive a sixty days' notice under the act of June 21, 1879, which was served on claimant September 28, 1893, by mailing the same to his address.

I am of the opinion that where the record shows that the statutory notice was duly issued and mailed to claimant's address, and is not returned to your Bureau, the presumption is that the notice was duly received by claimant, and this presumption is not outweighed by the affidavit of claimant first made in his appeal, but in such a case the Department will, on its own motion, examine into the merits of the claim to ascertain if any injustice has been done claimant in the action complained of.

The action of your Bureau allowing claimant a rating of $12 under the act of June 27, 1890, for disability due to rheumatism and piles, and subsequently reducing this rate of $6, will therefore be reviewed for the purpose of ascertaining whether said actions are authorized by the law and the evidence.

Claimant filed his first application under said act, July 14, 1890, in which he alleged permanent disability, due to rheumatism, piles, and sprain of right ankle.

He was first medically examined June 25, 1890 (under his old law claim), when the board reported his pulse rate as 104; respiration, 18; temperature, 98½; height, 5 feet 6 inches; weight, 150 pounds, and age 44 years. Well nourished, with skin, liver, and spleen normal; rectum engorged; 3 small internal piles one-third inch, sensitive, but not bleeding or ulcerated; distinct crepitus in both shoulders and left hip. No swelling or atrophy of the joints; muscles and tendons normal; motion not limited; all other joints normal. Heart is enlarged 5½ by 4 inches. Area of dullness, apex beat 2 inches to left and 1 below the ensiform cartilage. In action it is strong, rapid, and at times tremulous; believe to be hypertrophied as the result of rheumatism. No other disabilities. The board rated claimant two eighteenths for piles and ten-eighteenths for rheumatism and disease of heart. Claimant was thereupon rated at $12 by your Bureau on account of rheumatism and piles, and this result appears to have been reached by combining the ratings of the board, regardless of the fact that neither the claimant nor any of his witnesses testified or contended that he was totally incapacitated for labor.

Acting Secretary Bell in 1879 decided in the case of Abram McCullum (6 P. D., o. s., 111), that—

Unless specifically provided for, there is no law by which disabilities can be considered separately and compound, so as to allow for all, the pension which each considered separately would aggregate.

See also the decisions of Assistant Secretary Bussey in the following cases: Michael Kelly (3 P. D., 240); Theodore De Tar (4 P. D., 130); Albert Marshall (5 P. D., 226); Hiram H. G. Brandt (5 P. D., 282), and Henry H. Meike (6 P. D., 192).

The act of June 27, 1890, neither in terms nor by implication authorizes a combination of ratings to establish a pensionable degree of disability, but, in plain and unmistakable terms, states the condition which renders a claimant pensionable under section 2 of said act, i. e., incapacity to earn a support by manual labor.

Claimant in his application contended that he was "greatly disabled," while all of his witnesses estimated his inability to labor not to exceed one-half. Said action was also in disregard of the plain terms of the law, which provides pensions for those suffering from a mental or physical disability of a permanent character which incapacitates them from the performance of manual labor in such a degree as to render them unable to earn a support, at not exceeding $12 dollars per month or less than $6, proportioned to the degree of inability to earn a support, upon making due proof of the fact.

It is plain, therefore, that the action of December 10, 1890, was not justified by the law or the facts as disclosed by the evidence in the case.

In reference to the action reducing his rate, the medical referee, on March 20, 1895, reported as follows:

September 19, 1893, after a test medical examination, preliminary action looking to reduction of rating to $6 per month was taken by the board of revision of this Bureau, in accordance with the order of the Secretary of the Interior, dated May 27, 1893, which followed upon the decision in the case of Charles T. Bennett. February 7, 1894, the action of reduction to $6 per month was completed, to date from January 4, 1894.

The basis of the reduction was, of necessity, the certificate of medical examination made August 16, 1893, which showed conclusively that the soldier was not entitled to the maximum rate under the act in question, in view of the decision in the Bennett Case, and the claimant having failed to file any evidence, after notification, to show his title to said rate.

In conclusion, it may be proper to add that the present rating of $6 per month is, under the basis of rating determined by the decision in the Bennett Case, commensurate with the degree of incapacity for earning a subsistence by manual labor, described in the certificate upon which the original allowance was made, and in that of the test examination.

The board who examined claimant August 16, 1893, report that they believe claimant to be one-half disabled for the performance of manual labor, and their description of claimant's condition shows that their estimate was not too low.

At his last examination, September 2, 1896, he was rated but four-eighteenths for rheumatism, four-eighteenths for piles, four-eighteenths for chronic diarrhea, and two-eighteenths for catarrh, with no evidence of any other disability.

I am of the opinion that the evidence in this case shows that claimant was improperly pensioned at the rate of $12 per month under the act of June 27, 1890, and that his disability did not entitle him to a rate in excess of the minimum rate under said act.

The action appealed from is accordingly affirmed, and the papers in the case are herewith returned.

PRACTICE—DECLARATIONS—ACT JUNE 27, 1890.

MARY HAFFNER (WIDOW).

This widow's declaration for pension under section 3 of the act of June 27, 1890, executed in 1897, can not be held to be a duplicate of a declaration filed in 1893 under the same act and rejected, but should be treated as a new original declaration. The mere statement by the Commissioner in a communication to claimant that her claim had been previously rejected is not a rejection of the new claim nor such final action as furnishes a basis for a new appeal.

Assistant Secretary Webster Davis to the Commissioner of Pensions, January 8, 1898.

Claimant, as widow of Christian Haffner, late of Company I, Ninth Ohio Infantry, on July 17, 1897, appealed from the action of your Bureau of May 25, 1897, holding that her declaration, executed March 30, 1897, and filed April 1, 1897 was a duplicate of claim rejected January 23, 1894 (No. 577458).

It is contended that this declaration should be considered as a new claim.

Under the present construction of section 3 of the act of June 27, 1890, there would appear to be no limitation upon the right of the widow to file additional or new declarations for a widow's pension under section 3 of the act of June 27, 1890, as often as her previous declaration is rejected on the ground that she was not dependent under said act.

It was held in the case of Frances Kendall (8 P. D., 197) that the right of a widow to a pension under said act must be determined by her condition at the time she seeks to establish her right, and is in no way dependent upon or connected with her previous condition.

It is true the language of the grant of pension to the widows named in the act is, that if the officer or soldier designated in the act "had died, or shall hereafter die, leaving a widow without other means of support than her daily labor." It might be said that where the soldier died leaving a widow with other means of support than her daily labor, his widow would not be within the letter of the statute, and therefore not pensionable if she subsequently was without other means of support than her daily labor; but the statute has been construed as if it read, "has died, leaving a widow who may at any time thereafter be without other means of support than her daily labor," and it was accordingly held, in the case of Margaret O'Neill, widow (8 P. D., 333), that where the widow had squandered her means of support left her by her husband that she was entitled under said act to receive pension from the date of her application, deducting the period during which she possessed "means of support" independent of her labor.

Claimant filed her first application under section 3 of the act of June 27, 1890, for a widow's pension May 29, 1893, which was rejected by your Bureau January 23, 1894, on the ground that she was not dependent within the meaning of said act.

This action was affirmed on appeal March 18, 1896, and a motion for reconsideration was denied June 6, 1896.

On March 30, 1897, she executed a new declaration for widow's pension under said section 3 of said act, which was filed in your Bureau April 1, 1897.

On May 25, 1897, you addressed to the attorney of claimant the following communication:

> You are informed that the declaration of Mary Haffner, lately filed by you, is a duplicate of claim rejected January 23, 1894, on the ground that claimant was not dependent within the meaning of the act of June 27, 1890.
>
> Claim twice appealed to the honorable Secretary of the Interior, and twice the action of this Bureau in the rejection of this claim affirmed.

A widow's declaration for pension under section 3 of the act of June 27, 1890, executed in 1897, can not under the present decisions be held to be a duplicate of a declaration, or claim, filed in 1893, under the same act and section, and which had been rejected on the ground that she was not dependent under said act, but should be treated as an original or new declaration. The communication by the Commissioner, above quoted, can not be regarded as a rejection of said last declaration, or such final action by your Bureau as furnishes a basis for a new appeal.

This appeal is accordingly dismissed, and the papers in the case are herewith returned.

––––––

FEE—ATTORNEYS.

JOHN A. BURGESS (CLAIMANT).
MILO B. STEVENS & CO. (ATTORNEYS).

As but one fee can be certified on each issue to allow pension in a claim, where an attorney refuses to refund a fee which was erroneously paid him, action refusing another fee to the attorney entitled to the one so paid is proper.

Assistant Secretary Webster Davis to the Commissioner of Pensions, January 8, 1898.

Milo B. Stevens & Co., of Washington, D. C., September 30, 1897, appealed in the matter of fee on the issue of September 4, 1890, in the claim (certificate No. 381969) for increase, under the general law, of John A. Burgess, late of Company C, Sixteenth Wisconsin Infantry.

The soldier was pensioned at $10 per month under the general law, when, in his behalf, on November 13, 1889, the appellants filed a claim for straight increase. The claim was allowed September 4, 1890, and the fee was inadvertently certified and paid to Beardsley & Soule, of Tomah, Wis., who filed a power of attorney July 22, 1889.

The Bureau, under date of October 12, 1894, conceded appellants' title to the fee, and on the same date called upon H. S. Beardsley, of Tomah, Wis., the surviving member of the firm, for refundment of the $10 erroneously paid. No answer being received to this demand, November 13, 1894, a second call was made. On November 24, 1894, a letter was received from Mrs. H. S. Beardsley stating that her husband died March 3, 1893, and that he left no estate.

The question presented is discussed and decided in the case of William H. Moore (26 Fee P. L. Bk., 455). The conclusion there reached was approved October 9, 1897, in the case of Matilda A. Thompson (30 Fee P. L. Bk., 70). In said case the Department held that—

As but one fee can be certified on each issue to allow pension, where an attorney refuses to refund a fee which was erroneously paid him, action refusing another fee to the attorney entitled to the one so paid is proper.

The facts in the cases cited are similar to those arising in the one under consideration, and the foregoing rule is applicable.

The record shows that a fee on the issue of September 4, 1890, in this claim has been certified. It follows that, inasmuch as one fee has been paid, another can not be allowed. It also appears that the Bureau has exhausted its power to obtain a refundment of the fee paid to Beardsley & Soule. As the appellants were denied a fee upon the grounds indicated, the action of the Bureau is affirmed.

PENDING CLAIM—ACCRUED PENSION.

SAMUEL FITZPATRICK (DECEASED).

Where soldier's application was not filed with the Commissioner of Pensions until after his death, he can not be said to have had an application pending, and his widow is not authorized under any existing law to prosecute soldier's claim for pension.

Assistant Secretary Webster Davis to the Commissioner of Pensions, January 8, 1898.

Claimant, on July 2, 1897, appealed from the action of your Bureau of December 19, 1895, rejecting her application (certificate No. 364808) to prosecute her husband's pending claim, on the ground that soldier's application was not filed until after his death, and that she therefore had no title.

Claimant contends that it is immaterial when soldier's application was filed; also that the application was presented to the Commissioner of Pensions nearly one year prior to the time shown by the stamp, and that the Commissioner neglected to stamp the application.

Soldier's application appears to have been executed January 23, 1879, and was filed in your Bureau, as indicated by the file stamp on the application, June 28, 1880. Soldier died January 18, 1880, nearly five months before the application was filed.

The law authorizes the widow to prosecute her husband's pending application. (Act of March 2, 1895.)

Where soldier's application was not filed with the Commissioner of Pensions until after his death, he can not be said to have had an application pending, and his widow is not authorized under any existing law to prosecute such soldier's claim for pension.

The contention that the application was presented to your Bureau prior to soldier's death is not supported by any evidence in the case. It is the duty of your Bureau to file every application, when duly executed, the day it is received or presented, and the presumption is that officers perform their duty.

As the evidence shows that the soldier's application was filed after his death, the action of your Bureau of December 19, 1895, is affirmed.

POWELL'S BATTALION, MEXICAN WAR–ACT JANUARY 5, 1893.

ZACHARIAH WINKLER.

The provisions of the act of Congress of January 5, 1893, providing an increase of the rate of pension granted on account of services in the Mexican war to survivors of said war, are applicable to survivors of Powell's Battalion Missouri Mounted Volunteers, Mexican war, who are pensioned under the provisions of the act of March 3, 1891, for service during the war with Mexico, and such surviving members of said organization are entitled to receive the increased rate of pension provided by said act of January 5, 1893, under the same conditions, limitations, and regulations as other Mexican-war survivors who are pensioned under the provisions of the act of January 29, 1887. Departmental decision of June 16, 1896, on Brookman's appeal (7 P. D., 260) overruled, and ruling No. 237 of the Commissioner of Pensions modified.

Assistant Secretary Webster Davis to the Commissioner of Pensions, January 15, 1898.

This appellant, Zachariah Winkler, late private Company C, Powell's Battalion Missouri Mounted Volunteers, is a pensioner under the provisions of the act of March 3, 1891 (certificate No. 10681), as a survivor of said organization, at the rate of $8 per month, "for service during the war with Mexico," and on August 24, 1896, he filed in your Bureau an application for the increase of pension provided by the act of January 5, 1893, for Mexican-war survivors, which was rejected on September 2, 1896, upon the ground—

that claimant is not provided for by the act of January 5, 1893, his present pension having been granted under the special act of March 3, 1891, instead of the act of January 29, 1887.

From said action appeal was taken on December 5, 1896.

The act providing what has usually been denominated a service pension of $8 per month, for survivors of the Mexican war, was passed by Congress on January 29, 1887. On January 5, 1893, an act was passed providing for an increase of this pension from $8 to $12 per month upon certain conditions, therein designated. This latter act is as follows:

Be it enacted by the Senate and House of Representatives of the United States of America in Congress assembled, That the Secretary of the Interior be, and he is hereby, authorized to increase the pension of every pensioner who is now on the rolls at eight dollars per month on account of services in the Mexican war, and who is wholly disabled for manual labor and is in such destitute circumstances that eight dollars per month are sufficient to provide him the necessaries of life, to twelve dollars per month.

On March 3, 1891, an act was passed entitled "An act granting pension to Powell's Battalion Missouri Mounted Volunteers," and is as follows:

Be it enacted by the Senate and House of Representatives of the United States of America in Congress assembled, That the Secretary of the Interior be, and he is hereby, authorized and directed to place on the pension roll the names of all of the honorably discharged surviving officers and enlisted men of Powell's Battalion of Missouri Mounted Volunteers, raised under the act of Congress of May thirteenth, eighteen hundred and forty-six, for service during the war with Mexico; and the names of the surviving widows of such officers and enlisted men, subject to the limitations and regulations of the pension laws of the United States for pensioning the survivors of the war with Mexico.

The question presented for consideration and decision by this appeal is whether or not the provisions and benefits of the act of January 5, 1893, are restricted and confined exclusively to those Mexican-war survivors who are pensioned under the provisions of the act of January 29, 1887, or are the surviving members of Powell's Battalion, pensioned "for service during the war with Mexico," under the act of March 3, 1891, also included therein.

In defining the scope and intendment of statutory legislation, and in the endeavor to definitely ascertain who or what is embraced within its provisions, it is often necessary to take into consideration the events and reasons which influenced the legislature, and the surrounding circumstances which brought the statute into existence.

It has been contended, and it is so held by this Department (7 P. D., 260), that the words "on account of services in the Mexican war," used in the act of January 5, 1893, are to be construed and interpreted strictly and literally, and that said act refers only to such persons as are or may be pensioned under the provisions of the act of January 29, 1887, as Mexican-war survivors, and, inferentially, that it does not include or apply to members of Powell's Battalion, who are pensioned under the provisions of the act of March 3, 1891.

Shortly after the passage of the act of January 29, 1887, a member of Powell's Battalion filed in your Bureau a claim for the pension provided by said act. His claim was rejected by your Bureau, and, on appeal to this Department, its rejection was affirmed December 28, 1887 (Brockman's appeal, 1 P. D., 453), upon the ground that said organization "did not serve in Mexico, nor on either the coasts or frontier thereof or en route thereto," neither had the claimant been "personally named in any resolution of Congress for any specific service in said war." It was held by the Department at that time that only those whose Mexican service strictly and literally fulfilled the conditions of the statute were embraced by its provisions.

A mistake having been made in a report by the War Department of the facts shown by the official military records relative to the organization of said battalion, the case again came before the Department on motion for reconsideration, but the former holding and rejection was sustained October 27, 1888 (2 P. D., 239), upon the ground that—

The act of January 29, 1887, providing service pension for survivors of the Mexican war, requires that claimant shall have either actually served in said war, or been en route to Mexico and to the seat of war, or ordered away from their place of rendezvous and organization for that purpose.

This adverse holding by your Bureau and the Department occasioned application by the survivors of said battalion to Congress for relief and for legislation giving them a pensionable status as Mexican-war survivors. As a result of this movement in their behalf, in the Fiftieth Congress, Senator Davis, from the Committee on Pensions, presented to the Senate a bill granting pensions to Powell's Battalion Missouri Mounted Volunteers. In presenting the bill he submitted a report, narrating the service of the said battalion, and closing as follows:

The Pension Office declines to place any of the members of said battalion on the pension roll, on the technical grounds that "they were not in Mexico, on the frontier thereof, or en route thereto." Your committee think that there is no just ground for any discrimination against the few survivors of this battalion, and therefore, to avoid applications to Congress for special relief, recommend the passage of the accompanying bill.

The bill passed the Senate on September 25, 1888, was finally reported by the Committee on Pensions to the House on February 13, 1889, but no further action had thereon at that session. On July 28, 1890, the bill was again before the Senate of the Fifty-first Congress, and a somewhat detailed report accompanied it. The action of the Pension Bureau and the decisions of the Department affirming the same were quoted at length, together with certain data regarding said battalion, as well as some correspondence between Senator Cockrell and the War Department. The report closes as follows:

It is therefore manifest that this battalion was organized under the same law and in the same manner and for the same purposes as all the other volunteer soldiers in the Mexican war, and the fact that the Government placed them in a service somewhat different from the service of the other volunteers should not militate against their rights. They were mustered into the service during the war with Mexico, and were bound to obey the orders of the Government, and they obeyed them, and at the close of the war were regularly mustered out of the service, just as the other volunteers were, and they are clearly entitled to the same rights and privileges, and should be placed upon an equality with all other volunteer soldiers of the Mexican war under the general law granting pensions to them.

Your committee therefore report the bill back to the Senate and recommend that the words "nineteenth" and "for services in the Army of the United States in the establishment of military posts, and for services on the frontier during the war with Mexico" be stricken out, and in lieu thereof the word "thirteenth" be inserted in lieu of "nineteenth," and in lieu of the words "for services in the Army of the United States in the establishment of military posts, and for services on the frontier during the war with Mexico," there be substituted the words "for service during the war with Mexico," and as so amended recommend the passage of the bill.

The bill passed the Senate. On September 8, 1890, the same report and bill were before the House and ordered to be printed. On February 24, 1891, the bill was again before the House and the following discussion took place.

POWELL'S BATTALION MISSOURI VOLUNTEERS.

Mr. NORTON. I ask unanimous consent that the Committee of the Whole House be discharged from the further consideration of the bill which I send to the desk, and that it be now put upon its passage.

The bill was read as follows:

A bill (S. 1826) granting pensions to Powell's Battalion of Missouri Mounted Volunteers.

Be it enacted, etc., That the Secretary of the Interior be, and he is hereby, authorized and directed to place on the pension roll the names of all of the honorably discharged surviving officers and enlisted men of Powell's Battalion of Missouri Mounted Volunteers, raised under the act of Congress of May thirteenth, eighteen hundred and forty-six, for service during the war with Mexico, and the names of the surviving widows of such officers and enlisted men, subject to the limitations and regulations of the pension laws of the United States for pensioning the survivors of the war with Mexico.

The SPEAKER. Is there objection to the present consideration of this bill?

Mr. BURROWS. I think we should have some explanation of this measure. The proposition appears to be to put a whole battalion on the pension roll.

Mr. NORTON. When the act of 1887, granting a pension to survivors of the Mexican war, was passed there was no question in the mind of the committee who presented the bill that it embraced this battalion. Afterwards, when the application of a member of that battalion was made to the Pension Bureau, the matter was referred to the War Department, which reported that this battalion had not been organized under the act of May 13, 1846, authorizing the organization of volunteers for the Mexican war, but under an act providing for the raising of troops to be assigned to duty on the Oregon frontier.

On account of this report from the War Department the application for pension was rejected. It was afterwards discovered that a mistake had been made; that this battalion had been organized under the act of May 13, 1846, providing for the enrollment of volunteers for the Mexican war. These men were organized under the same law as all the others who have received pensions on account of the Mexican war; they were in all respects the same soldiery as served in the Mexican war, and they performed similar service. Originally there were only four hundred of them. A great many of them have died, and a great many have been pensioned by private acts, so that now comparatively few are left.

Mr. HEARD. After being enrolled for service in Mexico they were detailed to do service elsewhere?

Mr. NORTON. Yes, sir; after being enrolled for service in Mexico they were detailed by the proper authorities to do service on the Oregon frontier, and they kept that line open.

Mr. BAKER. How long were they in the service?

Mr. NORTON. During the entire Mexican war. They performed the same service as that performed by other soldiers of the Mexican war.

Mr. CANNON. They did go to the Oregon frontier?

Mr. NORTON. Yes, sir.

Mr. CANNON. And were there a year, or something like that?

Mr. NORTON. During the entire war.

I will add that this bill passed the Senate in 1888, but was not acted on in the House, although favorably reported at the time by the Committee on Pensions. In this Congress it has again passed the Senate, and it has been unanimously reported by the Committee on Pensions of this House.

Mr. DOCKERY. I hope there will be no objection to the bill.

The SPEAKER. Is there objection?

Mr. JOSEPH D. TAYLOR. I demand the regular order. (Cries of "Oh, no.")

Mr. Taylor withdrew his demand and the bill was read the third time and passed. It became a law on March 3, 1891.

Two things are to be observed in a review of these legislative proceedings by which this bill became a law. In the first place, the clear intent and purpose of the lawmakers is evident, as expressed in the reports of the committees, and the language used by Mr. Norton in the discussion on the bill in the House, to wit:

They are clearly entitled to the same rights and privileges and should be placed upon an equality with all other volunteer soldiers of the Mexican war, under the general law granting pensions to them.

And

When the act of 1887, granting a pension to survivors of the Mexican war, was passed. there was no question in the mind of the committee who presented this bill that it embraced this battalion.

Legislative action taken in pursuance of language such as this could mean but one thing—that it was the intent and purpose of Congress that members of Powell's Battalion should be considered and held by those intrusted with the administration and execution of the pension laws as entitled to the same rights and privileges, and be placed on the same footing, so far as the act of January 29, 1887, was concerned, as all other volunteer soldiers of the Mexican war; and this is further emphasized and rendered conclusive by the Congressional action striking out of the bill, as originally introduced and reported, the words "for services in the Army of the United States in the establishment of military posts, and for services on the frontier during the war with Mexico," and in substituting therefor the words "for services during the war with Mexico," thus recognizing by legislative enactment the military service rendered by said battalion as "service in the Mexican war."

In the second place, the omission of a specified rate of pension in said act of March 3, 1891, is extremely suggestive and highly important in this connection. This appellant is at present in receipt of a pension at the rate of $8 per month, granted him under the provisions of said act. But why was this particular rating granted him; from whence was it obtained, and where was the authority for granting it derived ? From the act of January 29, 1887, alone, and solely because that was the rating therein prescribed and allowed for the " survivors of the war with Mexico."

If the act of January 5, 1893, instead of increasing, had reduced, the rate of the Mexican war service pension to $6 per month, could mem- bers of Powell's Battalion, claiming a pensionable status by reason of the provisions of the act of March 3, 1891, successfully maintain the position that such reduction of rate would not affect their pensionable rights or apply to them ? Such a contention would be absolutely untenable, and would scarcely meet with serious consideration. If the rate of pension were thus reduced, the members of Powell's Battalion would be affected thereby, as survivors of the war with Mexico, for such is unquestionably their pensionable status by fair and necessary implication.

If a reduction of the rates of pension for survivors of the Mexican war by said act would have the effect of diminishing the amount of pension received by the members of said battalion under the act of March 3, 1891, then, e converso, an increase of such pension by said act must necessarily result in an augmentation of the amount of pension of such persons.

It is very clear to my mind, in view of the foregoing facts, that it was the manifest intent and purpose of Congress in passing the act of March 3, 1891, to place the members of Powell's Battalion upon the pension roll as survivors of the Mexican war, just the same in all re- spects as if they had been specifically included and named in the act of January 29, 1887. It necessarily follows that any subsequent and further legislation affecting those embraced by said latter act would likewise, and in the same manner, affect the surviving members of Powell's Battalion.

It has heretofore been asserted and contended that the act of March 3, 1891, was in the nature of a special or private act, and in one sense this is undoubtedly true. It is a private act in distinction from an act of a general public character, and it is special in so far as its provisions relate to a certain limited class of individuals; but it can be considered and construed as private and special only in so far as its provisions defined the pensionable status of members of Powell's Battalion, and, that being done, it leaves their pensionable rights and benefits to be governed and controlled by the general " limitations and regulations of the pension laws of the United States for pensioning the survivors of the war with Mexico."

If, however, it should be admitted, for the sake of the argument, that the act of March 3, 1891, was purely and strictly a special act in every sense of the term, how would the pensionable rights of Powell's Bat- talion thereunder be affected by such a construction ? Section 4720, Revised Statutes, provides as follows:

When the rate, commencement, and duration of a pension allowed by special act are fixed by such act, they shall not be subject to be varied by the provisions and limitations of the general pension law; but when not thus fixed the rate and continuance of the pension shall be subject to variations in accordance with the general laws, and its commencement shall date from the passage of the special act, etc.

The act of March 3, 1891, did not fix either the rate, commencement, or duration of the pension provided for therein. Is it not, then, true beyond all controversy that the rate and continuance of the pension of beneficiaries under said act "shall be subject to variation in accordance with the general laws?" In fact, section 4720, Revised Statutes, has already been invoked by this Department, and properly so, to fix and control the date of commencement of the pensions granted to members of Powell's Battalion under the provisions of the act of March 3, 1891. (Lee's Appeal, 6 P. D., 149.) Would it not be the height of inconsistency to invoke and apply this section for the purpose of fixing and determining the date of commencement of such pensions and refuse to apply it for the purpose of controlling the rate of such pensions? I am unable to reach any other conclusion.

It is therefore held that the surviving members of Powell's Battalion Missouri Mounted Volunteers who are now pensioned under the provisions of the act of March 3, 1891, are entitled to the benefits of the act of January 5, 1893, upon proof that their condition and circumstances are such as are required to give title to the increase of pension provided by said latter act; and the decision of this Department of June 16, 1894, on the appeal of George H. Brookman (7 P. D., 260), holding the contrary view, and under which this claim was rejected, is hereby overruled, reversed, and set aside, and you are requested to so modify ruling No. 237 of the Commissioner of Pensions that it may conform to the views herein expressed.

The rejection of this claim upon the ground stated is also reversed and set aside, and you are requested to reopen and readjudicate the same in accordance herewith and upon its merits.

SERVICE—INDIAN WARS, ACT JULY 27, 1892.

SUSAN C. PENISTON (WIDOW).

As the report from the War Department shows that the military organization in which this soldier served from August 26, 1832, to September 30, 1832, cooperated with the main body of troops in the suppression of the Indian hostilities during the Black Hawk war, his service is held to be sufficient to comply with the requirements of the act of July 27, 1892.

Assistant Secretary Webster Davis to the Commissioner of Pensions, January 15, 1898.

This claim for widow's pension was filed January 5, 1893, wherein it was alleged that Theodore Peniston, claimant's husband, enlisted about the 1st of April, 1832, in Captain Pollard's company, Missouri Volunteers, in the Indian war of 1832, and that he was honorably discharged June 1, 1832, and that he died in Daviess County, State of Missouri, November 9, 1892.

The claim was rejected February 24, 1894,

on the ground that there is no provision under the act of July 27, 1892, for service as shown; that his company was called out for the purpose of protecting the frontier of Missouri against the Indians; service not rendered in Black Hawk war. The detachment operated on the frontier of Missouri, hence not at seat of Black Hawk war.

The appeal, filed October 29, 1897, relates to the ground of rejection, with the contention that it is a matter of family history that Theodore Peniston was a soldier in Captain Pollard's company in the Black Hawk war, and was discharged at the close of the war; that he was granted a land warrant on account of such service, and that his brother and others who enlisted in the same company and performed the same service had been pensioned.

It is observed from the records that Robert P. Peniston, a brother of this soldier, also enlisted in Captain Pollard's company about the same time; that he performed the same service, and was also discharged September 30, 1832. He was granted a land warrant, and was pensioned under the provisions of the act of July 27, 1892, as a survivor of the Black Hawk war.

It is also observed that in the communication of the Commissioner of Pensions to this claimant under date of January 29, 1896, she was informed that pensions allowed to survivors of Captain Pollard's company were granted under a misapprehension as to the nature of the service rendered; that said company was not engaged in the Black Hawk war, but that it was called into service by order of the governor of the State of Missouri for the protection of that State.

The records of the War Department show that Theodore Peniston enlisted August 26, 1832, in Pollard's company, Fourth regiment Missouri Mounted Volunteers, war of 1832, and was discharged September 30, 1832. It is shown by a report from the Second Auditor Treasury Department that he was paid "from August 26 to September 30, 1832, one month and six days; no travel pay."

It is also stated in this report that "the company was called out for the protection of the frontier of Missouri against the Indians."

Doubtless rejection of this claim was based principally upon this report from the office of the Second Auditor of the Treasury, and yet this official record, showing merely that "the company was called out for the protection of the frontier of Missouri against the Indians," is not sufficiently definite as to whether the command to which this soldier belonged actually cooperated with or formed any part of the military operations during the Black Hawk war in 1832 for the suppression of the Indian hostilities.

It was therefore deemed proper to address the Secretary of War on November 3, 1897, as to the character of the service performed by the command in which this soldier was a member during the period of the Black Hawk war, as follows:

First. Whether, in view of the best information available, the organization to which this soldier belonged was called into service at that time for the specific purpose of protecting the people of said territory from the hostile Indians.

Second. Whether the service of said organization had direct connection with and formed part of the military operations immediately preceding and leading up to said war.

Third. Whether it can reasonably be assumed that this soldier, Theodore Peniston, rendered thirty days' military service in connection with the Black Hawk war.

In response the report of Colonel Ainsworth, Chief Record and Pension Office of the War Department, to the Secretary of War was forwarded to this Department under date of November 18, 1897, as follows:

RECORD AND PENSION OFFICE,
WAR DEPARTMENT,
Washington City, November 18, 1897.

The honorable the SECRETARY OF WAR.

SIR: In returning herewith the letter of the Acting Secretary of the Interior, dated November 3, 1897, relative to the pension claim of the widow of Theodore Peniston on account of service rendered by him in the Black Hawk war, I have the honor to advise you as follows:

From data obtained from the official records and other reliable historical sources, it appears that in April, 1832, there was an outbreak of Indian hostilities on the northwestern and western frontiers of Illinois, afterwards known as the Black Hawk war, and that these hostilities continued until some time in September of 1832.

The forces actually in conflict with the main band of Indians under Black Hawk at the seat of war were composed of a detachment of regular troops and a body of Illinois militia, called out by the governor of Illinois, which were accepted into the United States service and were under the immediate command of Brig. Gen. Henry Atkinson, United States Army.

In addition to the forces under General Atkinson a portion of the Missouri militia, called out by the governor of Missouri (Miller), served during a part of the Black Hawk war, concerning which militia force the governor, in a letter to the Secretary of War, dated June 28, 1832, stated as follows:

"I deem it proper to make you acquainted with the measures adopted by me for the protection of the northern frontier of this State, on being apprised of the movements and hostile intentions of the Black Hawk and his party in the State of Illinois.

"Soon after the defeat of the Illinois militia small parties of hostile Indians, passing to and from the main body under Black Hawk on Rock River, showed themselves on the northern frontier of this State, and in one or more instances drove off some cattle and perhaps some stock to aid, as was supposed, in subsisting the Black Hawk and his party. In consequence of these depredations and the hostile indications manifested by the Indians, the people residing on that frontier became alarmed and fled from their homes to more interior parts of the State. On being apprised of these hostile movements on the part of the Indians, I ordered to that frontier, with the least possible delay, four companies of mounted men. Two of these companies, under the command of a major, were instructed to range from the Des Moines to the main Chariton, so as to include within their line of march all the frontier settlers between these two points. The two other companies, under command of an officer of the same grade, were ordered to range from the main Chariton to the western branch of Grand River. Since the adoption of these measures the greater portion of our citizens who had abandoned their farms have, I am informed, returned to them.

"Under such circumstances I flatter myself that the troops thus raised and ordered into service will be considered by the General Government as being employed to repel invasion, and that they will be paid by the United States accordingly."

At that time, it must be remembered, the territory north of Missouri and west of Illinois was all practically Indian territory, unoccupied, or very sparsely occupied, by white settlers, the border line of white settlements being probably somewhere about the northern boundary line of Missouri. In addition to protecting the settlers, therefore, any force operating along the northern frontier of Missouri must have rendered material service to the main body of troops actually engaged with Black Hawk's band, and must have aided in the suppression of the hostilities by preventing the band on its retreat from penetrating southward and attacking the white settlers in that direction, as well as by preventing them from obtaining supplies by depredations on those settlers.

While it is not specifically shown that Capt. William C. Pollard's company of Missouri militia was one of the four companies referred to by the governor of Missouri in his letter of June 28, 1832, it is shown by the records that of the force called out by the governor four companies, of which Captain Pollard's company was one, were paid for their services by the United States, (1) it having been decided, on the opinion of the Attorney-General (Taney), dated October 26, 1832, that militia-called out under such circumstances which in the opinion of the President were sufficient to justify such call were entitled to be paid, (2) the President having recognized such militia as having been in the United States service, and (3) the governor of Missouri having certified that the four companies had actually performed the service stated in their respective muster rolls.

Theodore Peniston, the soldier whose case is under consideration, is shown by the pay roll of Captain Pollard's company to have been a private in that company, and to have been paid as such by the United States for thirty-six days' service.

It is therefore concluded—

(1) That the organization to which this soldier, Theodore Peniston, belonged was called into service for the purpose of protecting the settlers along the northern frontier of the State of Missouri from hostile Indians;

(2) That the services of said organization, by cutting off the supplies of Black Hawk's band and preventing its retreat southward, thus cooperating with the main body of troops in the suppression of the Indian hostilities, had direct connection with and formed a part of the necessary military operations during a part of the Black Hawk war; and

(3) That this soldier, Theodore Peniston, rendered thirty-six days' military service in connection with said war.

Very respectfully,

F. C. AINSWORTH,
Colonel, U. S. Army, Chief Record and Pension Office.

WAR DEPARTMENT, OFFICE OF THE SECRETARY,
November 18, 1897.

Respectfully returned to the honorable the Secretary of the Interior, inviting attention to the inclosed report of the Chief of the Record and Pension Office, whose views are concurred in.

R. A. ALGER, *Secretary of War.*

This report is quite conclusive upon the question at issue.

It may, therefore, be safely assumed that the command to which this soldier belonged had direct connection with the military operations for the suppression of Indian hostilities during the Black Hawk war; that Theodore Peniston having enlisted in said service August 26, 1832, and having been discharged September 30, 1832, his service was sufficient to comply with the requirements of the act of July 27, 1892.

The grounds of rejection of this widow's claim are, therefore, held to be erroneous. Said action is accordingly reversed and the case is remanded for readjudication in accordance with the foregoing.

————

WILLIAM B. WATSON.

1. A service of ninety days or more during the war of the rebellion in actual coopera-tion with the Navy under the orders of the President, and an honorable discharge from such service is sufficient to give the officers and seamen of the United States Revenue-Marine Service a pensionable status under the provisions of section 2. act of June 27, 1890 (Roger's appeal, 9 P. D., 96).
2. The Departmental ruling in Oliver's appeal (7 P. D., 597) overruled and set aside; and the decision in Schaffer's appeal (6 P. D., 137) reaffirmed.

Assistant Secretary Webster Davis to the Commissioner of Pensions,
January 15, 1898.

William B. Watson, late fireman United States revenue cutter *Tiger*, United States Revenue-Marine Service, filed in your Bureau on July 29, 1890, an application for pension under the provisions of section 2. act of June 27, 1890, which was rejected on January 31, 1894, upon the ground that "the officers and men of the Revenue-Marine Service, not being enlisted in the Navy, have no title under the act of June 27, 1890."

From said action this appeal was taken on June 24, 1897. The official record from the Treasury Department of this appellant's service in the Revenue-Marine Service shows that he served on board the United States revenue cutter *Tiger*, as a fireman, from February 1 to May 23, 1864, when he was discharged; and it is further certified by the honorable Secretary of the Treasury that during the entire period of his service thereon said vessel was under orders, by the President, to cooperate with the Navy. The sole question presented for consider-ation by this appeal is whether or not the service above indicated by the record is such as would give to this appellant a pensionable status under the provisions of section 2, act of June 27, 1890.

This question has engaged the attention of this Department on sev-eral former occasions, and has been most carefully considered and thoroughly discussed. with the result that a contrariety of opinion has been expressed, opposing conclusions reached, and conflicting decisions rendered thereon at different times.

In the case of Louis Schaffer, decided on appeal December 6, 1892, by Assistant Secretary Bussey (6 P. D., 137), the pensionable status of the officers and seamen of the Revenue-Marine Service, when cooperating with the regular naval forces of the Government in time of war, by order of the President, under the provisions of section 2757, Revised Statutes. both under the provisions of sections 4693 (paragraph 2) and 4741,

Revised Statutes, and under the act of June 27, 1890, was considered with great care, and after a very full discussion of the legislation and the historical facts bearing on the subject it was held that a service of ninety days or more in the Revenue-Marine Service in actual coopera- tion with the Navy, under orders by the President, during the war of the rebellion and an honorable discharge therefrom fully met the con- ditions of service required by the provisions of sections 2 and 3 of the act of June 27, 1890, and was sufficient to give a pensionable status to such persons and to their widows and minor children under said sec- tions. This ruling continued to control in the adjudication of claims of this character until June 22, 1895, when, the question being again before the Department on an appeal from the rejection of the claim of David Oliver, it was held by Assistant Secretary Reynolds (7 P. D., 597) that the provisions of sections 2 and 3 of the act of June 27, 1890, were appli- cable to and embraced only such persons, and their widows and minor children, who had been regularly enlisted men, or duly appointed and mustered officers in the military or naval establishments of the United States, and that those who served in the Revenue-Marine Service on vessels which cooperated, by direction of the President, with the Navy, as provided in section 2757, Revised Statutes, were not regularly appointed or mustered officers or enlisted men in the naval service, were not in the Navy or the naval establishment of the United States, and, consequently, neither they nor their widows and minor children had any pensionable status under the provisions of said sections of said act. So much of the decision in Schaffer's appeal (supra) as conflicted with the foregoing ruling was thereby overruled.

This same question was recently brought to my attention, and received very careful consideration in connection with the appeal of William F. Rogers, an officer of the Revenue-Marine Service, who served on board the revenue cutter *Forward* during the Mexican war, and on August 9, 1897, I held (9 P. D., 96) that said vessel while engaged in cooperating with the Navy under orders of the President during said war was embraced within and constituted a part of the naval establishment of the United States, and the officers and men serving thereon under said conditions for a period of sixty days or more occupied a pension- able status under the provisions of the act of January 29, 1887.

Although this latter case arose under the provisions of the act of January 29, 1887, the question presented and decided therein is iden- tical with that passed upon by my predecessors in the decisions herein- before referred to and with that presented by the present appeal. Notwithstanding the fact, which is mentioned in my decision of August 9, 1897, that the special terms and conditions of military or naval service required by the provisions of the act of January 29, 1887, to entitle to pension thereunder are essentially and radically different from those prescribed by sections 2 and 3 of the act of June 27, 1890, the requirements and provisions of both acts as to the general nature and character of such service are practically the same. The benefits of both acts are expressly limited to the same class of persons and to their widows and minor children, viz, officers and enlisted men in the Army or Navy of the United States who served, the former during the Mexican war, the latter during the war of the rebellion. The act of January 29, 1887, authorizes the Secretary of the Interior "to place on the pension roll the names of the surviving officers and enlisted men, including marines, militia, and volunteers of the military and naval services of the United States, who, being duly enlisted, actually served, etc., * * * and were honorably discharged," etc. The second section of the act of June 27, 1890, provides a pension, under certain conditions, for "all persons who served ninety days or more in the military or naval service of the United States" for the length of time therein prescribed, and "who have been honorably discharged therefrom;" and the third section of said act provides a pension for the widow and minor children of any deceased "officer or enlisted man who served ninety days or more in the Army or Navy of the United States during the late war of the rebellion and who was honorably discharged," etc., under the conditions therein named.

Hence it necessarily follows that if an officer or seaman of the Revenue-Marine Service whose service on board a vessel of the Revenue Marine while such vessel was acting in cooperation with the Navy under orders of the President during the Mexican war was such as to meet and fulfill the conditions of pensionable service required by the act of January 29, 1887, is to be considered an officer or enlisted man in the naval service of the United States and to occupy a pensionable status under said act, then an officer or seaman of the Revenue Marine who served under like conditions during the war of the rebellion, and whose service otherwise complied with the conditions of pensionable service prescribed by the act of June 27, 1890, must also be held to be, during the period of such service, an officer or enlisted man in the naval establishment of the United States, and would have a pensionable status under section 2, and his widow and minor children under section 3, of said latter act. The arguments and reasons by which the conclusion and holding above stated were reached by me in the case of Rogers (supra) were so fully and exhaustively stated in my decision on the appeal of said case, and by Assistant Secretary Bussey in his decision in the case of Schaffer (supra), that it would be useless to burden this opinion with a restatement of them at this time.

Although it was not positively and distinctly so stated in the decision on the appeal of Rogers, yet the practical effect of my ruling in that case was to overrule the decision of Assistant Secretary Reynolds in the case of Oliver, and to reaffirm the holding of Assistant Secretary Bussey in the case of Schaffer, which, I am convinced, was more in accord with the spirit and manifest intent of the law than the somewhat harsh and technical construction announced in the Oliver decision. In order, therefore, that there may be no doubt on this subject, and that nothing may be left to implication or construction, the holding of the Department in the case of David Oliver is hereby overruled and set aside, and so much of the decision of the Department in the case of Louis Schaffer as was overruled thereby is hereby reaffirmed and announced as the present views of the Department on this subject.

It follows, therefore, from the foregoing that the ground upon which this claim was rejected is not considered tenable or sound, and said action of rejection is hereby reversed and set aside, and you are requested to cause this claim to be reopened and readjudicated upon its merits, in accordance with the views relative to the proof to be required of actual cooperation with the Navy for the period necessary to give pensionable title under the act of June 27, 1890, as announced in the decision of the Department in the case of Louis Schaffer (supra).

EVIDENCE IDENTITY.

CHRISTOPHER COLUMBUS YANCEY.

One witness, in the absence of a record, whose statement is inconsistent with claimant's allegations, is insufficient to establish the incurrence of an injury on board of the *Naumkeag*, as alleged. Furthermore, the record shows that the Christopher Columbus who served on said vessel was at date of enlistment, December 12, 1864, 19 years old, 5 feet 5¼ inches tall, and by occupation a soldier; while claimant is shown to be 6 feet 3 inches tall, swears that he never was a soldier, and that in 1896 he was 40 years old.

Assistant Secretary Webster Davis to the Commissioner of Pensions, January 15, 1898.

This appellant filed in your Bureau on July 8, 1889, an application for pension under the provisions of the general law, based on an injury to left foot, alleged to have been incurred in line of duty during his service in the United States Navy, which was rejected on May 29, 1897, upon the ground that the service origin of said alleged disabling cause had not been established.

From said action appeal was taken on July 2, 1897.

The appellant alleges that he enlisted and served in the Navy, under the name of Christopher Columbus, on board of the gunboat *Naumkeag*, also called gunboat *No. 37*, from some time in the fall of 1864 to some time in 1865, when he was discharged from that vessel, never having served on any other. He can not fix the date of the incurrence of his alleged injury to left foot, but states that he thinks it was a few months after his enlistment, when said vessel was at New Orleans, La., loading with supplies, and that a barrel of mess pork was rolled or slipped down suddenly upon him, while he with others was engaged in stowing away the packages in the hold of the vessel, and before he could get out of the way the "chine," or edge, of the barrel head caught his left heel, inflicting a severe and painful wound, for which he was treated by the surgeon of the vessel, which developed into a bad sore, occasioned his discharge from the service, and has rendered him very lame ever since.

The official record in the Navy Department of the service in the Navy of Christopher Columbus as first-class boy on board the *Naumkeag* and other vessels furnishes no evidence whatever of the origin and incurrence of the alleged injury, or of medical or hospital treatment therefor in service or at date of discharge.

This claim has been most thoroughly and carefully investigated by a special examination, and in his statement before a special examiner the appellant gave the names of several officers and shipmates, with whom he claims to have served on board the *Naumkeag*, as witnesses upon whom he relied to prove the service origin of said alleged injury to left foot, and who, he asserted, were present and could testify to the circumstances of its incurrence.

All of these persons now living were seen and interviewed, and but one witness was found who corroborated appellant's allegations in any particular. This witness, whose name is Crowther, but who served on board the *Naumkeag* as a first-class boy under the name of Frey, testifies that he served with appellant on board said vessel, and corroborates appellant's allegations that he was injured in his left foot, or heel, while at work helping to take in and stow away stores and supplies, but his account of the circumstances of the incurrence of said injury differs very materially from that given by appellant, and it clearly appears from the papers in the case, as well as from his own testimony, that this witness had been carefully and systematically coached by the appellant relative to his statement and evidence in this case. The other witness upon whom appellant chiefly relies, Dr. Draper, who was surgeon on board said vessel at the time, fails to identify the appellant at all. He states that there was a colored boy on board the *Naumkeag* named Christopher Columbus, but he is unable to swear that this appellant was that boy. He also testifies that he has a recollection of a negro on board of said vessel who had his heel injured in some way, but is unable to state that it was this appellant, or the boy Christopher Columbus that he remembered. He sums up the extent of his knowledge and recollection in the matter as follows:

About all I can remember concerning the case is that there was a Christopher Columbus on the *Naumkeag*, and that there was a colored boy who had a sore heel.

The remaining survivors of the crew of the *Naumkeag*, during the time the appellant alleges he served thereon, who were referred to by him, or who were discovered and interviewed by the special examiners, have no knowledge of the appellant or of the incurrence of any such injury by him or by any member of the crew. They testify that there was a colored boy on the vessel named Christopher Columbus, but they never knew of his being injured in any way, or that he was lame at any time or from any cause, nor did they ever hear the boy they knew called Yancey, or know that he had any other name than Christopher Columbus. It is furthermore stated by several of these witnesses that the appellant could not have been injured at the time and place alleged by him, for the reason that the vessel was not at New Orleans, La., during that time for the purpose of taking in stores, or for any other purpose. Although this appellant has been accepted by the Navy Department as the Christopher Columbus who served as first class boy on board the *Naumkeag*, and granted a discharge from the Navy, the proof in this case gives rise to a very grave doubt as to his identity with the Christopher Columbus of record.

The descriptive list of Christopher Columbus shows that he was at date of enlistment, December 12, 1864, 19 years old, 5 feet 5¾ inches tall, and by occupation a soldier. The record shows that he served first on the *Great Western*, next on the *Naumkeag*, and last on the *Peosta*, from which vessel he was discharged. The witnesses who served on board the *Naumkeag* with Christopher Columbus testify that he was then of slight build, about 5 feet 5 inches tall, rather prepossessing in appearance, of amiable disposition and manners, and fail to remember any distinguishing marks or scars about him at that time.

This appellant is shown to be a man of herculean proportions, a giant in strength, nearly 6 feet 3 inches in height, and of rather a sinister and forbidding cast of features, which is increased by a prominent scar, that, he swears, resulted from an injury incurred long before his alleged enlistment in the Navy. He is, furthermore, shown to be a man of dangerous and revengeful disposition and very pugnacious, who has frequently been in prison for assaults and fights, and has the reputation of being an "all around tough" character in the community where he lives, so much so, in fact, that it was found difficult to procure evidence in his case at that place, except such as was entirely in his favor, because of the fear that he would learn of anything said to his discredit and revenge himself upon the witnesses by assaulting them on the first favorable opportunity. The appellant himself swears that he never was a soldier, and never had any service except in the Navy, and never served upon any vessel except the *Naumkeag*, and that he was discharged from this vessel.

Leaving out of view the irreconcilable discrepancies between the record of Christopher Columbus's naval service and the appellant's sworn statement as to his alleged naval service, it is most unreasonable, if not absolutely incredible, that this appellant should have grown after he was 19 years of age nearly 7 inches in height, and have developed from a slight and rather delicately formed youth into the physical giant he is now said to be, and that his character and disposition should have undergone so radical a metamorphosis from the amiable, good tempered, popular, and obliging young man to the sinister, revengeful, pugnacious, and even dangerous character that it appears from the evidence he is at the present time. Furthermore, if the appellant was correct in estimating his age at 40 years in 1896 he could not have been the Christopher Columbus who enlisted in the Navy at the age of 19 years in December, 1864.

It is useless, however, to further consider the question of identity since it is clear that the evidence in this case, taken in connection with all the adverse and suspicious circumstances above mentioned, is entirely insufficient to establish the service origin of the alleged injury to heel of left foot, even if it be conceded that the Christopher Columbus shown by the record to have served on the *Naumkeag* and this appellant are one and the same person.

I am, therefore, of the opinion that the rejection of this claim upon the ground stated was not error, and said action is affirmed accordingly.

ARMY NURSES—SERVICE.

MILLIE, ALIAS MINNIE, HOWARD (NOW PAYNE).

Claimant admits, and the evidence shows, her work while in the hospital at Washington, D. C., during the war, was cleaning said hospital; gathering, washing, and putting away for use the bandages and bedclothing used therein; carrying out slops, and such general work as directed; the personal attendance upon and care for and administering of medicines to the inmates being by white nurses only. Claimant is colored.

Held: Claimant's services were not "nurse" services as contemplated by the act of August 5, 1892.

Assistant Secretary Webster Davis to the Commissioner of Pensions, January 22, 1898.

In 1896 this appellant was allowed pension under the act of August 5, 1892, as a nurse. On June 11, 1897, after due notice, she was dropped from the rolls, on the ground that the service rendered by her was that of a laundress and scrub woman, and not that of a nurse; and she appealed July 21, 1897, contending her services during the war should be held, under a liberal construction of the law, as nurse and not laundry or scrub woman services.

Previous to dropping special examination was had, which shows claimant was employed, with other colored women, by Dr. Bliss, of Armory Square Hospital, Washington, D. C., in cleaning said hospital, gathering up, washing, rolling, folding, and putting away for use the bandages and bedclothes used therein, carrying out the slops, and performing any other general work which she and they were told to do; but that all the administering of medicines to and personal attendance upon and care for the sick were done by white nurses. Claimant herself admits all this.

The law herein provides pension for those women who were employed " as nurses" and who rendered " actual service as nurses in attendance upon the sick or wounded," etc. It is manifest, I think, that this appellant's services in said hospital were not such as may be included within the terms of said law, as having been within the contemplation of the law. They were not "nurse" services in any ordinary acceptation of the word nurse, but those of a mere laborer. The law evidently had in view those who were, directly or indirectly, in personal attendance upon the sick and wounded, administering to the latter's necessities as invalids.

I see no reason for dissenting from the grounds of dropping herein, and dropping is affirmed accordingly.

COMMENCEMENT, ACT JUNE 27, 1890—MINORS.

MINORS OF DAVID S. SHARER (DECEASED).

1. Pension to minors under section 3, act of June 27, 1890, must commence from date of application therefor.
2. Where one or more minors is insane, idiotic, or otherwise permanently helpless he shall not be deprived of his share of the joint pension upon arriving at the age of 16 years while there are other children under that age, but shall continue to receive the same as if he were still under 16. But this rule shall apply only to future payments.

Assistant Secretary Webster Davis to the Commissioner of Pensions, January 22, 1898.

I have carefully considered the questions submitted in your communication of October 1, 1897, arising in connection with the pension claims of the widow and minor children of David S. Sharer, sometime a soldier in Company G, One hundred and seventy-seventh Ohio Infantry Volunteers.

It appears that the widow was pensioned under the act of June 27, 1890, at the rate of $8 per month, commencing July 16, 1890, and $2 per month additional for each of three children—Effie, Freddie E., and Lula O. Effie became 16 years of age February 21, 1893; Freddie E. became 16 July 27, 1895, and Lula O. will attain that age June 10, 1898. The widow remarried May 11, 1895, and all pension then ceased.

On March 15, 1897, the widow, as guardian, filed a claim on behalf of Lula O. for a minor's pension, and on the same date she made application on behalf of Freddie E. under the provision of section 3, act of June 27, 1890, relating to insane, idiotic, or otherwise permanently helpless children.

Both claims were allowed and both pensions were made to commence on the date of filing application therefor—March 15, 1897. The minor, Lula O., was pensioned at $10 per month, by reason of her minority, while the helpless child, Freddie E., was allowed but $2 per month, to continue until June 10, 1898 (when Lula O. will become 16 years old), and $10 per month thereafter, but with the proviso that if the minor, Lula O., should die prior to attaining the age of 16 years, the pension should cease at the date of her death. The purpose of this proviso was to reissue the helpless child's certificate so as to make the $10 rate begin from the date of the minor's death instead of from the date at which she would have become 16.

It further appears that the youngest child, Lula O., is also helpless (idiotic), and will be entitled to the continuance of pension should she survive her sixteenth birthday.

Your action in the premises was in accord with instructions relative to the adjudication of claims of insane, idiotic, or otherwise helpless minors under the third section of the act of June 27, 1890, issued by Assistant Secretary Reynolds on April 5, 1894, supplemental to his decision previously rendered upon the appeal in the case of the minor of Jacob Loeb (7 P. D., 167).

Said instructions, so far as they relate to the case now under consideration, were as follows:

> Where more than one minor has been pensioned under either of the above-cited acts or prior laws, and the pensionable period of one or more of said minors has not expired when an insane or helpless copensioner has attained its sixteenth year, said minors are entitled to receive their pension until the expiration of their pensionable minority. the pension of the insane or helpless minor to continue at the rate of $2 until the youngest child attains its pensionable majority, at which date title to the continuance provided by the statute under consideration attaches, and at the rate provided by the law under which pension was originally granted.

The questions suggested by you are:

First. Whether, under the provisions of the act of June 27, 1890, under which this widow was pensioned, such pension should have been paid to the two surviving minor children of the soldier from the date of the widow's remarriage—in which event they would have shared such pension pro rata—and such pension continued to be paid to them until the minor, Freddie E., became 16 years of age, and then reissue made to continue his pension by reason of his helpless (idiotic) condition.

Second. Whether his continued pension should have been at the same rate that he had when a minor under 16 years of age.

Third. Whether, in the event that the minor, Lula O., survives her sixteenth birthday, her pension shall be continued, and, if so, from what date and at what rate.

You state that in your opinion the pension should have been paid to the minors, Freddie E. and Lula O., from the date of the widow's remarriage to the date at which the former became 16, during which time they should have shared the whole pension pro rata, and that from the day Freddie E. became 16 his pension should have been continued, by reason of his helpless condition, at the same rate he received as a minor.

You are also of the opinion that in case the minor, Lula O., survives her sixteenth birthday her pension should continue from that date "at a rate pro rata with the other helpless child."

Section 3 of the act of June 27, 1890, provides, inter alia, that in case of the death or remarriage of the widow, leaving a child or children of the soldier under the age of 16 years, the pension which the widow received, or to which she may have been entitled, under said act—

shall be paid to such child or children until the age of 16: *Provided*, That in case a minor child is insane, idiotic, or otherwise permanently helpless, the pension shall continue during the life of said child, or during the period of such disability, and this proviso shall apply to all pensions heretofore granted or hereafter to be granted under this or any former statute, and such pensions shall commence from the date of application therefor after the passage of this act.

The question first to be considered is whether the pension which the law directs shall be "paid" to the child or children under 16 years of age, upon the death or remarriage of the widow, should commence from the date of the widow's death or remarriage or from the date of application therefor.

Assistant Secretary Bussey, construing this law, on September 12, 1892, held that in the case of the death or remarriage of a widow pensioner under the act of June 27, 1890, the minor's pension would begin from the date of the widow's death or remarriage, and this "by operation of law, whether at that date a formal application be made therefor or not," but that in case the soldier died leaving no widow, but leaving a child or children under 16 years of age, the pension to such child or children could only commence from the date of filing the application therefor (6 P. D., 40).

A contrary view was taken by Assistant Secretary Reynolds, who held that all pensions under the act of June 27, 1890, must commence from the date of filing application therefor after the passage of the act, and in the case of minors after the death or remarriage of the widow. (Timothy L. Carley, 7 P. D., 12; Minor of Ernst Rieckoff, 8 P. D., 324; Mary E. Bronoel, Minor, 8 P. D., 387; Minor of George W. Good, 8 P. D., 407.)

It can not be denied that the law is somewhat ambiguous. It nowhere, in express terms, makes provision for a minor's pension as such. It prescribes the conditions upon which a widow may receive pension, and then declares that in the case of the death or remarriage of the widow "such pension" shall be paid to the soldier's child or children under the age of 16 years.

It might be argued, from the language, that the intent was not to make a separate grant of pension to the minor or minors, but to simply continue the pension which had formerly been paid to the widow, and pay the same to the minor child or children until the age of 16.

The more reasonable view, it appears to me, is to hold that the intent was (as in the old law) to make provision for two distinct classes of pensions, viz, widow's pensions and minors' pensions. The Department, in fact, adopted this view when it held that said section authorized the allowance of pension to minors in cases in which the soldier left no widow.

As the act does not grant pension to minors in express terms, but only by implication, it makes no express provision for the commencement of such pension; but inasmuch as all other classes of pensions provided for by said·act are made to commence from "the date of application therefor, after the passage of the act," and there is nowhere manifest an intent to establish a different date of commencement for minors' pensions, I am of the opinion that the same rule was intended to apply to them. This has been the rule in cases where no widow survived the soldier, and I can see no good reason why it should not also be the rule in cases where there was a widow. The minors are required to make an application in the latter class of cases as well as in the former. Their application is not for a continuance of the widow's pension, but for an original grant to them of a minor's pension; and in support of such application they must furnish proof that the widow's title is extinct.

For these reasons I am unable to concur in your opinion as to the date at which the minors' pension in this case should have begun, but hold that, in that respect, the adjudication was correct.

The question next to be considered relates to payments in case one or more of several minor children are insane, idiotic, or otherwise permanently helpless. Under the instructions given in connection with the decision in the Loeb case, heretofore quoted, the helpless minor, who is one of several copensioners, loses his right to any part of the pension except the $2 per month, upon arriving at the age of 16 years, and does not regain it until the youngest minor has passed its pensionable period. I am of the opinion that this is not a proper compliance with the requirements of the statute. Both the old law and the act of June 27, 1890, pension the minor children jointly where there are two or more, and when one dies or reaches the age of 16 his joint interest goes to the others. But the proviso to section 3 of the act of June 27, 1890, says that in case a minor is insane, idiotic, or otherwise permanently helpless the pension (i. e. the pension he receives as a minor, which, if there are several minors pensioned jointly, is his share of the joint pension) shall *continue* during his life or disability. This, being a later provision of the law, must prevail if there is any repugnance between it and the preceding general grant to minors as joint pensioners.

I am therefore of the opinion that an insane, idiotic, or otherwise permanently helpless child under 16 years of age who is pensioned jointly with minors does not lose his share in the joint pension on arriving at the age of 16, but is entitled to the same in like manner as if he were still under that age. In contemplation of law he is still a minor.

This appears to have been the later view of Assistant Secretary Reynolds. See his decision rendered April 18, 1896, in the case of the minor of Joseph Disbrow, in which, after quoting the provision of section 3 of the act of June 27, 1890, relative to the continuance of the pension of an insane, idiotic, or otherwise permanently helpless minor child, he said:

It was the manifest intent of this proviso to make continuous the right to pension which exists or has existed on account of a child's minority; and the law clearly applies, by its express terms, to all cases where the right to pension on account of minority has been adjudged and pension allowed accordingly. In all such cases where said child was, on reaching its sixteenth year, insane, idiotic, or otherwise permanently helpless, the age limitation is removed and such child should thenceforth be regarded, in legal contemplation, as in a continuing state of minority or infancy. (8 P. D., 142.)

The logical effect of this holding, however, appears to have been overlooked, as the instructions previously given in the Loeb case were not only not expressly modified, but were cited as embodying the rules to be followed in the execution of the provision of law referred to.

In the case submitted by you a reissue should be made to allow pension to Lula O. and Freddie E. jointly, but the payments which have been made to them under a different construction of the law will not be disturbed, the purpose of the reissue being only to secure to Freddie E. his pro rata share of all payments made hereafter.

Both children being helpless, the pension will of course continue during their lives, or during the period of disability.

WIDOW'S PENSION—ANTEREBELLION SERVICE.

ELIZABETH FRITZ (WIDOW).

It appearing that the alleged death cause of the soldier was contracted prior to March 4, 1861, in time of peace, and not in service during any war, there is no provision of law granting pension to his widow. (See Digest 1897, p. 500, 2 (a), and decisions there cited.)

Assistant Secretary Webster Davis to the Commissioner of Pensions, January 22, 1898.

This appellant filed in your Bureau on May 27, 1897, an application for pension under the provisions of the general law as widow of Peter Fritz, deceased, late private, artillery detachment, United States Army, at West Point, N. Y., alleging the death of said soldier on April 24, 1897, from disease contracted in line of duty during his military service, and for which he had been pensioned, which was rejected on June 28, 1897, upon the ground that the alleged death cause of the soldier having originated prior to March 4, 1861, in time of peace, and not having been contracted in service during any war, there was no provision of law under which his widow could be pensioned.

From said action appeal was taken on July 17, 1897.

The deceased soldier was pensioned under the provisions of the general law, for myalgia, alleged by him and proved to have been contracted in the winter of 1848–49, while he was serving as a private in the artillery detachment, United States Army, stationed at the United States Military Academy, at West Point, N. Y. This claim of his widow for pension is based solely upon the theory that the pensioned myalgia was the cause of the soldier's death, or at least that it contributed very materially to the fatal termination of his last illness.

Accepting, for the sake of argument in this case, the theory upon which this claim is based, this appellant has no title to pension whatever under the law as the widow of said deceased soldier. There is no law providing a pension for the widows of soldiers who died of disease contracted in the service in time of peace prior to March 4, 1861. The provisions of law pensioning the widows of soldiers whose death has resulted from disability contracted prior to March 4, 1861, apply only to cases where the death cause was incurred or contracted while in the performance of military service during certain wars specifically named and designated in the several acts granting such pension.

The provisions of section 4702, Revised Statutes, which makes provision for pensioning the widows of soldiers under the general law, are restricted by its express terms to the widows of soldiers who have died since March 4, 1861, from wound, injury, or disease incurred or contracted in the service and line of duty subsequent to that date, and the provisions of section 4713, Revised Statutes, to which reference is made in this appeal, refer only to invalid claims by and on behalf of soldiers themselves, and have no application whatever to widows' claims.

The question presented by this appeal is not a new one. It was held by Secretary Schurz, on May 4, 1877, on the appeal of the widow of William Silvey (4 P. D., o. s., 174), that—

Where disability of soldier was contracted prior to March 4, 1861, in time of peace, widow's claim was properly rejected upon the ground that under existing laws there was no provision for granting such pension.

And Secretary Kirkwood held, on June 21, 1881, on the appeal of the widow of Michael Heron (8 P. D., o. s., 294), that—

The widow of a soldier who has died or hereafter dies of disease contracted in the military service prior to March 4, 1861, is not entitled to pension unless the death cause originated in some war and produced disability prior to that date.

See also appeal of Mary Kelly (8 P. D., 382).

In view of the foregoing, it is clear that this appellant has no title to pension as the widow of said deceased soldier under the provisions of any existing law, and that the rejection of her claim upon the ground stated was not error.

Said action is therefore hereby affirmed.

SERVICE—CIVILIAN EMPLOYEES.

E. S. LEONARD.

Appellant claims pension for disability alleged to have been contracted while performing service as contract surgeon in connection with the recruiting service of the Twenty-seventh Michigan Volunteers.

Held: That as his service was as a resident private physician, and not rendered with any military force in the field, in transitu, nor in hospital, it was not such service as entitles him to pension under the fourth subdivision of section 4693 of the Revised Statutes.

Assistant Secretary Webster Davis to the Commissioner of Pensions, January 27, 1898.

This appellant filed in your Bureau, on May 12, 1892, a declaration for pension under the provisions of the fourth subdivision of section 4693, Revised Statutes, based on chronic bronchitis alleged to have been contracted in line of duty, while performing service in the United States Army as a contract or acting assistant surgeon, which was rejected on June 27, 1897, upon the ground that the service rendered by him was as a civilian physician, and was not of such a character as would be pensionable under the provisions of the law.

From said action appeal was taken on July 16, 1897.

The appellant alleges that he contracted his disability about January 30, 1864, while engaged in performing the duties of a contract surgeon in connection with the recruiting service of the Twenty-seventh Regiment of Michigan Volunteer Infantry, at Ovid, Mich., which was the place of his residence at that time.

The official records of the War Department show the following facts relating to this appellant's alleged service during the war of the rebellion.

The Surgeon-General's Office reports, under date of June 29, 1896:

The records of this office do not show any paym nts to the within-named E. S. Leonard. In a letter dated December 13, 1895, on file, Dr. Leonard states that he was employed as acting assistant surgeon for the recruiting service of the Twenty-seventh Michigan Volunteers from about the 20th of January to the 1st of June, 1864, for which services he was paid in full at Detroit, Mich.

Under date of July 6, 1895, the Record and Pension Office of the War Department reported as follows:

It appears from the records of this office that E. S. Leonard contracted as an acting assistant surgeon United States Army (contract surgeon), with Col. D. M. Fox, Twenty-seventh Michigan Volunteers, January 5, 1864, at Ovid, Mich., for duty at that place. No record of the date of the termination of this contract or of any payment to Dr. Leonard on account of it has been found. Herewith inclosed is a copy of a letter from Charles S. Tripler, surgeon, United States Army and medical director, Northern Department, to Lieut. Col. B. H. Hill, United States Army, acting assistant provost-marshal-general, Detroit, Mich., and a copy of Lieutenant-Colonel Hill's reply thereto, dated March 15, 1864, both referring to contracts with private physicians for attendance upon men of the Twenty-seventh Michigan Infantry Volunteers, at Ovid, Mich., in 1864.

The correspondence referred to in the foregoing report is as follows:

MEDICAL DIRECTOR'S OFFICE, NORTHERN DEPARTMENT,
Columbus, Ohio, March 12, 1864.

COLONEL: Contracts with private physicians for attendance upon 180 men at Ovid and 130 men at Kalamazoo, signed by Col. D. M. Fox, Twenty-seventh Michigan

Volunteer Infantry, and approved by you, having been referred to me by the Surgeon-General, I have to request that you will inform me what troops these are, whether permanently stationed at these points, whether they were recruits gradually enlisted for the regiment, and now either en route for their regiment or in depot, and any other circumstance in reference to them, that will enable me to furnish the report required by the Surgeon-General.

Very respectfully, your obedient servant,

CHARLES S. TRIPLER,
Surgeon, U. S. A., and Medical Director.

Lieut. Col. B. H. HILL, U. S. A.,
Acting Assistant Provost-Marshal-General, Detroit, Mich.

MARCH 15, 1864.

Dr. C. S. TRIPLER,
Surgeon and Medical Director, Columbus, Ohio.

DOCTOR: Your letter of the 12th instant is received. The contracts you refer to were for two companies of the Twenty-seventh Regiment Michigan Infantry and for other recruits of that regiment.

About 500 men were raised in all and were rendezvoused at Ovid and Hillsdale, respectively. There were no medical officers, either to attend the sick or examine the recruits, and it was necessary to make contracts with private physicians. The two companies raised and the recruits were for an old regiment.

Very respectfully, your obedient servant,

B. H. HILL,
Lieutenant-Colonel Fifth Artillery, Acting Assistant Provost-Marshal-General.

The only law under which this appellant could be pensioned as a contract surgeon is the fourth subdivision of section 4693, Revised Statutes, which reads as follows:

Any acting assistant or contract surgeon disabled by any wound or injury received or disease contracted in the line of duty while actually performing the duties of assistant surgeon with any military force in the field, or in transitu, or in hospital.

It clearly appears, not only from the foregoing official record, but also from the testimony of the appellant and others in this case, that appellant was temporarily employed as a resident private physician of Ovid, Mich., to examine and furnish medical attendance to certain recruits for the Twenty-seventh Michigan Volunteer Infantry, who were rendezvoused in that town prior to being sent to the front to join the regiment, and only for such time as they were at said rendezvous, and that he was paid by the Government for such medical attendance rendered them.

This was the character and the sum total of the service rendered by the appellant, and it is manifest that it does not meet or comply with the conditions of pensionable service by a contract surgeon required by the terms of the fourth subdivision of section 4693, Revised Statutes, to give title thereunder. He was never regularly attached to any military force "*in the field or in transitu or in hospital*," but was simply employed to give medical attention to and to attend upon these recruits when his professional services were needed, so long as they remained in the place of his residence, and no longer, and was paid for his services so rendered, just as in the case of other patients in the ordinary practice of his profession.

It is very evident that the terms of the fourth subdivision of section 4693, Revised Statutes, were made as express and explicit as they are, relative to the kind and character of service to be rendered, and in the prosecution of which a disability must have been contracted to give pensionable title to a contract surgeon, with the express purpose and intent of preventing pension being granted, in cases like the present one, for disability contracted while rendering professional services under a contract with the Government which did not differ in any essential particular from ordinary medical practice not connected with the military service.

I am therefore clearly of the opinion that the rejection of this claim upon the ground stated was not error, and said action is affirmed accordingly.

———

PAYMENT OF PENSION—WIDOW—GUARDIAN.

JOSEPHINE BURNS (WIDOW).

Appellant filed an application in behalf of herself and minor children, and at the same time procured a next friend to file application as guardian for said minors. Her application was denied and that of the guardian allowed. After the youngest child arrived at the age of 16 years, her case was reopened and allowed to begin from the time said youngest child became 16 years old. Claimant now asserts title to that which was paid to the guardian.

Held, Her contention is untenable because she procured the filing of the application by the guardian, received the money paid thereunder, and disbursed the same.

Assistant Secretary Webster Davis to the Commissioner of Pensions, January 27, 1898.

On April 14, 1896, Josephine Burns, widow of Elihu G. Burns, late of Company B, Seventeenth Iowa Volunteers, appealed from the action of your office, May 20, 1884, in rejecting her claim for widow's pension (certificate No. 239454) upon the ground that she was not the legal widow of soldier, she having been divorced from him on February 24, 1876.

The fact that claimant was so divorced appears of record. It appears also that almost immediately after having obtained a divorce from her husband she returned to him and lived with him as his wife until the day of his death, on September 14, 1877.

It appears also that after the death of soldier, upon claimant's application, the decree in divorce was vacated and set aside on September 28, 1881.

The original application of the claimant was filed on May 2, 1879, in which she alleged title to widow's pension, including that for four minor children left by soldier under 16 years of age at the time of his death.

Her claim was, although at first rejected, reopened on December 28, 1887, and allowed as to the widow's claim, to begin on April 15, 1887, the day after the youngest of said minor children reached the age of

16 years. She was also allowed her claim as to one of the minor children, to wit, Edwin, from the death of her husband to February 20,
1881, on which day said minor child had died.

It appears further that on the same day upon which the claimant's
application was filed, one J. M. Anderson also filed a declaration in
behalf of said minor children; which claim was approved June 6, 1884.
The pension due to the minor Edwin who had died in 1881, as heretofore mentioned, was not paid to the guardian, but was subsequently
paid to the widow. At the time when the widow's claim was allowed
the pension of the other children had been paid to the guardian.

The contention in the appeal before the Department now is, that the
minors' pension was illegally paid to the guardian, and that claimant
being now acknowledged as the legal widow of the soldier, should
receive the amount which was illegally paid.

Just why said guardian was appointed does not clearly appear, but
is left to conjecture.

The guardian appeared before a special examiner in October, 1883,
and testified that he was appointed guardian by the request of J. M.
Reid, the attorney in the case, and that he had never done anything
further than to make the application; that he had not in any manner
had the care or custody of the children; that they were in the custody
of the mother who was supporting them.

The claimant herself testifies that she had the custody of the children
until they arrived at the age of 16 years, with the exception of one,
who married a short while before arriving at that age. Nothing is said
as to the custody of the children subsequent to that time.

It does not appear that any proceeding such as is contemplated in
section 4706, Revised Statutes, has been had before a court having
probate jurisdiction to abrogate the guardianship of the mother. She
was the natural and lawful guardian of said minors, and no other
guardian could have been legally appointed except by her consent or
by due process of law, showing either that she had abandoned her
children, or, by reason of immoral conduct, was not a suitable person
to have the custody of the same.

The alleged guardian who represented the children was induced to
file the application in their behalf, it appears, at the request of J. M.
Reid, the attorney of appellant. The widow's claim and that of the
guardian were both filed on the same day, each of them asserting title
to the pension provided by law for the said minors.

From the above-mentioned facts it seems reasonable to infer that the
intervention of the acting guardian was procured through the solicitation of the claimant. It is clearly shown that her attorney induced
that supplemental proceeding, and the acts of the attorney that came
within the legitimate scope of that relation are the acts of the client.
Besides, if claimant is the legal widow of soldier (and if not she would
have no title to any pension whatever), the slightest objection on her

part would have operated to terminate the functions of the acting guardian.

Appellant's attorney being apprehensive, doubtless, that her claim would be rejected because of the fact that she had procured a divorce from her husband, induced the filing of the supplemental claim in behalf of the minors, in order to meet, as far as possible, that contingency.

Both claims, in so far as they relate to the minors, are one and the same, and the satisfaction of one is the satisfaction of both.

She is, therefore, in my opinion, bound by the action of the guardian, and estopped from denying the legality of any payment of pension made to him in behalf of her minor children.

In addition to what has been said before, since it appears that appellant did retain the custody and control of her children, exercising all the functions of real guardianship, and since it further appears that the alleged guardian was acting merely in the capacity of a next friend at her solicitation, the presumption arises that all pension money received by him in behalf of said children was by him in turn paid over to the appellant.

Even if her claim was sound and otherwise free from legal objection (which is not the case), it would be incumbent upon her to rebut that presumption by competent proof.

The action appealed from is without error, and is hereby affirmed.

LEGITIMACY—MARRIAGE.

KATIE SMITH (MINOR).

It appearing that the marriage of the parents of this minor was "absolutely void" under the laws of the State of New York, where all the parties resided both before and after said marriage, she was not a legitimate child of said deceased sailor, and has no title to pension as a minor under the provisions of the pension laws.

Assistant Secretary Webster Davis to the Commissioner of Pensions, January 27, 1898.

This appellant filed in your bureau on January 25, 1895, an application for pension, under the provisions of the general law, as guardian of Katie Smith, a minor child of William Smith, deceased, late seaman, United States Navy, alleging the death of said sailor, on December 5, 1894, from disease contracted in line of duty during his naval service; the death of the mother of said minor on October 9, 1887; that said sailor had never remarried after the death of the mother, and that at the date of the death of the sailor, as aforesaid, said minor was under the age of 16 years. Said claim was rejected, on April 5, 1897, upon the ground that said minor was not a legitimate child of said deceased sailor. From said action appeal was taken on July 22, 1897.

It appears from the undisputed and admitted facts in evidence in this case that the sailor and the mother of this minor were married in

Buffalo, N. Y., on January 10, 1880. The mother of minor, whose maiden name was Mary J. La Grue, had been previously married in the State of New York to one Garret S. Snell. On December 4, 1878, Snell obtained a decree of divorce from her at a special term of the supreme court of Buffalo, held in and for the city of Buffalo on the 4th day of December, 1878, at the city and county hall in said city. It is shown by a duly certified transcript of said decree of divorce, on file in this case, that permission was therein granted to the plaintiff, Snell, to marry again; but the court decreed and adjudged that "it shall not be lawful for the said Mary J. Snell, the defendant, to marry again until the plaintiff is actually dead."

The grounds upon which said divorce was granted are not set out in the decree; but, presumably, it was on account of adultery of the defendant, since, under the laws of the State of New York, such a prohibition against remarriage by the defendant is granted upon that ground.

It is admitted that the first husband of the mother of said minor, Garret S. Snell, is still living, and that no modification of said decree or removal of said prohibition was ever obtained.

It furthermore appears that all the parties resided up to the time of the respective deaths of the parents of said minor in the city of Buffalo, State of New York.

Section 49 of the Revised Statutes of New York, vol. 3, page 2334, provides as follows:

Whenever a marriage has been, or shall be dissolved, pursuant to the provisions of this article, the complainant may marry again during the lifetime of the defendant, but no defendant convicted of adultery shall marry again until the death of the complainant, unless the court in which the judgment of divorce was rendered shall in that respect modify such judgment, which modification shall only be made upon satisfactory proof that the conduct of the defendant since the dissolution of said marriage has been uniformly good.

Section 5, Revised Statutes of New York, vol. 3, page 2332, provides as follows:

No second, or other subsequent marriage shall be contracted by any person during the lifetime of any former husband or wife of such person, unless,

First. The marriage with such former husband or wife shall have been annulled or dissolved for some cause other than the adultery of such person; or,

Second. Unless such former husband or wife shall have been finally sentenced to imprisonment for life.

Every marriage contracted in violation of the provisions of this section shall, except in the cases provided for in the next section, be absolutely void.

The "next section" referred to in the foregoing has reference only to cases in which presumption of the death of husband or wife would arise from continued and unexplained absence, etc., and has no application whatever to the facts of this case.

It is apparent from the foregoing that the marriage of the parents of this minor was, under the laws of the State of New York, where said marriage was consummated, and where the parties resided all their lives, absolutely null and void.

In the administration of the pension laws it is provided:

That marriages, except such as are mentioned in section 4705 of the Revised Statutes, shall be proved in pension cases to be legal marriages according to the law of the place where the parties resided at the time of marriage, or at the time when the right to pension accrued. (Section 2, act of August 7, 1882.)

The legitimacy of minor children is to be determined in pension cases in accordance with the provisions of section 4704, Revised Statutes, which provides as follows:

In the administration of the pension laws, children born before the marriage of their parents, if acknowledged by the father before or after the marriage, shall be deemed legitimate.

Under this section it is obvious that a valid legal marriage must have been contracted by the parents, either before or after the birth of the minor seeking pension, before such minor could occupy a pensionable status under the law.

In this case it is clear that the parents of this minor never contracted a valid legal marriage at any time; she does not come within the provisions of said section, and can not be considered the legitimate child of the deceased sailor for pensionable purposes. Consequently, she has no pensionable status, and no title to pension, as a minor child under 16 years of age, under the provisions of the pension laws.

In view of the foregoing I am clearly of the opinion that the rejection of this claim upon the ground stated was not error, and said action is affirmed accordingly.

PRESUMPTION OF DEATH—ACT MARCH 13, 1896.

MATILDA L. KELLY (WIDOW).

The evidence in this case satisfactorily establishes the continued and unexplained absence of the above-named soldier from his home and family since November, 1877, since which date no intelligence of his existence has been received, and, therefore, his death should be considered "as sufficiently proved," in accordance with the provisions of the act of March 13, 1896.

Assistant Secretary Webster Davis to the Commissioner of Pensions, February 2, 1898.

This appellant filed in your Bureau on October 18, 1890, an application for pension under the provisions of section 3, act of June 27, 1890, as the widow of James H. Kelly, late quartermaster-sergeant, Twenty-first Independent Battery, Ohio Light Artillery, which was rejected on February 7, 1896, upon the ground that she was unable to establish, by proof, either the fact or date of the soldier's death.

From said action appeal was taken on July 16, 1897.

The soldier never filed an application for pension in his own behalf.

This claim has been carefully investigated by special examination, and apparently all available sources of evidence have been exhausted. The facts in evidence in the case are few and simple, and are as follows:

The appellant and the soldier were married in Green County, Mo., in October, 1860, or 1861, there appears to be some doubt about the year, and shortly after their marriage, in December, 1861, the soldier enlisted in Company D, Sixth Missouri Cavalry, and served therein for some months, but just how or when he left said organization does not appear from the record or the testimony.

After the soldier left this service he rejoined his wife, who was living with her father in Green County, Mo., and accompanied his wife, her father, and his family to Illinois, where they all remained about six months or a year and then the appellant and her father's family moved back to Green County, Mo., leaving the soldier in Vandalia, Ill.

This was the last time any of them ever saw the soldier, as he never rejoined his wife again. He afterwards enlisted, on April 1, 1863, in the Twenty-first Independent Battery, Ohio Volunteer Light Artillery, and served therein until June 16, 1865, when he was mustered out of the service with his company. There is on file, as an exhibit to one of the special examiner's reports in this claim, a letter written by the soldier from Knoxville, Tenn., to his wife's father dated June 16, 1865, in which he states that he had been that day mustered out of the service (which corresponds with the record) and would start for Missouri the next day, and would be at home as soon as possible. He did not go home, however, but appears to have been of an adventurous and roving disposition, and went to Mexico, where he took service against Maximilian, and remained some years in that country. He next turned up in San Francisco, Cal., where he lived until November, 1877, clerking, so he wrote his wife and family, in a drug store. During all this time, however, he appears to have kept up a regular correspondence with this appellant, and to have regularly sent her money for her support. A number of the letters written by the soldier to this appellant during this period were exhibited by her to a special examiner of your Bureau, who states that they had every appearance of genuineness and authenticity, and were couched in endearing and affectionate language toward the appellant, and filled with expressions of his intention to return to her as soon as he could make enough money to settle down in the drug business, or the practice of medicine. No intention to desert the appellant, or to permanently abandon his family is to be gathered from this correspondence, but just the contrary. On November 25, 1877, the soldier wrote the appellant a letter from San Francisco, Cal., approving of a contemplated move on her part from Missouri to Kansas, and stating that he was on the point of setting out on a voyage to China as surgeon of a sailing vessel. He states that he proposed to take some merchandise on the ship on his own account, which he would exchange in China, or Japan for tea, silks, and other valuable goods, and that he would leave the vessel at Liverpool, England, where he would dispose of his merchandise and return to New York by steamer and join her in Kansas in the course of a year from that date. He states that he hopes, with his wages as surgeon and the profits he expects to make on his goods, he will be able to return with enough money to set himself up in the drug business in Kansas, after which he intends to cease his wanderings and remain permanently at home with his wife and daughter. In this letter, as in others, he speaks in the most affec-tionate and endearing terms of this appellant and their only child, a daughter, and makes suggestions as to their welfare and comfort during the intervening period until he expects to rejoin them. This is the only letter the genuineness of which has been questioned, but it is, undoubtedly, in the same handwriting as a letter on file written in June, 1865, to the father of appellant, which was unquestionably written by the soldier, and its authenticity is conclusively established by the testi-mony of a brother of the soldier in Tennessee, who is reported to be of undoubted credibility, and who never saw or had any communication with this appellant; who swears that he had seen and read a letter from the soldier to his mother in Tennessee, written about the same date from San Francisco, Cal., in which he gives his mother the same account of his intended movements, and makes the same statements relative to his intention of rejoining his wife and daughter in Kansas upon the conclusion of his voyage around the world that he does in this letter.

There is not a scintilla of evidence in this case which tends in the remotest degree to indicate any intention on the part of the soldier to desert, or permanently abandon his wife and child, or to show any dis-agreement between himself and this appellant, or any cause whatever of marital infelicity. On the contrary, the testimony shows that the soldier and the appellant lived happily together, that she was and has always been a woman of good character and unblemished reputation, and the evidence clearly indicates that during his long absence from appellant, prior to his final disappearance in 1877, his affection for her continued undiminished, and that he intended to return to her as soon as he could succeed in accumulating sufficient means to secure for her a comfortable home, and enable him to make a start in business, and in the practice of the medical profession.

It is shown beyond dispute that he disappeared and has not been heard from since November, 1877, just before he stated he was about to start out on a long and more or less dangerous voyage around the world, and that he never has returned from that voyage according to his expressed intention at his departure. No explanation whatever of his failure to carry out his intention or of his continuous absence and silence for twenty years is afforded by the evidence in this case, other than the natural presumption under the circumstances that he died before he completed his voyage and was never able to carry out his intentions.

Since the rejection of this claim the act of March 13, 1896, was passed by Congress, which provides as follows:

That in considering claims filed under the pension laws, the death of an enlisted man or officer shall be considered as sufficiently proved if satisfactory evidence is produced establishing the fact of the continued and unexplained absence of such enlisted man or officer from his home and family for a period of seven years, during which period no intelligence of his existence shall have been received. And any pension granted under this act shall cease upon proof that such officer or enlisted man is still living.

It is manifest and indisputable that the proof in this case fully meets and fulfills the conditions and requirements of the foregoing act, and, therefore, the death of this soldier should be accepted "as sufficiently proved" as therein provided.

In view of the foregoing considerations, I am clearly of the opinion that the ground upon which this claim was rejected is not tenable under the evidence on file, and, consequently, said action of rejection is hereby reversed and set aside, and you are requested to reopen and readjudicate the same upon its merits, accepting the death of the soldier "as sufficiently proved" under the act of March 13, 1896.

SPECIFIC DISABILITY—INCREASE.

GIBHART KURTZ.

Soldier is pensioned at the rate of $30 per month on account of the loss of a forearm. Upon an application for increase the evidence shows that soldier's arm was amputated at the elbow, and he is entitled to increase under the act of August 4, 1886.

Assistant Secretary Webster Davis to the Commissioner of Pensions, February 2, 1898.

On May 25, 1896, Gibhart Kurtz, late of Company K, Eighteenth Missouri Veteran Volunteers, filed a declaration for increase of pension (certificate No. 63825), alleging that he was borne upon the pension rolls at the rate of $30 per month for disability from gunshot wound, causing amputation of right arm near the elbow joint; that he believes himself to be entitled to an increase of $6 per month for the reason that the amputation is so close to the elbow joint that it has affected the elbow joint and upper arm.

This claim for increase was by your office rejected on the 18th day of May, 1897, on the ground that the present rating for claimant's disability—the loss of a forearm—is fixed by the statutes.

Appeal was taken on the 17th of July, 1897, resting upon the contention that the evidence shows that claimant is entitled to the rating provided in the act of August 4, 1886, which provision is as follows:

That all persons now on the pension rolls, and all persons hereafter granted a pension, who in like manner shall have lost either an arm at or above the elbow, or a leg at or above the knee, or been totally disabled in the same, shall receive a pension of thirty-six dollars per month.

The certificate of medical examination executed on September 1, 1897, reveals the following objective conditions of the wound and amputation of claimant's right arm:

The right forearm is amputated at the elbow joint, except 2 inches of the ulna, which is completely flexed and immovably fixed on the anterior surface of arm. For this reason we are unable to determine whether the coronoid process is present or not, but it probably is not. All of the radius, even the head, is absent.

The olecranon process forms the lowest portion of the stump. Stump thinly covered and the cicatrix is irregular, depressed, tender, and adherent. Claimant has tried to wear an artificial limb, but could not on account of the pain it caused. We consider the stump much less satisfactory than it would be if amputation had occurred immediately at the joint.

The advisory opinion of the medical referee, dated September 30, 1897, is as follows:

This man is pensioned at $30 per month for loss of right forearm. He filed a claim for increase September 23, 1892, which was rejected September 20, 1893, on the ground that amputation is not at or above the joint. On May 25, 1896, he filed another claim for increase, which was rejected May 18, 1897, and from this latter action he appeals. If the amputation in this case was through the joint on a line drawn around the elbow joint at the base of the head of radius, soldier would be entitled under the act of August 4, 1886, to the $36 rate for loss of arm at or above the elbow. In this case it is impossible to determine the exact point of amputation for the reason that the head of the radius was removed at time of amputation, and the fragment of the ulna remaining is permanently flexed upon the arm. The landmarks, therefore, by which the point of amputation may be determined are absent or inaccessible. It would appear that the amputation was below the joint, because 2 inches of the ulna remain, but there is no way by which this can be accurately determined. The present condition of the elbow joint appears to be as great a disability as an amputation through the joint. With this description of the conditions, I believe the honorable Assistant Secretary will be able to decide whether soldier is entitled to specific rate allowed for amputation through elbow joint.

The issue in the case is thus limited to one single question of fact—Was the amputation of soldier's arm at or above the elbow?

This case is controlled by that of William W. Scott (7 P. D., 417).

In that case the issue was precisely the same as in this. The claimant was pensioned at the rate of $30 per month on account of the loss of a forearm, and was seeking an increase based upon the contention that the amputation of his arm was, in legal contemplation, at the elbow, which brought his claim within the provisions of the act of August 4, 1886.

It thus having become material to ascertain the limits of the elbow, the Department adopted the definition found in Gray's Anatomy, which is as follows:

The vertical extent of the elbow joint is limited above by a line drawn from one condyle to the other; below, by a line corresponding to the lowest part of the head of the radius.

While the board of examining surgeons and the medical referee are unable to fix the exact point of amputation, still they agree that the head of the radius was removed in said process.

In the case of William W. Scott, above mentioned, the Department held as follows:

I hold, therefore, in harmony with the case of Lawrence Gates, that the word elbow in said act was used in the conventional rather than the technical sense, and, in harmony with the rule mentioned in Gray's Anatomy, that the word elbow covers that portion of the arm included between the upper edge of the condyles of the humerus and the lowest part of the head of the radius. A line drawn around the arm immediately below the head of the radius marks the lower limit of the elbow.

The evidence in this case, viewed in the light of the above ruling, shows that soldier's arm was amputated at the elbow, and, for this reason, your office decision is reversed, with directions to readjudicate the case accordingly.

SERVICE—INDIAN WARS—ACT JULY 27, 1892.

CATHARINE WATERS (WIDOW).

The official records show that the soldier did not serve the required time in the Florida war to entitle his widow to pension under the act of July 27, 1892.

Assistant Secretary Webster Davis to the Commissioner of Pensions, February 2, 1898.

The appellant filed a declaration under the act of July 27, 1892, as the widow of James L. Waters, late of Captain Holland's company, Florida war, June 28, 1894, which was rejected by your Bureau September 20, 1894, on the ground of insufficient service.

From this action an appeal was filed March 18, 1896, and by decision of this Department, dated May 16, 1896, your action rejecting the claim on the grounds stated was affirmed.

This motion for reconsideration, filed September 22, 1897, contends that the appellant is entitled to pension under the act of July 27, 1892, citing the decision of this Department in the case of the widow of William F. Young, Company H, Fourth Illinois Volunteer Infantry, Mexican war, as covering her case.

The act of July 27, 1892, requires thirty days' service in the Black Hawk war, the Creek war, the Cherokee disturbances, or the Florida war with the Seminole Indians.

In the decision of David J. Bailey (7 P. D., 173), Assistant Secretary Reynolds held that under the provisions of the act of July 27, 1892, period of service commences from the date when a claimant appeared at the place of battalion, regimental, or brigade rendezvous designated in proper orders, and ends at the date when he reached said rendezvous on his return, or (section 4701, Revised Statutes) the date of the individual discharge, or the date when the organization to which he belonged was disbanded.

In this case the official records show that the soldier was enrolled April 8, 1836, and was discharged April 14, 1836, and that he was paid for seven days' service as a soldier.

It also appears that he received travel pay for fifty-eight days' travel, being 600 miles to place of rendezvous of said organization and 560 miles from place of discharge home.

The facts shown by the records are conclusive upon this Department as to the length of service rendered by the soldier in the Florida war, which in this case is seven days' actual service.

The travel pay allowed the soldier to and from the point of rendezvous was not pay for actual military service, but was pay for time and expenses allowed recruits and discharged soldiers, and precludes their being considered as in actual military service during the time they were entitled to receive it.

The soldier's service in the Florida war was not of sufficient length to entitle his widow to pension under the act of July 27, 1892, and the motion is therefore overruled.

SERVICE—ACT JUNE 27, 1890.

HENRY BOEDEKER.

Soldier enlisted in the Regular Army December 9, 1865, and was discharged December 9, 1868. He was stationed at Harts Island, New York Harbor, from December 14, 1865, to April, 1866, and at Camp Wright, near Galveston, Tex., from April, 1866, to May, 1866, and at Richmond, Tex., from May, 1866, to August 20, 1866.

Held, That his enlistment and service were not in or for the "war of the rebellion," within the meaning of the act of June 27, 1890. (See Edward Farrell, et al., 7 P. D. 532; John Barleyoung, 7 P. D., 453; Jeremiah Butler, 7 P. D., 214.)

Assistant Secretary Webster Davis to the Commissioner of Pensions, February 2, 1898.

Claimant, on July 29, 1897, appealed from the action of your Bureau of June 5, 1897, rejecting his claim (No. 1181865), filed October 12, 1896, under section 2 of the act of June 27, 1890, on the ground that soldier was not in rebellion service, he having enlisted December 9, 1865.

It is contended on behalf of claimant that as he enlisted December 9, 1865, and served until December 9, 1868, and as the war of the rebellion did not end until August 20, 1866, as held by the Supreme Court of the United States in the cases of United States *v.* Anderson (9 Wall., 56), *The Proctor* (12 Wall., 702), and McElrath *v.* United States (102 U. S., 438), it was error to hold that soldier was not in rebellion service.

This question was fully considered in the case of Edward Farrell et al. (7 P. D., 532), wherein it was held that—

Enlistments in loyal States after April 13, 1865, will not be deemed enlistments in or for the war of the rebellion, and any service rendered under such enlistments will be presumed not to have been rendered in the war of the rebellion, and to establish the contrary the claimant will be required to show affirmatively that his said subsequent service was rendered in direct connection with active military duty in aid of suppressing the rebellion.

In discussing the question of the service pension granted under the
act of June 27, 1890, it was stated in said case of Edward Farrell et
al., above cited, that—

Service pensions have been uniformly granted by Congress only in view of the
fact that the services were rendered in some necessary connection with, and in pursuance of the objects sought to be attained by, the particular war under consideration; and it is not believed Congress intended in this case to depart from such
uniformity so as to create the anomalies and incongruities in practice which would
necessarily result therefrom, as in the case mentioned.

It is a well-known historical fact that the war was practically ended, so far as
actual belligerency was concerned, in July, 1865. (Case of Jeremiah Butler, 7 P. D.,
214.) Active hostilities then ceased, as they ceased in the case of the Mexican war,
on February 2, 1848, at the signing of the treaty (ibid., 240). The war still subsisted, however, and pensionable service may have been rendered thereafter, both
in and during the war, until it was finally terminated as a status which will be
held, in accordance with the decision of the Supreme Court cited, to be August 20,
1866. But the question, in any case, whether service rendered was connected with
the war as part of its operations is one of fact, and as such is governed, in proof, by
legal presumptions, the same as in other cases. In view of the fact that belligerent
hostilities had ceased in July, 1865, it will, therefore, be presumed that any service
rendered after that date was not rendered in, although during, the war of the rebellion, and the burden of proof is upon claimants to show by direct and positive evidence that their service rendered thereafter was a part of the operations of the war,
and made for the attainment of the purpose declared in the proclamation of August
20, 1866, to have been finally attained.

Upon the subject of enlistments, it should be borne in mind that enlistments for
service in the war of the rebellion were suspended immediately after Lee's sur-
render in April, 1865, and that instead of enlisting men in the volunteer service,
they were being mustered out of the service.

On April 13, 1865, the assistant adjutant-general of the War Department sent the
following telegram to superintendents of the volunteer recruiting service of the
loyal States:

" By direction of the Secretary of War, all recruiting of troops by volunteer enlistments is hereby suspended.

"Please so instruct all mustering officers, provost-marshals, and other officers under
your orders without delay, and acknowledge the receipt of this by telegram."

Claimant in this case enlisted after the issuance of General Orders,
No. 99, which was as follows:

I. In order to recruit the ranks of the regular regiments as soon as possible, the
Adjutant-General will open recruiting stations at such points as offer a reasonable
prospect of enlisting good men.

II. Volunteers honorably discharged from the United States service who enlist in
the Regular Army within ten days from date of discharge will be allowed a furlough
of thirty days before joining their regiments. They will be paid all pay and allowances to which they may be entitled on being discharged from the volunteer service.

By order of the Secretary of War:

                                        E. D. TOWNSEND,
                                    Assistant Adjutant-General.

May 9, 1865, the President issued his proclamation announcing the
reestablishment of the United States authority in the State of Virginia.
(13 Stat. L., 777.)

As to those volunteers who enlisted in the Regular Army after the cessation of armed hostilities, it can not be truthfully said that their enlistment was for the war of the rebellion, nor should their service be deemed service "during the war of the rebellion" within the meaning of the term in the act of June 27, 1890, unless it is made to appear that their service was for the suppression of the rebellion, or rendered in the theater of war, and having immediate connection with the belligerent operations of said war. This service must be shown to be a war service. Many soldiers desired to continue in the military service, and instead of being mustered out of service with their organizations reenlisted in the Regular Army after all organized hostile operations on the part of the enemy had ceased. Their enlistments should not be treated as enlistments in, for, or during the war of the rebellion, within the meaning of the act of June 27, 1890.

While, therefore, soldier's enlistment was prior to the final termination of the war, as announced by the President in his proclamation of August 20, 1866, yet his enlistment was not for service in the war of the rebellion, as the Government was making no contract of that character at that time, but for a term of years in the Regular Army. His service was not a war service; he was engaged in no battle or other active service in connection with the operations of the war of the rebellion.

The action appealed from is accordingly affirmed, and the papers in the case are herewith returned.

MARRIAGE OF COLORED TO WHITE PERSONS IN TEXAS.

MARY A. MILLER (COLORED).

A colored woman, and former slave, who married and cohabited with a white man and ex-soldier in the State of Texas, has no pensionable status as his widow for the reason that such marriage was in violation of the laws of that State, and null and void. (Article 2843, Revised Statutes, Texas.)

Assistant Secretary Webster Davis to the Commissioner of Pensions, February 10, 1898.

The soldier, John Backer, was pensioned under the act of June 27, 1890, at the rate of $12 per month. He died February 9, 1893.

The claimant, a colored woman and a former slave, filed a declaration as his widow, July 20, 1893, under the act of June 27, 1890, which was rejected May 14, 1897, on the ground that the claimant is not the legal widow of the soldier. The claimant, being of African descent, married the soldier, a German, in Texas, and both resided there until his death. The statutory law of said State makes the claimant's marriage to the soldier null and void.

From this action an appeal was filed, August 13, 1897, contending that the ignorance of the parties to said marriage should be considered and operate as an excuse.

A well-known legal maxim is that ignorance of the law excuses no one, and to permit a party to plead ignorance of the law in excuse for violation of it would be to permit him to take advantage of his own wrong, which would be a violation of another well-known maxim.

Article 2843 of the Revised Statutes of Texas, in which State the said marriage took place, reads as follows:

It shall not be lawful for any person of European blood or their descendants to intermarry with Africans, or the descendants of Africans, and should any person of the aforesaid violate the provisions of this article such marriage shall be null and void.

The marriage of the claimant to the soldier being clearly in violation of the statute of the State in which the same took place, she has no pensionable status before this Department as the widow of the soldier in accordance with the act of August 7, 1882, amending section 4702, Revised Statutes, United States, which reads as follows:

SEC. 2. That marriages, except such as are mentioned in section forty-seven hundred and five of the Revised Statutes, shall be proven in pension cases to be legal marriages according to the law of the place where the parties resided at the time of marriage, or at the time when the right to pension accrued.

The action of your Bureau rejecting this claim on the grounds stated was proper, and the same is hereby affirmed.

PRACTICE—RESTORATION—RENEWAL.

JAMES W. MURRAY.

Pensioner was receiving $12 per month on account of loss of sight of left eye, was dropped from the rolls in 1895. He filed claims for renewal and was restored to the rolls from October 20, 1896, at $6 per month, for the same disability. medical referee expresses the opinion that he should not have been dropped, his rating only reduced. Refusal to restore him from date of dropping at reduced rating is based on the fact that he has only filed claim for renewal and not restoration. It is held that this action is chiefly technical, that the words "renewal" and "restoration" in applications are generally interchangeable and that this claimant, having applied for renewal, and admitted to be entitled to restoration, should be restored from the date of dropping without other application.

Assistant Secretary Webster Davis to the Commissioner of Pensions, February 10, 1898.

In the case of James W. Murray, late of Company H, Ninth United States Veteran Volunteers (Certificate No. 735195), an appeal has been filed July 22, 1897, from the refusal of your Bureau to restore his name to the pension rolls from the date of dropping, and at the original rate—$12 per month. As your report upon this appeal recites the material facts and defines the issue in the case, it is quoted in full:

SIR: In response to your request for a report on the appeal in the above-mentioned claim, I have the honor to submit the following:

Pensioner was in receipt of $12 per month under the act of June 27, 1890, on account of loss of sight of left eye, when, on November 1, 1895, he was dropped from the rolls on the ground that the same was not a ratable disability under said act, as then construed.

December 26, 1895, he filed a claim for renewal of his pension, alleging the same disability and impaired vision of right eye, and other disabling causes; which claim was rejected April 20, 1896, on the same ground of no ratable disability.

October 20, 1896, he again filed a claim for renewal, based on substantially the same allegations, which claim was allowed for loss of sight of left eye, pension to commence from said date of filing, October 20, 1896.

From the actions taken pensioner appeals, contending that he should have been restored to the rolls from the date of dropping, November 1, 1895.

It will be observed that the appellant has never applied to this Bureau for restoration. Neither his application of December 26, 1895, nor that of October 20, 1896, was an application for restoration. Both were in form new claims for original pension alleging loss of sight of left eye, and also other disabling causes.

Although the action of dropping November 1, 1895, and the rejection of April 20, 1896, were not in accord with the present practice, it is not believed that the claimant could properly be restored to the rolls without having filed a proper claim for restoration.

The report of the medical referee herewith, dated December 7, 1897, sustains the claim for restoration from a medical standpoint. But in the absence of a claim for restoration, the action of this Bureau in fixing the date of commencement is believed to be proper and the same is adhered to.

The opinion of the medical referee referred to is as follows:

This soldier was originally pensioned under the act of June 27, 1890, from October 3, 1890, at $8 to December 4, 1891, and then $12 on account of "loss of sight of left eye."

May 28, 1895, the case was revised under the practice at that time and dropping was proposed, which was carried out November 1, 1895, after proper notice to the claimant.

On December 26, 1895, he filed a declaration for pension under the act of June 27, 1890, in which was alleged "loss of sight of left eye, partial loss of sight right eye, kidney and lung disease, and rheumatism." Claim was rejected April 20, 1896, on the ground of "no ratable disability shown under the act of June 27, 1890." He filed another declaration under the same law October 20, 1896, alleging "loss of sight of left eye and cataract on right eye, kidney trouble, and disease of lungs." A rate of $6 was allowed from October 20, 1896, date of filing declaration for "loss of sight of left eye." Now the soldier, through his attorney, contends that rate should have commenced at date of dropping, and that he was entitled to a greater rate during this period.

After a careful examination of all the papers in the case, it is my opinion, in view of the permanent character of the disability and the subsequent granting a rate for same, the action of dropping was error. Reduction to $6 would have been proper, thus providing a rate commensurate with the degree of disability shown from pensioned causes.

The certificates of examination fail to describe any other disability which would affect the rate.

The question here involved, in the present aspect of the case, and in so far as it requires present consideration, is simply one of practice under the rules and regulations. The Bureau having admitted that the appellant is entitled to pension for the original disability alone, although at a reduced rate, and that upon proper application the pension would be restored to him at such reduced rate from the date of dropping, and the medical referee having expressed the opinion that there should only have been a reduction of rating in the first instance, and not a dropping from the rolls, it is only necessary to determine by what method he may be restored to his proper status. Inasmuch as this appellant was deprived of his pension by the act of the Bureau, and afterwards, under a change of practice as to ratings, he was declared entitled to his pension again upon the same basis as before, it is doubtful whether any declaration by him was necessary to restore his name to the rolls. But, admitting that some sort of declaration was essential, for the sake of regularity and as indicative of his acquiescence, it seems superfluous to require of him anything more than a formal statement that he desires to receive his pension again.

Then again, in ordinary cases where renewal or restoration of pension is sought, and where the rights of the claimant have not been developed and passed upon, as in this case, there does not appear to be any warrant for such a differentiation in the character of the application as is made in your report. Under the regulations prescribing how applications shall be made, and the proof to be furnished thereunder, there is no rule laid down as to an application for restoration except as it may have been intended to be included in the provision as to claims for renewal. In fact, from the readings of the whole provision (pp. 129 and 130, Laws and Regulations, 1896), the words "renewal" and "restoration" would seem to be largely interchangeable, and in an application where either word is used the character of the application, or the thing sought, would be determined by the facts in the particular case.

That this is true could probably be demonstrated in many instances from the files of the Bureau, where claimants, not understanding the technical difference between a renewal and a restoration of pension, have applied for the one when properly entitled the other, and the Bureau, with all the facts before it, has doubtless adjudicated the claims on the basis of the title involved. At any rate, as pointed out, the regulations do not recognize such a difference in applications for renewal and restoration, whatever the difference in proof required in each case, as would give standing to the position taken in this case as anything more than a technicality, and in view of the admissions made it seems somewhat inconsistent to refuse appellant restoration upon this application for "renewal."

It is unnecessary to discuss the merits of the claim and the propriety of what has been done and what is proposed, further than to state that the opinion of the medical referee to the effect that appellant is entitled to restoration at the reduced rate from the date of dropping is sustained by the evidence. It is directed, therefore, that the case be readjudicated in accordance with that opinion.

ATTORNEYSHIP—FORFEITURE—FEE.

ELIZA JACOB (CLAIMANT).

J. H. VERMILYA & CO. (ATTORNEYS).

As the appellants have, under rule 12, forfeited the attorneyship by neglecting the case for more than one year, they are not entitled to further recognition.

Assistant Secretary Webster Davis to the Commissioner of Pensions, February 14, 1898.

J. H. Vermilya & Co., of Washington, D. C., October 26, 1897, appealed in the matter of recognition in the claim for a widow's pension under the general law, of Eliza Jacob.

George E. Lemon, of Washington, D. C., October 3, 1885, filed the original declaration. The claim was rejected March 28, 1887, on the ground of no record and inability of claimant to furnish evidence of soldier's death to be in any way due or connected with his military service.

The appellants, July 11, 1890, filed a power of attorney. They filed evidence November 14 and December 28, 1892; January 10 and 21, 1893. Under date of July 10, 1893, they were notified that the evidence filed by them did not change the status of the case and that the Bureau adhered to its former action of rejection.

The Bureau states in its report accompanying the appeal of Messrs. Vermilya & Co. that—

Appellants then apparently abandoned the claim, and became in neglect under rule 13. June 10, 1897, they filed a call-up slip and requested permission to examine the papers, which privilege, in accordance with the practice, was denied. They subsequently appealed to me from this action, and the proper officer for that purpose was directed to examine the case and advise them of their status as attorneys. In compliance with these instructions appellants were informed, under date of September 20, 1897, that they would be recognized and given the status, upon calling up the case, and that they would be continued in the attorneyship, provided they file material evidence before another person files another power of attorney. They were also advised that the courtesy extended by recognizing them to call up the case and obtaining its status did not give them the right to examine the case in person until after they shall have filed material evidence in the case. From this action they have appealed, contending that by reason of the limit thus placed upon the recognition, they are unjustly deprived of the privilege of exercising their rights as attorneys, and thereby inflicting a hardship upon the claimant.

The action of the Bureau in this case was in harmony with the practice in cases of this character. These appellants had apparently abandoned the claim and were in neglect during the period of four years. They were accorded recognition by courtesy of the Bureau and the requirement that they should file material evidence before being permitted to make a personal examination of the papers in the case was within the discretionary powers of the Bureau and is adhered to.

It is manifest, as the Bureau had notified the appellants of the effect of the evidence filed by them, and over three years thereafter they neither called up the case nor filed any evidence, that they were clearly chargeable with laches. Hence, under their power of attorney they can make no demand upon the Bureau, for their title to recognition has been forfeited. However, as they have not been superseded, they can be accorded recognition through the courtesy of the Bureau; but it is manifest that recognition under these conditions is wholly within the discretion of the Bureau.

In this particular case the Bureau has informed the appellants that they will be accorded recognition under said rule provided they render material service before they are superseded. Such action is proper. While it is within the province of the Bureau to inform the attorneys as to the particular service required—that is, give them the requirements of the claim—it is wholly within the discretion of the Bureau to withhold such information for the reason that appellants have forfeited their rights to recognition. Furthermore, if they were given the requirements it would still be necessary for them to render material service prior to the appearance of another attorney in the case, and within the time allotted by the rules of practice before they would have any title to recognition under their present power of attorney. As they are without title to recognition, it follows that they have no right to inspect the papers in the case.

As the case stands the appellants under rule 12 forfeited their rights by neglecting the case for more than one year. Under these conditions the action of the Bureau in refusing to accord them further recognition is proper.

Action affirmed.

———

EVIDENCE—NEW DISABILITY.

SHADRICK LEE.

Whenever, in a claim for increase under the general law, an applicant, after long and unexplained silence, alleges a new disability of which there is neither record nor medical evidence, the adverse presumption arising from the absence of such evidence may be rebutted, but can be overcome only by direct and positive proof of incurrence and existence, or by satisfactory evidence as to facts and circumstances from which such incurrence and existence may be naturally, fairly, and reasonably inferred. (See case of Thomas H. Strange, 7 P. D., 36.)

Assistant Secretary Webster Davis to the Commissioner of Pensions, February 17, 1898.

In 1887 this appellant became a pensioner on account of scurvy. On March 10, 1888, he alleged also heart disease and disease of kidneys, which were rejected January 28, 1892, on the ground of no record and no satisfactory proof of incurrence in service.

On June 21, 1897, this appeal was filed, alleging that since said rejection additional evidence had been filed, and that appellant was notified April 9, 1897, that rejection was adhered to, as said evidence related to scurvy only; and he contends, however, that the evidence establishes the claim as to heart and kidney disease.

The only record of any action on April 9, 1897, is a jacket indorse ment of letter of notification that "evidence filed does not change the status of the claim for rheum.," which latter disability had been alleged May 9, 1893, and rejected April 13, 1896. No action as to heart and kidney diseases appears to have been had since January 28, 1892.

On November 15, 1897, accordingly, the Department returned the papers to you for a report as to what, if any, action had been taken as to alleged heart and kidney diseases since said rejection thereof in 1892, and the retransmitted papers contain a statement, dated January 11, 1898, attached to the brief face, to the effect that said rejection is adhered to, as the additional evidence mentioned is insufficient to reopen said claim on account of heart and kidney disease because but one affiant is at all definite as to either of said diseases, and there is no other testimony, original or new, conforming to claimant's allegations.

The claimant in his appeal cites as in support of the claim the testimony of William R. Brummit, William J. McKaney, E. B. Hudson, J. H. Farmer, Saul Barger, L. T. Evans, and Henry C. Seaser as to service origin, and of neighbors generally as to continuance.

He alleges in his declaration herein that he contracted heart disease and kidney disease in 1865, while in Andersonville prison. The records show he was captured in January, 1864, and was in confinement there-after at Richmond, Va., and Andersonville, Ga., at which latter place he was treated in August, 1864, for diarrhea, was paroled April 28, 1865, and mustered out May 29, 1865, to date April 17, 1865.

As stated in your letter, none of the original testimony—that of Hudson, Brummit, and McKaney—conforms to claimant's allegations as to origin. All of these testify as to incurrence in June, 1862. Said Farmer testified, in 1894, generally as to scurvy, and added merely that he had "heard said Lee complain of heart and kidney troubles." Barger stated, in affidavit filed in February, 1897, that he was captured November 6, 1863, and taken to Belle Island; that claimant was there at same time, and was sent from there to Andersonville; that he met him again in 1866, when he complained of heart and kidney disease. Henry C. Slover states in his affidavit, filed in March, 1897, that claimant had scurvy and some other diseases, which he can't name, and complained of stomach or heart troubles. C. T. Dickerson and D. B. Collins are alike general and meager in their statement, and, as stated, only Lafayette F. Evans, of all these, testifies positively as to actual existence in service of either heart or kidney disease, and his testimony is weak and far from being satisfactory.

Your rejection was clearly warranted by the evidence and in accord-ance with the well-established rule in such cases, which is as follows:

Whenever, in a claim for increase of pension under the general law, an applicant, after long and unexplained silence, alleges a new disability of which there is neither record nor medical evidence, the adverse presumption arising from the absence of such evidence is open to rebuttal by the testimony of officers, comrades, and neighbors, but such presumption is not outweighed by the mere recital under oath of assertions made long since by the soldier himself or by general and vague statements of the witnesses, and can be overcome only by direct and positive proof of incurrence and existence, or by satisfactory evidence as to facts and circumstances from which said incurrence and existence are to be naturally, fairly, and reasonably inferred. (Thomas H. Strange, 7 P. D., 36.)

Rejection is affirmed accordingly.

COMMENCEMENT, ACT JUNE 27, 1890—INCREASE.

ROLLIN LEWIS.

Pension under the second section of the act of June 27, 1890, must commence from the date of filing of the declaration, provided a pensionable degree of disability is shown to have existed on that date; but where such pensionable degree of disability did not exist at date of filing the declaration, but it appears that subsequent to the filing of such declaration and before a medical examination was had an applicant became pensionably disabled, another declaration must be filed.

Assistant Secretary Webster Davis to the Commissioner of Pensions February 17, 1898.

On July 20, 1890, Rollin Lewis filed an application for pension (certificate No. 46287) under the provisions of the act of June 27, 1890, alleging gunshot wound of right leg, rheumatism, chronic diarrhea, obesity, age, asthma, heart trouble, and general debility.

The claim was rejected on May 26, 1897, on the ground that no ratable disability was found to exist.

Appeal was taken August 13, 1897, based upon the contention that the evidence on file, together with the reports of examining boards, shows his condition to be such as to entitle him to a higher rating than he is receiving under the general law; that he is now 67 years old, which, with his disabilities, should entitle him to the full rating of the new law.

Soldier was pensioned under the general law at the rate of $4 per month on account of disability resulting from gunshot wound of right leg, which rate was increased to $6 per month under the provision of the act of March 2, 1895.

The material facts disclosed by the record of the case that are necessary to an intelligent consideration thereof are set forth in the advisory opinion of the medical referee of October 30, 1897, which is as follows:

An appeal is taken in this case from the rejection of the claim under the act of June 27, 1890. The declaration was filed July 22, 1890; but the claim was not adjudicated until March, 1897.

The claimant was examined September 21, 1892, when some evidence of asthma and rheumatism were described, in addition to the gunshot wound of the right leg, for which he is pensioned. The claimant was reported as very muscular; obesity was not excessive; there was no evidence of debility.

Another examination was made May 15, 1895, when the evidences of asthma and rheumatism were somewhat more marked, but there was no other disability that was shown at the former examination. The claimant's age at that time was given as 65 years.

The former certificate does not show a ratable degree of disability under the act of June 27, 1890, from any cause or causes. The last certificate does not show a ratable degree of disability independent of the effects of age. In accordance with the case of Francis Frank (9 P. D., 68), this claimant should now be deemed entitled to the minimum rating, but it is evident that the rating could not be allowed from the date of filing the first declaration, and, as no other declaration is on file, there is no legal date from which the pension could begin. The claimant is now in receipt of $6 per month under the provision of the act of March 2, 1895. In view of these facts the rejection of the claim is believed to have been proper.

In the case of Francis Frank the Department ruled that an applicant for pension under act of June 27, 1890,

who has attained the age of 65 years shall be deemed entitled to at least the minimum rate of pension provided by that act,

unless the evidence and medical examinations disclose an unusual vigor and activity for the performance of manual labor.

The Department in formulating rules to promote

a safe, speedy, and uniform system of adjudicating claims that arise under the second section of the act of June 27, 1890,

(Instructions, 9 P. D., 93), relating to disabilities which are incurred subsequent to the time of filing the declaration and prior to medical examinations, says:

Should it be found, however, not to have existed at the time when the original application was filed, but from a subsequent date prior to medical examination, the degrees of the disability of the application being below the maximum rating, pension may be increased accordingly from the date when such wound or injury was incurred or disease contracted, provided the degree of disability from all contributory causes is thereby enhanced to a sufficient extent to justify a higher rating.

Should it be found impossible to fix the exact date when such wound or injury was received or disease contracted, the higher rating shall commence from the date of the certificate of medical examination showing its existence.

When the last medical examination was had claimant had arrived at the age of 65 years. This fact might have been considered in connection with other disabilities in order to determine what rating might be given to claimant under the act in question. It might have been properly considered as a supplemental factor, to augment the rating authorized by preexisting disabilities, the increase thus arising to take effect from the date at which soldier reached that age.

This rule applies, however, only in cases where some ratable disability under said act did exist at the time of filing the original declaration. If no ratable disability whatever existed at that time, the claimant can not base a title to pension upon a disability of subsequent incurrence.

Eliminating the factor of age from the case at bar, the evidence fails to show title to any rating under the act of June 27, 1890, and for that reason the rejection was proper. Besides, from a medical standpoint the pension which appellant is now receiving is shown to be commensurate with existing disabilities.

The action appealed from is therefore affirmed.

RES JUDICATA—STARE DECISIS—RECONSIDERATION.

JAMES DUVAL.

Neither the doctrine of res judicata nor stare decisis is strictly applicable to claims for pension, and when adopted by the Department, simply becomes a rule which each administration prescribes for itself as a matter of policy or convenience, and may be waived, suspended, or ignored, as justice, policy, or convenience requires. (Case of Mary E. Eastridge, 8 P. D., 5.)

Assistant Secretary Webster Davis to the Commissioner of Pensions, February 23, 1898.

Claimant's attorney on September 15, 1897, filed a motion for reconsideration of departmental decision of November 7, 1896, affirming the action of your Bureau of August 24, 1896, which in effect rejected his application for renewal and increase of pension, filed August 12, 1896, under section 2 of the act of June 27, 1890.

It is contended, in brief, that claimant should have been restored to his pension under section 2 of the act of June 27, 1890, at $8 per month, from the date at which he was dropped from the roll under said act. Also, that his claim having been adjudicated, and claimant having been granted a pension under said act at $8, a subsequent Commissioner of Pensions had no legal right to review the decisions of his predecessor.

The question as to the degree of his disability under said act of June 27, 1890, was fully considered in the decision of November 7, 1896, and no valid reason appears for receding from the conclusion then reached, affirming the action of your Bureau. While the effect of the action of your Bureau of August 24, 1896, was to deny the application for restoration and increase, yet the claim was adjudicated allowing his claim for pension under said act of June 27, 1890, at $6 on account of rheumatism, varicose veins of both legs, and disease of eyes, no certificate to issue unless the claimant so elected. While the action did not in terms state the date of commencement, yet the claimant, not having elected to accept a pension under the act of 1890 in lieu of his pension at the same rate under the old law, the question as to when his pension under the new law would commence has not been passed upon by the Commissioner. The Department will not assume in advance that your Bureau would err in properly dating the commencement, should claimant elect to accept a pension under the act of June 27, 1890.

In reference to the second point raised, that a subsequent commissioner has no legal right to review the action of his predecessor, this is but another form of invoking the doctrine of res judicata.

The reasons why the rule as applied by the courts or to cases in which the rights of third parties are involved was discussed and passed upon in the case of Mary E. Eastridge (8 P. D., 5), wherein it was held that—

While the doctrine of res judicata and stare decisis is not strictly applicable to claims involving the title to pensions or increase or rejection of rates, so long as claimant or pensioner survives, the right of third parties not being involved, yet as was said by Judge Cox in the case of Long *v.* The Commissioner of Pensions, decided February 28, 1894:

"There is no statute which excludes the right of an executive officer to review the action of his predecessor in any unsettled or inchoate matter. * * * The doctrine of stare decisis is simply a rule which each administration prescribes for itself, without being constrained to do so by any statute or general principle of law, but simply as a matter of policy or convenience. * * * I infer that it has been the usage of the Department of the Interior not to apply the doctrine of res adjudicata to the rating of a pensioner, and in the absence of statutory provisions I should consider this usage the controlling authority on the subject. I think, however, that it also has the support of statute law. * * * No title passes by the admission of an applicant to the pension roll as in the case of a patent to land, which can not be recalled. Pensions are the bounties of the Government which Congress has the right to give, withhold, or recall at its discretion. * * * It is the duty of the officers of the Government to see that its bounty is not abused. It is the duty of the Commissioner, on a proper application, to decide what share of that bounty the law intends to bestow upon the applicant. Whatever is paid to him under that decision is gone beyond recall, but if the succeeding Commissioner should be satisfied that the pensioner was wrongfully rated, why should he not correct the error as to further payments? The pensioner has no contract rights to future payments. He has no vested rights in an erroneous construction of the law. The Government can not bring suit to set aside a mere erroneous decision of an ex-officer. * * * Its only remedy is in its own hands, and that is to stop the abuse, and the Commissioner, for the time being, is its organ to do that."

In the case of Harrison *v.* United States (20 C. Cls. Rep., 122), which was a suit to recover a pension which had once been allowed, but discontinued because its allowance had been obtained through fraud, the court said:

"If the placing of the name of an applicant upon the roll is to be considered a judicial act, it should only be considered a judgment nisi. The proceedings are largely ex parte, and from the vast number of applicants the work must be performed and the roll made up for the most part by the clerks."

Where cases are tried before a judicial tribunal, the parties interested are before the court and confronted with the witnesses who are subject to examination and cross-examination, and the facts of the case thus duly ascertained and finally determined, become, as a general rule, conclusive, subject only to be reviewed by an appelate court. The judgment must be a valid and final judgment.

It is, therefore, to such proceedings only that the doctrine of res judicata or stare decisis is strictly applicable. The doctrines, when adopted by the Department in pension cases, simply become rules which each Administration prescribes for itself as a matter of policy or convenience, and may be waived, suspended, or ignored as justice, public policy, or convenience requires.

The general policy regarding the application of the doctrine of res adjudicata, as applied to pension cases, was announced in the case of Jackson Martin, 7 P. D., 265, as follows:

While it has been held that "no pensioner has a vested right to his pension" (United States *v.* Teller, 107 U. S. Rep., 64), yet I also hold that cases long since adjudicated by previous administrations should not be reopened, reconsidered, nor adjudicated, except (1) upon discovery that the pension was procured through fraud, (2) when under the statutes the pension is required to be increased or reduced in accordance with the degree of the pensionable disability, (3) when indisputable or manifest error in law or fact is apparent in the record, or (4) when on presentation of new and material evidence it is indubitably shown that through mistake the pension was in whole or in part illegally refused or granted.

The act of December 21, 1893, provides that pensions granted under any law authorizing the granting of pensions, on application made and adjudicated upon, shall be deemed and held by all officers of the United States to be a vested right in the pensioner to the extent that payment of the pension should not be withheld or suspended until after due notice to the pensioner of not less than thirty days, the Commissioner, after hearing all the evidence, shall decide to annul, vacate, modify, or set aside the decision on which such pension was granted. The foregoing provision is, however, to be construed in pari materia with the provisions of the act of June 21, 1879, which provided—

That the Commissioner of Pensions shall have the same power as heretofore to order special examinations whenever, in his judgment, the same may be necessary, and to increase or reduce the pension according to right and justice; but in no case shall a pension be withdrawn or reduced except upon notice to the pensioner and a hearing upon sworn testimony, except as to the certificate of the examining surgeon.

The pensioner in this case was dropped from the rolls under the act of June 27, 1890, on a medical examination had under his application for increase, which action appears to have been according to right and justice.

The motion for reconsideration is therefore denied.

————

ANTEREBELLION SERVICE—DISABILITY—ORIGIN.

MATTEO BIANCHI (DECEASED).

1. Evidence alone that a claimant was treated in the service for the disease causing the disability for which pension is claimed is not sufficient to establish a claim: the continuance of the disease and the extent to which it disabled for the performance of manual labor must be shown.
2. As it appears that the disease causing the disability on account of which pension was claimed was contracted prior to March 4, 1861, claimant in this case is not pensionable, for the reason that his application was not filed within three years from the date of his discharge and was not completed prior to his death, as required by section 4713 of the Revised Statutes.

Assistant Secretary Webster Davis to the Commissioner of Pensions, February 26, 1898.

The soldier, Matteo Bianchi, late sergeant Battery K, Third United States Artillery, filed a claim for pension on the 31st of January, 1889, alleging that while in the United States military service and in the line of duty, at Alexandria, Va., on or about March 10, 1862, he contracted neuralgia in his back and hips from exposure. He died October 1, 1894, while said claim was yet pending. The prosecution of said claim was continued by his widow. It was finally rejected June 25, 1896, on the ground that there was no period for which pension could be allowed, the records of the War Department showing that the soldier's disability originated prior to March 4, 1861, and the claim not having been filed within three years after his final discharge from service, and the evidence requisite to establish the same not having been filed until after his death.

The law which your Bureau held to be applicable to the case is contained in section 4713, Revised Statutes, which reads as follows:

In all cases in which the cause of disability or death originated in the service prior to the fourth day of March, eighteen hundred and sixty-one, and an application for pension shall not have been filed within three years from the discharge or death of the person on whose account the claim is made, or within three years of the termination of a pension previously granted on account of the service and death of the same person, the pension shall commence from the date of filing by the party prosecuting the claim the last paper requisite to establish the same. But no claim allowed prior to the sixth day of June, eighteen hundred and sixty-six, shall be affected by anything herein contained.

It is contended in the appeal, filed July 7, 1897:

First. That the evidence necessary to complete a claim of this character is proof of origin of the disability claimed for in the service and line of duty, and that such evidence was furnished by the records of the War Department and was in the case long prior to the soldier's death.

Second. That your Bureau is not justified in setting up section 4713, Revised Statutes, as a bar to the admission of the claim, it being a reasonable assumption, in view of all the evidence, that the soldier's disability was due to exposure subsequent to March 4, 1861.

The records of the War Department show that he was in the military service continuously from December 20, 1853, to November 1, 1862, when he was discharged for disability, and that he again enlisted May 24, 1866, and was finally discharged May 31, 1869. During his service he received medical treatment as follows:

June 18, 1858, to July 2, 1858, for fistula; April 19, 1859, to April 23, 1859, for ophthalmia; July 17, 1859, to July 21, 1859, for rheumatism; March 19, 1860, to March 24, 1860, for ambustio; June 6, 1860, to June 10, 1860, for cholera morbus; April 17, 1861, to April 22, 1861, for subluxatio; August 4, 1862, to August 14, 1862, for sciatica, and August 17, 1862, to November 1, 1862, for coxalgia.

He was also treated for rheumatism in October, 1866, and March, 1867; for acute diarrhea in August and September, 1867; for a boil in November, 1867, and for constipation in January, 1868.

The disabilities for which he was discharged on November 1, 1862, were coxalgia, caused by a wrench of the hip, and persistent constipation.

It is argued, in support of the appeal, that it is unreasonable to hold that a man can not recover from an acute attack of rheumatism; that the records and other evidence in this case tend to show that the soldier completely recovered from the attack of rheumatism prior to March 4, 1861; and that—

the fact that he underwent greater hardship and exposure subsequent to March 4, 1861, than he ever did at any time prior thereto, and that after a year's active service in the field he was taken down with what he termed neuralgia of the back and hips. is good evidence that said attack was due to the exposure he underwent subsequent to March 4, 1861.

The medical referee to whom the case has been referred for an advisory opinion touching some of the issues involved says:

While it is not to be denied that a person may recover from an attack of acute rheumatism, so far as sensations and outward appearances may be concerned, yet it is never safe to conclude that a perfect recovery has taken place. An attack of rheumatism tends to predispose to further attacks of rheumatism. In fact the establishing of the continuance of rheumatism does not necessarily imply that unmistakable evidence of the disease must be shown present at all times and continuously. I do not think it possible to establish beyond a doubt, by any testimony, whether the rheumatism for which soldier was treated in 1867 was a continuance of the disease of 1859 or whether it was a new and separate attack of the same disease.

There is no evidence that the soldier was free from sensations of or outward manifestations of rheumatism between July, 1859, and March, 1862. We are asked to assume that he had recovered from said disease because there is no record of treatment for it during that period. Such an assumption, if made a general rule, would defeat the great majority of claims for pension on account of rheumatism.

There is no evidence on file that this soldier suffered from rheumatism between 1862 and 1866, or between 1867 and 1869, but no question has been or will be raised as to the continuance of the disease during those periods. I see no good reason why the same rule should not apply to the interval between 1859 and 1862.

Admitting that the soldier underwent greater hardship and exposure subsequent to March 4, 1861, than he ever did at any time prior thereto (as to which there is no evidence), it does not follow that he did not undergo sufficient exposure prior to 1861 to cause chronic rheumatism.

In the absence of positive evidence to the contrary, I think it is fair to presume that the rheumatic trouble for which he claimed pension originated in 1859.

In regard to the other point raised by the appeal, I would say that something more is necessary to complete a claim of this character than evidence that the soldier was treated for the alleged disease while in the service. The continuance of the disease and the extent to which it disabled him for the performance of manual labor must be shown. It was held by Attorney-General Wirt that—

evidence is not complete while anything of form or of substance is wanting, nor until it comes in such shape that its admissibility is unquestionable. (10 Op., 562.)

The evidence necessary to complete this soldier's claim was not filed until after his death.

The action of your Bureau is affirmed.

DECLARATIONS ACT JUNE 27, 1890—DISABILITY—EVIDENCE.

GEORGE ELLIS (DECEASED).

It being shown that the deceased soldier was, at the date of filing his application for pension and up to the date of his death, incapacitated for earning a support by manual labor in a pensionable degree, under the provisions of section 2, act of June 27, 1890, by disabling causes not alleged by him in his application, but shown not to be due to vicious habits, his claim should be admitted under instructions of this Department of July 28, 1897. (P. D., 93.)

Assistant Secretary Webster Davis to the Commissioner of Pensions, February 26, 1898.

The deceased soldier filed in your Bureau on July 31, 1890, an application for pension under the provisions of section 2, act of June 27, 1890, alleging inability to earn a support by manual labor from scurvy and chronic diarrhea. The soldier died on March 4, 1891, leaving said claim pending and unadjudicated, and this appellant was permitted to continue the prosecution of the same to completion as his widow.

Said claim was rejected on May 20, 1896, upon the ground that a degree of incapacity to earn a support by manual labor from the disabling causes alleged by soldier in his application, which was pensionable under the provisions of said section, had not been shown to exist. From this action appeal was taken on July 19, 1897.

The deceased soldier was medically examined under his said application by the board of surgeons at Frankfort, Ky., on February 4, 1891, who certify and describe his physical condition and existing disability as found by them as follows:

Upon examination we find the following objective conditions: Pulse rate, 120; respiration, 20; temperature, 101.5; height, 6 feet; weight, 120 pounds; age, 45 years. Claimant has a worn, emaciated appearance. Tongue coated and red at edges and tip. Throat and nasal cavities congested. Stomach tender. Abdomen full; ascites present, legs and feet œdematous from pressure of fluid on vena cava. Cirrhosis of liver. Edges hard. Spleen enlarged. Auscultation and percussion reveal mitral insufficiency, with hypertrophy, displacement upward from pressure. Vesicular murmur in lungs obscured from same cause; no cavities; no pain. Considerable dyspnœa on least exertion. Diarrhea chronic. Examination of rectum shows congestion. Vessels engorged. Three large ulcers on posterior wall and two internal hemorrhoids near anal orifice, size bean, tender and bleeding. Claimant suffers great pain from introduction [of] speculum.

It is the opinion of the board that the claimant is entitled, in his present condition, third-grade rating.

On August 18, 1897, this claim was submitted to the medical referee for his consideration and opinion, who replied, on September 22, 1897, as follows:

From an examination of this case it appears that the invalid claim under the act of June 27, 1890, which had been rejected on legal grounds in June, 1894, was "reopened for further consideration under recent departmental decisions." It was then submitted, under date of May 14, 1896, for a statement as to whether deceased soldier was ratably disabled from the date of filing by chronic diarrhea and scurvy. The claim was rejected May 16, 1896, on the ground of "no ratable disability shown from cause alleged under the act of June 27, 1890." This action appears to have been correct, for neither the medical testimony nor the certificate of examination dated February 4, 1891, shows any disability from those causes, or which can be medically accepted as covered by the allegation.

Relative to your inquiry under date of August 18, 1897, it can not be stated that there was no disability under act of June 27, 1890. The certificate dated February 4, 1891, one month before the death of soldier, showed a serious disease of the heart and liver and general dropsy, and the testimony appears to show that he was laid up for about a year before he died. The certificate of examination, dated July 3, 1889, showed the soldier to be then in excellent physical condition, and the heart and liver and other organs were normal. The cause or origin of the fatal illness attributed to disease of the heart is not shown by the testimony on file. If a legal approval to cover the disability shown can be justified by the soldier's allegation and the testimony on file, with the elimination of vicious habits, a rating may be allowed.

It is clearly shown by the evidence in this case that the disease of heart, liver, and dropsy referred to in the foregoing medical opinion by the medical referee, and on account of which he holds "a rating may be allowed," had existed in a marked degree and to a very disabling extent for more than a year prior to the death of the soldier, consequently a pensionable condition of inability to earn a support by manual labor due to said causes antedated the filing of his declaration for pension in July, 1890. The rejection of his claim, then, was based solely, as is expressed in terms by your Bureau, upon the ground that the soldier had failed to specifically name and designate in his declaration for pension the several causes of disability to which his existing condition of pensionable incapacity was found to be due, and not because of the failure of the evidence to show the existence of such pensionable condition from any cause not the result of vicious habits.

This action was taken under and in accordance with certain decisions of this Department which, in my opinion, announced too narrow and technical a rule for the adjudication of claims for pension under the provisions of section 2, act of June 27, 1890, and to prevent and correct the apparent hardship and injustice to claimants often arising in its application, I, on July 28, 1897, promulgated certain "instructions" for the guidance and regulation of the practice of your Bureau relative to the essential requirements of the law in declarations for pension under said section and in the adjudication of said claims. (9 P. D., 93.)

The first, third, and fourth of said "instructions" apply directly to the facts of this case and are as follows:

1. Every application for pension under the second section of the act of June 27, 1890, should state that the same is made under said act, the dates of enlistment and discharge, the name or nature of the diseases, wounds, or injuries by which the claimant is disabled, and that they are not due to vicious habits: *Provided, however,* That the omission of any of these averments shall not invalidate the application (the intent to claim pension being manifest and the declaration being executed in accordance with law), but such application shall be subject to amendment by means of a supplemental affidavit in the particulars wherein it is defective; said supplemental affidavit or affidavits to be read in connection with and as a part of the

application itself: *And provided further,* That a declaration *in the terms of the act* shall be sufficient.

3. Should the medical examination disclose the existence of any disease, wound, or injury not alleged in the original or amendatory application which is a factor in the applicant's inability to earn a support by manual labor, the claimant shall be called upon to state, under oath, the time, place, and circumstance, when, where, and under which such wound or injury was received or disease contracted, and whether it was in any manner caused by vicious habits.

4. Should the wound, injury, or disease not specified in the original or amendatory declaration, but discovered on medical examination, be shown to have existed at the time when the original declaration was filed, and it is found not to be due to vicious habits, it shall be taken into account the same as if formally specified in the original application in estimating the degree of the permanent mental or physical disability to which it contributes.

It is clear that under these "instructions" the rejection of this claim for the reason given would be erroneous, since it is therein stated that a declaration "in the terms of the act," that is merely alleging an inability to earn a support by manual labor not due to vicious habits without naming any disabling cause producing such condition would be sufficient. Under said instructions, upon the medical examination disclosing the existence of a disabling cause not named or alleged by the soldier in his declaration for pension, he should have been called upon, and if he had lived would have have had the right, to supply any omission therein relative thereto by amendatory affidavit or by proof. Furthermore, the fourth instruction provides that a disabling cause not alleged but discovered on medical examination, if shown to have existed at the date of filing original declaration for pension and found not to be due to vicious habits, shall be taken into account the same as if specifically alleged in estimating the degree of a claimant's pensionable disability under said act.

The right of this appellant under the law to continue the prosecution and complete the claim of her deceased husband for the accrued pension that might be found due him upon its allowance carried with it and conferred upon her the right to take any steps and to do anything in the prosecution of said claim that the soldier might have done had he lived. She could not change the basis of said claim, nor enlarge its scope, nor introduce any new element therein not covered by and included in the claim as originally made by the soldier, but in so far as the prosecution and completion of the claim made by him was concerned she stood in the shoes of the deceased soldier, and was entitled to all the rights and privileges under the law and the rules and regulations of your Bureau that he would have had or might have exercised.

The claim of the soldier was for pension on account of an alleged inability to earn a support by manual labor not due to vicious habits. It was not necessary under said "instructions" for him to have alleged anything more than this relative to the disability upon which his claim was based, but he could and would have been permitted to supply by proof the necessary facts showing the origin and causes of the alleged disabling condition pensionable under said section. Necessarily, therefore, this appellant as his widow, completing said claim, should be permitted, under the allegations of the soldier's declaration for pension, to prove the existence of any disabling cause producing inability on the part of the soldier to earn a support by manual labor at the date of filing his declaration which might have been alleged by him in amendment or explanation of said declaration or which he might have established by proof. She should also have been accorded the privilege of supplying any omissions or making any corrections that the soldier would have had under the third of the foregoing "instructions."

In the present case the existence of a pensionable condition of inability to earn a support by manual labor, due to the disabling causes for which the medical referee states "a rating may be allowed," is clearly shown at and prior to the date of filing the soldier's declaration for pension, and there is no evidence on file tending to show that said disabling causes were either produced by, or aggravated in their effects by vicious habits.

Therefore the rejection of this claim upon the ground stated is hereby set aside and reversed, and you are requested to cause the same to be reopened and readjudicated in accordance with the views herein expressed.

———

COMMENCEMENT OF HELPLESS MINOR'S PENSION UNDER ACT OF JUNE 27, 1890.

MINOR OF JONATHAN TALBERT.

Pension to an insane, idiotic, or otherwise permanently helpless minor under section 3 of the act of June 27, 1890, can not be made to commence prior to the date of filing the declaration therefor after the passage of said act.

Assistant Secretary Webster Davis to the Commissioner of Pensions, February 26, 1898.

On March 27, 1897, this appellant's application, filed February 26, 1897, to change date of commencement of his pension as a helpless minor child from date of filing claim therefor, August 27, 1890, to date his original pension under the general law ceased, September 4, 1878, when he became 16 years of age, was rejected on the ground that he had no title to pension as a helpless child prior to the passage of the act June 27, 1890, and such pension was properly commenced from date of applying for same after that date; and he appealed, by guardian, August 18, 1897, contending that, under the law and the decisions of the Department, said pension as helpless child should commence as above claimed for.

Said act of June 27, 1890, provides expressly that continuance of pension on account of a minor child's insanity, idiocy, or helplessness, shall be "from the date of application therefor after the passage of (said) act." In view of this express provision of the statute as to commencement of pension thereunder on account of such condition of a child, it is not apparent upon what reasons appellant's contention is based. There is no occasion for construction, for the law is positive and explicit.

Rejection of this application to change date of commencement was clearly proper and is affirmed.

LINE OF DUTY—ON A PASS TO HUNT.

MARGARET M. HOFFMAN (WIDOW).

The War Department reports that soldier was accidentally killed in line of duty while on a pass to hunt; that hunting is encouraged in the Regular Army, and regarded as improving the soldiers as marksmen, and as much in the line of duty while on such pass to hunt as while undergoing small arms practice at the target range, and that a soldier killed or wounded while so engaged, not in consequence of any willful neglect or improper conduct on his part, is considered in line of duty.

Held:

1. That in view of the fact that the records of the War Department are usually accepted as conclusive upon all other questions relating to a soldier's service, the contemporaneous record made by the proper medical officer that soldier was in line of duty when killed should be regarded, in the absence of evidence to the contrary, as controlling upon that question.

2. In cases where such record does not appear, the question of line of duty must be determined by the best obtainable parol evidence in each case, showing the facts or circumstances under which the disability was incurred.

Assistant Secretary Webster Davis to the Commissioner of Pensions, February 26, 1898.

I am in receipt of the following communication from Acting Commissioner of Pensions Davenport, viz:

DEPARTMENT OF THE INTERIOR,
BUREAU OF PENSIONS,
Washington, D. C., September 3, 1897.

The honorable the SECRETARY OF THE INTERIOR.

SIR: I have the honor to forward herewith the papers in the claim of Margaret M. Hoffman, widow of Oskar Hoffman, band, Twenty-third United States Infantry, original No. 625659, together with correspondence from the Adjutant-General's Office, dated April 9, 1897, and August 28, 1897.

The question raised is one of vital importance, and is submitted for your consideration and decision, and the War Department has this day been advised that the matter has been transmitted to you for this action.

The War Department desires that some rule issue, or some decision be made relative to line of duty cases, where the soldier or sailor was engaged in athletic sports, or in pursuit of health or enjoyment, upon permission of the proper authorities, and in what might be considered line of duty, when disabilities had been contracted or death had resulted from such sports or athletic games.

The matter is submitted for your consideration and decision.

Very respectfully,

J. L. DAVENPORT,
Acting Commissioner.

The claim referred to was rejected by the Bureau, March 13, 1896, on the ground—

That the evidence fails to satisfactorily establish the service origin of fatal disability; soldier was accidentally killed while on pass, hunting, and it does not appear that he was under orders connected with the service.

On behalf of the widow, the adjutant of deceased soldier's regiment addressed the following communication to the Adjutant-General of the Army:

FORT CLARK.
Brackettville, Tex., March 11, 1897.

The ADJUTANT-GENERAL OF THE ARMY,
Washington, D. C.

(Through post headquarters.)

SIR: On behalf of Mrs. Margaret M. Hoffman, widow of Oskar Hoffman, late principal musician of the Twenty-third Infantry Band, I have the honor to submit the following statement, and to request that such action be taken as may be deemed proper:

Principal Musician Oskar Hoffman of the band, Twenty-third Infantry, was formally granted permission to hunt, and furnished with one regulation shotgun for hunting purposes, on September 7, 1895. In the afternoon of that date, and within four hours of his start from the post, he was shot and killed, and in due course of time Mrs. Margaret M. Hoffman, now residing at No. 314 Vinton street, San Antonio, Tex., made application for pension, case No. 625659.

On March 24, 1896, the Acting Commissioner of Pensions addressed a letter, a copy of which is hereto attached marked "Exhibit A," wherein the decision is made that the evidence fails to establish the service origin of the fatal disability.

In view of the fact that the evidence seems to have been complete to establish the identity of the claimant, and the circumstances under which her husband died in the military service, I have agreed to make this representation to the Department, in the hope that the worthy widow of one of the best musicians and most faithful soldiers that ever served in our regiment should not, through some technicality or misapprehension, go unrecognized in her just claim for relief. Aside from all existing orders and regulations, the theory of the military service has always been (and is more so now than ever) to encourage officers and enlisted men in hunting in the vicinity of their station. Passes or permission to hunt are never recorded as leaves of absences in the general acceptation of the term, either against enlisted man or officer, and in this particular case late Principal Musician Hoffman, who was to be absent for a few hours only, according to the official records, does not appear to have been entered either as absent from duty, or absent at all, on September 7, 1895, when he was furnished a band shotgun and granted permission to hunt in the vicinity of this post. Contrary to the opinion of the Commissioner of Pensions, paragraph 58, Army regulations distinctly makes an officer on any hunting expedition assume, or continue in, the status of duty while hunting, and requires of him an official report, which is an act of official duty, and if he be killed or injured during the period of hunting I do not believe that it could be legally held that his status was not one of duty. Therefore, reasoning by analogy, even should that become necessary, and with nothing whatever specified against it, the inference would clearly seem to be that the private soldier or noncommissioned officer who is granted permission to hunt (similar to permission for officers to hunt), assumes a status of duty similar to that of the officer, and any different ruling would not only work manifest injustice and hardship, as seems to be threatened now in this particular case, but would be contrary to Army regulation customs. Indeed, the late Principal Musician Hoffman, with a comrade, had been supplied with a quartermaster's hunting wagon, kept for hunting purposes, and in this connection the fact might be noted that in a letter of instruction received from headquarters of Texas, concerning practical instruction in drill and military and athletic exercises, it is distinctly set forth that hunting should be encouraged among officers and enlisted men whenever it is possible to organize parties without interfering with drills and other exercises. Although this letter bears date subsequent to the death of Principal Musician Hoffman, the letter itself bears evidence of that general progressive policy encouraging outdoor sports and athletic exercises among soldiers, especially hunting, which results in giving most useful information and knowledge to the soldier of the country adjacent to his military station.

Attention is respectfully invited to the important fact that on the muster roll of the field staff and band, Twenty-third Infantry, for the months of September and October, 1895, the remarks entered opposite the name of Principal Musician Hoffman in reporting his death are as follows:

"Died near Fort Clark, Tex., September 7, 1895, of shotgun wound left thigh, accidental, in line of duty, while on pass, hunting."

To this remark no exception was taken by the reviewing authority of the War Department; and in this connection it is respectfully maintained not only that the proper military authority is entitled to define duty status of a soldier, but the records of the War Department, and above all the muster rolls of military organizations, always so carefully guarded, must be considered the best evidence of the military history of officers and soldiers.

As the immediate commander of Principal Musician Hoffman, I desire to state that so far as I was aware at the time he had permission to hunt upon the same rules and regulations that governed the officer, and on the day he was killed was officially regarded as on duty. From time to time sergeants and other non-commissioned officers of organizations of this post have been granted permission to hunt which have never been recorded against them as absentees from duty, and, so far as I am aware, I believe it must be conceded that any member of this command, be he commissioned officer or enlisted soldier, at the time of his acceptance of permission to hunt has always been regarded on a status of duty, and I respectfully request that the fullest opportunity be given to this paper by its submission to the highest legal authority to test the question in dispute between the Acting Commissioner of Pensions and the claimant.

Very respectfully,

J. A. DAPRAY,
First Lieutenant and Adjutant, Twenty-third Infantry.

Said communication bears the following indorsements:

[First indorsement.]

FORT CLARK, TEX., *March 16, 1897.*
Respectfully forwarded through the adjutant-general, Department of Texas.

The question herein raised as to the status of soldiers while hunting, being one of such general and vital interest, affecting the entire service, it is respectfully recommended that such action be taken as will meet the purpose of the within communication, the statements and arguments of which are approved and indorsed.

SAML. OVERSHINE,
Colonel Twenty-third Infantry, Commanding Post.

[Second indorsement.]

HEADQUARTERS DEPARTMENT OF TEXAS,
San Antonio, March 18, 1897.
Respectfully forwarded to the Adjutant-General of the Army.

ARTHUR MACARTHUR,
Assistant Adjutant-General in the absence of the Department Commander.

[Third indorsement.]

WAR DEPARTMENT,
ADJUTANT-GENERAL'S OFFICE,
Washington, March 29, 1897.

Respectfully referred, by direction of the Secretary of War, to the Surgeon-General, United States Army, for any remarks he may desire to make on the subject herein referred to.

J. B. BABCOCK,
Assistant Adjutant-General.

[Fourth indorsement.]

WAR DEPARTMENT,
SURGEON-GENERAL'S OFFICE,
March 30, 1897.

Respectfully returned to the Adjutant-General of the Army.

Questions relating to "line of duty" come so frequently before officers of the medical department that, as an aid to them in the formation of an opinion for entry on the medical records of a case, instructions were published November 5, 1896, by authority of the Secretary of War. (See marked paragraphs of the accompanying inclosure.)

In view of these instructions the medical officer was right in recording the death of Oskar Hoffman, late principal musician Twenty-third Infantry, as having occurred in the line of duty. The man was killed while on pass, hunting, and it does not appear that his death was due to willful neglect or immoral conduct. How far the officers of the Pension Bureau of the Interior Department should be influenced on questions of line of duty by the War Department record is a subject for others to discuss, but I may be permitted to state that when such questions come before me in adjudications under the laws relating to artificial limbs (R. S., 4787) I decide the case by the War Department record and wholly irrespective of the view taken by the Interior Department in decisions relating to pensions.

I respectfully suggest that these papers be referred to the Judge-Advocate-General of the Army for his views on the subject.

GEO. M. STERNBURG,
Surgeon-General, United States Army.

The marked paragraphs of the instructions referred to in the preceding indorsement of the Surgeon-General of the Army are as follows:

In Column XIII the opinion of the medical officer, based on a full consideration of all the facts as to whether the disease or injury occurred in the line of duty, should be explicitly stated as *yes* or *no*. In forming and recording this opinion medical officers will be guided by the following instructions:

(*a*) All diseases contracted or injuries received while an officer or soldier is in the military service of the United States may be assumed to have occurred in the line of duty unless the surgeon knows, first, that the disease or injury existed before entering the service; second, that it was contracted while absent from duty on furlough or without permission, or, third, that it occurred in consequence of willful neglect or immoral conduct of the man himself.

(*b*) When a soldier is disabled while on pass or in confinement, the question of line of duty must be determined by the circumstances attending the incurrence of the disability, but the fact of being on pass or in confinement should be stated.

(*c*) When a medical officer expresses the opinion that an injury occurring during athletic sports, properly indulged in, was received in the line of duty, the opinion is accepted by the Surgeon-General as satisfactory and final.

(*d*) In all cases in which the opinion is expressed by *no* the circumstances attending the incidence of the disability and on which the negative opinion is based should be stated in Column XII, or across the face of the columns on its left if space can be economized in that way.

The communication referred to and the indorsements quoted were referred to the Judge-Advocate-General of the Army by the following indorsement:

[Fifth indorsement.]

ADJUTANT-GENERAL'S OFFICE,
April 1, 1897.

Respectfully referred to the Judge-Advocate-General of the Army, with request that these papers be returned to this office with an expression of his views on the subject in question.

By order of the Secretary of War:

J. B. BABCOCK,
Assistant Adjutant-General.

The following indorsements express the opinions of the Judge-Advocate and Adjutant Generals of the Army and the Secretary of War on the subject submitted to this Department for an opinion:

[Sixth indorsement.]

WAR DEPARTMENT, JUDGE-ADVOCATE-GENERAL'S OFFICE,
Washington, D. C., April 3, 1897.

Respectfully returned to the Adjutant-General.

Principal Musician Oskar Hoffman, band, Twenty-third Infantry, was accidentally killed while on pass hunting, and his widow's claim for pension has been rejected by the Bureau of Pensions for the reason, as stated, that—

"The soldier was accidentally killed while on pass hunting, and it does not appear that he was under orders connected with the service."

I invite attention to my views, as stated, for the information of the Chief of the Record and Pension Office in the case of Joseph Shoemaker, October 15, 1896, a copy of which was, I understand, furnished to the Adjutant-General.

By the practice of the War Department a soldier on pass is held not to be taken out of the line of duty by that fact, and this, it would seem, includes the hunting pass. There is no reason why it should not, and in fact, hunting being encouraged, there would seem to be a very good reason for holding that in doing what he is encouraged to do the soldier is not taken out of the line of duty thereby. It is so held by the Board of Commissioners of the Soldiers' Home.

But the Interior Department has its own rulings in regard to what constitutes line of duty for pension purposes, and in the case of James E. Harrison held, under date of December 22, 1893, that the claimant, having received permission to hunt for his own recreation and while hunting having been shot in the hand by an accidental discharge of his gun, he was not in the line of duty. (7 Decisions Department of the Interior.)

G. NORMAN LIEBER,
Judge-Advocate-General.

[Seventh indorsement.]

ADJUTANT GENERAL'S OFFICE, *April 9, 1897.*

Respectfully submitted to the Secretary of War.

Permission to hunt is not held by the Government as leave of absence. The object of this absence is to improve the soldier as a marksman. While hunting he is held to be as much on his way to the position of a sharpshooter as he is while on the target range. For this reason the military authorities hold that a soldier absent from his post with permission to hunt is as much on duty as he is while undergoing small-arms practice at the target. It may be held that hunting is a recreation; it may as well be held that target practice is a recreation, for to certain men it is found to be so. Shooting at moving game is better practice for the soldier than firing at a stationary target.

In view of the importance to the service of a mutual agreement between the two Departments on the question, it is recommended that this case be referred to the Commissioner of Pensions for consideration in relation to the rulings of the former Commissioner of Pensions.

GEO. D. RUGGLES, Adjutant-General.

[Eighth indorsement.]

WAR DEPARTMENT,
Washington, April 13, 1897.

Respectfully referred to the Commissioner of Pensions.

I concur in the views expressed by the Adjutant-General in regard to the status of men absent from their posts with permission to hunt.

R. A. ALGER, Secretary of War.

From these papers two principal facts will be noted. The first is that the War Department does not regard an officer or soldier while on pass, hunting, as on leave of absence from his command, and while no order, general or special, is ever issued requiring them to engage in such sport or occupation, it is permitted and encouraged, as being for the good of the service and the improvement of the soldier's marksmanship. The second fact is that before alluded to, that when a soldier is disabled or killed while engaged in such sport, it is left to the medical officer to inquire into all the facts connected with the incurrence of disability or death and to determine whether he was in the line of duty: but these pertain exclusively to the rules and methods of that Department, and are binding only within its jurisdiction.

It has always been the settled conviction of this Department, as enunciated in many decisions, that in the administration of the pension laws the Bureau of Pensions is charged with determining for itself and upon all the evidence before it whether a soldier incurred his disability or death in the line of duty before allowance of pension can be made on account of his service. And in the pursuance of this policy the records of the War Department, in so far as they show facts, are accepted as evidence to be considered with other evidence on the subject. Due consideration is also given to the manner in which that Department regards the status of a soldier under certain circumstances, but mere opinion expressed where facts are not fully stated have no force to control the action of the Bureau.

In short, just as the War Department has a method of its own for ascertaining whether the disability or death of a soldier was incurred in line of duty, by leaving it to a medical officer to inquire into all the facts and circumstances and accepting his report as conclusive, so the Bureau of Pensions has the right to know all facts connected with the incurrence of disability and death, and is free to form its own conclusions without reference to an expression of opinion from the War or other Department. This right or duty has never been disputed, and is recognized by the Surgeon-General and Judge-Advocate-General of the Army in their reports quoted.

Furthermore, in the adjudication of claims of similar import to the one under consideration certain general propositions have controlled in deciding the question as to line of duty. Among these may be mentioned the general definition of what constitutes line of duty for pensionable purposes, contained in an opinion by Attorney-General Cushing (7 Op., 149), from which I quote the following:

Every person who enters the military service of the country—officer, soldier, sailor, or marine—takes upon himself certain moral or legal engagements of duty, which constitute his official or professional obligations. While in the performance of those things which the law requires of him as military duty he is in the line of his duty. But, at the same time, though a soldier or sailor, he is not the less a man and a citizen, with private rights to exercise and duties to perform; and while attending to these things he is not in the line of his public duty. In addition to this, a soldier or sailor, like any other man, has the physical faculty of doing many things which are in violation of duties, either general or special; and in doing these things he is not acting in the line of his duty. Around all those acts of the soldier or sailor, which are official in their nature, the pension law draws a legislative line, and then they say to the soldier or sailor: If while performing these acts which are within that line you thereby incur disability or death, you or your widow or children, as the case may be, shall receive a pension or other allowance; but not if the disability or death arise from acts performed outside of that line—that is, absolutely disconnected from and wholly independent of the performance of duty. Was the cause of disability or of death a cause within the line of duty or outside of it? Was that cause appertaining to, dependent upon, or otherwise necessarily and essentially connected with duty within the line, or was it unappertenant, independent, and not of necessary and essential connection? That, in my judgment, is the true test criterion of this class of pension cases under consideration.

The proposed criterion is deduced from the nature of things. Congress, if it had so pleased, might have prescribed an arbitrary general rule; as, for example, pension to all cases of disability or death in service, except in the contingency of misconduct; or pension for all cases, except where the cause of disability or death should occur while the party is in arrest or under sentence, on furlough, or leave of absence. Such a rule, like all other rules of an assumed arbitrary standard, might have been easier to administer than a natural rule, for the latter demands, in use, discriminating examination and just appreciation of the nature of the included subject matter; but the natural rule is the only just and equitable one, whether as regards the right of persons in the service and their families, or the policy of the Government.

The proposed criterion may shut out some cases of a class admitted heretofore through inadvertence, or from the absence of any definite rule whatever to work by, and the scope thus afforded for the action of biases and for mere discretion; as, for instance, disabilities or deaths produced by causes of disease or casualties having no relation whatever to the military service. True; and to pension disabilities or deaths occurring in the mere course of nature, and having no relation of casualty in duty, or disabilities or deaths produced by diseases or casualties happening to an officer or soldier in the prosecution and pursuit of his private affairs and amusements, or while employed on furlough in lucrative occupation, not official, is not required by any consideration of public service. On the other hand, the criterion proposed will bring in many cases heretofore excluded unjustly, and through disregard or nonperception of the true theory of reason or right, and of public policy in these matters, which is to bestow disability or death pensions only in these cases, but in all those cases where the cause of disability or death is the logical incident or provable effect of duty in the service.

Allow me, dismissing all further discussion of the cases thus excluded, to recall attention to the cases thus included.

When it is remembered that no commissioned officer or enlisted soldier, seaman, or marine has power to cast off his obligation at will; that whether he be on duty or off, in glory or disgrace, still the banner of his country is over him and its oath upon his conscience; when this great fact shall be remembered, it must be inevitable to concede that any rule based upon the assumption of its being impossible for an officer or soldier on furlough, on leave of absence, in arrest, under sentence, to perform acts, suffer casualties, receive wounds, or incur causes of disease, in the line of his duty, is not a truth, and, like all things not true, can not be conformable to justice or wisdom. As, while on active duty, he may do or suffer things not in the line of his duty, so while off duty, or on furlough, or under censure, he may do and suffer things which are in the line of duty. The letter of the law prescribes that the quality of the act or condition, as whether in the line of duty or not in it, shall determine the question of pension. That alone is just and wise, and that is the thought which, according to my reading of the statutes, has, from the beginning of this course of legislation to the end, held its place with unchangeable constancy in all the acts of Congress.

The idea that furlough or leave of absence must of necessity exclude an officer from all benefits of the pension laws may have arisen from the fact that officers are furloughed or put on leave of absence from time to time for the purpose of enabling them to enter into lucrative private pursuits, or for some other cause which implies negation of public duty. In such cases the officer will of course be excluded from the purview of the pension laws, not because of the furlough or leave of absence per se, but because of the special occasion or consequences thereof.

In regard to arrest, again, suppose that on march, in camp or garrison, or on a voyage, an officer is put in arrest on charges. In the first place those charges may not be substantiated, and then it would be manifestly unjust that the mere fact of his being charged would operate to deprive himself or his family of pension. Or, while he is in arrest, he dies of camp fever or ship fever, and then it is unjust to presume a criminality not proved in the course of law. Or, whether guilty or not, if he dies of wounds, casualty, or disease contracted while in arrest, still the death is not the consequence of the arrest, but of the public service. If not dying in arrest, and on trial being convicted and sentenced, that sentence being of death or dismissal for some grave military crime, that of course terminates the question of pension; but if his offense be a light one, with a sentence of reprimand, for instance, and he shall have happened to contract disability or mortal disease while in arrest, as by the hazards of a long march or voyage, it seems not just to add to his legal sentence the serious indirect aggravation of incapacity of pension. All these difficulties are avoided or conciliated by directing inquiry to the question, was the cause of disability or death, or was it not, an act of his official military duty?

I believe that the views thus presented constitute a reply to the compound question proposed by the Commissioner, in all its parts, except such as are questions of evidence. All these questions are referable to settled principles, and may be disposed of in a few words.

In the first place, casualty is a question of fact, to be proved according to the ordinary rules of evidence and to the reasonable satisfaction of the inquiring and deciding mind. That mind is entitled to have the very facts before it, and is not bound to accept as final the opinions even of an expert. Such opinions are evidence, but neither conclusive nor exclusive proof. Every person of judicial training well knows that the opinions of medical or other scientific or practical experts often differ, and that they sometimes err in a body as if by some epidemic contagion. There is a judicial case involving scientific inquiry, in the printed record of which are the answers of twenty-three experts to the same question; twenty-two of them give decision one way, and a single one of them gives a reverse decision; and, in the conclusion it was proved beyond all controversy that he alone was right, and that all the others erred. In general the opinions of an expert are of more or less weight and value, according to the person's constitution of mind and the degree of completeness of the collection of pertinent facts on which his mind acts. But it may happen that the great body of the wisest and most learned men of science shall be possessed by an erroneous opinion, while the true secret of nature is revealed to some discoverer who, as yet, is unknown to the world, and is painfully struggling up into the sunlight of greatness and of fame. In a word, no witness, whether expert or not, can rightfully claim to have his opinion take the place of the facts, and so to substitute his judgment for that of the Commissioner.

In the second place, the question of the quality or degree of proof requisite is a question clearly for the conscience of the Commissioner. If called upon to suggest any rule for the guidance of his discretion in the matter, it would be obvious for you to say that the pension laws are beneficial in their nature, and therefore to be construed beneficially in matters of inevitable doubt. In this view it seems to me not that the mere fact of an officer having died in the service and with utter absence of proof as to the origin or cause of his death suffices to raise a pension, but that where the proofs are balanced and it is impossible to determine by them as to the fact of "disease contracted" and the fact of "line of duty," found in juxtaposition, whether this collocation be of contiguity only or of actor and subject, of contemporaneity or sequence only, or of cause and consequence, it would be reasonable to presume in favor of the pension, and also to presume in favor of the pension in cases where the line of duty appears to enter potentially into the causes of the death, although it should happen not to be certainly provable that it was the exclusive or predominant cause; so that a possible error of absolute and mere uncertainty shall not be suffered to defeat the liberal intentions and beneficial policy of the Government.

In consonance with this statement of the law, it has been held also that a soldier while in the pursuit of his own pleasure and recreation, or engaged in private business, and not in the performance of those things which the law requires of him as a military duty, can not be considered in the line of duty, whether he was acting with permission or not. Many examples in point might be cited from former decisions, but it is sufficient to state that, as a general rule, in all cases rejected because disability or death was not incurred in line of duty, the soldier was not engaged in anything connected with his military duty or that could be considered a part of such duty.

And this leads up to the consideration, in the case referred by you, of the question whether a soldier, engaged as this one is shown to have been, should be regarded as in the line of duty. Usually, and in some particular cases heretofore decided, where a soldier has been given permission to hunt and engaged in that sport for his own pleasure and recreation, he was held to be acting outside of his military duty, and when injured or killed while so engaged, it was declared that no title to pension existed in him or his representatives. But the statements of the Adjutant General and the other officers, whose reports are herein quoted, present the question in a new phase, and in view of the aspect in which a soldier while on pass hunting is regarded by the War Department, it may be assumed that the sport or occupation has become something of a quasi-military duty, and when pursued under the circumstances reported by Adjutant Dapray, includes not only the consideration of the soldier's own pleasure, but the development of his efficiency as well. Being supplied with a regulation shotgun and with a quartermaster's hunting wagon, kept for hunting purposes, and it being further true that hunting is distinctly encouraged among officers and men, thus becoming a custom almost amounting to a regulation of the Army, it would seem that the soldier was largely relieved of the responsibility attaching to a voluntary act, and was virtually in the position of obeying instructions in going out to hunt.

Just how long it has been the policy of the War Department to permit and encourage such sports for the purposes stated is not known, but it is presumed to antedate the time of this soldier's death. It is a fact, however, as shown by Adjutant Dapray's letter, that the special instructions in this regard in the Department of Texas were given subsequent to the soldier's death. But this may not be important in view of the general policy which prevailed and of the opinions expressed by the Adjutant-General of the Army and the Secretary of War.

This case is not parallel with the James E. Harrison case (7 P.D., 97, referred to by the Judge-Advocate-General of the Army.

In that case the claimant testified that he was detailed as a cook, and was excused from all guard or picket duty or duty of a military character. At the time soldier was wounded hunting was not encouraged by the Army, nor was it the custom to engage in target practice. No guns for hunting purposes were furnished by the Government, as is now the case in time of peace at frontier posts. In fact, soldier was acting in violation of orders, as there were strict orders against carrying arms about except when on duty.

This case is analogous to that of Henry Newman (8 P. D., 532), wherein the rejection of the claim on the ground that soldier " did not incur the alleged injury in line of duty, as he was playing base ball at the time for his own amusement, and was not engaged in the performance of any military duty," was reversed.

In this case Assistant Secretary Reynolds used this language:

The soldier was not disobeying any order or command of the Army while engaged in the game of base ball which resulted in his injury; but, upon the other hand, he was performing an exercise calculated to strengthen his body and make him a more efficient soldier. Surely an exercise of that kind, when properly indulged in, was appurtenant to his line of duty, although not compelled in its performance by any rule or regulation of the Army.

It is evident from the foregoing that no definite or unvarying rule as to line of duty can properly be laid down, but each case must rest upon the particular facts appearing therein.

In view of the fact, however, that the records of the War Department are usually accepted as conclusive upon all other questions relating to the soldier's service, I see no good reason why the contemporaneous record made by the proper medical officer to the effect that in a given case the disability alleged was incurred in the line of duty should not be regarded in the absence of evidence to the contrary as controlling upon that question.

In cases where such record does not appear the question of line of duty must be determined by the best obtainable parole evidence in each case, showing the facts or circumstances under which the disability was incurred.

On the basis, then, already stated, that the soldier was engaged in a quasi-military duty, and not strictly in pursuit of his own business or pleasure, and also from the fact that the contemporaneous record distinctly states he was in the line of duty, it is concluded that the action of the Bureau in rejecting this claim on the ground stated, that soldier's death while on a pass hunting had no connection with his military service was error, and it is accordingly reversed.

EVIDENCE—INCURRENCE—ELLET'S RAM FLEET.

NOAH PERRY.

Appellant claims pension for disability from being scalded with hot water and steam while serving on the ram *Lancaster* in an engagement with the Confederate ram *Arkansas*. There is no record of incurrence of said disabling cause, of service on the *Lancaster*, nor of the *Lancaster* herself; but it is an accepted historical fact that said ram was disabled in July, 1862, by the ram *Arkansas* and that many of her men were scalded; and it is shown that appellant served on said ram, and was injured in line of duty as alleged, but the evidence of the existence and continuance since his discharge of any permanent disabling effects of said injury not being satisfactorily shown the case is returned for a special examination.

Assistant Secretary Webster Davis to the Commissioner of Pensions, February 28, 1898.

This appellant, Noah Perry, Company I, Sixty-third Illinois Volunteer Infantry, is a pensioner under the provisions of the general law (Certificate No. 294975) at the rate of $12 per month for malarial poisoning, chronic diarrhea, and resulting piles, and on June 24, 1891, he filed in your Bureau an application for additional pension, based on disease of lungs, throat, and heart, alleged to have been contracted in line of duty during his military service, which was rejected on May 23, 1895, upon the ground of the insufficiency of the evidence to establish the service origin or existence at discharge of said alleged additional disabling causes.

From said action appeal was taken on January 26, 1898.

The appellant alleges and contends that he was injured in July, 1862, while serving on detail in the "Mississippi Marine Brigade," or "Ellet's Ram Fleet," on board the ram *Lancaster*, a vessel of said organization, during an engagement between the *Lancaster* and the Confederate ram *Arkansas* on the Mississippi River, near the mouth of the Yazoo, above Vicksburg, by being scalded with hot water and steam about the head and chest, and inhaling superheated steam, to which he attributes the alleged disease of lungs, throat, and heart for which he claims additional pension.

The official military record in the War Department of the appellant's service shows that he was enrolled as a private of Company I, Sixty-third Illinois Volunteer Infantry, on December 1, 1861, at Olney, for three years, and was mustered into service on April 10, 1862, at Jonesboro, Ill. He appears to have been present with his company until May 17, 1862, on which date he is reported to have been detached for service with the "Mississippi Ram Fleet." It does not appear that he was ever returned to duty with his regiment, but he was borne upon the rolls thereof as on detached service until he was formally transferred to the "Marine Brigade," on February 11, 1863, by Special Orders, No. 69, from the War Department. His name was borne upon the rolls of the *Switzerland* company, Mississippi Marine Brigade, until August, 1864, when it was taken upon the rolls of Company A, Marine Regiment, United States Volunteers, to which he was transferred with other members of the first-named company who were not entitled to muster out of service when that company was discontinued by orders dated August 3, 1864. He was mustered out of service with Company A, Marine Regiment, United States Volunteers, at Vicksburg, Miss., on January 18, 1865, under Special Orders, No. 431, of the War Department, dated December 5, 1864, because the services of the organization were no longer required.

The record fails to show that the appellant served on the *Lancaster*, or that he was injured in the manner alleged by him, the only record connecting him in any way with that vessel being a hospital record showing that on August 4, 1862—

Noah Perry, seaman, ram *Lancaster*, entered Overton General Hospital, Memphis, Tenn., with typhoid fever; no disposition stated.

The Surgeon-General reports that no hospital records of the Mississippi Marine Brigade were ever on file in his office. In a communication from the Chief of the Record and Pension Office of the War Department, dated May 17, 1894, and on file with the papers in this case, he states: "There are no records of the ram *Lancaster* on file in this office;" and in a subsequent communication, dated January 3, 1898, also on file, he states:

There are no rolls or other records on file in this office showing the names of the men who served on the *Lancaster*, and it is impossible, therefore, to verify the allegation that Perry served on that vessel. It should be remarked, however, that it is not improbable that he served on the *Lancaster* before he was formally transferred to the Marine Brigade and assigned to duty on the *Switzerland*.

The Navy Department reports that there are no records whatever pertaining to the Mississippi Marine Brigade, or the vessels composing it, or the men serving thereon, on file in that Department. It was this absence of a record of service on the *Lancaster*, of the *Lancaster* itself, of the engagement and disabling of said vessel by the Confederate vessel *Arkansas*, and of the consequent injury alleged by the appellant from the explosion and escape of steam from her boilers, occasioned by a shot from the enemy piercing them, of medical or hospital treatment for said injuries, and of medical testimony showing the existence of said alleged injuries during service, that appears to have been one of the principal causes of the rejection of this claim upon the ground stated by your Bureau. It is shown by the record, however, that at the time he alleges he was injured, the appellant was serving on detached duty with the Mississippi Marine Brigade, also called "Ellet's Ram Fleet," and it is a well-established fact that owing to the peculiar and anomalous character of this organization, which was a naval flotilla operating on the Western rivers, organized by the Quartermaster-General's Office of the War Department, and under the nominal control of that Department, but at the same time cooperating with the naval forces, and, more or less, under the command and direction of the naval commanders in those waters, there is almost an entire absence of the usual official rep :rts and records relating to its organization and operations during the war of the rebellion, or any reliable or complete record of the vessels composing said flotilla, or of the service of the men who served thereon. This peculiar characteristic of the "Mississippi Marine Brigade" or "Ram Fleet" was called to the attention of this Department and carefully considered in connection with the case of John G. Coney (3 P. D., 200), decided September 30, 1889. In that case the claimant for pension had been an engineer on board the *Diana*, one of the vessels composing said "Ram Fleet," and the question involved was as to the character of said vessel, and in deciding his case on appeal the Depaitment stated (3 P. D., 202) as follows:

The claimant served as first engineer on board the steamer *Diana* from March 1, 1861, to July 9, 1864. The steamer *Diana* was a vessel attached to what was known as the Mississippi Marine Brigade, sometimes called "Ellet's Ram Fleet," which was organized during the war of the rebellion for service upon the Mississippi River and upon its tributaries. Said command or "fleet" appears to have occupied a rather peculiar and anomalous position, the exact status of the several vessels composing it being difficult to determine. It was organized under the War Department, and was under the command, first, of Col. Charles Ellet, who was fatally injured by the enemy in the battle of Memphis, in which the "fleet" was engaged; and afterwards of Col. Alfred W. Ellet, both officers having been detailed from the Army for that purpose. The vessels composing said "fleet" or "Marine Brigade" were purchased by the Quartermaster-General of the Army under direction of the Secretary of War. Each vessel was officered and manned by civilians, who were hired and paid by the Quartermaster's Department of the Army, and had on board, in addition to its regular crew, a detachment of enlisted men, under command, in some instances, of an officer or two, detailed from the Army. Some of these vessels were designated as "rams" and were fitted up and armed for offensive and defensive operations against the enemy; others were denominated as "transports;" but it is impossible to determine from the designation given in the records of the War and Treasury Departments what vessels composing said command were strictly "war vessels," and what not, some of those designated as "transports" appearing to have been as well armed, and, in the capacity of "gunboats," as actively employed in warlike operations, as those designated as "rams." In fact, owing to the peculiar circumstances connected with the organization of this command and to the anomalous position which it occupied in the service, the information to be derived from the official records as to the exact status of the officers and men composing the crews of these vessels in contradistinction from the detail of enlisted men of the Army that each had on board, as well as to the status of any one particular vessel of said command or "fleet," is both meager and unsatisfactory.

And again (on p. 205, same case), the Department states:

As a matter of course, if there were an official record of the War Department stating with distinctness and giving with certainty the character of said vessel and the nature of the service in which she was employed, such record would, under the long established rulings of the Department, have to be accepted as conclusive, and any error contained in such record could be corrected only by the Department from which it emanated; but amid the uncertainty which exists in this case, when the official records disclose absolutely nothing definite from which a satisfactory conclusion can be drawn, this Department would be certainly justified in determining for itself the character and service of said vessel from the next best evidence that could be obtained.

A striking illustration of this singular lack of official reports and records relative to the most important events and circumstances connected with the operations and service rendered by the Mississippi Marine Brigade is presented in this case. In reply to a communication from the Hon. Charles F. Manderson, a Senator from the State of Nebraska, requesting information concerning the engagement between the ram *Lancaster* and the Confederate ram *Arkansas*, about July 16, 1862, in which the boilers of the *Lancaster* were injured, resulting in an explosion by which this appellant alleges he was injured, the superintendent of Naval War Records of the Navy Department states, in a communication dated January 24, 1895, and on file in this case, as follows:

I regret to say that while this event appears, according to numerous responsible histories, a well-established fact, still there are no official reports in this office from the Union side pertaining to it. At the time of the passage of the Confederate ram *Arkansas* through the Federal fleet above Vicksburg, July 15, 1862, the ram fleet (of which the *Lancaster* was a part), under command of Brig. Gen. Alfred W. Ellet, was under the direction of the War Department; and although copies of General Ellet's papers are on file in this office, there is no report of the particular affair desired. The War Department also appears to have no report from him on the subject, nor do Flag Officers Farragut or Davis, both of whom were present, make any mention of the explosion of the *Lancaster's* boiler in their official reports. * * * The only explanation I can offer for the omission of the official reports of this affair is the fact that the correspondence pertaining to it is very incomplete, owing to the dual command of the ram fleet, which, although under the original control of the War Department, was still, more or less, cooperating with the naval forces in those waters.

And yet, the engagement between the *Lancaster* and the *Arkansas* on the Mississippi River near Vicksburg in July, 1862, and the disabling of the *Lancaster* by a shot piercing her boilers, causing an explosion by which many of her crew were scalded and disabled, is an established and accepted historical fact, as well authenticated as any other event during the war of the rebellion.

In the third volume of the series "The Navy in the Civil War," published by Charles Scribner's Sons, New York, 1883, entitled "The Gulf and Inland Waters," Capt. A. T. Mahan (United States Navy), describing the passage of the Confederate ram *Arkansas* through the Federal fleet on the Mississippi River above Vicksburg in July, 1862, states, on page 102, as follows:

She fought her way boldly through, passing between the vessels of war and the transports, firing and receiving the fire of each as she went by, most of the projectiles bounding harmlessly from her sides; but two 11-inch shells came through killing many and setting on fire the cotton backing. On the other hand, the *Lancaster* of the ram fleet which made a move toward her, got a shot in the mud receiver which disabled her, scalding many of her people, two of them fatally. The whole affair with the fleets lasted but a few minutes, and the *Arkansas*, having passed out of range, found refuge under the Vicksburg batteries.

Since this appellant is shown by the record to have belonged to that portion of the force serving in the Mississippi Marine Brigade, composed of enlisted men detailed from the army, the character of the vessel upon which he was serving when he alleges he received his injuries becomes an immaterial question for pensionable purposes, but it may be as well to state in passing that in a communication on file with the papers in this case, dated January 3, 1898, from the Chief of the Record and Pension Office of the War Department, the following statement is made:

Reports and correspondence that are on file in this Department, and are printed in the Rebellion Records show conclusively that the ram *Lancaster* was not a transport, but was an armed vessel.

In view of the conditions indicated by the foregoing it is clear that an official record of the service of this appellant on board the *Lancaster*, of the incurrence of the injuries alleged by him thereon, and of subsequent medical and hospital treatment for the same upon the hospital boat attached to said "ram fleet," could hardly be expected, and the absence of such record should not have been permitted to militate against the allowance of his claim, if his allegations relative to the incurrence of his disability are corroborated by other competent evidence.

That appellant was serving on the *Lancaster* in July 1862, that he was on board of said vessel during her engagement with the *Arkansas*, and that he was among the number of her crew who were badly scalded and injured by hot water and by inhaling steam escaping from her boilers when they were pierced by a shot from the enemy, is shown by the testimony of the first master and executive officer of the *Lancaster*, the second mate of that vessel, and three comrades of his company and regiment who were also members of the detachment and serving with him on the *Lancaster* at that time. The service of the two officers on board the *Lancaster* at the time of said engagement does not appear to be questioned, and the record shows that the three other witnesses were detailed at the same time with the appellant from Company I, Sixty-third Illinois Volunteer Infantry for service in the "Mississippi Marine Brigade." These witnesses are all reported to be of good character and credibility, and no reason whatever appears in the papers in this case for doubting the truthfulness of their statements. They state that the appellant was first sent to Overton General Hospital, Memphis, Tenn., for treatment for his injuries, and was subsequently treated therefor on board the hospital boat attached to said "Ram Fleet," at that time the *Queen of the West*. A comrade of appellant's company states in an affidavit filed in his claim for original pension in March

1884, that about July 1862, between Vicksburg and Memphis, he waited upon and nursed the appellant on board the *Queen of the West*, who was then totally disabled, but he failed to remember the nature of his disability.

The three comrades who served on board the *Lancaster*, and subsequently on the *Switzerland* of the "Ram Fleet" with the appellant, testify that he complained during his subsequent service, and suffered with some affection or disease of his throat and lungs, which he attributed to his having inhaled hot steam at the time he was injured and scalded on board the *Lancaster*.

I am clearly of the opinion that the evidence is sufficient to establish the fact that the appellant was injured in the service and in line of duty, as he alleges, but the evidence of the existence at and continuance since his discharge from the service of any permanent disabling effects of said injury is extremely weak and unsatisfactory. The appellant is shown by medical examinations to have suffered since the date of filing this claim for additional pension with some bronchial and catarrhal troubles, somewhat in the nature of bronchial asthma, but a pathological connection between these later affections and the injury he received on board the *Lancaster* in 1862 has not been satisfactorily established. The testimony relative to his physical condition in service subsequent to his injury and at the time of his discharge is both meager and inconclusive, failing to indicate clearly that he was at that time suffering from any severe disability, or the nature of his disability, if any. But one witness testifies to the existence of throat or lung disease soon after appellant's discharge, and his affidavit is so indefinite and states so few facts that it throws but little light on this phase of the case. There is no positive evidence showing existence of throat or lung trouble prior to about 1868, and no medical evidence showing the existence of these diseases or treatment therefor prior to 1870. The medical examinations of appellant show that no pensionable disability from heart disease has existed since the date of filing declaration for additional pension, and the evidence fails to indicate its existence prior to that time.

Although the evidence now in the case can not be accepted as establishing a connection between appellant's present disease of throat and lungs and the alleged injury in service, I am clearly of the opinion that an injury from scalding of head and chest and from inhaling hot steam in service and line of duty has been proved, and that this claim should not have been rejected without further investigation relative to the existence and continuance of the alleged results of said injury. No special examination of this case appears ever to have been made, which unquestionably should have been done. The physical condition and state of health of the appellant, the nature of his disabilities, if any, during the period of more than two years that he served in the Mississippi Marine Brigade, subsequent to July, 1862, when he was injured, and at the date of his discharge, should be ascertained if possible, by careful inquiry among the surviving officers and comrades with whom he served in said organization. His condition from discharge, and the nature of any disability suffered by him, as well as when throat and lung trouble was first observed by those most intimately associated with him, and how long it has continued since discharge should be ascertained, and the evidence thus obtained should be submitted to and carefully considered by the medical officers of your bureau, who should be called upon to state, in the light of the information thus obtained, whether the present bronchial and catarrhal affection of the appellant could be accepted as a pathological result of injury from scalding and inhaling hot steam in 1862.

In order, therefore, that this claim may be investigated and adjudicated upon the lines above indicated, your action rejecting the same is hereby reversed and set aside, and you are requested to cause the same to be reopened and readjudicated, in accordance with the suggestions herein contained.

EVIDENCE—PRESUMPTION OF DEATH—MARRIAGE.

ANNIE DENNIS, FORMERLY RENO (WIDOW).

Claimant's first husband left her in Missouri, in 1873, to go to Chicago, Ill., for medical treatment, and a few months later she received a letter from his sister informing her that he was dead. Relying on the truth of this statement, she married one Holmes in December, 1877, who procured a divorce from her on the ground of desertion in 1882. In April, 1883, claimant married the soldier who died in July, 1890. Her first husband has never been heard of in that community since 1873.

Held: These facts are sufficient to raise the presumption that claimant's first husband had died prior to her marriage to Holmes, and her marriage to the soldier was legal, and she is his widow.

Assistant Secretary Webster Davis to the Commissioner of Pensions, March 7, 1898.

Claimant on September 13, 1897, filed a motion for reconsideration of Departmental decision on March 4, 1895, affirming the Bureau action of January 9, 1894, rejecting her widow's claim (No. 753052), filed August 22, 1890, under section 2 of act of June 27, 1890, on the ground that the evidence, after special investigation, failed to prove the death of claimant's first husband.

Claimant contends that the Department erred in applying the law of presumption of death, and cites the cases of Marie Sharpe (8 P. D., 175); Caroline A. Sickles (6 P. D., 164); Sarah Gorby (4 P. D., 298); Davie v. Briggs (97 U. S., 628); Greenleaf on Evidence, paragraph 42; Rice on Evidence, pp. 764 and 1223; 49 Ill. S. C. Rep., 470; 3 Bibb Ky., 233; 52 Maine, 465; 34 Mich., 34; 42 Pa., 159; and the act of Congress approved March 13, 1896,

The testimony in this case shows that claimant was married to Charles Harmer, at Kahoka, Clark County, Mo., in 1869, and lived and cohabited with him as his wife until the spring of 1873, when he left her to go to Chicago for medical treatment, he having previously been absent from her for medical treatment for about a year. Two children were born as the issue of this marriage, a boy about one year after the marriage and a girl some few months after claimant's said husband last left her.

Claimant testified that she had letters written for her to her husband. and received letters from him while he was in Chicago; that when he left he kissed her and their boy, and said he would return when he got cured; that their relations were pleasant; that her girl was born August 15, 1873; that some five months before this child was born she received a telegram and letters from her husband's sister, Mary Harmer, in Chicago, stating that her husband was dead; that he had died in hospital; that these letters and the telegram were burned when her father's house was destroyed by fire. Two of her brothers testify that they heard of her said husband's death, but deny having read letters to claimant of her husband's death.

Walter DeWit, one of claimant's brothers, testifies that her husband worked for N. F. Givens, deceased, who thought a good deal of him, and that he heard of Harmer's death through Mr. Givens. He further testified that he knew of but one thing that caused him to go away— that he had a running sore on his hip, and he thinks he went to Chicago to be treated. Other witnesses testified to his having a fistula, and claimant testifies his trouble was a cancer at lower end of spine. An examination of neighbors shows that the general understanding was that Harmer was dead; that he died about 1873, in Chicago.

It further appears that claimant, relying upon the truth of the report of her said husband's death, married one John W. Holmes, at Kahoka, Clark County, Mo., December 1, 1877, over three years after she had been informed of her first husband's death; that said Holmes was also informed of the death of claimant's first husband.

Claimant was divorced from Holmes on a bill filed by him, in which he charged desertion and a former husband living at date of his marriage to claimant. The bill appears to have been filed September 6, 1879, and charged desertion from September 1, 1878. A decree appears to have been granted April 21, but the clerk has omitted to set forth the year in the transcript. Holmes testified that it was in 1882. In this decree the following language is used:

> But nothing in this decree shall be held to prevent the defendant from marrying again, but express leave is hereby given her to marry again at any time after this day.

Holmes testified that the decree was granted on the ground of desertion alone; that he testified in court in the case that he did not know and did not believe that her former husband was alive at the time of his marriage, but that he believed him dead.

While this decree is not conclusive on this Department in this case and is not very material, in view of the conclusion which I reach, yet it indicates that the court found as a matter of fact and law that claimant's first husband was dead at the date of her second marriage, and that the claimant had a right to believe that there was no legal impediment to another marriage.

Claimant was married to soldier, William O. Reno, in Lee County, Iowa, April 6, 1863, and lived and cohabited with him as his wife until his death, July 13, 1890, in said State.

The question of the validity of this marriage is to be tested by the laws of Iowa, as required by the act of August 7, 1882.

The question of presumption of death was involved in the case of Tisdale r. Conn. Mutual Life Ins. Co. (26 Iowa, 170). In that case Edgar Tisdale left his wife to visit Chicago and was last seen in that city September 25, 1866. No reason was shown for his absenting himself from his wife. Letters of administration were issued upon his estate December 18, 1866. His wife brought suit against the defendant on a policy of insurance, and the company defended on the ground that her husband was not dead, and that the facts did not justify the presumption of his death. Under the charge given by the district judge, the verdict and judgment was for the defendant, and plaintiff appealed.

It was held on appeal by Beck, J. (syllabus): That the death of an absent person may be presumed in less than seven years from the date of the last intelligence from him, from facts and circumstances other than those showing his exposure to danger which probably resulted in his death. Also that the granting of letters of administration is prima facie evidence of death of the party on whose estate they are issued, and the judgment of the district court was reversed. The case was retried in the district court, resulting in a verdict and judgment for the plaintiff for the full amount of the policy, and defendant appealed (28 Iowa, 12). In affirming the judgment, the supreme court affirmed the correctness of the charge of the district judge in substance as follows:

The bare fact that a man who has disappeared, and whose death is contested, was seen alive within three years prior to the granting of letters of administration upon his estate, will not be sufficient to overcome the presumption of death arising from the issuing of such letters.

It would appear from this decision that the supreme court of Iowa liberalizes rather than restricts the common-law rule of presumption of death.

In discussing the question in the first hearing, Beck, J., said:

The first instruction (of the district judge) announces the rule that "the death of an absent person can not be presumed except upon evidence of facts showing his exposure to danger, which probably resulted in death, before the expiration of seven years from the date of the last intelligence from him; and that evidence of long absence without communicating with his friends; of character and habits, making the abandonment of home and family improbable, and want of all motive or cause for such abandonment which can be supposed to influence men to act is not sufficient to raise a presumption of death." The instruction is not in accordance with the true rule of evidence, and is erroneous. The error is evidently the result of an improper construction of the familiar rule of evidence that where a person has not been heard of for many years the presumption of duration of life ceases at the end of seven years (2 Starkie's Ev., 361), and an attempt to apply it to the facts in this case. The rule by no means limits the presumption of death to an absence of the person whose existence in life is a question, without tidings from him for a space of seven years; nor does the modification of the rule laid down in the cases cited by defendant's counsel—that such absence for a shorter period, if the person is shown to have been in peril, will raise a presumption of death—exclude evidence of other facts and circumstances which tend to establish the probability of death.

In the Iowa case above cited the plaintiff was not aided, as is the claimant in this case, by another and stronger presumption than that of death—i. e., that of innocence. The presumption is in favor of the validity of marriages, and where, in a case involving the validity of a marriage, the presumption of innocence is confronted with the presumption of continuance of life the latter presumption must give way to the stronger presumption of innocence. See Bishop on Marriage and Divorce, par. 951; Jennette Burton (9 P. D., 31).

At the time the decision of March 4, 1895, was rendered there was a tendency on the part of the Department to restrict the rule of presumption of death, as announced in the case of Davie v. Briggs (97 U. S., 628), and to apply the rule of the criminal law requiring the fact of death to be shown beyond a reasonable doubt; and on March 6, 1895, two days after the decision in this case, the doctrine was announced in terms in the case of Melinda L. Crider (7 P. D., 462). It was stated in that case that "it may happen that a person's death may be presumed 'to have happened within a period of time even shorter than seven years if the inference is deduced from well-authenticated facts of such a nature as almost to preclude the possibility of a mistake.' * * * I therefore feel it incumbent upon me to lay down the rule that, independent of absence for any period of time, it must be held in pension cases that the facts attending the absence must show beyond a reasonable doubt that the party is dead."

On March 13, 1896, Congress passed the following act:

That in considering claims filed under the pension laws the death of an enlisted man or officer shall be considered as sufficiently proved if satisfactory evidence is produced establishing the fact of the continued and unexplained absence of such enlisted man or officer from his home and family for a period of seven years, during which period no intelligence of his existence shall have been received. And any pension granted under this act shall cease upon proof that such officer or enlisted man is still living.

This act in effect reestablishes the common-law rule of presumption of death as announced by the Supreme Court in Davie v. Briggs (97 U. S., 628).

(See case of Marie Sharpe, 8 P. D., 175.)

I am of the opinion that claimant has established a valid marriage under the laws of the State of Iowa. I am also of the opinion that the

Bureau erred in the action rejecting her claim upon the ground that she had not proved the death of her former husband, thus placing the burden of proof of establishing the death of her first husband prior to her last marriage upon the claimant. (See Blanchard v. Lambert et al., 43 Iowa, 228; Jennette Burton, 9 P. D., 31.)

In the Iowa case above cited the plaintiff brought suit against the executor of her husband's estate, and the defense was interposed by the heirs that she was not the legal widow of her husband Blanchard, she having at the time of her marriage a former husband living; that she was incompetent to contract a valid marriage with Blanchard, as she was at the time of her marriage to Blanchard the legal wife of H. N. Musgrave, to whom she was married in 1857. Plaintiff denied the allegations of the answer, and on the issue thus joined the parties proceeded to trial. The evidence disclosed the following facts: Plaintiff's name was formerly Mrs. E. K. Lord; that on May 24, 1857, married to Horatio N. Musgrave in Hardin County, Ohio, and soon thereafter moved with him to Indiana, and cohabited with him as his wife about one year; they then returned to Ohio about the same time and lived in the same county, but not as man and wife; that some years before she left Ohio it was reported that Musgrave was again married and lived with a woman as his wife; that plaintiff lived near and knew these facts. In March, 1867, plaintiff, under the name of E. K. Lord, married I. D. Blanchard and lived with him as his wife until his death, August 14, 1872, being treated and regarded by the community as his wife. Musgrave died in June, 1871.

The court found, on these facts, that the plaintiff was the legal widow of Blanchard, and entitled to dower; from which decision defendants appealed. The supreme court of Iowa, June 6, 1876, held that the decision of the court below was clearly right, and affirmed it on two grounds:

First. Upon the ground that the presumption of innocence overrides opposing presumptions, and that the law presumed that Musgrave had obtained a divorce from plaintiff prior to his cohabitation with his second wife, citing and following the doctrine on this point as announced in the cases of Carroll v. Carroll (20 Texas, 731); Yates v. Houston (3 Texas, 433); Lockhart v. White (18 Texas, 102), and The King v. The Inhabitants of Twining (2 B and Ald., 387).

Second. That the cohabitation of plaintiff with Blanchard as his recognized wife, after the death of Musgrave in June, 1871, to the date of Blanchard's death in August, 1872, raised the presumption of a subsequent marriage after the removal of all legal impediments by the death of Musgrave; that under section 2526, of the Iowa Code (which provides that marriages solemnized, with the consent of parties, in any other manner than as prescribed in that chapter, are valid; but that the parties shall forfeit to the school fund the sum of $50 each), a common law marriage was valid; that it was a settled rule of the common law that any mutual agreement between the parties to be husband and wife in presenti, followed by cohabitation, constitutes a valid and binding marriage, if there is no legal disability on the part of either to contract matrimony.

The court cited and followed the rule on this subject as announced in Rose v. Clark (8 Paige Ch. Rep., 573); Fenton v. Reed (4 Johnson, 51); Jackson v. Claw (18 Johnson, 347), and cited the cases of Starr v. Peck (1 Hill, 270), and Wilkinson v. Payne (4 Durn and East's Rep., 468).

The doctrine announced in the case of Blanchard v. Lambert appears to be the settled law in Iowa, and that case is cited in the 51 Iowa, 570; 58 Iowa, 720; 69 Iowa, 398, and 78 Iowa, 502, where the facts did not bring these cases within the rule of Blanchard v. Lambert. In the case of G lman v. Sheets (76 Iowa, 502), the court by Robinson, J., said:

> It is claimed that even if a marriage was contracted, as alleged, yet, under the facts of the case, a divorce will be presumed under the rule announced in Blanchard v. Lambert (43 Iowa, 229). We do not think this case is within that rule. In that case each party to the first marriage claimed to have contracted a subsequent marriage, and it was held that it would be presumed that the relation created by the first marriage had been dissolved. It was held in Ellis v. Ellis (58 Iowa, 720)—a case similar to this—that "there must be something based on the acts and conduct of both parties inconsistent with the continuance of the marriage relation before the presumption should be indulged" that a divorce had been granted. Nothing of that kind on the part of the appellee is shown in this case.

The case of Blanchard v. Lambert is a leading case and cited by most, if not all, elemental law writers in connection with other Federal and State decisions, in support of the general rule that after a marriage is proved every presumption favors its validity, and that a rebuttable presumption is never sufficient to outweigh, overcome, or disprove a fact.

See Lawson on Presumptive Evidence, 576; Gilpin v. Page (18 Wall., 3 54); Whittaker v. Morrison (1 Fla., 29); Van Buren v. Cockburn (14 Barb., N. Y., 122); Neitz v. Carpenter (21 Cal., 456); Patterson v. Gaines (6 How., 550); Powell v. Powell (27 Miss., 783); Fleming v. People (27 N. Y., 329); Ward v. Dulaney (23 Miss., 410); Ferrie v. Pub. Adm. (4 Barb., N. Y., 28).

In the case under consideration the claimant proves a ceremonial marriage with soldier in the State of Iowa on the 6th day of April, 1883, and has filed a certified transcript of her marriage certificate, and the validity of this marriage can not be impeached by the presumption that her first husband, who was last heard from in 1873, and who was then reported dead, is still alive, or that he is presumed to have been alive at the time of her marriage to soldier in 1883.

The motion is accordingly sustained, and the Departmental decision of March 4, 1895, and the Bureau action of January 9, 1894, are reversed.

The papers in the case are herewith returned.

DEPENDENCE—WIDOW—ACT JUNE 27, 1890.

MATILDA HELVE (WIDOW).

The soldier, prior to his death, deeded certain real estate owned by him in Chicago, and valued at $8,000, to his brother-in-law, without consideration, who deeded it to the soldier's eldest daughter, without consideration, the purpose of these transfers being to save the property from his creditors. After his death the widow applied $2,500 of her own money to the cancellation of a mortgage upon the aforesaid property. She and her three children (all grown) live together and use the rents and profits of the property for their common support. They have a home and net income of $270 per year, independent of their earnings.

Held: That claimant is not without other means of support than her daily labor within the meaning of the law.

Assistant Secretary Webster Davis to the Commissioner of Pensions, March 7, 1898.

This widow's claim for pension (No. 636025) under the act of June 27, 1890, was rejected by your Bureau in July, 1897, on the ground that she had other means of support than her daily labor. From that action an appeal was taken on August 6, 1897, the contention of which is that the evidence shows her to be possessed of no property whatever and to have no income from any source, except the voluntary contributions of her children and that derived from her daily labor.

The facts developed by special examination were as follows:

Some years before his death the soldier, being in financial difficulties, conveyed certain real estate owned by him in the city of Chicago to his brother-in-law, who deeded it to the soldier's eldest daughter. There was no actual money consideration for either of these transfers, the object being to place the property beyond the reach of the soldier's creditors.

This property still stands in the name of the daughter. It consists of two "two-flat" buildings, with the lot 50 by 125 feet on which they stand, and two unimproved lots, the total value of which is estimated at $8,000. Three of the flats are rented; the fourth is occupied by the claimant and her three children.

The soldier possessed no property at the time of his death, but held a life insurance policy for $3,000, payable to his widow. She collected this money after his death and used $2,500 of it in paying off a mortgage on the real estate which had been deeded to her daughter. The remaining $500 went for outstanding debts, funeral expenses, etc. A new mortgage for $1,000 has since been placed upon the improved real estate and the money expended for repairs. The income derived from the property is $35 per month and is used for the general expenses of the family. Interest on the borrowed money, taxes, and insurance consume $150 per annum, leaving the family a net income of $270 per annum, with no rent to pay. The two younger children are employed and contribute to the general support. A few citations from the testimony may serve to throw further light upon the question at issue. The claimant deposed as follows:

Question. What understanding had you with your daughter Frances, or anyone else, at the time you used $2,500 of your insurance money to pay the mortgage indebtedness, as to your status or rights and interest in the property?

Answer. None whatever; I never had an agreement, or understanding, or contract, either written or verbal, with Frances or anyone else to the effect I should have a life support from the property, or that I should be provided with a home or living. I have nothing to show that I paid the mortgage debt with my money. I handed the money to Frances. She attended to the business.

Question. Is it not true, as a matter of fact, that you are expected to and that it is your intention to make the property your home and that you expect to derive an income from the property sufficient for a comfortable living?

Answer. Yes, that is true; but I don't know that I have a legal right to any of the benefits I have thus far enjoyed and expect to enjoy in future.

Question. What understanding had you with your husband or daughter Frances at the time the property was transferred to her—Frances?

Answer. Well, I don't know that there was any, except that it was known that he was financially embarrassed and conveyed the property to Frances for no other purpose than to save the property. It was not understood by any of us that it was a gift to her.

The daughter Frances testified as follows:

Question. Do you regard the property as yours absolutely?

Answer. Well, yes; legally it is mine absolutely; morally it is not. I expect to divide it with my brother, W. Edgar, and sister, Corrie May, and that mother shall have the income from it as long as she lives. I have no intention of ever depriving her of the income from the property.

Question. Why was the property transferred to you by your uncle?

Answer. Well, father did the business. My understanding is, and always has been, that he thought mother would not live long, as she was then in very poor health, and thought it best to make the transfer to me direct.

Question. Do you consider the income—the $35 per month rent from the three flats—belongs to your mother?

Answer. Yes, I do. I do all the business, though; but the income from the property is used entirely for the expenses of the family. Mother has no other income from any source and if the buildings should burn down she would be dependent upon her children for support. As it is, the property gives us a comfortable home and $35 per month.

It is clear that while the claimant has no legal interest in the valuable property formerly owned by her husband she has an equitable interest, which is recognized by the person in whom the legal title is vested. The transfer of the property to the eldest daughter (to which the claimant was a party) was simply a device for preserving it for the use and benefit of the whole family. That the claimant regarded herself as having a rightful interest in said property is manifest from the fact that she applied $2,500 of her own money to the cancellation of the mortgage thereon; and that she is regarded by her children as enjoying what of right belongs to her and not as dependent upon their bounty is manifest from their testimony. In view of these facts it is immaterial what her legal rights are. So long, at least, as the existing arrangement continues she must be regarded as having other means of support than her daily labor, and as, consequently, not entitled to pension under the act of June 27, 1890. The action of your Bureau is affirmed.

MARRIAGE—REMARRIAGE—ACT JUNE 27, 1890.

Lucy P. Potter (widow).

The evidence in this claim shows that claimant remarried subsequent to the death of soldier and prior to the passage of the act of June 27, 1890, and fails to show that said second marriage was void or invalid. In the absence of direct proof that her said second husband had a wife living from whom he was not divorced at the date of his marriage to claimant, or that his former marriage was void, claimant has no title to pension under said act.

Assistant Secretary Webster Davis to the Commissioner of Pensions, March 7, 1898.

Claimant's attorney, on August 12, 1897, appealed from the Bureau action of July 16, 1897, rejecting her widow's claim No. 633277, filed May 7, 1896, under section 3 of the act of June 27, 1890, on the ground that claimant had remarried prior to the passage of the act of June 27, 1890.

It is conceded that claimant remarried after the death of soldier and prior to the passage of the act of June 27, 1890, but it is contended that her said second marriage was void, for the reason that at the date of said marriage her second husband had a former wife then living from whom he had not been divorced.

The difficulty with this proposition is that it is not shown that her said second husband had a former wife living at the date of his marriage to claimant, the proof on this point being the testimony of claimant as to the statements of her said second husband and mere rumors that he had a former wife and family.

There is no proof that said second husband was previously married, or that if previously married that such marriage was legal, or that if previously married that such former marriage had not been dissolved previous to his marriage to claimant. Claimant, if relying on the validity of her second marriage, would be entitled to all these presumptions in her favor and in support of the validity of her second marriage.

Such are the decisions of the courts of Illinois, the State in which claimant was married to her second husband.

It was held in the case of Schmisseur v. Beatrice (147 Ill., 210) that—

Evidence that a man had a previous wife living at the time of his second marriage is not sufficient to prove the marriage invalid, since it will be presumed that the previous marriage had been dissolved by divorce. The presumption that a wife from whom her husband had not heard for some time is still alive yields to the presumption in favor of the innocence of a second marriage by the husband.

So, also, in the case of Harris *v.* Harris (8 Ill., App., 57) it was held that—

> After a lapse of time, less than nine years even, the law treats the presumption of the legality of the second marriage as overcoming that of the continuance of life, and requires that direct proof should be made that the former husband or wife was living at the date of the second marriage.

See also Johnson *v.* Johnson (114 Ill., 611) and Angel *v.* People (96 Ill., 209).

The evidence in this claim shows that claimant remarried subsequent to the death of soldier and prior to the passage of the act of June 27, 1890, and fails to show that said second marriage was void or invalid. Claimant is therefore not entitled to pension under the provisions of the act of June 27, 1890, and the action appealed from is accordingly affirmed.

VICIOUS HABITS—EVIDENCE—ACT JUNE 27, 1890.

MORRIS HESS.

> There being nothing in the case to arouse a suspicion that the disability was in any way due to vicious habits, or that the claimant has ever been addicted to vicious habits, or that his statement as to the circumstances under which the disability was incurred is untrue, rejection was not warranted. (Citing John Martin. 7 P. D., 578.)

Assistant Secretary Webster Davis to the Commissioner of Pensions, March 7, 1898.

This is a claim under the act of June 27, 1890. The claimant enlisted as a private in Company F, Seventy-first Regiment of New York Infantry, April 25, 1861, and was mustered out with his company July 30, 1864. He again enlisted in Company F, Fifteenth New York Engineers, September 15, 1864, and was mustered out with said company June 13, 1865. On December 29, 1865, he enlisted in Company H, Sixth United States Infantry, and served until honorably discharged, December 29, 1868. He filed his claim for pension under the act of June 27, 1890, on January 12, 1892, alleging inability to earn a support by manual labor by reason of rupture and disease of the kidneys and lungs. Subsequently he alleged other causes of disability, viz. disease of the bladder, lumbago, and rheumatism. The claim was rejected first in January, 1896, again in December, 1896, and again in June, 1897, on the ground that a ratable disability was not shown independent of the rupture, and the claimant was unable to prove that the latter was not due to vicious habits. From that action an appeal was taken August 6, 1897, in which it is contended that the evidence on file is sufficient to warrant a presumption that the disability (rupture) was not caused by vicious habits.

The claimant has stated under oath that his rupture first appeared a few days after his discharge from the Regular Army, in 1868, and that he does not know when or how it was caused, but believes that it was due to a strain received while unloading commissary stores three days before his discharge. His statements on this point appear to be consistent throughout. Assuming his statement to be true, it is, of course, impossible for him to prove the time, place, and circumstances of incurrence of the disability. He has filed the following testimony:

James W. Sears, being duly sworn, states that about January, 1868, (?) the claimant came to his house, having, as he said, just been discharged from the Regular Army. He remained there and worked for affiant two or three years, during which time he complained a good deal of rheumatism and lame back, and was often compelled to refrain from labor for a day or two. He was a man of good habits.

Frederick Kimmer testified that he became acquainted with the claimant in the winter of 1868, about the time he came to work for James W. Sears, and knew him, during the time he worked there, as a man of good habits and a good citizen. Affiant does not believe that any injuries alleged by him were due to vicious habits.

J. H. Hill testified that he has known the claimant for about four years, and has found him to be a man of good character and reputation and of ordinary habits.

Dr. H. H. McDonough has known claimant for the same length of time, and states that while he has known him he has always been a civil, quiet, good citizen. Affiant has frequently known him to be seriously ill from the effects of rupture.

I am of the opinion that the claim should not have been rejected upon the ground stated. There is nothing in the character of the disability or in the claimant's allegations concerning it to arouse a suspicion that it was caused by vicious habits. I do not know of any vicious habits which would have a direct tendency to cause such a disability, and there is nothing whatever in the case to suggest that it resulted indirectly from any vicious habit. On the other hand, it is well known that such injuries are of frequent occurrence among men of good habits.

In the case of John Martin (7 P. D., 578) Assistant Secretary Reynolds announced, as a rule susceptible of general application to cases of this kind—

that where the circumstances of the incurrence of the disability can not be proved, and there is apparently no valid ground for attributing the same to vicious habits, and the claimant has always, so far as can be ascertained, been a man of good repute for credibility, it would be reasonable to presume in favor of the claim.

I think the rule is a sound one and should be followed in this case. The rejection is set aside, and you are respectfully requested to readjudicate the claim in accordance with the views above expressed.

This decision is not intended to preclude your Bureau from making further investigation in regard to the claimant's habits or the origin of his disability, if deemed expedient, but, as the case now stands, rejection is not warranted.

BARBARA TROTTER (WIDOW).

A widow who owns the house in which she lives, which is assessed at $930, and valued, according to her statement, at $1,600, and has $1,800 loaned out at 6 per cent interest, is not "without other means of support than her daily labor" within the meaning of section 3 of the act of June 27, 1890.

Assistant Secretary Webster Davis to the Commissioner of Pensions, March 7, 1898.

The appeal in this case was filed August 6, 1897, and was taken from your action of November 9, 1895, rejecting the claim, under the act of June 27, 1890, of Barbara, widow of Louis Trotter, private, Company E, One hundred and eleventh Ohio Infantry. (Original No. 612413.)

The soldier was a pensioner under said act at $6 per month, for disease of heart and neuralgia. He died March 27, 1895.

The widow's application was filed April 15, 1895.

In an affidavit filed August 7, 1895, she states that—

She owns lot 52, Barker's addition, Toledo, Ohio, on which she lives; that said property is assessed at $930, and is worth about $1,600; that she has no other property, personal or real, except her household goods; that she has no income of any kind, and that no one is legally bound to support her.

In an affidavit filed October 3, 1895, she states as follows:

My means of support are: I room and board my daughter and her husband, renting them one room; they pay $5 per week. I have $1,800 loaned out at 6 per cent; the interest ($9) is paid to me monthly. I have no other income. My taxes, insurance, and repairs are nearly $60 per annum.

A certified transcript from the record of property assessments of Lucas County, Ohio, shows that property standing in the name of Barbara Trotter, and designated as lot 52, Barker's addition, was assessed at $930 for the year 1895.

The marriage of the widow to the soldier and the death of the latter are both shown by duly certified transcripts from the marriage and death records, respectively, of said county and State.

Charles P. Schaefer and John Geigel state, in a joint affidavit filed October 3, 1895, as follows:

We know claimant; she is a near neighbor. Her house and lot is worth $1,500, and would rent for about $144 per annum. The house is small and is occupied by herself; she rents one room and boards her daughter and son-in-law, to help support her. She owns no other real estate. She has $1,800 invested at 6 per cent per annum, from which she receives the interest, $9, monthly. A mortgage of $200 against her property is held by the Toledo Loan Company, bearing 8 per cent. She is 53 years of age; can not support herself by manual labor; does what she can by boarding her daughter and son-in-law; has to pay taxes, insurance, and repairs, amounting to about $55 per annum.

The claim was rejected November 9, 1895, on the ground of non dependence, the claimant having other means of support than her own labor.

She appealed to your Bureau for a reconsideration of her claim and filed some evidence as to her financial condition, which evidence, however, is practically of the same character as that heretofore filed in her claim, and she was advised by you, under date of July 23, 1897, that the said evidence did not change the status of her claim, the rejection of which was considered proper and would be adhered to.

From this action the pending appeal was entered at this Department, August 6, 1897, the contention therein being—

That the claimant's income from all sources, after paying her taxes, insurance, and repairs, amounting to about $50 annually, is insufficient to afford her a support.

Inasmuch as this claimant is shown by the evidence, including her own testimony, to be in possession of property, real and personal, valued at over $3,400, which is encumbered by a mortgage of but $200, and from which an annual income of over $250 could be derived, she is not, in my judgment, entitled to a pension under the third section of the act of June 27, 1890. See cases of Jennie D. Lewis (6 P. D., 294), Katharine Klein (7 P. D., 278), and Susan Landgraff (7 P. D., 380).

The action appealed from having been in accordance with the rules and practice in cases of this character, the same is hereby affirmed.

DESERTION—DISCHARGE—SECTIONS 4692, 4693, AND 4694, R. S.

JAMES McCALLAN.

Desertion from the general service during the late war of the rebellion is no bar to pension on account of disability contracted in the United States service while serving under a contract of enlistment entered into since the close of said war, from which late service sailor was honorably discharged.

Assistant Secretary Webster Davis to the Commissioner of Pensions, March 12, 1898.

I have considered yours of December 30, 1897, requesting the further consideration of the claim of James McCallan, late seaman, United States Navy, No. 39896, in which the rejection of the same by your Bureau was affirmed by this Department November 15, 1897.

In your communication you say:

The facts in this case seem to distinguish it from the case of George Lessor (8 P. D., 114), cited in your decision, and no decision has been found in which the exact question at issue in this case has heretofore been decided. In the said case of Lessor a general rule as to the effect of desertion is announced in the following language: "A claimant against whom there stands a charge of desertion under an enlistment for service in the war of the rebellion, which charge the War Department declines to remove, has no title to pension under any existing law on account of disability incurred in said war or service performed therein."

It will be observed that this ruling, which has been announced in numerous other cases, applies only to claims on account of services performed or disabilities incurred in the "war of the rebellion." On the other hand it is held, uniformly, that desertion from a service either prior or subsequent to the war of the rebellion does not bar a claim on account of services rendered in that war. (Digest of 1897, p. 161.)

Thus it is held that desertion from Mexican war service is no bar to pension on account of disability incurred in the war of the rebellion; and that desertion prior to the war of 1812 was no bar to pension for disability incurred in that war. (Digest of 1897, "Desertion," pp. 163-164.)

In the case of Bridget Kelley (7 P. D., 128), Assistant Secretary Reynolds held that desertion from service in the war of the rebellion was no bar to pension to soldier's widow on account of his prior service in the Mexican war.

The question arises, therefore, whether the desertion of this claimant during the war of the rebellion should bar his claim on account of disabilities incurred subsequent to said war in the United States Navy. Claimant's service in the Navy, in which he claims to have incurred disability, was under an enlistment in 1871, and had no connection whatever with the war of the rebellion.

While no decision has been found that is exactly in point, the trend of the decisions above referred to would seem to lead to the conclusion that desertion during the war of the rebellion should not bar a claim on account of disability incurred in a subsequent service which had no connection with that war.

The distinction between this case and that of Lessor, above referred to, is that Lessor's several terms of service were all during the war of the rebellion.

As this distinction does not appear to have been considered, or is not alluded to in your decision, herewith, it seems proper to invite your attention to the same, and to submit whether the desertion shown by the record should bar this claim.

Where the statute under which pension is claimed requires an honorable discharge from the service on account of which pension is granted in any particular war, it has been held that a deserter from the service during that war who had never been discharged was not pensionable.

Thus, under section 4736, R. S., which provides for placing on the pension roll the names of all such persons—

* * * who served sixty days in the war with Great Britain, of eighteen hundred and twelve, and were honorably discharged * * *

it was held by Secretary Delano that—

a soldier in the war of 1812 who deserted from service therein and was never discharged is not pensionable as a survivor of said war. (Daniel McAlpine, 2 P. D., o. s., 390.)

So, in the case of the widow of Albert Wilson (8 P. D., o. s., 184), Secretary Kirkwood held that—

the widow of a soldier of the war of 1812 is not pensionable if he is marked on the rolls a deserter, although he obtained a bounty-land warrant for such service. it appearing that the record of desertion was not reported in the bounty-land claim.

And under section 4730, R. S. (acts of May 13, 1846, and July 21, 1848. which provides pension to soldiers who were—

disabled by reason of injury received or disease contracted while in the line of duty in actual service in the war with Mexico, or in going to or returning from the same, who received an honorable discharge,

it was held by Acting Secretary Bell that—

an honorable discharge is essential to entitle soldiers of the Mexican war to pension for disabilities; and a soldier whose final record was that of desertion is therefore not pensionable. (John G. Kelley, 8 P. D., o. s., 229.)

The act of June 27, 1890, likewise makes an honorable discharge a prerequisite to pension under the second section thereof, and it has beeu uniformly held that to entitle a claimant to pension under said act he must have been honorably discharged from all service contracted to be performed during said war. (Isaac N. Babb, alias Dunlap, 8 P. D., 59; Henry Davinney, 7 P. D., 233.)

It is also held that au honorable discharge of the soldier from all service he contracted to perform during the war of the rebellion is a prerequisite to widow's pension under said act. (Sarah Bush, 9 P. D., 144; Bessie Wheeler, 9 P. D., 155.)

But it has been held that desertion from service prior to the war of 1812 is no bar to pension on account of service in such war (James Barnes, 2 P. D., o. s., 442); and that desertion from service during the Mexican war was no bar to pension based on service in the war of the rebellion (Jacob Bowersmith, 3 P. D., 303); also that desertion from the Regular Army subsequent to the war of the rebellion is no bar to pension under the act of June 27, 1890. (Catherine Tubah, 8 P. D., 82; James W. Miller, 8 P. D., 316.)

It was held in the case of Bridget Kelley (7 P. D., 128) that—

under the provisions of the act of January 29, 1887, the widow of a soldier entitled to pension by reason of her husband's service and honorable discharge in the Mexican war is not barred by reason of her husband's desertion from service in the war of the rebellion.

These decisions were in claims filed under laws which specifically made an honorable discharge a prerequisite to pension.

Sections 4692, 4693, and 4694, under which this claim must be adjudicated, contain no such restriction, and the decisions thereunder have not been harmonious, it being held in some cases that a deserter is constructively in the service and that section 4724, R. S., was a bar. (Cases of Elizabeth A. Gannon, 3 P. D., 67; William T. Coburn, 7 P. D., 182; Peter Kenney, 7 P. D., 588.)

And in the case of George Lessor (8 P. D., 114) it was held that—

A claimant against whom there stands a charge of desertion under an enlistment for service in the war of the rebellion, which charge the War Department declines to remove, has no title to pension under any law on account of disability incurred in said war or services performed therein.

On the other hand, it has been held that—

When a soldier incurs a disability in the service and has been discharged, but subsequently reenlists and deserts, there is no authority for withholding the pension granted on account of said disability other than the provision (section 4724, R. S.) of law that a pensioner shall not for the same period receive his pension and the pay of his rank or station in the service. (Benjamin Robbins, 6 P. D., o. s., 486.)

In the above case Secretary Schurz restored claimant's name to the roll, deducting payments from the date of second enlistment to the date when he was last paid.

In the case of Henry Davinney (7 P. D., 233) it was held that claimant, having been disabled in the line of duty during his first term of service in the war of the rebellion, from which he was honorably discharged, though he subsequently reenlisted and deserted, having filed his claim prior to July 1, 1880, was pensionable for the period between his discharge to the date of his reenlistment; but his claim under the act of June, 27, 1890, was rejected on the ground that he had not been honorably discharged from all service contracted to be performed in that war. And in the case of James H. Brush, alias Jesse L. Judd (7 P. D., o. s., 72), it was held that desertion from a service prior to that in which the disability was incurred is not a bar to pension. In that case soldier deserted from the Ninth Iowa Cavalry and enlisted in the Regular Army, where he was accidentally wounded in 1866, in consequence of which his limb was amputated, for which he had been pensioned, but his name had been dropped from the roll on information that he had deserted from a former service.

The facts in the case under consideration and the one cited are nearly identical, and are identical in principle. Brush was pensioned for disability incurred in the Regular Army under an enlistment subsequent to the war of the rebellion, notwithstanding that he deserted from the service under an enlistment to serve in the war of the rebellion, and the same point is involved here.

I am of the opinion that the decision in the Brush case was proper in view of the present rulings of the Department holding that desertion from the service prior to the war of 1812 is no bar to pension as a survivor of said war; that desertion from the service in the war with Mexico is no bar to pension based on service in the war of the rebellion, and that desertion from the service during the war of the rebellion is no bar to pension on account of service in the Mexican war.

The claimant referred to in your communication enlisted in the Regular Army September 13, 1860, was transferred to the general service and deserted from said service at Governors Island, New York, July 30, 1862, and on the next day enlisted in the One hundred and thirty-second New York Infantry, in which he served until mustered out, June 29, 1865, having been continuously in the service during the whole war. He subsequently served in the United States Navy from May 17, 1866, to April 23, 1870, and from August 12, 1870, to June 30, 1871. He claims pension for disability contracted during his last service in the United States Navy.

I hold that sailor's desertion from the general service in 1862, during the war of the rebellion, is no bar to pension on account of disability incurred in the United States Navy, under an enlistment in 1870, since the close of the war of the rebellion.

The former decision in this case of November 15, 1897, is therefore reconsidered and set aside, and the action of your Bureau rejecting claimant's case on the ground of desertion in 1862 is reversed.

COMMENCEMENT—SECTION 4698½ R. S.—GRADE RATE.

CHARLES H. FLOURNEY.

Appellant pensioned for rheumatism and resulting disease of heart filed a claim for increase September 12, 1895, which was allowed at third grade ($24 per month) from November 27, 1895, date of the certificate of the medical examination made under the pending claim. He contends the increased rate should commence from October 24, 1891, as the evidence of two physicians showed that on that date his disability was equivalent to the loss of a hand or a foot. It is held, that as claimant's disability is not permanent and specific his increase of pension was properly made to commence from the date of the certificate of medical examination made under the pending claim, showing the increased disability as provided by section 4698½ of the Revised Statutes.

Assistant Secretary Webster Davis to the Commissioner of Pensions, March 12, 1898.

Claimant on November 20, 1897, filed a motion for reconsideration of departmental decision, affirming the Bureau action of January 14, 1896, commencing the increase of his pension from November 27, 1895, in his increase claim, certificate No. 349957, filed September 12, 1895.

The contention is, in brief, that his third-grade rate should have commenced October 25, 1891, instead of November 27, 1895; that the act of March 3, 1883, stands as an independent act, and is mandatory, and that pensioners "shall receive a pension of $24 per month" from and after the passage of said act when the proof shows the claimant's disability equivalent to the loss of a hand or a foot; and that said act is not affected by section 4698½, but repealed said section by implication; that as the evidence shows claimant's disability equivalent to the loss of a hand or a foot on October 24, 1891, he should be pensioned at that rate from that date.

I am of the opinion that the contention of claimant is not well taken. Repeals by implication are not favored, and there is nothing in the terms of said act of March 3, 1883, implying an intention to repeal any act or section of the pension laws, except a portion of section 4698, although it modifies section 4699.

The fact that the act provided—

that nothing contained in this act shall be construed to repeal section forty-six hundred and ninety-nine of the Revised Statutes of the United States, or to change the rate of eighteen dollars per month therein mentioned to be proportionately divided for any degree of disability established for which section forty-six hundred and ninety-five makes no provision,

lends no color to the construction that all other sections of the Revised Statutes were therefore repealed. The reason for referring in terms in said act to said section 4699 is apparent.

As the act substituted the $24 for the $18 rate, provided by section 4698, it repealed so much of said section as provided for the $18 rate, and but for the proviso section 4699 would have become nugatory, as the $18 rate was superseded by the $24 rate, but it was desirable to retain the $18 for future use as a denominator (in cases when rank rate under section 4695 was not involved), indicating a degree of disability greater than total, or $8, and less than $18, or a degree of disability less than that equivalent to the loss of a hand or a foot, and for which section 4695 made no provision. By operation of law the third-grade rate became $24 instead of $18 per month.

See cases of Thomas Stapleton (3 P. D., 48); John P. Besser (7 P. D., 146).

Had claimant's disability been permanent and specific, the date of commencement would not have been dependent upon a surgeon's certificate, but not being "permanent and specific" within the meaning of section 4698½, the date of commencement is controlled by that section.

A "permanent specific" disability is one that is due to wounds, injuries, or disease contracted in the service, and in line of duty, and which is unchanging and fixed and permanent in character, and which, when once established, does not require subsequent medical examinations to determine its existence or continuance, and which disability is particularly enumerated and classified by law, and for which a fixed and definite rate of pension is named in the law, as the loss of both feet, both hands, one foot, and one hand, as provided in section 4697, Revised Statutes, the loss of an arm at or above the elbow, or a leg at or above the knee, etc.

See case of William H. Parker (8 P. D., 198).

Claimant's disability for which he is pensioned is due to rheumatism and resulting disease of heart, and is clearly not specific in character. The fact that disability resulting from said diseases may become equivalent to a "permanent specific disability" does not render it "specific" within the meaning of that term in the pension laws.

To determine the degree of disability, and when it becomes equivalent to the loss of a hand or a foot, requires medical examinations as required by section 4698½.

So, too, said act is to be construed in connection with section 4698½, in pari materia. As was held in the case of Sarah H. Ozborn (7 P. D., 318):

It is a well-established rule that where various statutes relate to the same subject they are all to be taken into consideration in construing any one of them, and that all acts in pari materia are to be taken together as if they were one law. If a thing contained in a subsequent statute be within the reason of a former statute, it shall be taken to be within the meaning of that statute. United States v. Freeman (3 Howard, 565) and authorities therein cited. See also case of Adolph Bernstein, decided May 19, 1894 (7 P. D., 229).

The various statutes upon the subject of pensions enacted by Congress from time to time comprise our system of pension laws, in the nature of a code relating to one subject and governed by one spirit and policy. They are to be construed together like our revenue laws, banking laws, land laws, mining laws, patent laws, admiralty, and other similar laws upon a specific subject. And where the later statutes fail to repeal a former in express terms or by necessary implication, such later statutes operate cumulatively, and not by way of substitution or repeal.

A reference to the medical examinations shows that prior to November 27, 1895, claimant's disability was not established by any examining surgeon's certificate as equivalent to the loss of a hand or a foot. His pension at third-grade rate was therefore properly made to commence from that date.

The motion is accordingly denied, and the papers in the case are herewith returned.

MEDICAL EXAMINATION—EXAMINING SURGEONS.

ISAAC GOODIN.

A certificate of a medical examination, not sworn to, made by a person who had ceased to be an examining surgeon or a member of a board of examining surgeons, can not be considered the certificate of a civil surgeon, but is without authority of law and null and void; and a claimant, having submitted to such examination under protest, should have the benefit of an examination by a duly authorized examining surgeon or a board of examining surgeons.

Assistant Secretary Webster Davis to the Commissioner of Pensions, March 12, 1898.

The appellant, Isaac Goodin, first lieutenant Company I, Thirty-fourth Indiana Infantry, is now pensioned at $24 per month for chronic diarrhea and resulting disease of rectum.

His original certificate was issued August 5, 1884, at $4.25 (one-fourth of rank) from December 28, 1861, and $8.50 (one-half of rank) from June 28, 1882, for chronic diarrhea.

A certificate granting increase to $12.75 (three-fourths of rank) was issued October 14, 1887, and the third issue was made June 6, 1890, allowing increase to $17 (total of rank) from November 20, 1889, for chronic diarrhea and resulting disease of rectum.

The certificate of the present rate, third grade, was issued July 20, 1894. A claim for increase on account of pensioned causes and alleged resulting disease of heart was filed June 18, 1897, and a "home examination" was requested on the ground that the claimant was physically unable to appear before the board of examining surgeons. An order for said examination was issued September 13, 1897, and sent to Dr. Joseph Simecek, at Wilber, Nebr., notwithstanding the fact that Dr. Simecek had ceased to be a member of the board of examining surgeons at said place on the 31st of August, 1897.

The claimant submitted to an examination, under protest, by Dr. Simecek on the 21st of September, 1897, the certificate of which examination describes the following objective conditions:

Pulse rate, 77; respiration, 20; temperature, 97; height, 6 feet; weight, 131 pounds; age, 80 years.

Applicant is very weak, but, considering his age, the weakness is due to the old age. He is anæmic; muscular system weak; he can walk without help, but not more than one block at a time; he does not need the attendance of another person; he is not confined to bed at present.

Chronic diarrhea: Tongue is coated and fissured; stomach distended; bowels tympanitic; skin jaundiced and dry. 10/18.

Urine contains abnormal amount of phosphates; no blood; no sugar; no albumen. No disease of rectum. No rating. No disease of heart; it is weak, but, considering his age, it could not be expected to be stronger; no murmurs; no dilatation; no hypertrophy. No rating. General condition is one of poor health; there is general debility, for which no cause, except old age, can be found. 17/18.

All organs healthy, as above stated. No vicious habits.

In support of said claim for increase the evidence of the claimant's family physician and of two neighbors was filed on the 18th of June, 1897, the date of filing said application.

Dr. John B. Foss, of Crete, Nebr., testifies as follows:

I have been his family physician for the last six or seven years, visiting and prescribing for him at short intervals, as it has been necessary for him to take medicine constantly to relieve his suffering consequent upon having the following diseases and disorders: Chronic diarrhea and resulting disease of rectum; heart disease and vertigo; and by reason of the above named diseases and disorders, enfeebled by old age (he being 80 years of age), and increasing vertigo and organic disease of the heart his disability for performing manual labor is total. It requires almost constant attention of one person to care for him.

John H. Gruben and William L. Lovell, of Crete, Nebr., testify to the fact that the claimant is wholly disabled for the performance of manual labor, confined to the house most of the time, and requires the almost constant attention of another person.

The claim for increase was rejected November 27, 1897, on the ground that no increase was warranted on account of pensioned causes, and that disease of heart and vertigo were not shown to be results thereof.

From this action the claimant, through his attorneys, entered an appeal February 1, 1898, contending therein as follows:

That the claimant had not been accorded a fair and impartial examination by a duly qualified and sworn medical examiner, or board of examiners, as provided by law and the rules of the Bureau of Pensions; that an order was issued for the claimant's examination at his residence, which order was sent to Dr. Joseph Simecek, of Wilber, Nebr., who was not a sworn, qualified medical examiner, but on the contrary he, the said Simecek, had but a few days prior to said appointment [designation probably meant] been removed from the board of examining surgeons at Wilber, Nebr., and that at the time he was so appointed [designated] there was a duly sworn, qualified, and competent full board of examiners in the said town; that the claimant, through his attorney, sent to the Commissioner of Pensions a written protest against said Dr. Simecek being allowed to make the examination, on account of his prejudice, but notwithstanding said protest no change was made and he had to submit to an examination by Dr. Simecek, and that he has good reason to believe, and does believe, that the said Simecek was so prejudiced that he did not make a fair report according to the facts, and that by reason thereof his claim was rejected.

The said appeal was referred to your Bureau on the 2d ultimo for report thereon.

The papers in the case were transmitted to this Department on the 1st instant, with the opinion—

That the action of rejection of the claim for increase was proper, and should be adhered to. The pensioner's advanced age is unquestionably the principal cause of his disability.

Without entering into the question as to whether or not the claimant is entitled to an increase by reason of pensioned causes, or any pathological sequelæ thereof, which fact, however, can only be determined after the claimant shall have been examined by a properly authorized examining surgeon or board of surgeons, there does not appear to be any room for doubt but what the order for the medical examination held in consequence of the claim for increase was issued to a physician whose official connection with your Bureau, as an examining surgeon, had terminated some time prior to the date on which said order was issued; and that the examination made by him on the 21st of September, 1897, in accordance with said order, was without warrant of law; and that his certificate of the same should be regarded as null and void.

Neither can the said certificate be looked upon in the light of that of a civil surgeon, as it is not sworn to, nor was the order issued with that object in view.

I fully concur in the contention of the appellant that he is, at least, entitled to an examination by a duly constituted examining surgeon or board of surgeons, for which purpose the claim should be reopened, and an order issued to the secretary of the board at Wilber, Nebr., to proceed to the claimant's home and make a thorough examination for all disabilities alleged in his claim for increase, and to make a careful differential diagnosis between the same and any manifest results of senility.

As this action involves reconsideration in the light of additional evidence it is regarded as a reversal of the action taken, and a final disposition of the pending appeal.

If, in the light of the new evidence, your final action is still adverse, the claimant has the right of further appeal.

As this claim has been made special you are requested to direct that prompt action be taken, in accordance with the views set forth herein.

DISABILITY—ACT JUNE 27, 1890—PRACTICE.

JOHN W. HIRD.

The evidence, the certificates of examination, and the concurrent opinion of the medical referee show the existence of a degree of disability warranting a rate under the act of June 27, 1890. Under the present rules as to rating, the action of rejection is reversed, notwithstanding that it was in accordance with the practice at the time the claim was adjudicated.

Assistant Secretary Webster Davis to the Commissioner of Pensions, March 12, 1898.

The appeal in this case was filed at this Department February 15, 1898, and was taken from the action of your Bureau, dated December 20, 1895, rejecting the claim under the act of June 27, 1890.

The appellant, John W. Hird, Company K, Twenty-eighth Maine Infantry, was formerly pensioned under the general law at $4 per month for "nervous debility." His name was dropped from the rolls by reason of his failure to claim his pension during a period of three years. He filed a claim for restoration May 9, 1895, which claim was rejected December 7, 1896, on the ground that a ratable degree of disability from the alleged "nervous debility" had not been shown to exist since date of dropping.

On the 19th of March, 1892, the soldier filed a declaration under the act of June 27, 1890, in which "malarial poisoning and nervous debility" were the only disabilities alleged.

A medical examination was held under this application at Fitchburg, Mass., September 11, 1892.

No objective symptoms of either malarial poisoning or nervous debility were manifested at said examination, but an incomplete right inguinal hernia was shown to exist, and a rating of 6/18 was recommended therefor.

A supplemental application under the said act was filed May 16, 1894, in which the disabilities alleged were "disease of throat, torpid liver, chronic constipation, piles, hernia, nervous debility, spinal weakness, and rheumatism."

Dr. L. W. Baker, of Baldwinsville, Mass., states, in an affidavit filed May 11, 1893, as follows:

I have never treated Mr. Hird professionally; but his history is a very clear one, and his nervous debility and the irregular muscular twitching of the right sterno-mastoideus muscle (sufficient to rotate the head) is, in my opinion, entirely due to a severe nervous shock received in 1863. * * * He has also suffered from malarial poisoning contracted during the war, as a result of which there is now, and has been for several years, severe constipation, necessitating the daily use of enemas, the use of cathartics having been abandoned by medical advice.

The hernia from which he now suffers was probably caused by this constipation. The disabilities above stated have existed continuously since March 19, 1892.

At a medical examination, held July 24, 1895, at Fitchburg, Mass., the following objective conditions were manifested:

Pulse rate, 72; respiration, 18; temperature, 98; height, 5 feet, 8¼ inches; weight, 145 pounds; age, 53 years.

General appearance good; hands smooth; muscles hard; tongue has thin greenish coat; skin clear; nasal and throat passages highly irritated and streaked with mucus, which drops down from posterior nares; larynx considerably irritated and congested. /18.

Torpid liver and chronic constipation; liver dullness extends from sixth rib to margin; no tenderness over liver; splenic area normal. No indications of liver trouble. Bowels are somewhat loaded.

Piles.—The internal veins are considerably enlarged and quite congested: no external piles. 4/18.

Hernia of right side: tumor size of a hen's egg, which only comes into the canal: does not protude through the external ring, which readily admits tip of index finger. It is easily reduced and, apparently, easily retained. 8/18.

There is no evidence of hernia on the left side. Nervous debility and spinal weakness; complains of some tenderness along spinal column, but no tangible symptoms of any other spinal weakness.

Rheumatism.—No enlarged joints and no limitation of motion; complains of some pain in the sciatic region.

Heart.—Apex   visible, but in normal position; area normal; no murmurs. No vicious habits.

No other disability found.

The claim was rejected November 9, 1895, on the ground that a ratable degree of disability on account of causes alleged was not shown to exist.

From this action the pending appeal was entered February 15, 1898, the contentions therein being that an injustice had been done the claimant in the rejection of his claim, as he was shown "to be disabled by reason of pharyngitis, enlarged prostate gland, chronic constipation, and incomplete right inguinal hernia."

Inasmuch as it did not appear that your Bureau had ever been asked by the claimant to recede from the action appealed from, the appeal was referred to you for an advisory opinion of the medical referee as to whether or not he adhered to said action.

The medical referee states, in said opinion, as follows:

This appellant, on March 19, 1892, filed a claim under the act of June 27, 1890, and on May 16, 1894, he filed a supplemental declaration under said act   Claims were rejected November 9, 1895.   From this adverse action an appeal is filed.   The soldier alleged, among other disabilities, hernia.   The certificates of examination made under the claim show that the appellant suffers with an incomplete inguinal hernia of the right side.   The papers are returned by the Department for the opinion of the medical referee as to whether or not said action should be adhered to in view of the fact that an incomplete inguinal hernia is now held to be ratable under said act.

As it is now held that an incomplete inguinal hernia incapacitates for the performance of manual labor in a degree warranting the minimum rate under the act of June 27, 1890, the action of rejection of this claim must be receded from.

If there be no legal objections, the disability will be rated as indicated, if case is again submitted to this division.

In view of the fact that the evidence, the certificates of medical examination, and the concurrent opinion of the medical referee all show the existence of a degree of disability on account of right inguinal hernia, which warrants allowance of the minimum rate under the act of June 27, 1890, the action appealed from is reversed, and the papers in the case are remanded for a readjudication of the claim under said act in accordance with said fact.

As this case has been made special, you are requested to direct that prompt action be taken in the premises.

DEATH CAUSE—COMBINATION OF CAUSES.

SARAH J. SMITH (WIDOW).

The sailor was pensioned for disease of heart. The attending physician certified that death was caused by "pneumonia, exhaustion, and purulent infiltration," after an illness of three months' duration. The widow's claim was rejected on the ground that the alleged cause of death was not due to the disability for which the sailor was pensioned.

Held: That inasmuch as the principal desideratum in a case of lobar pneumonia is the maintenance of the proper action of the heart, to which the treatment is mainly directed; and in view of the fact that the sailor was pensioned for disease of that most important viscus, and that the evidence in the case shows that said disease, as well as pneumonia, was an important factor in the death cause, the question as to the relation of the acute disease of lungs to the preexisting chronic disease of heart is one of complication, not of pathology, the claim is reopened and submitted for readjudication and allowance.

Assistant Secretary Webster Davis to the Commissioner of Pensions, March 19, 1898.

The attorney in this case filed on the 5th instant a motion for reconsideration of departmental decision of December 7, 1897, affirming the action of your Bureau, dated April 11, 1895, rejecting the claim of Sarah J., widow of Henry C. A. Smith, late second-class fireman United States Navy (original No. 14434).

The sailor at the time of his death was a pensioner under the general law at $12 per month for disease of heart.

He died April 1, 1894. The cause assigned, according to a certified transcript from the record of deaths in the District of Columbia, was "pneumonia, exhaustion, and purulent infiltration."

The attending physician of the sailor, Dr. William B. French, of Washington, D. C., who rendered the certificate of death, states, however, in an affidavit filed June 19, 1894, as follows:

On January 3, 1894, I found Mr. H. C. A. Smith, of this city, in the first stage of pneumonia, his heart intermitting and weak, and his general condition poor. He stated then and several times subsequently during rather violent attacks of pain in region of the heart (angina pectoris?) that he had had trouble with that organ while in the Navy and had been treated for it.

Its condition contributed largely to the fatal termination of his pneumonia some three months from the beginning of his disease.

The widow's claim was rejected, as above stated, April 11, 1895, on the ground that the sailor's death resulted from "disease of lungs (pneumonia)" not due to the cause for which he was pensioned.

From this action an appeal was taken June 11, 1897, the contentions therein being—

That the sailor was a pensioner for heart disease; that the death cause, or one of the causes which it appears caused his death, lung disease, is held by all the medical authorities to be sequela or result of heart disease, and if the sailor was affected by lung disease, and there is a pathological connection between heart disease and lung disease, the fact that pneumonia was one of the causes of death is nothing against allowance of the claim.

The medical referee, in an advisory opinion, dated September 30, 1897, states as follows:

There is nothing in this case to warrant the contention of appellant that there was a disease of lungs in this case independent of the pneumonia (inflammation of the lungs).

The medical certificates do not show it, the evidence on file does not show it, and the medical approval rejecting the widow's claim does not show it.

The word pneumonia, inserted in the medical approval of rejection, was simply to explain the form of disease of lungs to be understood, and not that there was pneumonia in addition to some other disease of lungs. If there was some other disease of lungs (chronic in character) due to disease of heart or of service origin, which could be legally accepted, the widow's claim could not be rejected on medical grounds.

As the case now stands, pneumonia (an acute disease) would have to be accepted as a pathological result of disease of heart, in order that the widow's claim be admitted, and this we can not do.

That disease of heart adds materially to the gravity of an attack of pneumonia can not be denied, and if it were shown in this case that the prominent symptoms during the last illness were manifestly those due to the complicating disease of heart (which has not been done in this case) the cause of death could be accepted as due to disease of heart complicated by pneumonia, and the widow's claim admitted.

As the case now stands, the action rejecting the widow's claim was proper.

Under date of December 7, 1897, this Department affirmed the action appealed from.

It was held in the decision of that date that—

The evidence in this case fails to establish the existence of any reasonable or probable connection between the death of the sailor and his service in the Navy.

This decision appears to have been rendered without full consideration of all the facts in the case, and without reference to the rules laid down in prior departmental decisions in analogous cases.

The facts in this case are, that the sailor was pensioned for organic disease of heart; that he contracted pneumonia; that said disease did not run its usual course, and end, by crisis and recovery at the usual periods, or by death, as occurs in one case out of every four or five, but it appears to have been a case of delayed resolution, as the sailor was confined to his bed some two months; that he became somewhat better and was able to go out of doors occasionally during a period of three weeks, when he was again obliged to take to his bed and died within two weeks.

There have been several decisions handed down in cases involving similar questions to the one at issue within the purview of which it would seem that this case might have been considered at the time it was adjudicated.

Assistant Secretary Bussey held in the case of Mary A. Cox (3 P. D., 313) that—

Where the evidence, lay and medical, goes to show that the cause for which pension was granted to a soldier was complicated with a disease which was the immediate cause of his death, the Department will sustain the widow's claim for pension on account of the soldier's death from said complication of causes, holding the same, for pensionable purposes, to be due to the line of duty in the service.

In my opinion of August 21, 1897, in the claim of the minors of Napoleon B. Trask, I held that the rule laid down in the above-cited case had not been amended, qualified, recalled, or annulled by other or contrary decision, and reaffirmed the same.

I also held in the Trask case that, in my opinion, the decision in the case of Mary A. Cox fully met the issue presented by the medical referee in the said Trask case, and laid down a proper rule for the guidance of your Bureau in the adjudication of kindred cases. In the said opinion I also cited the decision of Assistant Secretary Bussey in the case of the widow of Ernest Bierbaum (4 P. D., 172), which is as follows:

> The true rule would seem to be that the case should hinge upon the predominating cause of death, provided the question as to what was the predominating cause is susceptible of proof; but if several causes combine to produce death, only a part of which are due to service and none to fault of the soldier, and from the obscure character and effect of the diseases the extent to which each contributed toward producing death can not be determined, the question should be: Would the disability not due to the service have probably produced death independently of the disability of army origin? If not, the claimant should be given the benefit of the doubt.

I also referred in said opinion to the case of Alma Neidhammer (8 P. D., 276), in which Assistant Secretary Reynolds held as follows:

> Soldier, during his fatal illness, suffered from disease of heart, for which he was pensioned, and also from disease of lungs, which is not conclusively shown to be due to the service, though the evidence strongly tends to establish the same. Both disease of lungs and disease of heart were factors in causing death, but it can not be determined with any degree of certainty which of the two diseases was the predominating cause or contributed most toward producing death, and it is held that from the evidence it is more reasonable to assume that death was due to the soldier's military service than to assume that it was not, and the doubts in the case will be resolved in favor of the claimant.

In an advisory opinion, dated July 7, 1897, in the Trask case, the medical referee states as follows:

> * * * The soldier was pensioned for rheumatism and resulting disease of heart. It appears that death was due to suppurative disease of lungs, and that disease of heart was also present.
>
> It is not medically established that there was a pathological connection between the lung lesion and the heart affection, although it may be admitted that both were factors in the death cause, yet the former, disease of lungs, was the most prominent.
>
> It is a well-established theory that the existence of disease of heart seriously complicates any lung lesion, and if we can be authorized to admit this class of cases it is believed that justice will be done to many claimants whose cases would be rejected if we adhere to the requirement of a strictly pathological connection between the fatal disease and the disability of service origin.

Ample authority appears to have been given in my said opinion, and in the decisions referred to therein, for the allowance of claims in which a logical complication could be demonstrated between the cause of death and the disability accepted as of service origin, although no pathological connection existed between the same.

I also stated in the said opinion—

That the rule laid down by Assistant Secretary Bussey in the case of Mary A. Cox is based upon reason and good judgment, and is in accord with the long and unvaried holding of the Department that "the pension laws should be construed in the liberal and generous spirit which prompted their enactment, and where doubts can not be resolved by evidence, presumption should incline toward claimant."

If it be necessary, therefore, to reaffirm the departmental decision in the cited case of Mary A. Cox (3 P. D., 313), and the rule laid down therein by Assistant Secretary Bussey, the same is hereby reaffirmed, and the action of your Bureau should be governed accordingly in cognate cases.

The medical referee appears to have been willing to admit that a complication existed between the chronic disease of lungs and existing disease of heart in the Trask case, yet refuses to recognize a similar condition in the case at bar between the acute disease of lungs shown to have been contracted three months prior to the sailor's death and the valvular disease of heart from which he had suffered ever since his discharge from the service, although, as Osler states in his admirable work on The Principles and Practice of Medicine, page 531:

The progressive cardiac weakness is, after all, the important enemy to fight in pneumonia.

Relative to the nature of said disease, the same author states, on page 529, that—

Pneumonia is a self-limited disease, and runs its course uninfluenced in any way by medicine. It can neither be aborted nor cut short by any means at our command. Even under the most unfavorable circumstances it will terminate abruptly and naturally without a dose of medicine having been administered.

As to the prognosis of said disease he states, on page 526, that—

Many circumstances of course influence prognosis, particularly the extent of the disease, the height of the fever, the presence of other diseases, and the occurrence of complications.

One of the most frequent complications, according to said author, is endocarditis. He states that—

It may be said that with no acute febrile disease is endocarditis so frequently associated.

It is much more common in the left heart than in the right. It is particularly liable to attack persons with old valvular disease.

As to treatment, he states that "the indications are to lower the temperature and support the heart."

If it is necessary to "support the heart" when there is no preexisting lesion of said organ, of how much more importance is it to maintain its proper action when it is already so seriously diseased as to endanger life without the occurrence of any complication.

The condition of the sailor's heart is best shown by the certificate of the last medical examination, which was held in this city September 1, 1890, and which shows the following objective conditions:

Pulse rate, 108; respiration, 24; temperature, normal; height, 5 feet 4¼ inches; weight, 133 pounds; age, 58 years. Weak and tremulous. Area of cardiac dullness increased in all directions; apex beat felt under eighth rib, near sternum; auscultation reveals a loud-blowing apex murmur, and one at aortic valve of same character, both systolic; action rapid; rhythm irregular as to force and frequency. Lungs normal. No rheumatism. No œdema. We recommend †⅜.

The testimony of Dr. J. W. Bayne, of this city, is also of importance as showing the serious nature of the heart lesion. He states, in an affidavit filed July 23, 1890, as follows:

Did not know Mr. Henry Smith while in the service, but have frequently been called upon the last five or six years to render him professional services.

I have made a careful physical examination of his chest, and find considerable enlargement of the heart, so much so, indeed, that there is a noticeable distension of the left side of the chest. This is due to valvular disease of the heart, which trouble is much aggravated by any violent or active exercise.

The medical referee states in his advisory opinion that—

As the case now stands, pneumonia (an acute disease) would have to be accepted as a pathological result of disease of heart in order that the widow's claim be admitted, and this we can not do.

This is stating an impossibility, as pneumonia "is now almost universally regarded as a specific infectious disease, depending upon a micro-organism." (Osler's Practice of Medicine, p. 512.)

It can not, therefore, be regarded as a pathological sequence of any other disease whatever, but must be considered as an independent disability, and in this case be regarded as either the sole cause or a contributing cause of the soldier's death.

Inasmuch as neither the claimant nor her attorney can be presumed to have any technical knowledge of disease, or of the pathological relation between any two diseases, the fact that an untenable allegation or contention is made in the claim should not be allowed to operate against the interests of the former, but rather should she receive the benefit of the professional knowledge of those passing upon the merits of her claim, be advised of any error of contention, and be given the opportunity to cure the same.

The medical referee also states in his said advisory opinion—

That disease of heart adds materially to the gravity of an attack of pneumonia can not be denied, and if it were shown in this case that the prominent symptoms during the last illness were manifestly those due to the complicating disease of heart (which has not been done in this case) the cause of death could be accepted as due to disease of heart complicated by pneumonia, and the widow's claim admitted.

Inasmuch as the only statement made by the attending physician of the sailor as to the objective symptoms manifested during the fatal illness referred almost entirely to the existing disease of heart, and the symptoms thereof exhibited; and as he stated that "its condition contributed largely to the fatal termination of his pneumonia," it is not quite clear why the medical referee should state that the prominent symptoms manifested during the last illness were not due to the complicating disease of heart.

If he was not satisfied upon that point, it would seem that due consideration of the rights of the claimant would have prompted the calling for a full clinical history of said illness before taking final action in her claim. It does not appear that any such call was made. In view, however of the well-established fact, not theory, that organic disease of heart must necessarily complicate, to a greater or less extent, an attack of pneumonia, it is not apparent why any special testimony on that point should be required before considering the possibility of any existing complication between the two diseases when both are shown to be present, although it is well that the extent of the complication should be shown.

A motion for reconsideration of departmental decision of December 7, 1897, was filed on the 5th instant.

It is contended in said motion that this claim is admissible under the rule laid down in the case of Mary A. Cox, which rule was reaffirmed in the opinion rendered in the case of the minors of Napoleon B. Trask, under date of August 21, 1897.

Accompanying said motion was an additional affidavit of Dr. William B. French, relative to the objective symptoms manifested during the sailor's fatal illness. The doctor states as follows:

I was first called to treat Mr. H. C. A. Smith the 2d day of January, 1894, and found him suffering from an attack of pneumonia, complicated with some affection of the heart, which greatly increased the danger of his pneumonia. The exact character of the heart lesion I can not now recall, but it was a prominent symptom, that I well remember. To control the heart's action digitalis was necessary, together with other remedies addressed particularly to that organ. He remained under my care until February 27, 1894, when he rallied sufficiently to be up and about the house. On March 20, I was again called and treated him until his death, April 1, 1894. While his death was primarily due to pneumonia, it is no doubt probable that the heart lesion was largely instrumental as a cause of death.

An affidavit of the claimant was also filed with the pending motion in which she sets forth at great length the facts; that the soldier was pensioned for disease of heart, from which he suffered severely at times; that he was taken sick January 2, 1894; that the attending physician pronounced said sickness to be pneumonia; that she nursed him from the time he was taken ill until he died; that the prominent symptoms manifested during said illness were referable to the heart; that she supposed that the actual cause of death was disease of heart, until the attending physician stated that death was due to pneumonia, or inflammation of the lungs; but that she is still satisfied that death was caused by the complicating disease of heart.

Taking into consideration the facts that the evidence of the attending physician of the sailor, and of the claimant, who was his wife and nurse, tends to show that the disease of heart, for which he was pensioned, was an important factor in the death cause; that both the aortic and mitral valves of the heart were shown to have been diseased; that disease of heart is not only one of the most common but also one of the most serious complications occurring in a case of lobar pneumonia, and that the Department laid down a rule, in the case of Mary A. Cox, that—

Where the evidence—lay and medical—goes to show that the cause for which pension was granted to a soldier was complicated with a disease which was the immediate cause of his death, the Department will sustain the widow's claim for pension on account of the soldier's death from said complication of causes, holding the same. for pensionable purposes, to be due to the line of duty in the service,

which rule was reaffirmed in the case of the widow of Ernest Bierbaum. in the case of Alma Neidhammer, and in the case of the minors of Napoleon B. Trask, there is sufficient ground, in my judgment, to warrant allowance of this claim, on account of the sailor's death being due to the complications of the pensioned and alleged death causes.

The motion for reconsideration of departmental decision in this case. under date of December 7, 1897, is sustained, the said decision is rescinded and set aside, and the action of your Bureau rejecting the widow's claim is hereby reversed.

In view of the fact that the claimant is shown to be in destitute circumstances her claim has been made special, and you are requested to direct that prompt action looking to its allowance be taken, for which purpose the papers in the case are herewith returned.

DECLARATIONS—ACT JUNE 27, 1890.

JOHN H. SHARON (DECEASED).

As declaration is substantially in the terms of the law, and the claimant in his statement to the examining board alleged the disabilities he claimed for, said claim is held to be valid.

Assistant Secretary Webster Davis to the Commissioner of Pensions, March 19, 1898.

On January 22, 1896, claim for pension of John H. Sharon, now deceased, filed August 23, 1892, under the act of June 27, 1890, was rejected on the ground that no valid claim was on file, the claimant having alleged no disability; and his widow, he having died October 15, 1896, filed this appeal August 20, 1897, contending the claim filed by her said husband is valid under the decisions of the Department.

The declaration in this case appears to be formal in all respects except that it alleges no disability whatever. It reads as follows, after statement of service and discharge:

That he is now unable to earn a support by manual labor by reason of—reenlistment in Company I, Thirty-second Regiment Pennsylvania Cavalry, January 5, 1864, and discharged at Cumberland, Md., October 31, 1865—that said disabilities are not due to his vicious habits, and are, to the best of his knowledge and belief, of a permanent character, etc.,

concluding with the other essential averments of title under said act. The portion above included between dashes, as to reenlistment and discharge, is inserted in the blank space of the form used left for insertion of allegations as to disabilities.

While this declaration thus appears to be incomplete in its formal allegations, yet it appears that when the claimant was examined thereunder on March 29, 1893, he stated to the examining board, and it is so recorded in their certificate:

I have paralysis. I have no power in my left arm. I have rheumatism. I had measles and took cold, followed by rheumatism. I have catarrh;

and he was examined accordingly upon these allegations.

In my letter of instructions of July 28, 1897 (9 P. D., 93), I held that "a declaration in the terms of the act shall be sufficient." The declaration in this case is substantially in the terms of the law—it alleges an inability to earn a support by manual labor, and that his disabilities are not due to vicious habits. It does not state expressly that this inability to earn a support by manual labor was due to disabilities, but such is a natural and necessary inference, and the expression may properly be supplied by intendment.

The statement to the examining board may also, in this case, be accepted as sufficiently supplying the omitted specification or allegation of disabilities, although such statement was not under oath, and can not be held, therefore, to be an amendatory "affidavit." It is a matter of record, however, which was properly recorded by Government agents in the performance of their duty, and is certified to by them as required by the rules of their office.

I am, therefore, of the opinion that the claim filed by the deceased may be accepted as a valid claim under said act, and his widow be allowed to complete same as provided by law.

Rejection is reversed accordingly, and you will please readjudicate the claim in conformity herewith.

RECORD, AMENDMENT OF SAME—JURISDICTION.

GEORGE W. DRAKE.

The official records of the War and Treasury Departments fail to show that this appellant was in the military service of the United States at any time during the war of the rebellion, and all testimony offered to controvert the record should be filed in the War Department, as the Bureau and this Department are bound by such record.

Assistant Secretary Webster Davis to the Commissioner of Pensions, March 19, 1898.

George W. Drake filed in your Bureau on November 12, 1892, an application for pension under the provisions of section 2, act of June 27, 1890, alleging that he had served for ninety days and more during the war of the rebellion as a private in Company B, Fourth Provisional

Enrolled Missouri Militia, and had been honorably discharged from said service, which was rejected on November 25, 1893, upon the ground that the official records in the War and Treasury Departments failed to show that he had served in said organization or had rendered any military service whatever during the war of the rebellion.

From said action appeal was taken on September 3, 1897.

The War Department has no record of the appellant's alleged service or of the organization to which he states he belonged.

The Auditor of the Treasury for the War Department reports that—

the name of George W. Drake is not found upon the rolls of Capt. James Tuggle's company, B, Fourth Provisional Regiment Enrolled Missouri Militia, or on the rolls of any company of said regiment on file in this office.

There is on file an affidavit from Moses C. Brown, of Gallatin, Mo., who swears that he was first lieutenant of Company B, Fourth Provisional Enrolled Missouri Militia, and that the appellant enlisted and served in said company from April, 1864, to October, 1864.

This testimony would be good evidence to submit to the proper officials of the War or Treasury Department in support of an application by the appellant to correct his military record, but it can not avail him here or in your Bureau. Neither your Bureau nor this Department have any authority or jurisdiction whatever to enlist a man into the military service of the United States, or to grant him an honorable discharge therefrom, or to supply or correct his military record, or to hear and consider evidence filed for that purpose.

Such evidence should be presented to the officials of the War Department having custody and control of such records, who alone have jurisdiction and authority to consider the same and grant the relief desired.

The appellant must present himself with a record of enlistment, service, and discharge before he can occupy a pensionable status or his claim for pension be considered on its merits either in your Bureau or by this Department.

The rejection of this claim for the reason stated was clearly not error, and is affirmed accordingly.

LINE OF DUTY—PERSONAL ALTERCATION.

ADOLPHUS LIMOGES.

Claimant having taken a pocketbook from a drunken comrade while the latter was asleep, and having refused to return it upon demand, was assaulted with a club, and sustained permanent injury of the left shoulder.

Held, That the injury was not incurred in the line of duty.

Assistant Secretary Webster Davis to the Commissioner of Pensions, March 26, 1898.

This soldier, on May 23, 1883, filed a claim for invalid pension on account of an injury of the left shoulder, alleged to have been caused

by being struck thereon with a club by a comrade. In April, 1891, he
filed a claim under the act of June 27, 1890. The claim under the old
law was rejected in May, 1895, after a special examination, on the
ground that the alleged injury was not received in the line of duty.
The claim under the act of June 27, 1890, was rejected on the ground
that the principal cause of disability (injury of left shoulder) was due
to vicious habits. On appeal the action in the latter claim was reversed
by Assistant Secretary Reynolds in a decision rendered July 20, 1895.
In that decision the following language was used:

> The injury to claimant's shoulder was inflicted by a comrade, Thomas Cuthbertson,
> who struck him with a stick. It does not appear that the claimant was intoxicated
> at the time, or had given Cuthbertson any good cause for assaulting him. The eye-
> witnesses to the affair agree that Cuthbertson was "fighting drunk." It is also
> fairly established that the claimant while in the service was a dissipated character
> and has been since his discharge. The evidence does not tend to show that the
> claimant was injured while engaged in a personal encounter, but is to the effect that
> he was assaulted and injured before he had time to defend himself, and did not try
> to resist his assailant.

The claimant, through his attorneys, Milo B. Stevens & Co., now
appeals from the rejection of his claim for pension under the old law,
contending that the decision above referred to virtually held that the
soldier was injured in the line of duty.

The claimant has given the following account of the circumstances
under which he was injured:

> Cuthbertson and I had some words about some money I was keeping for him. He
> was lying down on some hay, drunk. His pocketbook was halfway out of his
> pocket. I went to the corporal of the guard and told him to come and look at Cuth-
> bertson. The corporal told me to take the pocketbook and keep it for him till he
> sobered up. He knew Cuthbertson and I were very warm friends. About an hour
> afterwards Tom got up and came to me, asking for his money. I told him I had it
> and it was safe, and when he got sober he could have it. I was afraid he would
> lose it. He got mad and went away. He came back in a few minutes and struck me.

The statement that he was told by the corporal of the guard to take
charge of Cuthbertson's pocketbook is not corroborated. In other
respects his account of the affair agrees substantially with what is told
by other witnesses, none of whom, however, are very reliable. Cuthbertson says he thought the claimant intended to steal his money.

Conceding the facts to be as stated, it is evident that the assault
upon claimant was not wholly without provocation, as in the cases of
William M. Ammerman (3 P. D., 1), William H. Brockenshaw (3 P. D.,
11), and John Dean (4 P. D., 392), which are cited in the appeal. The
assault grew out of an altercation concerning some property belonging
to Cuthbertson which had been taken from him by claimant. It was a
controversy about a purely personal matter, having no connection with
the performance of any military duty. The fact that claimant, at the
time the assault was made, was engaged in the performance of duty
(cleaning his horse) does not settle his status as to "line of duty" with
the respect to the injury. We have to take into consideration the

circumstances which led up to the assault. If the claimant had done nothing whatever to provoke an assault, or if what he did do had been done in the course of his duty as a soldier, he would unquestionably have been in the line of duty. But in taking Cuthbertson's pocketbook he stepped outside of the limits of his duty as a soldier and acted solely in his capacity as a private individual. Whether his motives were good or bad is immaterial. In the case of Alexander Gillespie (2 P. D., 16) the Department held that the fracture of claimant's skull by an enraged comrade in retaliation for an alleged personal offense can not be construed into a legitimate incident of the line of military duty or as having any proper relation thereto. And in the case of Mary A. McManus (4 P. D., 346) it was held that while the Government is bound to protect a soldier from unnecessary harm, yet it is not bound to protect him from the consequences of a quarrel entered into voluntarily on his part and having no connection with the performance of any military duty. Also in a case where the claimant was shot by a civilian in consequence of remarks made by him relative to a quarrel then in progress between such civilian and another officer of the claimant's regiment, the wound was held not to have been incurred in the line of duty, regardless of the question as to whether or not his remarks were sufficient provocation for the shooting. (Bowman H. Peterson, 8 P. D., 56.) These citations are sufficient to show the general tenor of the decisions in cases of this kind. After careful consideration, I am of the opinion that the appellant's claim for pension under the old or so-called "general" law was properly rejected, and the rejection is accordingly affirmed.

ACCRUED PENSION—ACT MARCH 2, 1895.

ALLEGED MINORS OF WILLIAM B. WEYANT.

Under the act of March 2, 1895, no payment of accrued pension (except in reimbursement cases) can be made to any person other than the widow or a child of the soldier.

Assistant Secretary Webster Davis to the Commissioner of Pensions, March 26, 1898.

I have considered the appeal filed July 8, 1897, on behalf of the minor children of Louisa A. Weyant, deceased, late an applicant for pension under the act of July 14, 1862, as the widow of William B. Weyant, formerly a soldier in Company D, Eighty-second Regiment of Pennsylvania Infantry. The facts in this case are as follows:

The soldier died November 1, 1869, without having made any claim for pension, leaving a widow, but no children under the age of 16 years. The widow remarried February 4, 1883, and on August 8, 1890, filed a claim for pension from the date of the soldier's death to the date of her remarriage. She died January 17, 1892, while her claim was still pending, leaving children under 16 years of age by her second hus-band. The guardian of these children, on January 9, 1896, made application to continue the prosecution of the widow's claim with a view to having the accrued pension found to be due thereon paid to her minor children under the provisions of the act of March 2, 1895. Said application was rejected by your Bureau on March 31, 1897, on the ground that the children are not the children of the soldier, and therefore have no status to apply for accrued pension under the act of March 2, 1895. From that action the appeal is taken, the conteu-tion therein being that the law makes no distinction between a widow's children by the soldier and her children by another person.

The law in question reads as follows:

Be it enacted by the Senate and House of Representatives of the United States of America in Congress assembled, That from and after the twenty-eighth day of September, eighteen hundred and ninety-two, the accrued pension to the date of the death of any pensioner, or of any person entitled to a pension having an application therefor pending, and whether a certificate therefor shall issue prior or subsequent to the death of such person, shall, in the case of a person pensioned, or applying for pen-sion, on account of his disabilities or service, be paid, first, to his widow; second, if there is no widow, to his child or children under the age of sixteen years at his death; third, in case of a widow, to her minor children under the age of sixteen years at her death. Such accrued pension shall not be considered a part of the assets of the estate of such deceased person, nor be liable for the payment of the debts of said estate in any case whatsoever, but shall inure to the sole and exclusive benefit of the widow or children. And if no widow or child survive such pensioner, and in the case of his last surviving child who was such minor at his death, and in case of a dependent mother, father, sister, or brother, no payment whatsoever of their accrued pension shall be made or allowed except so much as may be necessary to reimburse the person who bore the expense of their last sickness and burial, if they did not leave sufficient assets to meet such expense. And the mailing of a pen-sion check, drawn by a pension agent in payment of a pension due, to the address of a pensioner, shall constitute payment in the event of the death of a pensioner subsequent to the execution of the voucher therefor. And all prior laws relating to the payment of accrued pension are hereby repealed.

The appellant rests his case upon the words of the statute, "to her minor children under the age of sixteen years at her death," contending that the same do not properly admit of an interpretation confining their application to her children by the soldier.

The act of March 2, 1895, may be said to have been an act to revise, consolidate, and amend the previously existing provisions relative to the payment of accrued pension contained in section 4718 of the Revised Statutes and the act of March 1, 1889. Much of the language of these former statutes was retained in said act, and where so retained without any new qualifying words or phrases, it may be presumed that it was intended to have the same meaning which had been accorded it in the practical construction of such former statutes by your Bureau and the Department; for if it had been the intention to exclude any known con-struction of the previous statutes the legal presumption is that the lan-guage would have been so changed as to effectuate that intention. (See Sutherland on Statutory Construction, secs. 309 and 333.)

Section 4718, Revised Statutes, reads, in part, as follows:

SEC. 4718. If any pensioner has died or shall hereafter die, or if any person entitled to a pension, having an application therefor pending, has died or shall hereafter die, his widow, or if there is no widow, the child or children of such person under the age of sixteen years shall be entitled to receive the accrued pension to the date of the death of such person.

The act of March 1, 1889, provided, inter alia, that—

* * * the amount which may have accrued on the pension of any pensioner subsequent to the last quarterly payment on account thereof and prior to the death of such pensioner shall, in the case of a husband, be paid to his widow, or if there be no widow, to his surviving minor children or the guardian thereof, and in the case of a widow, to her minor children.

In the act of March 2, 1895, these provisions are consolidated and amended to read as follows:

* * * the accrued pension to the date of the death of any pensioner, or of any person entitled to a pension having an application therefor pending, and whether a certificate therefor shall issue prior or subsequent to the death of such person, shall, in the case of a person pensioned, or applying for pension, on account of his disabilities or service, be paid, first, to his widow; second, if there is no widow, to his child or children under the age of sixteen years at his death; third, in the case of a widow, to her minor children under the age of sixteen years at her death.

It will be observed that that part of the act relating to the accrued pension of a widow is taken, ipsissima verba, from the act of March 1. 1889. It becomes proper to inquire, therefore, what construction was given by the Pension Bureau to the words "to her minor children" in the execution of the latter act. This question is answered by a statement from the former chief of the board of review incorporated in your report of February 8, 1898, in which he says:

* * * and in the act of March 1, 1889, the clause "and in the case of a widow to her minor children" was also construed as relating only to the children of the soldier.

It must be presumed the Congress was cognizant of that construction, and that when it used the same words in the act of March 2, 1895, it intended them to have the same effect.

Approaching the question from another point of view, it seems reasonably clear from an examination of all the provisions of the act that it was designed to restrict the payment of accrued pension (except in the way of reimbursement for expenses of last sickness and burial) to those persons who would succeed to the soldier's pensionable rights under the provisions of section 4702, Revised Statutes—i. e., to his widow and his minor children under 16 years of age. It shuts out the grand children of the soldier, his nephews and nieces, and even his parents and minor brothers and sisters. Can it be supposed that Congress intended, while excluding these relations from benefit under said act, to let in persons having no blood connection whatever with the soldier?

It may be said that the accrued pension "in the case of a widow" is simply so much money which was owing to her at the time of her death, and that it is but right and proper that the Government should pay the same to her minor children, who would have enjoyed a share of the benefits of it if she had lived. But any reasoning of this kind, based on the equities of the case, would apply with equal force to the accrued pension of a mother, or father, or brother, or sister who may have died leaving a child or children under 16 years of age. Yet the law expressly declares that—

in case of a dependent mother, father, sister, or brother, no payment whatsoever of their accrued pension shall be made or allowed except so much as may be necessary to reimburse the person who bore the expense of their last sickness and burial, if they did not leave sufficient assets to meet such expense.

If the widow in this case had died leaving minor children (under the age of 16 years) by the soldier and also minor children by the second husband, it is clear that no part of the accrued pension could be paid to the latter, as the soldier's children would have a right under section 4702, Revised Statutes, to apply for and receive pension in their own right from the date of the soldier's death. From this it is apparent that the law is solicitous only for the minor children of the soldier, and takes no cognizance of any seemingly equitable rights on the part of other children.

The theory upon which the act of March 2, 1895, seems to have been based is that a pension is a provision made solely for the maintenance of the person to whom it is granted, and that upon the death of such person all right and title to the pension, or any part thereof, ceases. Any unpaid balance due at the time of death should revert to the Government, since its payment would not subserve the purpose for which the pension was granted.

It is easy to see why an exception to this general rule should be made in favor of the soldier's minor children and in favor of persons who have paid the expenses of a pensioner's last sickness and burial. It is not easy to see why an exception should be made in favor of children who are wholly unrelated to the soldier.

After the most careful examination, I am of the opinion that the construction given to the law by your Bureau was correct, and your action is therefore affirmed.

———

DISLOYALTY—SECTION 4716, REVISED STATUTES, AND ACT JUNE 27, 1890.

GEORGE W. GILBERT.

1. Claimant was in the Army of the Confederate States from May, 1861, to September, 1863, and was afterwards in the Army of the United States from October, 1864, to July, 1865. Having voluntarily engaged in and aided and abetted the rebellion against the authority of the United States, he is not entitled to pension under said act of June 27, 1890, his title being barred by the provisions of section 4716, Revised Statutes.

2. Said section 4716, Revised Statutes, has application to the act of June 27, 1890, as well as to that of July 14, 1862, or any other law, except as its operation is suspended by the act of March 3, 1877, in the case of those disabled in a service subsequent to the disloyal service, or as exemption from its operation is specifically provided for in other laws granting pensions for service in prior wars. No repeal of said section 4716, Revised Statutes, or exemption from its operation is provided in the act of June 27, 1890, and it is construed in *pari materia* with other laws to be subject to the inhibition of said section.

Assistant Secretary Webster Davis to the Commissioner of Pensions, March 26, 1898.

This is a motion, filed January 10, 1898, requesting reconsideration of decision of this Department of November 20, 1897, affirming on appeal the rejection by your Bureau of the claim (No. 967943) of George W. Gilbert, late private Company I, First Tennessee Mounted Infantry, for pension under the provisions of section 2, act of June 27, 1890, upon the ground that he had voluntarily served during the war of the rebellion in the Confederate Army, and his title to pension under said section was barred by the provisions of section 4716, Revised Statutes.

This claim was most carefully considered by me on appeal, and the questions presented were thoroughly and fully discussed, and the former departmental rulings and decisions bearing thereon collated and reviewed at length in the decision above referred to by which its rejection was affirmed. Said decision is as follows:

George W. Gilbert, late of Company I, First Tennessee Mounted Infantry, filed his application December 16, 1890, for pension under the act of June 27, 1890, and while said claim was still pending he filed another, February 25, 1897, alleging additional disability. The final action was taken on these claims May 7, 1897, on the ground of "no title under said act of June 27, 1890, claimant having served voluntarily in the Confederate States Army, as shown by the records at the War Department. Barred by section 4716, Revised Statutes." From this action appeal has been entered. May 21, 1897, by S. Jerome Smith, attorney, the sole contention being that section 4716, Revised Statutes, has no application to the act of June 27, 1890, which is a law unto itself, directing payment of pension to all persons who served ninety days in the Army or Navy of the United States, and were honorably discharged therefrom, without regard to the record of any other service.

The records of the War Department show that claimant first enlisted May 12, 1861, in Company B, Sixteenth Tennessee Infantry Confederate States Army, and continued in said service until September 19, 1863, when he was captured at the battle of Chicamauga. The prisoner of war records contain no information about him, but it is shown that he afterwards enlisted, October 9, 1864, in the service of the United States, in Company I, First Tennessee Mounted Infantry United States Army, and was discharged July 22, 1865.

There are no complications in this case on the score of the claimant's service in the Confederate States Army. He admits the service and that it was voluntary. The only difference between the record and his statement as to this service is that instead of being captured, as the records show, he avers that he left his command soon after the battle of Perryville and never returned to it again. The record may be in error as to his capture, and the presumption is that he remained about his home in Tennessee after his desertion from the Confederate service until his enlistment in October, 1864.

The only matter to be determined, then, is the issue raised in the appeal as to whether claimant's title to pension under the act of June 27, 1890, is affected by the operation of section 4716, Revised Statutes. The same question has been before the Department many times in other cases, and decisions, pro and con, have been rendered upon it. Said section 4716, Revised Statutes, is as follows:

"No money on account of pension shall be paid to any person, or to the widow, children, or heirs of any deceased person, who, in any manner, voluntarily engaged in or aided or abetted the late rebellion against the authority of the United States."

This was amended by the act of March 3, 1877, as follows:

"That the law prohibiting the payment of any money on account of pensions to any person, or to the widow, children, or heirs of any deceased person, who, in any manner, engaged in or aided or abetted the late rebellion against the authority of the United States, shall not be construed to apply to such persons as afterward voluntarily enlisted in the Army of the United States, and who, while in such service, incurred disability from a wound or injury received or disease contracted in the line of duty."

Prior to the passage of the act of June 27, 1890, the uniform rulings in departmental decisions had been that said section 4716, Revised Statutes, from the date of its enactment, February 4, 1862, had application to all laws granting pensions, and that disloyalty, in the sense therein defined, of voluntarily aiding and abetting the late rebellion against the authority of the United States, was a bar to title, except as the operation of said section was modified by the act of March 3, 1877, in the cases of those who received wounds or injuries or contracted disease in the service subsequent to the disloyal service, and except in such cases as exemption from the operation of said section was made, in express terms, in any law.

The only exceptions thus made are as follows: Act of March 9, 1878, granting pensions to soldiers and sailors of the war of 1812; act of January 29, 1887, granting pensions to soldiers and sailors of the Mexican war; act of July 27, 1892, granting pensions to survivors of certain Indian wars. In the first-named act, that of March 9, 1878, the exempting clause is as follows:

"That the Secretary of the Interior be, and he is hereby, authorized and directed to restore to the pension rolls the names of all persons now surviving heretofore pensioned on account of service in the war of 1812 against Great Britain, or for service in any of the Indian wars, and whose names were stricken from the rolls in pursuance of the act entitled 'An act authorizing the Secretary of the Interior to strike from the pension rolls the names of such persons as have taken up arms against the Government or who have in any manner encouraged the rebels,' approved February 4, 1862; and that the joint resolution entitled 'Joint resolution prohibiting payment by any officer of the Government to any person not known to have been opposed to the rebellion and in favor of its suppression,' approved March 2, 1867, and section 4716 of the Revised Statutes of the United States shall not apply to the persons provided for by this act: *Provided*, That no money shall be paid to any one on account of pensions for the time during which his name remained stricken from the rolls."

In the other two acts, those of January 29, 1887, and July 27, 1892, section 5, of the one, and section 6, of the other, reads as follows:

"That section forty-seven hundred and sixteen of the Revised Statutes is hereby repealed so far as the same relates to this act or to pensioners under this act."

From a careful reading of the laws from which these quotations are made, it will be observed that Congress, having an appreciation of the full import of section 4716, Revised Statutes, was careful of the limitation of its operation to be authorized, and of the class of cases in which such limitation should apply. Thus, in the act of March 3, 1877, the limitation goes only to the extent of removing the disability, imposed by said section, of those who, having participated in the rebellion, have subsequently enlisted in the *Army* of the United States, and *become disabled in such subsequent service.* This exemption does not extend to any other persons or class of persons, nor to the widows, children, or dependent relatives of the persons named, nor was it extended to those who, since their disloyal service, served in the Navy, until August 1, 1892. Furthermore, this exemption has reference to a service rendered subsequent to and entirely independent of all disloyal service, and was intended to give recognition to such service because of actual disability contracted therein, and untainted by any suspicion of disloyalty.

So, in relation to the beneficiaries in the other acts referred to, their services were rendered in wars long prior to the war of the rebellion, and were in all respects loyal and wholly meritorious. But what is more strictly to the point in relation to all of these acts, whatever the purpose may have been in enacting them, the exemption from the operation of section 4716, Revised Statutes, is expressly made, and is not left to implication or construction.

It was subsequent to the passage of the act of June 27, 1890, that a different interpretation was given to the applicability of section 4716, Revised Statutes, to the pension laws in general, and especially to that act, the principal feature of such interpretation being that said section had been in effect repealed by the act of March 3, 1877, and if not, that the exemption which was expressly made in other laws was, by implication, applicable to said act of June 27, 1890. The decisions on this line, and which sustain the view contended for in this appeal, were rendered between 1890 and 1893. These are principally the decisions in the cases of George W. Coffey (4 P. D., 285) and Daniel B. Garrison (6 P. D., 289), and others therein cited. In the decision in the Coffey Case it is stated that "the only essential conditions precedent to pension under the act of June 27, 1890, are service of not less than ninety days, an honorable discharge, and proof of the fact that claimant's disabilities are not due to his own vicious habits." And it was further held, in reference to the act of March 3, 1877, that—

"This act is obviously applicable to the claimant in this case. It operates expressly as a repeal of the act of February 4, 1862 (now section 4716), so far as the latter act might otherwise relate to him. It exempts the claimant, and all persons similarly situated, from the inhibition which section 4716 contains."

So also, in the decision of the Garrison Case, overruling a previous decision holding a different view, in the same case, and adopting the decision in the case of Henry L. Hayman, of March 19, 1891 (not published), a similar ruling was made. After quoting the second section of the act of June 27, 1890, the decision states:

"The foregoing provision expressly states that proof of service for ninety days in the naval service of the United States during the late rebellion, and of an honorable discharge therefrom, shall be sufficient as a basis for invalid pension under the act of June 27, 1890. This provision is made regardless alike of section 4716 and of the act of March 3, 1877; it is made without reference to any other condition than those distinctly named in the act of which it forms a part, and it may be added that even if there be aught in preceding legislation in conflict with this provision it would be held by the Department as repealed, in conformity with the accepted rules of statutory construction—the latest expression of the legislative will is necessarily the law until the same be amended or revoked. The claim of Mr. Hayman must, therefore, be adjudicated under section 2 of the act of June 27, 1890, and not in pursuance of section 4716, Revised Statutes, which has, in fact, no bearing upon the case. The Government accepted Mr. Hayman as a suitable person for the naval service of the United States, and nothing that he had done prior to his authoritative admission into that service can invalidate his claim for pension under the act of June 27, 1890."

It will be observed that besides the inconsistency between the position here taken and that taken in the decision of the Coffey Case, and besides the peculiar and arbitrary construction by which section 4716, Revised Statutes, is ruled out of all application to the act of June 27, 1890, the attempt is made to sustain the claimant's title on a sort of plea of quantum meruit—that is, that inasmuch as the service of ninety days was rendered as stated, the Government has no right to inquire into claimant's past conduct of disloyalty so as to deprive him of a pension.

Decisions sustaining the contrary view to the above have been rendered since 1893. These hold that the act of June 27, 1890, is a part of the pension code and must be construed in conjunction with all general pension laws; that section 4716, Revised Statutes, has a direct bearing on the title of beneficiaries under said act of June 27, 1890, there being no exemption provided therein from the operation of said section. (See cases of Adolph Bernstein, 7 P. D., 229; Milo Ousterhout, 7 P. D., 270; Job White, 7 P. D., 312; Sarah H. Osborn, 7 P. D., 317; Angustus H. Longee, 7 P. D., 386; Anastatio Capella, 8 P. D., 308; Emma H. Seymour, 8 P. D., 325.)

In these decisions cited the subject has been discussed in all its bearings, and the decisions in the Coffey and Garrison cases were distinctly overruled. It is unnecessary to rehearse all the reasoning by which the conclusions of these decisions were sustained. It will be enough to make one or two citations which appear pertinent to the precise issue involved. Thus, in the Bernstein decision the construction to be given to the act of June 27, 1890, was stated as follows:

"This act of June 27, 1890, is a part of the pension code and is to be construed, like all similar acts, in *pari materia*. The various statutes upon the subject of pensions enacted by Congress from time to time comprise our system of pension laws, in the nature of a code, relating to one subject and governed by one spirit and policy. They are to be construed together, like our revenue laws, banking laws, land laws, mining laws, patent laws, and other similar laws upon a specific subject; and where the later statute fails to repeal a former in express terms or by necessary implication, such later statutes operate cumulatively and not by way of substitution or repeal.

"'It is a well-established rule that where various statutes relate to the same subject they are all to be taken into consideration in construing any one of them, and that all acts in *pari materia* are to be taken together as if they were one law. If a thing contained in a subsequent statute be within the reason of a former statute it shall be taken to be within the meaning of that statute. (U. S. r. Freeman, 3 Howard, 565, and authorities therein cited.)'

"The law upon this subject is concisely and correctly stated by Sutherland in his work on the Construction of Statutes (section 283), as follows:

"'All consistent statutes which can stand together, though enacted at different dates relating to the same subject, and hence briefly called statutes in *pari materia*, are treated prospectively and construed together as though they constituted one act.' * * *

"As stated by Sutherland, in his work already cited:

"'The legislatures are presumed to know existing statutes and state of the law relating to the subjects with which they deal, hence they would expressly abrogate any prior statutes they intended to be repealed by new legislation.' (Sec. 297.)

"So, in the Job White decision, it was held:

"'Section 4716, Revised Statutes, prohibits the payment of any money on account of pension to any person, or to the widow or children or heirs of any deceased person who in any manner voluntarily engaged in, or aided or abetted the late rebellion against the authority of the United States, except in cases where pension is granted on account of disability due to a wound or injury received or disease contracted in the service of the United States, under a contract of enlistment entered into subsequent to the time such person was engaged in aiding or abetting the late rebellion, and in certain classes of pensions granted on account of service in wars prior to the war of the rebellion, which are expressly excepted from the operation of said section.'"

These rulings are in harmony with the decisions of the Department made previous to 1890, as already noted, and are clear in giving uniform interpretation to all laws, without forcing a construction unwarranted by the text and inconsistent with sound reasoning. The act of June 27, 1890, in these rulings is considered as much subject to the inhibition of said section 4716, Revised Statutes, as the act of July 14, 1862, or any other law containing no express clause of exemption from that inhibition.

After giving full consideration to the purpose for which the section 4716, Revised

Statutes, was enacted, and to its relations to other laws, due regard being had to that construction which will preserve the force and consistency of each law, without inharmony, I am constrained to agree with the views expressed in the later decisions referred to, and to hold that the disloyalty defined in said section 4716, Revised Statutes, is a bar to title under the act of June 27, 1890, as it is under all other laws providing pension for service in and during the war of the rebellion, or where express exemption from its operation is not made.

And I can see no reason or good purpose in trying to place a strained construction on the act of June 27, 1890, by holding that it is *sui generis*, disconnected from any relationship to other laws, and unaffected by this section 4716, Revised Statutes, to which it makes no specific reference, and of which it contains no repeal or exemption. Said act provides pension upon certain conditions therein named, but in so far as those conditions are not inconsistent with the enforcement of other laws the pension is subject to the provisions of the laws in general.

Furthermore, there is to my mind no ground for the statement that the act of March 3, 1877, operates expressly as a repeal of section 4716, Revised Statutes. The plain language of that act shows that it was only intended to exempt from the application of said section a certain class of persons therein specifically designated and described, while as to all others the section remained in full force and effect. Neither can I lend approval to the idea intended to be conveyed in the quasi plea of *quantum meruit*, as contained in the decision of the Coffey Case, supra, wherein it is stated:

"The very act of accepting the claimant's services, if unaccompanied by fraud on his part, subjected the Government to an estoppel against any and every denial to him of equal pensionable rights with all the rest of its soldiers. And hence the claimant, from the moment of his enlistment in the Army of the United States, stood upon an equal footing before the law with all other soldiers in the same Army."

Because the claimant rendered service to the United States does not of itself entitle him to a pension. Being a gratuity and not a debt, pensions are only granted when the persons to receive them have brought themselves in consonance with the spirit and intent of the laws and complied with the requirements of those laws as to proof of title. And in the execution of these terms claimant must not only prove that the service was rendered, but that all other requirements have been met, including the fact of his loyalty. And whatever may be said in the line of this last quotation from the Coffey Case, and in favor of the equity of allowing pension to those who, although having committed such act of disloyalty, afterwards atoned for the same as far as possible, and rendered faithful service to the Government in the war of the rebellion, the fact yet remains that the law as it stands is against such allowance, and can not be evaded or changed except by the Congress itself.

The claimant having voluntarily engaged in and aided and abetted the rebellion against the authority of the United States is not entitled to pension under the provisions of the act of June 27, 1890, and the rejection of his claim was proper. That action is affirmed.

The present motion does not attempt to assign any errors in said decision or to refute or combat any of the reasons therein set forth for the conclusions and ruling thereby announced, but simply enters a general and unqualified denial of the fact, conclusively and positively proven by the official military records and his own sworn statements and repeated admissions that the claimant had voluntarily served in the Confederate Army.

It therefore presents no reason and affords no basis or ground whatever for a change or modification of said decision, which is believed to be thoroughly sound, and to correctly state the law applicable to this case, and is in entire accord with the present view and holding of this Department upon this question.

Therefore the decision upon the appeal of this claim of November 20, 1897, and the action of your Bureau thereby affirmed, will be maintained and adhered to, and this motion is overruled.

PRACTICE—INCREASE—ORDER 352.

JOHN W. GRANLESS.

Order No. 352, issued by the Commissioner of Pensions December 24, 1897, which prohibits the consideration of increase claims within one year of date of last adjudication in the case, is revoked and set aside, and the rule contained on page 52 of Walker's Treatise on the Practice in the Pension Bureau, holding that such claims would not be adjudicated until six months after the allowance of the original claim, though when declarations therefor were filed claimants should be ordered for examination as soon as practicable, reestablished.

Assistant Secretary Webster Davis to the Commissioner of Pensions, March 30, 1898.

I have considered the appeal in behalf of John W. Granless, late of Company K, Twenty third Pennsylvania Infantry, from your action of January 6, 1898, refusing to consider his claim for increase of pension, filed October 5, 1897, within twelve months from a prior adjudication, September 23, 1897.

In your action above referred to you say:

You are advised that your claim was adjudicated September 23, 1897, and that you are now drawing $8 per month under the act of June 27, 1890. By a recent order of this Bureau, claims for increase of pension will not be considered within twelve months from the allowance of the claim or a prior adjudication.

The order referred to says "increase claims will not be *considered* within one year," etc. This was substituted for the rule laid down in Walker's Treatise on the Practice of the Pension Bureau (p. 52). Said rule was as follows:

Claims for increase will not be *adjudicated* until six months shall have elapsed after the allowance of the original claim; though, when declarations are filed therefor, the claimants should, as soon as practicable, be ordered for examination, for the reason that the increase must commence at the date of the medical examination made pending such claim, except in cases of permanent and specific disabilities.

There is a vast difference between these two rules aside from the period mentioned during which the claims would not be adjudicated. The old rule says: Claims will not be *adjudicated* within six months from allowance of the original claim, but that claimant should be ordered for a medical examination as soon as practicable; while your order says such claims will not be *considered* within one year; thus arbitrarily depriving a meritorious claimant of a medical examination for one year at least, and thus depriving him of one year's increase of pension.

By section 4698½, Revised Statutes, the increased rate of pension, when allowed, begins from the date of the examining surgeon's certificate showing an increase in a claimant's disability.

Pensioners have a right to apply for an increase of pension when they believe themselves entitled thereto, and no discrimination should be made against them substantially affecting their rights.

It is a fundamental rule of practice in the Bureau and the Department that claims shall be considered in the order of filing; but it is true that this is not always practicable in the numerous individual claims for pensions, and it should be remembered that one class of claimants can not be expected to willingly concede the right of precedence to another class, especially when this affects the amount of pension a claimant may receive.

For instance: A person receiving a pension at a low rate for a nervous disease which suddenly results in paralysis, rendering him entirely helpless, and entitling him, on establishing his claim, to a rate of $72 per month. If, immediately on filing his claim, he should be ordered for an examination and appeared for examination, his increased rate would begin from the date of the surgeon's certificate of such examination; but under your order (No. 352) he is deprived of the benefit of an examination for at least one year from filing his claim.

It is believed that the practical effect of Order No. 352 will result in great injustice to a great number of claimants for increase. Practically, the limitation extends far beyond the twelve months prescribed. Claimants are not prohibited from filing their claims when they choose, and it follows that a large number will be filed and will be filed away, and many of them will not be considered until called up. Then a medical examination will be ordered, which still further prolongs the adjudication and materially affects the claimant's interests, since the increase, if allowed, must commence in most cases from the date of the medical examination. It will thus be observed that the adjudication of increase claims under this order is indefinitely postponed.

I am informed that you have so arranged the business in your Bureau that four days in each week are set apart for the adjudication of original claims and two days each week for adjudicating increase, rerating, and restoration claims.

Under this arrangement no injustice will be done claimants for original pensions, and no reason appears for refusing to adjudicate increase claims in the order in which filed, as near as practicable.

In this case claimant filed in July, 1890, a claim under the act of June 27, 1890, which was rejected August 26, 1893. He filed another claim September 9, 1895, which was allowed September 23, 1897, at $8 per month. It thus appears that in claims to which said order does not apply it requires from two to three years to reach them for adjudication, and, on this basis, if Order No. 352 is followed, no medical examination would be ordered within three years from date of filing the claim. Five months have now elapsed since this claim for increase was filed and no medical examination has been ordered.

After carefully considering this question, I am free to say Order No.

352, if enforced, will result in great injustice to a large number of claimants, and the same is therefore revoked and set aside, and hereafter you will please adjudicate increase claims in accordance with the rule found on page 52 of Walker's Treatise on the Practice in the Pension Bureau, approved by Commissioner of Pensions Dudley, November 15, 1882, and followed from that time until the promulgation of your said order, December 24, 1897.

PRESUMPTION OF DEATH EVIDENCE.

JULIA BOYLE (MOTHER).

The continued unexplained absence of the soldier for more than twenty years, though sufficient to raise the presumption of death, does not entitle his mother to pension, as it must be further shown that such soldier died of a wound or injury received or disease contracted in the United States service and in line of duty.

Assistant Secretary Webster Davis to the Commissioner of Pensions, March 31, 1898.

Julia Boyle filed a claim for pension, under the general law, on the 29th day of December, 1890, as dependent mother of William Boyle, late of Company B, Fifth Michigan Cavalry, alleging, among other things, that her said son was captured at the battle of Trevilian Station, June 11, 1864, and sent to Andersonville Prison, Georgia, where he remained a prisoner of war for about nine months, and, while in prison aforesaid, he contracted chronic diarrhea, fever, and rheumatism, which resulted in disease of stomach, bowels, liver, kidneys, heart, piles, scurvy, and general nervous debility, and suffered therefrom until after his discharge from the Army, and finally died while en route to San Francisco, Cal., soon after February 18, 1875.

Her claim was rejected November 2, 1891, on the ground that the evidence fails to show the date and cause of the soldier's death, and that his death was due to his military service, the claimant having stated under oath her inability to furnish such evidence.

This appeal therefrom was entered September 10, 1897, the appellant contending that she has made diligent search for said son, and has been unable to find his whereabouts since February 18, 1875.

In order to grant a pension to a dependent mother, under section 4707, Revised Statutes of the United States, it must appear that the soldier upon whose death the claim is based died of a wound, injury, casualty, or disease contracted in the military or naval service of the United States while in the line of his duty.

In this case the appellant has testified that she is unable to state when, where, or of what disease the soldier died, or in fact that he is actually dead.

It would be useless to hold that the continued unexplained absence of the soldier for more than twenty years had raised the presumption of his death, because that fact alone would not be sufficient to satisfy the conditions named in the statute, as it would be necessary to further show that said death was due to his army service, which in the nature of the case would be impossible.

Therefore, after a careful review of the evidence, I am of the opinion that the proof in the case is wholly insufficient to establish the claim.

Rejection affirmed.

PRACTICE–RESTORATION–INCREASE.

CHARLES I. REED.

A claim for restoration can not be regarded as a claim for increase. (Thomas Mallon, 8 P. D., 208.)

Assistant Secretary Webster Davis to the Commissioner of Pensions, March 31, 1898.

Charles I. Reed, of Company I, One hundred and twenty-eighth Indiana Volunteers, enlisted February 22, 1864, and was discharged April 10, 1896. He was pensioned under the act of June 27, 1890, at the rate of $10 per month, from July 11, 1890 (Certificate No. 548453), on account of disability resulting from rheumatism and disease of heart. His rating was subsequently reduced to $6 per month, commencing June 4, 1895.

On December 26, 1895, claimant filed a declaration asking restoration to his former rating, to commence from date of reduction. He alleges the same disabilities as were declared in the original application, namely, rheumatism, heart disease, and dyspepsia. The claim was adjudicated on August 12, 1897, and approved for a rating of $8 per month, commencing March 4, 1896, the date of last medical examination.

From this action appeal was taken on September 9, 1897, upon the following assignment of error:

I appeal from the action of the Pension Office in adjudicating the claim as an increase claim instead of as a claim for restoration of pension to the original rate, commencing from date of reduction. The claim cited was not a claim for increase of pension and in the application for restoration he did not ask increase, but did ask to be restored to his original rate from the date he was reduced.

In the letter of transmittal from your Office the following statement occurs:

Pension appears to have been erroneously increased on a declaration for restoration. It is not believed, however, that said allowance should now be disturbed.

The claimant asks that the action be reversed and that his application be adjudicated as a claim for restoration of pension, and that his former rate be restored to him to commence from the date on which the same was reduced.

The action of your Office in treating the pending claim as an application for increase was an irregularity which might work a hurtful detriment to the rights of the claimant.

In the case of Thomas Mallon (8 P. D., 208) it is substantially held that the adjudication of a claim for restoration to a rate from which claimant had been reduced as a claim for increase is error. In that case the facts are very similar to those disclosed by the record of the case at bar. The claimant had been pensioned at the rate of $12 per month under the act of June 27, 1890, which rate had been reduced to $6 per month. An application for restoration presents the contention that claimant is entitled to his original rate from the date of reduction, and therefore relates back, to take effect at some time which antedates the filing thereof. A claim for increase, except in case of specific disability, is conditioned upon the disclosures of a medical examination made subsequent to the filing. The successful conditions of a claim for restoration are precedent; those of a claim for increase are subsequent.

Inasmuch as the pending claim for restoration has been adjudicated as a claim for increase instead of a claim for restoration, the action appealed from is reversed.

SERVICE, LENGTH OF—TRAVEL PAY.

PHILIP E. RYAN.

From date of enrollment to discharge soldier served eighty-five days. He claims that his term of service should be held also to include the time required to go from place of discharge to place of enlistment. This claim is untenable.

Assistant Secretary Webster Davis to the Commissioner of Pensions, March 31, 1898.

On March 2, 1896, Philip E. Ryan filed a declaration for pension (No. 1174811) under the act of June 27, 1890, alleging that he was enrolled on October 20, 1862, in the Mercantile Battery, Illinois Light Artillery, from which he was discharged on May 13, 1865. His claim was rejected on May 6, 1896, on the ground that claimant did not serve ninety days in the war of the rebellion within the meaning of said act, as shown by the records of the War Department.

Soldier's military history, as disclosed by the records of the Department of War, is as follows:

It is shown by the records that this soldier, while in confinement in the guardhouse of his command at Memphis, Tenn., escaped from confinement on the night November 23, 1862, and deserted to the enemy. The records of prisoners of war show that he was captured by the enemy in west Tennessee, and paroled November 26, 1862. No subsequent record has been found of him under military control until March 28, 1865, when he surrendered as a deserter at Tod Barracks, Columbus, Ohio, under the President's proclamation of March 11, 1865. He was discharged the service May 13, 1865, with loss of all pay and allowance due at date of desertion, together with that which had accrued since, in accordance with the instructions of the Secretary of War of May 3, 1865.

From the action of rejection claimant appealed on August 30, 1897, contending that the record shows that he was with his command eighty-five days from date of enlistment to date of discharge, and adds:

To this must be added pay or allowance for travel from place of discharge to place of enlistment, as provided by law, a distance of 350 miles by the shortest route at that date. This is equal to fourteen days of time, making a grand total of ninety-nine days of service, according to law and rules of practice of Pension Bureau.

The plain and unambiguous provision of section 4701, Revised Statutes, is that the period of service of all persons entitled to the benefit of the pension laws—

shall be construed to extend to the time of disbanding the organization to which such persons belonged or until their actual discharge for other cause than the expiration of the service of such organization.

In the case of George W. Hill (7 P. D., 235) the contention of claimant was precisely similar to that in the case at bar. His term of service, if measured by the period from enrollment to muster out, was eighty-five days, but if measured by the time for which he was paid it was one hundred and one days. Under these facts the Department in the Hill case held:

The rule that pay determines the length of service is not a sound rule for general application. It may be safe as applied to some cases, especially of service in earlier wars where the records are incomplete, but would certainly be often unsafe and inaccurate if applied uniformly in the administration of the pension laws. No law extends the period of service beyond the date of actual discharge or of disbandment of the organization. But the law does, in many instances, authorize pay for a limited period after either of these dates.

It is very clear that appellant did not serve ninety days in the war of the rebellion, within the meaning of the act of June 27, 1890, and for that reason the action of your office is affirmed.

———

PRACTICE—INCREASE—ORDER NO. 352.

GEORGE BUCK, JR.

As order No. 352, from the enforcement of which this appeal was filed, has been revoked and set aside, the contentions of appellant are no longer tenable. The appeal is therefore dismissed.

Assistant Secretary Webster Davis to the Commissioner of Pensions, April 2, 1898.

This claimant was pensioned from the date of discharge, July 15, 1865, at the rate of $4 per month for fistula in ano. The rate was increased to $8 per month from June 14, 1880. It appears that on May 19, 1869, he also filed application for pension for chronic diarrhea, alleged to have been contracted in the service.

As final action had not been taken upon this claim for chronic diarrhea, it was renewed in a claim for increase, which was filed March 21,

1888. Said claim for increase was disposed of in August, 1888, it having been held that the pensioner was not entitled to increase for fistula in ano, and the portion of the claim based upon chronic diarrhea was held in abeyance under ruling 97, and was not disposed of until June 25, 1897, when it was held there had been no disability from chronic diarrhea since date of discharge.

On September 12, 1896, a claim for increase was filed, in which new disabilities of service origin were alleged, viz, disease of ankles and knees. This claim was also rejected June 25, 1897, on legal grounds—claimant's inability to connect said causes with his military service.

Another claim for increase was filed October 1, 1897, renewing the claim based upon chronic diarrhea contracted in Virginia in the summer of 1862; also for disease of kidneys contracted in March, 1862, disease of heart, and indigestion, and again for soreness or disease of knees and ankles.

It appears that claimant was informed November 20, 1897, and January 14, 1898, through Hon. R. D. Sutherland, House of Representatives, who had three times requested a medical examination, that said application for increase, filed October 1, 1897, would not be considered until reached in its turn after twelve months from the date of the last adjudication of his claim (June 25, 1897).

. This action was evidently based upon your order No. 352, dated December 24, 1897, which reads as follows:

Hereafter claims for increase of pension will not be considered within twelve months from the last action—allowance or rejection.

An appeal in this case from the enforcement of said order was filed March 27, 1898, with the contention that the order—

is without precedent, is unreasonable, arbitrary, and unjust in the extreme, and should be set aside and each case considered upon its own merits—

and that the order should be revoked, and that the claimant be ordered for medical examination at an early date, with the view of final adjudication.

The appeal does not call for an examination of the merits of the claim only so far as it may be affected by the order referred to.

The evident purpose of the repeated calls for status and requests for medical examination was to preserve the claimant's rights under the law as to the date of commencement of increase for pensioned causes, should it be allowed.

But the enforcement of the order referred to involved more than this, since it indefinitely postponed the adjudication of that portion of the increase claim based upon new and additional disabilities.

The effect of order No. 352 was fully discussed in the departmental decision rendered March 30, 1898, in the case of John W. Granless, Company K, Twenty-third Pennsylvania Infantry, certificate numbered 943069, in which it was held that its enforcement would result in great injustice to a large number of claimants; therefore it was deemed proper to revoke and set aside said order, and reestablish the rule laid down in Walker's Treatise, page 52, of November 15, 1882, which had been the practice until your order No. 352 was promulgated.

As said order has been revoked, there is no longer any ground for the contention contained in this appeal.

It is therefore dismissed, and the case is returned for adjudication accordingly.

SERVICE—DRAFTED MAN—DISCHARGE.

OBEDIAH P. HANKINSON.

The official military record of this appellant's service during the war of the rebellion shows that he did not render any pensionable service whatever in the Army of the United States during said war.

Assistant Secretary Webster Davis to the Commissioner of Pensions, April 5, 1898.

Obediah P. Hankinson, late unassigned private, Pennsylvania Volunteer Infantry, filed in your Bureau, on May 29, 1897, an application for pension under the provisions of section 2, act of June 27, 1890, which was rejected on July 12, 1897, upon the ground that he had rendered no pensionable military service during the war of the rebellion.

From said action appeal was taken on August 24, 1897.

The official military record in the War Department of this apellant's military service during the war of the rebellion shows that he was drafted on September 27, 1864, failed to report, and was arrested as a deserter on March 6, 1865, and delivered at the military post at Harrisburg, Pa., on the 8th of said month. He was tried by court-martial for desertion, convicted, and sentenced to forfeit all pay and allowances then due, or that might become due to the date of promulgating said sentence, and to be assigned to some regiment in the field to serve one year from the date of joining the same, and to forfeit $12 per month for the entire term of service.

The proceedings, findings, and sentence of the court-martial that tried him were approved and promulgated June 28, 1865, in "General Orders, No. 80, Headquarters Department of Pennsylvania," but that part of the sentence of the court relative to assignment to some regiment in the field was not carried into effect. By "Special Orders, No. 407, paragraph 2, War Department, Adjutant-General's Office, July 29. 1865," he was ordered to be dishonorably discharged without pay or allowances, and he was so discharged August 1, 1865.

The War Department further reports:

As this man was convicted of desertion by a general court-martial, the proceedings, etc., of which were approved and promulgated by competent authority, the *charge* of desertion no longer stands against him; the record of the *fact* that he was absent in desertion from September 27, 1864, to March 6, 1865, can not, however, be expunged.

So much of paragraph 2, of Special Orders 407, War Department, Adjutant-General's Office, July 29, 1865, as directed the dishonorable discharge of this soldier is canceled.

It is contended in this appeal that the cancellation of the order directing the dishonorable discharge of the soldier had the effect of restoring him to the service, and giving him an honorable and pensionable service of ninety days or more.

This contention is wholly untenable. During the time the appellant was in desertion, from September 27, 1864, to March 6, 1865, it will surely not be seriously contended that he was in an honorable or pensionable service, and from and after March 6, 1865, when he was apprehended, up to the time of his discharge, he is shown by the record to have been held first as a prisoner awaiting trial, and undergoing trial, and after conviction, as a convict awaiting the carrying out of his sentence. That the period of his detention, either before or after trial and conviction, under such circumstances would not constitute a pensionable service under the provisions of section 2, act of June 27, 1890, does not admit of argument.

Furthermore, this Department has already passed upon the identical question raised by this appeal. This appellant filed a claim for pension under the provisions of the Revised Statutes, which was rejected by your Bureau, and on appeal from said action this Department held on May 5, 1894 (7 P. D., 227), as follows:

It may be further stated, as a general proposition, that where a claimant, who was drafted for one year's service, failed to appear and was arrested as a deserter, tried, convicted, and sentenced to forfeit all pay and allowances then due or to become due to the date of the promulgation of the sentence, and then assigned to some regiment in the field to serve one year from the date of joining the same, the legal effect of said sentence was to postpone the commencement of his pensionable military service, for which he was drafted, until the assignment to some regiment in the field in accordance with said sentence; and where so much of said sentence, as directed him to be assigned to some regiment in the field, was never carried into effect, the man's military service, for which he was drafted for one year, never commenced.

The foregoing ruling was altogether sound, and correctly states the law applicable to the facts disclosed by this applicant's military record, and it is apparent therefrom that he never rendered any pensionable service whatever during the war of the rebellion.

Therefore, the rejection of this claim upon the ground stated was not error, and is affirmed accordingly.

DISLOYALTY—SECTION 4716, R. S.—RESTORATION.

BARNABAS SARVER.

It clearly appearing from the official military record in the War Department of this
appellant's army service during the war of the rebellion that he had voluntarily
served in the Confederate army during said war, and the adverse presumption
created by said record being unrebutted by any sufficient or satisfactory evidence that said Confederate service was involuntary, payment of pension to him
under the provisions of section 2, act of June 27, 1890, is expressly and positively prohibited by the provisions of section 4716, Revised Statutes, United
States.

(Job White, 7 P. D., 312; Sarah H. Ozborn, ibid., 317; Augustus H. Longee, ibid., 586;
Emma H. Seymour, 8 P. D., 325; Anastatio Capella, ibid., 308; William C. Couch,
ibid., 39; Aaron T. Bush, ibid., 254.)

It being shown by the record and the testimony that the incapacity to earn a support by manual labor, for which this appellant was formerly pensioned under the
act of June 27, 1890, is a direct result of disability contracted while confined as
a Confederate prisoner of war at Camp Douglas, Illinois, the effect of restoring
him to the rolls under said act would be to grant him a pension for disability
contracted while serving in the ranks of the Confederate army, in open rebellion
against and hostility to the authority of the United States.

*Assistant Secretary Webster Davis to the Commissioner of Pensions, April
8, 1898.*

Barnabas Sarver, late private, Company F, Fifth United States Volunteer Infantry, was formerly pensioned under the provisions of section
2, act of June 27, 1890, at the rate of $8 per month, for partial inability
to earn a support by manual labor from disease of eyes, and on July
29, 1895, he was, after due and legal notice, dropped from the rolls, upon
the ground that he had rendered voluntary service in the Confederate
army during the war of the rebellion, and payment of pension to him
was prohibited by the provisions of section 4716, Revised Statutes.

On April 27, 1896, he filed in your Bureau an application for restoration of said pension, which was rejected on June 6, 1896, upon the same
grounds upon which he had been dropped from the rolls.

From this action appeal was taken on September 7, 1897.

The official record in the War Department of this appellant's military
service during the war of the rebellion shows that he was enlisted as a
private, for three years, in Company K, Fifty-fourth Virginia Infantry,
Confederate States army, by Captain Deyerle, of that company, on
May 26, 1862, and served in said organization until sometime in the
spring or summer of 1864 (the exact date does not appear), when he
was captured by the Union forces, and confined as a Confederate prisoner
of war at Camp Douglas, Illinois, until April 1, 1865, when he enlisted
as a private in Company F, Fifth United States Volunteer Infantry
("Rebs."), United States Army, and served therein until October 15,
1866, when he was mustered out of the service with said company, and
honorably discharged.

The foregoing record of the appellant's service in the Confederate army very clearly and unmistakably indicates upon its face that it was not forced and involuntary service rendered by him therein, but was entirely voluntary on his part.

It shows that he was not conscripted or drafted into the Confederate service, but was enlisted by the captain of the company that he joined, and that he served therein faithfully for at least two years without absence or default of any kind and as a prisoner of war for about one year after his capture before he ever exhibited any disposition whatever to embrace the Union cause.

It thus appears that this appellant was in the Confederate service for a period of certainly not less than three years before his tardy loyalty and love for the Union, which he now so earnestly and vigorously protests animated him all the time, manifested itself in any way whatever, and when he did finally make up his mind to espouse the Union cause it was at a date only about thirty or sixty days prior to the utter collapse and final and complete overthrow of the rebellion, and he then enlisted in an organization composed of men who, like himself, had been in the Confederate service and prisoners of war and were unwilling to fight against the Confederacy, for military service against the Indians in the far Western States and Territories.

The strong and almost conclusive adverse presumptions which naturally and obviously are created by the military record of this appellant are unrebutted by any evidence whatever other than the unsupported and uncorroborated assertions of the appellant himself that his Confederate service was forced and involuntary on his part, and that he was conscripted into the Confederate service and kept there against his will and desire.

Clearly such unsupported statements by the party in interest are utterly incompetent and wholly insufficient to controvert the plain and indisputable facts of his military service shown by the official record, or the legitimate and unavoidable inference to be drawn therefrom that his Confederate service was voluntary in every sense of the word.

This Department has repeatedly held that the provisions of section 4716, Revised Statutes, which absolutely and expressly prohibit the payment of any money on account of pension to any person, or to the widow, children, or heirs of any deceased person, who in any manner voluntarily engaged in or aided or abetted the late rebellion against the authority of the United States applied as well to pensions granted under the provisions of the act of June 27, 1890, as to those granted under the provisions of the Revised Statutes. (Job White, 7 P. D., 312; Sarah H. Ozborn, *ibid.*, 317; Augustus H. Longee, *ibid.*, 586; William C. Couch, 8 P. D., 39; Aaron T. Bush, *ibid.*, 254; Anastatio Capella, *ibid.*, 308; Emma H. Seymour, *ibid.*, 325).

In the case of Augustus H. Longee (*supra*) it was also expressly held:

Where the record shows that a claimant voluntarily engaged in, or aided and abetted the rebellion, his claim, under the act of June 27, 1890, should be rejected under section 4716, Revised Statutes.

The facts of this case afford a striking illustration of what would be the inevitable result of a departure from the above cited departmental rulings.

The pension formerly granted to this appellant under the provisions of section 2, act of June 27, 1890, was on account of partial inability to earn a support by manual labor resulting from disease of eyes. Disease of eyes, and consequent failure of vision, was the only disabling cause ever alleged or proven by the appellant to have produced a condition of disability pensionable under the provisions of said act. Prior to claiming pension under the act of June 27, 1890, the appellant had made a claim for pension under the provisions of the act of March 3, 1877, which exempts from the operation of section 4716, Revised Statutes, pensions granted on account of wounds or injury received or disease contracted in line of duty while serving under a voluntary enlistment in the United States Army subsequent to a disloyal Confederate service, which was also based upon disease of eyes. This claim was rejected by your Bureau on February 6, 1892, upon the ground "that the disease of eyes for which pension is claimed was contracted while he was serving in the Confederate army." That the ground upon which this claim was rejected was absolutely sound and correct is not only abundantly shown by the proof, but is practically admitted by this appellant.

The hospital record of the appellant, while in confinement as a Confederate prisoner of war at Camp Douglas, Illinois, shows that he was treated in "prison hospital" from November 17 to 29, 1864, for smallpox. It is to this attack of smallpox, contracted while in the service of the Confederacy, and months prior to his enlistment in the United States Army, that the appellant admits, and the evidence tends to show, his present disease of eyes is directly attributable.

To hold, therefore, in accordance with the contention and prayer of this appeal, that the provisions of section 4716, Revised Statutes, have no application to this claim, and to restore appellant to the rolls under the act of June 27, 1890, would be, in effect, to grant and pay him a pension for a disability contracted while he was serving in the ranks of the Confederate army in open rebellion against and hostility to the Government of the United States. That Congress would by legislative enactment authorize such a travesty upon justice and common sense as this would be is not to be for an instant entertained, much less then can the same result be attained by implication and construction, opposed alike to sound reason and the plain letter of the law.

The rejection of this claim for restoration of pension upon the ground stated was therefore clearly not error, and is affirmed accordingly.

SERVICE—SPECIAL ACT—ACT JUNE 27, 1890.

JAMES THREET.

The members of Captain Beaty's Company of Independent Scouts, never having been legally mustered into the United States service, are not pensionable under the act of June 27, 1890, notwithstanding the act of July 14, 1870, recognizing said organization as a part of the military force of the United States, and granting them pay and pension on making proof of actual service.

Assistant Secretary Webster Davis to the Commissioner of Pensions, April 11, 1898.

On August 13, 1890, this appellant, James Threet, filed a claim, No. 916887, for pension under the act of June 27, 1890, as a member of Captain Beaty's company, Independent Tennessee Scouts. The claim was rejected March 29, 1894, on the ground he was not regularly mustered into the United States service, and he appealed September 11, 1897, contending rejection is on a ground merely technical.

The records of the War Department show this claimant was enrolled January 25, 1862, in said company, and was discharged June 1, 1865.

It appears from the papers herein that this record of service was based upon an act of Congress, approved July 14, 1870 (16 Stat. L., p. 653), reading as follows:

AN ACT for the relief of Captain Beaty's company of Independent Scouts.

Whereas David Beaty, of Fentress County, Tennessee, did, on the twenty-fifth day of January, eighteen hundred and sixty-two, organize a company of independent scouts, numbering one hundred and two men, including himself as captain, and his first and second lieutenants; and whereas said company was on continuous duty engaged in the work of suppressing the rebellion from the date of its organization until the first day of June, eighteen hundred and sixty-five, serving under the orders of the commander of the army in Tennessee; and whereas said company was never legally mustered into the service of the United States by any properly authorized mustering officer, and neither officers or privates of said company have ever received any compensation for said services from the Government of the United States: Therefore

Be it enacted by the Senate and House of Representatives of the United States of America in Congress assembled, That the organization set forth in the foregoing preamble be, and the same is hereby, recognized as a part of the military force of the United States engaged in suppressing the recent rebellion, and the members thereof, on making proof of actual service, are declared to be entitled to the same pay, pensions, as though they had been regularly mustered into the service of the United States as cavalry; *Provided,* That there shall be filed in the War Department a roll of said company, which shall be sworn to by the captain and two lieutenants of said company; *And provided further,* That each soldier, upon applying for payment under this act, shall be required to make oath as to the length of his service in said company.

Pursuant to the passage of said act the War Department in June, 1871, detailed Lieut. W. H. Clapp to investigate as to the service of this organization, and on August 18, 1871, that officer made a full report in regard to it.

It appears that Captain Beaty's company was an irregularly composed organization, made for mutual protection, and existed independently of any portion of the Federal Army. Prior to the passage of said act it had no military status whatever. As stated in the preamble of the act,

it was never legally mustered into the service of the United States by any properly authorized mustering officer;

nor is there, in fact, any showing made anywhere in the records that it, or any of its members, was ever employed in any way by any officer of the Federal Army. Lieutenant Clapp's report shows, on the contrary, that its members were largely engaged in marauding for individual gain, instead of being employed continuously in the work of suppressing the rebellion.

Some desultory and occasional connection with the Federal forces appears, however, from the preamble of said act to have existed, and the law was manifestly enacted in order that any member who may have incurred a disability while so employed might secure, on account thereof, the benefit of the pension laws then in force relating to disabilities incurred in line of duty in service.

Such being the inducement to and purpose of this special act, the question is: May its provisions be extended so as to allow the members of this organization pension under any other law, particularly the act of June 27, 1890?

I am of the opinion the scope of a special act, such as the act of July 14, 1870, is, can not be thus broadened. The act of June 27, 1890, sets up conditions of title to pension wholly different from those which, it must be presumed, were in the contemplation of Congress when it enacted the law of July 14, 1870; and it can not be supposed that Congress would have declared that the questionable general service of these men is service which is pensionable under the conditions expressed in the act of June 27, 1890. Pensionable title under the latter act is predicated upon service actually rendered for ninety days or more, and an honorable discharge from such service; while the service of these men was so broken and questionable in every way that no certain character can be attributed to any of it.

It is, therefore, held that the members of this company are not pensionable under the act of June 27, 1890; and rejection of this claim is affirmed accordingly.

MARY A. CLARKSON (WIDOW).

Claimant owns lots in Detroit, Mich., worth $1,000 and has $3,605.63 in bank drawing 4 per cent interest. She earns enough by keeping boarders to support her comfortably. *Held:* That she is not without other means of support than her daily labor within the meaning of the law. Accumulated savings of a widow's labor can not be excluded in estimating her means of support.

Assistant Secretary Webster Davis to the Commissioner of Pensions, April 21, 1890.

I have considered the appeal filed September 7, 1897, from the action of your Bureau in rejecting the claim of Mary A. Clarkson for pension under the act of June 27, 1890, as the widow of Isaac L. Clarkson, late captain of Company B, Seventeenth Michigan Infantry. This claim was filed December 7, 1894, and was rejected in June, 1896, after a special examination, on the ground that the claimant was not without other means of support than her daily labor.

It is stated in the appeal that the claimant's property consists of unproductive lots worth not over $1,000 and unproductive money in bank amounting to between $1,000 and $1,200. It is contended that this property, even if invested, is not a sufficient means of support to debar her from pension; and moreover, that being wholly the proceeds of her own labor during the past fifteen years in keeping a boarding house, such property is expressly excepted by the act of June 27, 1890, in estimating her means of support.

The claimant stated to the special examiner who investigated her case that she paid $1,800 for certain lots owned by her in the city of Detroit, Mich., but that she had been unable to borrow $800 on them and would sell them for $1,000. They were assessed, it appears, at $1,230. She submitted statements from various banks in Detroit showing that she had at that time (April 14, 1896) deposited to her credit $3,605.63, upon which she drew 4 per cent interest. The real estate was free from incumbrance, but she owed $800.

She did not say that her property represented the savings of her own labor. She did say that a part of the money in bank had been bequeathed to her by a sister. However, I am of the opinion that it is immaterial how the property was acquired. The essential question is, Has she other means of support than her daily labor? The evidence shows that she has property worth nearly or quite $4,000 over and above her indebtedness, from which she derives an income of $144 per year. This is in addition to what she earns by keeping boarders which, she says, is sufficient to maintain her. It should be stated that about $2,000 of her money has come to her (by bequest as above stated) since her claim for pension was filed, but prior to that addition to her possessions she was obviously in easy circumstances with respect to the procurement of a support.

I can not assent to the theory that the accumulated savings of a widow's industry or skill should not be considered "other means of support than her daily labor," within the meaning of the act of June 27, 1890. By "her daily labor" the law undoubtedly has reference to her earnings from day to day which are consumed in her support. When any portion of such earnings in excess of what is needed for her support is laid by it becomes capital, which is capable of yielding income independent of her labor, and therefore constitutes "other means of support" than her labor. The claimant's "means," in this case, being sufficient, under rulings of the Department, to exclude her from the benefits of the act of June 27, 1890, the action of your Bureau is affirmed.

SERVICE—DRAFTED MAN—CIVILIAN EMPLOYEE.

BASIL T. RIDGEWAY.

It appearing that this appellant was drafted and accepted but not held to military service under said draft, and detailed and employed as a mechanic in the Washington Navy-Yard at regular wages during the whole time of his service, he is held by the authorities of the War Department not to have been in the military service of the United States, and not entitled to recognition as a soldier for any purpose, and is, therefore, not entitled to pension under any existing law.

Assistant Secretary Webster Davis to the Commissioner of Pensions, April 23, 1898.

Basil T. Ridgeway, late unassigned drafted recruit, Maryland Volunteers, filed in your Bureau on August 28, 1886, a declaration for pension (No. 618884), under the provisions of sections 4692 and 4693, Revised Statutes, which was rejected on June 26, 1891, upon the ground that he had rendered no service in the Army or Navy of the United States, having been drafted but not held to military service.

On July 5, 1890, he filed an application for pension under the provisions of section 2, act of June 27, 1890, which was also rejected upon the same date and on the same grounds above stated.

From the rejection of both claims, as aforesaid, this appeal was taken on September 7, 1897.

It is shown by the official military records of the War Department that this appellant was drafted on the 9th day of July, 1864, in the Fifth district of Maryland, and was discharged on a detachment muster-out roll, dated December 11, 1865, at Washington, D. C., with remark—

Accepted and detailed in Washington Navy-Yard, under Circular No. 28, Provost-Marshal-General's Office, Series 1864.

The certificate of discharge furnished appellant when he was discharged the service, which is on file with the papers in this case, recites that he was enrolled on July 9, 1864, to serve one year, or during the war, and is discharged "from the service of the United States"

July 9, 1865, at Washington, D. C., by reason of expiration of term of service. It also bears the following indorsements:

Detailed under provisions of Circular No. 28, Pro. Mar. Genl's Office, Series of 1864.

P. M. G. O. D. R. C., *June 15, 1865.*

This man served as a mechanic in the U. S. Navy-Yard from date of draft to discharge. Is not entitled to pay or bounty, never having been in the Army.

H. P. WALCOTT, *Payer., U. S. A.*

It is admitted by the appellant that as soon as he reported to the provost-marshal in Washington, D. C., under the draft, he was detailed to work in the Washington Navy-Yard, and was employed there as a mechanic at regular wages continuously until he was discharged.

The military status of men of this class, whose enrollment, employment, and discharge were identical in all respects with that of this appellant, has been very carefully considered and passed upon by the officials of the War Department in the following communication from the Chief of the Record and Pension Office of the War Department, prepared by direction and authority and with the approval of the honorable the Secretary of War:

WAR DEPARTMENT,
Washington City, January 14, 1891.

The SECOND COMPTROLLER,
    United States Treasury.

SIR: In reply to your letter of the 3d instant, transmitting discharge certificate in the case of Samuel R. Turner, a drafted man of the District of Columbia, and requesting to be furnished with his military history and other information concerning this class of men; also if held to service, what stood in the way of their drawing rations, clothing, fuel, etc., in kind, in the city of Washington, in 1865 and 1866, I am directed by the Secretary of War to inform you as follows:

The records show that Samuel R. Turner was drafted September 27, 1864, in sixth district, District of Columbia, for one year, reported to the provost-marshal, District of Columbia, September 29, 1864, and was released from personal service under the draft in accordance with the provisions of Circular No. 28, of July 25, 1864, from the Provost-Marshal General, which reads as follows: "Skilled mechanics and operatives employed in the armories, arsenals, and navy-yards of the United States who shall be drafted, and, on examination, held to service, will not be required to report for duty under such draft so long as they remain in the aforesaid service, provided the officer in charge shall certify that their labor as mechanics or operatives is necessary for the naval or military service."

This man at the date of his draft was employed in the navy-yard of this city as a mechanic, and having complied with the requirements of above-named circular was permitted to continue his labor in a civil capacity without constraint from military authority.

Neither rations, clothing, nor arms were issued to him by military authority.

The object of reporting to the provost-marshal was to determine his physical qualification for service under the draft, and having been found so qualified he was released from personal service, as set forth above.

This man (as was the case with all others who were at date of draft employed in the navy-yard) was never forwarded to a rendezvous for drafted men, but had he been held to actual service he would have been released by virtue of the order of April 14, 1865, from the Provost-Marshal-General, which reads as follows: "All men drafted under the call of December 19, 1864, who have not been forwarded to general rendezvous will be released. This order is not to apply to substitutes already mustered in."

The attention of the provost-marshal of the District of Columbia was specially drawn to this order by the following letter, dated May 1, 1865: "The Provost-Marshal-General directs relative to drafted men who were detailed for service as skilled mechanics, in accordance with Circular No. 28, dated July 25, 1864, from this office. whose services as such are no longer required, that you will discharge them as drafted men under the orders issued from this office April 14, 1865."

The wording of above letter referring to these men as "detailed for service," and directing them "discharge as drafted men" is misleading, inasmuch as they were not detailed by military authority, and the circular of April 14, 1865, directs the release of drafted men.

On various dates in November and December, 1865, Lieut. H. C. Strong, mustering officer, Department of Washington, mustered out of service and furnished discharge certificates to men of this class, but indorsed their muster-out rolls as follows: "Acknowledge receipt of pay as citizen employees since date of enlistment."

This action was taken under a misapprehension of the facts in the case, and has not been recognized by this Department. Any military status which may have attached to the class of persons referred to was terminated by the provisions of the circular of April 14, 1865, from the office of the Provost-Marshal-General.

Following is a copy of a letter from this Department addressed to the attorney of a claimant in a case of this nature:

"WAR DEPARTMENT,
"*Washington City, April 5, 1884.*

"SIR: The Department duly received your letter of the 19th ultimo, appealing from the action of the Adjutant-General in declining to grant a discharge certificate to one Philip Hutchinson, who was drafted on March 2, 1865, and who it is alleged was detailed to attend to the telegraph wire extending over the Eastern Branch bridge, this city.

"In reply I beg to inform you that upon an examination of the case it is found that said Hutchinson was drafted on March 2, 1865, but was not mustered into military service of the United States, he having been detailed at the navy-yard bridge in the capacity of 'bridge builder,' under the provisions of Circular No. 28, from the Provost-Marshal-General's Office, dated July 25, 1864, as follows: * * *

"Such military history as may have attached to the classes of persons referred to in the above-quoted circular was closed by the provisions of circular from the office of the Provost-Marshal-General, dated April 14, 1865, a copy of which is herewith inclosed.

"In view of the facts stated, the action of the Adjutant-General in declining to grant a discharge in the case is sustained by this Department.

"Very respectfully,

"ROBERT T. LINCOLN,
"*Secretary of War.*"

On January 7 this case was referred to the Acting Judge-Advocate-General of the Army, with a request for his opinion in the matter, and on the 13th it was returned to this Department with the following remarks:

"Samuel R. Turner was drafted September 27, 1864, in Washington, D. C.—that is, his name was put on a list of names of civilians prepared by the proper officers of the Government from which to draw, under the law, a certain number for military service, and it transpired that it was one among those that were drawn.

"After his name was so drawn he was notified of the fact, and, in obedience to the notice, he reported to the proper officer September 29, 1864, for examination, etc., and to submit to being mustered into the military service. His examination showed him to be subject to do military duty, but he was at the time a civilian employee of the Government and his services were needed in that capacity. On this account he was not mustered into the military service, but was excused therefrom under Circular No. 28, of July 25, 1864, so long as he should remain in the civil service in which he was then employed.

"He remained in that service until November 28, 1865, and, it may be, longer. But at this time he was discharged from the obligation to enter the military service (in case he should quit the civil service) which rested on him on account of his name having been drawn as aforesaid and his having been excused only on the condition above mentioned.

"He was given a certificate of discharge such as is given to a person discharged from the military service, but this certificate does not state that he was discharged from the military service; nor would it have been true if it had stated this. The man had never been in the military service and could not have been discharged from it unless he had been. The Government had it in its power to muster him into the military service, and had him ready to muster him in, but without doing so it offered him the privilege of continuing in the employment he was then in, with the understanding that if he abandoned it he would have to enter the military service, and he accepted the offer.

"I concur in the former decisions of the Department in this class of cases, as shown by the indorsement hereon of December 30, 1890, and the statements and decisions in the brief herewith."

I am further directed to state that the Secretary of War has personally reviewed this case and has decided that men of this class can not be considered as having been in the military service of the United States, and are not entitled to recognition as soldiers.

Very respectfully,

F. C. AINSWORTH,
Captain and Assistant Surgeon, United States Army.

It has long been held by this Department that the holdings and rulings of the War Department should govern and control all questions relating to the military status and service of applicants for pension. The official military records of that Department are held to be conclusive as to all matters of enlistment, kind and character of service, discharge therefrom and kindred subjects, and the holdings and rulings of its officials as to whether or not a particular individual was in the military service of the United States, or as to what constituted military service in the Army of the United States in any given case, are entitled to and have always been given the greatest weight and consideration by this Department in the adjudication of pension cases. (George W. Hill, 7 P. D., 235, and decisions therein cited.)

The foregoing ruling of the War Department relative to the status of men whose enrollment, service, and employment were similar to this appellant's, is in entire consonance and accord with the well-settled holding of this Department that service by enlisted or drafted men in the "general military service" of the United States, as clerks, in the Executive Departments of the Government, or in other capacities or employments not military in their nature, was not a military or pensionable service within the meaning of the law. (Digest 1897, page 470, subtitle 5, "General Service.")

It is also held by this Department that—

Pension under section 2, of the act of June 27, 1890, is limited to persons regularly enlisted or mustered into the military or naval service of the United States, who served therein for ninety days or more during the late war of the rebellion, and were honorably discharged therefrom. (James M. Barnes, 8 P. D., 94; Annie E. Few, Ibid., 95; Andrew J. Shannon, 7 P. D.. 64.)

It is clear, from the foregoing, that the service of this appellant can not be held to have been a pensionable service under either the provisions of sections 4692 and 4693, Revised Statutes, or of section 2, act of June 27, 1890, and that the rejection of both of said claims, for the reasons given, was not error, and said action is affirmed accordingly.

SERVICE—PILOT—ACT JUNE 27, 1890.

HENRY N. HAYNIE.

Service as a pilot does not entitle to pension under section 2 of the act of June 27, 1890. (Citing Susannah, widow of Francis Mackey, 8 P. D., 535, and William P. Gordon, unpublished.)

Assistant Secretary Webster Davis to the Commissioner of Pensions, April 23, 1898.

I have considered the appeal filed August 7, 1897, from the action of your Bureau in dropping from the pension roll the name of Henry H. Haynie, formerly a pilot on the U. S. S. *Resolute.* Mr. Haynie was granted a pension under the act of June 27, 1890, in March, 1892, and drew the same until July 23, 1895, when his name was dropped from the roll on the ground that he was not an enlisted man in the Navy but only a civilian employee, and hence not entitled to pension under the provisions of the act of June 27, 1890. From that action the appeal is taken.

In August, 1894, the Pension Bureau requested the Navy Department to inform it whether one Moses Kirkpatrick, an applicant for pension who rendered some service as a pilot during the war of the rebellion, was regarded as a civilian, officer, or enlisted man. The question was referred to the Judge-Advocate-General of the Navy, who rendered the following opinion, which was approved by the Secretary of the Navy:

In view of the fact that pilots were not enlisted men or appointed as officers by the Department, that its records do not show their entry into the service, or their conduct while serving as such, and that such appointments were made by the commanding officers of the squadrons, subject to the approval of the Department, and held during the pleasure of the appointing officer, I am of the opinion that pilots can not be regarded as officers or enlisted men in the Navy, and therefore must be regarded as civilians employed under the authority of the Navy Department.

SAM. C. LEMLY,
Judge-Advocate-General.

In accordance with that opinion Assistant Secretary Reynolds held in the case of Susannah, widow of Francis Mackey (8 P. D., 535), that—

A pilot serving on a vessel of the Navy is not an officer or enlisted man but merely an employee for the time being and is not entitled to pension under the second section of the act of June 27, 1890.

That decision was cited and reaffirmed by me on November 15, 1897, in the case of William P. Gordon (Certificate No. 16495). The view then taken is still adhered to. The action in the case now under consideration is, therefore, affirmed.

___

SERVICE—SUBSTITUTE—ENLISTMENT.

MARY BRADY (WIDOW).

It appearing from the evidence that the deceased husband of this appellant served in the above-named organization as a substitute for and under the name of one Thomas F. Jessup, who had been drafted into the service, and by a private arrangement with Jessup took his place in the ranks and answered to his name, but was not sworn in, nor mustered into the military service, he was not in the military service of the United States, his service was not a pensionable service, and would not entitle his widow to pension under any existing law. (Christian, alias Ernest Ulrich, 4 P. D., 411.)

Assistant Secretary Webster Davis to the Commissioner of Pensions, April 30, 1898.

Mary Brady filed in your Bureau on January 17, 1879, an application for pension under the provisions of section 4702, Revised Statutes, as widow of James H. Brady (deceased), alleging that he had served as a private in Company E, Sixth Provisional Enrolled Missouri Militia, during the war of the rebellion, and had died while in the service, on January 25, 1864, of disease contracted in line of duty.

On May 11, 1891, she also filed an application for pension under the provisions of section 3, act of June 27, 1890, as widow of said alleged deceased soldier.

Both of said claims were rejected on March 12, 1897, upon the ground that it was shown by the official military records of the War Department and the evidence in this case that the deceased, James H. Brady, had served as a substitute for one Thomas F. Jessup, and was never sworn in, accepted, or mustered into the military service of the United States.

From this action appeal was taken on August 7, 1897.

This case was before the Department and considered under said appeal on March 12, 1898, but the reasons then given for affirming the action of your Bureau were erroneous, and therefore the decision rendered herein on that date has been recalled and canceled, the appeal reinstated on the docket, and the claim will now be considered on appeal de novo.

There is no record in either the War or Treasury Department of the alleged military service of said James H. Brady, or that he was ever at any time in the military service of the United States.

The Auditor of the Treasury for the War Department reports, under date of October 22, 1895, that the records of his office show that one Thomas F. Jessup served as a private in Company E, Sixth Provisional

Enrolled Missouri Militia, from June 15, 1863, to February 29, 1864, a period of 259 days of actual service.

The testimony of the captain and other surviving members of Company E, Sixth Provisional Enrolled Missouri Militia, obtained by a special examination of this case, shows clearly that from October, 1863, to January 25, 1864, the date of his death, the service in said company credited on the record to Jessup was in fact performed by Brady as his substitute. It does not appear that Brady was ever regularly enlisted, sworn into the service, and accepted as a substitute for Jessup, or that he was ever mustered into the military service of the United States as such, but that in pursuance of a private arrangement with Jessup and with the tacit consent and acquiescence of the captain of said company he simply took Jessup's place in the ranks, answered to his name, and performed his duties.

There can be no question about the fact that had Brady been regularly and legally sworn in, accepted, and mustered into the service as Jessup's substitute his service in Company E, Sixth Provisional Enrolled Missouri Militia, would have been a pensionable service, both under the Revised Statutes and under the act of June 27, 1890, as is expressly provided by section 4722, Revised Statutes, and by the act of February 15, 1895, but it is equally as clear from the foregoing undisputed facts that he was not during the time he served in said company, and never was, in the military service of the United States. It is manifest that if Brady had left the company and absented himself without leave, or had committed any other breach of military discipline, however flagrant or outrageous, he could not have been lawfully arrested or punished therefor, nor have been held amenable to military discipline or control, but that Jessup, and he alone, could have been held answerable for the failure to carry out and perform the military service for which he (Jessup) was held liable. Brady, under such an arrangement, was only answerable to Jessup for violation of his private contract with him, not to the Government, which was no party to the transaction, and had never legally accepted Brady's service in lieu of that Jessup was bound by law to render.

Under the circumstances it is self-evident that Brady was not in the military service of the United States during the period he served in said company under his agreement with Jessup.

In the claim of Christian, alias Ernest Ulrich (4 P. D., 411), this Department, on February 25, 1891, passed upon and decided on appeal a case in which the material facts were almost precisely similar to the one now under consideration. That was a case in which a son, with the consent of his officers, took the place of his father in the ranks, answered to the father's name, and performed the military service which the father had enlisted and contracted to perform. On January 24, 1864, upon the expiration of the term for which the father had enlisted, the son, still under his father's name, reenlisted and was sworn in as a veteran volunteer, and continued to serve under his father's name until discharged. It was held by the Department that up to the time that the son reenlisted and was sworn in as a veteran volunteer, his service, under the arrangement to take his father's place, was not a pensionable service, and that during said time he could not be held to have been in the military service of the United States, but that from and after his reenlistment he was in the military service, and his subsequent service was pensionable, for the reason that, although he still went under his father's name, he, the son, was, as a matter of fact, the actual person who reenlisted for another term and was sworn into the service, and that this fact alone put him regularly and legally into the military service of the United States from and after that date, no matter under what name such service was rendered.

I am, for the foregoing reasons, firmly of the opinion that the alleged service of the deceased husband of appellant was not a pensionable service; that he was never at any time in the military service of the United States, and that the rejection of this claim upon the ground stated was not error.

Said action is accordingly affirmed.

·——

AID AND ATTENDANCE—RATE—DISABILITY.

IRA W. HAYFORD.

When it is established, beyond any reasonable doubt, that, on account of pensioned cause or causes, or any pathological sequelæ thereof, the pensioner is not only "totally incapacitated for performing manual labor," but can neither dress nor undress himself without the aid and attendance of another person, as is shown by the evidence and certificate of medical examination in this case, the Department will construe the said aid and attendance as such "frequent and periodical personal aid and attendance of another person" as is contemplated by the provisions of the act of July 14, 1892, and as warranting the allowance of the rate prescribed in the said act.

Assistant Secretary Webster Davis to the Commissioner of Pensions, April 30, 1898.

The appellant in this case, Ira W. Hayford, Company G, Fourth Wisconsin Cavalry, is now pensioned at $36 per month for "injury of right knee, resulting in total disability of right leg."

His original certificate was issued February 21, 1889, at $24 per month from October 12, 1886, for "injury to right knee." This rate was subsequently increased to $30 per month from January 29, 1890, and on February 24, 1892, the certificate for the present rate and disability was issued, the increase dating from April 1, 1891.

Claims for increase filed April 25, 1893, August 3, 1894, September 6, 1895, and January 25, 1897, respectively, were all duly rejected.

The claims filed August 3, 1894, and September 6, 1895, respectively, were rejected without medical examination, on the ground that inasmuch as the evidence filed did not show that the claimant required the aid and attendance of another person an examination looking to an increase to the $50 rate was not warranted.

In support of the claim of the appellant that he is not only totally incapacitated for performing manual labor by reason of pensioned causes, but is also disabled thereby in such a degree as to require the frequent and periodical personal aid and attendance of another person, the following evidence has been filed:

Minnie F. and Sarah T. Hayford, the wife and daughter, respectively, of the pensioner, testify:

That they are attendants of the soldier, and that his right leg is in such a condition that he can neither dress nor undress himself; that his limb is so painful a portion of the time that he can not sleep, and they are compelled to apply liniments and baths to relieve him; that if he falls to the floor he can not rise without assistance; that he can neither stand nor move without crutches or other support, and that he requires and receives their personal aid and attendance regularly.

Dr. John Lord testifies:

That the claimant is totally disabled for the performance of all manual labor requiring the use of his legs by reason of a diseased condition of the right kneejoint, which renders him unable to walk without the aid of crutches; that the said joint is enlarged and anchylosed, and, in his present condition he requires aid and assistance in dressing and undressing.

Dr. Henry Remy states:

That he has examined the claimant, and finds him to be entirely disabled by reason of injuries in his right knee; that there is chronic hypertrophy and anchylosis of the joint; that the parts are very painful at times, and there is considerable œdema; that it is impossible for him to get along without daily attendance, and there is no hope of improvement.

Dr. Samuel Bassford testifies:

That the soldier has a disability of the right kneejoint which renders the limb, in his opinion, permanently useless; that he is unable to use the right leg for support or in walking; that he must use a crutch and cane, and he can neither dress nor undress himself.

Albert R. Goodwin testifies:

That the claimant is a cripple from an injury of the right knee, and can walk only with crutches; that he is cared for by his wife and daughter, upon whom he is dependent for aid and attendance; that he is not able to dress or undress himself, and that he requires the regular personal aid and attendance of another person every day.

This evidence tends to show, at least, that the claimant requires the frequent and periodical aid and attendance of another person.

In pursuance of the claim filed January 25, 1897, a medical examination was held before the board of surgeons at Alfred, Me., on the 5th of May, 1897, although no additional evidence had been filed.

The following objective conditions were manifested at the said examination:

Pulse rate, 80; respiration, 24; temperature, 98; height, 5 feet 4 inches; weight, 150 pounds; age, 50 years.

We find the right lower extremity swollen and œdematous from the foot to the hip joint, the foot being swollen and the hip joint involved in the inflammation of and disease of the entire limb.

There is fibrous anchylosis of knee and hip joints. He seems to have no control of the limb but to drag it along. He says there is a sense of numbness in the limb a great part of the time, and at other times suffers severe pain in the knee.

He is unable to dress and undress himself without assistance of another person.

Circumference of limb around kneejoint is 15 inches; that of left limb at same location, 14 inches; other parts of limbs in about the same proportion.

The help of a second person is necessary a part of the time, beyond question.

We would therefore recommend him for the intermediate grade rate of $50 per month.

The pending appeal was taken from your action of September 24, 1897, rejecting this latter claim for increase.

The contention of the said appeal is:

That the evidence on file shows that the pensioner requires and receives the frequent and periodical personal aid and attendance of another person by reason of pensioned causes.

In an advisory opinion under date of March 5, 1898, relative to the action appealed from, the medical referee states as follows:

This appellant is now pensioned at $36 per month for injury to right knee, resulting in total disability of right leg. He contends that he is entitled to $50 per month because he requires some assistance in dressing and undressing.

The certificate of examination which was made under the claim showed the right leg to be swollen and œdematous, with fibrous anchylosis of the knee and hip joints. The claimant walks with the aid of a crutch and cane.

No other disability is shown to exist.

The rating which claimant now receives is the specific rating for the total disability of one leg.

The assistance required because of this disability in dressing and undressing does not appear to be such frequent and periodical aid and attendance as is contemplated in the act of July 14, 1892.

The rejection of the claim was proper and should be adhered to.

It is observed that the medical referee does not deny that the soldier requires the aid of another person in dressing and undressing, by reason of the pensioned disability, but that he does not consider such assistance as warranting the allowance of the rate prescribed in the act of July 14, 1892.

As to just what degree of disability, or amount of aid and attendance is required in consequence thereof, so as to bring the case within the purview of the provisions of the act of July 14, 1892, can not be defined in any general rule, it is not my purpose, nor do I deem it necessary, to lay down any special rule for guidance in all cases of this character, other than that which is to be found in the language of the said statute.

In departmental decision of January 6, 1898, in the case of Harrison
B. George (certificate 69860), I held that:

The words "frequent and periodical" are in express terms contradistinguished
from the words "regular and constant," and clearly indicate that periods of time
may occur when aid is not required, and yet the soldier be entitled to the rate
named.

The conditions named in the act must occur at stated intervals; the length of time
between the recurrence is largely a question of judgment as to the intent of Congress.

The medical referee invites attention to the fact that the claimant is
now pensioned at the specific rate for total disability of one leg, and he
is of the opinion that the rejection of the claim was proper and should
be adhered to.

In this opinion I do not concur.

It is true that the soldier is now receiving all that the law allows for
"total disability of one leg;" but, in my judgment, the fact that the
claimant's right leg is totally disabled is not the only question to consider in this case.

The term "totally disabled in the same," used in the act of August
4, 1886, has been "construed to mean such a disability as renders the
limb or member of no practical use or convenience—a disability as great
as if the limb had been actually amputated." (Christian Miller, 4 P.D.,
351; and William Cline, 7 P. D., 119.)

In my judgment, the disability shown in this case is not only as great,
but much greater than "if the limb had been actually amputated," even
at the hip joint.

If the limb had been amputated "at the hip joint, or so near the joint
as to prevent the use of an artificial limb," on account of the disability
of service origin, the $45 rate would, of course, be warranted; but
the said amputation, without complications of any kind, would not constitute a degree of disability requiring the aid and attendance of another
person.

In this case both the evidence and the certificate of the medical
examination held on the 5th of May, 1897, show that by reason of the
anchylosis of the right knee joint, the adhesions in the right hip joint,
and the generally inflamed and diseased condition of the whole right
lower extremity, all of which have been accepted as due to the disability of service origin, the claimant not only has but requires the
frequent and periodical personal aid and attendance of another person
in dressing and undressing, and in otherwise administering to his personal wants and comfort.

The whole right lower extremity is not only shown to be useless, but
worse than useless, as, in addition to being a source of great pain and
discomfort, it interferes with locomotion and prevents the pensioner
from performing the necessary function, unaided, of dressing and
undressing, and attending to many other personal wants and requirements.

The aid and attendance of another person, shown to be necessary in this case, is, in my opinion, such "frequent and periodical personal aid and attendance" as is contemplated by the provisions of the act of July 14, 1892.

The action appealed from is reversed, and the papers in the case are herewith remanded for readjudication and allowance, in accordance with the views herein set forth.

HONORABLE DISCHARGE—DEATH IN SERVICE—ACT JUNE 27, 1890.

ELSIE HUMMEL (WIDOW).

When soldier has served a term of ninety days or more in the military or naval service of the United States during the late war of the rebellion and has been honorably discharged therefrom, reenlists, and dies during his subsequent term of service, his death not being the result of a violation of any law, rule, or regulation of the military or naval service, the requirements of the act of June 27, 1890, as to length of service and honorable discharge are fulfilled, and his widow is entitled to pension on compliance with the other conditions of the act.

Assistant Secretary Webster Davis to the Commissioner of Pensions, April 30, 1898.

Claimant's attorney on September 27, 1897, filed a motion for reconsideration of departmental decision of April 27, 1893, affirming the Bureau action of August 10, 1891, rejecting her widow's claim No. 290661, filed July 17, 1890, under section 3 of the act of June 27, 1890, on the ground that her husband, the soldier, "was not finally honorably discharged, he having died in service."

It is contended that:

Soldier entered the service as a member of Company F, One hundred and seventy-second Pennsylvania Volunteers, October 22, 1862, and was honorably discharged from service July 31, 1863. This—a service of ninety days during the war of the rebellion and an honorable discharge—it is claimed perfects the claimant's title to pension in so far as length of service and honorable discharge are concerned.

The soldier reentered the service as a member of Company I, Two hundred and second Pennsylvania Volunteers, in September, 1864, and was drowned July 26, 1865, prior to receiving a discharge.

The Bureau held that he was drowned "while absent without leave," but the War Department, when asked to amend the soldier's record and to grant an honorable discharge under the law which directs that soldiers who served faithfully until May 1, 1865, having previously served six months, and who left their command without proper authority, shall be honorably discharged, refused a discharge on the ground that "certificates of discharge are not furnished in the cases of soldiers who died while in the service," thereby holding that the soldier had not severed his connection with the service, but that he "died while in the service."

Under this decision of the War Department it must be held that the soldier's final service had an honorable termination.

It is true that the soldier's death, from accidental drowning while he was outside the limits of the camp, was not a death in line of duty, but at the same time the fact that the soldier, after having completed his first service, reentered the service and met an accidental death should not be a bar to the pension of his widow under the act of June 27, 1890.

Claimant's attorney files with his appeal a communication from the War Department under date of October 3, 1895, in which it is stated that "Certificates of discharge are not furnished" (by the War Department) "in cases of soldiers who died while in the service."

In the departmental decision of April 27, 1893, it was said:

The facts as alleged by the claimant are these: Her husband first enlisted October 28, 1862, in Company F, One hundred and seventy-second Pennsylvania Volunteers, and was honorably discharged therefrom July 31, 1863. He again enlisted as a member of Company I, Two hundred and second Pennsylvania Volunteers, August 30, 1864, and was drowned on the 26th of June, 1865, while on his way home on a leave of absence.

The record of his alleged service in the One hundred and seventy-second Pennsylvania Volunteers has not been obtained from the War Department, but it may, for present purposes, be admitted that the facts are as stated by the claimant.

The record of his subsequent service in the Two hundred and second Pennsylvania Volunteers shows that at the time he was drowned he was "absent without leave."

The transcript of the War Department on file in this case reports that Frederick Hummel, a private of Company I, Two hundred and second Regiment Pennsylvania Volunteers, was enrolled on the 30th day of August, 1864, at Lewisburg, Pa., for one year, and is reported on roll to October 31, 1864, present, so borne to April 30, 1865. May and June, 1865, absent without leave; muster-out roll of company dated August 3, 1865, reports him "Drowned in the West Branch of the Susquehanna River, Northumberland, Pa., June 26, 1865."

As soldier had died five days prior to the last day of June, that fact readily accounts for his being reported absent without leave, if the company officer making out the bimonthly returns for May and June had no knowledge of his death, and the records showed that he had not been granted a pass or furlough. No necessary connection is shown between soldier's death and his absence from his command, nor is it shown that at the time of his death he was violating any law, rule, or regulation of the military service.

Section 3 of the act of June 27, 1890, provides:

That if any officer or enlisted man who served ninety days or more in the Army or Navy of the United States during the late War of the Rebellion, and who was honorably discharged has died, or shall hereafter die, leaving a widow without other means of support than her daily labor, or minor children under the age of sixteen years, such widow shall, upon due proof of her husband's death, without proving his death to be the result of his Army service, be placed on the pension roll from the date of the application therefor under this act at the rate of eight dollars per month, etc.

The facts in the case of Mary E. Walker, widow of Samuel H. Walker (7 P. D., 197), were similar to those presented in this case. Walker had served more than ninety days and had been honorably discharged. He reenlisted and was killed during his second term of service, not in line of duty, but not in violation of any law, rule, or regulation of the service.

After considering the line of decisions which hold that the "honorable discharge" named in the act of June 27, 1890, had reference to all the service in the Army or Navy during the war of the rebellion, and not to any particular term of service, it was held that:

Even though the words "honorably discharged" be interpreted in their broadest sense and held to mean an honorable discharge from each and every term of service, yet death in the second term of service should be construed as equivalent to an honorable discharge, unless occurring under circumstances which would have warranted a dishonorable one. To hold otherwise is to defeat a meritorious class of claimants who bring themselves within the plain letter and spirit of the act by proving every essential requirement of law. I am of the opinion when soldier has served a term of enlistment of ninety days or more and has been honorably discharged therefrom, reenlists and dies during his subsequent term—which death is not the result of a violation of any law, rule, or regulation of the military or naval service—the requirements of the act of June 27, 1890, as to length of service and honorable discharge are fulfilled, and his widow is entitled to pension on compliance with the other conditions of the act.

I am of the opinion that the same rule is applicable to this case, and while not passing on the merits of this case, as the evidence is too meager, yet the rejection of the claim on the grounds stated is not tenable.

The motion for reconsideration is, therefore, sustained, the former departmental decision of April 27, 1893, is reconsidered, and the Bureau action of August 10, 1891, is reversed.

The case is remanded for further investigation and readjudication in accordance with the facts, and the rule of construction as herein announced.

———

COMMENCEMENT OF INCREASE—NEW DISABILITY.

STEPHEN HIETT.

Where a pensioner under the law of July 14, 1862, files an application for additional pension, based on a newly alleged cause of disability, not specific, such claim, if allowed, dates from the time of filing such application, and not from the date of the examining surgeon's certificate establishing a pensionable degree of disability from said newly alleged cause.

In such cases the date of commencement is governed by the proviso in section 2 of the act of March 3, 1879, and not by section 4698¼, Revised Statutes.

Assistant Secretary Webster Davis to the Commissioner of Pensions, April 30, 1898.

Claimant's attorney, on December 2, 1897, filed a motion for reconsideration of departmental decision of November 30, 1896, affirming the Bureau action of March 31, 1896, adjudicating his claim certificate No. 175872, for increase and additional pension based on an old and newly alleged disability, filed August 20, 1890, and August 12, 1893, and granting him an increase to third-grade rate from August 20, 1896, the date of the last medical examination.

Claimant, Stephen Hiett, enlisted August 8, 1862, and was discharged May 20, 1865. He was pensioned from date of discharge at $8 per month for gunshot wound of left hand and breast.

It is contended in support of said motion, as was also contended in the former appeal, in brief, that it was error to adjudicate the claim for additional pension based on newly alleged causes of disability, non-specific in character, as a straight increase, and date the commencement of increase from the last medical examination instead of from the date of filing the application.

The solution of this question involves the question as to whether the admission of the new cause of disability affected the rate of pension to which he was entitled, or whether his increased rate was on account of increased degree of disability arising from the causes for which he was pensioned, at the date of filing his application for increase on account of old and new disabilities.

At the time of filing his application of August 20, 1890, for increase on account of pensioned causes and weak eyes and partial blindness resulting from smallpox, loss of teeth, result of scurvy of service origin, he was in receipt of a pension at $18 per month on account of gunshot wound of left hand and breast, and resulting disease of lungs, allowed August 3, 1888.

His application of August 20, 1890, not having been adjudicated, he filed a second application August 12, 1893, by another attorney, in which he claimed increase on account of pensioned causes, and he alleged again the new disability, i. e., impaired vision, resulting from smallpox contracted in service at New Orleans in 1864.

Instead of adjudicating these claims the Bureau, on December 20, 1895, five years and four months after he had filed his first application for additional pension, notified claimant that the rate of $18 per month was abolished by the act of March 3, 1883, and $24 substituted therefor, and calling upon him for evidence to show that his disabilities were equivalent to the loss of a hand or a foot, and in case of his failure to furnish said evidence, his pension would be reduced to $17 per month.

At this time all the evidence as to incurrence and continuance of disease of eyes and mouth was filed in the case that was on file when the case was adjudicated March 31, 1896, when claimant was adjudged entitled to a rating of six-eighteenths on account of disease of eyes and mouth. Combined rating not to exceed $24 per month from February 26, 1896.

So, also, all the certificates of medical examinations except the last, of February 26, 1896, were then on file.

Considering now the question of soldier's disabilities from the causes for which he was pensioned, and rated, by the action of March 31, 1896, and subsequent to August 20, 1890, the date of filing his application for new disabilities and increase, it appears that he was first medically examined under said application November 25, 1890, when the board at Sullivan, Ind., reported his condition as follows:

Pulse rate, 70; respiration, 20; temperature, 97; height, 5 feet 4 inches; weight, 112½ pounds; age, 54 years.

Tongue red, smooth, and slightly furred. Skin anæmic and body is poorly nourished. The middle finger of left hand has been removed about the middle of first phalanx and the stump is firmly adherent to third finger. There is firm anchylosis of joint formed by the first and second phalanges of first finger and partial anchylosis of all other joints of first and third fingers. Muscular tissue is wasted and tendons drawn so that the hand is not of very much use in the performance of manual labor. There are five or six small cicatrices over anterior and lower portion of left lung where claimant says that buckshot entered, and claimant says that it is very tender over ribs on left side about 2 inches below left nipple. There is a small scar 1 inch to right of third lumbar vertebrae that is very tender, and claimant says that a shot was removed from there. Left side of thorax does not appear as full as right one, and we find left side of thorax 1 inch smaller than right. Measurement of chest at rest 31 inches, on expiration 29½, and on inspiration 32½ inches.

Percussion resonance impaired over entire left lung, vesicular murmur indistinct and some bronchial breathing. Heart appears normal. Claimant has five teeth above and eight below, and half of them are so loosened that they could be removed with the fingers. Gums are spongy and fauces and pharynx are very red and blood vessels are enlarged. Mucous membrane is thickened and considerable pus on posterior part of pharynx. The margins of both upper and lower lids of each eye are inflamed and thickened, and especially of right eye. Claimant can read at 20 feet the letters on Snellen's card that should be read at 120 feet.

He is, in our opinion, entitled to eight-eighteenths rating for the disability caused by gunshot wound of left hand, four-eighteenths for that caused by scurvy and loss of teeth, and four-eighteenths for that caused by disease of eyes; eight-eighteenths for gunshot wound of left breast and resulting disease of lung.

He was next medically examined September 20, 1893, when the board reported his condition as follows:

Pulse rate, 72; respiration, 20; temperature, 99; height, 5 feet 6 inches; weight, 110 pounds; age, 56 years. Circumference of chest on expiration, 29½ inches; on inspiration, 31½ inches.

He has a number of scars (9) on the left side, ranging from an inch above the nipple to the lower border of the rib.

Part of the shot were taken out in front, and three were taken out, as the scars show, to the right of spine.

There is one shot supposed to be lodged in the lungs.

The heart sounds are about normal. There is an asthmatic condition of the respiratory organs.

There has been a flesh wound on the inside of the lower third of the left leg, which was not done at the same time that the wounds on the right side were.

There is varicose veins of both legs, most prominent just below popliteal spaces.

The middle finger of left hand has been amputated through first phalanx and the other three fingers are so injured as to be useless, or almost so.

There is chronic conjunctivitis and granulation of both eyes, worse on the right side.

There is some entropion.

The disease of eyes is of long standing, and he states that it is the result of an attack of measles and smallpox which he had while in the service.

There is irritability of the bladder produced by enlarged prostate gland. He suffers from nasal and pharyngeal catarrh.

He was next medically examined by the board at Vincennes, Ind., June 27, 1894, which reported his condition as follows:

Pulse rate, 60; respiration, 18; temperature, 98¾; height, 5 feet 4 inches; weight, 127 pounds; age, 57 years.

Applicant has scurvy. His gums are inflamed and ulcerated and recede from the teeth. His stomach is dilated, liver torpid, and bowels are constipated. His skin is sallow and his entire system shows signs of malnutrition. There is no evidence of his having had smallpox; there are no pits or other indication. Applicant has received an injury of left hand, the second finger having been shot away, and the functions of the first and third fingers are destroyed. The tendons of these fingers are adhered to surrounding tissues and the injury is equal to the loss of the first, second, and third fingers. He has four scars in right side just above the spine of the ischium. The scars are about one-fourth inch in diameter and adherent and give the appearance of gunshot wounds. He also has two scars in left breast just 1 inch below left nipple. Scars are adherent and about one-third inch in diameter. The scars on breast and in left side do not interfere with function of parts. Applicant's heart and lungs are normal. He has a chronic catarrhal inflammation of the lids of both eyes, but there is no pannus of the cornea of either eye, and all of the deeper structures are normal. His vision, according to Snellen's test, is one-half. He can distinguish the letters F, D, T, G at a distance of 20 feet. He is totally unable to earn a living by manual labor as a result of scurvy and injuries from gunshot wounds. We believe him to be a man of good habits. We attribute the condition of his stomach, liver, and nutrition to his scurvy and do not believe he has chronic diarrhea.

The gunshot wounds just over hip show signs of occasionally suppurating, and while they do not include surrounding tissues they are tender and painful and thereby interfere slightly with function of parts. There is no limitation of motion, and function of parts are but slightly interfered with. Wound under left nipple does not interfere to any marked degree with function of parts.

He was last medically examined by the board at Terre Haute, Ind., February 26, 1896, which reported his condition as follows:

Pulse rate, 108; respiration, 24; temperature, 99; height, 5 feet 5¼ inches, weight, 115 pounds; age, 59 years.

The second finger of left hand has been removed just below articulation of first and second phalanges. The end of stump is very tender. The hand is weakened sixth-eighteenths. We find five or six small scars on left side of chest, anterior aspect. The scars are nonadherent. (See diag.) His chest is narrow, and he is very much emaciated; is able to do but little work. Full inspiration, 31¼; forced expiration, 30 inches. There is diffused flatness over entire chest and dullness over lower and posterior portion of left lung. The vesicular murmur in entire left lung is feeble, at base almost lost. In spaces we find crackling rales more marked on left side. He has a moist cough, and expectorates mucus pus. Fourteen-eighteenths.

Claimant denies a history of chronic diarrhea. His emaciation, in our opinion, is due to results of scurvy and disease of lungs. Has but four teeth in upper jaw and two in the lower. Mucous membrane of mouth is very vascular, and gums are swollen and spongy. The stomach and bowels are tympanitic. Six-eighteenths.

No evidence of disease of kidneys. Has a well-marked lumbago. Is unable to bend forward and touch the floor. Motion of back painful and limited one-half. Four-eighteenths. There is no evidence of hemorrhoids or disease of kidneys. He has an enlarged prostate gland.

No evidence of wound of left hip. . Lids of each eye inflamed and thickened; conjunctiva filmy. Pupils equal in size and partially dilated. Media clear; fundus somewhat hazy. Disc outlined, normal in size. Reads Snellen with both and each separately at 13 feet. Four-eighteenths.

Heart's action rapid and somewhat irregular, otherwise normal. Rapid action of heart may be attributed to disease of lungs and result of scurvy (indigestion).

The man is unable to earn a support at manual labor. He is emaciated and broken down.

On May 1, 1889, prior to filing his application for additional pension on account of disease of eyes and mouth, he was rated eighteen-eighteenths for gunshot wound of left hand, eight-eighteenths for rheumatism, four-eighteenths for disease of lungs, and 2 grade on account of disease of eyes. This board certified vision of left eye, five-twentieths; right eye, three-twentieths (Snellen's types); that there was tenderness in ciliary region, right most so; pterygium at inner canthus of left eye; depressed and whitened optic papillæ in both eyes.

James A. Catlin testified September 12, 1894, from an acquaintance of thirty-five years:

That claimant had suffered from disease of eyes and scurvy; that he had been, for the last ten years or more, entirely incapacitated and unable to perform manual labor, from his personal knowledge of his physical condition.

George W. Dooley testified September, 1894:

That he had been intimately acquainted with claimant since his discharge, and has seen him every few days; that he had been seriously afflicted with disease of eyes, scurvy of the mouth, and other ailments, and that for the greater part of the time he had been able to perform but little, if any, manual labor.

John M. Sauth testified June 1, 1895:

That he saw claimant on his return from the Army; that he has known him prior to and since service; that he had been continuously afflicted with sore mouth, which the doctor called scurvy, and disease of eyes; that, in his judgment, the claimant has not been able to do a half a day's work since he came home from the Army, and at present and for some time past he has not been able to do any work at all; that he has lived near claimant since his return from service.

William McClure testified April 27, 1895:

That he was with claimant and lived in the same neighborhood about a year after he came home from the service; that he was troubled with his eyes and had to keep a handkerchief over them all the time; that he lived near him about seven years and then did not see him again until in the fall of 1894, when he was in such poor health that he was wholly unable to do anything, and at the present time is not able to do any kind of work at all.

Dr. John S. Murphy testified October 11, 1894:

That he had known claimant for the last fifteen years and treated him for chronic sore eyes in 1881, at which time he was "in a very broken-down condition;" also treated him for scorbutus; treated him in August, 1894; that claimant is a man of good habits.

On January 6, 1896, three witnesses testify to claimant's condition:

That it was greater than the loss of an arm or a leg; that he was unable to work, but is confined to his house and bed for weeks at a time.

In the Bureau action of March 31, 1896, claimant was rated six-eighteenths for disease of eyes and mouth by the medical referee, who also held that there was no ratable disability from buckshot wound of left hip, chronic diarrhea, and alleged piles and disease of kidneys shown since filing claim.

This would indicate that, from a medical standpoint, claimant's disability is due to his pensioned causes.

It also appears that claimant established his claim based on newly alleged disabilities—disease of eyes and mouth—and that he was accorded a rating therefor. It is also clear from the evidence that these disabilities materially add to the disability due to the gunshot wounds and disease of lungs for which he had previously been pensioned at $18 per month. It is also clear to my mind that claimant should have been accorded the benefit of a rating for his new disabilities from August 20, 1890, the date of filing his application therefor.

Where a pensioner under the law of July 14, 1862, files an application for additional pension, based on a newly alleged cause of disability, not specific, such claim, if allowed, dates from the time of filing such application and not from the date of the examining surgeon's certificate establishing a pensionable degree of disability from said newly alleged cause.

In such cases the date of commencement is governed by the proviso in section 2 of the act of March 3, 1879, and not by section 4698½, Revised Statutes. (See Digest of 1885, p. 327; Digest of 1897, p. 102.)

I am of the opinion that this motion should be allowed; the departmental decision of November 30, 1896, and the Bureau action of March 31, 1896, should be reversed. It is accordingly so ordered, and the papers in the case are herewith returned.

DEPENDENCE—ACT OF JUNE 27, 1890.
SARAH C. THOMPSON (WIDOW).

The evidence shows that claimant was, at the time of filing her declaration, in possession of ample means of support other than her daily labor, having been allowed $300 from her husband's estate for support for one year, and she is not pensionable under the act of June 27, 1890, under the declaration filed, though she may now be dependent.

Assistant Secretary Webster Davis to the Commissioner of Pensions, April 30, 1898.

Edward L. Thompson, late of Company D, Thirty-ninth Iowa Volunteers, died on the 19th day of January, 1896, leaving a pending claim for pension under a declaration filed July 7, 1890. Upon the intervention of his widow, Sarah C. Thompson, said claim was adjudicated and approved on August 22, 1896, at the rate of $6 per month.

On February 8, 1896, said widow also filed a declaration for widow's pension (No. 628428), under the provisions of the act of June 27, 1890, in behalf of herself and four minor children under 16 years of age.

The claim was rejected on May 19, 1897, on the ground that it is not shown by the evidence adduced upon special examination that claimant was, at date of filing her application, dependent within the meaning of the said act.

Assigning said action as error, appeal was taken on September 3, 1897, resting upon the contention which is substantially set out in the grounds of the motion as follows:

The estate of her late husband, which is unsettled and now in court, was only invoiced at fourteen hundred and forty-four dollars ($1,444.00), goods and cash on hand at time of his death, and according to the laws of Iowa the widow is only entitled to one-third ($\frac{1}{3}$) of the late husband's estate after all cost of administration is paid, and in this case claimant was allowed three hundred dollars ($300.00) for support of claimant and her minor children for the year she had to settle the estate in.

By order of the court claimant was allowed to sell said stock of goods and invest the proceeds, with about four hundred dollars ($400.00) that she received of her late husband's pension, in an eighty (80) acre farm, valued at two thousand ($2,000.00), she, as administratrix, assuming a mortgage on said land at six hundred dollars ($600.00), bearing 8 per cent interest, and payable annually.

In addition to the facts recited in the appeal, which are approximately borne out by the evidence in the case, it is material to add a portion of claimant's testimony, as follows:

December 8, 1896, I bought 80 acres of land, where I now live, for $2,000. I paid $1,400 cash and gave mortgage of $600. I bought in my own name, Sarah C. Thompson. The money paid for the land was all I had, both my own and that of the estate. I now have this 80 acres of land, mortgaged for $600, four horses, three cows and three heifers, two hogs and two little calves, and a colt. That is all the stock I have.

The evidence in the case does not fix any value upon the live stock above mentioned. The interest of the claimant in the farm, it appears, is about one-third of $1,400, and it may be assumed that the value of her estate, both real and personal, would not exceed $600. The ques tion then arises, Does a widow, with a "means of support" equivalent to $600, occupy a pensionable status under the act of June 27, 1890?

In the case of Susan Landgraf (7 P. D., 380) it is said:

A strict construction of the language of the statute would exclude from its benefits a widow who has any means of support whatever other than the proceeds of her labor. It is not believed that such a construction would be in harmony with the spirit and intent of the law.

In the same case it is also held:

Without undertaking to lay down an inflexible rule it may be said that, in general, where a widow is said to have, from sources independent of her labor, an income considerably in excess of the amount which the act of June 27, 1890, provides for widows who have no income or means of support outside of their earnings, such widow does not come within the class for whose benefit said act was intended.

It will thus be seen that the line which determines the pensionable or nonpensionable status of a widow is only approximately fixed, and each case must stand somewhat upon its own peculiar conditions.

Since it is held, substantially, that an applicant who has a "means of support" which, aided by reasonable effort on her part, will produce an income considerably in excess of the amount which the act provides, is not pensionable, it seems equally logical to hold that an applicant is pensionable whose "means of support," although aided by reasonable effort, will only yield an income considerably less than the amount provided by the act.

The "means of support" of the applicant in this case is limited in value to about $600, an amount which manifestly can not by the exercise of reasonable effort on claimant's part be made to produce an income that is not considerably less than $8 per month.

There is, however, another question in this case. The claimant filed her application in less than one month after the death of her husband, during the same year in which she was awarded $300 by the court as a support for herself and minor children. If she should be pensioned under her pending application it must take effect, under the law, from the date of filing the same. But during the period of one year immediately following the death of her husband she had ample means of support. For the reason that claimant at the time of filing her declaration did not occupy a pensionable status the action appealed from is affirmed.

DEPENDENCE—ACT JUNE 27, 1890.

ISABELLE VARCO.

As the evidence in this case fails to show the value of claimant's means of support, the motion is sustained, and departmental decision of March 13, 1897, reversed, and a special examination ordered.

Assistant Secretary Webster Davis to the Commissioner of Pensions, April 30, 1898.

Claimant's attorney, on October 26, 1897, filed a motion for reconsideration of departmental decision of March 13, 1897 (9 P. D., 1), affirming the Bureau action of September 28, 1895, rejecting her widow's claim No. 591143, filed February 20, 1894, under section 3 of the act of June 27, 1890, on the ground that she had "other means of support than her daily labor, it appearing that she had a life lease of valuable property, and is therefore not dependent within the meaning of the act of June 27, 1890."

It is argued on behalf of claimant that—

The contention of the appeal was that the rejection of the case is error because as a matter of fact the income derived by her from the property (farm land) which she occupies is not hers by right but by sufferance of another person who is legally entitled thereto but allows the claimant to freely occupy and enjoy the benefits of the property. The decision is based upon a misconception of the views upon which the appeal was based, as there was no contention that because the property occupied and used by the widow was not left to her or for her use by the soldier, she should be regarded as entitled to the benefits of the act of June 27, 1890.

What is contended is that if the view expressed in the decision rendered were correct, then the claimant would be equally independent if she were the guest of her State in its penal institution or an inmate of one of the county almshouses, because here, too, it would be a question as to the actual circumstances of the claimant, and it would be shown that she was being comfortably housed and clothed and fed at the public expense. In the case at bar, the Bureau rejected the claim on the ground that the claimant has "a life lease in valuable property," which statement does not appear to be true, unless free occupancy by sufferance constitutes in law a life lease. The fact appears to be that whatever interest the claimant has in the property in question is subject to the prior interest of her mother-in-law, continuing during the latter's life.

"Means of support" within the meaning of the law, we submit, is not charity, whether public or private in character. It is that support to which the claimant has a *right* and can maintain in law or equity. It is not questioned, we believe, in the case at bar but that the person having the right to what the claimant enjoys may dispossess her at any day; and if this is true it can hardly be said that the property is to her a "means of support" within the meaning and intent of the law.

The finding of facts in said decision were as follows:

Claimant has a dower interest in 80 acres of land, and there appears to be no contention but this would take her outside the statute invoked were it not for the reason that the dower is subject to the life estate of her mother-in-law. It is shown, however, that claimant has the free use of the land, her interest, in fact, being not that of her dower interest, but that of a free tenant by permission of the holder of the life estate. The real question involved is not as to the means the claimant's husband left her, but it is rather what means of support did this widow actually have when she filed her declaration.

The question asked in said decision, i. e., "What means of support did this widow actually have when she filed her declaration?" does not appear to have been answered, and from an examination of the evidence in the case it appears to be impossible to answer; yet this is the main question in the case, and on which the decision must turn.

The following is all the evidence in the case bearing on the question of value of claimant's means of support:

Edgar P. Spooner and J. F. Prouty testified in a joint affidavit June 15, 1895, that—

claimant has a life lease in 80 acres of land situate in the town of Austin, Mower County, Minn., which amounts not to exceed $200 per year. She also owns two cows, which constitute the character and value of all property possessed by her and the amount of her income from all sources.

J. C. Hawkins testified, December 26, 1896, that soldier left claimant a life estate, subject to the life estate of his mother, and two cows, nothing more, and that her friends have been obliged to help her; that—

said mother-in-law's estate comes first, but up to the present time she has allowed the said Isabelle Varco the free use of said land after paying all taxes and expenses of keeping up the same. The title to said land stands as follows: First, a life estate to the mother of the deceased; then a life estate to the widow of deceased, subject to the mother's estate, and at the death of the mother and widow the title goes to the son of the deceased.

J. E. Parmeter testified, December 26, 1896, that soldier left claimant as her only means of support—

a life estate in 80 acres of land, subject to a life estate of Mrs. E. U. Varco, her mother-in-law, the fee going to a son of the deceased on the death of his mother and grandmother. Her mother-in-law has suffered her thus far to have the free use of said land, after paying all the taxes and expenses of running the same. She also has two cows, and I know of nothing more. She is really in needy circumstances.

Claimant testified that the only property left her by her husband, George W. Varco, was two cows and a life estate in 80 acres of land, his homestead. That the mother of deceased has a prior life estate in said land, and that the title of said land, subject to said life estates, is in a son of said George W. Varco; that the mother of her husband has allowed her to occupy said land since the death of her husband, on account of the need and destitute condition of affiant.

The foregoing evidence fails to state the value of the real estate or any facts from which its value can be approximately estimated. The witnesses who estimate the value of claimant's life lease at not exceeding $200 per annum do not indicate what they mean by this estimate, whether this is the net or gross income from the 80 acres per annum, or whether the $200 is their estimated value of her contingent estate, which has never vested, and may never vest title in claimant.

It would appear from all the evidence that claimant has no vested title to the land, her estate in expectancy being but a contingent remainder, and that her benefits derived from said land is but the voluntary contribution of her mother-in-law.

The decision of March 13, 1897, was, therefore, hardly responsive to the question presented, nor in harmony with the decisions of this Department in similar cases of this class. (See cases of Evaline Davis (widow), 9 P. D., 2; Emma T. Wangelin (widow), 9 P. D., 76.)

The main question to be determined in this case was, and is, what was claimant's means of support at date of filing her application? and this it is impossible to determine from the evidence.

I am, therefore, of the opinion that the motion should be sustained, the departmental decision of March 13, 1897, reversed, and a special examination directed; and it is accordingly so ordered.

The papers in the case are herewith returned.

COMMENCEMENT—INCREASE—ACT OF JANUARY 5, 1893.

DANIEL WEBSTER LEVAN.

The date of commencement in Mexican war claims for increase under said act is in each claim the day on which the case is legally approved by the Board of Review.

As this rule was followed in the action upon this claim, the same was proper, and is affirmed.

Assistant Secretary Webster Davis to the Commissioner of Pensions, May 7, 1898.

Daniel Webster Levan, a Mexican war survivor, was pensioned as such in 1887, under the act of January 29, 1887, his pension being $8 per month, commencing from the date of the passage of said act. He filed January 21, 1893, an application for increase under the act of January 5, 1893, which provides as follows:

Be it enacted, &c., That the Secretary of the Interior be, and he is hereby, authorized to increase the pension of every pensioner who is now on the rolls at eight dollars per month on account of service in the Mexican war and who is wholly disabled for manual labor, and is in such destitute circumstances that eight dollars per month are insufficient to provide him the necessaries of life, to twelve dollars per month.

This claim for increase was rejected January 25, 1894, on the ground that pensioner was not wholly disabled for manual labor, as shown by a medical examination held December 26, 1893. This action was communicated to claimant and his then attorney January 30, 1894. Subsequently, or on January 14, 1897, the pensioner filed another claim for increase under the same act, in which another attorney was appointed. Said attorney was informed April 23, 1897, of the rejection of January 25, 1894, and he filed an appeal April 30, 1897. Before the same was acted on, however, the claim of January 14, 1897, was allowed, the rating being increased to $12 per month, and the said appeal was dismissed.

In this allowance the increased rate was made to commence June 11, 1897, the date of the approval of the same by the Board of Review of the Bureau. The attorney then filed, August 17, 1897, another appeal, assigning said date of commencement of increase as error, and contending that the higher rate should have been commenced from the date of filing the application therefor. The arguments he presents in support of his position have all been considered in previous cases of similar nature.

The action commencing the increase of pension from the date of approval by the Board of Review was based on an order of the Commissioner, No. 231, dated July 6, 1893, as follows:

The date of commencement in Mexican war claims for increase under the act of January 5, 1893, shall in each claim be the day on which the case is legally approved by the Board of Review.

This order and the action of the Bureau in pursuance thereof in claims for increase under said act of January 5, 1893, have been approved by the Department in a number of decisions. Among the first of these decisions is that in the case of Edward C. Collins, alias Edward Crossweight, late of Company I, Twenty-sixth Ohio Volunteers (Mexican war), and dated May 19, 1894. It is therein pointed out that although the provision of the act is to give a pension of $12 per month instead of $8 to such Mexican war pensioners as were then on the rolls and receiving the latter amount, yet the act does not direct that the higher rating, or increase, shall be given from the date of the passage of the act, but title to the same is made contingent upon the establishment of certain facts or conditions by proof, to the satisfaction of the Commissioner. It is then stated:

There is no question about when the act took effect. But that does not bear on this inquiry, as the act itself grants no increase of pension, but only authorizes the

Secretary to act when cases are brought before him and the necessary facts proven. It is this action that grants the increase in each case, and the increase can not have an existence until he acts and grants it.

In short, as no specified time is fixed by said act when the increased rate of pension shall commence (as is the case with other laws, which designate the date of passage, or the date of medical examination, as the date of commencement), and as the granting of said increased rate at all is made to depend, first, on the proof that certain conditions exist—viz, entire disability to perform manual labor, and destitution—and, second, upon the declaration of the Bureau that such proof is satisfactory, it must necessarily follow that title does not exist until such declaration or approval is given, and the increase or higher rate begins from that time—that is, from the date of approval of the case by the Board of Review.

Other decisions on the line of the one herein cited have been since rendered, and in each the Bureau order No. 231 has been upheld. The arguments made in the appeal that this claim is not affected by section 4713, Revised Statutes, nor by section 4698½, Revised Statutes, but that the increase would properly begin from the date of filing the application therefor if the proof showed the conditions imposed by the act existed at said date, have been all considered in the several decisions referred to, and the Department has preferred to interpret the law in the manner herein set forth for the reasons given.

This claim being entirely similar to those heretofore passed upon, it must be held that the commencement of increase was properly fixed as from the date when approval was given by the Board of Review, viz June 11, 1897, and the action is affirmed.

It should be remarked that the pensioner died July 14, 1897, and this appeal was really filed on behalf of the widow, who has been since pensioned in her own right.

———

ADULTEROUS COHABITATION—ACT AUGUST 7, 1882.

ELIZABETH SMITH (WIDOW).

The evidence shows that from 1887 to about 1893 the appellant and one Daniel Boston lived together in a small tenement consisting of two rooms; that a part of the time they lived there alone and the remainder of the time a small boy lived with them; that it was the general opinion among their immediate neighbors that they were living as man and wife; that on several occasions the appellant stated that Boston was her husband; and that they, in fact, were not legally married.

Held: That the facts are sufficient to justify the action of dropping her name from the pension roll under the act of August 7, 1882.

Assistant Secretary Webster Davis to the Commissioner of Pensions, May 14, 1898.

I have considered the appeal filed August 23, 1897, from the action of your Bureau in dropping from the pension roll the name of Elizabeth

Smith, widow of Lewis Smith, formerly a soldier in Company D, Thirty-fifth Regiment, United States Colored Troops. It appears that the appellant was, in July, 1892, granted a pension under the act of June 27, 1890, and that she continued in receipt of the same until July 6, 1896, when the pension was terminated on the ground that she had since the passage of the act of August 7, 1882, lived in open and notorious adulterous cohabitation with one Daniel Boston. From that action she appeals, contending that she has furnished abundant evidence that the charge against her was false and that she is a woman of good moral character.

The first information that the appellant was living in adultery came to your Bureau through a special examiner who, in September, 1895, forwarded seven depositions made before him, with the recommendation that the papers in the case be sent to the field for a special examination. A special examination was made in May, 1896.

The evidence shows that from 1887 to about 1893, the appellant rented a couple of rooms in a tenement house in Charleston, S. C., and that during all that time a man named Daniel Boston made his home with her. It is not conclusively shown that they occupied the same bed or sleeping apartment. She says he was simply a boarder and that he slept in one room and she slept in the other. He says the same. One of the rooms was used as a kitchen, but the evidence tends to show that there was a small bed or lounge in it. A boy named Thomas Johnson, a relative of the appellant, lived there part of the time.

The appellant swears that Boston and the boy slept in the bed in the kitchen and they both corroborate her. One witness swears that the bed in the kitchen was too small for two persons. All agree that it was a single bed. There is no evidence of any familiarity between Boston and the appellant on which to base a positive inference that they were living in the relation of man and wife, but it was undoubtedly the opinion of the majority of their near neighbors that they were so living, and there is apparently trustworthy evidence that on several occasions the appellant stated that Boston was her husband. There is also some evidence that on one occasion he declared that she was his lawful wife.

On the other hand, the appellant has introduced testimony from persons living in the neighborhood, who say they always supposed that Boston was only a boarder and never saw or heard anything to indicate otherwise. As to the majority of these persons, however, it is clear that they had not so good an opportunity to know the actual state of affairs as those who testified adversely. An exception may be made in the case of J. B. Wethers, who lived in the same house, but he admits that there was "a neighborhood rumor" that the appellant and Boston were cohabiting as man and wife. There is considerable testimony of a general nature to the effect that the appellant has always been a woman of good moral character. She is a member of the Morris Street

Baptist Church (colored) in the city of Charleston, and well spoken of by her pastor.

There is no doubt that the person who first directed the attention of your special examiner to this case was actuated by malice, and I should not be inclined to attach much weight to his testimony were it not amply corroborated by other persons who are not shown to have had any motive for desiring to injure the appellant. As the case stands, I am of the opinion that the evidence establishes the following facts:

1. That the appellant and Daniel Boston, from 1887 to 1893 or thereabouts, lived together in a small tenement consisting of two rooms.

2. That during a part of that time they were the only occupants of the rooms. During the remainder of the time a small boy also lived there.

3. It was the general opinion in the immediate neighborhood that they were living as man and wife.

4. The appellant stated on more than one occasion that Boston was her husband.

5. That they, in fact, were not legally married.

The appellant is about 43 years old at the present time and Boston is about 62. Taking all the facts together, I think they establish with reasonable certainty the open and notorious adulterous cohabitation of the parties during the period referred to.

Much of the testimony favorable to the appellant relates to more recent years, during which her relations with Boston appear to have been less intimate.

The act of Congress approved August 7, 1882, declares that— .

The open and notorious adulterous cohabitation of a widow who is a pensioner shall operate to terminate her pension from the commencement of such cohabitation.

After careful consideration I am constrained to hold that the action appealed from was correct, and the same is accordingly affirmed.

RATE OF PENSION—DEAFNESS—PRACTICE.

HILKIAH P. NICHOLS (DECEASED).

The rating of pension on account of total deafness of one ear was, in accordance with established practice, during the period covered in this case (from 1865 to 1870) one dollar per month.

Assistant Secretary Webster Davis to the Commissioner of Pensions,
May 21, 1898.

On December 17, 1866, Hilkiah P. Nichols, who was a member, during the late war, of Company M, First Vermont Infantry, filed a claim for pension on account of deafness, which was yet pending when he died, February 22, 1870, and was completed by his widow, Mary H. Nichols, this appellant. It was allowed, and certificate No. 934179, issued in June, 1897, granting pension accordingly at $1 per month for total deafness of right ear.

On September 7, 1897, said widow appealed, contending the rate allowed is less than others receive for the same degree of disability.

The rate of pension allowed in this case is in accordance with the established practice as to pension for the period over which the pension in this instance runs, i. e., from discharge in 1865 to the soldier's death in 1870. Thirteen dollars per month is the rate allowable for this period for total deafness of both ears, and total deafness of one ear is considered to entitle to but $1 per month. (See Pension Laws, Decisions and Rulings, 1882, pp. 151-152.)

The medical referee states in his advisory opinion herein:

> The rate of one-eighteenth (or $1) was the recognized rate for deafness of one ear from discharge until April 3, 1884, when the first change was made in the rate for this disability. The same rate was allowed as has been given others for this same disability, and under the practice of the Bureau a higher rate could not have been allowed.

No injustice to appellant appears, therefore, in the adjudication of her deceased husband's claim. The rating was in accordance with established practice, and is affirmed.

ADULTEROUS COHABITATION—ACT AUGUST 7, 1882.

MATILDA AGUE.

1. The provisions of section 2 of the act of August 7, 1882, are applicable to widows' claims under section 3 of the act of June 27, 1890.
2. Adulterous cohabitation of a soldier's widow, on or subsequent to August 7, 1882, terminates her pensionable status as effectually as her remarriage.
3. Section 2 of said act of August 7, 1882, is in no sense a penal statute, nor is it to be construed according to the rules of construction of penal statutes, but is remedial and is liberally construed.

Assistant Secretary Webster Davis to the Commissioner of Pensions,
May 24, 1898.

Claimant's attorney on October 5, 1897, appealed from the Bureau action of August 16, 1895, dropping claimant's name from the rolls (widow's pension, certificate No. 301629) under section 3 of the act of June 27, 1890, on the ground that she had violated the provisions of the act of August 7, 1882, having lived in open and notorious adulterous cohabitation with one Cary Wallace since date of soldier's death.

The following is the brief and argument in support of the appeal:

> I. The last clause of section 2 of the act of August 7, 1882, under which Mrs. Ague was dropped from the pension roll, is as follows:
>
> "The open and notorious adulterous cohabitation of a widow who is a pensioner shall operate to terminate her pension from the commencement of such cohabitation."
>
> This section declares a forfeiture of property or rights to property, and is, there-

fore, to be construed strictly, the same as a penal statute. (Endlich, Int. of States, 343; Russell v. University, 1 Wheat., 432; United States r. Athens University, 35 Ga., 344; Sutherland, Stat. Cons't, 208, 358, and notes.)

What is meant by a strict construction of the statutes? On this point see Sutherland, Stat. Cons't, 352 and notes, 348; Potter's Dwarris, 245; Andrew r. United States, 2 Story, 203; 2 Curtis, 502; 2 Paine, 162; 1 Blatch., 151; 2 Wheat., 119; Sutherland, Stat. Cons't, 350–353, and notes; Endlich, 329, 330; Potter's Dwarris, 21 Am. Rule; 29th Rule of Vattell; 26 N. Y., 523; 95 N. C., 434. A few quotations will be given.

"Those who contend that a penalty may be inflicted must show that the words of the act distinctly express that, under the circumstances, it has been incurred. They must fail if the words are merely equally capable of a construction that would and one that would not inflict the penalty." (Sutherland, 352.)

"The difference between a liberal and a strict construction of a statute is this: That a case may come within one unless the language excludes it, while it is excluded by the other unless the language includes it." (Sutherland, 348.)

"It is our duty to expound and not to make acts of Parliament. We must not extend a penal law to other cases than those intended by the legislature, even though we think they came within the mischief intended to be remedied." (Per Lord Kenyon in Jenkesson v. Thomas, 4 T. R.)

(See also, as especially applicable, 329 Endlich Int. Stats.)

II. Applying the rules of law and the principles above enunciated to the facts of this case, as disclosed by the record, it must be held that the dropping of Mrs. Ague from the pension rolls was reversible error, which this Department has the power to correct and ought to correct for the following reasons:

(1) At the time of the passage of the act of June 27, 1890, under which her right to pension originated, she was a widow who was not living in 'open and notorious adulterous cohabitation.' At that time she had led an exemplary and virtuous life for at least four years. (2) This condition continued and existed when she made application for pension, when her pension was granted, when it was taken from her, and continued down to the present time.

At no time did she come within the act of August 7, 1882, as "a widow who is a pensioner" living in "open and notorious adulterous cohabitation." To rule otherwise is to read into the statute language which Congress did not place there, which is not permissible. Her right to a pension under the act of 1890 is determined by her condition or status at the time of her application. (Frances Kendall, 8 P. D., 197.)

With respect to the ruling of the Department in the case of Eliza Fain, (7 P. D., 572), and kindred cases, wherein a different construction is placed upon the statutes from what is herein contended for, it is sufficient to say that that ruling is believed to be incorrect and not capable of being sustained in law or in equity. It is, moreover, not in harmony with previous rulings of the Department in similar cases. (See especially Sarah E. West, 3 P. D., 115, a decision by Assistant Secretary Bussey, well considered and ably sustained by reason and logic.)

Soldier enlisted October 31, 1861, and was discharged February 21, 1863. He reenlisted February 1, 1864, and was discharged June 29, 1865. He was married to claimant in 1863, and died November 6, 1882. Claimant kept a house of prostitution from 1882 to 1886, and had two illegitimate children since the death of her husband, one born in 1884 and the other in 1886, as the result of her adulterous cohabitation with one Cary Wallace. She subsequently maintained illicit relations with one James Sullivan for several years—just how many or for what exact time, does not appear; but claimant testifies that since her pension was allowed under the act of June 27, 1890, she has had nothing to do with any man, and has never remarried. John H. Kelly, a police officer, testified before a special examiner, June 3, 1893, that claimant had kept a house of ill fame which he raided twice, and he had heard of its being raided by other officers; that for the last four or five years she had not been so notorious.

Claimant was first pensioned August 12, 1891, under act of June 27, 1890, from July 14, 1890, and her name was dropped from the rolls August 29, 1895, on the ground that she had violated the provisions of the act of August 7, 1882. The evidence in the case shows no specific act of open and notorious adulterous cohabitation since the passage of the act of June 27, 1890, nor does it satisfactorily appear when said acts ceased.

The special examiner on June 10, 1895, reported that since claimant has been in receipt of a pension she has abandoned her former habits and led a very good life; that her condition is now deplorable enough, yet if deprived of her small pension it would be worse, and she would either be forced back in her former avocation or fall a charge on the community where she resides.

Soldier at date of his death left a pending claim for pension, which was rejected June 19, 1895, on the ground that his death was not shown to be due to his service.

Claimant filed a claim as widow, under section 4702, Revised Statutes, which was rejected June 19, 1895, on the ground that soldier's death was not shown to be due to the service.

Assuming that claimant has not been shown guilty of notorious adulterous cohabitation since she was granted a pension, the question raised by the appeal turns upon the construction of the phrase "who is a pensioner" as used in said section 2 of the act of August 7, 1882.

The statute in question has been the subject of frequent contention and discussion before this Department, resulting in numerous decisions, often inharmonious, and some of which are in direct conflict with each other. As showing the difficulty in ascertaining the intent of Congress in the use of the language employed, conflicting decisions have been rendered by the same Secretary and same Assistant Secretary in an effort to correctly interpret the law in question (see collocated cases, Digest of Pension Decisions of 1897, pp. 15 to 19), and in one case, at least, conflicting rules of construction appear to have been applied to said act in the same decision. See the case of Sarah E. West, widow (3 P. D., 115).

In that case it was said, in discussing said section 2 of the act of August 8, 1882, page 119, that—

it was somewhat akin to a penal statute, and as such its terms must be literally enforced. The operation of penal laws can not be safely enlarged by interpretation. New penalties can not be created by construction without endangering the whole system of statutory punishments.

The discussion of this subject is closed on page 120 in the following language:

While, therefore, the forfeiture in question is somewhat akin to a penalty, it is, in truth, only a legal recognition of the fact that to all proper intents and purposes the widow's pensionable condition has legally ceased.

It was further said, on page 117 of said case, that—

The language of the section is that "the open and notorious adulterous cohabitation of a widow who is a pensioner shall operate to terminate her pension from the commencement of such cohabitation." The language is explicit and emphatic. It explicitly defines the crime upon which the forfeiture of pension shall be based as the "open and notorious adulterous cohabitation of a widow." It applies the penalty for the crime thus described to only a "widow who is a pensioner."

That case was affirmed by Assistant Secretary Bussey, who rendered the decision in the West case, in the case of Cynthia A. Evans (5 P. D., 188), wherein he defined the "crime" mentioned in the West decision as follows:

The adulterous cohabitation which the law thus makes the ground of forfeiture is a living together in the apparent, though not lawful, relationship of husband and wife, involving "the voluntary sexual intercourse of a married person with a person other than the offender's husband or wife," the theory of the law being that a widow who is a pensioner is a "married" person within the legal definition of "adultery" and within the meaning of the inhibitory clause of section 2 of the act of August 7, 1882.

It would thus appear that in order to sustain the construction given to the statute in the West case the "widow who is a pensioner" was declared to be a widow who is a pensioner and a married woman, thus adding a fourth condition to the three conditions of forfeiture enumerated in the West case. The language of section 2 of said act of August 7, 1882, which was held in the West case to be "explicit and emphatic," and "explicitly defined the crime upon which the forfeiture of pension was based," required a construction in the Evans case which changed the widow to a married person without a remarriage of the widow.

In the case of Jennette Thompson (7 P. D., 262) it was held that the act of August 7, 1882, was in no sense a penal statute; that it neither commands nor forbids the doing or omission of any act; that it simply provides a condition which renders the widow of a soldier nonpensionable from the date of the passage of the act; that it prescribed no penalty any more than does the provision that a widow's pension shall cease upon her remarriage, or that a minor's pension shall cease upon the minor attaining the age of 16 years, or that a dependent parent's pension shall cease when dependency ceases.

I am of the opinion that Congress did not attempt to define a crime in stating the condition which should terminate the widow's pensionable status. As was held in the case of Alice Gray (7 P. D., 134):

It is clear that Congress, by the use of the words "adulterous cohabitation of a widow," did not employ the word "adulterous" in its technical signification. To hold otherwise would render the provision inoperative.

So, also, to hold strictly to the phrase "who is a pensioner" would lead to an equally absurd conclusion, and result in pensioning a widow who, if she were in receipt of a pension, would be dropped from the rolls under said act. The construction of the language of said act, "who is a pensioner," was fully considered in the case of Sarah J. Grooms (7 P. D., 207), where the absurdity of a strict or literal construction was illustrated by the facts in that case. The words "who is a pensioner" were held to include a widow who was an applicant for a widow's pension, and the Sarah E. West case (3 P. D., 115) and the case of Cynthia Evans (5 P. D., 188) and other similar cases, so far as they were in conflict with the Grooms case, were in terms overruled. It was said in the concluding paragraph of the Grooms case that—

> The act in terms simply operates to forfeit the right to continuance of the pension when the conditions named in the statute are established, and if found to exist when the application is made, or while pending, such forfeiture is destructive of all title to pension.

In the case of Eliza Fain (7 P. D., 572) the material facts were substantially the same as in the case under consideration. Claimant had been pensioned under section 3 of the act of June 27, 1890, and dropped from the rolls for violation of section 2 of the act of August 7, 1882. The evidence showed adulterous cohabitation subsequent to 1882 and up to 1890, and in June, 1890, claimant had given birth to an illegitimate child. In that, as in this, case, violation of the provisions of the act of August 7, 1882, was admitted subsequent to 1882 and prior to June 27, 1890; but in both the Fain case and the case under consideration the claimants contended that they had not violated the act of 1882 since June 27, 1890, and, as they were not pensioners at the time they violated the act of 1882, they did not come within the provisions of said act of 1882, but were pensionable under the act of June 27, 1890. The Fain case was decided on the theory that it was unnecessary to show that her adulterous cohabitation had continued after she became a pensioner, for the reason that open and notorious adulterous cohabitation of a widow destroys her right to pension from the date of the commencement of such cohabitation as effectually as if she had remarried on that date.

As was said in that case (7 P. D., 575):

> The gravamen of the widow's offense does not lie in the fact that she was a *pensioner* when she committed the adulterous acts, but in the fact that her conduct was subversive of public decency and law and of such a character as would have caused her to forfeit all claim to support by the husband if he were living. The law does not say if a widow whose pension has been terminated by reason of open and notorious adulterous cohabitation thereafter reforms and lives chastely she may have her pension restored. She forfeits not only the pension then due, but the *right* to such pension for all time. But no reason can be given why such conduct should work permanent forfeiture of a pension already granted that is not an equally strong reason why it should be a bar to the allowance of any future claim for pension. It is not to be believed that Congress when it declared, in effect, that the open and notorious adulterous cohabitation of a widow pensioner should operate to annihilate her right to pension, intended that a widow who was not a pensioner might indulge in such cohabitation as long as suited her interest or inclination and then, whenever she so desired, exchange a paramour for a pension. The purpose of the law was to prevent the pensioning of widows after they were found to have been guilty of open and notorious adulterous cohabitation. From the time that such cohabitation is established (since August 7, 1882) their right to pension is gone.
>
> If this appellant had married in 1886, when she began to cohabit with the father of her illegitimate children, and that fact had not been discovered until 1895, there

would be no question as to the propriety of dropping her name from the rolls; but the law relative to remarriage is in almost the same language as that relating to open and notorious adulterous cohabitation. It says: "On the marriage of any widow, dependent mother, or dependent sister, *having a pension*, such pension shall cease" (sec. 4708, R. S.).

The same question raised in this case was squarely presented in the case of Ellen J. Pipes (7 P. D., 489), and after careful consideration the conclusion was reached that the existing conditions named in section 2 of the act of August 7, 1882, worked a forfeiture of the pensionable status and is a bar to pension for those who may become applicants for pension; that the law makes no provision for restoring the pensionable right when once forfeited under said act, and that the inhibition therein contained applies with equal force to applicants and pensioners, whether under the act of June 27, 1890, or under prior laws; that the act of June 27, 1890, is incomplete in itself, and depends in many respects upon prior legislation for its enforcement; that it in no respect abrogates, repeals, amends, or modifies the act of August 7, 1882, and that Congress therefore intended that the provisions of the act of 1882 be applied to the act of June 27, 1890.

I gave this question careful consideration in the case of Ann Fagin, decided July 7, 1897 (9 P. D., 62), and, with the various decisions before me, I reached the conclusion that the adulterous cohabitation of a widow subsequent to the passage of the act of August 7, 1882, works a forfeiture of her pension or right to a pension under the act of June 27, 1890. In that case the adulterous cohabitation was shown to have ceased long prior to the act of June 27, 1890.

From what has been said it is clear to my mind, first, that the act of August 7, 1882, is in no sense a penal statute and should not be construed, under the rules, applicable to statutes that declare the forfeiture of property or property rights; second, that a strict or literal application of the language of the act of August 7, 1882, would defeat the object of the law and lead to absurd conclusions; third, that the act of August 7, 1882, is a remedial statute and should be liberally construed, so as to correct the mischief at which it was aimed and effectuate the remedy.

It is urged by claimant's attorney that this Department held in the case of Francis Kendall (8 P. D., 197) that the right of a widow under said act of June 27, 1890—

must be determined by her condition at the time she seeks to establish her right, and is in no way dependent upon or connected with her previous condition.

This language, it must be conceded, is not strictly correct, nor was it necessary in determining the question presented in that case, which was merely that of dependence of the widow at the date of filing her application. The law requires the condition of dependence of a widow under section 3 of the act of June 27, 1890, to exist at the date of filing her declaration, as her pension, if allowed, must commence from that date. She may not seek to establish her right for many years after filing her application, and her dependence is not determined solely by her dependence then, but it must be shown to have existed at the time she filed her claim. Her right to pension is also so far dependent upon and connected with her previous condition that she must show a legal marriage to the soldier, and continuous widowhood, and even then her right is forfeited if she is shown to have lived in open and notorious adulterous cohabitation subsequent to the death of her husband—after August 7, 1882. So much, therefore, of the language of that case as is contained in the second paragraph of the syllabus is overruled as an incorrect statement of the law.

In conclusion, I am of the opinion that the case of Sarah E. West (3 P. D., 115), and other cases in conflict with the case of Sarah J. Grooms (7 P. D., 207), were properly overruled, and that the constructions of the act of August 7, 1882, and its application to claims under the act of June 27, 1890, as announced in the cases of Jennette Thompson (7 P. D., 262), Alice Gray (7 P. D., 134), Ellen J. Pipes (7 P. D., 489), Eliza Fain (7 P. D., 572), and the case of Ann Fagin (9 P. D., 62), are correct, and the same are hereby reaffirmed.

The action appealed from is accordingly affirmed, and the papers in the case are herewith returned.

INCREASE—CERTIFICATES OF MEDICAL EXAMINATIONS.

ROBERT W. MATTHEWS.

Inasmuch as the evidence on file, including the last two certificates of medical examination, is unsatisfactory as to the degree of disability existing at the date of said examinations, on account of pensioned causes alone, a special examination is deemed advisable, for which purpose the papers in the case are remanded.

Assistant Secretary Webster Davis to the Commissioner of Pensions, May 24, 1898.

The appeal in this case was entered at this Department January 14, 1898, against your action of December 23, 1897, rejecting the claim for increase filed May 22, 1897.

The appellant, Robert W. Matthews, Company G, Eleventh Indiana Infantry, certificate numbered 101637, is now pensioned at $17 per month for gunshot wounds of right lung and both thighs.

He was originally pensioned for the said disabilities at $6 per month from July 27, 1865, which rate was increased to $12 per month from February 14, 1883, and on January 30, 1891, the certificate for the present rate, to date from July 9, 1890, was issued.

An application for increase on account of pensioned causes and alleged resulting paralysis of right side was filed March 7, 1896, and rejected June 19, 1896, on the ground that the disability due to the said pensioned causes had not increased, and that the right hemiplegia, which on medical examination was shown to exist, was not a pathological sequence of any disability for which the soldier was pensioned.

A similar claim was filed May 22, 1897, and similar action was taken in said claim December 23, 1897.

It is from the action declining to accept the right hemiplegia as a pathological sequence of any pensioned cause that the pending appeal was taken.

The appellant contends that an injustice has been done him, as he honestly believes that the paralysis of his right side was the direct result of the wounds for which he is pensioned, and was not caused by any other trouble, which fact is certified to in the evidence of Drs. A. P. Fitch, William H. Schultz, Jesse S. Reagan, and S. C. Alexander, now on file in his claim.

Dr. A. P. Fitch testifies that it is "possible and probable" that the shock the claimant received when wounded, especially the wound through the body—

Has weakened his vital force, disturbed reflex action, and hastened decay to the extent of weakening arterial coats, especially the arterioles of the brain, therefore contributing in some extent to the breaking of the vessel and hemorrhage, which cause brought about the paralyzed condition of this unfortunate and helpless man.

Dr. Jesse S. Reagan testifies that the soldier is partially paralyzed, and that the said paralysis was "perhaps caused by or resulted from the wounds" for which he is pensioned.

Dr. William H. Schultz states that he believes the paralysis from which the claimant is suffering to be the result of his wounds, and that he further believes "that either of two of his wounds may have contributed to his present condition through the process of an emboli. the neoplasm giving way at the time of hemorrhage."

Dr. S. C. Alexander testifies as follows:

On December 5, 1895, I was called to see Mr. Robert W. Matthews, who was then partially paralyzed, which paralysis continued to complete hemiplegia of the entire right side. I attended Mr. Matthews continually for eight days. Said Matthews was then totally disabled, and, in my opinion, the disability is permanent. Said paralysis is due, I think, to the effect of the gunshot wounds received in the late war.

In a joint affidavit, filed October 8, 1896, Drs. H. M. Skillman and F. O. Young, of Lexington, Ky., testify to the fact that on or about December 5, 1895, the claimant was stricken with apoplexy, and that he is now suffering from paralysis of the right side; but the said affiants do not even hazard a guess as to the cause of the said apoplectic stroke and the hemiplegia resulting therefrom.

Dr. M. H. Rose, of Thorntown, Ind., testifies, in an affidavit filed September 18, 1897, that he "thinks it possible, and very probable," that the wounds for which the soldier is pensioned "caused deranged. irregular, reflex nervous action, and thus became the bottom cause of Mr. Matthews's apoplexy and paralysis."

The claimant was medically examined under each application for increase filed by him as above stated.

He was examined May 6, 1896, by the board of surgeons at Lebanon,

Ind., the certificate of said examination showing the following objective conditions:

Pulse rate, 94; respiration, 16; temperature, 98; height, 5 feet 10 inches; weight, 117 pounds; age, 54 years.

Tongue, slightly coated gray; protrudes, deflected slightly to right; conjunctiva, icteric; poorly nourished; in health was plethoric, and weighed 195 pounds.

Pulse, 94; standing, 110; fair volume and regular; chest measures, 37, 37½, 38½; bilateral measurements at third rib, right side 18½ inches, left side 19 inches; at ensiform, right 18 inches, left 19 inches; percussion note is clear over lungs, except lower portion of right; apex beat of heart apparent on palpation at fifth interspace; dullness sixth rib to nipple line; heart sounds normal.

Gunshot wound of right lung; ball entered center of sternum 1 inch above ensiform cartilage; from the condition of the scar and lung it appears the ball ranged to the left; no mark of exit; no injury to spine has ever been apparent; scar, size of a silver quarter, depressed, adherent, and tender; disability resulting from gunshot wound of right lung rated at seven-eighteenths.

Gunshot wound of right thigh, upper middle third, penetrating; entered anteriorly in center of thigh; exit almost directly in line posteriorly; ball passed inner side of femur; a depression shows considerable destruction of bone in line of wound.

Gunshot wound, penetrating outer aspect, upper middle third of right thigh; exit inner aspect; opposite entrance, passed posterior to femur.

Gunshot wound outer aspect, lower third of right thigh; this scar is size of a silver half dollar, irregular, adherent, dragging, and tender; femur injured at this point, and several pieces of bone have been removed; the leg is smaller than left; muscles shrunken, soft, and flabby; right thigh at junction of middle and upper thirds measures 17 inches; left, 18½ inches; middle and lower thirds of right, 15 inches; left, 17 inches; above patella, right, 14½ inches; left, 15 inches; calf, right, 12½ inches; left, 13½ inches; disability resulting from gunshot wounds of right thigh, ten-eighteenths.

Gunshot wound of left thigh; upper middle third, inner aspect, not penetrating; scar irregular, size of a silver half dollar, not adherent or tender; no disability.

Hemiplegia of right side; complete loss of motion in arm and leg, with little sensation; hand and foot œdematous and cold; fingers contracted slightly in palm; aphasia; requires aid to dress and undress and to answer calls of nature; when helped up can by the aid of crutch on left side swing the right leg so as to move around a room, and is improving; the lesion is central; no pathological relation between the gunshot wounds and the paralysis. No rale. No other disability. Disabilities not the result of vicious habits.

The description of the character and locations of the gunshot wounds for which the soldier is pensioned is practically the same in the certificate of the medical examination held September 8, 1897, as in the foregoing certificate, except in regard to the wound of chest, as the board which made the latter examination was of the opinion that the ball lodged somewhere in the posterior wall of the chest and injured one or more of the spinal vertebræ and the spinal cord.

It is also stated in the certificate dated September 8, 1897, that—

The board is of the opinion that gunshot wound of right lung has contributed to the paralysis of claimant by embolia in the brain at time of injury, forming lesions in the vessels of the brain by adhering to their inner walls.

The certificate of examination dated May 6, 1896, states that the—

Percussion note is clear over both lungs, except lower portion of right; apex beat of heart apparent on palpitation at fifth interspace; dullness sixth rib to nipple line; heart sounds normal.

Relative to the condition of the thoracic viscera at the examination of September 8, 1897, the following statements are made in the certificate of that date:

Lungs normal, with the exception of dullness by percussion and osculation (auscultation) of lower part of middle lobe of right lung, well defined on the posterior wall.

Heart: Plain of dullness, 5 by 5½ inches; apex murmur most distinct 1½ inches below and to left of left nipple; impulse very weak; arhythmic and intermittent; cyanosis, dyspnœa, vertigo, and œdema of both upper and lower eyelids.

An addendum to the said certificate has the following statement:

The president of the board has personal knowledge of the claimant suffering in years past frequent attacks of severe pain in left side and posterior part of his head. and vertigo, he having been his family physician a number of years.

By a comparison of the statements embraced in the said certificates, as quoted above, it will be observed that they differ very materially as to the existence of any organic disease of the heart, which disease, if it did exist prior to the occurrence of the stroke of apoplexy in December, 1895, may prove to be a very important factor in determining the cause of the said apoplexy and the hemiplegia resulting therefrom.

The statements as to the condition of the right lung are also somewhat at variance. In the certificate dated May 6, 1896, it is stated that the "percussion note is clear over both lungs, except lower portion of right," while it is stated in the certificate dated September 8, 1897, that the dullness is over the middle lobe, well defined on the posterior wall.

The boards also disagree as to whether or not the right hemiplegia. from which the soldier is now shown to be suffering, is a pathological sequence of the disabilities for which he is pensioned.

The claimant alleges that the said paralysis resulted from the wounds for which he is pensioned, and he is supported in this allegation by the evidence of several physicians who claim to have more or less personal and professional knowledge of the existence of the said wounds, and are of the opinion that the paralysis resulted therefrom, although no two of them appear to have the same theory as to the pathological relation between the wounds and the paralysis.

It is noted that the certificate dated May 6, 1896, has the following statement in regard to the claimant's general appearance: "Poorly nourished; in health was plethoric and weighed 195 pounds."

The said plethoric condition might have been indicative of what has been termed the apopleptic habitus, and have thus accounted in a measure for the stroke of apoplexy which occurred.

It is also observed that although both certificates describe the locations and condition of the various cicatrices of the several wounds received by the soldier, and name the structures injured or pierced by the missiles inflicting the said wounds, neither of them shows to what extent the said structures were injured, nor the degree of disability resulting therefrom.

In view of this fact, and in order that no possible injustice may be done this claimant, the claim for increase should, in my judgment, be reopened and sent to the field for a thorough special examination under special instructions, to be prepared in accordance with the views hereinafter set forth.

I deem this course advisable by reason of the fact that the questions at issue can be more readily and satisfactorily determined upon evidence adduced upon special examination, when the affiants shall have been properly cross-questioned, than upon that secured by correspondence.

The certificate of examination dated July 9, 1890, shows the existence at that time of flatness and dullness over the entire lower portion of the right lung, with absence of all respiratory murmur in that region, and entire restriction of expansion in the right lung; but it is not shown whether or not the conditions described were, in the opinion of the board, caused by the wound of chest. Dullness over the middle and lower lobes, respectively, of the right lung is also shown in the two more recent certificates, heretofore referred to, but in neither of them is it stated to what cause the boards ascribed the said conditions.

The special examiner should be instructed to take the deposition of each member of the Lebanon, Ind., board of surgeons, both in 1896 and in 1897, and to request them to state in detail the amount of damage done by each wound received by the soldier, and to what extent it contributes toward the present degree of disability.

Inasmuch as the present board of surgeons at Lebanon, and by which the claimant was last examined, expressed the opinion that the missile which made the wound of chest "injured one or more of the spinal vertebræ thereby injuring the spinal cord," the members of said board should be cross-questioned as to the symptoms upon which they based a diagnosis of injury to the cord. If the cord was injured at the time the wound was received, why was the paralysis not immediately manifested, and would not the said paralysis have been paraplegia instead of hemiplegia?

Each member of the said board should also be closely cross-questioned in regard to the following statement found in their certificate of examination:

The board is of the opinion that gunshot wound of right lung has contributed to the paralysis of claimant by embolia in the brain at time of injury, forming lesions in the vessels of the brain by adhering to their inner walls.

If "embolia," or, more properly speaking, embolism, was produced in the brain at the "time of injury," why did not paralysis immediately follow instead of occurring over thirty years thereafter?

How could an embolus carried along in the blood current adhere to the inner coat of the vessel instead of pursuing its course until it reached an arteriole whose diameter was too small to admit of its further passage where it would cause an infarction?

But more important still is the question, How would it be possible for an embolus of sufficient size to cause cerebral embolism to pass through the capillaries of the lungs, as it would have to do before it reached the left heart from whence it would be carried to the brain?

Dr. A. P. Fitch should be asked to explain how it is possible for shock, which is generally a temporary condition, and either terminates in healthy reaction or passes into fatal sinking, to cause any special pathological lesion, either in the brain or elsewhere; and upon what grounds he bases the opinion expressed in his affidavit?

The other physicians who have testified in this case, with the exception of Drs. Skillman and Young, of Lexington, Ky., as they have not attempted to show any relation between the wounds and the stroke of apoplexy, should be cross-questioned as to the opinions expressed in their affidavits, and which are set forth herein, relative to the paralysis resulting from the wounds.

The physicians who had professional knowledge of the claimant prior to the date on which the stroke of apoplexy occurred should be questioned as to whether or not he had valvular disease of heart at that time, and if so, to what cause, in their opinion, the said disease was due.

The primary object of this examination is, however, to obtain a careful differential diagnosis as to the degree of disability due to pensioned causes alone, or any probable pathological sequelæ thereof, toward which the special examiner should bend his best endeavors. But inasmuch as no additional expense will be involved, and in order that the claimant may be afforded every reasonable opportunity to establish his claim that the right hemiplegia from which he is now suffering is a result of his army service, the examination should be conducted with that object in view also, for which purpose the papers in the case are herewith remanded.

As this action involves consideration in the light of additional evidence, it is regarded as a reversal of the action taken and a final disposition of the pending appeal.

If, in the light of the new evidence, your final action is still adverse the claimant has the right of further appeal.

Inasmuch as this claim has been made special you are requested to direct that prompt action be taken in the premises.

ATTORNEYSHIP—POWER OF ATTORNEY—PRACTICE.
ANNA L. McBRIDE (CLAIMANT).
H. D. PHILLIPS (ATTORNEY).

As the appellant never filed any instrument which conferred upon him any rights in the case, action denying him a fee was proper.

Assistant Secretary Webster Davis to the Commissioner of Pensions, May 24, 1898.

H. D. Phillips, of Washington, D. C., March 31, 1898, appealed in the matter of fee on the issue of May 29, 1897, in the claim for a widow's pension under the act of June 27, 1890, of Ahna L., widow of Robert D. McBride, late of Company C, Fifteenth Ohio Volunteer Infantry.

B. M. Veatch, of Coldwater, Kans., April 6, 1893, filed the claimant's original declarations under said act, and also under the general law, which contained powers of attorney in his favor. As said declarations were executed before Mr. Veatch as notary public, it was held that the powers of attorney contained therein did not confer any valid authority upon him to prosecute the claims. (Lydia A. Miner, 8 P. D., 104.)

The appellant, September 28, 1894, filed in the claim under the act of June 27, 1890, a power of attorney; the claimant's signature thereto was not attested by two witnesses. The appellant was notified October 27, 1894, that said power was not valid under rule 4 of the Rules of Practice. On April 13, 1895, he filed another power of attorney which, however, did not specify the claim to which it was to apply.

The signature of the claimant to the power of attorney filed September 28, 1894, was attested by one witness only; this witness was the notary before whom the power of attorney was executed.

Rule 4 of the Rules of Practice before the Commissioner of Pensions provides that—

No power of attorney purporting to be executed by a claimant will be recognized as good and valid authority unless the same be signed in the presence of two witnesses. * * *

In the case of Obed A. Patterson (8 P. D., 452), the Department held that—

A power of attorney to which the signature of the claimant is not attested by two witnesses confers no authority upon an agent or attorney to appear in a pension claim, and without such authority a person can have no title to a fee.

Under the authorities cited, the power of attorney filed by appellant September 28, 1894, conferred upon him no authority to prosecute the claim in which it was filed, as the claimant's signature to the same was not attested by two witnesses.

The power of attorney filed by appellant April 13, 1895, in which was not set forth the claim it was to apply, was properly held to relate to the claim filed under the general law. Prior to the decision in the case of R. H. Clark (8 P. D., 202), dated May 16, 1896, a power of attorney which does not specify the claim to which it was intended to apply only conferred authority upon an attorney to prosecute the claim of the grantor of the power filed in his behalf under the general law. This rule was modified in the case cited, but the new rule was not intended to be retroactive. (See case of Oscar Love, certificate 890,141, 26 Fee P. L. Bk., 419, decided April 22, 1896.)

It does not appear that the appellant ever filed any instrument which, under the rules of practice, conferred upon him any authority to prosecute the claim under the act of June 27, 1890, and upon that ground was denied a fee.

Action affirmed.

ATTORNEYS—PRACTICE—EVIDENCE.

Thomas J. Edwards (claimant).

C. E. Foote (attorney).

Where two or more claims for pension are pending in behalf of the same person, instruments of evidence filed by an attorney will not inure to his benefit as material service rendered in more than one claim unless he indorses upon said instruments, or sets forth in their contents, the several claims to which they are intended to apply.

Assistant Secretary Webster Davis to the Commissioner of Pensions, May 24, 1898.

C. E. Foote, of Kalamazoo, Mich., October 26, 1897, appealed in the matter of fee on the issue of September 14, 1897, in the claim (Certificate No. 941459), under the general law, of Thomas J. Edwards, late of Company C, First Michigan Volunteer Infantry.

L. O. Wood, of Washington, D. C., August 13, 1890, filed the original declaration under the general law alleging gunshot wound of thumb of left hand as a cause of disability of service origin, and on March 25, 1891, filed evidence which prima facie established the case. February 2, 1893, the claim was rejected upon the ground of no pensionable disability since date of filing.

The appellant, September 20, 1895, filed a power of attorney and fee agreements. On the same date the appellant in behalf of the soldier filed a claim for pension under the act of June 27, 1890; he filed in said claim October 5, 1895, three medical affidavits showing claimant's physical condition at that time.

The claim under the general law was reopened, as appears by slip attached to the brief face, upon recent medical examinations showing a ratable disability under old law, and allowed.

The appellant contends that the medical evidence filed by him was material, and therefore he should be paid a fee.

It is true that the evidence filed by the appellant is the kind usually required for the purpose of securing a new medical examination in a claim under the general law which stands rejected upon the ground of no pensionable disability shown to be due to cause alleged. But there is nothing to indicate that it was considered at all, and as it was filed in the claim under the act of June 27, 1890, it can not be presumed that it was considered in the claim under the general law. An attorney is at liberty to file an affidavit in two or more claims pending in behalf of the same claimant, but it must be set forth in the contents of the affidavit to what claims it is to apply or the claims must be indorsed upon the affidavit; the intention will not be presumed from the fact that the evidence is germane to the issues presented in the several claims. I do not wish to be understood that evidence will be considered as applying only to the particular claim or claims mentioned in the evidence or indorsed thereon; but that the filing thereof will inure to the benefit of the attorney in the claim or claims in which he designates its application in the manner above indicated.

I am of the opinion that where two or more claims for pension are pending in behalf of the same claimant, instruments of evidence that are filed by an attorney will not inure to his benefit in more than one claim unless he indorses upon said instruments, or sets forth in their contents, the several claims to which they are intended to apply.

It is frequently contended upon appeal in claims for fees or for recognition that evidence filed in a claim under the general law should be deemed as material service rendered in a claim under the act of June 27, 1890, because said evidence is material to each claim and was considered in the adjudication of them, although there is nothing to show that said evidence was intended by him to apply to more than one claim. Also it is manifest in many instances that such a contention partakes more of the nature of a happy afterthought than of an intention. All doubt can be allayed by proper indorsements when the evidence filed is intended to apply to more than one claim. The indorsement mentioned is mere clerical work; and therefore a requirement that papers be properly indorsed entails no hardship whatever. Furthermore, where there is a contest concerning the fee, as in this case, the question will not turn upon an intent as to which there may reasonably be grave doubt. So far as I am informed and have observed, the rule herein stated has been followed in the practice and I am unable to assign any good ground for an exception to it in this case.

The medical affidavits mentioned were filed by the appellant in the claim under the act of June 27, 1890, and were limited by him by an indorsement thereon in their application to that claim. It can not, therefore, be held that the filing of said affidavits constitutes material service in the general law claim; and as appellant filed no evidence in the general law claim, nor otherwise rendered any material service therein, action denying him a fee was proper.

TITLE, ACT JANUARY 29, 1887—DISABILITY.

CHARLES W. JOHANNES.

In order to be allowed pension under the act of January 29, 1887, an officer or enlisted man is not required to show that he is subject to a disability equivalent to some cause recognized by the pension laws as sufficient reason to allow pension under those laws at the rate of $8 per month; said officer or enlisted man may be entitled to the benefits of said act if it appear that he is subject to such disability as would be recognized by those laws as sufficient reason for the allowance of pension for any rate less than $8 per month.

Assistant Secretary Webster Davis to the Commissioner of Pensions, May 27, 1898.

The appellant, Charles W. Johannes, served as landsman on United States ship *Congress* from August 30, 1845, to February 5, 1849.

April 28, 1887, he applied for pension under the act of January 29, 1887, granting pensions to the survivors of the Mexican war. The claim was allowed March 28, 1889, at $8 per month, to commence November 12, 1888, the date on which the claimant completed the sixty-second year of his age. In his declaration he alleged that he was subject to some disability equivalent to some cause prescribed or recognized by the pension laws of the United States as a sufficient reason for the allowance of a pension, to wit—that he now suffers from chronic rheumatism in a heart affection.

July 13, 1891, the soldier applied for reissue of pension. In his application he alleged that the evidence on file showed at the time of the approval of the act of January 29, 1887, he was subject to a disability equivalent to some cause recognized by the pension laws as a sufficient reason for the allowance of pension, and requested that certificate issue to allow him pension from January 29, 1887, to November 12, 1888, the date pension was allowed to commence on the original issue in his case. This claim was rejected March 26, 1897, upon the ground that a recognizable disability at date of act was not established. From this action an appeal was entered August 19, 1897.

The appellant also served on the United States ship *Harriet Lane*, as seaman, from August 27, 1861, to September 28, 1864. On January 27, 1882, he filed a claim for pension under the general law on account of chronic rheumatism. Medical examinations were held August 2, 1882, and September 12, 1883, and the claim was rejected November 13 following, upon the ground of no pensionable disability.

Also, on September 5, 1893, the appellant filed a claim for increase under the act of January 5, 1893. A medical examination was held July 25, 1894, and the claim was allowed August 29, 1894, at $12 per month, to commence August 27, 1894, the date the claim was legally approved.

The foregoing sufficiently explains the contents of the slip signed by the reviewer who adjudicated the claim for reissue. Said slip reads as follows:

Although so greatly disabled by heart in '94; although he applied for rheumatism, as Gibson, in '82; although Drs. Linthicum, Hollyday, and Chew find some of the above in *May*, '83; yet in view of the 2d medical examination several months later, or in *September*, '83, agreeing with the one of '82, I do not think it is established that, so early as the date of the act, he was disabled to the degree required by the act of January 29, '87. (The chief of the board of review holds that the degree meant in that act is one that would be rated at $8.)

He has alleged 4 years' service, which we have not got—from 1857 to 1861—on the *Plymouth, John Adams* and *Niagara*. In calling for it both his names should be stated.

   (Signed)   C. H. *Ber.*
March 26, '97.

Section 1 of the act approved January 29, 1887, provides—

That the Secretary of the Interior be, and he is hereby, authorized and directed to place on the pension roll the names of the surviving officers and enlisted men, including marines, militia, and volunteers, of the military and naval services of the United States, who being duly enlisted, actually served sixty days with the Army or Navy of the United States in Mexico, or on the coasts or frontier thereof, or en route thereto, in the war with that nation, or were actually engaged in a battle in said war, and were honorably discharged, and to such other officers and soldiers and sailors as may have been personally named in any resolution of Congress for any specific service in said war, and the surviving widows of such officers and enlisted men: *Provided*, That such widows have not remarried: *Provided*, That every such officer, enlisted man, or widow who is or may become sixty-two years of age, or who is or may become subject to any disability or dependency equivalent to some cause prescribed or recognized by the pension laws of the United States as a sufficient reason for the allowance of a pension, shall be entitled to the benefits of this act; but it shall not be held to include any person not within the rule of age or disability or dependence herein defined, or who incurred such disability while in any manner voluntarily engaged in aiding or abetting the late rebellion against the authority of the United States.

The opinion expressed in the foregoing slip that a soldier must be suffering from a cause of disability that would entitle him to a rating of $8 per month under some other law in order to be allowed pension under the act of January 29, 1887, before he has attained the sixty-second year of his age, is based apparently upon the portion of said act hereinafter discussed, and is accepted as its true meaning, for the reasons that one of the classes of persons therein enumerated—viz, widows of soldiers—would, if entitled to pension under some other act, as dependent relatives of a soldier, receive no less than $8 per month; and that such degree of dependency as would give a dependent relative title to pension under some other act must be shown in a widow's claim before she would be entitled to pension under the act of January 29, 1887, prior to completing the sixty-second year of her age.

Therefore, the conclusion is accepted that, as the rate of $8 per month is provided by the act of January 29, 1887, on account of the dependent condition of a widow before she is 62 years of age, the disability which a soldier must have, when entitled to pension under said act before arriving at 62 years of age, is such disability as would warrant a rating of at least $8 per month under some other pension law.

The particular portion of the act to be discussed reads thus:

Provided, That every such officer, enlisted man, or widow who is or may become 62 years of age, or who is or may become subject to any disability or dependency equivalent to some cause prescribed or recognized by the pension laws of the United States as a sufficient reason for the allowance of a pension, shall be entitled, etc.

Officers, enlisted men, and widows are entitled to pension under said act upon becoming 62 years of age; then follow the conditions upon which they are entitled when under that age. These conditions are disability or dependency. I know of no instance where the law provides for the allowance of pension to a soldier for the reason that he is dependent upon another for support. Nor has my attention been called to any law providing for the allowance of pension to widows or dependent relatives on account of any cause of disability from which they may suffer. It is scarcely necessary to mention the numerous laws providing pension for soldiers on account of wounds, injuries, or

disease they have received or contracted. In view of these underlying principles of pension legislation, and the specific provision of the
act approved January 29, 1887, that disability or dependency, when
required to be shown in a claim thereunder shall be equivalent to some
cause prescribed or recognized by the pension laws of the United States
as a sufficient reason for the allowance of pension, and in the light
afforded by investigation as to the degree of disability thus recognized
by those laws for granting pensions to soldiers, it is my opinion that in a
soldier's claim for pension under the act of January 29, 1887, when he
has not become 62 years of age, such degree of disability must be shown
to give him title to pension thereunder as is recognized under any law
as pensionable. Under the general law, the rate of $2 per month is paid
to a soldier on account of a slight degree of disability, and when such
degree of disability is shown in a soldier's claim under the act of January 29, 1887, he may be entitled to pension under that act although he
is under the age of 62.

This conclusion is reached regardless of any view that may be entertained as to the conditions required to be shown by the act of January
29, 1887, for the allowance of pension to widows before they become 62
years of age, as the language of the act when taken in connection with
the provisions of other laws to which reference is specially made affords
ample means for ascertaining the rights of all soldiers without any
attempt to determine the rights of such widow claimants.

I am, therefore, of the opinion that any officer or enlisted man
mentioned in the act approved January 29, 1887, under the age of 62
years may be entitled to its benefits, when disabled by any cause of
disability, upon making application for pension thereunder, that would
entitle him to a rating therefor under any other law providing for the
allowance of pension. As this fact was not determined in appellant's
case the action of the Bureau is reversed with request that the claim be
readjudicated in accordance with the views herein expressed.

REDUCTION—RATE—ACT JUNE 27, 1890.

THOMAS MALLON.

Soldier was pensioned at $12 per month in August, 1890, which rating was reduced
to $6 per month in March, 1895. The contention is that his original rating was
fixed in harmony with regulations which obtained at that time, and can not
legally be affected by regulations formulated subsequent thereto.
Held: It is the statute, not the regulations, which determines his rights.

*Assistant Secretary Webster Davis to the Commissioner of Pensions.
May 27, 1898.*

Thomas Mallon, formerly of Company I, Seventy-second New York
Volunteers, was borne upon the pension roll under the provisions of the
act of June 27, 1890, from August 27, 1890, until March 4, 1895, at the

rate of $12 per month, by reason of disability resulting from rheumatism and disease of the heart (Certificate No. 732,361). On the last-mentioned date, due notice having been previously given, his pension was reduced to $6 per month, which has been his rating since that time.

On June 21, 1895, claimant filed an application for restoration to the roll at the maximum rating, to take effect from date of reduction.

His claim was adjudicated on October 28, 1895, and rejected, on the ground that the reduced rating was commensurate with existing disability, the same being treated as a claim for straight increase. Upon appeal being taken from this action, the Department, on February 8, 1896 (8 P. D., 208), reversed the same, upon the sole ground that it is error to adjudicate a claim for restoration as a claim for increase. In accordance with said departmental decision the claim was readjudicated on March 23, 1896, and rejected on the ground that his present rating is commensurate with the disability which existed at and from the date of claimant's reduction. From said action appeal was taken on September 17, 1897, in which the contention is embodied in the following assignment of error:

We claim first, that the action reducing the soldier's pension was illegal and unjust, for the reason that at the time his pension was granted him at $12 per month his rate was legally fixed under rulings then in force. We believe that whatever rulings may have been made subsequent to the rulings under which his rate of pension was granted could not legally be made retroactive, but could only apply to claims adjudicated in future. We claim second, that the action of the Pension Office in rejecting his claim for restoration upon proper application was error for the same reason as above cited.

It will be observed that the assignment of error set forth in the appeal does not involve the contention that appellant was unable to earn a support by manual labor at the date of reduction of his pension, but rests upon the legal proposition that his original rating, fixed in harmony with regulations which obtained at that time, can not be legally affected by regulations formulated subsequent thereto. The contention substantially involves the proposition that claimant has a vested right not only to a pension, but to the degree of rating originally estimated, provided the same was done in harmony with regulations then existing. This contention is manifestly untenable. It is the statute, not the regulations of the Pension Bureau, which determines the rights of a claimant for pension. If regulations are made in harmony with statutory provisions they are valid; if formulated in contravention of the express provisions of the statute, then the regulation, not the statute, must fall. The second section of the act of June 27, 1890, relative to the continuance of a pension, provides that—

Such pension shall commence from the date of the filing of the application in the Pension Office, after the passage of this act and upon proof that the disability then existed, and shall continue during the existence of the same.

Since the pension terminates when the disability ceases, it necessarily follows that when total disability ceases the maximum rating corresponding thereto should terminate regardless of any regulation formulated in contravention thereof.

The act of December 21, 1893, which, by its own provisions applies to pensions which had been granted prior to that time as well as to those thereafter granted, sets forth the conditions and limitations under which the Bureau of Pensions may reduce or modify any existing pension. The statute declares that pensions shall be deemed and held—

to be a vested right in the grantee to that extent that payment thereof shall not be withheld or suspended until, after due notice to the grantee of not less than thirty days, the Commissioner of Pensions, after hearing all the evidence, shall decide to annul, vacate, modify, and set aside the decision upon which such pension was granted.

In the case at bar the pension has been modified after due compliance with all the requirements of that statute.

This disposes of the contention set forth in the appeal, and no error being shown in the action of which complaint is made, the same is hereby affirmed.

SERVICE—CIVILIAN EMPLOYEES—ACT JUNE 27, 1890—PILOT.

ANNA M. WHALEN (WIDOW).

The widow of a pilot is not pensionable under the act of June 27, 1890; as he was not an officer or an enlisted man in the Army or Navy of the United States. (Susannah, widow of Francis Mackey, 8 P. D., 535.)

Assistant Secretary Webster Davis to the Commissioner of Pensions, May 27, 1898.

In 1894 this appellant, Anna M. Whalen, was allowed pension under the act of June 27, 1890, Certificate No. 9591, as the widow of Adolph C. Whalen, who was a pilot serving on several vessels of the Navy during the late war. On February 14, 1896, her name was dropped from the rolls on the ground that said pilot's service was not pensionable under said act, as he was not an enlisted man or officer in the Army or Navy, but a contract pilot.

She appealed August 13, 1897, contending said ground of dropping is erroneous in law and fact.

The Fourth Auditor of the Treasury Department reports herein that said Adolph C. Whalen, pilot,

was appointed on the *Pensacola* November 1, 1863, and served thereon to February 29, 1864; on the *Stockdale* to July 26, 1864; on the *Corypheus* to November 26, 1864; on the *Potomac* to December 21, 1864; on the *Rose* to August 22, 1865; on the *J. C. Kuhn* to September 30, 1865; on the *Rose* to January 8, 1866, and on the *Cowslip* to July 31, 1866, when discharged.

A report from the Navy Department also shows his service as "1st Class Pilot, U. S. N.," on U. S. S. *Rose* from November 1, 1865, to January 1, 1866, and on the *Cowslip* from March 1, 1866, to June 1, 1866, when he went on leave.

On March 16, 1898, I addressed a communication to the Secretary of the Navy requesting a report as to the status in the Navy of pilots serving as above.

The reply of the Secretary of the Navy, dated May 7, 1898, is as follows:

Your letter of March 16, 1898, requesting to be informed whether a pilot serving in the United States Navy during the war of the rebellion is considered by this Department to have been an enlisted man, or what official status, if any, such pilot occupied therein, for use in pension claim certificate No. 9591, has been received.

In reply I have the honor to inform you that an opinion has been rendered by the Judge-Advocate-General of the Navy holding, that as pilots were not enlisted men or appointed as officers by the Department, that its records do not show their entry into the service or their conduct while serving as such, and as such appointments were made by the commanding officers of the squadrons, subject to the approval of the Department, and held during the pleasure of the appointing officer, pilots can not be regarded as officers or enlisted men in the Navy, and therefore must be regarded as civilians employed under the authority of the Navy Department.

The reports containing the record of service in this case, inclosed in your letter, are herewith returned.

It is manifest, therefore, that dropping of pension in this case was proper, pilots not being in either of the two classes, officers and enlisted men, which only are pensionable under the act of June 27, 1890. Rejection of this claim was in accordance with the decision in Susannah, widow of Francis Mackey, 8 P. D., 535, and is affirmed.

SERVICE—CIVILIAN EMPLOYEES—ACT JANUARY 29, 1887.

HENRY BARLOW.

The record of claimant's grant of bounty-land warrant shows he was a civil employee merely, and not an enlisted man. Claim for pension was, therefore, properly rejected.

Assistant Secretary Webster Davis to the Commissioner of Pensions, May 27, 1898.

On March 29, 1897, this appellant, Henry Barlow, filed a claim, No. 24,927, for pension under the act of January 29, 1887, alleging service en route to Mexico, during the Mexican war, as a member of Captain Smith's company, in which he says he enlisted at Cincinnati, Ohio, on August 17, 1847, for the war, and was honorably discharged therefrom in November, 1847, at San Antonio, Tex.; said service being on detail as guard of train and stock.

The claim was rejected April 14, 1897, on the ground that claimant was not an enlisted man, but a civilian employee of the quartermaster, rejection being based upon the papers on file in the claimant's bounty-land claim, under which he was granted a warrant for 160 acres of land. He appealed September 14, 1897, alleging, merely, that his service was as an enlisted man.

On April 27, 1898, I returned the case to your Bureau for transmittal of the papers in said bounty-land claim; there appearing to be, in this claim, no other evidence of service that what may be contained in said bounty-land claim.

The papers, including those in said bounty-land claim, are now retransmitted with a slip by the chief of the old War and Navy division of your Bureau, calling attention to the enrollment paper as to muster and to the report of the Quartermaster-General on back of the declaration in that claim, also stating the allowance of the bounty-land warrant was under the fourth paragraph of section 2426, Revised Statutes, which provides specifically for wagon masters and teamsters.

The enrollment paper here referred to is a certificate signed by S. H. Drum, assistant quartermaster, dated Cincinnati, Ohio, August 17, 1846, to the effect that—

The bearer, Henry Barlow, has been engaged by me as a teamster for the service of the United States in Texas and Mexico for the period of six months from this date, unless sooner discharged by proper authority.

This certificate is attached to the declaration dated March 22, 1855, in which bounty land is claimed, under the act of March 3, 1855, on account of service as a teamster. This declaration bears the endorsement:

H. Barlow served in the Quartermaster's Department as herdsman under Lieut. W. I. Newton and as a teamster under Capt. S. H. Drum at San Antonio, Tex., from August 17, 1846, to October 8, 1846.
(Signed)   O. P. Thomas, *D. Q. M. G.*
January 15, 1856, Q. M. G. O.

It is manifest, therefore, from this evidence that appellant was an employee merely of the Quartermaster's Department, and not an enlisted soldier in the army of the United States, and that he was allowed bounty-land warrant under the special provision of section 1 of the act of March 3, 1855 (now the fourth paragraph of section 2426 of the Revised Statutes of the United States), that—

The benefits of this section shall be held to extend to wagon masters and teamsters who may have been employed under direction of competent authority in time of war in the transportation of military stores and supplies.

The act of January 29, 1887, under which this claim is filed, provides:

That whenever any person has been granted a land warrant under any act of Congress, for and on account of service in the said war with Mexico, such grant shall be prima facie evidence of his service and honorable discharge, but such evidence shall not be conclusive and may be rebutted by evidence that such land warrant was improperly granted.

While the grant of bounty-land warrant in this case is not shown to have been improper, the record shows it was made under a special provision of the bounty-land act as to a class of unenlisted employees which is not provided for in the pension act of January 29, 1887; and, therefore, such grant may not be accepted as prima facie evidence of pensionable service and discharge under the latter act. The whole record of the grant of a bounty-land warrant must be considered; and when such record shows the grant was based upon other service than is made the basis of pensionable title under the act of January 29, 1887, no presumption as to such title can arise from the fact such warrant had been granted.

Said act of January 29, 1887, provides pension for the "surviving officers and enlisted men * * * who, being duly enlisted," etc. As this appellant was not of either of these classes he may not be pensioned under this act. Rejection of his claim is, therefore, affirmed.

AID AND ATTENDANCE—RATE.

JOHN JOHNSON.

The soldier is now pensioned at $45 per month for loss of right arm at the shoulder joint.

It is both claimed and shown that the wound which caused the loss of the right arm also caused destruction of the tissues about the shoulder joint to such an extent that it is necessary for the claimant to wear a pad or some other means of protection, in the adjustment of which the services of another person are required.

Held, That inasmuch as the services of another person are required at least twice daily, in the adjustment of the pad which the pensioner is compelled to wear over his right shoulder for its protection, the said services are considered as such "frequent and periodical personal aid and attendance of another person" as is contemplated by the act of July 14, 1892, and warrants allowance of the rate prescribed by the said act.

Assistant Secretary Webster Davis to the Commissioner of Pensions, May 31, 1898.

The appellant in this case, John Johnson, Company D, Second Wisconsin Infantry, is now pensioned at $45 per month for loss of right arm at shoulder joint.

He was originally pensioned at $8 per month from April 10, 1863, which rate was subsequently increased to $15 from June 6, 1866, to $18 from July 25, 1872, to $24 from June 4, 1874, to $30 from March 5, 1883, to $37.50 from March 3, 1879 (under special act of Congress, approved February 14, 1885), and to $45, the present rate, from August 21, 1886.

A claim for increase and rerating, filed July 19, 1889, was rejected July 29, 1890.

A similar claim filed May 13, 1897, was rejected March 11, 1898.

It is from the latter action that the pending appeal was entered March 25, 1898, the contentions therein being that the said action was error, both as to the claim for increase as well as to that for rerating, and—

That there are other conditions in this particular case that were produced by the wound that carried away both the arm and the shoulder joint that should be considered in reaching a conclusion as to whether or not the claimant is entitled to greater consideration, in the matter of rating, than has been given him.

It is also contended, in the said appeal, that it is a question of fact to be determined from all the evidence in the case, including the report of the board of examining surgeons, as to whether the applicant's case falls within or without the acts of Congress approved March 4, 1890, and July 14, 1892, respectively.

The said contentions were duly considered by the Department, and it was thought that, perhaps, your Bureau might, upon a thorough reconsideration of all the facts in the case, recede from the action appealed from; so the papers in the case were, on April 11, 1898, remanded for a personal opinion of the medical referee as to whether or not the said action was proper and should be adhered to; and, at the same time, it was suggested that the last certificate of medical examination be returned for further report as to the conditions manifested at the said examination.

The objective conditions described in the said certificate were as follows:

Pulse rate, 76-84-92; respiration, 20; temperature, normal; height, 5 feet, 5 inches; weight, 204 pounds; age, 56 years.

Right arm taken off by a piece of shell at shoulder joint; comparative measurements show acromion process and coracoid process also partially gone, acromion about line of neck, coracoid about point of attachments of biceps; bilateral measurements show atrophy of about 2 inches; measurements shown on diagram.

There is a large irregular cicatrix over seat of amputation about its middle, tender and sensitive, he states; this scar is 5 by 2¼ inches. He wears a large pad as a protection; worn over under shirt.

The claimant can dress and undress, except so far as adjusting pad, which is held in position by safety pins and cords, which he can not adjust. Rate, $45.

Heart: The heart's action is regular; good quality; apex normal; no organic lesion.

Chronic pharyngitis; mucous membrane congested. Rate, two-eighteenths.

Urine, sp. gr. 1,018; no sugar, no albumen. Rate, nothing.

We think he requires frequent aid and attendance, and entitled to such rate. $50. No other disability. No evidence of vicious habits.

The said certificate was returned to the board of surgeons, as suggested, for amendment.

The amendment was made April 25, 1898, and is embodied in the opinion of the medical referee, which was called for, as above stated, and which is as follows:

The soldier, John Johnson, Company D, Second Wisconsin Infantry, is now pensioned at $45 for loss of right arm at shoulder joint, the specific rate for such disability. He claims increase on the ground that the amputation in his case included the removal of bone other than that belonging to the arm, and that owing to the walls of the chest being unprotected at that point, and the sensitiveness of the stump, it is necessary for him to wear a pad or appliance to protect the parts from exposure and injury, and he requires the personal and regular aid of another person in applying this pad. Other needs of assistance, such as in preparing and cutting his food, tying his neck-tie, and such like services referred to in the testimony, are common to all persons who have lost an arm. The only point in controversy, therefore, appears to be the question whether the soldier requires a pad worn on his shoulder, and the regular and personal aid of another person to apply it.

In compliance with your suggestion as contained in your communication of April 11, 1898, the certificate of examination of November 15, 1897, was returned to the board for amendment, by compliance with all the instructions embodied in the order of November 12, 1897. The amended certificate is now with the papers in the case. The report shows entire loss of right arm, with a portion of acromion and coracoid processes; no portion of clavicle gone; right shoulder measures 2 inches less than left; cicatrix 5 by 2½ inches, and middle portion alleged to be tender and sensitive; wears a pad over the stump, which is held in position by safety pins and cords, which he can not adjust; claimant undressed and dressed in the presence of the board. In summing up the board say: "We think he requires the use of a pad, based upon the (subjective) tenderness over wounded area. He requires aid and attendance to properly adjust pad, *as worn by claimant*, but we believe a protective pad could be worn, said pad forming a portion of shoulder to coat on wounded side, thereby offering same protection and doing away with necessity of aid."

The degree of disability shown in this case is greater than that resulting from the "specific disability," loss of arm at shoulder joint, and the frequent and periodical aid made necessary in the adjustment of the pad is believed to come within the provisions of the act of Congress approved July 14, 1892, creating the intermediate rate of $50 per month, and this pensioner should be so rated from date of medical certificate made November 15, 1897. Further rerating is not warranted.

The pensioner also claimed rerating on the ground that the rates heretofore allowed have not been in accordance with the provisions of the various acts of Congress relative to "total disability;" and that he not only now requires, but has required ever since the date of his discharge, the regular aid and attendance of another person, by reason of the wound of his right shoulder.

In an affidavit filed December 18, 1897, he states as follows:

That he is now a pensioner at $45 per month, the specific rate for loss of an arm at the shoulder joint; that to treat his case as a shoulder-joint amputation or its equivalent is to clearly misconstrue both the evidence and the law; that his case not only involves loss of the entire arm, but also a part of the shoulder and body on right side, thus exposing vital organs to such a degree as to require the wearing of a pad or some other means of protection, and that in the preparation and adjustment of the said pad or means of protection he is compelled to have the daily and frequent aid and personal attendance of another person.

The fact that the claimant is not only compelled to wear the said pad for the protection of his injured shoulder, but that he also requires and has the assistance of another person in the proper adjustment of the same, is testified to by several physicians of this city and by members of his immediate family.

It is observed that in the amendment to the certificate of examination, heretofore referred to, the board states:

We think he requires the use of a pad, based upon the (subjective) tenderness over wounded area. He requires aid and attendance to properly adjust pad, as worn by claimant, but we believe a protective pad could be worn, said pad forming a portion of shoulder to coat on wounded side, thereby offering same protection and doing away with necessity of aid.

The question raised by the board of surgeons as to the necessity for the aid and attendance of another person being avoided by the claimant having the protective pad which he is compelled to wear form a portion of the shoulder of his coat on the wounded side is a contingency which does not appear to have been considered by the act of July 14, 1892, to the benefits of which the claimant appears to be entitled by reason of the necessity for the said aid and attendance; nor is there any other law by which he could be compelled to use any other method for the protection of his shoulder than that which he himself elects.

The claimant, however, appears to be under the impression that he is entitled to the benefits of the various acts of Congress providing for the degree of disability requiring the "regular aid and attendance" of another person, under which impression he filed his claim for both increase and rerating.

In this contention the claimant is clearly in error, as at no time has it been shown that he ever required more than the frequent and periodical aid and attendance of another person by reason of the disability for which he is pensioned.

In his advisory opinion, above quoted, the medical referee states that—

The degree of disability shown in this case is greater than that resulting from the "specific disability," loss of an arm at shoulder joint, and the frequent and periodical aid made necessary in the adjustment of the pad is believed to come within the provisions of the act of Congress approved July 14, 1892, creating the intermediate rate of $50 per month, and this pensioner should be so rated from date of medical certificate made November 15, 1897.

Further rerating is not warranted.

I concur in the views set forth in the said opinion, both as to title to increase and to lack of title to rerating.

In a recent decision, rendered in the case of Ira W. Hayford (9 P. D. 307), I held that—

When it is established beyond any reasonable doubt that, on account of pensioned cause or causes, or any pathological sequelæ thereof, the pensioner is not only "totally incapacitated for performing manual labor," but can neither dress nor undress himself without the aid and attendance of another person, as is shown by the evidence and certificate of medical examination in this case, the Department will construe the said aid and attendance as such frequent and periodical personal aid and attendance of another person as is contemplated by the act of July 14, 1892, and as warranting the allowance of the rate prescribed in the said act.

The services of a second person shown to be necessary in each of these two cases, although not identical, are believed to be analogous, and as being sufficient to bring them both within the purview of the act of July 14, 1892.

The action appealed from is, therefore, reversed, and the papers in the case are herewith remanded for readjudication and allowance, in accordance with the views herein set forth and the concurrent opinion of the medical referee.

ELLIE MORRIS (WIDOW).

A child who is an incurable epileptic, having a falling fit once a week, on an average, and nervous attacks much oftener, who is vigorous in body but dull mentally, who is able to attend to his personal wants except when suffering from an epileptic seizure, and can perform some remunerative labor but not nearly sufficient to afford him a support, is "permanently helpless" in the contemplation of the law, and the pension on his account should be continued.

Assistant Secretary Webster Davis to the Commissioner of Pensions, May 31, 1898.

Ellie Morris, widow of Elwood Morris, late of Company A, Sixth Pennsylvania Cavalry, was, in April, 1893, granted a pension of $8 per month under section 3 of the act of June 27, 1890, with $2 per month additional for each of four children then under 16 years of age. The second child, Warren L. Morris, became 16 years of age on the 17th of March, 1896, and the additional pension allowed on his account then ceased. On March 25, 1897, the widow filed a claim for its further continuance under the proviso to section 3 of the act of June 27, 1890, which declares that—

* * * in case a minor child is insane, idiotic, or otherwise permanently helpless, the pension shall continue during the life of said child, or during the period of such disability, etc.

This claim was rejected by your Bureau in September, 1897, on the ground that the child referred to was not "insane, idiotic, or otherwise permanently helpless." From that action an appeal was taken on September 23, 1897.

The evidence shows that the child is afflicted with epileptic fits and has been for several years. A board of surgeons who examined him on May 19, 1897, reported:

We find claimant presents an ordinary healthy appearance. Muscular system well developed; but we find mental faculties are not in perfectly normal condition. He answers simple questions, but does not appear to concentrate his mind on any subject.

In a supplemental report made July 21, 1897, the board says:

The claimant presents a very favorable appearance. He is not helpless. He can dress and feed himself and attend to the calls of nature unassisted, and is able to do light work. He has attended school, but makes very little progress beyond spelling and reading. He can read the newspaper and is able to go about and away from home unattended. He is robust in appearance, with evidence of good health. During this examination he is perfectly quiet, with no evidence of nervousness.

With a view to ascertaining the frequency, duration, and severity of the epileptic attacks, and the extent to which they incapacitated the child for self-help and self-support, a special examination was had in September, 1897. The only person found who could state positively how frequently the seizures occurred was the boy's mother, who testified that he had a fit about once a week, lasting from ten minutes to half an hour, during which he would fall, foam at the mouth, and shake violently. After the paroxysm was over he would sleep for an hour or two and would be drowsy the rest of the day. Besides these falling fits she stated that he had frequent spells, when he would throw his head back and shake violently. These spells occurred three or four times a day and sometimes a dozen times a day.

The testimony of the mother and of the neighbors who were interviewed shows that he was able to attend to all of his personal needs, did not require an attendant, but went about alone, and was able to do some remunerative labor, such as digging in a garden, lawn-mowing, whitewashing, etc. The mother said that his earnings during the past two years would not amount to $10, and that she supported him.

E. P. Barber, a neighbor, in answer to a question as to his opinion of the boy's earning capacity, said: "I would not have him for his board. All he earns is a little pin money." Thomas Fries, another neighbor, testified that he employed him two or three weeks in the summer of 1896 at whitewashing and helping around the farm, and paid him 50 cents a day. During that time he had two epileptic fits. Witness did not consider him able to earn a living for himself.

With reference to the meaning of the words "permanently helpless" in the first proviso to section 3 of the act of June 27, 1890, Assistant Secretary Reynolds, in the case of John M. Laughlin (8 P. D., 52), said:

We may judge of the meaning of the term "permanently helpless" by its conjunction with the words "insane," "idiotic," with which it is relatively synonymous, as shown by the connecting adverb "otherwise," this identity of meaning having special reference to the ability of the beneficiary to earn a support. That is, in the sense that an insane or idiotic person would be incapable of earning a living, or attending to his personal comforts, so one suffering from permanent injuries or disease of body in a degree that would prevent him from performing any labor or from caring for himself would be helpless, and entitled to the benefits conferred by the said proviso.

In a case somewhat analogous to the one now under consideration, in which the evidence showed that the child (a girl) for whom continuance of pension was claimed was afflicted with incurable epilepsy, rendering her liable to frequent spasms and spells of unconsciousness, which had made her weak and of low vitality, so that she could perform only the lightest household duties and no remunerative labor, besides causing her to be the subject of constant watchfulness and some aid and attendance, it was held that she was permanently helpless in the contemplation of the law and that the pension on her account should be continued. (Frances Stetzell, 9 P. D., 9.)

In this case the child is vigorous in body, though dull in intellect, and he can perform some manual labor. It is evident, however, that what he earns is a very small fraction of what is necessary for his support. In fact, it may be safely said that so far as his ability for self-support is concerned it is not above that of an ordinarily healthy boy 12 years of age. He is still a burden upon his mother—still in need of her help—to as great a degree as when he was under the age of 16 years.

In addition to the effect of his disease in unfitting him for regular work, we have to take into consideration the fact that persons ordinarily do not like to employ an epileptic. As one of the witnesses says:

There are many people who would like to employ him out of sympathy, but are afraid of his having those fits.

There is, apparently, no probability that his condition will improve. All things considered, I am of the opinion that the case presented is one to which the provision for the continuance of pension may well be held to apply. The action of your Bureau is, therefore, reversed.

———

FEE AGREEMENTS—RESTORATION.

JOHN R. GOARD (CLAIMANT).

JOHN L. SPRINGSTON (ATTORNEY).

Where the Bureau, upon evidence procured by special examination, has approved action for dropping a pensioner's name from the roll upon the ground that his disability was not incurred in line of duty, and notice has been given him to show cause why his name should not be dropped, he may properly file a claim for restoration of pension, whether or not his name has been actually dropped from the pension roll. Such a claim is one in which the law directs that valid fee agreements be recognized if filed.

Assistant Secretary Webster Davis to the Commissioner of Pensions, May 31, 1898.

John L. Springston, of Fort Smith, Ark., April 16, 1898, entered a motion for reconsidering the decision of the Department of July 11, 1895, affirming the action of the Bureau denying him a fee for services rendered by him in the pension claim of John R. Goard.

From the time of his discharge, November 30, 1864, to December 3, 1872, the claimant was allowed pension under the general law on account of gunshot wound. Further payment of pension to the claimant and to all other pensioners on the Fort Gibson roll was suspended under order of the Secretary of the Interior "per office letter April 25, 1873." No grounds are assigned, nor does any further reason for suspension appear in this claim at the time said action was taken.

April 19, 1877, an application for restoration of pension was filed. The claim was specially examined in May, 1883. Action was approved for dropping claimant's name from the rolls. Further action in the case is indicated by letter of August 25, 1883, to the chief of agent's division, directing suspension of payment of pension "upon evidence showing that disability from gunshot wound was not incurred in line of duty." On the brief attention was called to the fact that claimant's

name was still on the rolls. This would impart, at least, that payment
of pension had been continued, though such was not the fact.

On December 5, 1883, notice was given the claimant that he would
be allowed thirty days to show cause why his name should not be
dropped from the rolls.

On January 4, 1884, action of dropping was adhered to—"evidence
filed does not change action as formerly indicated to drop."

Applications for restoration were also filed October 10, 1887, and
February 17, 1890. The claim was rejected November 14, 1893, upon
the ground that his wound was not received in line of duty.

In 1894 the appellant filed fee agreements and an appeal from the
foregoing action of rejection. On appeal the Department held, March
23, 1895, that claimant's wound was received in line of duty, reversed
the action of the Bureau, and directed that claim should be readjudicated in accordance with the facts in the case. Thereupon payment of
accrued pension since December 3, 1872, was made to the claimant.
No fee was certified to the appellant. From action denying him a fee
he entered an appeal June 20, 1895. The decision of the Department
relative to appellant's right to a fee was rendered July 11, 1895. The
following is the text thereof:

> It appears that the case was treated throughout as a claim for restoration. This
> was error, however, for upon investigation it was found that the pensioner's name
> had never been dropped from the rolls, the action simply relating to suspension and
> to continue the payment of pension. There was no dropping from the rolls, and
> therefore no restoration. For the payment of a fee for services rendered in prevent-
> ing the dropping of a pensioner's name from the rolls the law makes no provision.

The proceedings were not instituted with the view of preventing the
dropping claimant's name from the rolls. His name had been on the rolls
for many years, but had resulted in no benefit to him. Furthermore,
the Bureau had determined he had no title to pension. The proceedings had resulted not only in a removal of suspension of payment of
pension, but in establishing his claim for pension. So the decision of
the Department upon the right of the appellant to a fee was not responsive to the issue arising upon the facts, any further than to deny him a
fee upon wholly irrelevant grounds.

In this particular it may be proper to note that on October 14, 1897,
in a communication to the Commissioner of Pensions (9 P. D., 1897), I
held, in substance, that a fee may be allowed an attorney for services
rendered under a rule to show any cause why a claimant's name should
not be dropped from the rolls. Therefore the reason assigned for
denying the appellant a fee in this case is no longer tenable were the
proceedings instituted in behalf of the claimant such as are described
in the decision of the Department herein.

Many reasons may be advanced for calling the proceedings a claim
to secure the removal of the suspension of payment of pension, but all
of them would rest for support upon the fact that there was no reissue
to allow pension and no brief was made evidencing action to allow

pension anew. However, were the claim such proceeding the appellant would be entitled to a fee under the decision of the Department in the case, George D. Hilton (8 P. D., 182). It was there held that—

Services rendered by an attorney in securing the removal of suspension of payment of pension in a case comes within the provisions of section 4 of the act of July 4, 1884 (amended section 4786, Revised Statutes), authorizing the Commissioner of Pensions to recognize fee agreements in certain classes of claims, and in such other cases of difficulty and trouble as the Commissioner may see fit to allow.

But upon full review of the record in the case I am of the opinion that the claim was for restoration of pension. It appears that further payment of pension to the claimant was suspended under a general order of the Secretary of the Interior. No cause appears from the record for issuing the order, although properly made. It does appear, however, that payment of pension to all other persons on the Fort Gibson roll was suspended at the same time and for a reason common to all. Upon application for restoration of pension filed in 1877 (which upon adjudication was properly treated by the Bureau as an application for the removal of suspension of payment of pension, as claimant's right to pension had not at that time been finally adversely determined) it was adjudged August 21, 1883, upon evidence secured by a special examination, that his wound was not incurred in the line of duty, thus denying claimant's title to pension in the first instance. So long as that action stood the claimant was absolutely without any title to pension, whether his name was on the rolls or not. Following that action suspension of payment was directed and claimant was given notice December 5, 1883, to show cause why his name should not be dropped from the rolls. Upon evidence filed pursuant to this notice action for dropping was adhered to January 4, 1884. Nothing remained to do but the formal act of striking the claimant's name from the rolls. From that date the claimant had no more right to pension than he would have had if his original claim had never been admitted. It is true there was some deviation from the practice usually observed in dropping a pensioner's name from the rolls upon the ground that his disability was not incurred in the line of duty. This deviation consisted in holding the special examination in a claim for restoration—in reality a claim looking to the removal of suspension of payment of pension. But no error was committed, as the special examination was conducted for the purpose of determining whether claimant's wound was incurred in line of duty. The evidence thus secured would properly serve for the purpose of action of dropping his name from the rolls upon the ground indicated, and accordingly such action was directed.

It can not be presumed that payment of pension was suspended in 1872, for the same reason that action for dropping was approved in 1883. In the first instance the cause for suspension was common to all cases included in the order of the Secretary of the Interior; in the second the evidence adduced on special examination was deemed to show a special cause, viz, that claimant's wound was not received in the line of duty.

So, when in 1887 the claimant filed a declaration for restoration of pension, the conditions were entirely different from those that existed in 1877, when he filed an application which was treated as looking to the removal of suspension of payment of pension. In 1887 his pensionable status was denied; it had been determined that his disability was not incurred in the line of duty. There remained nothing further to do except to strike his name from the rolls. The omission of this perfunctory and formal act pursuant to action approved for dropping did not confer any benefit upon nor deprive him of any right he might have had his name actually been dropped from the rolls. As a matter of law his name was dropped from the rolls to all intents and for all purposes. Under the action of the Bureau the claimant stood without pensionable status and the retention of his name upon the pension roll was a mere nullity. Under these conditions the claimant was at liberty to file a claim for restoration or enter an appeal from the action of the Bureau dropping his name from the rolls; he chose the former course and prosecuted the claim to a successful issue.

Section 4786, Revised Statutes, as amended by section 4 of the act of July 4, 1884, provides that:

The agent or attorney of record in the prosecution of a case may cause to be filed with the Commissioner of Pensions duplicate articles of agreement without additional cost to the claimant setting forth the fee agreed upon between the parties. * * * And such articles of agreement as may hereafter be filed with the Commissioner of Pensions are not authorized nor will they be recognized except in * * * claims for restoration where a pensioner's name has been or may hereafter be dropped from the pension rolls on testimony taken by a special examiner showing that the disability * * * on account of which pension was allowed did not originate in the line of duty. * * *

The object of a claim for restoration mentioned in the foregoing enactment is not restoration of a person's name to the pension rolls; that is but an incident to the real object, when secured, which is the restoration to the claimant of his pension. So, in this case, as claimant's name, as a matter of law, "was dropped from the pension roll," and in fact as well as in law, "on testimony taken by a special examiner showing that the disability * * * on account of which pension was allowed did not originate in the line of duty," his claim for restoration was one coming within the purview of the statute, it follows that the fee agreements filed by him, if valid, should have been recognized, and, under the rules of practice and the law as construed by the Department, the total amount of fee stipulated in them should have been certified to the appellant. (See case, John Schoepf, 7 P. D., 19.)

It may be urged that action refusing to certify a fee as in a claim for restoration was proper, for the reason there was no reissue to allow pension, and, therefore, the record upon which the question of fee is determined does not show that appellant is entitled to a fee. It will be remembered that the claim was considered by the Bureau as for restoration and was so considered by the Department upon appeal; therefore such reissue was proper as is usually made in claims for restoration. Although upon appeal in the matter of fee it was held error to consider the proceedings as a claim for restoration, in this motion it is held that it was proper to so consider them. Therefore that which should have been done will be considered as done so far as the question of allowing fee is concerned.

It may also be urged that under the rule laid down in the case, George W. Amos (8 P. D., 271), action denying the appellant a fee can not now be reconsidered. In that case the Department declined to disturb a departmental decision made by a former administration when the decision was based upon all the facts appearing in the case which were necessary to be considered in determining the question at issue.

In this case it appears that a fee was denied the appellant not in view of the facts, but under a misapprehension of them, and no decision was reached upon the facts as they appear, but upon an assumption wholly unsupported by the facts.

For the foregoing reasons this motion for reconsideration is sustained. The appellant's claim for fee should be determined in accordance with facts as herein set forth and approved.

DEATH CAUSE.

NANNA J. SMITH (WIDOW).

The word "complicated," as used in the case of Napoleon B. Trask (9 P. D., 113), means involved, interwoven, or connected with, and to entitle a widow to a pension under section 4702, Revised Statutes, she is required to show that the disease, wound, or injury of soldier of service origin, in line of duty, had some probable connection with or relation to death cause, and was a contributing and presumptive predominating factor in producing death.

Assistant Secretary Webster Davis to the Commissioner of Pensions, May 31, 1898.

Nanna J., widow of John S. Smith, late private, Company F, Sixth Tennessee Infantry, by her attorney, on December 27, 1897, filed a motion for reconsideration of departmental decision of September 25, 1897, affirming the Bureau action of November 7, 1896, rejecting her widow's claim No. 613528, filed April 29, 1895, under section 4702, Revised Statutes, on the ground that death resulted from disease of heart, not due to chronic diarrhea.

It is contended on behalf of claimant that said departmental decision is in conflict with the rule announced in the case of Napoleon B. Trask (9 P. D., 113).

I am of the opinion that the evidence in this case fails to show that the cause for which pension was granted was " so complicated with the disease which caused death" as to bring this case within the ruling in the Trask case.

Soldier enlisted December 2, 1862, was discharged July 26, 1865, and died March 29, 1895, of heart failure and chronic disease of heart of long standing, as testified by the attending physician.

Soldier was pensioned at $2 per month for chronic diarrhea due to the service, but the attending physician testified that it was not his intention when testifying to leave the impression that soldier's death was due to chronic diarrhea or any form of bowel trouble.

The word "complicated" in the Trask case is used in the sense o-being involved, or interwoven, or connected with the disease which was the immediate cause of death, and to entitle a widow to a pension under section 4702, Revised Statutes, she is required to show that the disease for which soldier was pensioned, or which originated in the service and in line of duty, had some probable connection with and was a contributing and presumptive predominating factor in death cause. (See Alma Neidhammer 8 P. D., 276.)

In the case under consideration there is no reasonable doubt raised as to the cause of soldier's death, and for that reason the rule announced in the Trask case that "where doubts can not be resolved by evidence presumption should incline toward claimant" has no application in this case, for, as there was no "complication" of chronic diarrhea with disease of heart, death could not have resulted from a "complication" of said causes. I find no valid or satisfactory reason for reversing or in any manner modifying the former departmental decision in this case, and the motion is accordingly overruled.

SERVICE—CIVILIAN EMPLOYEES—PILOT.

WILLIAM B. TAYLOR.

A pilot is not an officer or enlisted man in the Army or Navy, and he is not entitled to pension under the act of June 27, 1890.

Assistant Secretary Webster Davis to the Commissioner of Pensions, May 31, 1898.

William B. Taylor, late second-class pilot, U. S. S. *General Grant* United States Navy, appealed on May 22, 1897, from the Bureau action of January 27, 1896, dropping his name from the rolls as a pensioner under section 2 of the act of June 27, 1890, certificate No. 18256, on the ground that he was not regularly enlisted or mustered into the service of the United States.

Claimant contends that having served as second-class pilot and attached to the Mississippi Squadron July 13, 1864, until June 21, 1865, when discharged by Acting Rear-Admiral S. P. Lee, commanding said squadron, he is entitled to a pension under the act of June 27, 1890, and was improperly dropped from the roll.

This appeal was considered in part July 10, 1897, and the papers were returned to the Bureau for a further report from the Navy Department. The papers are now returned with the following report:

NAVY DEPARTMENT,
Washington, December 1, 1897.

SIR: Referring to your communications of July 27 and November 18, 1897, in which you make the following inquiries in connection with the claim of William B. Taylor on account of service as a second-class pilot on the U. S. S. *General Grant,* viz:

"What was the 'Mississippi squadron,' and of what vessels was it composed, and whether this squadron was composed of armed vessels?"

"How were second-class pilots received into the service, and especially how was the claimant so received?"

I have to inform you that—

(1) The Mississippi squadron consisted of armed vessels under the command of naval officers, and included also, in ordinary reference, Ellet's ram fleet and the Mississippi Marine Brigade, which served for a portion of the time under the command of the senior naval officer of the Mississippi squadron. Its limits extended northward from New Orleans, on the Mississippi River, and its tributaries located in the States in insurrection.

This Department has no prepared list of this squadron. The preparation of such a list would be impracticable, as it would involve a constant change of names of ships and dates every recurring month for a period of three years or more. If urgent, the Department can prepare a list of all the vessels which were at any time connected with the Mississippi squadron, and can also furnish specific information with reference to the vessels of the squadron at any specific date.

(2) Pilots were received into the service for duty in the several squadrons by authority of the commanding officers of the squadrons, subject to the approval of the Department, such appointments being held during the pleasure of the appointing officers. In view of this and the fact that pilots were not enlisted men or appointed as officers by the Department, together with the further fact that the Department's records do not show their entry into the service or their conduct while serving as such, an opinion has been rendered by the judge-advocate-general of the Navy to the effect that pilots can not be regarded as officers or enlisted men in the Navy, and therefore must be regarded as civilians employed under the authority of the Navy Department.

There does not appear anything on the records of the Department to indicate that the status of William B. Taylor was different from that of other second-class pilots appointed in the manner above referred to.

As the evidence in this case fails to show that claimant was an officer or enlisted man in the Army or Navy, in the war of the rebellion, he is not shown to be entitled to pension under the act of June 27, 1890.

See cases of Andrew J. Shannon (7 P. D., 64); David Oliver (7 P. D., 597); Susannah Mackey (8 P. D., 535), and Henry N. Haynie (9 P. D., 304).

The action appealed from is affirmed, and the papers in the case are herewith returned.

SERVICE—HOME GUARDS.

ABNER ROBINSON.

Hall's company. West Virginia Home Guards, to which this appellant belonged, and in which he alleges his military service was rendered during the war of the rebellion, was a State militia organization that was never in the military service of the United States, and the officers and enlisted men thereof are not pensionable under any existing law.

Assistant Secretary Webster Davis to the Commissioner of Pensions, June 4, 1898.

Abner Robinson filed in your Bureau on August 25, 1890, a declaration for pension under the provisions of sections 4692 and 4693, Revised Statutes, alleging that he had served from 1862 to 1865 as a private in Captain Hall's company of West Virginia Home Guards (miscellaneous), and had contracted disability from exposure in line of duty during said service, which was rejected on October 15, 1892, upon the ground that he was not in the military service of the United States.

From said action appeal was taken on September 21, 1897.

Neither the War nor Treasury Departments have any record of the organization in which this appellant alleges his military service was rendered.

Said organization appears to have been a State militia organization, raised for temporary service and local defense, under the orders of the provisional and loyal governor of the State of Virginia at that time, and was never in the military service of the United States at any time, either actually or constructively.

It is clear, therefore, that the officers and enlisted men of said organization have no pensionable status or title under any existing law at the present time, and the rejection of this claim upon the ground stated was not error, and is affirmed accordingly.

ATTORNEYSHIP—POWER OF ATTORNEY—ATTESTATION.

REBECCA C. VINING (CLAIMANT).

A power of attorney to which the signature of the claimant is not attested by two witnesses confers no authority upon an agent or attorney to appear in a pension claim, and without such authority a person can not have title to a fee.

Assistant Secretary Webster Davis to the Commissioner of Pensions, June 10, 1898.

W. H. Love, of Plymouth, Ind., October 28, 1897, appealed in the matter of fee on the issue of August 26, 1897, in the claim for a widow's pension under the act of June 27, 1890, of Rebecca C. Vining, widow of Minor Vining, late of Company F, Fortieth Ohio Volunteer Infantry.

The claimant, October 25, 1892, filed the original declaration. The appellant, April 8, 1897, filed a power of attorney. On the allowance of the claim a fee was not certified the appellant for the reason that the claimant's signature to the power of attorney was not attested by any witnesses.

Section 5 of the act of July 4, 1884, among other things provides:

That the Secretary of the Interior may prescribe rules and regulations governing the recognition of agents, attorneys, or other persons representing claimants before the Department.

Pursuant thereto, Rules of Practice have been promulgated by the Secretary of the Interior, and attorneys, agents, or other persons have been accorded or denied recognition in claims in which they have appeared as representing claimants.

Rule 1 of Rules of Practice before the Commissioner of Pensions provides in substance that a person admitted to practice before the Department of the Interior upon filing a power of attorney from the claimant will be held authorized to prosecute his claim for pension.

Rule 4 of said rules provides that:

No power of attorney purporting to be executed by a claimant will be recognized as good and valid authority unless the same be signed in the presence of two witnesses and acknowledged before an officer duly authorized to administer oaths for general purposes whose official character is certified under seal.

There are many ways by which a claimant can authorize an attorney to prosecute his case. The contract could be shown by letter, by admission, or by cooperation. It may be expressed or implied. All these methods are recognized in courts of justice; in fact, the authority of an attorney to represent a party in any matter pending before the courts is taken for granted unless called in question by some interested person.

In pension claims, however, it was deemed expedient that the authority of an attorney to prosecute a case should appear by a power of attorney, and that he should not be entitled to recognition unless he was thus authorized. Having approved of this form of evidence of contracts between attorneys and claimants, I do not think there can be any doubt as to the authority of the Secretary of the Interior in requiring that the power of attorney must be executed in accordance with a particular formula. It is true that a power of attorney may confer authority upon a person to do acts in the place and stead of another, and said power would be deemed valid for all purposes though the signature of such other was not attested by two witnesses, or its execution acknowledged before some particular officer; but these principles of law do not govern where there are specific rules regulating the execution of powers of attorney and fee agreements.

The question primarily turns upon the fact whether the Secretary of the Interior has any warrant in law to require attorneys to obtain a power of attorney from a claimant. If he has not, then any other evidence of such authority is all that is necessary. This feature of the case is disposed of by the statute cited. I do not think it can be reasonably maintained that the Secretary of the Interior can require a person to file a power of attorney before his authority will be recognized to prosecute a claim and not require said power of attorney to be executed in a particular manner; in other words, declare what form of its execution shall be necessary in order for a power of attorney to be deemed valid.

Claimants and attorneys in most instances reside many miles apart. They are not associated in any way except in the prosecution of a pension claim. By the laws the Commissioner of Pensions is authorized to certify to an attorney a fee for securing the allowance of pension in behalf of some claimant. The pension agent upon the authority of the certificate of the Commissioner pays the fee as the agent of the claimant. The person to whom the fee is to be paid is made known to the Commissioner by the contents of the power of attorney. He authorizes the pension agent to pay the claimant's money is discharge of an obligation. His authority to do so, if good business methods are observed, should be an instrument executed in accordance with a formula approved by the Department, and affording reasonable assurance that the claimant has authorized the payment of a fee to the attorney named in said instrument. If the law permitted the claimant to settle with his attorney in the same manner as he would with his attorney for service in conducting proceedings in a court of justice, the high class of evidence now required to establish an attorney's authority to prosecute a pension case could, and doubtless would, be dispensed with.

In the case of Valerie S. Murray (8 P. D., 247), the question decided was in many particulars like the one arising on this appeal. In considering that case Assistant Secretary Reynolds used the following language relative to the necessity of observing rule 4 of the Rules of Practice in the execution of a power of attorney:

It is hardly necessary to call attention to the fact that your Bureau in the adjudication of pension claims, as to the authority and identity of attorneys and claimants, relies almost wholly upon statements contained in written instruments of evidence. It is rarely that a claim is specially examined for the purpose of obtaining additional information upon these points. Therefore, there is attached to these instruments a value independent of their weight as evidence, either as to the claimant's right to pension or of the contract existing between the claimant and his attorney, namely, as means of satisfying the Bureau that claimants and attorneys are the persons they represent themselves. This value is dependent upon and grows out of the fact that these instruments are executed in accordance with a formula prescribed by the rules of practice and the law governing their execution.

I am convinced that rule 4 contemplates an attestation of the signature of the claimant to a power of attorney by persons other than the attorney taking under said power, as the Bureau is thereby better assured of the genuineness of the instrument, and also that one of the avenues of fraud is thereby closed.

Upon the issue of certificate to allow pension the question of payment of fee is at once determined. It must be settled before payment of pension is made. Therefore, the Commissioner is required to act upon a question where delay is not, and should not be, allowed. Under these conditions the evidence of attorneyship should be of a character that admits of no doubt, and can be overcome only upon the ground of fraud. Such evidence when documentary (as is always the case in a claim for pension), as a rule, can furnish no safeguards unless executed in accordance with a formula prescribed for the execution of instruments which are then accepted without further proof of their genuineness than is afforded by the contents of the instruments themselves.

It may be urged that the rule will result in the deprivation of an attorney of his fee because of his failure to observe a mere formality, when he has fairly earned it, and there is no person who disputes his title.

This question was discussed in the case of Eliza Shank (8 P. D., 486), where completing evidence of the due execution of fee agreements was not filed until after the issue of certificate to allow pension. Relative to the rule there laid down, Assistant Secretary Reynolds said:

The statute (4786, R. S.) does not contemplate any condition other than the filing of the evidence of such agreements and of their proper execution prior to the issue of the certificate.

The statutes and the rules are plain, and it is so manifest that any oversight in the proper execution of the agreements or of the filing of evidence of their proper execution can not in any measure be due to the requirements of the law or rules of practice, but wholly due to the carelessness or neglect of the attorney, that no other pretext or excuse can be assigned for permitting such evidence to be filed after the issue of the certificate of pension.

The foregoing applies with equal effect where the evidence as to an attorney's authority to appear in a case has not been executed in manner and form required by the Rules of Practice. Those rules have been in force for many years, and have been given as widespread publication as the usual methods permit. In no instance has an attorney on appeal to this Department plead his ignorance of the requirements of the rules nor any misunderstanding of them, but has sought to disregard them. The rules should not be subverted by the oversight and neglect of persons claiming rights under powers of attorney where evidence is wanting of their proper execution in accordance with those very rules, and this due to the oversight and neglect of such persons.

So in this case, as the signature of the claimant to the power of attorney in favor of the appellant is not attested by two witnesses, in accordance with a long line of decisions laid down in cases on appeal before the Department it is held that—

A power of attorney to which the signature of the claimant is not attested by two witnesses confers no authority upon an agent or attorney to appear in a pension claim, and without such authority a person can not have title to a fee.

Action affirmed.

EDWARD H. LIGON.

Claimant at the age of 19 years voluntarily left his home in Tennessee and spent two months in a Confederate camp in the State of Alabama.

Held: That he voluntarily aided and abetted the late rebellion against the authority of the United States within the meaning of section 4716, Revised Statutes, and is not entitled to pension under the act of June 27, 1890.

Assistant Secretary Webster Davis to the Commissioner of Pensions, June 10, 1898.

Edward H. Ligon, late private in Company G, Fourth Tennessee Mounted Infantry, appealed September 23, 1897, from the Bureau action of March 12, 1897, dropping his name from the roll as a pensioner under section 2 of the act of June 27, 1890, Certificate No. 791026, on the ground that he aided and abetted the late rebellion by his voluntary service in the Confederate army, as shown by his own statement and other evidence.

He contends that it is a fact that in the month of May, 1861, his uncle, Thomas Ligon, persuaded him to leave his father, who was a Union man residing in the State of Tennessee, and go to a Confederate camp in the State of Alabama; that he rode his own horse and went unarmed, and staid in said camp several weeks, but never had a gun in his hand while there; that he never drilled or did any service of any kind while in said camp, and was never sworn into said Confederate service; that he never gave any aid or comfort to the enemies of the Government; that he left said Confederate camp and returned home to Smith County, Tenn., of his own volition and remained with his father at home until October, 1864, when he left home and joined said Fourth Tennessee Mounted Infantry, from which he was honorably discharged.

He further says that his full name is Edward Harney Ligon, and that he had a cousin named Edward Harrison Ligon who did at the beginning of the war enlist and serve in the Confederate army, and that the Department has mistaken the acts of Edward Harrison for those of Edward Harney.

He also contends that his disabilities for which he was pensioned were incurred in the service while a member of said Fourth Tennessee Mounted Infantry.

This last contention is immaterial so far as his right to pension under the act of June 27, 1890, is concerned. See cases of Adolph Bernstein (7 P. D., 229); Ellen J. Pipes (7 P. D., 289); Sarah H. Ozborn (7 P. D., 317); Isaac N. Babb, alias John Dunlap (8 P. D., 59); Anastatio Capella (8 P. D., 308); Miles F. Fullbright (9 P. D., 146); George W. Gilbert (9 P. D., 279), and Barnabus Sarver (9 P. D., 294).

His second contention also becomes immaterial in view of the admissions of claimant.

In an affidavit filed February 8, 1897, he testified that he was persuaded by his uncle in 1861 to go in the rebel army; that he had three brothers in the Confederate service with Forest and two with Morgan; that he also had an uncle and cousin in the Confederate service; that he went as far as South Florence, Ala., and was gone about two months; that he was then 19 years of age.

It is not necessary that a man should have been sworn in and rendered service in the Confederate service to debar him from pension under the act of June 27, 1890, under section 4716, Revised Statutes, which provides that—

No money on account of pension shall be paid to any person, or to the widow, children, or heirs of any deceased person, who in any manner voluntarily engaged in, or aided or abetted the late rebellion against the authority of the United States.

Section 4716, Revised Statutes, is a broad declaration of the governmental policy, and forbids in terms the payment of any money on account of pensions to any of the class of persons therein named, unless expressly excepted from the provisions of said section.

The act of June 27, 1890, contains no provision that the inhibition of section 4716 should not apply to applicants for pension under said act, and if claimant comes within the class of persons designated by said section 4716 he is clearly not entitled to a pension under said act of June 27, 1890.

Chief Justice Marshall, in the case of Bollman v. Swartwout (4 Cranch 126), used the following language:

It is not the intention of the court to say that no individual can be guilty of this crime (levying war against the United States) who has not appeared in arms against his country. On the contrary, if war be actually levied—that is, if a body of men be actually assembled for the purpose of effecting by force a treasonable purpose—all of those who perform any part, however minute, or however remote from the scene of action, and who are actually leagued in the general conspiracy, are to be considered as traitors. Crimes so atrocious as those which have for their object the subversion by violence of those laws and those institutions which have been ordained in order to secure the peace and happiness of society are not to escape punishment because they have not ripened into treason.

So, also, the court in the case of Respublica v. Abraham Carlisle (1 Dallas, 35) said:

By joining the armies of the enemy, or by enlisting or procuring others to enlist for that purpose, constitutes treason.

Again, in the case of United States v. Vigal (2 Dallas, 346), the court said:

Loss of property by waste or fire, or even by slight or remote injury to the person, is no excuse for joining an insurrection.

Justice Field, in the case of United States v. Greathouse (4 Sawyer 472), said:

Whatever overt acts are committed, which in their natural consequence, if successful, would encourage and advance the interests of the rebellion, in judgment of law, aid and comfort are given.

In the foregoing cases the courts were considering the question of the crime of treason, but it is not necessary that the acts of claimant should amount to treason as defined by the constitution in section 3, article 3, and by the courts, in order to bring him within the purview of section 4716, Revised Statutes.

The language of this section is very broad, and includes "any person who in any manner voluntarily aided or abetted the late rebellion." By the phrase "aiding and abetting" is meant to support, assist, connive at, second, further, stand by, countenance, encourage, or assist. To abet is to encourage by aid or approval. (See Century Dictionary.)

In criminal law, aiding and abetting is an offense committed by one who, though not directly perpetrating a crime, is yet present at its commission and renders aid or encouragement and assistance to the perpetrator. (See 1 Russell on Crimes, Chap. II.)

As held in the case of Timberlake r. Brewer (59 Ala., 108)—

the words aid and abet, in legal phrase, are pretty much the synonyms of each other. They comprehend all assistance rendered by acts, words of encouragement, or support, or *presence*, actual or constructive, to render assistance should it become necessary. No particular acts are necessary.

It is immaterial, therefore, whether claimant was a principal in the first or second degree, or was an accessory before or after the fact, in aiding or abetting the late rebellion, as in either case he would come within the provision of section 4716, Revised Statutes.

As stated by Mr. Chief Justice Waite in Young v. United States (97 U. S., 62), there may be aid and comfort without treason.

It was held by Assistant Secretary Otto, May 9, 1864, in the case of James A. Sewers, that encouragement of the rebels or sympathy with their cause, bars claim for pension under said section 4716, Revised Statutes. (See Digest of Pension Decisions, 1897, p. 181.)

So, also, it was held by Secretary Delano that making clothes and tents for rebel soldiers, or voting for the ordinances of secession in 1861, were acts of disloyalty which bar pension. (See Digest of Pension Decisions, ibid.)

It was held by Acting Secretary Cowen, in the case of Henry L. Davis (3 P. D., o. s., 56), that payment of taxes to the Confederate government was disloyalty, which barred the right to pension.

It was held by Secretary Schurz that presumption of disloyalty was raised by payment of taxes to the Confederate government, or furnishing food and clothing to sons in the Confederate army, but such presumption may be rebutted. (See case of Phillip Hoppel, 5 P. D., o. s., 151.)

He also held in the case of John W. McDonald (5 P. D., o. s., 104), that holding the office of postmaster and performing the duties thereof under the Confederate government was aiding and abetting the rebellion.

In the case under consideration the claimant at the age of 19 years left the home of his father, in the State of Tennessee, and went into camp with the Confederates, in the State of Alabama, taking his horse with him, where he remained some two months. By so doing he voluntarily aided and abetted the late rebellion within the meaning of section 4716, Revised Statutes, and is not entitled to a pension under the act of June 27, 1890.

The action appealed from is accordingly affirmed, and the papers in the case are herewith returned.

SERVICE—MEXICAN WAR.

MARY E. POWERS (WIDOW).

To convey title to pension under the act of January 29, 1887, it must be shown that the soldier's military service was associated with the war with Mexico.

Assistant Secretary Webster Davis to the Commissioner of Pensions, June 10, 1898.

This soldier, John T. Powers, private, unassigned, United States Voltigeurs, enlisted April 3, 1848. He was discharged June 27, 1848. He was pensioned at $8 per month, under certificate numbered 16604, on July 12, 1888. He died December 21, 1896, and the widow filed her claim January 2, 1897. This claim was rejected March 29, 1897, on the ground that soldier was not in Mexico sixty days, or on the coast or frontier thereof, or en route thereto.

From this action an appeal was filed December 31, 1897, it being contended that soldier was taken to Fort McHenry, Md., as a rendezvous, and that while there he was en route for the war.

From date of enlistment to date of discharge covered a period of some eighty-four days. This is a longer period than the statute requires. Up to May 30, 1848, however, the date when the war with Mexico is held to have ended, the period of service was but fifty-seven days, a shorter time than that required by the statute.

While the soldier enlisted for the war with Mexico, he never left Fort McHenry, Md., where he was discharged by reason of expiration of service. The records of the War Department fail to show that soldier was ever en route to Mexico during the war.

Moreover, he remained unassigned, which would indicate he was never intended to have served in Mexico. He remained in the Army at a post remote from the seat of war after the war ended, and continued in the service until the term for which he enlisted had expired.

Then there is nothing to indicate that his service had any connection whatever with the Mexican war.

It may have been contemplated to use his services in this war if found advisable, but nothing appears to indicate that this was ever found necessary.

Certainly he did not serve (actually, the law requires) sixty days with the Army or Navy of the United States in Mexico. Nor did he serve on the coasts or frontier in that war, nor could he, even technically, or by the most strained or liberal construction, be regarded as having been en route thereto.

Why has Congress affixed these conditions to title, i. e., stipulating that there must be shown service in Mexico, engagement in battle, service on the coasts or frontiers, or a showing that the applicant was at least on his way to Mexico for service in the war with that country!

The reason is obvious. It was for the purpose of segregating those who entered the general military service of the United States during the progress of this war from those who, purposely, were attached to the forces operating or intended to be operated against Mexico.

There is nothing to associate this claimant's military service with the war with Mexico, either by his own record or that of his regiment. Indeed, claimant was never a fixed or designated factor in the regiment.

The practice of the Department in these cases has been to require testimony to support the requirements of the statute. No uniform rule can be laid down, but, generally, it may be stated that such facts must be presented as will indicate an intention on the part of the War Department to utilize the soldier's services in the war with Mexico.

Were it shown, however, that this soldier's service was associated with the war with Mexico, I should not regard it as just to deny title because a portion of the service was rendered after the 30th day of May, 1848, when such war is held to have ended. The difficulty lies in the fact that this particular soldier is not shown to have been associated in any manner whatever with the war in question. Possibly a more proper ground of rejection would be on this basis and not because he lacked sixty days' service.

Your action rejecting the widow's claim is sustained.

RATE—DISABILITY.

JOHN W. FELLOWS.

Seventeen dollars per month is deemed an adequate pension for disability due to rheumatism and resulting disease of heart, evidenced by atrophy of muscles of left shoulder, with motion much impaired and marked crepitation in both shoulder joints and both kneejoints, resulting in hypertrophy of heart, heart's beat being 120 per minute.

Assistant Secretary Webster Davis to the Commissioner of Pensions, June 14, 1898.

The appellant in this case, John W. Fellows, Company F, Fourth West Virginia Infantry, is now pensioned at $17 per month for rheumatism and resulting disease of heart and naso-pharyngeal catarrh.

He is also shown to be now suffering from locomotor ataxia, in consequence of which he is not only wholly disabled for manual labor, but requires, perhaps, the frequent and periodical, if not the regular, personal aid and attendance of another person.

He has made several statements in regard to the origin of the latter disability, a brief history of which is set forth in an advisory opinion of the medical referee, dated November 14, 1896, and which is as follows:

This claimant is now on the rolls for rheumatism and resulting disease of heart and naso-pharyngeal catarrh, at seventeen-eighteenths.

In his original declaration, filed September 23, 1879, rheumatism and disease of lungs are alleged.

In declaration filed October 12, 1889, he alleges "affection of lumbar and spinal column," as result of rheumatism.

In declaration of December 5, 1891, he alleges injury to spine from lifting logs and sunstroke and resulting disease of nervous system.

In declaration of September 13, 1895, he alleges locomotor ataxia and disease of spinal cord, as result of sunstroke and injury to spine.

It seems from this that the claimant attributed locomotor ataxia, or disease of spinal cord, to three distinct and separate causes, viz, to rheumatism, injury of spine and sunstroke.

The last two have been legally rejected, and the question is now raised whether the disease of spinal cord, or locomotor ataxia, can be medically accepted as a pathological result of rheumatism.

From careful review of all the evidence and medical certificates in the case the adverse medical action of September 14, 1896, is believed to be right. This conclusion is based on the following facts: All the earlier medical certificates in this case describe the existence of rheumatism beyond dispute. There were crepitus and swelling and stiffness of the joints, with a mitral murmur of the heart. These are characteristic symptoms of rheumatism.

In the earlier stages of locomotor ataxia, it is true, we often have sharp neuralgic pains in the muscles, and especially of the lower extremities, and these are sometimes mistaken for myalgia or muscular rheumatism, but crepitus, stiff and swollen joints, and, above all, valvular disease of heart are never present.

From these facts we may safely assert that the soldier was properly pensioned for rheumatism.

In regard to the second point—whether the locomotor ataxia is a probable pathological result of rheumatism—all that can be said is this: All medical authorities that I am acquainted with agree that locomotor ataxia is an organic disease of the spinal cord, having for its leading causes heredity, syphilis, traumatism, alcoholism, or other causes, but no pathologist, to my knowledge, holds or accepts the disease as a sequela of rheumatism.

On December 12, 1896, the papers in the case were again referred to the medical referee for a further advisory opinion as to whether or not—

From a medical standpoint his opinions of June 22 and November 14, 1896, vacate his action of April 3, 1895, relative to sunstroke and injury to spine and alleged results.

If not, does the evidence now on file in the claim, including that prefixed to the brief, warrant a change of any part of said action? Also, whether locomotor ataxia, or any other disability that may be shown or is alleged, is accepted as a result of injury to spine or sunstroke, as seems to be implied by the legal action of August 27, 1896.

The medical referee replied, under date of December 15, 1896, as follows:

The medical action of April 3, 1895, meant that neither sunstroke nor injury of spine, nor any disability which could be accepted as a result thereof, was shown in a ratable degree since the date when the claim therefor was filed.

The opinion of November 14, 1896, does not affect this action in any respect.

The opinion of June 22, 1896, was not intended to vacate this action, unless it should "be clearly shown that a diseased condition of the spinal cord has existed continuously since discharge," but in view of the history of the case, the early certificates of medical examination, and the well-known course of locomotor ataxia, it is, and will be, practically impossible to fulfill this requirement.

The evidence now on file does not warrant any change in the intended action of April 3, 1895.

A ratable disability is not shown from injury of spine, or sunstroke, or any disability which can be accepted a result of either of said causes in this case.

A ratable disability is not shown from disease of kidneys, but is described from disease of eyes and nervous system, which covers impaired memory.

In view of the whole history of the case the recent evidence as to the existence of "spinal trouble," "spinal disease," "lameness of back," "weakness of back," etc., soon after claimant's discharge must be understood as relating to the effects of the rheumatism for which he is pensioned.

The statement of S. W. Calvert, filed on October 21, 1896, can not be accepted as a correct history of the disease of nervous system, in view of the evidence and medical examinations in the case.

While a ratable disability is shown from disease of the nervous system and eyes since the date of filing claim in 1891, yet from a medical standpoint continuance since date of discharge is not established.

The action of April 3, 1895, referred to above, was the rejection of the claim on account of sunstroke, malarial poisoning, injury of spine and alleged results, on the ground that no ratable disability therefrom had been shown since the date of filing the claim therefor.

The medical opinion of June 22, 1896, referred to is as follows:

No disability has been shown since filing on account of malarial poisoning.

Locomotor ataxy is shown to have existed since March 29, 1891.

This is a possible result of sunstroke or injury to spine.

But in order for it to be accepted it must be clearly shown that a diseased condition of the spinal cord has existed continuously since discharge.

It is possible that the rheumatism for which pensioned has been simply the ataxic pains and not true rheumatism. If the legal approval can be changed to locomotor ataxia instead of rheumatism it will be of benefit.

I can find nothing in the case to warrant the statement that "locomotor ataxy is shown to have existed since March 29, 1891."

The date mentioned is, however, probably error, and was intended to be May 29, 1891, as the certificate of medical examination of that date states that the claimant " walks with a straddling gait—patella reflex poor," although this should hardly be regarded as sufficient evidence upon which to base a diagnosis of locomotor ataxia, especially when no evidence of said disease was manifested at the medical examination in February, 1892, nearly one year thereafter.

At the latter examination it was shown that the soldier could stand on either foot or walk in a straight line with the eyes closed, and that there was no areas of either hyperæsthesia or anesthesia; but both rheumatism and disease of the heart were found to exist.

The further statement in the said opinion of June 22, 1896, that—

It is possible that the rheumatism for which pensioned has been simply the ataxic pains, and not true rheumatism,

is fully controverted by the statements in the medical opinion of November 14, 1896, relative to the existence of the latter disease.

There does not appear to be any room for doubt but what this soldier is suffering from both rheumatism and paralysis (locomotor ataxia), and that the disability due to the latter has progressed to such an extent that it has so masked the disability due to the former that it is difficult to differentiate as to the exact degree of disability due to each cause, but it is believed that the present rate is fully commensurate with the degree of disability shown to exist on account of pensioned causes.

A claim for increase was filed May 20, 1897, and rejected December 16, 1897; the claim for additional pension was not reopened nor considered.

From this action the claimant entered an appeal at this Department February 5, 1898, contending therein that he is wholly disabled for all manual labor by reason of pensioned causes, and that the origin and continuance of sunstroke and results has been fully established by competent evidence, both medical and lay.

It is true that a large amount of evidence has been filed, and adduced upon special examination, but it is also true that the said evidence is more cumulative than effective.

It is alleged that the existing locomotor ataxia is of service origin, and is claimed to be due to either sunstroke or an injury of the spine incurred during the war, yet the first positive evidence of the existence of said disease was not manifested until January 21, 1896, on which date the soldier was examined by the board of surgeons at Chicago, Ill., although its existence was suspected at two prior examinations, both of which were held in Cincinnati, Ohio, the first on January 31, 1894, at which time the board made a diagnosis of "incipient sclerosis of the cord," on account of the claimant's inability to stand with his eyes closed, and the second on June 12, 1895, when the board found some lack of coordination of the lower extremities, which condition was aggravated when the claimant's eyes were closed.

The certificate of examination made at Chicago, Ill., October 20, 1897, has the following statement relative to the claimant's paralysis:

The claimant is suffering from an advanced stage of locomotor ataxia. He describes the girdle pain. There is muscular incoordination. The patella and other reflexes are not abolished, but ankle clonus is present. He describes cushions under his feet in walking.

There is marked hyperæsthesia over the entire body. The pupils are enlarged and very slow to react. Muscular incoordination is so marked that he can not dress himself or button his clothes. It is probable that he has suffered from this ataxia for a long time and that it has been called rheumatism.

His ataxic condition is so marked that it masks all other diseases. There is no deformity of the spine showing injury. There is no evidence of syphilis. The skin, glands, and genitals present no evidence of this disease.

He is unfit for manual labor, and needs an attendant to dress and undress him and to wait upon him. (Rating, first grade.)

It is observed that the board of surgeons which made the above-mentioned medical examination was inclined to believe that the rheumatism for which the soldier is and has been pensioned was but the earlier manifestations of the existing locomotor ataxia.

That this idea is erroneous is fully shown by the history of the case as set forth in the advisory opinion of the medical referee, dated November, 1896, heretofore referred to. The said idea was probably based upon the fact that the rheumatic symptoms, except the valvular disease of the heart, were completely obscured by the ataxic symptoms.

It is also observed that the said board states "the claimant is suffering from an advanced stage of locomotor ataxia."

In this event the progress of the disease must have been quite rapid, as it was only shown to exist in its preataxic stage at the medical examination of June 12, 1895.

With a view of showing that the existing locomotor ataxia was of service origin, a vast amount of testimony has been filed, which, however, is too voluminous to refer to in detail, but which is, as heretofore stated, principally lay evidence, and more cumulative than important.

Considerable medical evidence has also been filed, but it relates principally to existing conditions and has no important bearing upon the origin of the same.

In regard to the degree of existing disability, from pensioned causes alone, the most recent certificate of examination shows the following objective conditions:

Pulse rate, sitting, 100; standing, 110; respiration, 26; temperature, 98¼; height, 5 feet 10¼ inches; weight, 155 pounds; age, 58 years.

We find atrophy of muscles of left shoulder; by measurement from middle of sternum to spinal column is 1 inch smaller than right; motion in it is much impaired, almost immovable. There is marked crepitation in both shoulders and both knee joints.

Right leg at gluteo-femoral fold, and just above and just below knee, is 1 inch smaller than left.

Heart on exercise is 120, hypertrophied, impulse forcible, much dyspnœa, no murmur.

Rate for rheumatism and results, sixteen-eighteenths; pharnyx and posterior nares inflamed and discharging.

Rate for nasopharyngeal catarrh, eight-eighteenths.

The conditions described in this certificate on account of locomotor ataxia are practically the same as those described in the certificate dated January 21, 1896, although a rating of but $50 per month is recommended therefor.

The present rate of $17 per month is, in my judgment, fully commensurate with the degree of existing disability on account of pensioned causes, in view of which fact, and the fact that the evidence on file fails to show the existing disease of nervous system (locomotor ataxia) is in any way due to the soldier's service, the action appealed from was proper, and is hereby affirmed.

ATTORNEYSHIP—FEE.

WILLIAM BOATE (CLAIMANT).

MILO B. STEVENS & CO. (ATTORNEYS).

When in a claim for straight increase, an order for medical examination has not been obeyed, and the attorney of record has been so notified and takes no further action in the case, and makes no satisfactory explanation of such failure within ninety days from the date of such notification, he is held to be in neglect and his attorneyship forfeited; and where subsequently another attorney files a new application for increase, secures an order for medical examination, with which the claimant complies, upon the allowance of the claim from date of such examination the latter attorney should be paid the fee.

Assistant Secretary Webster Davis to the Commissioner of Pensions, June 16, 1898.

M. B. Stevens & Co., of Washington, D. C., April 19, 1898, appealed in the matter of fee on the issue of February 15, 1898, in the claim for increase under the act of June 27, 1890, of William Boate, late of Company M, Seventh Pennsylvania Volunteer Infantry.

The soldier was pensioned under the act of June 27, 1890, when, on September 26, 1894, L. C. Wood & Co., of Washington, D. C., filed a declaration for increase; an order for medical examination issued April 23, 1895, with which the claimant did not comply; Messrs. Wood & Co. were notified September 5, 1895; the claimant failed to appear for medical examination. On October 19, 1895, a second order for examination issued. On February 20, 1896, Messrs. Wood & Co. were notified that claimant again failed to appear. Thereafter they took no further action in the case.

On June 2, 1897, appellants filed a second declaration for increase, and on July 20, 1897, filed claimant's request for a medical examination; an order issued October 11, 1897, with which the claimant complied November 24, 1897. Certificate issued February 15, 1898, to allow increase to commence November 24, 1897. On this issue appellants were denied a fee upon the ground that they had rendered no material service in securing the pension allowed.

In the case of Robins E. Babcock (7 P. D., 285) it was held that—

,When, in a claim for increase, an order for medical examination is not obeyed, the attorney shall be notified of the fact, and, unless within ninety days from the date of the notice a satisfactory explanation of such failure is filed, the attorney shall be held in neglect and his attorneyship forfeited.

Under the foregoing rule Messrs. L. C. Wood & Co. became in default on the expiration of ninety days from February 20, 1896, the date on which they were notified of the claimant's failure to comply with an order for medical examination, after which they took no further steps in the prosecution of the case.

The appellants were entitled to recognition upon filing, June 2, 1897, a new declaration containing a power of attorney in their favor. However, a right to recognition does not alone give title to a fee; in addition, an attorney must render some material service in securing the pension allowed.

In the case of Mahlon D. Holcomb, certificate No. 92435 (19 Fee P. L. Bk., 244, decided September 29, 1894), it was held that—

Neither the transmittal of an order for examination nor the forwarding to the Bureau of claimant's explanation for not obeying said order is such service as will warrant the payment of a fee.

The reasons for this rule are set forth at some length in the decision, and the rule itself was approved by the Department in the case of John B. Thompson, certificate No. 584892 (26 Fee P. L. Bk., 384, decided August 22, 1896).

It is worthy of note that the cited cases were claims for additional pension awaiting only the claimant's medical examination before certificate issued to allow pension; the rule correctly states the practice in that class of claims. The rule has also been applied in straight increase claims. It has also been held that the filing of a duplicate declaration is not material service.

As procuring and forwarding orders for medical examination and filing a declaration for increase are all the services an attorney can render in a claim like the one under consideration, and procuring and forwarding such order and filing a duplicate declaration are held not to be material service in a claim for straight increase, the question arises whether a fee can be paid to any other attorney than the one who filed the original declaration for increase.

No single rule of practice covers the multiplicity of conditions upon which fees are denied and allowed to attorneys in claims for increase.

In the case of Edward H. Teeter, certificate No. 82029 (22 Fee P. L. Bk., 438, decided June 12, 1895), the facts were as follows:

P. J. Lockwood, August 27, 1886, filed a claim for straight increase. A medical examination was held November 17, 1886. Soule & Co., of Washington, D. C., October 16, 1888, filed another declaration for increase. Another medical examination was held February 20, 1889. Certificate issued August 17, 1889, to allow increase to commence from the date of the last medical examination, and the fee was paid to Soule & Co. Upon appeal entered by Mr. Lockwood, it was held that Soule & Co. were entitled to the fee, as the former had no connection with the claim allowed. Apparently the reason assigned for denying Mr. Lockwood a fee finds support in this, that increase would not have been allowed but for the services performed by Messrs. Cralle & Co., and these were services not required of nor expected to be performed by Mr. Lockwood; therefore these services were sufficient of themselves to secure increase, and, as the claim filed by Mr. Lockwood resulted in no benefit to the claimant, the fee should be paid to the attorney who instituted the proceedings which resulted in the allowance of pension, and without which pension would have been denied, although the claim filed by Mr. Lockwood was fully completed by him without any delay. The fact is, as shown by the date of the commencement of increase, that the claimant was not entitled to increase when Mr. Lockwood filed an application therefor. This of itself would be ample ground for denying him a fee. To all intents and purposes, the claim for increase filed by Mr. Lockwood was rejected. The practice as stated in the Teeter decision has been followed in claims in which the facts were similar to those arising in that case.

In this case, Messrs. Wood & Co., who filed the original declaration, became in neglect before any medical examination was held in the claim. Subsequently, and while Messrs. Wood & Co. were in neglect, the appellants filed a new declaration, secured a new order for medical examination, under which the claimant was examined, and increase was allowed to commence from the date of said examination. Under like condition of facts in other cases fees have been paid to the attorney who performed such services as were performed by the appellants in this case. I am therefore of the opinion they should be paid the fee.

The practice finds its support in this, that as the attorney who filed the original declaration became in default before any medical examination was held, and the claimant under these conditions executed a new application for pension and appointed another attorney to prosecute it, the first claim was abandoned by all interested parties; therefore the claim allowed is the one based on the new application, with the prosecution of which the first attorney had no connection. The rules followed in this and the Teeter case cover nearly all conditions arising in claims for straight increase upon which title to fee depends.

Action reversed.

FEE—ATTORNEYSHIP—REFUNDMENT.

GEORGE AAB, DECEASED (CLAIMANT).

H. D. PHILLIPS (ATTORNEY).

1. As there is no proper evidence on file of appellant's authority to secure the payment of accrued pension in the soldier's claim, he is not entitled to a fee.
2. The Bureau of Pensions has authority to demand the refundment of a fee or of any compensation purported to have been paid by a claimant to an attorney for services or expenses in a pension claim where the record shows a fee has been allowed by the Bureau and paid him when not entitled thereto, or where the receipt of compensation directly or indirectly from the claimant for such services or expenses is admitted by the attorney.

Assistant Secretary Webster Davis to the Commissioner of Pensions, June 16, 1898.

H. D. Phillips, of Trenton, N. J., August 5, 1897, appealed in the matter of fee in the claim under the general law (Certificate No. 174372) of

George Aab, deceased, late of Company B, Twentieth New York Volunteer Infantry, upon issue of September 28, 1896, to allow accrued pension to his widow.

At the time of the death of the soldier, January 21, 1895, he was a pensioner under the general law at the rate of $4 per month; he was last paid at the New York agency, to November 4, 1894.

The appellant February 5, 1895, filed the declaration of Louisa Aab for widow's pension under the act of June 27, 1890; the claim was allowed February 16, 1897, and appellant was paid a fee of $10. On March 26, 1895, the appellant filed in behalf of the widow an application for payment to her of accrued pension due the soldier at the time of his death; September 28, 1896, certificate issued for the same and the amount ($10) was paid to the widow. On this issue no fee was paid the appellant.

The foregoing is from the record. The report of your Bureau, accompanying the appeal of Mr. Phillips, reads:

> On February 27, 1897, immediately after the widow pensioner had received notice of the allowance of pension, one J. R. H. Potts, of Newark, N. J., called upon her and presented an order from appellant for the payment of $3 as his fee for service rendered in the claim for soldier's accrued pension; this, in addition to the $10 fee which had been certified in the widow's claim. It appears from the evidence obtained on special examination of the matter that pensioner paid the $3 under duress. The special examiner developed the fact that pensioner never knowingly authorized appellant to act as her attorney in either of her claims; that she employed one John A. Rodrigo, a notary public and justice of the peace of Newark, N. J., to prosecute her claim; that she paid Rodrigo fees from time to time as occasion required for the execution of papers before him, and did not know that appellant had anything to do with the matter in question. Rodrigo, in a sworn statement before the special examiner on March 29, 1897, states that he was subagent for appellant and received $2.50 for every case sent him; that he prepared and executed the declaration and most of the evidence filed in support of the widow's claim, and the declaration for accrued pension, all upon appellant's blanks. He also testified that Mrs. Aab paid him 50 cents for each declaration and affidavit prepared and executed, and forwarded the declaration for accrued pension to appellant.

In this appeal Mr. Phillips states that he received $3 direct from the claimant for his services in securing the payment of the accrued pension in the soldier's claim.

The appellant was required to refund the amount ($3), hence this appeal.

In the case of Mylon Angel (8 P. D., 35) it was held that—

> The Bureau has no authority to demand the refundment of a fee except when the record shows one has been allowed and paid through error, fraud, or mistake, or when one has been legally allowed but paid to an attorney not entitled thereto.

In that case the conflicting evidence gave rise to a question of fact in the particular whether the attorney, Martin Metcalf, had received any compensation whatever for his service in the claim. He testified that he received the sum of $10 from the claimant, but the amount was paid upon an account due him, and was intended by the latter to so apply. The claimant testified that the money was paid to Mr. Metcalf as a compensation for services in a pension claim and upon his demand. Thus an issue of fact arose which was not within the jurisdiction of the Pension Bureau to determine. In the case under consideration the attorney, Mr. Phillips, admits that he received money from the claimant as a compensation for service rendered by him in a claim for pension. The claimant states that she paid him money for such services. There is no question but what compensation for service in a pension claim was paid to this appellant by the claimant, and herein this case essentially differs from the claim of Mylon Angel. While the rule laid down in that case should apply under like conditions arising in any other case, I am of the opinion that it should be limited in its application to those cases where the issue presented is whether any compensation has been paid the attorney.

But where an attorney admits he has received compensation from a claimant an issue of law, not of fact, arises, and one which is within jurisdiction of the Bureau to determine. In such a case the Bureau may properly require an attorney to refund the compensation received upon the ground that the demand and receipt of it were violation of the pension laws, as to the commission of which there is no doubt arising upon the evidence.

Having reached this conclusion, the rule laid down in the case of Mylon Angel is modified so as to read as follows:

The Bureau of Pensions has authority to demand the refundment of a fee, or of any compensation purported to have been paid by a claimant to an attorney for services and expenses in a pension cla'm, where the record shows a fee has been allowed by the Bureau and paid him when not entitled thereto, or where the receipt of compensation directly or indirectly from the claimant for such services and expenses is admitted by the attorney.

Where an attorney has received compensation for service in a pension claim from a claimant under a misapprehension of the law it is reasonable to presume that he stands ready to return the money thus received. When this is done he is entitled to the respect and confidence due to him as an attorney practicing before your Bureau. A demand for refundment has met with all the requirements of the case and is a proceeding which can work no harm.

But where an attorney cloaks the unlawful receipt of compensation for services in a pension claim by any device, and a demand for refundment is made to which he pleads the device, it would be paradoxical for the Bureau to find the device, restore the money paid to the claimant, and permit the attorney to continue to practice. Furthermore, the attorney's statement should not be discredited in the particular case unless it is found that his practice has been in many cases to obtain fees illegally, and this of itself would and ought to work the attorney's disbarment.

It is apparent that the demand for refundment of a fee (compensation) should not be made unless the attorney admits the receipt thereof or the records show that payment of a fee has been made to him. The foregoing sufficiently indicates the steps which should be taken and what proof is necessary when information is received that an attorney has received compensation and he denies having received any.

In the Mylon Angel case it is stated that steps looking to prosecution of an attorney or his disbarment should be taken when it appears that he has received a fee in contravention of law or the rules of practice. It was not intended to prohibit the Bureau from making a full investigation by special examination or other means for the purpose of determining that an attorney has received an unlawful fee, whether he admits the receipt thereof or not. If it is disclosed by the evidence of the attorney that he has received money from the claimant to which he is not entitled a demand for refundment would be proper. But if the attorney denies having received any money from the claimant in the matter of his pension claim except disbursements, which the attorney has accounted for to the satisfaction of the Bureau, a demand for any refundment of any further amount which the attorney swears he received in a transaction not connected directly or indirectly with any pension claim would be an assumption of jurisdiction belonging to another tribunal and a threat to deprive the attorney of his practice if he sought the protection of the courts, and this upon the evidence of one interested person. As already said, the attorney's word should not be discredited because one pensioner has charged him with having taken fees illegally. If the attorney is practicing a device which is his method of obtaining illegal fees this practice can readily be established by the testimony of many witnesses, and when established should work his disbarment.

As to the action of the Bureau denying the appellant a fee, attention is called to a communication of the Department dated October 14, 1897 (9 P. D., 136), relative to the allowance of fees for services rendered by an attorney in preparing and filing evidence under a rule to show why a pensioner's name should not be dropped from the roll under the act of June 27, 1890.

It is there held that—

Such services may properly be included within the terms of the statute relative to the preparation, presentation, or prosecution of claims under the provisions of the act.

Then follows:

The term "prosecuting a claim" is not limited in its designation to initiatory proceedings; * * * and this term prosecuting a claim for pension is found in section 4785, Revised Statutes, as reenacted and amended by the act of July 4, 1884, and in section 4 of the act of June 27, 1890.

The import of the foregoing is that for services rendered in prosecuting a claim for pension, either under the general law or the act of June 27, 1890, a fee is provided.

Under the general provision of section 4785, Revised Statutes, relative to the allowance of fees, either one, ten, or more dollars may be allowed for services rendered in securing payment of accrued pension; that is, such amount within the statutory limit as the Commissioner of Pensions may see fit to allow and deem equitable and just.

In this case no power of attorney is found in favor of the appellant authorizing him, in behalf of the widow, to secure the allowance of accrued pension in the soldier's claim. Under well-known rules of practice he has no title to a fee. Had he filed such authority he would be entitled to a small fee—such amount as the Commissioner of Pensions might see fit to allow.

As his client had been allowed a widow's pension, that claim necessarily required proof of her marriage to the soldier and of the latter's death. As evidence of these facts were on file at the time application for the payment of accrued pension in the soldier's claim was made, there remained little if any service to perform except filing the application. In view of the small amount of service on the part of an attorney to secure the accrued pension under the foregoing conditions, in my opinion he should not be certified, were he entitled, a fee in excess of one dollar; but, as said before, the fee may be such amount as the Commissioner of Pensions may deem equitable and just.

The appellant submits that it was proper for him to collect a fee from the claimant for securing the payment of accrued pension in the soldier's claim.

He submits that—

The charge was proper. No law bears on the subject; no attorney is recognized in such matters and no power (of attorney) is filed. It does not constitute any pension case. It is simply scrivener's, notary's, and lawyer's work. The law does not expect one to work for nothing. The Department has allowed like charges in other and similar cases.

Section 4876, Revised Statutes, as re-enacted and amended by section 3 of the act of July 4, 1884, provides that—

No agent or attorney or other person shall demand or receive any other compensation for his services in prosecuting a claim for pension, or bounty-land, than such as the Commissioner of Pensions shall direct to be paid to him not exceeding twenty-five dollars.

Now, by the very terms of this section the payment of any fee in the prosecution of a claim for pension is forbidden except in the manner therein specified, and as the proceedings in this case constitutes the prosecution of a claim for pension, it follows that an attorney is thereby prohibited from collecting a fee from the claimant. The appellant's contention is nothing more than for a device to avoid the provisions of the act.

The appellant urges that the widow is permitted to engage an attorney in her behalf to secure the payment of accrued pension in her deceased husband's claim to her. It is so held, but the law has specified the manner in which the payment for these services shall be made. He also urges that the widow is not a pensioner by virtue of the provisions of the action of March 2, 1895. But the prohibition of section

4785, Revised Statutes, is not limited to the collection and payment of fee from claimants and pensioners; it is general. The language of the section is:

No * * * person shall demand or receive any other compensation for his services in prosecuting a claim for pension * * * than such (compensation) as the Commissioner of Pensions shall direct to be paid to him.

The prohibition relates to the attorney receiving a fee, not to his client paying one. Undoubtedly this particular objection of the appellant is suggested by one of the penal provisions of the act of July 4, 1884, in section 4, which reads:

Any agent or attorney or other person instrumental in prosecuting any claim for pension * * * who shall wrongfully withhold from a pensioner or claimant the whole or any part of the pension or claim allowed and due such pensioner or claimant, shall be deemed guilty of a misdemeanor. * * *

However, it is evident that this section contains no limitation upon any of the preceding sections of said act. As to whether the appellant would or would not incur the penalty thereby provided for the reason that his client was not a claimant for pension nor a pensioner is a question to be determined by the courts having jurisdiction of criminal prosecutions for the violation of the provisions of said section.

For the foregoing reasons the action of the Bureau is affirmed. This decision, in so far as authorizing the payment of fees in the class of claims specified, is not retroactive.

DESERTION—HONORABLE DISCHARGE.

JOHN NORTON.

1. In claims for pension under the acts of January 29, 1887, June 27, 1890, and July 27, 1892, an honorable discharge from all enlistments for service in the particular war to which these acts refer, is a prerequisite to pension.

2. In claims for pension under sections 4692 and 4693 Revised Statutes, on account of disability incurred in the line of duty during a term of enlistment from which the claimant deserted, the claim should be rejected, for the reason that there is no period from which the pension could commence, as claimant had never been discharged from such term of service; and for the further reason that claimant having violated and repudiated his said contract of enlistment he thus forfeited all right to any benefits that were incident to such enlistment.

3. If the claim for invalid pension under sections 4692 and 4693, Revised Statutes, is based upon disability incurred in the line of duty during a term of enlistment from which the claimant was legally discharged, a desertion from a subsequent enlistment, of itself, is not a bar to pension. If the claim was filed prior to July 1, 1880, the pension would commence from the date of discharge from the term of enlistment during which the disability was incurred, but such pension will cease upon reenlistment and can not be restored while claimant is in the service, nor while in desertion from such subsequent enlistment. (Case of Henry Davinney, 7 P. D., 234.)

4 If the disability was incurred in the service under a subsequent enlistment, while the claimant was a deserter from a prior enlistment which had not terminated prior to such reenlistment, the claim should be rejected on the ground that the disability was not incurred in the line of duty, but while claimant was absent from his proper command in violation of his former contract of enlistment.

5. The decision in the case of George Lessor (8 P. D., 114), in so far as the same conflicts with the rules laid down here, is overruled.

Assistant Secretary Webster Davis to the Commissioner of Pensions, June 21, 1898.

I have considered your communication of June 25, 1897, relative to the case of John Norton, late of Company B, First District of Columbia Cavalry, who is a pensioner under certificate No. 255335, from which I quote the following:

I have the honor to transmit herewith for your consideration the files of the admitted pension claim of John Norton, certificate No. 255335, and to invite your attention to the decision of Assistant Secretary Reynolds of March 30, 1896, in the case of George Lessor (No. 59, present series), for such action as you may deem proper.

Said Norton applied for pension October 18, 1865, on account of a gunshot wound of the head alleged to have been received at the battle of Bermuda Hundred, June 23, 1864, while a private of Company B, First District of Columbia Cavalry, and was pensioned December 31, 1883, at the rate of $2 per month from the day after his discharge, May 4, 1865, and subsequently increased to $24 per month from February 18, 1885, on account of said wound and resulting disease of the nervous system, which rate of pension he is now drawing.

This pension was allowed upon allegations and proof that he enlisted under the name of John Norton in Company B, First District of Columbia Cavalry, July 31, 1863, and that he was wounded as alleged and discharged from said service May 3, 1865.

During a special investigation of charges of withholding pension certificates, cashing pension checks, and withholding pension money made against one A. C. Andrews, of Gloucester, Mass., the pensioner Norton admitted that he had a prior service during the war of the rebellion, viz: In Company A, Ninth Massachusetts Infantry, under the name of John Brennan, and from a report of the War Department it now appears that he did enlist under that name as a private in Company A, Ninth Massachusetts Infantry, April 11, 1861, and deserted therefrom January 21, 1863. His service in the First District of Columbia Cavalry began July 31, 1863, and terminated by discharge on May 3, 1865.

Under the departmental decision in the case of George Lessor, above cited, it is now proposed to notify this pensioner that being in a status of desertion from the first service which he contracted to render during the war of the rebellion he had forfeited his right to pension for a disability contracted in a subsequent service from which he was, however, honorably discharged.

The decision in the case of George Lessor (8 P. D., 114), to which you refer in your communication, was based on the erroneous theory that sections 4692 and 4693 Revised Statutes, referred solely to pensions granted for service, or for disability incurred in the service during the war of the late rebellion, while it is a general pension law applicable to all claims on account of disability incurred in the line of duty since March 4, 1861.

The law under which Norton was pensioned provides that any officer of the Army, Navy, or Marine Corps, or any enlisted man in the military or naval service of the United States, or in its Marine Corps, disabled by reason of any wound or injury received, or disease contracted, while in the service of the United States and in the line of duty, shall, upon making due proof of the fact, be placed on the list of invalid pensioners. (Sections 4692 and 4693, Revised Statutes.) Two conditions, and two only, are thus established as necessary to create title to invalid pension: (1) Service as an officer or enlisted man in the Army, Navy, or Marine Corps; (2) incurrence in such service, and in the line of duty, of a disease, wound, or injury resulting in disability.

Neither in the fundamental act (of July 14, 1862) granting pensions on account of disabilities incurred in the service since March 4, 1861, nor in any of the various acts amendatory thereof or supplemental thereto, is there any express provision that desertion or the lack of an honorable discharge shall constitute a bar to pension. If, therefore, pensions are denied to persons who incurred disabilities in the service and in the line of duty since March 4, 1861, on the ground that they, either subsequent or prior to the incurrence of such disabilities, deserted the service, or were dishonorably discharged therefrom, authority for such action, if it exists, must be derived from the law by implication.

It has been argued (see case of Lessor, supra) that the intent of Congress to deny pensions to deserters is manifest (1) from the fact that in many of the acts granting pensions for service or disabilities incurred in the service prior to March 4, 1861, the grant is expressly limited to such soldiers as " did not desert the service" or who "received an honorable discharge;" (2) from the language of the act of July 19, 1867, which, while providing that certain soldiers and sailors shall not be taken or held to be deserters, declares that nothing therein shall operate as a remission of any forfeiture incurred by such soldiers or sailors of pay, bounty, pension, or other allowances; and (3) from various acts passed since the war providing for the removal of charges of desertion in certain cases.

The argument under the first head was summed up by Commissioner John C. Black, in his ruling September 4, 1885 (Digest of 1885, p. 195), as follows:

> Nor will the mind of the ordinary man believe, without convincing proof thereof, that it has been designed to exact of the soldiers of the Regular Army and of that great class of volunteers of other and honorable wars, the condition of an honorable discharge or release from service, and at the same time allow that the company of their equally honorable brethren of the war of 1861 should be degraded and lowered in the universal estimation of mankind by admitting to the high privileges of the pension rolls those not honorably discharged or released from service. Or, in other words, the Commissioner can not believe that the Government intends that the deserters of the war of 1861 should be placed upon a par with the faithful soldiers of that great war and all the wars that preceded it.

This argument, if it proves anything, proves much more than was contended for in the Lessor decision. It proves that in order to have a pensionable status under the act of July 14, 1862, and subsequent acts, a soldier must not only have a record free from the charge of desertion, but must also have an honorable discharge. This is what General Black contended; and in this he was consistent, for it is quite as inconceivable that Congress intended to put dishonorably discharged soldiers upon a par with those who received an honorable discharge as it is that they intended to put deserters upon a par with honorably discharged men.

But no one any longer contends that an honorable discharge is an essential element of title to pension under sections 4692 and 4693 Revised Statutes (act of July 14, 1862), for disability incurred in the service and line of duty since March 4, 1861.

In the case of the mother of James B. Conroy (2 P. D., o. s., 477), Secretary Delano held that the character of a soldier's discharge had no bearing whatever upon his right to pension for such disability, and this has been the position of the Department from that time (1875) to the present day, with the exception of a brief period from October 22, 1887, to August 17, 1889, the former date being that of the decision of Assistant Secretary Hawkins in the case of Daniel B. Kaufman (1 P. D., 383), and the latter that on which said decision was overruled by Assistant Secretary Bussey (3 P. D., 137). The holding of Secretary Delano and Assistant Secretary Bussey was reaffirmed by Assistant Secretary Reynolds in the case of Anne E. Bassett (8 P. D., 321).

The authority for withholding pensions from persons for services in ante-rebellion wars, or for disability received therein, is derived from the statute granting such pensions, as said laws distinctly and positively make an honorable discharge a prerequisite to pension, while sections 4692 and 4693, Revised Statutes, contain no such provision.

Thus under section 4736, Revised Statutes, which provides for placing the names on the pension roll of all such persons—

who served sixty days in the war of Great Britain, of eighteen hundred and twelve, and were honorably discharged—

it was held by Secretary Delano that—

A soldier in the war of 1812, who deserted from service therein and was never discharged, is not pensionable as a survivor of said war. (Daniel McAlpine, 2 P. D., o. s., 370; widow of Albert Wilson, 8 P. D., o. s., 181.)

And so under section 4730, Revised Statutes (acts of May 13, 1846, and July 21, 1848), which provides pension to a soldier who was—

disabled by reason of injury received or disease contracted while in the line of duty in actual service in the war with Mexico, or in going to or returning from the same, who received an honorable discharge —

it was held by Acting Secretary Bell that—

An honorable discharge is essential to entitle soldiers of the Mexican war to pension for disabilities, and a soldier whose final record was that of desertion is therefore not pensionable. (John G. Kelley, 8 P. D., o. s., 229.)

The act of June 27, 1890, likewise, makes an honorable discharge a prerequisite to pension under the second section thereof, and it has been uniformly held that a claimant thereunder must have been honorably discharged from all service contracted to be performed during said war. (Isaac N. Babb, alias Dunlop, 8 P. D., 59; Henry Davinney,

7 P. D., 233; Susan Colgin, 5 P. D., 127; Kate Eibel, 7 P. D., 179; James Cullen, 6 P. D., 72.)

The same is true of the act of January 29, 1887. (Bridget Kelley, 7 P. D., 128.)

But it has been held that desertion from service in the Mexican war was no bar to pension based on service in the war of the rebellion. (Jacob Bowersmith, 3 P. D., 303.)

It has also been held that desertion from the Regular Army subsequent to the war of the rebellion was no bar to pension under the act of June 27, 1890. (Catharine Tubah, 8 P. D., 82; James W. Miller, 8 P. D., 316.)

In the case of James McCallan (9 P. D., 255), it was held that desertion from an enlistment for service in the war of the rebellion was no bar to pension for disability incurred in the line of duty while serving under an enlistment in the Navy since the close of the war of the rebellion.

It was held in the case of Bridget Kelley (7 P. D., 128), that the widow was pensionable on account of her husband's service in the Mexican war, notwithstanding his desertion from his service in the war of the rebellion.

It has also been held that—

When a soldier incurs a disability in the service and has been discharged, but subsequently reenlists and deserts, there is no authority for withholding the pension granted on account of said disability prior to his reenlistment other than the provisions of law that a pensioner shall not for the same period receive his pension and the pay of his rank or station in the service. (Benjamin Robbins, 6 P. D., o. s., 486.)

In the above case, decided by Secretary Schurz, at the time of his second enlistment, Robbins was receiving a pension for disability which he incurred in his first service and in the line of duty in that service, from which he also had an honorable discharge. The Secretary held that his title to pension for that disability was not forfeited by his subsequent desertion from a second service, and when his pension was restored, under said decision, the period between the date of his enlistment and the date to which last paid as a soldier in said second service was deducted.

The same Secretary also held, in the case of James H. Brush, alias Jesse L. Judd (7 P. D., o. s., 73), that desertion from a service prior to that in which the disability was incurred is not a bar to pension. In that case soldier deserted in 1864 from the Ninth Iowa Cavalry and enlisted in the Regular Army, where he was accidentally wounded, causing the amputation of an arm, for which he had been pensioned, but his name was dropped from the roll upon receipt of information of his former enlistment and desertion. The Secretary took the ground that as the law sanctioned pensions to persons who served in the Confederate Army in the rebellion against the authority of the United States for disabilities subsequently received while serving in the United

States Army, it was certainly not the intent of the law to grant more to a soldier who had formerly participated in the rebellion than to one who had simply been guilty of a dereliction of duty in the service.

Sections 4692 and 4693, Revised Statutes, grant pensions for disability incurred in the service and line of duty since the 4th day of March, 1861, but unlike most other pension statutes, it is not conditioned on an honorable discharge, and it has therefore been held that a dishonorable discharge, though barring pension under the act of June 27, 1890, is no bar to pension for disability incurred in line of duty under sections 4692 and 4693, Revised Statutes. (Daniel B. Kaufman, 3 P. D., 137; Jane Conroy, 2 P. D., o. s., 477; Anne E. Bassett, 8 P. D., 321.)

In the case of Henry Davinney (7 P. D., 233), it was held that claimant having been disabled in line of duty during his first term of service, from which he was honorably discharged, though he subsequently reenlisted and deserted, having filed his claim prior to July 1, 1880, was pensionable from date of his discharge to the date of his reenlistment, but his claim under the act of June 27, 1890, was rejected because he was not finally honorably discharged from all service in the war of the rebellion.

So it has been held that the fact of desertion alone does not forfeit pension under sections 4692 and 4693, Revised Statutes.

Pensions are not withheld as a punishment for some military offense, but because the law does not authorize payment of the same.

Thus pensions under the act of June 27, 1890, for service in the war of the rebellion, and under the act of January 29, 1887, for service in the war with Mexico, are withheld from persons who enlisted for service in said war and deserted and were never discharged, because the law makes an honorable discharge from such service a prerequisite to pension. But there is no more reason for paying a pension to a person for service in the war of the rebellion who is a deserter at large from an enlistment for service in the Mexican war than to a person who is a deserter at large from any other service, except where the law requires an honorable discharge, when it is held that such discharge means an honorable discharge from all service contracted to be rendered in the war for which pension is granted, or for disability contracted during a term of enlistment from which claimant deserted and was never discharged, because in that case, having forfeited all rights under his enlistment by violating his contract, he could have no claim to any benefits thereunder. But there is no provision in sections 4692 and 4693, Revised Statutes, making an honorable discharge a prerequisite to pension.

The only condition, other than contained in section 4724, Revised Statutes, is that the claimant shall have been an officer or enlisted man in the Army or Navy or Marine Corps, disabled since the 4th day of March, 1861, by reason of any wound or injury received or disease contracted while in the service of the United States and in the line of duty. (See cases of Jane Conroy, 2 P. D., o. s., 477, and Henry Davinney, 7 P. D., 233; also Anne E. Bassett, 8 P. D., 321.)

Section 4724, Revised Statutes, however, provides that a person shall not draw both a pension and the pay of his rank and station in the service, and this occasioned the ruling, in force for a time, that pension should be denied to a deserter, because he was constructively in the service. (Case of William T. Coburn, 7 P. D., 182; Peter Kenney, 7 P. D., 588, and Elizabeth A. Gannon, 3 P. D., 67.)

This is based upon the theory that desertion, being a continuing offense, the act does not cease until the deserter is apprehended or surrenders himself up.   But Attorney-General Taft (15 Op., 157), in an opinion on the question when the statute of limitation for the trial and punishment of deserters commenced to run, entertained a different view.   He said, on pages 162 and 163:

Thus it seems that in our military service the contract of enlistment must, in all cases, even in that of desertion, be regarded as having expired when the last day of the term of enlistment therein fixed has elapsed.   And since the obligation to serve depends on the contract, and necessarily ceases therewith, the offense of desertion, on grounds already set forth, must be deemed to terminate at the same time.   In short, that offense may be viewed as continuing up to the end of the term of engagement, but not beyond.

The act of July 19, 1867, before referred to, which, while providing that certain soldiers and sailors shall not be taken or held to be deserters, declares that nothing therein shall operate as a remission of any forfeiture incurred by such soldiers or sailors of pay, bounty, or pension, or other allowance, relates only to the term of enlistment from which such soldier or sailor deserted, and not to a term of service which had been rounded out by an honorable discharge.   And the same may be said of the act of March 2, 1882, and that of March 2, 1891.

The acts of July 14, 1862, and March 3, 1879, provided that pensions for disabilities incurred in the service and in line of duty shall (under certain circumstances) commence from date of discharge.   It is a necessary inference, from this provision, I think, that the soldier or sailor seeking pension for disability incurred since March 4, 1861, must show a discharge.   This discharge, I take it, must be from the term of service during which the disability, on account of which pension is claimed, was incurred.

There is an obvious reason why desertion from a particular term of service should operate as a bar to pension for any disability incurred therein.   An enlistment is a contract wherein the enlisted man obligates himself to serve in the military, naval, or marine service for a certain period of time, and while pension may not be regarded as a part of the consideration for such service promised by the Government (being rather, as the courts have held, in the nature of a gratuity), it may reasonably be held that by the violation of his contract he justly forfeited all benefits which might otherwise have accrued to him from it, including the right to pension for disability incurred.   He can not found any claim on a contract which he has voluntarily repudiated. But, having faithfully performed his contract, his right to all the emoluments appertaining thereto becomes complete, and, in the absence of any express declaration of law on the subject, can not be forfeited by subsequent acts. A claim based on a performed contract can not be defeated by pleading that the claimant has violated some other contract

Forfeiture of pension can result from desertion only in one of two ways—either as an incident of the violation of a contract or as part of the punishment for a crime. The law nowhere makes forfeiture of pension one of the penalties for desertion, and the well-known rule as to construction of penal statutes forbids the increase of penalties by implication. Moreover, punishment can not be inflicted for a crime until after trial and conviction by a court of competent jurisdiction, which, in a case of desertion, is a court-martial. The cases we are now considering are those in which there is merely an unremoved charge of desertion on the records, no trial by court-martial having ever been had.

For these reasons any argument based on the peculiar heinousness of the crime of desertion must be regarded as irrelevant. However much we may abhor a crime, we have no authority to add anything to the penalty therefor imposed by law. But even in this purview it can not be said that desertion is a more heinous offense against the Government than mutiny or inciting to mutiny; nor is it a crime so revolting to the moral sense as assassination or incest; yet it has never been maintained that conviction of any of these offenses would debar a soldier from pension for disability incurred in the service and line of duty. Why should desertion, considered merely as a crime, be singled out as the only one which a man may not commit and retain his right to pension? Pension is not a reward for good conduct. It is a compensation for disability incurred in the line of military duty. The right of a soldier to receive it is not affected in the slightest degree by his character as a man or a soldier, whether the same be good or bad.

It has been argued that the discharge of such soldier from his second enlistment does not alter his status as a deserter under his first enlistment, and it is laid down as a fundamental principle that pension can not be lawfully granted to one who occupies the status of a deserter. This underlying principle is said, in the Lessor case, to be "evident from a review of the acts granting pensions to persons who performed service in the Army or Navy of the United States."

I have reviewed the acts referred to and find no such intent manifest. The acts prescribe certain conditions which shall entitle certain classes of soldiers to pension, and anyone who fulfills these conditions has pensionable status.

But, it is said, a soldier can not release himself from the service by his own act; hence a deserter is still constructively in the service, and the law does not permit the allowance of pension to persons in the service. The provisions of law on this point are the following:

Section 4724 provides that—

No person in the Army, Navy, or Marine Corps shall draw both a pension as an invalid and the pay of his rank or station in the service, unless the disability for which the pension was granted be such as to occasion his employment in a lower grade, or in the civil branch of the service.

The act of March 3, 1881, provides that—

Hereafter no pension shall be allowed or paid to any officer, noncommissioned officer, or private in the Army, Navy, or Marine Corps of the United States, either on the active or retired list.

It has been urged that they are " constructively in the service." But this is a mere fiction. Besides, the law does not prohibit payment of pensions to persons constructively in the service, but only to those who are receiving pay for such service or who are on the active or the retired list.

It has been said that a sound public policy forbids the pensioning of deserters. That is a matter for the law-making power to consider. If Congress has not seen fit to exclude deserters from the benefits of the pension laws, this Department can not do so. I would say, however, that in so far as public policy is urged as a reason for denying pension in this and similar cases, it seems to me to have no force whatever The question is not whether deserters shall be pensioned. That question has been settled. Deserters are pensioned—have been pensioned under every Administration—and no one now disputes their right to pension. I mean those deserters whose offense was condoned or pardoned, or who, having been apprehended, tried, and convicted of desertion, and served out their punishment, were afterwards discharged either honorably or dishonorably. All these classes of deserters are pensioned without question. I can not conceive of any sound reason based on public policy why pension should be given to the man who has been convicted of desertion and denied to the man who has never been brought to trial, but is only charged with desertion.

In view of the line of decisions before referred to, and not questioned, that desertion in 1848 was no bar to pension for disability contracted in 1871, I can not see how it can be held that the fact of desertion, of itself, can be set up to bar a claim for pension under sections 4692 and 4693, Revised Statutes.

As already said, if the desertion was from the term of service in which the disability was contracted pension would not be granted, as the claimant had not fulfilled, but violated, his contract—and for the further reason that he was not discharged; and as pension, when granted, must commence from date of discharge, there is no date from which it may commence.

Nor do I think a soldier would be pensionable for a disability contracted during a period when he was in desertion from a former enlistment, he having enlisted subsequent to such desertion in violation of the Articles of War, because while absent in desertion he was not in the line of duty, it being held that desertion is a continuing offense and may be committed from day to day up to and including the day on which his term of enlistment expires. (15 Op. Atty. Gen., 157.)

Neither do I think that pension may properly be paid for any period covered by an enlistment whether faithfully fulfilled or not. When a soldier who is a pensioner reenlists his pension is discontinued, but it may be restored on his discharge from such enlistment, whether he was discharged honorably in the usual course of military rules, or by reason of his term of service having expired, when he could no longer be held to service.

That is, no pension should be paid for any period during which a person was actually in the United States military or naval service, nor during a term of enlistment from which he deserted.

The views herein expressed may be summarized as follows:

1. In claims for pension under the acts of January 29, 1887, June 27, 1890, and July 27, 1892, an honorable discharge from all enlistments for service in the particular war to which these acts refer is a prerequisite to pension.

2. In claims for pension under sections 4692 and 4693, Revised Statutes, on account of disability incurred in the line of duty during a term of enlistment from which the claimant deserted, the claim should be rejected for the reason that there is no period from which the pension should commence, as claimant had never been discharged from such term of service, and for the further reason that claimant having violated and repudiated his said contract of enlistment he thus forfeited all right to any benefits that were incident to such enlistment.

3. If the claim for invalid pension under sections 4692 and 4693, Revised Statutes, is based upon disability incurred in the line of duty during a term of enlistment from which the claimant was legally discharged, a desertion from a subsequent enlistment of itself is not a bar to pension. If the claim was filed prior to July 1, 1880, the pension would commence from the date of discharge from the term of enlistment during which the disability was incurred, but such pension will cease upon reenlistment and can not be restored while claimant is in the service nor while in desertion from such subsequent enlistment. (Case of Henry Davinney, 7 P. D., 234.)

4. If the disability was incurred in the service under a subsequent enlistment, while the claimant was a deserter from a prior enlistment which had not terminated prior to such reenlistment, the claim should be rejected on the ground that the disability was not incurred in the line of duty, but while claimant was absent from his proper command in violation of his former contract of enlistment.

5. The decision in the case of George Lessor (8 P. D., 114), in so far as the same conflicts with the rules laid down here, is overruled and set aside.

In view of the foregoing, I should say that Mr. Norton, having enlisted in the First District of Columbia Cavalry while in desertion from Ninth Massachusetts Infantry, and while he was still a member of that organization, was not in the line of duty as a soldier when he is alleged to have received the disability for which pension is claimed, being at the time a deserter from the Ninth Massachusetts Infantry.

EVIDENCE-SUFFICIENCY OF-INCURRENCE.

GEORGE W. WARREN.

Appellant's allegation that he incurred sunstroke, or heat prostration, in August, 1862, while on a forced march with his command between Tullahoma and Manchester, Tenn., is fully sustained by the affidavits of three reputable comrades, who are shown by the record to have been present with their command and the claimant at the time and place alleged, and who, in correspondence with the Bureau, fully adhere to and sustain the statements made in their affidavits.

Held: That no reason appearing for discrediting their testimony, it is deemed sufficient to show incurrence of the disability alleged in the service and line of duty.

Assistant Secretary Webster Davis to the Commissioner of Pensions, June 22, 1898.

George W. Warren, late musician, band, Fifteenth Indiana Volunteer Infantry, is a pensioner under the provisions of sections 4692 and 4693, Revised Statutes, at the rate of $17 per month for chronic diarrhea and resulting piles and rheumatism, and on December 19, 1891, he filed in your Bureau an application for additional pension, based on sunstroke and alleged resulting nervous prostration, paralysis, epilepsy, and disease of eyes, which was rejected on November 18, 1895, upon the ground that the service origin of said alleged sunstroke was not established. From said action appeal was taken on September 17, 1897.

The official military records of the War Department show that the appellant enlisted on June 14, 1861, and was mustered out of the service with the band of said regiment on September 10, 1862, under general orders from the War Department. There is nothing in the official record to indicate that the appellant incurred, or contracted, or received medical treatment for any disability during his said term of service; neither is there any medical testimony on file showing the origin of sunstroke or the existence of any of the alleged results in the service, at discharge, or immediately thereafter.

The appellant alleges that he incurred a sunstroke, or heat prostration, in August, 1862, while on a forced march with his command between Tullahoma and Manchester, in the State of Tennessee.

This allegation is fully sustained and corroborated by the testimony of three comrades, Bennett, Pfafflin, and Gates.

The official military records show that these witnesses were members of said band with the appellant, and were present with their command at the time alleged. In their correspondence with your Bureau they fully sustain their original testimony, and their standing and credibility is reported good.

The record shows that the appellant was present with the band at the time when he alleges he incurred a sunstroke, and that the band was then on its way, under orders, to Nashville, Tenn., to be mustered out of the service, and the place where it is alleged he was prostrated by heat was directly on the route that would have been traveled by said band in obeying said orders. If, as appears from the record and the testimony, the band was separated from the regiment and on its way to Nashville to be mustered out when the alleged sunstroke was incurred by the appellant, such fact sufficiently accounts for the absence of any mention in the record of the incurrence and subsequent effects of said disability, and the fact that the band was so soon thereafter mustered out would render it extremely unlikely that any record of medical or hospital treatment of the appellant would be found. The appellant is now pensioned for diseases contracted in the service and line of duty concerning which there is no record evidence whatever.

I have been unable to discover in this case any good or sufficient reason whatever for discrediting the three witnesses testifying to the origin of the so-called sunstroke or heat prostration of the appellant in the service as alleged by him, and I am of the opinion that it should be accepted as sufficient to show that fact.

Whether or not said heat prostration, sunstroke, or whatever else it may properly be termed, produced the after effects alleged by appellant, and has disabled him in a pensionable degree since his discharge, or whether, if this should be found to be the case, it would ultimately result in increasing the rate of the pension he is now receiving for other cause, are matters to be considered by your Bureau upon a readjudication of this case, since the claim for additional pension was rejected solely upon the ground of lack of proof of service origin, and no medical action appears to have been taken therein.

The rejection of this claim upon the ground stated is, therefore, hereby reversed and set aside, and you are requested to reopen and readjudicate the same upon its merits, accepting service origin of sunstroke or heat prostration as sufficiently proved.

ACCRUED PENSION—ACT MARCH 2, 1895—MINOR GRANDCHILDREN.

MINOR OF ORANGE TRICE.

The grandchildren of a soldier have no title to accrued pension. Ruling No. 218 of the Commissioner of Pensions is abrogated by the act of March 2, 1895.

Assistant Secretary Webster Davis to the Commissioner of Pensions, June 22, 1898.

John W. King, as guardian of George and John, minor children of Rebecca King, deceased, who was the minor of Orange Trice, deceased, late corporal Company C, Seventeenth United States Colored Infantry, appealed September 21, 1897, from the Bureau action of August 4, 1897, rejecting their claim, No. 234376, filed February 23, 1897, on the ground that there is no law granting pension to grandchildren of soldiers.

It is contended that as soldier's widow died in 1864 Rebecca, the minor child of soldier, was entitled to a pension; that as she died in 1896, with her minor's claim pending, her minor children, George and John, are entitled to the accrued pension due their mother, and Ruling No. 218 of the Commissioner of Pensions, in the case of minors of James Robinson, private, Company E, Fourteenth Kentucky Infantry, No. 194148, is cited as authority in support of this contention.

Under that ruling the minors of a minor were awarded the distributive share of their mother's minor's pension.

It becomes unnecessary at the present time to discuss or consider the correctness or error of said Ruling No. 218, as it is now abrogated by the act of March 2, 1895.

Soldier enlisted February 6, 1864, and was discharged April 24, 1865, on which date he died, leaving a minor child, Rebecca, but no widow. Rebecca died in 1896, leaving her minor's claim pending, and which was rejected February 1, 1897, on the ground of " no one entitled to complete the claim." Her two children, George and John, now seek by their guardian to complete the claim.

The pension laws do not grant a pension to the grandchildren of soldiers, and the act of March 2, 1895, in express terms limits the right to accrued pension of the soldier to his widow, or in case of no widow, then to the child or children under 16 years of age. In case of the death of a widow having an application for pension pending, the act limits the right to her minor children under 16 years of age. In case of the death of a minor child who was a minor at the death of the soldier no payment whatsoever of the accrued pension is allowed to be made by said act except so much as may be necessary to reimburse the person who bore the expense of last sickness and burial of the deceased, in case of no sufficient assets to meet such expense.

This act in terms provides that—

All prior laws relating to the payment of accrued pension are hereby repealed.

The only portion of the minor's accrued pension which could, in any event, be recovered by the grandchild or grandchildren of this soldier would be the expenses of last sickness and burial of their mother where they incurred the expense, and their said parent, the minor of soldier, did not leave sufficient assets to meet such expense.

The action appealed from is accordingly affirmed, and the papers in the case are herewith returned.

SERVICE—REVENUE CUTTERS—ACT JUNE 27, 1890.

WILLIAM B. WATSON.

It appearing from the official records and from the testimony that the United States revenue cutter *Tiger*, upon which this appellant served, was, during the time of his service thereon, under orders by the President to cooperate with the Navy, and was stationed on Chesapeake Bay, and waters tributory thereto, in actual and active cooperation with the naval forces of the United States, guarding the approaches to the national capital, and "arresting rebel depredations on American commerce and transportation" in those waters, his service on said cutter under such circumstances for ninety days or more, and an honorable discharge from such service, are sufficient to meet the requirements of section 2, act of June 27, 1890, and give him a pensionable status thereunder if other pensionable conditions required by said section are shown to exist.

Assistant Secretary Webster Davis to the Commissioner of Pensions, June 28, 1898.

William B. Watson, late fireman United States revenue cutter *Tiger*, United States Revenue-Marine Service, filed in your Bureau on July 29, 1890, an application for pension under the provisions of section 2, act of June 27, 1890, which was rejected on June 9, 1898, upon the ground of—

claimant's inability to furnish satisfactory proof that the revenue cutter *Tiger* actually cooperated with the Navy during his service thereon.

From said action appeal was taken on June 17, 1898.

This claim was recently before this Department on appeal from a former rejection by your Bureau, at which time the issue then presented was carefully considered, and in a decision rendered January 15, 1898, the action of your Bureau was reversed and the claim remanded for reopening and readjudication. (9 P. D., 182.) At that time the claim had been rejected solely upon the general legal ground that—

the officers and men of the Revenue-Marine Service, not being enlisted in the Navy, have no title under the act of June 27, 1890.

This ground of rejection being, ex necessitate, preliminary and antecedent to any investigation or consideration of the merits of this particular case on the proof presented in support of this claim, it was, as a matter of course, alone considered and passed upon by the Department on the former appeal, and in the decision then rendered no opinion was expressed, either directly or indirectly, inferentially or constructively, as to the sufficiency or insufficiency of the evidence on any point, or the merits of this particular case in any respect, but all such questions were expressly remanded for the consideration and attention of your Bureau on the readjudication of this claim.

This Department then held that a service of ninety days or more during the war of the rebellion in actual cooperation with the Navy under orders of the President and an honorable discharge from such service is sufficient to give the officers and seamen of the United States Revenue-Marine Service a pensionable status under the provisions of section 2, act of June 27, 1890. This ruling followed the decision in the case of William F. Rogers (9 P. D., 96), overruled the decision in the case of David Oliver (7 P. D., 597), and reaffirmed the holding in the case of Louis Schaffer (6 P. D., 137), and in remanding the case for readjudication attention was called to the fact that proof of actual cooperation with the Navy for the period necessary to give pensionable title under the act of June 27, 1890, should be required in this case, in accordance with the directions contained in the decision rendered in the case of Louis Schaffer (*supra*). In accordance with the instructions of the Department this claim was reopened and readjudicated in your Bureau and has been again rejected upon the ground above stated.

In the Schaffer decision (*supra*) it was held that proof of ninety days' service in actual cooperation with the Navy under the orders of the President in " arresting rebel depredations on American commerce and transportation and in capturing rebels engaged therein," and of an honorable discharge from such service, must be made in each case to entitle officers and seamen of the Revenue-Marine Service to pension under the provisions of section 2, act of June 27, 1890; but it was also held therein that in the absence of an official record parole evidence was admissible, and the geographical location of the vessel at the time in question and all the surrounding circumstances should be taken into consideration in ascertaining the fact of such actual cooperation and in determining the character of the service rendered in each particular case.

The sole issue presented by this appeal, and the only question to be considered at this time relates to the sufficiency of the evidence to show actual cooperation with the Navy under the orders of the President, as above defined, during the time that this appellant served on board the United States revenue cutter *Tiger*. The evidence on this point is extremely meager. The official record of the Treasury Department shows that the appellant served on board the United States revenue cutter *Tiger* as a fireman from February 1 to May 23, 1864, when he was honorably discharged from the service, and that said vessel was under orders, by the President, to cooperate with the Navy during the entire period of his service thereon. It is furthermore certified by the honorable Secretary of the Treasury that during the period of the appellant's service thereon said vessel was stationed on the Chesapeake Bay and the waters tributary thereto, and was under orders, by the President, to cooperate with the Navy. In an official communication addressed to the honorable Secretary of the Interior on March 16, 1898, the honorable Secretary of the Treasury states as follows:

I have the honor to acknowledge the receipt, by your reference, of a communication of the Commissioner of Pensions dated the 12th ultimo, in which is requested a list of vessels and officers of the Revenue-Cutter Service performing duty in the Chesapeake Bay from March 4, 1861, to July 1, 1865, and in reply thereto I inclose the list desired.

The Commissioner in his letter states that the "information is requested with a view to enable the Bureau to determine what, if any, knowledge the officers may possess in relation to the fact, dates, and nature of any cooperation the revenue cutters may have had with the Navy during the period in question." As the determination of this question involves the pensionable status of the officers and men who served on these vessels, I respectfully submit the following for your consideration:

As stated in a communication addressed to the honorable Secretary of the Interior, dated February 14, 1891 (claim of Louis Schaffer, No. 14443), by the Acting Secretary of the Treasury, "the revenue cutters were, at the opening of hostilities in 1861, armed, manned, and equipped as naval vessels of like size, and were maintained upon that footing throughout the war." They were, in fact, "war vessels," and of the naval force available within their respective theaters of operation, and coequal with naval vessels in their responsibility as a "defensive and offensive force." It may not be susceptible of proof from the records of this Department that they (with a few exceptions) were actually in cooperation with the Navy, but that they were regarded and used in precisely the same manner as were their associate vessels of the Navy, and therefore as "war vessels," wherever performing duty, is so evident a fact that it can not be fairly questioned.

The fact that they were ordinarily engaged in their regular duties as "revenue cutters" did not militate against their warlike status, but, on the other hand, being thus engaged, and consequently ever in readiness for prompt response in emergencies, and regarding, as they at all times did, military exigencies as of the first importance, their efficiency in that regard was thereby enhanced.

In view of these facts it is respectfully submitted whether those serving on board the vessels of the Revenue-Cutter Service during the period in question, and their dependents, if not pensionable under section 4741 of the Revised Statutes, do not come within the meaning of the language of the second paragraph of section 4693.

Attached to said communication is a list of vessels of the Revenue-Cutter Service which performed duty on the Chesapeake Bay and the waters tributary thereto during the period from March 4, 1861, to July 1, 1865, and the specific dates between which such duty was performed, and in said list the *Tiger* is named as having performed such duty from September 11, 1861, to December 19, 1861, and from December 17, 1862, to July 1, 1865.

Some further information relative to the nature and character of the service rendered and the duty performed by the *Tiger* during this period is obtained from a report of the Superintendent of Naval War Records of the Navy Department, on file in this case, dated May 23, 1898, in which it is stated that there is on file in his office two letters from the Secretary of the Treasury to the Secretary of the Navy, dated, respectively, February 24 and July 1, 1863, the former stating that "the revenue steamer *Tiger* is at the Washington Navy-Yard with injured boilers," and asking "that orders be issued for immediate repairs," the latter asking "for revolvers and ammunition for revenue steamer *Tiger* at Washington Navy-Yard."

There is no parole testimony on file which tends to throw any additional light on the question of the actual cooperation with the Navy by the *Tiger*, or the character and nature of the duty performed by her during the time this appellant served thereon, and, apparently, none is obtainable.

The foregoing official records and documents, while extremely indefinite and inconclusive on the direct question under consideration, clearly show that during the period that this appellant served on board the United States revenue cutter *Tiger* said vessel was under orders from the President to cooperate with the Navy. The language of the order under which this duty was performed was that said cutter should cooperate in " arresting rebel depredations on American commerce and transportation, and in capturing rebels engaged therein."

It is also apparent that during said period the *Tiger* was attached to and formed a part of the naval flotilla of the United States operating in the Chesapeake Bay and its tributary waters during the war of the rebellion.

It is a well-known and indisputable historical fact that the duty performed by these naval forces was of a most important character and necessary for the protection of the National capital and the navigation and commerce of those waters from the depredations and assaults of the enemy. The naval vessels stationed in Chesapeake Bay and its tributary waters not only guarded and protected the water approaches to the capital, but were constantly engaged in preventing communication between the Maryland and Virginia shores of the Potomac, and between the Eastern Shore of Maryland and Virginia across Chesapeake Bay, and in arresting and capturing disloyal persons engaged in conveying men, supplies, and information to the Confederates at those points. It is an undoubted fact that a contraband trade of this character was carried on, to a more or less extent, during the war of the rebellion between the shores of Maryland and the Confederates in Virginia, by which the enemies of the Government were materially assisted, and it can not be denied or gainsaid that had it not been for the naval vessels of the United States stationed and cruising in Chesapeake Bay and its tributary waters at that time "American commerce and transportation " on those waters would have been seriously interfered with and imperiled, if not entirely prevented, by " rebel depredations." It sufficiently appears from the evidence in this case that during the time that the appellant served on her the *Tiger* was one of the vessels engaged in the performance of this duty, and that she was so employed by direct orders from the President. The conclusion, therefore, seems to me to be inevitable that during this period the *Tiger* was actually cooperating with the Navy under the President's order, and that the specific duty then performed by her was assisting in " arresting rebel depredations on American commerce and transportation and in capturing rebels engaged therein," thus fulfilling to the letter the terms and requirements of said order.

The decision in the case of Louis Schaffer (*supra*) merely requires that it should reasonably appear from the evidence in each case that there was a service of ninety days in actual cooperation with the Navy under the order of the President as therein defined and an honorable discharge therefrom, to entitle the officers and seamen of the Revenue-Marine Service to pensionable status under the provisions of section 2 of the act of June 27, 1890, and I am clearly of the opinion that the proof in this case fully meets said requirement, and that the service of this appellant on the United States revenue cutter *Tiger* from February 1 to May 23, 1864, was a pensionable service under the provisions of said section.

Therefore, the rejection of this claim upon the ground last stated by you is also reversed and set aside, and you are requested to again reopen and readjudicate the same in accordance with the views herein set forth, and with its merits in other respects.

It is needless to say that no question has been considered in this decision except that upon which the claim was rejected, and which was presented by this appeal, no opinion being expressed or implied herein relative to the physical condition of the appellant, or as to the existence of a pensionable incapacity to earn a support by manual labor. This branch of the case not being involved in the ground of rejection, and not having been passed upon by your Bureau, is necessarily remanded for your consideration upon the readjudication of this claim as herein directed.

PRACTICE APPEALS-DISABILITY.

WILLIAM ROGERS.

1. Rule 6 of Rules of Practice in appeals applies only to cases where clerical errors are made in rating, and not to cases where the question is one of judgment on the evidence (Charles Yokel, 8 P. D., 431).
2. This claimant's capacity for earning a support is not impaired in a degree entitling under said act to any higher rate than $6 per month, the rate of pension he is now receiving.

Assistant Secretary Webster Davis to the Commissioner of Pensions, June 28, 1898.

This appellant, William Rogers, was an acting ensign, during the late war, in the United States Navy, and was allowed pension in March, 1896 (certificate No. 23863), under the act of June 27, 1890, at $6 per month from October 22, 1895, on account of disability from rheumatism.

In April, 1896, his claim, filed January 29, 1886, under the general law, was approved for allowance, and certificate reissued accordingly, allowing pension at $2.50 per month to March 2, 1895, and at $6 per month thereafter, on account of disability from disease of left ear.

On June 20, 1896, he again claimed pension under said act, and claim was approved in May, 1897, for allowance at $6 per month on account of disability from rheumatism, and, on claimant electing, by letter of June 30, 1897, to receive that pension instead of pension under the general law, certificate reissued accordingly in November, 1897, the claim, however, being briefed as a claim for restoration of pension from October 22, 1895.

On September 8, 1897, the claimant appealed, contending the certificate of examination made under said claim of June 20, 1896, shows title to a higher rate of pension under said act than $6 per month.

The medical referee, when called on for an advisory opinion on the merits of the appeal, suggested only that appeal should be dismissed under rule 6 of Rules of Practice in appeals, citing Jacob Oiler (7 P. D., 411); and in your submission of papers you state this view is sustained by that decision and also by the decision in George A. Brown (8 P. D., 309), but that a contrary view is taken in Charles Yokel (8 P. D., 431).

Said rule 6 provides that—

If, upon the issue of certificate of pension the appellant claims that error exists as to the rate of his pension, he should present the facts to the Bureau of Pensions, and an appeal will not be entertained in such cases until after adverse action thereon has been taken by said Bureau.

The decision in the case of Charles Yokel makes a distinction between clerical errors in rating and cases where the determination of the rate is the result of judgment on the evidence, holding that the rule applies only to the former class of appeals and not to the latter. This, being the latest of the decisions on this rule, must be accepted as controlling the present practice; and as this appeal is within the second class, as distinguished in the Yokel decision, it is properly taken and will be entertained.

The certificate of the examination mentioned shows the claimant was a well-nourished man of 56, weighing 188 pounds (being 5 feet 11 inches in height), with normal lungs, heart, liver, spleen, and bowels, and with no disability appreciably affecting his capacity for earning a support except rheumatism, the evidences of which are described as follows:

There is contraction of middle finger of right hand to nearly an angle (right angle), and a tumor over first phalanx as large as a chestnut. The tumor is sensitive to pressure, and the tendon is much enlarged for some distance up palm of hand, perhaps as large as pipe stem. The finger can not be extended by passive movement, but is fixed.

There was also some neuralgic contraction of facial muscles on left side.

It is manifest this claimant's capacity for earning a support was not impaired in a degree entitling, under the act of June 27, 1890, to any higher rate than $6 per month. No injustice, therefore, is apparent in your action allowing pension under said act at that rate, and it is affirmed.

INCREASE RATE—ACT AUGUST 4, 1886.

ALEXANDER P. McELROY.

The first provision of the act of August 4, 1886, does not increase pensions for disability from other causes than the loss of a hand or foot or total disability in the same. It does not increase pensions for disabilities equivalent to the loss of a hand or foot.

Assistant Secretary Webster Davis to the Commissioner of Pensions, June 30, 1898.

The appellant, Alexander P. McElroy, who was a corporal, Company C, First Maryland Volunteers, has been in receipt of a pension since the 26th of June, 1865, on account of disability from a gunshot wound of left leg, which fractured the tibia. The pension was paid at the following rates per month: $8 from June 26, 1865; $15 from June 6, 1866; $18 from June 8, 1872; and $24 from March 3, 1883. It is now paid at the last-mentioned rate.

On the 22d of September, 1888, Mr. McElroy filed an application in which he alleged that he believed himself entitled to an increase of pension on account of total inability to perform manual labor, and entitled to the rate of $30 per month under the act of August 4, 1886. His claim was rejected on the 2d of August, 1889, on the ground that there had been no increase of disability. From the action rejecting the claim an appeal was taken on the 9th of November, 1897.

The pensioner was examined on the 14th of May, 1889, by a board of surgeons at Washington, D. C., who reported his disability as follows:

Ball passed across tibia from without inward and upward leaving a scar 3½ by 2 inches, depressed, adherent, and tender. There had been some loss of bone. Toes are firmly anchylosed in an extended position. On the lower third of leg and extending about two-thirds of the way around it, is a brownish discoloration, superficial in character. Measurements: Right ankle, 8 inches; left ankle, 8 inches; at level of wound right leg, 10 inches; left leg, 8½ inches; over calf right leg, 14 inches; left, 12 inches. Claimant uses the foot very well to-day, and, as it stands, we can not say that it is equivalent to total disability in the foot. It is but fair to claimant to say that he claims that we see the leg at its best. If so, it is unfortunate (to the claimant), as we are obliged to say that in our judgment there should be no increase of the rating in this case.

The pension law of March   , 1883, provides a pension of $24 per month for all persons—

who, while in the military or naval service of the United States and in the line of duty, shall have lost one hand or one foot or been totally and permanently disabled in the same or otherwise so disabled as to render their incapacity to perform manual labor equivalent to the loss of a hand or foot.

The act of August 4, 1886, provides a pension of $30 per month for all persons—

who, while in the military or naval service of the United States and in the line of duty, shall have lost one hand or one foot or been totally disabled in the same.

The pensioner in his appeal does not contend that he is so disabled as to be incapacitated for the performance of any manual labor. The only question raised by his appeal is whether he is totally disabled in one foot. He has not lost a foot, and unless he is totally disabled in the left foot for all practical purposes he is not entitled to the rate of $30 per month, the rate he claims.

The first provision of the act of August 4, 1896, does not increase the pensions of those who are disabled by causes other than the loss of a hand or foot or total disability in the same. It does not increase the pensions of those who have a disability equivalent to the loss of a hand or foot.

The pensioner in this case has not lost his foot. He has not total disability in his foot. The board by whom he was examined under the claim to which his appeal relates stated in their certificate that he used his foot very well on the day of the examination.

The board at Washington, D. C., by whom applicant was examined on the 3d of August, 1883, stated that his disability was, in their opinion, equivalent to the loss of a hand or foot "under a liberal construction of the law."

The degree of disability in a hand or foot for which the law of August 4, 1886, provides a pension of $30 per month is not only such as prevents the use of the hand or foot for ordinary manual labor, but precludes the use of the same for any practical purpose whatever. (William Cline, 7 P. D., 119.)

The action from which the appeal is taken is in accordance with the law and decisions thereunder and is affirmed.

FEE—NO FUND, NO FEE.

DORCUS DUGGINS (CLAIMANT).
JOHN H. DUFFIE (ATTORNEY).

As the only fee provided by law is to be deducted from the pension, it follows that when the payment of accrued pension is expressly limited to the defrayal of the expenses of a pensioner's last illness and burial there is no fund from which the payment of a fee can be made. (Case of Lawrence H. Davis, dec., 8 P. D., 406.)

Assistant Secretary Webster Davis to the Commissioner of Pensions, June 30, 1898.

John S. Duffie, of Washington, D. C., May 23, 1898, appealed in the matter of fee on the issue of September 23, 1897, in the claim for a dependent parent's pension under the act of June 27, 1890, of Dorcas Duggins (now Nance).

The soldier, Ephraim, alias Philip, Duggins, served in Company A. Sixty-eighth United States Colored Volunteer Infantry, from February 20, 1864, to May 19, 1864.

The claimant's original declaration for a dependent parent's pension under the act of June 27, 1890, was filed April 28, 1892, by P. C. Cooter, of Cape Girardeau, Mo.; said attorney on same date filed evidence.

September 12, 1892, the appellant filed a power of attorney, and filed evidence on April 24 and May 15, 1895, the last of which completed the claim. September 23, 1897, certificate issued to allow pension, and a fee was certified to the appellant; however, no fee was paid, as the claimant died without any payment of pension being made or any voucher being executed therefor.

The act of Congress approved March 2, 1895, provides that from and after the 28th day of September, 1892, in case of the death of a dependent mother who is a pensioner or entitled to a pension having an application therefor pending, no payment whatever of the accrued pension shall be made or allowed except so much as may be necessary to reimburse the person who bore the expenses of her last sickness and burial if she did not leave sufficient assets to meet such expenses.

In the case of Joseph Abbott, dependent father of William H. Abbott, decided May 4, 1895 (22 Fee P. L. Bk., 75), the Department held that—

as the only fee provided by law is to be deducted from the pension, it follows that when payment of accrued pension is expressly limited to the defrayal of the expenses of the pensioner's last illness and burial there is no fund from which the payment of a fee can be made.

The case of Abbott was recently approved by the Department in the case of Lawrence H. Davis (8 P. D., 406).

The facts in this case bring the question of the allowance of a fee within the foregoing rule, therefore the action of the Bureau denying the appellant a fee is affirmed.

RATE—ACT MARCH 19, 1886.

LAURA A. YOUNG (WIDOW).

1. As claimant was married to soldier after his discharge from the service, and after the passage of the act of March 19, 1886, which increased the pensions of widows and dependent relatives of deceased soldiers from $8 to $12 per month, her pension was properly allowed at the rate of $8 per month only, as said act contained a proviso limiting its application to widows who were married to soldiers prior to the passage of the act, or during the service of such soldier.
2. Appellant having filed her application under the misapprehension that her claim under the general law had been rejected, and that she was pensioned under the act of June 27, 1890, instead, said appeal is dismissed.

Assistant Secretary Webster Davis to the Commissioner of Pensions, July 15, 1898.

Laura A. Young, on September 13, 1897, filed an appeal stating that her claim for pension under the act of July 14, 1862, as the widow of

Walter T. Young, formerly a soldier in Company E, First Massachu-setts Cavalry, had been rejected by your Bureau on the ground that the soldier did not die of the diseases for which he was pensioned. As a matter of fact her claim was allowed, but it appears from a letter written by her on May 23, 1898, that she inferred it had been rejected and that she was pensioned under the act of June 27, 1890, because the rate allowed was only $8 per month.

The act of March 19, 1886, which increased the pensions of widows and dependent relatives of deceased soldiers and sailors from $8 to $12 per month contained a proviso limiting its application to widows who were married to the deceased soldier or sailor prior to its passage, or who should thereafter marry prior to or during the service of the soldier or sailor. The appellant was married to the soldier on July 25, 1888, and the latter was not then in the service; consequently there is no law which authorizes the allowance to her of a higher rate of pension than $8 per month. The appeal, having been filed under a misapprehension as to the action taken by your Bureau, is dismissed.

RATES—ACT JUNE 27, 1890.

DAVID WILSON.

1. The pension law, with the exception of the act of February 28, 1877, granting a pension for the loss of an arm and a leg, has never permitted the allowance of a pension made up of the sum of the rates allowable for disability from two or more causes considered separately. The rate must be based upon the combined effect of all the causes.

2. The rates of pension under the general law are much higher than those under the act of June 27, 1890, the highest rate under the latter act being $12 per month, which is allowable for about the same degree of disability for which the general pension law provides the rate of $30 per month.

Assistant Secretary Webster Davis to the Commissioner of Pensions, July 15, 1898.

The appellant, David Wilson, late of Company H, Eleventh Missouri Cavalry, was pensioned under the general law at the rate of $2 per month from November 18, 1886, and $4 per month from February 11, 1891, on account of disability from injury to right wrist. By a certifi-cate issued March 29, 1895, he was pensioned from June 27, 1891, under the act of June 27, 1890, at the rate of $8 per month on account of disability from injury to right wrist, rheumatism, and neuralgia. On the 6th of July, 1895, Mr. Wilson filed an application for increase of pension under the act of June 27, 1890, in which he alleged disability from injury to right wrist and arm, rheumatism, neuralgia, catarrh, weak eyes, and kidney disease. His claim for increase of pension was rejected on the 18th of January, 1897, on the ground that the rate of $8 per month was proportionate under the act of June 27, 1890, to the disability from injury to right wrist, rheumatism, and neuralgia, and that there was no ratable disability under said act from the other causes alleged. From this action an appeal was taken on the 27th of September, 1897, the pensioner contending that he is totally disabled and entitled to a rating of $12 per month under the act of June 27, 1890.

Applicant was examined on the 5th of February, 1896, by the board of surgeons at Hermitage, Mo., who reported his age as 49 years and his condition as follows:

Right wrist joint has been dislocated, and may have been broken at the same time. Ulna was dislocated backward and outward. Ulna and radius are separated at wrist joint. Slight limitation of motion of wrist. Some tenderness and loss of strength.

Can pronate and supinate with this arm. Can grasp 12 pounds with right hand and 20 with left. On injury to wrist we rate him four-eighteenths.

He has slight rheumatism in both shoulders and hip joints. Crepitus and tenderness on motion, but no swelling.

Urine is acid. No evidence of rheumatism in any other part of the body. Heart normal. On rheumatism we rate at four-eighteenths.

No evidence of neuralgia, but he may have it at times.

Slight catarrh of posterior nares. Some inflammation and slight discharge to back part of mouth. Throat inflamed some. On catarrh we rate him two-eighteenths.

He has general debility, on which we rate him two-eighteenths.

The board found no disability from disease of eyes or defect of vision. They found no evidence of disease of kidneys.

Upon review of the case on the 25th of February, 1896, the medical referee gave the opinion that the rate of $8 per month was proportionate under the act of June 27, 1890, to the degree of the pensioner's incapacity for earning a support by manual labor.

The ratings given by the board of surgeons at Hermitage, Mo., for the disability from the several causes stated, if added together, would give applicant the amount of pension he claims, but with the exception made in the pension law of February 28, 1877, which granted a pension for the loss of an arm and a leg at the rate made up of the sum of the rates for each disability, the law has never permitted the allowance of a rate of pension made up of the sum allowable for disability from two or more causes considered separately. The rate of pension must be based upon the combined effect of the several causes. Besides this, the ratings made by the board at Hermitage, Mo., were made under the general pension law, under which pensions are much higher than under the act of June 27, 1890. Under the general pension law the rate of pension for incapacity for the performance of any manual labor is $30 per month, while under the act of June 27, 1890, the rate for total incapacity for earning a support by manual labor is $12 per month. The degree of disability referred to in the act of June 27, 1890, as incapacity for earning a support by manual labor, is about the same degree of disability that is referred to in the general pension law as incapacity for the performance of any manual labor.

It is believed that the pensioner in this case is not more than two-thirds disabled for earning a support by manual labor within the meaning of the act of June 27, 1890. The pension for two-thirds disability under said act is $8 per month, the amount he is now receiving. The action from which the appeal is taken is therefore affirmed.

RANK—RATING ACT JUNE 27, 1890.

MARY ANN HURST (MOTHER).

Rank in the service is not to be considered in any application under the act of June 27, 1890.

Assistant Secretary Webster Davis to the Commissioner of Pensions, July 15, 1898.

Mary Ann Hurst, mother of Frederick Hurst, who was captain of Company E, Forty-eighth Regiment of New York Volunteers, is in receipt of a pension of $12 per month under the act of June 27, 1890.

From the action fixing the rate of pension at $12 per month an appeal is taken, the contention being that the first section of the act of June 27, 1890, does not fix a rate of pension and that it was the intention that persons pensioned thereunder should be allowed the rate to which they would be entitled under former laws; that the pensioner in this case should have been allowed a pension of $20 per month as the mother of a captain.

It is true that there is nothing in the first section of the act of June 27, 1890, as to the rate of pension, but the second proviso to the second section of the act directs that rank in the service shall not be considered in applications filed under this act. This proviso does not apply merely to applications under the section to which it is appended, but to all applications under the law. The officer himself, if he was now living and totally disabled, would not be entitled to a higher rate of pension under the act of June 27, 1890, than $12 per month, and it is not consistent with the spirit of said law, or any other pension law, that the mother should receive a higher rate of pension than the officer himself would be entitled to if living and totally unable to procure a support by manual labor.

The action from which the appeal is taken is affirmed.

DEATH CAUSE—LINE OF DUTY.

REBECCA J. GILLCOF (WIDOW OF JOHN BARTON).

Soldier, who had been home on a ten days' furlough for the purpose of voting at an election, while waiting at the wharf for passage on a steamer on which he was to return to his command got into an altercation with some persons, one of whom struck him on the head with a stone, killing him instantly.

Held: He was not in line of duty, and therefore his death was not due to the service, and his widow is not pensionable under the general pension laws.

Assistant Secretary Webster Davis to the Commissioner of Pensions, July 15, 1898.

John Barton was enrolled in Company I, One hundred and fortieth Indiana Volunteers, on the 10th of September, 1864, at Columbus, Ind. On the muster-out roll of his company, dated July 11, 1865, he is reported as having died of a wound of the head by a stone, received in a drunken row at Carrollton, Ky., September 16, 1864.

On the 27th of May, 1867, an application for pension was made by Rebecca Barton, in which she stated that she was married to John Barton on the 6th of September, 1862; that said John Barton died on the 16th of September, 1864, at Carrollton, Ky., of wounds.

Her claim was rejected November 15, 1870, and was reopened, and was finally rejected on the 13th of October, 1893, on the ground that the injuries of which her said husband died were not incurred in the line of duty, but in a drunken row. From this action an appeal was taken on the 15th of October, 1897.

It appears from an affidavit of claimant's that the soldier was at home on a furlough of ten days at the time he was murdered. The furlough was given to allow him to vote at a general election. He was at the wharf boat at Carrollton, Ky., with claimant and others, on the evening of the 16th of September, 1864, waiting to take passage on the mail boat, which was expected to arrive in a short time. While there he got into an altercation with some persons, one of whom struck him on the head with a stone, killing him instantly. The contest between these persons arose from some trifling matter, which is not clearly set forth in the evidence.

The applicant objects to the word "drunken" in the report upon the rolls of her husband's company, contending that he was not drunk at the time. It is not important to determine whether he was intoxicated at the time or not. He was absent by permission from his company and regiment for the time being and not for any purpose connected with his duty as a soldier. He was permitted to be out of the line of military duty for the time being. His death was not due to the performance by him of any military duty, or obedience, active or passive, on his part to any law, order, rule, or regulation of the military service. He was therefore not in the line of duty at the time he was killed. The action rejecting the claim of the widow on the ground that the injury which caused her husband's death was not incurred in the line of duty was proper and is affirmed.

DESERTION—DISCHARGE.

WILLIAM ROSS.

1. Claimant having enlisted for service in the war of the rebellion August 22, 1864, and deserted said service November 14, 1865, he can not be held to have been honorably discharged from his service in the war of the rebellion.

2. The fact that he served after July 1, 1865, does not warrant a holding that he was honorably discharged on said date, as he was never either actually or constructively discharged.

Assistant Secretary Webster Davis to the Commissioner of Pensions, July 19, 1898.

William Ross, late seaman, U. S. S. *Ohio, Brooklyn,* and *Iosco,* filed a claim for pension under the act of June 27, 1890, No. 41882, alleging that he entered the service during the war of the rebellion, on or about August, 1864, and was honorably discharged in September, 1865, by reason of illness. That he is now suffering from injured right arm and spine, varicose veins of both legs, defective and failing eyesight of both eyes, chronic lumbago, and general debility.

His claim was rejected July 10, 1897, on the ground of his desertion, November 14, 1865, as shown by the records of the Navy Department.

An appeal therefrom was entered August 5, 1897, and on the 20th day of November, 1897, I affirmed the same on the ground that claimant having enlisted for service in the war of the rebellion August 22, 1864, and deserted said service November 14, 1865, he can not be held to have been honorably discharged from his service in the war of the rebellion.

This motion for reconsideration was filed January 7, 1898, the appellant, by his attorney, contending as follows:

The docket number of this appeal is 35784, and from said appeal we quote: "It is contended in brief, that claimant's desertion after the close of the war of the rebellion in no manner affects his title to pension under section 2 of the act of June 27, 1890, he having served more than ninety days during the war of the rebellion, and his desertion having occurred subsequent to said war. Claimant enlisted in the United States Navy August 22, 1864, served until November 14, 1865, when he deserted, as appears from the records of the War Department." This statement accurately sets forth our ground of appeal, but it is apparent that error is made in the assertion that the records of the War Department afford any evidence as to this sailor's service; we concede, however, that the records of the Navy Department do show this man's desertion in November, 1865. Immediately following this quotation reference is had to the case of "Franklin S. Cowen, 7 P. D., 374," from the decision in which an excerpt is made, and then follows the extraordinary conclusion (after citing the case of James Cullen, 6 P. D., 72): "In accordance with said decision the action of your Bureau appealed from is affirmed."

In the case at bar the claimant was a member of the permanent establishment (United States Navy), while the cases cited for sustaining the adverse decision are those made in the cases of members of the volunteer forces of the Army. The rejections of the claims of Cullen and Cowen (cited) were proper, and were based on the fact that the organizations in which they enlisted grew out of, and had sole reference to, the war of the rebellion, and were expected to and did disappear when the said war ended. These conditions made every enlistment therein an enlistment for the war of the rebellion; but in the case of an enlistment in either the Regular Army or Navy (permanent establishment) it has been repeatedly and authoritatively held that the close of the war of the rebellion operated, eo instanti, to honorably discharge from the said war every person then in either the said Army or Navy (permanent establishment). See instructions of Mr. Reynolds to the Commissioner of Pensions, dated April 5, 1895, more than six months subsequent to the most recent (Cowen) decision quoted in support of the adverse action of November 20, 1897, heretofore referred to.

On page 540, P. D., 7, is exhaustively set forth the reasons for regarding the war of the rebellion at an end July 1, 1865, so far as the Navy is concerned, and comment is made on the fact that at that date only one vessel (privateer *Shenandoah*) of the Confederate navy was afloat, and that its existence "upon the high seas subsequent to July 1, 1865, could not create or continue the existence of the war of the rebellion." Further, in considering the case of James Locke, who had enlisted in the Navy June 14, 1865, there is used the language, "While, therefore, the enlistment of the said James Locke was in, for, or during the war of the rebellion, he would be regarded, for pensionable purposes, as having been discharged from said service July 1, 1865, in accordance with the decisions of the Supreme Court in the cases of the United States r. North and United States r. Emory (112 U. S. Rep., p. 510)."

Attention is also invited to the claim of Alfred S. Soper, late United States Navy, No. 23559 (docket No. 26971), wherein the facts are very similar to those in the case at bar. Soper entered the Navy January 25, 1864, and was dismissed therefrom July 28, 1865; he applied for pension under the act of June 27, 1890, and the claim was rejected by the Commissioner of Pensions on the ground that Soper had not been honorably discharged from the war of the rebellion. Upon appeal it was held, quoting the Locke decision and alluding to the Supreme Court cases before adverted to, that Soper was honorably discharged the war of the rebellion on July 1, 1865, by virtue of the close of said war as of that date, so far as the Navy was concerned, and the adverse action of the Commissioner of Pensions was reversed and the claim was allowed. This was on June 13, 1896, or nearly two years subsequent to the promulgation of the decision relied upon to support the findings of November 20, 1897, for which we now move a reconsideration.

In our appeal of August 5, 1897, we did not set forth in extenso the authorities upon which we relied to sustain our contention, as we believed that the practice in such claims was too well settled and too well known to necessitate a specific citation. Doubtless there are other decisions that might be quoted in support of this claim, but as the ones here relied upon (Locke, Soper, etc.) have not been overruled, we assume that they are sufficient to warrant a compliance with our request for a reconsideration.

The records of the Navy Department, Bureau of Navigation, show that William Ross enlisted August 22, 1864, at Boston, Mass., for three years, as seaman, and served on the *Ohio, Brooklyn, Iosco, Vermont,* and *Miantonomoh,* and deserted from the service November 14, 1865.

It appears, therefore, that the appellant has performed but a small part of the contract entered into between himself and the Government of the United States, to wit, a service of three years in the Navy, and that he has never been relieved in any manner from the binding force of said contract of enlistment, either by an honorable or a dishonorable discharge.

One prerequisite to title under section 2, act of June 27, 1890, has been established by the record evidence in the case, viz, service of ninety days in the United States Navy during the war of the rebellion, but an additional requirement, to wit, an honorable discharge therefrom, does not appear by the record; hence our inquiry will be directed to the latter question.

In order to understand correctly the ruling of the Supreme Court of the United States in the cases of United States *v.* North and United States *v.* Emory (112 U. S., 510), cited as authority in the case of James Locke (7 P. D., 532), it will be necessary to quote the language of the several acts of Congress under which the said suits were brought in the Court of Claims, and which received interpretation by the Supreme Court as aforesaid.　They are as follows:

Act of July 19, 1848, section 5:

And be it further enacted, That the officers, noncommissioned officers, musicians, and privates engaged in the military service of the United States in the war with Mexico, and who served out the time of their engagement, or may have been honorably discharged, and first to the widows, second to the children, third to the parents, and fourth to the brothers and sisters of such who have been killed in battle, or who died in service, or who, having been honorably discharged, have since died, or may hereafter die, without receiving the three months' pay herein provided for, shall be entitled to receive three months' extra pay: *Provided*, That this provision of this fifth section shall only apply to those who have been in actual service during the war.

Act of February 19, 1879:

Be it enacted, etc., That the Secretary of the Treasury be, and he is hereby, directed, out of any moneys in the Treasury not otherwise appropriated, to pay to the officers and soldiers engaged in the military service of the United States in the war with Mexico, and who served out the time of their engagement, or were honorably discharged, the three months' extra pay provided for by the act of July nineteenth, eighteen hundred and forty-eight, and the limitations contained in said act, in all cases, upon the presentation of satisfactory evidence that said extra compensation has not been previously received: *Provided*, That the provisions of this act shall include also the officers, petty officers, seamen, and marines of the United States Navy, the Revenue-Marine Service, and the officers and soldiers of the United States Army employed in the prosecution of said war.

These suits were brought in the Court of Claims, and the facts may be briefly stated as follows: James H. North was an officer in the Navy of the United States from May 29, 1829, to January 14, 1861, when he resigned.　He served in the war with Mexico, as lieutenant, on board the frigate *Potomac*, from February 10, 1846, until July, 1847, when his vessel sailed for the United States.

William H. Emory was an officer in the Regular Army of the United States most of the time from July 1, 1831, to July 1, 1876, when he was placed on the retired list.　He was appointed first lieutenant of topographical engineers July 7, 1838, and promoted to captain April 24, 1851.　On or about the 1st of October, 1847, while he was lieutenant of engineers, he was appointed by the President as lieutenant-colonel in the District of Columbia and Maryland volunteers, for service during the war with Mexico.　He took the oath of office in Washington about the 2d of October, and joined his regiment in Mexico, under the orders of the War Department, and served with it "in the war with Mexico" until mustered out of service as lieutenant-colonel, on the 24th of July, 1848.　Upon his muster out he resumed his former rank as lieutenant of engineers and continued his service as such.

Mr. Chief Justice Waite delivered the opinion of the court.　He recited the above facts and continued:

The questions are—

1. Whether the officers of the Navy and of the Regular Army who were employed

in the prosecution of the war with Mexico are entitled to the three months' extra pay provided for by the act of 1848; and if so, then,

2. What is the "pay" to which they are entitled?

We have no hesitation in answering the first of these questions in the affirmative. All the doubts there may have been upon that subject when the act of 1848 stood alone were, in our opinion, removed by the act of 1879. It is difficult to see why the proviso was added to that act, if it were not to make it plain that Congress intended to include "the officers, petty officers, seamen, and marines of the United States Navy, the Revenue-Marine Service, and the officers and soldiers of the United States Army employed in the prosecution of said war" among those who were entitled to the "extra pay" provided for.

The answer to the second question is, to our minds, attended with no greater difficulty. Those of the Regular Army and Navy who where engaged in the military service of the United States in the war with Mexico may be said to "have served out the term of their engagement," or to have been "honorably discharged" within the meaning of those terms as used in the act of 1848, when the war was over, or when they were ordered or mustered out of that service. Being in the Army and Navy, their "engagement" to serve wherever ordered for duty. Their engagement to serve in the war with Mexico ended when they were taken away from that service by proper authority.

The pay they were to receive was evidently that which they were receiving at the end of their engagement, or when they were honorably discharged. The language is, "shall be entitled to receive three months' extra pay," evidently meaning the same pay they would have received if they had remained in the same service three months longer. It follows that, as North was serving at sea when he was ordered away, he was entitled to three months' sea pay, and as Emory was mustered out of his service in the war as lieutenant-colonel of volunteers, his pay must be in accordance with that rank.

It will be observed that in the case of James H. North—an officer of the United States Navy—it was not held that he was discharged from his service in the war with Mexico nor that the end of the war with that nation was equivalent to an honorable discharge therefrom, but that he "served out the time of his engagement" when he was taken away from that service by proper authority, to wit, when his vessel sailed for the United States in July, 1847.

William H. Emory was an officer in the Regular Army and served therein until his appointment by the President as a lieutenant-colonel of volunteers for service during the war with Mexico, and was honorably discharged, within the meaning of the act of 1848, when mustered out of the volunteer service in the war with that nation.

Those persons of the Regular Army or Navy who remained in the service until the said war was over were not entitled to the three months' extra pay provided for in said act by reason of an honorable discharge resulting from the termination of the war, but on account of the first condition named in the said act, to wit, "served out the time of their engagement."

It was manifestly the intention of Congress, by the provisions of the act of 1848, to include all persons therein enumerated who had performed actual service during the war with Mexico and had served out the time of their engagement, or had been honorably discharged—special volunteers for the said war, as well as those of the Regular Army or Navy—hence it was necessary to name two conditions as contained in the act, the first one for the benefit of those who "served out the time of their engagement," members of the Regular Army and Navy; and the second one for those who "may have been honorably discharged," for the said war.

May 30, 1848, has been accepted as the date of the legal termination of the Mexican war (7 P. D., 240), although William H. Emory was not mustered out of service until the 24th day of July, 1848, one month and twenty-four days after the termination of the war; yet the Supreme Court held that he was entitled to three months' extra pay provided in said act, from the date of his muster out of the volunteer service, and not from the date of termination of the war. Therefore I think that it is manifest that the date of the legal termination of the war was never intended to be equivalent to an honorable discharge.

James Locke enlisted in the United States Navy, as landsman, on the U. S. S. *Vermont* June 14, 1865, and was discharged from the U. S. S. *Colorado*, to which he had been transferred, September 7, 1867, and it was in this case that Assistant Secretary Reynolds made the following statement:

> While, therefore, the enlistment of the said James Locke was in, for, or during the war of the rebellion, he would be regarded, for pensionable purposes, as having been discharged from said service July 1, 1865, in accordance with the decisions of the Supreme Court in the cases of the United States *v.* North and United States *v.* Emory (112 U. S. Rep., p. 510).

And after quoting a portion of said decision he made the further statement:

> As said James Locke enlisted June 14, 1865, he can not be said to have served ninety days or more in or during the war of the rebellion within the meaning of the act of June 27, 1890, and the action of your Bureau rejecting his application under section 2 of said act is therefore affirmed.

The authority cited, as I have endeavored to interpret, does not warrant the conclusion that Locke was discharged from service in the war of the rebellion at the date named, July 1, 1865, but, under the authority cited, the time of his engagement for said service had terminated, although he was not discharged until more than two years thereafter.

The doctrine as laid down in the Locke Case is correct, with the exception of the misuse of the word "discharge," as appears from the following quotation therefrom:

> That enlistments in the United States Navy after July 1, 1865, were not enlistments in or for the war of the rebellion, and that any service in the United States Navy rendered after that date, under any enlistment prior to July 1, is presumptively not service in the war of the rebellion, and the burden of proof to overcome the presumption is upon the claimant to show, by satisfactory evidence, that such service after July 1, 1865, was active war or naval service in aiding in the suppression of the armed forces of the Confederate army or navy.

In following the dictum in the Locke Case, Assistant Secretary Reynolds was further led into error in the case of Alfred S. Soper, No. 23569, Letter Book 206, page 81, in a decision under date of June 13,

1896, when he held that "in the absence of proof that claimant served in the war of the rebellion subsequent to July 1, 1865, he was, for pensionable purposes, discharged from his service in the war of the rebellion July 1, 1865."

The case of William B. Johns (2 P. D., 393) was also cited as authority in the Alfred S. Soper Case, and as it is based upon the decision of the Supreme Court of the United States, in the cases of North and Emory, comment thereon is deemed unnecessary.

It is manifest under the facts in this case that the appellant was never actually or constructively discharged from the naval service of the United States; therefore under section 2, act of June 27, 1890, he is not entitled to pension. Motion overruled.

RATE—ACT JUNE 27, 1890—DISABILITY—REDUCTION.

JOSEPH A. DUDGEON.

Disabilities which are pensionable under the second section of the act of June 27, 1890, must cause incapacity for performance of manual labor in such degree as to produce inability to earn a support, and the rate must, within the limits fixed, be proportioned to the degree of inability to earn a support.

The right to increase and the right to reduce rest upon the same basis; the only question to be considered is whether the increase or reduction was warranted by the law and the facts.

Assistant Secretary Webster Davis to the Commissioner of Pensions, July 22, 1898.

I have considered the appeal filed May 3, 1898, from the action of your Bureau in reducing the pension of Joseph A. Dudgeon, late of the United States Navy. It appears that the appellant was, in March, 1891, granted a pension under the act of June 27, 1890, at the rate of $8 per month, commencing from the date of his application, July 14, 1890. The rate was subsequently increased to $12 per month from December 4, 1891. In July, 1895, it was reduced to $6 per month to take effect from July 4, 1895. It is contended in the appeal that the reduction was unwarranted and illegal.

In his original application for pension the appellant alleged that he was incapacitated for earning a support by manual labor by reason of loss of the right eye and partial impairment of the sight of the left eye, disease of the kidneys, and nervous prostration. Medical examination, however, failed to disclose any cause of disability except total blindness of the right eye. It may be said, therefore, that the pension allowed was for loss of sight of the right eye. The rating was in accordance with order No. 164 of the Commissioner of Pensions, which directed that all claimants under the act of June 27, 1890, showing a mental or physical disability or disabilities of a permanent character not the result of their own vicious habits, incapacitating them for the performance of manual labor in such a degree as would be rated under former laws at or above $6 and less than $12, should be rated the same as if their disabilities were of service origin; and that all those showing a pensionable disability which, if of service origin, would be rated at or above $12 per month, should be rated at $12 per month.

The established rate for loss of the sight of one eye, in March, 1891, was $8 per month. By order No. 245 it was increased to $12 per month from December 4, 1891, and the appellant's pension was increased accordingly.

On May 27, 1893, order No. 164 was revoked by Secretary Smith and the Commissioner of Pensions was directed to prepare new rules and regulations covering the proof of the right to pensions and rates of the same, in accordance with the provisions of section second of the act of June 27, 1890, keeping in mind the fact that the disabilities which are pensionable under said section must cause incapacity for the performance of manual labor in such a degree as to produce inability to earn a support and that the rate must, within the limits fixed, be "proportioned to the degree of inability to earn a support."

The Commissioner was also directed to have an examination made to determine what pensions had theretofore been allowed under the second section of the act approved June 27, 1890, in disregard of the terms of said act and in conflict with the ruling of the Department in the case of Charles T. Bennett (7 P. D., 1).

The appellant's case was one of those which came up for examination under the Secretary's order. He asserts that he was reduced without having his "day in court;" but the papers show that he was notified of the proposed reduction on the 4th of February, 1895, and informed that he would have thirty days within which to show cause why he should not be reduced. On March 16, 1895, Hon. D. E. Sickles, inquiring on his behalf, was fully advised in regard to the reasons for the reduction; and on April 11, 1895, the pensioner was given thirty days more within which to file evidence. He does not appear to have availed himself of this privilege or to have taken any step to retard or prevent the proposed action.

He now claims that the Commissioner of Pensions or Secretary of the Interior had no right to reduce his pension because his disability was of a permanent character. But the reduction was not made on the ground that his disability had decreased, but on the ground that he had been illegally rated in the beginning.

It is unnecessary here to enter into any argument as to the legality of the action. The right of the Commissioner of Pensions (subject to the approval of the Secretary of the Interior), after due notice to the pensioner, to reduce or withhold pension which he may deem to have been improperly allowed has been repeatedly affirmed by the Department, by courts of law, and by act of Congress. (See James Duval, 9 P. D., 218; Harrison v. United States, 20 C. Cls. R., 122; Long v.

Com. Pens., Sup. Ct. D. C., February 28, 1894; and acts of June 21, 1879, and December 21, 1893.) There can be no more question as to the right of the Commissioner in 1895 to reduce the appellant's pension from $12 to $6 than there is as to the right of his predecessor, in 1891, to increase it from $8 to $12. The right to increase and the right to reduce rest upon the same basis. The only question to be considered is whether the reduction was warranted by the law and the facts.

The act of June 27, 1890, confers pensionable status upon the soldiers and sailors who (1) served ninety days during the war of the rebellion, (2) were honorably discharged, and (3) are suffering from a mental or physical disability (*a*) of a permanent character, (*b*) not the result of vicious habits, which (*c*) incapacitates them for the performance of manual labor to such a degree as to render them unable to earn a support. A soldier who served only eighty-nine days is not entitled. One who is only temporarily disabled is not entitled. One who is incapacitated for manual labor to some extent but not "in such a degree as to render him unable to earn a support" is not entitled.

The act further provides that the rate of pension shall be not more than $12 and not less than $6 per month and shall be "proportioned to the degree of inability to earn a support." This would seem to be a plain direction that a man who can earn nearly but not quite a support shall have $6 per month; that a man who can earn little or nothing shall have $12 per month; and that intermediate degrees of inability for self-support shall entitle to intermediate rates.

If this view of the law is correct, then it only remains to consider to what extent the appellant's ability to earn a support by manual labor is affected by the loss of sight of the right eye. Most of us probably have knowledge of men thus afflicted who by their manual labor earn a comfortable support for themselves and families. In fact it is well known that the loss of the sight of one eye does not materially diminish the ability to perform ordinary manual labor. It was at one time held by the Pension Bureau, with the sanction of the Department, that the disability was not sufficient to give title to even the minimum rate provided by the act of June 27, 1890. Recently a more liberal rule has prevailed, and loss of the sight of one eye is now considered ratable at $6 per month. The case of Jacob Rollison, to which the appellant has referred as analogous to his, was a case in which the soldier was originally pensioned at $12 per month for neuralgia, loss of sight of right (left) eye, and disease of left (right) eye. In March, 1894, his name was dropped from the rolls on the ground that he was not ratably disabled for earning a support by manual labor under the act of June 27, 1890. Pension under said act was renewed at $8 per month from January 2, 1897, for loss of sight of left eye and disease of heart. In his appeal he contended that pension should have been restored from the date of dropping. The holding of the Department was—

That inasmuch as the loss of sight of one eye is now considered as constituting a degree of disability warranting allowance of the minimum rate under the act of

June 27, 1890, and as it is shown by the medical evidence and all the certificates of medical examination on file in this case that all useful vision in the claimant's left eye has been wholly lost from a period antedating the filing of the original declaration under the said act, he is entitled to restoration at the said minimum rate for the loss of sight of left eye from the date of dropping his name from the rolls.

It will be seen that the decision affords no support to this appellant's contention that he is entitled to the maximum rate under the act of June 27, 1890, for loss of sight of right eye. If said rate were now allowed to him he would receive twice the amount that is allowed to others for like disability.

There is evidence tending to show that the appellant suffers to some extent from other causes of disability, and the report of an examination made June 3, 1896 (under an "old law claim"), indicates that the disability from all causes then existing would entitle him to a somewhat higher rate; but as there is no claim for increase pending, increase can not be lawfully allowed. It is not shown that he was entitled to a higher rate than $6 per month at the time the reduction was made. (See opinion of medical referee dated July 1, 1898.) After careful consideration, I find no sufficient reason for disturbing the action of your Bureau, and the same is therefore affirmed.

DESERTION—DISCHARGE.

SAMUEL B. DUMP.

During the whole period that appellant served in the One hundred and thirty-third Ohio Volunteers, in which he alleges he contracted his disability, he was a deserter from the United States Navy, and his disability was not therefore incurred in the line of duty, and he is therefore not pensionable under the general law nor under the act of June 27, 1890. (John Norton, 9 P. D., 382.)

Assistant Secretary Webster Davis to the Commissioner of Pensions, July 29, 1898.

Samuel B. Dump, alias Samuel Brown, filed a claim for pension under the general law on the 19th day of October, 1889, alleging that while a member of Company B, One hundred and thirty-third Ohio Infantry, in the military service of the United States and in line of duty, on or about the early part of or middle of May, 1864, he contracted measles, which resulted in deafness of right ear and disease of eyes and chest. He further alleged that he had not been employed in the military or naval service of the United States otherwise than as a member of Company B, One hundred and thirty-third Ohio Infantry.

On the 23d day of August, 1893, his claim was rejected on the ground of no disability from the alleged causes since date of filing claim.

The claim was reopened and after further consideration rejected the second time, January 28, 1896, on the ground of claimant's inability, though aided by special examination, to furnish the necessary evidence to established the existence of alleged results of measles at discharge and continuance since. On the 14th of August, 1897, an additional reason for rejecting the claim was entered on the face brief as follows:

Claimant deserted from the *Avenger*, United States Navy, on March 12, 1864, and was never discharged therefrom, as shown by the records of Navy Department.

The appellant's claim under the act of June 27, 1890, was rejected July 31, 1896, on the grounds that claimant deserted from a prior service in the United States Navy, as shown by the record, and is a deserter at large.

This appeal from both of the above-stated actions was entered July 21, 1897, the appellant, by his attorneys, contending that he received a final honorable discharge from the One hundred and thirty-third Ohio Infantry, and that a desertion from a former enlistment in the Navy is not believed to be a sufficient reason upon which to base a rejection of his claim under either law.

The records of the Navy Department show that Samuel Dump, seaman, enlisted on the *Grampus* February 20, 1864, and served to February 26, 1864; on the *Clara Dolsen* to March 4, 1864, and deserted from the *Avenger* March 12, 1864.

The records of the War Department show that Samuel Brown was enrolled in Company B, One hundred and thirty-third Ohio Infantry, May 2, 1864, and mustered out with company August 20, 1864.

The appellant made the following statement on special examination, September 23, 1895:

I am the identical Samuel P. Dump who served as a private in Company B, One hundred and thirty-third Ohio Volunteer Infantry, under the name of Samuel Brown. I only gave part of my name when I enlisted. My full name was and is Samuel Brown Dump. I enlisted in May, 1864, and was discharged in August, 1864. I served on the U. S. gunboat *Avenger* No. 4, from the spring of 1863. I served six months on this boat and was discharged at Cairo, Ill.

The record does not indicate the term of the seaman's enlistment in the Navy, but it may be assumed as a fact that it was for a longer period than two months and twelve days, the period of time from date of his enlistment in the Navy until his enlistment in Company B, One hundred and thirty-third Ohio Infantry.

I held in the case of John Norton (9 P. D., 382) that—

In claims for pension under the acts of January 29, 1887, June 27, 1890, and July 27, 1892, an honorable discharge from all enlistments for service in the particular war to which these acts refer is a prerequisite to pension.

It is evident, therefore, from the facts of this case that the appellant has no title under the act of June 27, 1890, for the reason that he did not receive an honorable discharge from all enlistments for service in the war of the rebellion.

The appellant has alleged in his claim under the general law that he contracted measles while a member of Company B, One hundred and thirty-third Ohio Infantry, and that deafness and disease of eyes and chest resulted therefrom.

In the case of John Norton, to which I have referred, I also held that—

If the disability was incurred in the service under a subsequent enlistment, while the claimant was a deserter from a prior enlistment which had not terminated prior to such reenlistment, the claim should be rejected on the ground that the disability was not incurred in the line of duty, but while claimant was absent from his proper command in violation of his former contract of enlistment.

The facts in this case indicate that the appellant was a deserter from his contract of enlistment in the Navy, and that the term of said contract had not expired when he reenlisted in Company B, One hundred and thirty-third Ohio Infantry, therefore he was not in the line of duty when the alleged disability was incurred.

Rejection affirmed.

EVIDENCE—PRESUMPTION OF DEATH.

SUSAN KELLY (WIDOW).

Soldier was seen in Denver, Colo., about four years after he abandoned his home and family in Ohio, by an acquaintance, whom he told that he had a wife in Ohio with whom he had some difficulty and that he wanted to go away from her.

Held, That his absence from his home and family for more than seven years is not unexplained, so that his death may be presumed under the act of March 13, 1896.

Assistant Secretary Webster Davis to the Commissioner of Pensions, July 30, 1898.

Joseph Kelly enlisted on May 15, 1861, in Company B, Twenty-fourth Ohio Volunteer Infantry, and was discharged on July 9, 1862. His widow, Susan Kelly, filed an application for widow's pension (No. 439123) on July 12, 1890, under the provisions of the act of June 27, 1890.

Her claim was rejected on August 10, 1897, on the ground that she is unable to produce satisfactory evidence of soldier's death, or to support the presumption of his death under the rule in the act of March 13, 1896.

From this action appeal was taken on October 7, 1897, presenting the contention that her husband has been absent twenty-one years, during which time she has heard nothing from him, in view of which she insists that the presumption of death obtains.

The issue raised by the appeal involves an application of the rule set forth in the act of March 13, 1896, to the proven facts in the case. Said act provides that—

The death of an enlisted man or officer shall be considered as sufficiently proved if satisfactory evidence is produced establishing the fact of the continued and unexplained absence of such enlisted man or officer from his home and family for a period of seven years, during which period no intelligence of his existence shall have been received.

It appears from the evidence adduced before a special examiner in the month of June, 1894, that the claimant and her husband were raised in Zanesville, Ohio, where they were married in the early part of the year 1868. At this place the soldier lived with his family, and was engaged in the grocery business until about the year 1875, when he moved to Columbus, Ohio. Here he secured a position as a guard in the penitentiary of that State, which position he held for about nine months and was discharged. Having lost his position he sent his family back to Zanesville and left Ohio, stating that he was going west to Indiana for the purpose of seeking employment. It appears that he did go to the State of Indiana, and secured temporary work at Logansport. During his stay at the latter place, which seems to have been not longer than three or four months, he wrote frequently to his wife, and occasionally sent her a little money. When he disappeared from Logansport he ceased writing and the widow has never heard from him since. It seems further that soldier was affected with heart disease, and that during his short stay in Indiana he visited a sister, who at that time resided in Michigan City. The sister, Mrs. Maggie Taylor, testified before the special examiner that while soldier was at her home he was attacked with heart disease and became unconscious. A physician was called in to see the soldier and restored him to consciousness. Several witnesses testified that soldier had a brother to die suddenly of heart disease and that he had a living sister who is now afflicted with said malady. The neighbors and friends of claimant testify that the relations between the soldier and his wife were cordial and affectionate, and that there was nothing observable in their lives which indicated any domestic infelicity. The claimant bears a good reputation and is highly spoken of in respect to industry and all domestic virtues.

John Miller, a witness before the special examiner, deposed that he, when a boy, lived in Zanesville and knew the soldier. Witness left Zanesville in 1880, and in 1882 went to Denver, Colo., and while there he saw soldier. He was not certain that it was Joseph Kelly, but recognized him by a scar which he had on his face. He knows that Joseph Kelly, the soldier, had a scar on his face and the man he saw in Denver had a scar on his face, but witness could not say that it was the same kind of scar.

John V. Hart deposed that he knew a man in Zanesville, Ohio, by the name of Kelly from 1854 to 1871 or 1872. He does not remember his given name. When he first knew Kelly he was a single man, and whether he had married afterwards he could not tell. This man Kelly witness saw in Denver, Colo., in 1880. They recognized each other and had frequent conversations for a period of about four weeks. Witness's recollection is that Kelly told him that he had a wife in Ohio with whom he had had some trouble and that he (Kelly) wanted to keep away from her on that account. He gave witness to understand that he did not wish it known in Zanesville, Ohio, that he (Kelly) was in Denver. Witness believes that soldier was called Joe Kelly.

The case turns upon the question as to whether the absence of soldier is explained or "unexplained" within the meaning of the act of March 13, 1896. There seems to be but little doubt that soldier was seen in Denver, Colo., in the year 1880, about four years after he had left his home in Ohio. He then desired, it seems, that his whereabouts should be unknown to the people of Zanesville, in which place his wife was then residing. This conduct of the soldier explains his absence both before and after the time at which he was seen in Denver. It is simply a case of desertion, in view of which it must be held that the evidence fails to show "the fact of the continued and unexplained absence" of the soldier.

The rule under which the presumption of death obtains is obviously based upon the assumption that a man when absent from his home would under normal conditions institute some sort of communication with his family, and a failure to do so, for as long as seven years, is so much at variance with the law of nature as to raise the presumption that such person has ceased to exist.

The absence, however, must be "unexplained" or the presumption of death does not obtain. The explanation in this case consists in the fact that the soldier abandoned his family, and would naturally have a motive for concealing the fact of his existence as far as possible.

The action of your office seems to have been without error, and is hereby affirmed.

DOUBLE PENSIONS—SPECIAL ACT.

EMMA A. PORCH (WIDOW).

This appellant is now in receipt of a pension of $20 per month, granted to her personally by a special act of Congress in recognition of services rendered by her individually to the Government during the war of the rebellion. She seeks, in addition thereto, a pension as widow of the deceased soldier under the general provisions of section 4702, Revised Statutes. The granting or payment of such pension to her is expressly and positively prohibited by the provisions of section 5 of the act of July 25, 1882, so long as she is in receipt of pension under said special act.

Assistant Secretary Webster Davis to the Commissioner of Pensions, July 30, 1898.

Emma A. Porch filed in your bureau on January 3, 1896, an application for pension under the provisions of section 4702, Revised Statutes, as widow of Allen B. Porch, deceased, late private Company D, Fifth Missouri State Militia Cavalry, alleging the death of said soldier on December 18, 1895, from disease contracted in line of duty during his military service, which was rejected on March 23, 1896, upon the ground that she was then in receipt of a pension of $20 per month under a special act of Congress.

From this action an appeal was taken to this Department on April 15, 1896, and this case was duly considered thereunder on June 30, 1896, and a decision rendered on that date affirming the rejection of the claim upon the ground stated. No subsequent proceedings have been taken in the case in your bureau, and the present appeal, which was filed on February 26, 1898, is in the nature of a motion for a review and reconsideration of the decision on the first appeal.

In her former appeal the appellant urged as a proposition of law that inasmuch as she was "specially provided for" by a special act of Congress, the provisions of law which prohibit one person from drawing more than one pension at the same time did not apply to her case.

The present appeal or motion, although quite lengthy, merely repeats this argument without adding any additional ground or reason for a reversal of the action of rejection, or assigning any other error in said decision affirming the same.

This appellant is now on the pension rolls at the rate of $20 per month under and by virtue of a special act of Congress, which recites that said pension is granted to her individually, in recognition of services rendered by the appellant to the Government during the war of the rebellion. She does not desire to surrender said pension of $20 under the special act and take in lieu thereof a widow's pension of $12 per month under the general provisions of section 4702, Revised Statutes, but seeks to obtain the latter pension in addition to the one she is now receiving under the special act, and enjoy both at the same time.

In the decision rendered in this case on the former appeal, which is hereto attached, it was clearly pointed out to the appellant that section 5 of the act of Congress approved July 25, 1882, expressly provides—

That no person who is now receiving, or shall hereafter receive a pension under a special act shall be entitled to receive in addition thereto a pension under the general law, unless the special act expressly states that the pension granted thereby is in addition to the pension which said person is entitled to receive under the general law.

The special act under which the appellant is at present pensioned contains no provision that the pension thereby granted shall be in addition to the pension which she might be entitled to receive under the general law.

There is no ambiguity or uncertainty whatever in the terms of said section 5 of the act of July 25, 1882, and no opportunity for implication or construction of its provisions, nor is there any room for discussion of this matter.

The law clearly, positively, and absolutely forbids and prohibits the receipt and enjoyment of both of these pensions by this appellant at the same time.

The rejection of this claim by your bureau upon the ground stated, and the decision of the Department of June 30, 1896, affirming said action, were manifestly without error and will be adhered to, and said action of rejection is hereby reaffirmed.

SERVICE—MILITIA.

JAMES W. ANDERSON.

A State militiaman, whose organization was not called into the United States service by the President, is pensionable only under subdivision three of section
4693 R. S., where his claim was prosecuted to a successful issue prior to July 4,
1874, notwithstanding he performed duty under the commander of the Department of Kansas.

*Assistant Secretary Webster Davis to the Commissioner of Pensions, July
30, 1898.*

On January 4, 1893, James W. Anderson filed his claim under the
general law, alleging gunshot wound and incurrence of rheumatism at
Westport, Mo., about the 1st day of November, 1864.

Claim was rejected on May 25, 1893, on the ground that applicant
was never in the United States service, and an appeal is filed on October 1, 1897, in which it is contended that soldier volunteered at the call
of the governor of his State, Kansas, who called for volunteers under
the orders of the President of the United States, and that therefore his
service was in the United States Army.

The records of the War Department have been searched many times,
but the name of James W. Anderson is not found as attached to any
regular military organization of the United States Army.

The following certificate shows, without doubt, his true status:

STATE OF KANSAS, ADJUTANT GENERAL'S OFFICE,
Topeka, June 16, 1896.

I hereby certify that it appears from the records on file in this office that J. W.
Anderson was enrolled on the — day of May, 1864, at Kennekuk, by M. C. Willie,
and ordered into active K. S. M. service as private in Company G, Twelfth Regiment
Kansas Volunteer Militia Cavalry, on the eighth day of October, 1864, at Atchison,
by Governor Thomas Carney; that the service was performed in pursuance of a
proclamation of Governor Thomas Carney, issued in compliance with General Orders,
No. 53, Department of Kansas, dated at Fort Leavenworth, October 9, 1864, promulgated by Maj. Gen. S. R. Curtis, U. S. A., commanding the department; and
also General Orders, No. 56, by General Curtis, dated Fort Leavenworth, Kans.,
October 10, 1864, declaring martial law throughout the State of Kansas, and ordering
all men, white or black, between the ages of 18 and 60 years into the militia service,
and that he was relieved from duty on the twenty-seventh day of October, 1864. By
order of Governor Thomas Carney.

(Signed)   S. M. Fox, *Adjutant-General.*

Section 4693, Revised Statutes, sets forth substantially the status
necessary to be shown, in order that one may come within the benefits
of the pension laws, and it is very clear that if soldier has any pensionable service status it must be by reason of the third subdivision of
said section, which is as follows:

Any person, not an enlisted soldier in the Army, serving for the time being as a
member of the militia of any State, under orders of an officer of the United States,
or who volunteered for the time being to serve with any regularly organized mili-

tary or naval force of the United States, or who otherwise volunteered and rendered service in any engagement with rebels or Indians, disabled in consequence of wounds or injury received in the line of duty in such temporary service. But no claim of a State militiaman or nonenlisted person, on account of disability from wounds or injury received in battle with rebels or Indians, while temporarily rendering service, shall be valid unless prosecuted to a successful issue prior to the 4th day of July, 1874.

Claimant can not come under subdivision 1 of the said section, for he was not "an enlisted man * * * in the military or naval service of the United States," which is a sine qua non under said section. I am aware that if soldier had been a member of a military organization which was called into the United States service by the President of the United States, that his status might have been different, for the President had the right to call State militia into the United States service. (Houston r. Moore, 5 Wheat., 1.) However, the declaring of martial law in the State of Kansas, and the ordering of all males between the ages of 18 and 60 years into the militia service, by the major-general commanding the Department of Kansas, was not, neither was it equivalent to, the calling of such militia into the United States service by its President. (See the various sections of Title XVI, Revised Statutes, for the power and method of calling State militia in the United States service.)

It is, then, as hereinbefore stated, only under the third subdivision of section 4693 that claimant can establish a pensionable status, and it is seen at a glance that if he ever had one under that section his claim has lapsed. His is a claim of a State militiaman, was not prosecuted to a successful issue prior to July 4, 1874, and as such, by the express terms of the statute in question, is barred in any event from an affirmative action after that date. For this reason, independent of any other, your rejection of his claim was the only thing possible under the law.

The action appealed from is affirmed.

AID AND ATTENDANCE—DISABILITY.

FREDERICK P. GOIN.

Inasmuch as the preponderance of the evidence on file in this case warrants the presumption that the pensioner is so disabled by reason of his military service as to require the frequent and periodical, but not regular and constant, personal aid and attendance of another person, the action of reduction from the $72 rate to second grade, instead of to the rate prescribed by the act of July 14, 1892, was error, and is, in so far as the amount of the reduction is concerned, reversed; the decision of October 24, 1896, affirming the said action and departmental letter of July 23, 1897, overruling a motion for reconsideration of the said decision, are rescinded and set aside, and the papers in the case are remanded for readjudication and allowance of a rate commensurate with the degree of disability shown to exist and believed to be of service origin.

Assistant Secretary Webster Davis to the Commissioner of Pensions, July 30, 1898.

On January 14, 1898, Hon. C. B. Landis, M. C., Ninth Indiana District, filed at this Department a motion for reconsideration of departmental decision dated October 24, 1896, affirming the action of your Bureau of August 11, 1896, in the claim for restoration filed May 5, 1896, by Frederick P. Goin, Company I, Seventy-fifth Indiana Infantry (certificate numbered 138719).

The soldier is now pensioned at $30 per month (second grade) for varicose veins of left leg and thigh and resulting ulcer.

He was formerly pensioned at $6 per month from December 23, 1875, for varicose veins of left leg, which rate was subsequently increased to $8 per month from November 1, 1877; to $12 per month from August 7, 1878; to $18 per month from July 9, 1879, for varicose veins of left leg and thigh; to $24 per month from June 28, 1888, for varicose veins of left leg and thigh and resulting ulcer; to $30 per month from August 15, 1883; to $36 per month from August 4, 1886, for varicose veins of left leg and thigh and resulting ulcer, with total disability of leg; to $50 per month from January 28, 1890, and to $72 per month from March 4, 1890.

On March 25, 1896, there was a reissue to drop for total disability of leg and to correct rate.

The certificate issued on the said date was for the disability for which the soldier is now pensioned and at the rate now allowed therefor.

The said claim for restoration, filed May 5, 1896, as above stated, was, however, treated by your Bureau as a claim for increase and rejected as such, notwithstanding the facts that, although an increase blank was used in making the claim, the word "increase" on both the face and the back of the blank was erased with red ink and the word "restoration" substituted therefor; that it was explicitly stated in the said declaration that the claimant believed himself to be entitled to restoration; that in a separate affidavit, filed at the same time, the claimant stated that he had required the aid and attendance of another person for the past ten years and begged that his former rate of $72 per month be restored to him, and that he filed medical evidence with the said claim corroborative of his allegation as to the necessity for the aid and attention of another person.

To treat the said claim as a claim for straight increase, as was done in this case, was obviously error; but inasmuch as an increase was denied, it is evident that had the claim been properly treated as a claim for restoration, title thereto would also have been denied; therefore, in view of the facts that the said claim was treated as a claim for increase and rejected accordingly; that the said action was on appeal affirmed by this Department; that a motion to reconsider the said affirmation was overruled, and that another motion for reconsideration is now pending, it is deemed inexpedient, as well as unnecessary, to remand the papers in the case for readjudication in accordance with the intent of the said application, and the question at issue, viz, Is the pensioner entitled to restoration to the rate provided by the act of March 4, 1890, which rate was formerly allowed him, or should he be given the benefit of the provisions of the act of July 14, 1892, in lieu thereof, will be determined upon the facts now before us and as presented herein.

Another claim for restoration was filed April 20, 1897, in which it is alleged that the claimant requires the constant aid and attendance of another person both day and night, and that he has required the same amount of attention ever since his pension was reduced from $72 to $30 per month. The claimant also requests in the said application that, instead of being ordered before some local board, he be permitted to come to Washington and be examined by the office board.

It appears from an indorsement on the jacket, dated September 29, 1897, that the claimant was called upon to furnish evidence showing whether or not he was disabled in such a degree as to entitle him to either the $50 or the $72 rate. No evidence appears to have been furnished in response to the said call.

It is believed, however, that there is sufficient evidence, including the several certificates of medical examination now on file in the case, upon which the question at issue can be intelligently and satisfactorily determined.

The claimant was first medically examined on January 24, 1876, since which time he has submitted to ten different medical examinations in his various claims for increase and restoration, the last examination having been made June 10, 1896.

The condition of the claimant's left leg at the examination of January 24, 1876, as described in the certificate of that date, was as follows:

The internal saphenous vein throughout the whole course is enlarged; from the knee to the saphenous opening it is not less than one-half inch in diameter; in the popliteal space the varix or tumor is as large as a turkey's egg; the superficial plexus of veins on the legs, both posteriorly and anteriorly, is as large as a crow's quill; no discoloration or ulceration exists.

The same conditions are described in several succeeding certificates of examination, except that both the veins and the tumor are shown to have been gradually increasing in size up to July 11, 1883, on which date the claimant was examined by the board of surgeons at Indianapolis, Ind., when the following objective conditions were manifested:

Varicose condition of entire left saphenous vein from groin to foot.

The vein is about 1 inch in diameter. There is an immense conical varicose tumor just above left popliteal space that measures 20 inches around apex of tumor and leg, and around base of tumor next to leg it measures 13½ inches.

It will be observed that the size of the veins and the tumor have increased simultaneously, the latter having reached an enormous size, as is shown by the measurements above noted.

The pensioner was examined by a single surgeon at Tipton, Ind., January 28, 1890, who made a diagnosis of popliteal aneurism, but upon his certificate of the said examination being returned to him for a full statement of all the objective symptoms upon which he based his said diagnosis, he acknowledged that he may have erred in concluding that the tumor was an aneurism of the popliteal artery, as he had been unable by the use of the stethoscope to detect any "arterial bruit or sound indicating aneurism," and amended his certificate by substituting the word "varix" where he had previously written "aneurism."

The soldier was next examined on July 24, 1895, at Noblesville, Ind. A diagnosis of aneurism of the popliteal artery was also made at this examination, but the certificate of the same was not returned for any further information on the subject; instead of which a test examination under special instructions was ordered August 28, 1895. The said examination was made November 27, 1895, by the board of surgeons at Tipton, Ind., which board was instructed to determine the nature of tumor in popliteal space.

Relative to the matter of the said tumor the certificate of the said examination states as follows:

There is a tumor in popliteal space; size around leg just above knee cap, 23 inches; circumference of tumor from above downward, 14 inches. Tumor soft and pliable, is sacculated, some of its deeper tissues are hard and rough to palpation, and tender on pressure.

Tumor slightly cold; we find no aneurismal thrill or pulsation on palpation or auscultation.

The legs above and below the knee are symmetrical in size. The knee is held at an obtuse angle; can almost straighten it.

Diagnosis: Varicose aneurism of veins and not of popliteal artery. * * *

This applicant is totally disabled for the performance of manual labor, and requires the frequent and periodical aid, though not regular, of an attendant. Claimant can feed himself, but can not clothe himself.

Under the said application for restoration, filed May 5, 1896, and which was treated as a claim for increase, as heretofore stated, another medical examination, under special instructions, prepared under the direction of the medical referee, was held June 10, 1896, at Anderson, Ind.

The certificate of the said examination describes the condition of the tumor and varicose veins of the claimant's left leg. and states that the former is a result of the latter.

It is also stated in the said certificate that the—

Claimant is disabled in such a degree as to require the frequent and periodical, though not regular and constant, aid and attendance of another person in walking, dressing, dressing the affected limb, etc., on account of debility and the hindrance caused by the tumor.

The testimony of several physicians who at different periods have made physical examinations of the claimant has from time to time been filed in this case. The said physicians appear to be about equally divided upon the question as to whether the tumor on the soldier's left thigh is an aneurism of the popliteal artery, and of course not due to pensioned cause, or whether it is a varix, and therefore due to or part and parcel of the pensioned disability.

It is noted that at only two of the eleven medical examinations held in the course of the prosecution of this claim has a diagnosis of aneurism been made, and that in one instance the diagnosis was subsequently receded from and changed so as to agree with the other diagnoses made in the case. This change was made by reason of the fact, as explained by the examining surgeon, that no pathognomonic symptoms of aneurism had been manifested at his examination of the claimant, and therefore a positive diagnosis of the same was not in his opinion warranted, although he thought it possible that those making a different diagnosis were as likely to err as himself.

The action of reduction of rate in this case appears to have been based principally upon the report and recommendations of a special examiner of your Bureau under date of April 20, 1895, and upon the ex parte testimony submitted therewith.

The special examiner reports that while in the neighborhood of the appellant's home, engaged upon the investigation of another claim, and having occasion to call upon the appellant for the purpose of securing his testimony as a witness in the said claim, he found him in his back yard cutting potatoes preparatory to planting them; that the soldier walked without the use of a cane or crutch, and with only a perceptible limp, and that his hands were hard and calloused from manual labor.

The recommendations of the special examiner were to the effect that the pensioner be given thirty days' notice in accordance with the provisions of the act of December 21, 1893, with a view to the reduction of the rate in his claim from $72 to $30; and that a competent and reliable United States examining surgeon should be detailed to examine pensioner at his home without giving him an opportunity of discoloring his leg with acids.

It is not quite clear as to what results the special examiner considered could be accomplished by the soldier by discoloring his affected limb with acids, especially in so far as making a diagnosis of the nature and cause of the tumor thereon, and which contributes so much to the degree of disability under which he is now and has been for some years past laboring, was concerned.

The testimony adduced by the special examiner and submitted with his said report and recommendations consists of the depositions of James T. Quear and Jacob Wilburn, respectively, neighbors of the pensioner—one a blacksmith, the other a farmer—and the facts to which they testify consist of answers to queries propounded to them by the special examiner as to the nature of the disability for which the soldier is pensioned, his exact physical condition, and the degree of disability resulting therefrom.

One deponent states that the soldier "is getting a pension for an injury to his left leg, causing an abscess or something of that kind. He gets $72 per month." The other witness states:

He receives a pension of $72 per month for an injury and resulting disability of left leg. He has some kind of a blood ulcer or tumor of the left leg, which requires the wearing of an elastic bandage of some kind.

It will thus be seen that neither of the said deponents has any personal knowledge even of the name of the disability for which the soldier is pensioned, and as both deponents are laymen they should not have been considered as competent to testify as to the soldier's "exact physical condition," as they were required to do by the special examiner.

Their testimony as to whether or not, as a matter of fact, the pensioner actually performed any manual labor would of course be entitled to consideration, but their opinions as to the nature of his disabilities or the degree of disability caused thereby hardly warrants the weight which appears to have been given to it.

The statement of the special examiner that the appellant's "hands were hard and calloused from manual labor" is fully controverted by the findings of three different boards of examining surgeons before which he has appeared for examination since the date of the said statement—two in 1895 and one in 1896—each one of which found that he was not only wholly disabled for the performance of manual labor, but required the frequent and periodical aid and attendance of another person. Furthermore, the soldier is now pensioned at $30 per month (second grade) by reason of the fact that he is wholly incapacitated for the performance of manual labor.

On September 2, 1896, the chief of the western division of your Bureau referred the papers in the case to the medical referee—

For his personal consideration and opinion as to whether he approves action of rejection of increase, August 11, 1896. The said rejection appears to have been based upon report of special examiner, but the statements and evidence therein contained are not sustained by the report of medical examination of June 10, 1896, in the opinion of this division.

If claimant is unable to use his leg—and he seems to be totally disabled therein for all practical purposes—is he not entitled at least to the rating of $36 per month, under the act of August 4, 1886? But the amended medical certificate (July 30, 1896) seems to fully indicate that the soldier is entitled to $50 per month under act of July 14, 1892.

The medical referee replied on the same date as follows:

The action rejecting increase from second grade in this case, for varicose veins of left leg and thigh and resulting ulcer, is proper. The tumor on his thigh and the discharging sinus, which probably leads to diseased bone, are not results of the pensioned disability, and they alone cause any need for aid in dressing or walking.

Moreover, the report of the special examiner in 1895 showed that instead of having total disability of the left leg the claimant walked " with only a perceptible limp," and performed considerable manual labor.

It may be further noted that his present condition is partly due to sciatica and varicose veins of right leg, which are not pensioned.

It is observed that although the medical referee states that the tumor on the soldier's left thigh "is not a result of the pensioned disability," and that it alone "causes any necessity for aid in dressing and walking," he carefully refrains from expressing any opinion as to the nature and origin of the same.

As before stated herein, there is a difference of opinion among the medical men who have made personal examinations of the said tumor as to whether it is an aneurysm or a varix, with the preponderance of opinion, however, in favor of its being the latter; but it is worthy of note that although the said tumor has been examined by a large number of physicians during the past twenty-three years this case has been under consideration in all its different phases, not a single one of them has expressed an opinion that there was any probability that it was other than an aneurysm or a varix, notwithstanding the great variety of abnormal growths known to the medical profession.

While I am willing to admit that it has not been established beyond the peradventure of a doubt that the tumor on the pensioner's left thigh is either part and parcel of the disability for which he is pensioned or a pathological sequence thereof, I do not believe that we would be justified in arbitrarily overriding the expressed professional opinions of so many physicians, whose diagnoses have been based upon the objective conditions manifested in their presence, and whose abilities as diagnosticians we have no good reason to question.

Most of these physicians have examined the soldier in their capacity as United States examining surgeons, and it is but fair to presume that they were not only competent to perform their duties, but were also as solicitous of the interests of the Government as they were of those of the claimant, and that their said diagnoses have been honestly and intelligently rendered; otherwise it would seem to be futile to order a claimant before a board of surgeons for the purpose of obtaining a differential diagnosis of the nature of his disabilities.

As before stated herein, the medical referee, in his said advisory opinion of September 2, 1896, contented himself with the statement that the said tumor "is not a result of the pensioned disability," gave no reason why he did not consider it a result, and made no attempt to show what he thought it really was or to what it was due.

Therefore, in view of the facts that the weight of the evidence in the case is in favor of the contention of the appellant that the condition of his left leg is due entirely to the varicose veins, of service origin; that the evidence on file to the contrary is not sufficient to justify the views expressed by the medical referee in his said advisory opinion, and that in the absence of such positive and conclusive evidence of the exact nature of the said tumor, which constitutes so great a degree of disability, as can probably only be obtained post mortem, the pensioner should, in my judgment, be given the benefit of what reasonable doubt may exist in this case, and be allowed a rate commensurate with the degree of disability which may properly be considered as due to his military service.

In this connection I deem it proper to state that while the contention of the appellant, and of his attorney and friends, that he requires the regular aid and attendance of another person—in fact, "has to be waited on as though he was a child"—may be true, I do not consider that the necessity for so much aid and attendance is due entirely to the pensioned cause or any results thereof, but I do consider that the amount of aid and attendance of another person made necessary by the degree of disability properly chargeable to his military service is such " frequent and periodical personal aid and attendance of another person" as is contemplated by the provisions of the act of July 14, 1892, and as warranting allowance of the rate prescribed herein.

In view of the further fact that the said degree of disability existed at the date the rate was reduced from $72 to $30 per month, the said action of reduction to second grade, instead of to the rate prescribed by the act of July 14, 1892, was, in my judgment, error, and the same is, in so far as the amount of reduction in the rate is concerned, reversed; the decision of October 24, 1896, affirming the said action, and departmental letter of July 23, 1897, overruling a motion for reconsideration of the said decision, are rescinded and set aside; the pending motion for reconsideration is sustained, and the papers in the case are herewith remanded for restoration from the date of reduction, at the rate of $50 per month.

RESTORATION-RATE.

JOSEPH C. KING.

Where the degree of disability shown at time of original allowance did not warrant the rate of pension named in the original certificate, and pensioner's name was dropped from the rolls by reason of his failure to claim the same for three years, upon application for restoration pension may be restored at a less rate than that originally allowed.

Assistant Secretary Webster Davis to the Commissioner of Pensions, August 6, 1898.

The appellant, Joseph C. King, late of Company B, Third New Jersey Infantry, was in the military service of the United States from May 25, 1861, to October 6, 1862, and filed a claim for pension on the 27th of August, 1868, alleging that during said service he contracted epilepsy. The claim was adjudicated in June, 1869, and a certificate issued for a pension on account of epilepsy at the rate of $5 per month, commencing May 25, 1869. It appears that the certificate never reached the appellant, and that no payment of pension thereunder has ever been made. In August, 1891, he applied for pension under the act of June 27, 1890, and then learned, for the first time, that he had been granted a pension under the old law, and that his name had been dropped from the rolls by reason of his failure to claim the same for three years.

The claim under the act of June 27, 1890, was rejected on the ground that he had not a ratable disability under said act. He then applied for restoration and payment of the pension under the old law, and on February 1, 1894, your Bureau issued to him a new certificate for pension on account of epilepsy and resulting disease of the nervous system, at the rate of $2 per month from the date of his discharge to October 19, 1892, and $8 per month thereafter. He protested against that action, contending that he was entitled to receive the rate named in his original certificate ($5 per month) from the date of his discharge to October 19, 1892. Your Bureau having declined to allow that rate, he. on January 11, 1898, filed an appeal.

The consideration of this appeal involves two questions:

1. Has the appellant a legal right, by virtue of the certificate issued to him in 1869, to demand and receive the rate of $5 per month during the period between October 6, 1862, and October 19, 1892, or during any portion of said period?

2. Is he, upon the evidence in the case, entitled to a higher rate than $2 per month during the period stated or during any portion thereof?

As the certificate issued in 1869 never came into the possession of the appellant and no payment of pension thereunder was ever made, he did not become, in fact, a pensioner. True, a judgment granting him pension was rendered by the Pension Bureau, but such a judgment was not final and conferred no vested right. As was said by Judge Cox in the case of Long *v.* Commissioner of Pensions (Sup. Ct. D. C., Feb. 28, 1894):

> No title passes by the admission of an applicant to the pension roll, as in case of a patent to land, which can not be recalled. It is the duty of the officers of the Government to see that its bounty is not abused. It is the duty of the Commissioner, on a proper application, to decide what share of that bounty the law intends to bestow on the applicant. Whatever is paid to him under that decision is gone beyond recall. But if a succeeding Commissioner should be satisfied that the pensioner was wrongfully rated, why should not he correct the error as to future payments? The pensioner has no contract rights to future payments; he has no vested right in an erroneous construction of law.

A similar view was taken by the Court of Claims in the case of Harrison *r.* United States (20 C. Cls. R., 122), which was a suit to recover a pension which had once been allowed, but discontinued because its allowance had been obtained through fraud. After referring to the statutes, the court says:

> Aside from these statutes, the power of revision, as the Government counsel have argued, may well be considered to be inherent in the nature of the first decision, as well as in the necessities of the Bureau. The pension is a gratuity. It involves no claim of right, no agreement of parties, and, as it is not assignable, no acquired rights of third parties. The law describes a class of persons upon whom it chooses to bestow its bounty. The Secretary and the Commissioner are directed to find out and make a list of the persons thus described. The proceedings and evidence are

largely ex parte. From the vast number of applicants the work must be performed and the roll made up for the most part by the clerks. If placing the name of an applicant upon the roll is to be considered a judicial act, should it not be considered a judgment nisi?

On the appeal of Alger J. Baldwin, whose name had been dropped from the pension roll for the reason that he had not claimed pension for three years, and whose application for restoration had been rejected by the Pension Bureau, Acting Secretary Cowen held:

> It is undoubtedly proper that, in the examination of claims for renewal or restoration of pension, the same scrutiny that is exercised in the examination of original claims for pension should be employed. In this case it appears that a reexamination of the evidence upon which the pension was originally granted develops the fact that the disability on account of which he was pensioned was not "incident to the service," and therefore that the claim was improperly allowed in the first instance. (1 P. D., O. S., 117.)

The action of the Bureau was accordingly affirmed.

The Treatise on the Practice of the Pension Bureau, compiled by order of the Commissioner of Pensions under the authority of the Secretary of the Interior, and approved by the latter April 9, 1898, states on page 45, section 3, as follows:

> In reviewing claims for restoration the same scrutiny is required as in original ones; and if for any reason it is found that the claim was improperly allowed in the first instance it should be specially examined or rejected, as the evidence in the case may indicate. The Bureau having the right to reject claims for restoration by reason of the original claims being improperly allowed, it must necessarily follow that the original action can be modified in accordance with the facts; therefore a claim may be restored at a less rate than that for which it was originally allowed.

In view of the foregoing, I am clearly of the opinion that the appellant is not entitled to restoration to the pension roll at the rate named in the original certificate as a matter of legal right.

Is he entitled, as a matter of justice, upon the evidence?

He was discharged from service because of epilepsy; origin not stated. A surgeon who examined him on October 10, 1868, reported:

> From all the facts gathered, the feebleness of intellect in loss of memory, the wild, empty, staring look in this applicant, no doubt of some diseased action going on in the brain. What it may terminate in, time only will tell. * * * In my opinion the said Jos. C. King is two-thirds incapacitated for obtaining his subsistence by manual labor from the cause above stated.

Another surgeon who examined him on May 31, 1869, reported as follows:

> Applicant states that symptoms of epilepsy first showed themselves while he was in camp, near Alexandria, Va., about June, 1862; that he does not recollect ever to have had anything of the kind during his life; that the attacks come on now about once a month, which is oftener than when in the service. He is unable to assign any reason for them, nor does a careful examination reveal any probable cause for them. He says they last generally about twenty minutes. He is 30 years of age; appears healthy. * * * In my opinion the said Joseph C. King is one-fourth incapacitated for obtaining his subsistence by manual labor.

When last examined, on October 29, 1892, he was suffering from nervous prostration; was thin and anæmic, with pale skin and flabby muscles; had muscular tremors, slight twitching of the facial muscles, and feeble heart action. The board rated his disability at eight-eighteenths. He stated that he had not fallen in a fit for ten years.

In view of his general appearance, and statement to the examining surgeon on May 31, 1869, the rate allowed in the certificate issued June 18, 1869, must be deemed excessive. I think the action of your Bureau in reducing it on reissue to $2 per month was correct. He was then having only one fit a month on an average, lasting only twenty minutes. This was more frequent, he said, than they were in the army. There is no evidence that they were more frequent or more severe at any time between the date of his discharge and the date of his examination in May, 1869. They had not affected his general appearance of healthfulness. There is no evidence upon which to base an increase of rate after 1869 until the examination in October, 1892. The fact that he made no effort to obtain pension during that period, prior to 1891, indicates that he was not very seriously incapacitated for earning a support. After careful consideration of all the evidence, I am inclined to think that he has received substantial justice under the law in the matter of rating, and must, therefore, decline to disturb the action of the Pension Bureau.

LINE OF DUTY—ACCIDENTAL WOUND.

JAMES E. HARRISON.

Soldier, by permission of his superior officer, was engaged in hunting with a gun for his own pleasure and amusement, and while so engaged received the injury alleged as a basis for pension, by the careless and negligent handling of his gun. *Held*, that he was not in line of duty.

Assistant Secretary Webster Davis to the Commissioner of Pensions, August 6, 1898.

On August 26, 1897, claimant filed a motion for reconsideration of departmental decision of December 22, 1893, in the case of James E. Harrison (7 P. D., 97).

Soldier was pensioned from August 19, 1869, under the general law for gunshot wound of left forearm and hand, and on April 19, 1877, was dropped from the roll on the ground that the disability for which he was pensioned was not incurred in line of duty. Assistant Secretary Bussey, in a decision rendered July 29, 1892, sustained an application for restoration to the pension roll, holding that the alleged disability was incurred in line of duty.

The Department, acting upon information conveyed in a communication from your office dated November 11, 1893, rendered the decision now under consideration, in which it is held that claimant has no pensionable status, for the reason that the injury alleged as a basis for pension was not incurred in line of duty. By virtue of this decision soldier was again dropped from the roll.

The contention presented in the motion is, that the injury alleged as a basis for pension was incurred in line of duty.

The facts in the case are few and without complication. The original declaration alleges that the wound of claimant was received about the 12th day of May, 1863. At this time the command to which claimant belonged was doing garrison duty at Centerville, Mo. Claimant at that time, with three others, was detailed to cook for the squad, and was excused from all guard or picket duty, or duty of any other character than that of cooking. On the day on which claimant received the wound he took his gun after serving dinner and went from the court-house yard, where the command was encamped, about 400 yards across an open piece of ground to a ravine containing water. He was alone, and the water being clear he concluded to get a drink, and placing the palm of his hand over the muzzle of his gun he attempted to lay it on the ground, when the hammer struck a stone and the gun was discharged, causing the alleged injury.

At the time of being thus injured he was not on duty, or acting in pursuance of orders from his superior officers, but was acting on his own volition. These are the circumstances under which claimant received the injury as detailed by himself before a special examiner. He further stated that the command was an outpost, and the orders were to keep arms about themselves.

Capt. Benjamin S. Jones, the officer in command, testifies in part as follows:

Claimant was along with us on this trip. He was detailed to cook for the whole squad. He did not do any picket or scout duty. There was no order for the men to carry their guns in camp or town. There were deer in that part of the country, and several of the men had permission from me to hunt. I remember particularly the blacksmith, F. Cowels, had such permission. I think I gave Harrison permission to go out and hunt on the evening he received the wound in his hand. I am positive that claimant was not doing any duty, guarding or picket duty, as he did not do anything of that kind. I know it was permission to hunt and nothing else. There was no necessity for anyone to hunt, as we had sufficient rations without it, and the blacksmith had to look out for the shoeing of the horses and the claimant only to cook, and the hunting was done only in their leisure time, to pass away the time and for their pleasure.

The claimant was outside the camp, under permission of his captain, engaged in hunting with a gun, which was accidentally discharged, causing the injury alleged as a basis for pension. The only question in the case is this: Was he then in line of duty as contemplated by the law?

The distinguishing feature of this case consists in the careless and negligent manner of the claimant at the time of the accident in placing his hand upon the muzzle of the loaded gun while laying it upon the ground. In this material respect this case is unlike that of Margaret Hoffman (9 P. D., 227), in which the soldier, while out on a pass, engaged in hunting, was killed by the accidental discharge of a gun. The proper medical officer recorded the death of soldier as having occurred in line of duty, for the reason that an examination of the facts and circumstances surrounding the fatal occurrence did not show any "willful neglect or immoral conduct."

There is a similar distinction between the case at bar and that of Henry A. Helmer (L. B., 286, p. 11), in which the claimant was injured by being thrown from a horse he was riding, in company with and at the request of one of his commanding officers, over the battlefield of Pea Ridge, Ark., looking after the dead and wounded of their command. In the Helmer case it was held:

He went over said battlefield with and at the request of his superior officer, when all were permitted and encouraged to go, and as the injury was not the result of his own misconduct, the records of the War Department, stating that he was in the line of duty at the time he was injured, will be accepted.

In the case of Henry Newman (8 P. D., 532) the Department announced the principle that an injury received by a soldier while engaged in playing a game of baseball may create a pensionable status, since the War Department encourages athletic sports, and an enlisted man, while engaged in such sport, in camp or garrison, is regarded as being in line of duty. The element of misconduct or negligence is not involved in the Newman case.

In the case of Diana B. Groff (8 P. D., 91) it is held:

Disability or death from a contributory or secondary cause, which could have been avoided by the exercise of ordinary care and discretion, does not confer the right to pension.

The claimant in this case, while in possession of a loaded gun, placed his hand upon the muzzle thereof and put it down upon a rock, thereby causing the injury which he received. This was not the conduct of a prudent man, and the consequence of such negligence might have been avoided by the exercise of the slightest care and prudence. It is therefore held that claimant at the time he received the injury was not in line of duty.

For the reasons above mentioned, the departmental opinion is adhered to and the motion overruled.

RATES—PRACTICE.

NIXON REES.

Where the basis of a claim under the act of June 27, 1890, is the loss of sight of one eye, which disabling cause is shown to have existed at the date of filing the declaration, and the claim was rejected under the prevailing practice on the ground that such condition did not constitute a ratable disability under said act, the subsequent adoption of the rule which allows a rate for such disability operates to vacate the former adverse action and to allow the claim.

Assistant Secretary Webster Davis to the Commissioner of Pensions, August 8, 1898.

The papers in this case were returned from the Bureau July 15, 1898, with the suggestion that the motion be further considered with a view to reopen the case, inasmuch as the loss of sight of one eye, which is shown in this case, is under present practice ratable in claims under the act of June 27, 1890. The report of the medical referee of February 25, 1898, in this case, to which you invite my attention, is as follows:

This appellant, on August 17, 1892, filed a claim under the act of June 27, 1890, which was rejected February 11, 1895.

He filed another claim April 5, 1895, which was also rejected, June 22, 1896, on the ground of no ratable degree of disability under said act.

On July 20, 1896, he appealed from these adverse actions. The Department, in a decision rendered October 24, 1896, affirmed the rejections. A motion for a reconsideration of departmental action was filed March 8, 1897, which was overruled April 10, 1897.

A second motion for reconsideration was received September 16, 1897, and the case is returned by the Department "for a report of the medical referee, and his opinion whether, from a medical standpoint, claimant was shown to be ratably disabled under the act of June 27, 1890. He will also please state whether the claimants under said act are now being rated as pensionably disabled on account of loss of sight of one eye and, if so, the reason and authority for such rating."

In the opinion of the medical referee, dated September 15, 1896, and attached to face brief, it was held that the rejections of claims under the act of June 27, 1890, were proper for the reason that there was no objective evidence that the soldier suffered with rheumatism as alleged, and that the rates recommended by the examining surgeons were not warranted. This opinion still obtains so far as rheumatism is concerned.

The certificates of examination in the case show that the soldier has lost the sight of his right eye. At the dates of the rejection and the affirmation thereof by the Department it was held that the loss of sight of an eye did not constitute a degree of disability under the act of June 27, 1890, which would warrant a rate.

On May 3, 1897, I instructed the medical examiners that hereafter the loss of sight of one eye should be rated under the act of June 27, 1890, at $6 per month. These instructions were based upon my knowledge that, as a matter of fact, the loss of sight of an eye does materially abridge a man's ability to earn a support by manual labor, and, in a degree, warranting the minimum rate under said act.

In accordance with this view, this appellant is entitled to a rate as indicated.

In view of the present practice, as announced on page 97, of Practice of the Pension Bureau, paragraph 13, approved April 9, 1898, the departmental decision of April 16, 1898, overruling the motion for reconsideration of departmental decision of October 24, 1896, affirming the Bureau action of June 22, 1896, rejecting claim No. 1126208, filed April 5, 1895, under section 2 of the act of June 27, 1890, on the ground that no ratable disability was shown, is hereby recalled and rescinded.

The motion for reconsideration is sustained, and the case is reopened and remanded for further adjudication in harmony with the present practice.

NONRESIDENTS—ADJUDICATION.

HENRY McFADGER.

The lawmaking power has made no distinction between applicants for pension by reason of their place of residence since the war, and there should be none in the execution of the law; and all orders or instructions which, in effect, suspend or prevent a prompt and impartial adjudication of claims filed by nonresidents are revoked, and there shall be no distinction between claims filed by those who reside in this country and those who reside in foreign countries.

Assistant Secretary Webster Davis to the Commissioner of Pensions, August 12, 1898.

On the 2d ultimo an appeal, filed by Taber and Whitman Company, from the practice in your Bureau denying to applicants for pension, and for increase of pension, residing without the United States, an order for their medical examination, and thus suspending indefinitely adjudication in such claims, was referred to you for report showing under what authority of law, or order of record, your Bureau was thus operating.

Appellants referred to the case of Henry McFadger, No. 42179, in which order for medical examination was withheld, and also to another claim in which they are the recognized attorneys, wherein action was suspended by authority of a chief of division of your Bureau, as follows:

By order of the Commissioner of Pensions, dated November 23, 1897, all claims referred to the medical referee for medical examination of claimants residing in foreign countries will be returned to the files of the adjudicating divisions without issuing orders for such examination, there to remain until further orders.

In response I have your report of the 6th instant, in which you devote considerable space to the conditions of the McFadger case, which are not under consideration only so far as such conditions may justify the delay in adjudication.

Your report pertinent to the question at issue is as follows:

Congress saw the excesses and the abuses, to some, extent in our pensioning those living abroad, who could not be found in this country, and accordingly took a most radical step by stopping payment for a time of all those pensioned under the law of 1890.

The attorneys point out to you how the way is open for your Commissioner to enlarge the pension business abroad, but they don't mention that the law is not mandatory. I have no satisfactory means at my command to identify a claimant with the service when he lives outside the jurisdiction of the United States.

I have issued no orders on this subject, but I did instruct the medical referee last November to return some foreign cases in his division to the files until I was ready to consider them. This matter has been the subject of discussion here in the Bureau among my most competent men and advisers, and I have had it carefully examined, too, from a legal standpoint, and I am convinced that my jurisdiction is limited to the United States, although the gentlemen cite you, or intimate, what was done in the past.

I am clearly of the opinion that so long as we have over 600,000 claims pending in this Bureau, claims of Americans, that live in America, that pay taxes in America, that fought to save America, and would do so again if necessary—I say I am clearly of the opinion that if there should be any preference given it should be given to Americans first, and not to men who have been disabled years after they rendered a a few months' service at their choice; and, as I said, I can not find any law that is mandatory on this subject to compel me to allow a case that is up on prima facie, ex parte, without examining the merits, to protect this Government.

It is presumed that no claim is allowed "without examining the merits, to protect this Government." The vital question at issue is whether there is authority vested in the Commissioner of Pensions to discriminate against a class of pensioners, or applicants for pension, because they reside without the limits of the United States; and, in doing so, is the spirit and letter of the law properly executed?

In a recent article for publication, you stated as follows:

Although so widely scattered. the pensioners who reside abroad are not numerous. There are something like four thousand in all, one-half of them in Canada.

These are already pensioners, some of whom have been placed on the roll under former Administrations, and include those who were pensioned before and after their departure to a foreign country. Many of these, doubtless, under former practice, have had their pensions increased while abroad; and their right to an adjudication of a claim for original, or au increase claim, has not hitherto been questioned. To do otherwise would, in effect, deny to a claimant a statutory right definitely conferred.

A temporary or permanent residence in a foreign country does not work a forfeiture of the rights of a soldier or sailor of the late war, under the pension laws. On the contrary, Congress has, from time to time, made provisions for granting nonresidents a pension, in the nature of special legislation in their behalf.

Section 21 of the act of Congress approved March 3, 1873, provides that declarations of claimants residing in foreign countries may be executed before a United States minister or consul, or before some officer of the country duly authorized to administer oaths for general purposes, and whose official character and signature shall be duly authenticated by the certificate of a United States minister or consul.

Also, in the act of July 25, 1882, provision was made for the medical examination of claimants residing in foreign countries, as follows:

The fee for the examination of claimants who reside out of the United States shall not exceed ten dollars, which shall be paid, upon the presentation of satisfactory vouchers, out of the appropriation for the payment of the examining surgeons. and through the United States consulate nearest to the claimant's place of residence.

It is true that in the act of Congress approved March 1, 1893, it was provided that—

From and after July 1, 1893, no pension shall be paid to a nonresident, who is not a citizen of the United States, except for actual disabilities incurred in the service.

This provision of law doubtless had reference to claims of nonresidents under the act of June 27, 1890, but even this was subsequently repealed in the act approved March 2, 1895. It is evident the pension laws apply with equal force to domestic and foreign applicants, with the distinction that additional regulations have been found necessary in the prosecution of claims of those who reside abroad.

Why this legislation on behalf of foreign claimants, except for the purpose of recognizing their just rights under the general pension system and providing a way for the prosecution of their claims?

To hold that an adjudication of such claims is not mandatory is to hold that any of the pension laws may be executed at the will of the administrative power, or that certain claimants may be granted their statutory rights and from another class such rights may be withheld.

You state—

I am convinced that my jurisdiction is limited to the United States. * * * Can not identify claimants, etc.

If the law be properly executed your jurisdiction will not be extended beyond the limits of the United States; and as you accept the identity of pensioners abroad upon the receipt of every payment of pension, I see no reason why the method adopted by your predecessors in identifying claimants should not be continued, with proper safeguards.

At least, the rights under the law of claimants residing in foreign countries should not be abridged, and every opportunity should be freely given to them to establish their claims without discrimination.

Some of these claimants are native-born American citizens, temporarily, perhaps, residing abroad; others, although of foreign birth, took the oath of allegiance to the United States Government and rendered valiant service in the Army or Navy.

The lawmaking power has made no distinction by reason of their place of residence since the war, and there should be none in the execution of the law.

For these reasons I deem it proper to direct that all orders or instructions which, in effect, suspend or prevent a prompt adjudication of claims filed by nonresidents shall be revoked, and that in this respect there shall be no distinction between claims filed by those who reside in this country and those who reside in foreign countries.

DEATH CAUSE—POISONING.

LAURA HALL, NOW GREGG (WIDOW).

Soldier's death from an overdose of opium, which he was in the habit of taking as a remedy for diarrhea contracted in the service, but which was probably accidental and not intentional, could not be considered to have been in any way a result of the disease or otherwise connected with his military service

Assistant Secretary Webster Davis to the Commissioner of Pensions, August 13, 1898.

In the claim for pension of Laura Hall, now Gregg, as widow of James Ladson Hall, late second lieutenant Company C, Ninety-ninth

Pennsylvania Infantry, a motion has been entered July 21, 1898, for the reconsideration of my decision of April 14, 1898, sustaining your rejection of said claim on the ground that soldier's death from opium poisoning was not the result of chronic diarrhea contracted by him in the service, nor otherwise connected with said service. The basis of that decision was that, although the soldier suffered from attacks of diarrhea, the only effective remedy for which was opium taken in some form, yet his death was not due to the disease, but to carelessness or mistake in the use of the remedy, and under the law it could not be regarded as the result of disability contracted in the service.

The contention of this motion is that soldier being accustomed to take laudanum to allay the pain caused by the attacks of diarrhea, he usually kept a vial of it near him, and the fact that he accidentally took an overdose of the drug, which resulted in his death, should not be attributed to carelessness or contributory negligence, but should be considered to have been unavoidable, and his death the result in effect of the disease contracted in service; that is, if it had not been for the existence of said disease the fatal dose would not have been taken. There is then cited the ruling in a decision by Assistant Secretary Hawkins in the case of the widow of Francis O. Miller (2 P. D., 214), to the effect that—

The relation of cause and effect must exist in the sense that the cause, i. e., wound, injury, or disease received or contracted in the service, must be the thing or condition without which the result, i. e., death, would not have occurred.

The material facts in this case were recited in the decision complained of, but may be again briefly summarized for the purpose of placing the exact circumstances of soldier's death clearly before the mind. During his service, in 1862–63, the soldier contracted chronic diarrhea and continued to suffer from it to the time of his death. The attacks of the disease were severe, and on the prescription of a physician he began using opium, usually in the form of laudanum, as the only remedy that would effectually relieve the pain. He kept a tobacco store in Philadelphia, Pa., and usually had a small bottle of the drug on his desk, to be used whenever the attacks of the disease came on or he had unusual distress in his stomach. About September 11, 1870, he complained of being ill and asked his clerk to get a carriage to take him to Woodbury, N. J., about 10 miles from Philadelphia, and where his wife was staying. During this trip it is supposed the soldier took the overdose of opium. On his arrival at his destination he told his wife not to let him go to sleep, and he seemed very ill. A physician was called, when it was discovered that he was suffering from narcotic poisoning, from which he died in three hours. It is not definitely shown just when the overdose of the drug was taken, that is, whether early in the journey or just before arrival at Woodbury, and it is not shown whether it was taken with suicidal intent or by accident, but it was presumed to be a mistake, because he had been in the habit of taking the remedy at such times as he wished or believed he needed it.

In the former decision it was stated that it was not important to determine whether the dose of the narcotic which caused death was taken intentionally or by mistake. The main point was that death was not caused by the disease contracted in service, but by some fault, carelessness, or mistake in the use of the remedy for that disease. Therefore the soldier's death could not be considered in any way connected with his military service. And this position seems altogether correct, while the contention that if the disease had not existed the fatal dose would not have been taken is by no means tenable. It may be perfectly legitimate to use any remedy prescribed by a reputable physician for a disease, but because so prescribed once, and because found effectual as prescribed, is no reason why carelessness or negligence or mistake from any cause in its use should make the taking of an overdose have the relation of cause and effect with the disease which it was designed to relieve. It would seem that the very nature of the remedy in this case, its deadly effects when taken in too large quantities, of which the soldier must have known, would have called for the exercise of all the more caution. It does not seem at all admissible to recognize such a connection between the cause of death and the military service as is here sought to be upheld.

Nor does the citation of the ruling in a former decision, as before quoted, help the case. That ruling contemplates that the wound, injury, or disease received or contracted in the service should be a direct contributing and predominating factor in the cause of death, and without which death would not have occurred. This can not be said to be true, in any sense, in the case of this soldier. It is nowhere stated or proven that he was ever in any precarious state or danger of dying from his attacks of diarrhea. All that is shown is that these were severe at times, and caused him considerable pain, which was relieved by the remedy he used. Said ruling could not have had reference to the relational effects of the misuse of a drug with the military service.

Other rulings, having a more direct bearing on this claim under consideration, will give a clearer understanding of the intendment of the law and the position of the Department in cases involving like facts. Some of these rulings are here quoted:

Where the soldier's death was caused by an overdose of morphine administered by himself upon his own responsibility but with no suicidal intent: *Held,* No basis for widow's claim. (Alice E. Travers, 1 P. D., 110.)

Death must be shown to have been the natural, direct, or proximate result of disease contracted in the service; and where death resulted from an overdose of laudanum, taken through mistake or carelessness, the death cause is too remote from the soldier's pensionable cause of diarrhea to be accepted. (Mother of John G. Stack, 2 P. D., 153.)

Soldier's death (after discharge) from poisoning in consequence of a mistake made by the physician who was treating him for a disease claimed to have been contracted in the service, or by the druggist in putting up the medicine, can not be accepted as being so directly connected with his military service as to warrant the allowance of

pension to his widow under section 4702, Revised Statutes. (Ellen Flynn. widow,
8 P. D., 54.)

Death resulting from the morphine habit, though contracted by using the drug to
relieve pain caused by a malady contracted in the service and in line of duty, not on
the advice of a physician but on soldier's own responsibility, can not be accepted as
due to the service in the line of duty. (Jessie M. Whallau, widow, 8 P. D., 131.)

Under these rulings and upon the facts as they appear in the evidence in this case the former decision upholding the rejection of the
claim was correct, and this motion is accordingly overruled.

· DESERTION—RESTORATION.

DANIEL McGRAW.

This appellant was pensioned for disability incurred during his first term of service,
from which he was honorably discharged May 24, 1862, from that date. He
was subsequently drafted and served until April 8, 1864, when he deserted.

Held, That he is entitled to restoration of his pension, deducting pension for the
whole period during which he could have been legally held to service under
the draft. (John Norton, 9 P. D., 382.)

Assistant Secretary Webster Davis to the Commissioner of Pensions.
August 13, 1898.

Daniel McGraw, late private, Company F, Eighty-sixth New York
Volunteer Infantry, and Company K, Seventy-sixth New York Volunteer Infantry, was formerly pensioned under the provisions of sections
4692 and 4693, Revised Statutes, from May 24, 1862, for disease of
heart, and was last in receipt of a rating of $24 per month.

On October 30, 1895, he was, after due and legal notice, dropped from
the rolls upon the ground that he was a deserter from his last term of
service during the war of the rebellion.

From said action appeal was taken on August 4, 1897.

The official military record in the War Department of this appellant's
army service shows that he first enlisted on October 16, 1861, in Company F, Eighty-sixth New York Volunteer Infantry, and served therein
until May 24, 1862, when he was discharged upon a surgeon's certificate
of disability, because of "chronic pericarditis." He was drafted on
July 13, 1863, and assigned to Company K, Seventy-sixth New York
Volunteer Infantry, and served in the latter organization until April 8,
1864, when he deserted.   He was never returned to his command, and
was never discharged from his last term of service, being borne on the
muster-out roll of said company as a deserter at large.   The War
Department reported on August 22, 1895, as follows:

The charge of desertion can not be removed upon the data now before this
Department. ·

The action dropping this appellant from the rolls was based upon the
facts shown by the foregoing official record relative to the second term

of service of appellant during the war of the rebellion and his desertion therefrom, and was in accord with the ruling of this Department in the case of George Lessor (8 P. D., 114), wherein it was held that a claimant against whom there stands a charge of desertion under an enlistment for service in the war of the rebellion, which charge the War Department declines to remove, has no title to pension under any existing law.

Since said action was taken, however, the rather arbitrary and sweeping decision and ruling in the Lessor case has been very materially modified and changed by me in a recent decision, rendered June 21, 1898, in the case of John Norton (9 P. D., 382), wherein, among other things, I held that—

If a claim for invalid pension under sections 4692 and 4693, Revised Statutes, is based upon disability incurred in line of duty during a term of enlistment from which the claimant was legally discharged, a desertion from a subsequent enlistment of itself is not a bar to pension. If the claim was filed prior to July 1, 1880, the pension would commence from the date of discharge from the term of enlistment during which the disability was incurred, but such pension will cease upon reenlistment and can not be restored while claimant is in the service, nor while in desertion from such subsequent enlistment.

This appellant was pensioned for a disability contracted during his first term of enlistment, and on account of which he was legally and honorably discharged from said term of enlistment upon a surgeon's certificate of disability. Consequently, under the foregoing decision and ruling in the Norton case, which distinctly and in terms overrules and sets aside the decision in the Lessor case, where it conflicts therewith, his desertion from his second term of service would not bar his title to said pension, except during the period covered by his second term of service, which, in this instance, would be the period during which he could have been legally held to service under the draft.

I also held in said decision in the case of Norton, following the opinion of Attorney-General Taft (15 Op., 157), that a soldier could not be considered as in desertion from a term of enlistment for military service beyond the date when such term of enlistment would expire, the contract of enlistment and the offense of desertion being deemed to terminate at the same time.

It is clear, therefore, that this appellant could not be held to be in desertion from his second term of service after the date when he would have been entitled to his discharge by reason of the legal expiration of said term of service, and that he would be entitled under the above cited ruling, to restoration of his pension from and after that date.

The action of your Bureau dropping this appellant from the rolls under the decision in the case of Lessor (supra) is, therefore, hereby reversed and set aside, and you are requested to restore him to the rolls, and cause his pension to be paid him from date of dropping, first deducting the whole amount of pension he received for the period covered by his second term of service, which is the period during which he could have been legally held to military service under the draft.

PATHOLOGICAL SEQUENCE—PRACTICE.

THADDEUS P. REIG.

The soldier is now pensioned at $16 per month for "rheumatism and resulting disease of heart, and total deafness of left ear."

He claimed increase on the ground that the rheumatism had affected his spinal column.

On examination he was shown to be suffering from locomotor ataxia. The claim for increase was rejected on the ground that disease of the spinal cord could not result from rheumatism.

From this action the claimant appeals, contending—

First. That he has established by competent evidence that the locomotor ataxia did result from the rheumatism for which he is pensioned.

Second. That the symptoms upon which the claim for rheumatism were both based and established were but the earlier manifestations of the cord lesion, and that the name of the pensioned disability should be changed by substituting locomotor ataxia for rheumatism.

Third. That he is suffering from both rheumatism and locomotor ataxia; that both disabilities are of service origin, and that the evidence upon which his claim on account of the former disability was established should be accepted as also showing the service origin of the latter.

Held, first. That although it is almost universally conceded by the medical profession that rheumatism and locomotor ataxia have one or more etiological factors in common, and also, in the preataxic stage of the latter disease, certain similar subjective symptoms, they are, nevertheless, universally considered by all recognized medical authorities as entirely separate and distinct diseases, with no similarity whatever in their pathological anatomy, and are not regarded by the most modern observers as having any casual relation to each other, either pathological or otherwise.

Second. That inasmuch as both rheumatism and tabes dorsalis are shown to exist, the contention that the latter was mistaken for the former is untenable.

Third. That in view of the fact that the Department does not take primary action in any claim for pension, the contention that the evidence on file also establishes the service origin of locomotor ataxia can not be considered until the merits of the claim shall first have been passed upon by the Bureau of Pensions.

Assistant Secretary Webster Davis to the Commissioner of Pensions, August 13, 1898.

On the 29th of July, 1890, the appellant in this case, Thaddeus P. Reig, Company G, Two hundred and eleventh Pennsylvania Infantry, filed an application for pension under the general law on account of "chronic rheumatism, neuralgia in head, and deafness of left ear."

On June 13, 1891, the certificate of his present pension of $16 per month on account of rheumatism and resulting disease of heart and total deafness of left ear was issued.

January 30, 1895, the soldier filed an application for increase on account of pensioned causes and alleged partial deafness of right ear, resulting from total deafness of left ear, and bronchitis, resulting from disease of heart, and stated that he required the frequent and periodical aid and attention of another person.

This claim was rejected December 16, 1895, on the ground that the disability due to pensioned causes had not increased, and that no special results of said causes had been shown to exist.

Another application for increase was filed April 20, 1897, in which the claimant alleges:

That he is informed and believes that the rheumatism has affected the spinal column and the muscles of his back; that he is incapacitated for all kinds of manual labor.

A medical examination was held under the said application, at Warren, Pa., on June 9, 1897, at which examination not only rheumatism, but a well-marked case of locomotor ataxia, was manifested.

In regard to the origin of the locomotor ataxia, the said board concluded that in the absence of any syphilitic history or dyscrasia the tabes was probably due to the long-continued and frequently acute rheumatic affection, and cited certain medical authors in support of that view of the case.

In an affidavit filed July 1, 1897, Dr. Willis M. Baker, of Warren, Pa., states, in part, as follows:

This is to certify that I have examined Mr. T. P. Reig many times during the past ten years. * * *

I am fully convinced that the muscular pains from which he has suffered for so long a time have been largely due to the disease of his spinal cord, and not to rheumatism. Yet he has well-defined rheumatic disease present. Both shoulder joints are involved; rheumatic crepitation is present in both, and motion is at least limited to one-half normal motion. Right knee joint is also rheumatic; motion only slightly affected. Its circumference is three-fourths of an inch greater than the left knee. * * *

I regard the disease of his spinal cord as posterior spinal sclerosis. He has not yet reached the stage of paralysis, and yet that stage is rapidly approaching. * * *

His condition then, to sum up, is practically this: Locomotor ataxia, well defined, leaving no doubt whatever as to its existence. Rheumatism present at this time in both shoulders and right knee.

It appears from the papers in the case that, upon the advice of Dr. Baker, the claimant's family physician, the soldier went to Buffalo, N. Y., to consult Dr. J. W. Putnam, who, it is stated, is a specialist in diseases of the nervous system, and who made an examination of the claimant, the results of which are set forth in his letter to Dr. Baker, under date of June 7, 1897, which letter is now on file in the case.

Nothing additional is shown as a result of Dr. Putnam's examination. Dr. Baker's diagnosis of locomotor ataxia was confirmed by him.

Relative to the origin of the said disability Dr. Putnam states in his said letter:

As to the causation, I can find no history of any disease except rheumatism. As you know, this is referred to in Dercum's book on Nervous Diseases as one of the causes of locomotor ataxia.

It is observed that Dr. Putnam abstains from stating whether or not he indorses Dercum's theory, leaving it to be inferred perhaps, if so desired, that rheumatism was one of the accepted causative factors in tabes dorsalis.

The said claim for increase, filed April 20, 1897, was rejected July 14, 1897, on the ground that the degree of disability from pensioned causes had not increased, and that locomotor ataxia (disease of spine) could not be accepted as a result of any disability for which the soldier was pensioned.

Subsequent to the date on which the said adverse action was taken, affidavits of the claimant and of his family physician, respectively, were filed, with a view to showing that the locomotor ataxia from which the claimant is now suffering is of service origin, and that the objective symptoms upon which the claim on account of rheumatism was both based and established were but the earlier manifestations of the existing lesion of the spinal cord.

In view of the fact that the appellant is undoubtedly suffering from both rheumatism and locomotor ataxia, and that the degree of disability due to the latter disease far exceeds that due to the former, it is evident that the claim now set up, that what was supposed to be rheumatism was in reality locomotor ataxia, is made in consequence of the fact that a much higher rating would be warranted in the event that the name of the pensioned cause could be changed from rheumatism to locomotor ataxia, and also the futility of endeavoring to establish the original contention that the latter disability is a pathological sequence of the former is, perhaps, recognized.

The claimant makes the following statement in his said affidavit:

* * * That he contracted rheumatism in the service and has been troubled with it from discharge up to the present time; that he has doctored unceasingly since discharge, and has visited some of the most famous resorts in Europe, and has been treated by two of the foremost German physicians as well as by physicians in his own country for rheumatism, but has found no relief from his pain; that the physicians who have prescribed for him until recently have done so diagnosing his disease as rheumatism and it has been rheumatism he has been treated for, but he has found no relief, although having tried the cures at watering places in Europe and America as aforesaid, and this fact caused him to think that there must have been some mistake made in diagnosing his case, for had he only had rheumatism he must have found some measure of relief after having tried so many remedies; that about three months ago he called on Dr. W. M. Baker, of Warren, and was by him carefully examined, as a result of which examination the said Dr. W. M. Baker told affiant he had some spinal trouble and suggested his going to Buffalo to consult Professor Putnam; that affiant soon after went to Buffalo and was examined by the said Professor Putnam, who told affiant that he was suffering from progressive locomotor ataxia.

Affiant further states that he has undoubtedly had and still has rheumatism, yet he believes that he was suffering from progressive locomotor ataxia when he left the service, and that the symptoms of said disease were mistaken by his comrades and himself for symptoms of rheumatism, and this belief is based on the following facts, namely:

First. At the time of his discharge very little was known of locomotor ataxia even among professional men, and the disease had hardly been heard of by affiant and his comrades who have hitherto testified in this case.

Second. Affiant being an especially healthy man, of sound physique, the disease remained in its first stage for many years, until increasing age and consequent breaking up of the system rendered affiant less able to withstand the disease.

Third. Had it been rheumatism alone (as was then supposed) that affected affiant, it is reasonable to suppose that some measure of relief and respite from pain would have been gained by the efforts that were continually and at all times made to get rid of the disease and consequent disability; but, on the contrary, affiant continued to suffer lightning pains in his body, arms, and legs, some slight disturbances of sensibility in the lower extremities, etc., from the time of his discharge up to the present time.

Affiant further states that in his present condition he is unable to perform manual labor; that he suffers pain continually and that he has difficulty in walking, and that such difficulty is steadily increasing.

Affiant further states that he has never had syphilis nor is his present condition due to his own vicious habits, but was incurred in the line of duty; and that his post-office address is Warren, Pa.

Dr. Baker's affidavit is as follows:

* * * That he has known the claimant, T. P. Reig, for about sixteen years and has treated him off and on since that time up to within six years ago for rheumatism; that some three or four months ago the said Reig came to his office and complained of sharp pains in his back, arms, and legs, inability to obtain sleep or rest on account of such pains, etc.; that affiant stripped the said Reig and carefully examined him and found the reflexes on one side to be entirely absent; that he went up and down the said Reig's body with needles, and found that in some spots the said Reig was extremely sensitive, while in others there seemed to be no sensation; that affiant informed the said Reig that he had spinal trouble, and suggested that he go to Buffalo to see Professor Putnam, a noted specialist; that claimant did go to Buffalo and was treated by said Putnam; that said Putnam has since written to affiant stating that said Reig has progressive locomotor ataxia, and thus verifying affiant's opinion in the matter.

Affiant further states that he has watched the said Reig since his return from Buffalo, and that he is constantly getting worse and is totally incapacitated for the performance of manual labor, and it is affiant's opinion that the said Reig will soon become a helpless invalid.

Affiant further states that while the said Reig undoubtedly had some rheumatism when he first commenced treating him, he is now of the opinion that claimant was suffering from locomotor ataxia, and that, as no careful physical examination of claimant was made at the time he first commenced prescribing for him, the very common mistake was made in supposing that claimant's affection was principally rheumatism and that his condition and suffering were due to rheumatism. Affiant is satisfied now that the said Reig contracted locomotor ataxia in the service—due to exposure, cold and wet, and excessive bodily exertions, and that this first stage—the stage of invasion—lasted until within a few months ago, and that while in this stage claimant showed symptoms easily confounded with rheumatic symptoms, although there is no doubt claimant suffered from rheumatism to some degree. Affiant believes that claimant is now in the second stage of locomotor ataxia—the stage of full development—and that it is only a question of time before the disease results fatally.

Affiant further states that the claimant's condition is in no way due to syphilis or vicious habits of any kind, as he has never found any sign or trace of syphilis in any form, although he has examined the claimant carefully.

It would appear from the allegations of both the claimant and his family physician that any idea of attempting to establish the original claim of the former that the locomotor ataxia from which he is now shown to be suffering resulted from the rheumatism for which he is pensioned had been abandoned; and that he intended to prosecute his claim for increase on the ground that the additional disabling cause, locomotor ataxia, was an independent disability of service origin, as it is still maintained that he also has rheumatism. As further evidence of this fact, attention is invited to a joint affidavit of C. A Waters and A. B. Nesmith, comrades of the claimant, who have heretofore testified in his claim, and who state as follows:

That they were comrades of Thaddeus P. Reig and have seen him almost daily since being discharged, with the exception of the time said Reig has been absent from home being treated for his health; that they have hitherto made affidavits to the fact that said Reig incurred rheumatism while in the service and has suffered from it ever since, and such affidavits are now on file in the Pension Bureau with the other papers in said Reig's case; that affiants state from their own personal knowledge, gained from daily intercourse with said Reig, that in the last few months his condition has been steadily growing worse, and that he exhibits symptoms not usually found in persons suffering from rheumatism; that affiants have talked with both Reig and Dr. Baker, who has been the said Reig's physician for many years, and they are satisfied that the said Reig's disability was principally due to locomotor ataxia contracted in the service, the symptoms of which are so much like the symptoms of rheumatism that the affiants confounded them and ascribed the said Reig's condition as due to rheumatism, while they now are convinced that the main trouble with the said Reig was incipient locomotor ataxia, although affiants know that the said Reig did suffer more or less from rheumatism.

Affiants further state that they have seen the said Reig almost daily since discharge, as aforesaid, and they know that the said Reig incurred some disability while in the service which they thought was rheumatism, but which they are now convinced is locomotor ataxia; that since discharge the said Reig's condition has grown steadily worse, and that the disability which some time ago the doctors called rheumatism, and was supposed to be rheumatism, is unmistakably locomotor ataxia, and has developed in such a way that it can not longer be confounded with or mistaken for rheumatism.

Affiants further state that they know the said Reig is and always has been a man of good habits and are satisfied that the disability from which he is now suffering—locomotor ataxia—is not the result of syphilis or any vicious habits.

An additional letter, dated September 2, 1897, from Dr. Putnam to Dr. Baker has been filed in the case, and inasmuch as an opinion is expressed therein as to the probable cause of the soldier's disease of the spinal cord, the letter is given in full herein, and is as follows:

I have examined Thaddeus Reig as you requested.

My opinion is that the slight rheumatism which he has is not sufficient to account for all the pain from which he suffers.

You know as well as I do that it is a common thing to find that patients suffering with disease of the spinal cord (locomotor ataxia) have been treated by some doctor for rheumatism. It certainly has been my experience to find patients have been treated for chronic muscular rheumatism for a number of years when during all that time the patient was suffering from the lightning pains of ataxia.

As to the cause of the ataxia in Reig's case I am unable to give a definite, positive opinion. There is no history or evidence of syphilis. My only opinion is that it is probable that the exposure to fatigue and damp during the army life was a contributing factor in the case.

This letter is deemed to be of importance, as it fully controverts one of the contentions of the pending appeal, as will hereafter be shown.

On the 5th of October, 1897, the medical referee rendered the following advisory opinion in regard to the said additional evidence:

The papers in this case have been carefully reviewed. It is now claimed that the rheumatism originally alleged and now pensioned was in reality locomotor ataxia, and it is desired that the name of disability be changed accordingly.

The evidence originally filed clearly established a claim for rheumatism, and from the medical certificates it is clear that soldier has some rheumatism. He also has locomotor ataxia.

There is testimony on file tending to show that the locomotor ataxia was also of service origin. It can not be accepted as a result of rheumatism, yet it is possible that he has suffered from both diseases, and if he can show to the satisfaction of the legal division that he also contracted disease of spinal cord (locomotor ataxia) in the service, and a claim therefor can be legally submitted for admission, a rate will be allowed commensurate with the degree of disability from both causes. It is observed that disease of heart has been accepted as a result of rheumatism, and that total deafness of left ear has also been pensioned.

The claimant not being satisfied with the action of your Bureau in his case, appealed therefrom to this Department on January 4, 1898.

It is contended in the pending appeal that—

The medical referee erred in holding that locomotor ataxia could not be accepted as a result of rheumatism. On this point applicant desires to call attention to the report of the examining board at Warren, Pa., in which report reference is made to certain standard authorities to the effect that locomotor ataxia not only can be, but frequently is, the result of rheumatism.

Attention is also invited to the report of that medical board and their opinion expressed therein.

The affidavit of Professor Putnam, the noted specialist in nervous diseases, of Buffalo, N. Y., is on file expressing his opinion that the locomotor ataxia from which claimant is suffering is a direct result from rheumatism.

Relative to the contention in regard to an opinion expressed by Dr. Putnam in his affidavit on file that the locomotor ataxia from which the claimant is suffering is a direct result from rheumatism, attention is invited to the fact that Dr. Putnam has never made an affidavit in this case, and his only statements therein are embraced in his two letters to the claimant's family physician, both of which have been heretofore referred to. In his letter of September 2, 1897, the Doctor states:

As to the cause of the ataxia in Reig's case, I am unable to give a definite, positive opinion. There is no history of syphilis. My only opinion is that it is probable that the exposure to fatigue and damp during the army life was a contributing factor in the case.

As to the contention that your Bureau erred in holding that loco-motor ataxia could not be accepted as a result of rheumatism, it may be stated that although it is almost universally conceded by the medical profession that rheumatism and locomotor ataxia have one or more etiological factors in common, and also, in the preataxic stage of the latter disease certain similar subjective symptoms, they are, nevertheless, universally considered by all recognized medical authorities as entirely separate and distinct diseases, with no similarity whatever in their pathological anatomy, and are not regarded by the most modern observers as having any causal relation to each other, either pathological or otherwise.

In view, however, of the fact that it is further contended by the appellant that inasmuch as he has never had syphilis, and has never been exposed to cold, over exertion or great fatigue, has never had any acute disease, except rheumatism, and has never been given to alcoholic excesses, it is unreasonable to suppose that the locomotor ataxia from which he is suffering is due to anything except rheumatism, and as certain authors, "whose authority can not be successfully questioned," it is claimed, are cited, it may be advisable to consider what these authors, as well as others, have to say upon the subject.

The authors cited are as follows:

I have several times had occasion to point out the rheumatic origin of ataxia. (Rosenthal, Diseases of the Nervous System, Wood's edition, 1879, vol. 1, p. 244.)

There seems to be no doubt that there is a causative relation between rheumatism and locomotor ataxia. (Bartholow's Practice, seventh edition, p. 672.)

"Overexertion, great fatigue, exposure to damp and cold, some acute diseases (acute rheumatism ——), and alcoholic excesses have been mentioned as causes. (Dercum's Nervous Diseases, 1895, p. 633. Topinard, De l'Ataxie Locomotrica, Paris, 1864, p. 363.)

The views of Rosenthal were published in 1866, as a result of his experience in the Vienna general hospital, and as he expressed the opinion that cold was the most frequent cause of posterior spinal sclerosis (tabes dorsalis—locomotor ataxia), and opposed the idea that specific disease was the chief cause thereof, it is hardly probable that, in the light of subsequent investigation, his views would meet with the indorsement of the medical profession.

The opinion credited to Bartholow will be found on page 609 instead of 672, as stated, and is not given as the views of the author, but is charged to Topinard.

Neither does Dercum hold of his own motion that any causal relation exists between rheumatism and ataxia. What he does state in regard to the etiology of the latter disability in his book on Nervous Diseases, page 633, is as follows:

Syphilis is by far the most important etiological factor in tabes.

Fournier places the percentage of syphilis in causes of locomotor ataxia as 91 to 98 per cent; Erb, at 88 per cent; Rumpf, at 80 to 85 per cent; Sachs, at over 90 per cent. Gowers found only 58 per cent of his private cases as syphilitic, but assumed 80 per cent among the lower classes. In eighty cases of locomotor ataxia observed by me at the Vanderbilt clinic, in which this factor was carefully investigated, a specific history was verified in 71 per cent. * * *

Concussion of the spine from falls is sometimes the cause. Overexertion, great fatigue, exposure to damp and cold, some acute diseases (acute rheumatism, typhoid fever, pneumonia, diphtheria, and typhus), and alcoholic excesses have been mentioned as causes.

It will be observed that he states certain acute diseases have been mentioned as causes, thus throwing the responsibility for the views expressed on some other writer. Special attention is also invited to the fact that only acute diseases were mentioned, not, as in this case, an old chronic affection of thirty-two years' standing.

Topinard stated in 1864 that among the diatheses which predisposed toward progressive locomotor ataxia the rheumatismal was the only one the influence of which was incontestable.

He would find much difficulty in getting any modern neurologist to coincide with any such view.

Having considered the etiology of tabes, it would probably be well to consider for a moment its morbid anatomy, which, as Osler states (p. 840), consists of—

Sclerosis of the posterior columns of the cord, foci of degeneration in the basal ganglia, and sometimes chronic degenerative changes in the cortex cerebri.

The said lesions are persistent and characteristic of the disease in question.

Relative to the morbid anatomy of chronic rheumatism, the same author states (p. 278), that—

The synovial membranes are injected, but there is usually not much effusion. The capsule and ligaments of the joints are thickened, and the sheaths of the tendons in the neighborhood undergo similar alterations, so that the free play of the joints is greatly impaired. In long standing cases the cartilages also undergo changes and may show corrosions. Even in cases with the severest symptoms the joint may be only slightly altered in appearance.

Important changes take place in the muscles and nerves adjacent to chronically inflamed joints, particularly in the monoarticular lesions of the shoulder or hip. * * *

As to the etiology of the latter disease, Osler states (p. 278)—

This affection may follow an acute or subacute attack, but more commonly comes on insidiously in persons who have passed the middle period of life. In my experience it is extremely rare as a sequence of acute rheumatism. It is most common among the poor, particularly washerwomen, day laborers, and those whose occupations expose them to cold and damp.

It will thus be seen that while it is commonly admitted that prolonged exposure to cold and wet, such as belongs to certain occupations, may be responsible for either rheumatism or locomotor ataxia, the lesion is of an entirely different character, attacks different structures, is manifested differently, except that pain is, subjectively, characteristic of each. and it is not, therefore, believed to be susceptible of demonstration that either disease bears any causal relation to the other.

It will be observed that in his various contentions in the pending appeal, as enumerated herein, the appellant is hardly consistent.

First. He contends that it was error not to accept locomotor ataxia as a pathological sequence of rheumatism.

Second. That what was originally supposed to be rheumatism was in reality locomotor ataxia, and the name of the disability for which he is pensioned should be changed from the former to the latter.

Third. That he is suffering from both rheumatism and locomotor ataxia, and that his claim on account of the latter disability should be allowed upon the evidence furnished in the original claim.

In regard to the first contention, the reasons given herein are, in my judgment, ample for sustaining the action appealed from.

The second contention is untenable, by reason of the fact that the appellant is shown to be suffering from both rheumatism and locomotor ataxia.

The third contention is not properly before the Department for consideration on its merits, as primary action in the claim on account of locomotor ataxia as an independent disability of service origin has not yet been taken by your Bureau.

Therefore the action appealed from is, in so far as the refusal of your Bureau to accept the existing locomotor ataxia as a result of the rheumatism for which the appellant is pensioned is concerned, hereby affirmed.

The papers in the case are herewith remanded for such action as may be necessary looking to the adjudication of any existing claim on account of locomotor ataxia as an independent disability of service origin.

HELPLESS MINOR—ACT JUNE 27, 1890.

MINOR OF WILLIAM JOHNSON.

Claimant is 24 years old, has been since 1885 an inmate of an asylum for feeble-minded persons, does not know her age, is unable to comprehend numbers above 5, is capable of receiving only the most elementary instruction, and, in the opinion of the surgeon detailed to examine her, is permanently incapacitated for earning a living and requires the care and attendance of another person daily.

Held, That she is entitled to continuance of pension as claimed.

Assistant Secretary Webster Davis to the Commissioner of Pensions, August 17, 1898.

Eva F. Johnson, daughter of William Johnson, deceased, formerly a soldier in Company B, One hundred and third Ohio Infantry, was in 1881 pensioned jointly with two other minor children of said soldier. She became 16 years of age May 20, 1882, and the youngest minor became 16 November 11, 1883. On July 14, 1890, an application was filed by guardian for continuance of pension to Eva F., under the first proviso to section 3 of the act of June 27, 1890, it being alleged that she was an imbecile. Said application was rejected in June, 1898, on the ground that she was not "insane, idiotic, or otherwise permanently helpless" within the meaning of the law. From that action an appeal was taken July 15, 1898.

It appears from the evidence that the claimant has been since September 5, 1885, an inmate of the Asylum for Feeble Minded at Columbus, Ohio. Dr. Gustavus A. Doren, of that institution, certifies that her physical condition during that time has been fairly good, but that she is mentally deficient, and will never be able to support or care for herself.

A pension surgeon who examined her on April 23, 1898, reported as follows:

Claimant is unable to make any intelligible statement about condition or history. She does not know her age and can not tell how long she has been in the institution. Says she has six fingers on both hands. Unable to comprehend numbers above 5. Can not read in books higher than First Reader. General appearance good. * * * There is no appreciable debility except cerebral. She is feeble-minded and has probably always been so. She goes to school in the institution in the forenoons and works in the laundry in the afternoons, and seems happy and contented. * * * She is not insane; she has no delusions or any insane stigmata. She is feeble minded, properly classed as idiotic, capable of receiving a small amount of instruction. * * * No evidence of disease of spine, or meninges, or brain, except the imperfect development of the brain cortex. Contour of head normal. Claimant is so disabled from mental and physical debility as to be permanently incapacitated from earning a living, though not entirely helpless. She requires the frequent and daily (periodical) aid and attendance of another person.

The law under which continuance of pension is claimed reads as follows:

Provided, That in case a minor child is insane, idiotic, or otherwise permanently helpless, the pension shall continue during the life of said child or during the period of such disability, and this proviso shall apply to all pensions heretofore granted or hereafter to be granted under this or any former statute, and such pensions shall commence from the date of application therefor after the passage of this act.

As the disability in this case is altogether mental, and is not of the character designated as insanity, the only question to be considered is whether it amounts to idiocy as contemplated by the statute.

A very full and clear exposition of the subject of idiocy in its legal aspects is to be found in the decision of Assistant Secretary Reynolds in the case of Clarence Loveitt (7 P. D., 405), from which I quote the following:

Idiocy in law "is an imbecility or sterility of mind, and not a perversion of the understanding. When a man can not count or number 20, nor tell his father's or mother's name, nor how old he is, having been frequently told it, it is a fair presumption that he is devoid of understanding." (Bouvier's Law Dictionary, vol. 1, p. 679.)

Blackstone defines an idiot to be one "who hath had no understanding from his nativity." (Blackstone's Com., p. 303.)

With the English jurists "idiot is a legal term signifying a person who has been without understanding from his nativity, and whom the law therefore presumes never likely to attain any. If a man has any glimmering of reason, so that he can tell his parents' age, count 20, or understand the like common matters, it is said he is not an idiot." (Laws of Idiots and Lunatics, Collison, vol. 1, p. 3.)

According to Lord Coke an idiot "is one which from his nativity, by a perpetual infirmity, is non compos mentis." (Collison, vol. 1, p. 118.)

Under the English procedure persons non compos mentis are divided into two classes—idiots and lunatics. (Ibid., p. 122.)

Chancellor Kent laid down the following rule: "Thus imbecility of mind is not sufficient to set aside a contract where there is not an essential privation of the reasoning faculties or an incapacity of understanding and acting with discretion in the ordinary affairs of life. This incapacity is now the test of that unsoundness of mind which will avoid a deed at law." (Kent, vol. 2, p. 573.)

There are degrees of idiocy, and Dr. Howe makes the following classification:

"Idiots of the lowest class are mere organisms, masses of flesh and bone in human shape, in which the brain and nervous system have no command over the system of voluntary muscles, and which consequently are without power of locomotion, without speech, without any manifestations of intellectual or affective faculties.

"Fools are a higher class of idiots, in whom the brain and nervous system are so far developed as to give partial command of the voluntary muscles; who have, consequently, considerable power of locomotion and animal action, partial development of the intellectual and affective faculties, but only the faintest glimmer of reason and very imperfect speech.

"Simpletons are the highest class of idiots, in whom the harmony between the nervous and muscular system is nearly perfect; who, consequently, have normal powers of locomotion and animal action, considerable activity of the perceptive and affective faculties, and reason enough for their simple individual guidance, but not enough for their social relations. (Wharton and Stille's Medical Jurisprudence, section 685.)"

In the same work it is stated that, "Though we may fail to discover a definition of idiocy thoroughly comprehensive, we are justifitd in saying that where there is even a low degree of intelligence idiocy can not be said to exist. The test is comparatively simple. If the pretended idiot can be shown to have intelligently performed acts of business during the period in which idiocy be claimed to have existed, the allegation of the incompetency on this ground falls, unless fraud or constraint be shown."

I can not believe that it was the intent of Congress to limit the benefits of the proviso to section 3 of the act of June 27, 1890, to idiots of the first class under Dr. Howe's division or to idiots of the first two classes. The provision was undoubtedly made for the benefit of such children over 16 years of age as are mentally or physically incapable of taking care of themselves, and hence have to be assisted and cared for by parents or guardians.

In the case of Frances Stetzell (9 P. D., 9) in which the child for whom continuance of pension was claimed was afflicted with epilepsy, Assistant Secretary Reynolds said:

The whole matter, then, resolves itself to this:

That this child has an incurable physical malady, which, judged by its past history, is liable to become more and more severe, and which, besides rendering her weak and unable to do remunerative labor, keeps her also in a constant state of liability to attacks or spasms, requiring aid and attention from others. Thus, while said child can dress and undress herself and attend to her personal needs, she could not probably obtain employment that would give her a support, by reason of the liability to fits, even if she were physically able to work, which she is not, except in the lightest employment, and guided by her mother.

Taking all the evidence together, and considering the sex of this child as well as her afflicted condition, I am disposed to the opinion that she is permanently helpless in the sense intended by the law, and that the pension on her account should be continued.

Following this decision I held in the case of Ellie Morris (9 P. D., 353) that—

A child who is an incurable epileptic, having a falling fit once a week on an average and nervous attacks much oftener, who is vigorous in body but dull mentally, who is able to attend to his personal wants except when suffering from an epileptic seizure, and can perform some remunerative labor, but not nearly sufficient to afford him a support, is "permanently helpless" in the contemplation of the law, and the pension on his account should be continued.

In this, as in the Stetzell case, the gist of the holding was that the helplessness contemplated by the statute in question was not absolute incapacity for self-help in performing the ordinary daily functions of life, but inability to do business or to earn a livelihood; not the helplessness of the paralytic, but the helplessness of the child of tender years and immature mind.

It is evident that the claimant in this case is an idiot of the highest class according to Dr. Howe's classification, but nevertheless an idiot. She does not know her age; is unable to comprehend numbers above 5; is capable of receiving only the most elementary instruction; is permanently incapacitated for earning a living, and requires the frequent and daily attendance of another person. I am clearly of the opinion that she is entitled to continuance of pension under the proviso to section 3 of the act of June 27, 1890; and you are respectfully requested to have action taken in accordance with that opinion.

Action reversed.

———

FRAUD AND MISTAKE—REIMBURSEMENT.

ALEXANDER W. DEES.

1. It appearing that the disability of this appellant from disease of eyes can not be attributed to the results of sunstroke in service, and said disease of eyes not being shown by the evidence to have been otherwise due to his military service, the action terminating the pension granted him on account thereof, and rejecting his claim for restoration of the same was proper and is affirmed, although the ground stated for said action was erroneous.

2. It being shown that the nervous affection of face, from which this appellant suffered prior to his enlistment, was not a factor in the disability from disease of eyes for which he was first erroneously pensioned, and had no connection therewith, pathologically or otherwise, all basis for a charge of fraud in obtaining said pension is eliminated from this case, the same having been granted, not through fraud on his part, or a mistake of fact on the part of the Pension Bureau, but merely as the result of an erroneous judgment on the evidence, and no legal grounds exist for withholding payment of his present pension to reimburse the Government for former payments made to him under his original pension certificate as a result of such erroneous judgment. (Christian May, 8 P. D., 71).

Assistant Secretary Webster Davis to the Commissioner of Pensions, August 20, 1898.

This claim was carefully considered by me on appeal May 27, 1898, upon which date the papers were returned to your Bureau, with a communication requesting an advisory opinion from the medical referee, setting forth a full history of the case, and stating all material facts and evidence therein, as follows:

Alexander W. Dees, late captain Third Battery, Michigan Volunteer Light Artillery, was originally pensioned under the provisions of sections 4692 and 4693, Revised

Statutes, for disease of nerves and eyes, results of sunstroke, from date of discharge, November 20, 1862, to June 4, 1887, when he was dropped from the rolls upon the ground that the disease for which he had been pensioned was due to a nervous affection of face and eyes originating and existing prior to his entering the military service. At the date when he was dropped from the rolls he was in receipt of a "second grade" rating of $30 per month. On September 14, 1887, he applied for restoration of his said pension, and also alleged rheumatism as an additional disabling cause of service origin. On November 15, 1888, this claim was rejected, and on October 19, 1894, he renewed application for restoration, and on June 25, 1892, and February 26, 1895, he renewed his claim for rheumatism, and also alleged dyspepsia, dropsy, and dysentery as further additional disabling causes contracted in service and line of duty.

On July 20, 1897, his claim on account of rheumatism, dyspepsia, and dysentery was admitted, and pension allowed him for said diseases at $10 per month from September 14, 1887, and $15 per month from June 15, 1892, and $20 per month from January 30, 1895, but payment of said pension to him was withheld, and is now being withheld, to reimburse the Government for money erroneously paid him on his original pension. At the same time his application for restoration of his original pension was again rejected.

From the rejection of said claim for restoration, and the action withholding payment of his present pension, as aforesaid, this appeal was taken on September 20, 1897.

The appellant alleged in his original declaration, filed August 11, 1863, that he had received a sunstroke in service on the 28th of May, 1862, while his battery was in action before Corinth, Miss. The fact that he was overcome by heat and contracted some disability in the nature of a sunstroke at the time and under the circumstances alleged appears to be well, if not conclusively, established by contemporaneous official medical evidence on file, no less than five army surgeons certifying that they had examined and treated him during the summer and fall of 1862, and found him suffering with effects of sunstroke. The certificate of medical examination, upon which his resignation and application for discharge from the service was based, states, explicitly, that he had incurred a sunstroke on May 28, 1862, for which the examining surgeon had treated him during the following summer. The officer who succeeded him in the command of the battery certifies, on November 26, 1863, that the appellant incurred a sunstroke on the date and under the circumstances alleged by him that rendered him nearly insensible for several days, and that he was near appellant at the time and helped to carry him off the field. An army surgeon, who examined appellant for pension on August 11, 1863, certifies that he had received a sunstroke on the date alleged while in action with his battery before Corinth, Miss., which had affected his eyes.

Furthermore, there is on file a more recent affidavit, filed on December 20, 1897, from Edward Batewell, who signs himself "late surgeon 14th Michigan V. V. Infantry and division surgeon, 2nd Div., 14th A. C." wherein he states that he was called to treat and attend on the appellant on May 28, 1862, before Corinth, Miss., "who whilst his battery was engaged with the enemy was overcome by sun." He minutely describes the appellant's symptoms and physical condition at the time, as he recollects it.

The evidence upon which the appellant was dropped from the rolls was obtained by a special examination of his case, made in 1885 and 1886, and consists of the testimony of numerous witnesses that for some years prior to his entering the service, and during his service prior to the alleged incurrence of sunstroke, he was afflicted with some sort of a nervous affection evidenced by a twitching or jerking of the facial muscles on one side. It does not clearly appear on which side of the face this condition was manifested, but it is abundantly proven that it did exist, and that there was an involuntary contraction of the muscles about one of his eyes and on one side of his face for several years at least prior to his entering the Army. This nervous affection of the face seems to have been accepted as the cause and source of the appellant's disease of eyes, and the fact that he has on several occasions emphatically denied under oath that it existed prior to the incurrence of sunstroke in the service constitutes the basis of the charge of fraud, upon which the action withholding his present pension is founded. Attention is invited to the fact that although the existence of a nervous twitching or jerking of the muscles of one eye and one side of the face is shown prior to enlistment, it does not appear that his vision was in any way affected thereby at that time, all the witnesses who testify to the existence of said twitching of the face stating that his eyesight was then good, and his eyes appeared to be sound. The only evidence appearing in the case tending to show any disease or affection of the appellant's eyes, independent of said nervous affection, prior to his service, is to the effect that a number of years before he entered the service he had suffered from granulated lids for a short time, and from which he had fully recovered long before the civil war.

In view of the foregoing facts appearing in evidence, it is deemed advisable before finally passing upon this case on appeal that the papers be submitted to the medical referee, whose careful and thorough consideration of all the evidence is requested, and whose professional advisory opinion, in aid of this Department, is desired upon the following points:

(1) Is there presented by the proof in this case any good ground or reason, from a medical standpoint, why the evidence should not be accepted as establishing the incurrence of a sunstroke by appellant in the service as alleged?

(2) If the service origin of sunstroke be accepted as proved, can it be medically accepted as the primary cause and source of appellant's disease of eyes, independent of the nervous affection of face antedating his service?

(3) Is it possible to differentiate in this case between the results of sunstroke and said nervous affection of face?

(4) Does the proof in this case afford a just and reasonable ground for ascribing to said nervous affection of face the disease of eyes and loss of vision for which this appellant was originally pensioned rather than to the effects of sunstroke incurred in the service?

In this connection it is suggested that it would be advisable, if not absolutely necessary to a proper consideration of this case, to cause a careful examination of this appellant to be made by a competent and expert oculist, who should be requested to give a full and accurate description of the present condition of his eyes and a differential diagnosis of the disease or diseases with which they are affected.

Upon the receipt of the opinion of the medical referee, as herein requested, you will please transmit the same, with the papers in this case, to this Department for further consideration and final disposition of the case on appeal.

The medical referee replied, as requested in the foregoing, on July 13, 1898, and the papers have again been transmitted to this Department for final disposition of the case on appeal.

The opinion of the medical referee is as follows:

This claimant was originally pensioned (August 6, 1864) for "disease of eyes, resulting from sunstroke," at the rate of $15 per month, which rate was increased to $20, from April 8, 1870, for "disease of eyes and nerves."

His name was dropped from the rolls from June 4, 1887, upon the ground that the disability for which pensioned was due to a nervous affection of face and eye, existing prior to enlistment.

Claimant appeals now for restoration to the rolls and for continuance of pension for this disability.

In considering this appeal, the honorable Secretary requests an advisory opinion of the medical referee upon the following points:

1. Is there presented by the proof in this case any good reason, from a medical standpoint, why the evidence should not be accepted as establishing the incurrence of a sunstroke by appellant in the service, as alleged?

2. If the service origin of sunstroke be accepted as proved, can it be medically

accepted as the primary cause and source of appellant's disease of eyes, independent of the nervous affection of face antedating his service?

3. Is it possible to differentiate in this case between the results of sunstroke and said nervous affection of face?

4. Does the proof in this case afford a just and reasonable ground for ascribing to said nervous affection of face the disease of eyes and loss of vision for which this appellant was originally pensioned, rather than to the effects of sunstroke incurred in the service?

As suggested by the Department, an expert eye examination was directed, which examination, made June 15, 1898, shows quite defective vision in each eye, not improved by glasses (the left eye being only able to count fingers at 3 feet); slight conjunctivitis of lids. Right eye, slight haziness in upper part (of cornea); iris and lens normal; vitreous full of large stringy floating bodies; other deep structures and vessels normal. Left eye, diffused haziness of cornea; deep structures, as far as could be seen, all normal; marked astigmatism, evidently due to corneal irregularities and not corrected by cylindrical lenses.

From this showing, each cornea is notably hazy, and the right vitreous full of floating bodies; but all other eye structures are normal. The twitching is shown to effect the muscles of the right side of face.

Replying specifically to the questions propounded, it may be stated that—

1. From a medical standpoint, the incurrence of sunstroke in service is not established by the evidence in the case for the reason that the distinctive symptoms thereof, as will be more particularly described hereafter, are not shown.

2. Even if service origin of sunstroke were proved, it has no probable connection with appellant's disease of eyes. This disease of eyes, on expert examination, is shown to be limited to the conjunctiva and cornea of each eye and the vitreous humor of right eye. Claimant admitted to Special Examiner Beble (No. 4, p. 6) that he had "granulated lids" about 1857, for which he treated himself with zinc sulphate, copper sulphate (bluestone), and rose-water. This inflammation (the so-called "granulated lids") is evidently identical with, or the cause of, complainant's existing opacities of cornea, and possibly, also, of the opacities in right vitreous. It has no probable connection with the alleged sunstroke.

3. The differential diagnosis between results of sunstroke and, in this case, the nervous affection of face, presents no difficulty. The latter is the so-called "habit chorea," a spasmodic affection of a single muscle, or an associated group of muscles, of the right side of face. No constant pathological nervous change has been found associated with such affection. The results of a bona fide sunstroke are generally readily recognized. The only constant pathological sequel observed is chronic inflammation of the cerebral meninges, or, in very severe cases, of the adjacent gray matter of the brain, the symptoms of which are marked inability to endure heat, persistent headache, impairment of memory and mental faculties, and, in some cases, insanity. Fayrer (Tropical Diseases in India, pp. 303-313) shows that in many cases, where marked sequelæ and insanity were clearly traceable to sunstroke, the only constant pathological change found on post-mortem examination was inflammation of the cerebral meninges, "the skull plates thickened, dense, and heavy, and their diploe obstructed." A pathological connection between claimant's affection of face and the results of sunstroke can not on medical grounds be admitted.

4. The proof in this case does not afford any ground for ascribing claimant's disease of eyes and loss of vision to his affection of face.

It will be at once observed that the scientific and expert investigation of the condition of this appellant's eyes, and the nature of the disease or lesion with which they are affected, made pursuant to the suggestion in my foregoing communication, together with the professional opinion of the medical referee based upon the facts thereby developed, puts an entirely new aspect upon this case and changes entirely the issues involved and the questions to be considered.

It now appears that the nervous affection of face, which antedated the appellant's enlistment, and was supposed to have been the original cause, or to have been pathologically connected with the origin of the disease of eyes for which he was originally pensioned, is not and has never been a factor in his disability from that cause and never had any connection whatever with his disease of eyes, pathologically or otherwise. It is apparent, therefore, that the action dropping this appellant from the rolls was based upon an erroneous diagnosis of his disease of eyes and upon improper and untenable grounds.

It does not follow, however, that the action dropping the appellant from the rolls was itself wrong, although it may have been and was based upon improper grounds. Unquestionably the evidence in this case shows that this appellant suffered some sort of a severe attack during his military service on May 28, 1862, which was pronounced and supposed by the medical officers who examined and treated him about that time and soon afterwards to have been a sunstroke or something of that nature, resulting from exposure to the rays of the sun. The medical referee refuses to accept this attack as a genuine or pronounced sunstroke, for the reason that the evidence fails to show that it was accompanied or followed by any of the distinctive or recognized symptoms or sequelæ of sunstroke; but, however this may be, it now appears that this also becomes an immaterial question in this case, since it has been demonstrated by the expert examination of appellant's eyes that the disease affecting them can not be accepted as a pathological result of sunstroke, or any attack of a similar nature, and is, from its inherent nature and characteristics, precluded from being attributed to any such cause. Therefore, not only was this appellant dropped from the rolls upon improper and erroneous grounds, but the original grant of pension to him for disease of eyes was based upon a mistaken diagnosis of his disease and a wrong conception of the origin of his disability.

The medical referee attributes the origin of appellant's present disease of eyes to an attack of sore eyes, or an inflammation of the eyes and lids, with which he admitted he suffered in 1857; but whether this be true or not, the fact remains that if sunstroke, or the attack, whatever it was, which he is shown to have suffered in service on May 28, 1862, be eliminated as the primary cause and origin of the disease of eyes for which he was pensioned, there is no evidence in this case showing the origin of said disease of eyes in his military service, or connecting it therewith in any way whatever. The appellant never alleged or attempted to establish the service origin of his disease of eyes except as a result of a sunstroke, and there is not a particle of evidence which tends to give rise to or support any other theory upon which it could be attributed to his military service.

It is clear, therefore, that the original grant of pension to the appellant for disease of eyes having been erroneous, the action dropping him from the rolls and terminating said pension and subsequently rejecting his claim for restoration of said pension was correct, notwithstanding a wrong and indefensible reason was given for said action. If, as a matter of fact, the disease of eyes for which appellant was pensioned was not shown to be of service origin, he was not entitled to pension on account thereof under the provisions of the law, and it was right to drop him from the rolls, although the reason given for terminating said pension was mistaken and erroneous.

Therefore said action, dropping appellant from the rolls on account of disease of eyes and subsequently rejecting his claim for restoration, will be affirmed, not upon the grounds stated by your Bureau for said action, but because the evidence in this case fails to establish the service origin of said disease or to connect it in any way with his military service.

It is far otherwise with the action withholding the payment of the appellant's pension subsequently granted him to reimburse the Government for payments of his original pension made on account of disease of eyes.

It is and always has been the ruling of this Department, that such action was never warranted except in the two instances where actual fraud on the part of the pensioner was shown in procuring the allowance of the erroneous pension, or where such allowance had resulted from clear mistake of fact on the part of your Bureau, and it is unnecessary to cite authorities in support of so well settled a proposition. In the present case, as was remarked in my foregoing communication of May 27, 1898, the only basis for a charge of fraud against this appellant in connection with the grant of his original pension presented by the evidence consists of the fact that he at first concealed, and afterwards denied, under oath, the existence prior to his service of the nervous affection or twitching of the muscles of his face, which was supposed to be pathologically connected with the pensioned disease of eyes. It having now been ascertained and determined that said nervous affection of the face was not a factor in the disability for which the appellant was originally pensioned, and never had anything whatever to do with his disease of eyes, every element of fraud has been eliminated in this case, and the only ground or reason ever given for withholding payment of his present pension utterly fails. It is an elementary legal proposition that fraud, to be effective, must be material. Some deception, or other evidence of bad faith on the part of the pensioner relative to some material issue involved in his case, must be shown before he can be properly charged with fraud which would justify the withholding of his present pension. Since the nervous affection of the muscles of his face never had any connection with, and was neither a superinducing cause of, nor an element in his disability from disease of eyes, it is wholly immaterial to the issues involved in this case whether it originated prior or subsequent to his military service, or whether he concealed its existence and afterwards denied it.

Leaving out of view the nervous affection of the appellant's face as an element in his disability from disease of eyes, there is certainly no ground whatever afforded by the evidence in this case for charging him with fraud in the prosecution of his original claim for pension.

The evidence establishes beyond question the fact that he suffered some sort of a severe attack in the service and line of duty, which was supposed by the army medical officers who attended him at the time to have been a sunstroke, and the medical evidence tended very strongly to show that said attack of illness had affected his eyes. The evidence afforded ample ground for an honest belief on the part of the appellant that the disease of eyes on account of which he first applied for pension was due to said attack in service, and in this belief the adjudicating officers of your Bureau appear to have shared, since, with this evidence all before them, they admitted his claim on this theory and granted him a pension for disease of eyes as a result of sunstroke.

Nor does the fact that the appellant suffered with an attack of sore eyes, or inflammation of the eyelids, in 1857, prior to his enlistment, to which the medical referee now attributes the origin of his present disease of eyes, afford any basis for charging him with fraud. It does not appear that he ever concealed this fact; on the contrary, it first and only became known by his voluntary statement to a special examiner. He can not be charged with bad faith in not having previously mentioned this antebellum attack of sore eyes, since all his testimony relative thereto must be taken together; and he states that it was of short duration, temporary in its effects, that he fully recovered therefrom, and his eyesight was not subsequently affected thereby; and the other evidence in the case, showing that his vision was apparently unimpaired for some years previous to and at the time of his entering the military service, would seem to corroborate his statements in this respect. All we know about said first attack of sore eyes is what the appellant has told us himself, and, judging from that, he had no reason to believe that it had any relation to his present disability, or was a material factor in his case, which it would be bad faith on his part to fail to mention.

The evidence in this case fully warrants the conclusion that the allegations and statements of the appellant in his original claim for pension were based upon an honest mistake as to the origin of his disease of eyes, and that the allowance of said claim was the result of a mistaken judgment on the evidence by the adjudicating officers of your Bureau, and not of any deception, fraud, or bad faith on the part of this appellant. The fact that the pension thus allowed was erroneously granted affords no ground or warrant whatever under the law for withholding the payment of the pension which was subsequently properly granted to the appellant, and to which he is legally entitled.

This case is very similar, both in facts and principle, to the case of

Christian May (8 P. D., 71), decided by this Department February 8, 1896, in which it was held that—

the Government can not withhold the pension granted under the act of June 27, 1890, to reimburse itself for moneys erroneously paid as pension under the general law when such pension was not procured through fraud or mistake, but was allowed as the result of an erroneous judgment on the evidence.

In said case the claimant, May, was first pensioned, under the provisions of the Revised Statutes, for disease of eyes, and was dropped from the rolls upon the ground that said disease had existed prior to his enlistment. He was subsequently pensioned under the act of June 27, 1890, but payment of this pension was withheld to reimburse the Government for erroneous payments of his first pension.

The decision rendered in said case contains a well-considered discussion of the grounds upon which payments of pension can be withheld for reimbursement, and sets forth the nature of actual or positive fraud, and the character of the proof required to establish it, such as it is necessary to establish to warrant such action withholding payment of pension, with a full citation of authorities bearing on the subject. (8 P. D., 73 and 74.) It was held in said decision that although the action dropping May from the rolls was correct and should be affirmed, yet, inasmuch as your Bureau had before it evidence showing that disease of eyes existed prior to enlistment at the time his original claim for pension was adjudicated and admitted, and it was not shown that he had been guilty of any deception or bad faith in procuring its allowance, but that its allowance was the result of an erroneous judgment on the evidence, the payment of his pension under the act of June 27, 1890, could not properly or legally be withheld from him, and the action withholding such payments was reversed.

The reasoning and holding of said decision applies absolutely and with equal force to the facts of the present case, and there is no question as to the soundness and legality of the ruling therein made.

In view of the foregoing the action withholding payments of the pension at present granted to this appellant is hereby reversed and set aside, and you are requested to cause a reissue of his present pension certificate to be made to pay him the money that has been improperly withheld from him on his present pension

---

SERVICE—MILITIA.

WALTER MORRIS.

The fact that the organization to which the claimant belonged was not regularly mustered into the service of the United States does not debar him from pension for disability incurred in the line of duty, it appearing that said organization was called into service by the authority of the President, turned over to the United States officers, and by them ordered outside the State for duty, and that the members were paid by the General Government at the time of muster out.

Assistant Secretary Webster Davis to the Commissioner of Pensions, August 17, 1898.

I have considered the appeal filed August 7, 1897, from the action of your Bureau in rejecting the pension claim of Walter Morris, late a private in Joseph M. Knap's Battery A, Pennsylvania Militia. This is a claim under the provisions of sections 4692 and 4693 of the Revised Statutes. The appellant filed his declaration March 12, 1894, alleging that he was enrolled in the above-named organization June 27, 1863, and honorably discharged August 15, 1863, and that while in the service and line of duty at Hancock, Md., in July, 1863, he sustained an injury of the left foot by a cannon running over it. His claim was rejected in February, 1896, on the ground that the organization in which he was serving when the injury was incurred was not mustered into the service of the United States. From that action he appeals, contending that although not regularly mustered he was nevertheless in the military service of the United States and entitled to pension for disability incurred in the line of duty.

The officer in charge of the Record and Pension Office of the War Department reports that it does not appear from the records of that office that such an organization as Knap's Battery of Pennsylvania Artillery was mustered into the service of the United States in 1863. The appellant makes, in his appeal, the following statement in regard to his service:

The day I enlisted I was told by the recruiting officer that the service was to be outside the State, consequently under United States officers and beyond the control of the State; in corroboration of which the next day we were transported at Government expense to West Virginia, thence over the Baltimore and Ohio Railroad to Cumberland, Md. There, if not before, we were brigaded with an infantry regiment (of which State I now forget, but it was not from Pennsylvania). This brigade was commanded by Brigadier-General Kelley, then in the United States service (since dead). While under General Kelley, at Hancock, Md., the injury was incurred. It was understood and agreed both by myself and those who enlisted me that I was enlisting in the service of the General Government, and in accordance with that agreement and understanding my services were duly rendered to the United States and not to the State of Pennsylvania or any other State or Government.

The adjutant-general of the State of Pennsylvania reports that he was enrolled as a private in Capt. Joseph M. Knap's Battery of Pennsylvania Volunteer Militia June 27, 1863, and was mustered into the service of the State for the period of ninety days, unless sooner discharged, and that he was mustered out with the battery August 16, 1863.

In reply to an inquiry as to what order or call the battery was recruited under and at what places and under whose command it served, the adjutant-general of the State says:

All the Pennsylvania militia were called into service in accordance with a call of the President and turned over to the United States for service. Only muster-in and muster-out rolls are filed here, which do not state where the service was rendered.

The Auditor of the Treasury for the War Department reports that the records of his office show that the appellant served as a private in Capt. Joseph M. Knap's Battery A, Pennsylvania Emergency Militia, from June 27, 1863, to August 16, 1863, and was paid on the muster out of his company.

The appellant's statement that the battery was ordered outside the State of Pennsylvania is corroborated by the following "Special orders," which will be found in the official publication, The War of the Rebellion, Official Records of the Union and Confederate Armies, volume 27, series 1, part 3:

Special orders, }   HDQRS. DEPT. OF THE MONONGAHELA,
    No. 8.   }   *Pittsburgh, Pa., July 9, 1863.*

I. In accordance with instructions from Headquarters of the Army, July 7, the following troops will proceed without delay and report at the places indicated:

II. Lieut. Col. J. C. Lininger's battalion six months volunteers will report at Hancock, Maryland, via Wheeling and Cumberland.

III. Col. S. B. Dick's three months militia will report at New Creek Station, Baltimore and Ohio Railroad, Maryland.

•   •   •   •   •   •   •

V. Capt. J. M. Knap, Battery A, Pennsylvania Militia, will report at Beverly, Virginia.

The commanding officers, when they arrive at their respective designations, will report by telegraph to Brig. Gen. B. F. Kelley, Hancock, Md.

By command of Major-General Brooks:

                                            WM. R. HOWE,
                                        Assistant Adjutant-General.

It appears, therefore, that the organization to which the soldier belonged was called into service by the authority of the President; that it was turned over to the United States officers and by them ordered outside the State for duty, and that the members were paid by the General Government at the time of muster out.   Does the fact that they were not regularly mustered into the service of the United States debar them from pension under the general pension laws now in force?

In the case of Randolph M. Manley (5 P. D., 295) it was held that a person who enlisted in a regiment of the Pennsylvania militia pursuant to the President's proclamation for six months' volunteers, even if the regiment was not mustered into the service of the United States, but was engaged in its service, has a pensionable status under the first subdivision of section 4693, Revised Statutes.

The question was at that time very fully and carefully considered and the decision, prior to its promulgation, was submitted to and concurred in by the Assistant Attorney-General for the Department of the Interior and by the Attorney-General.   I quote from said decision part of the argument which is peculiarly applicable to the case now under consideration:

Now the question arises, Was appellant, while a member of the Pennsylvania militia serving in the State of Maryland, where he incurred his sunstroke, in the service of the United States or in the service of the State of Pennsylvania alone?

If he was not "in the service of the United States," but in the service of the State of Pennsylvania only, I conclude he has not a pensionable status under the first subdivision of section 4693, Revised Statutes.

The Acting Judge-Advocate-General of the Army, in a communication dated January 23, 1890, and addressed to the Commissioner of Pensions, relative to the status of certain Pennsylvania militia, has said:

"I infer from this that, although in the case of a volunteer soldier, the muster in necessarily fixes the commencement of the term of actual service, in the case of a militia organization it is not absolutely necessary that there should be this formality in order to place it in the actual service of the United States. There seems to be good reason for this. The volunteer, before his muster in, has not bound himself to any service; the militiaman is already enrolled in the service of the State, and is simply transferred for a certain time and for a certain purpose to that of the United States. If he is mustered into the latter service, this will determine its commencement, and it was probably partly on account of the convenience of having it so determined that the act of 1862 required it; but it would seem that any act which would fix it would also be given that effect. It might be that, in a case of great emergency, no formal muster in could be had, but that the militia were nevertheless received by the authorities of the United States, placed under the command of its officers, and used for its purpose. It could hardly be held that they were not in the service of the United States because this formality had not been complied with. So I am of the opinion that this requirement of the act of 1862 should properly be regarded as directory only, and that in the case under consideration the fact that there was no muster in would not, of itself, absolutely preclude its being held that the Thirteenth Regiment Pennsylvania Militia was in the actual service of the United States."

The following quotation taken from page 774, volume 1, Military Law, by Lieut. Col. W. Winthrop, a work now recognized as the highest authority on the principles and rules involved in American military law, and relating to the form and evidence of "enlistment," is deemed pertinent here:

"Form and evidence of enlistment: The statute law not having defined in what enlistment shall consist, or what shall constitute evidence of enlistment in general, it follows that the existence of a contract of enlistment in any case may be proved in the same manner as any other contract for service. Article 47 provided, in substance, that in the special case of a deserter the receipt of pay shall be equivalent to, i. e., evidence of an enlistment, so far as to estop the offender from denying that he is duly in the Army. So, in any other case, the fact that the party has accepted pay or a pecuniary allowance as a soldier, has been provided as such with arms, clothing, rations, etc., by the military authorities, or has voluntarily performed military service under the orders of a superior for any considerable period, would ordinarily constitute prima facie evidence that he has entered into a contract of enlistment with the United States."

Whether a militiaman was in the United States military service does not depend so much upon the fact that he was mustered into such service as it does upon the fact that he was actually in the service, doing duty in the body of the Army, subjected to the Articles of War, and amenable to the United States for any violation of orders given by authority of the United States.

Again, it is said:

In this case there were organization, rendezvous, marching, drilling, guard and picket duty—acts performed both inside and outside of the State of Pennsylvania, under the command of the regular officers of the Army, and appellant's disability was contracted while he was serving not the State of Pennsylvania, nor while under the command of the governor of said State, but the United States, and while doing military duty in the State of Maryland, where he had gone in obedience to the orders of the President of the United States, as conveyed through his officers.

As a further evidence that the members of this militia regiment were at that time regarded as in the United States service, their muster-in and muster-out rolls were filed in the War Department of the United States, and they were paid for their services by the United States.

The governor of Pennsylvania had no jurisdiction or authority in Maryland and could not legally be operating his troops in that State. The men did not merely cross the State line in pursuit of the enemy and return immediately, but were ordered there by the United States officers as a body of United States troops in contradistinction from mere State militia. This was not the temporary service, or service for "the time being as a member of the militia of any State under orders of an officer of the United States," described in subdivision 3 of section 4693, but the service of enlisted men employed in the military service of the United States. They were subject to the orders of the President, being under his command as Commander in Chief of the Army of the United States and amenable to the Articles of War.

It is clear, I think, from the foregoing that Manley's status and that of this appellant were identical so far as their relation to the "service of United States" is concerned. The action of your Bureau from which the appeal is taken is therefore reversed, and the case is remanded for further consideration.

———

SERVICE—CIVILIAN EMPLOYEE—ACT JUNE 27, 1890.

JOHN LAUGHLIN.

1. The words "all persons" in section 2 of the act of June 27, 1890, are limited by the context to those persons who have been "honorably discharged" from "the military or naval service of the United States during the war of the rebellion." and do not include a person who served in the capacity of a civilian employee or as a nonenlisted person.

2. The record evidence in this case shows that the claimant was a civilian employee and nonenlisted person of the Quartermaster's Department.

Assistant Secretary Webster Davis to the Commissioner of Pensions, August 17, 1898.

John Laughlin, late cook on the ram *Horner*, Quartermaster's Department, by his attorney, filed a motion for reconsideration, June 30, 1898, of the departmental decision of February 23, 1898, reversing the Bureau action of November 22, 1894, rejecting his claim (No. 1,056,234). filed August 24, 1891, under section 2 of the act of June 27, 1890, on the ground that he was not an enlisted man, but served as a civilian.

The contention is that it was error to hold that "before the case can be properly adjudicated it must be determined whether or not the applicant was an enlisted man," as was held in said departmental decision; that it is a well-established rule that laws should be so construed as to give force and effect to the purpose for which they were enacted: that the decision illegally injected the phrase "enlisted man" into the first line of the second section of the act of June 27, 1890; that these words do not occur in said section; that the language of the section is "all persons," which is in perfect harmony and accord with the broad and justly liberal terms of the act of July 14, 1862, and the resolution of July 16, 1862, which seem to have been intended for the very class of persons of which the applicant in this case was a member; that said section 2 is easily understood and needs no rule of construction to ascertain the plain intent of Congress, and that claimant is beyond question one of the volunteers for whose benefit the act of June 27, 1890, was enacted.

It is admitted by the attorney for claimant that the words "all persons" are limited, first, to those who served ninety days or more in the military or naval service during the war of the rebellion; second, who were honorably discharged, and third, who are suffering from a mental or physical disability of a permanent character, not the results of their own vicious habits, and which incapacitates them from earning a support by manual labor. He virtually concedes that the phrase "all persons" is not used in its broad, general sense, but is limited to a certain class of persons by the context.

What persons, then, did Congress intend to pension under said section 2 of the act of June 27, 1890?

The title of the act is:

An act to grant pensions to soldiers and sailors who are incapacitated for the performance of manual labor, and provide pensions to widows, minor children, and dependent parents.

The first section provides for the dependent parents; the third section provides for the widows and minor children; the fourth section relates to attorneys' fees and the wrongful withholding of pensions, and if Congress intended to provide for "soldiers and sailors" in the act, that intent is found in the second section, as these four sections comprise the act.

The argument of the attorney for claimant indicates that his construction of the words "all persons" in said section was not only soldiers and sailors, but also civilian employees, who served with the Army or Navy as such.

The natural interpretation of "all persons" suggested by the title of the act is that the phrase was intended to designate "soldiers and sailors"—not civilians or persons who were not soldiers and sailors.

It is true the title of an act is but a formal part, and can not be used to extend or restrain any positive provisions in the body of the act, as was announced by Mr. Justice Field, in Hadden v. Collector (5 Wall., 112), but if the meaning of the act is doubtful the title, if expressive, may have the effect to resolve the doubts, and is entitled to consideration, as was held in case of Deddrick v. Wood (15 Pa. St., 9), citing the case of United States v. Fisher (2 Cranch, 358). See also Commonwealth v. Marshall (62 Pa. St., 328).

But in my opinion we are not required to invoke the aid of the title of the act in this case, although it must be conceded that the title is clear and expressive, as the context furnishes a stronger and more satisfactory method of ascertaining the intent.

The class of pensioners included in the phrase "all persons" is by the plain language of the same sentence limited to those who served "in the military or naval service, * * * and have been honorably discharged therefrom."

Men serve in the military or naval branch of the service by virtue of their enlistment, muster, or commission. No civilian, as such, can legally serve in the Army or Navy. When he enters the service he ceases to be a civilian, he surrenders many of his legal and natural rights as a civilian, and becomes a soldier or a sailor or marine, subject to military and naval rules, laws, and regulations. So also no civilian can be "honorably discharged" from the military or naval service in the sense in which that word is used in the Army, the Navy, and in the pension laws. See cases of George W. Fleck (7 P. D., 343); Margaretha Arendes (8 P. D., 425); Sarah Bush (9 P. D., 144).

It has accordingly been held that a contract surgeon, provost-marshal, enrolling officers, teamsters, and pilots, were civilian employees, and not entitled to pension. See cases of Henry Cushman (7 P. D., 408); Annie E. Few (8 P. D., 95); E. S. Leonard (9 P. D., 194); Isaac N. Philips (3 P. D., 377); Andrew J. Shannon (7 P. D., 64); John W. Reynolds (1 P. D. (o. s.), 223); James M. Barnes (8 P. D., 94); Tryphene (5 P. D. (o. s.), 291); Samuel P. Tate (1 P. D., 449); Basil T. Ridgway (9 P. D., 300); Henry N. Haynie (9 P. D., 304); Mary Brady (9 P. D., 305; Henry Barlow (9 P. D., 347); Anna M. Whalen (9 P. D., 346), and Wm. B. Taylor (9 P. D., 360).

The argument that civilian employees were granted pension under the act of July 14, 1862, and the resolution of July 16, 1862, and that Congress therefore intended to pension them under the act of June 27, 1890, loses its force when we consider said act and resolution of 1862, as amended by the acts of July 27, 1868, and March 3, 1873 (sec. 4693, Revised Statutes), provide that no claim of a nonenlisted person on account of disability from wounds or injury received in battle while temporarily rendering service should be valid unless prosecuted to a successful issue prior to July 4, 1874, and this was the law at the time Congress enacted the law of June 27, 1890, and is still the law.

It is hardly reasonable to suppose that Congress intended to pension a nonenlisted man under the act of June 27, 1890, while at the same time they refused him pension for wounds received in battle in the war of the rebellion. If they so intended it is natural to conclude that they would have manifested it by different language than was employed in section 2 of that act. It is true that the words "man," "men," or "enlisted" do not occur in the section, but neither do the words "civilian employee" or "nonenlisted man."

The courts have frequently had occasion to construe the words "all" and "all persons," and limit their application to all of a particular class, intended to be included or excluded as shown by the context and subject-matter to which they relate, thus ascertaining and carrying into effect the legislative intent.

In the Maine poor law the words "all persons" were limited to those persons who could legally obtain the benefit of the act, and did not include a person who could not legally make a settlement. (See Hallo-well *v.* Gardiner, 1 Me., 93; Milo *v.* Kilmarnock, 11 Me., 455.)

So in a statute which provided that "in all cases," etc., the word "all," was limited to a certain class of cases. (See Philips *v.* State, 15 Ga., 518.)

The court in that case in commenting upon the use of the word "all," use the following language:

One is amazed in casting a glance over our statute books to find how often this form of expression occurs, frequently signifying as here, not absolutely "all," but "all" of a particular class only. Indeed it seems to be common to all writings, lay as well as legal, sacred as well as profane, and the generality of the phrase is frequently to be restrained in an act, not only by the context, but by the general form and scheme of the statute, as demonstrative of the intention of the legislature.

In the case of Keiffer *v.* Ehler (18 Pa. St., 388), the court, by Lowrie, J., said:

In acts of assembly as well as in common parlance the word "all" is a general, rather than a universal term, and is to be understood in one sense or the other according to the demands of sound reason, and an act which authorized the attachment of "all debts," was held not to include debt due by bill of exchange and promissory notes.

In the ex parte case of T. W. Ball (41 Cal., 29), the court in construing the phase, "all persons," occurring in the State constitution which provided that—

All persons shall be bailable by sufficient sureties, unless for capital offenses, when the proof is evident or the presumption great,

held that it did not apply to or include a person who had been convicted of an offense less than capital in degree.

As stated by Sutherland on Statutory Construction, paragraph 279—

The sense in which general words or any words are intended to be used furnishes the rule of interpretation, and this is to be collected from the context, and a narrower or more extended meaning will be given according as the intention is thus indicated.

In the case of Reed *v.* Bush (5 Bin., 455) the words "all actions" in a stipulation included only actions, ex contractu, and not torts, as held by the court in construing the words according to their intent.

Assistant Secretary Bussey, in construing the act of June 27, 1890, in his communication to Commissioner Raum, November 22, 1890, named the conditions on which pensions were allowed, and the second condition was, in case of a soldier, that he should have received a final honorable discharge from the service. (See The Commissioner of Pensions, 4 P. D., 225.)

The previous instructions issued by the Commissioner under said law clearly show that he construed the words "all persons" as applying to those who were enlisted or commissioned. In the blank form of application the claimant was required to state the date when he was "enrolled" and "honorably discharged."

From the date of the passage of said act of 1890 to the present the words "all persons" in section 2 of said act have uniformly been held to apply to those persons who were enrolled in the service, as soldiers, sailors, or marines. (See Pension Decisions heretofore cited.)

It is well settled that the contemporaneous and uniform interpretation of the statutes by those charged with that duty is entitled to great weight, and in cases of doubt ought to turn the scale. (See cases of Brown v. United States, 113 U. S., 568; United States v. B. and Mo. Riv. R. R., 98 U. S., 334–341; Douglas v. Pike, 101 U. S., 677; United States v. Graham, 110 U. S., 219–221; The Laura, 114 U. S, 441; Philbrick v. United States, 120 U. S., 52–59; United States v. Hill, 120 U. S., 169; United States v. Johnston, 124 U. S., 236; Robertson v. Downey, 127 U. S., 607; Edward Lesser v. Darby, 12 Wheaton, 207, and United States v. Gilmore, 8 Wall., 330.)

As stated by Sutherland on Stat. Con., paragraphs 307 and 309:

If there is ambiguity in the language, the understanding of the application of it when the statute first goes into operation, sanctioned by long acquiescence on the part of the legislature and judicial tribunals, is the strongest evidence that it has been rightly explained in practice. The practical construction given by the Interior Department of the General Government in reliance upon the uniform opinions of the Attorney-General's office, of a statute granting lands, should be followed by the State authorities until reversed by the Federal courts. * * * The legislature is presumed to be cognizant of such construction, and after long continuance without any legislation evincing its dissent, the courts will consider themselves warranted in adopting that construction. Contemporary construction and official usage for a long period, by the person charged with the administration of the laws, are among the legitimate aids in the interpretation of statutes.

All aids to interpretation of this section of the act of June 27, 1890, lead naturally and forcibly to the conclusion that the words "all persons" used in the first line of the section were not intended to include any person who was not regularly in the military or naval service of the United States, and a civilian employee or nonenlisted person is therefore excluded from the benefit of the act.

The record evidence of the Third Auditor's office shows that claimant served as a cook on the ram *Horner* from May 1, 1862, to August 28, 1862. This report is dated January 27, 1892.

The pay rolls of the office of the Auditor for the War Department, in the Treasury Department, show that claimant served from May 1, 1862, to July 26, 1862, when said vessel was laid up on account of low water in the Ohio River.

The Auditor of said last-named office reported on March 11, 1898, as follows:

The steam rams were constructed under the supervision of the officers and crew employed by the Quartermaster's Department. There were no regular enlistments and no fixed term of service. Men were employed and discharged at the discretion of the quartermaster in charge of the ram fleet.

This last report shows a service of less than ninety days, and assuming it to be correct, the claimant would not be entitled to a pension under section 2 of said act, even if he had been duly enlisted and honorably discharged.

No valid or satisfactory reason appears for reversing the former departmental decision, and the motion is accordingly overruled.

***

ATTORNEYS—EXAMINATION OF RECORD.

H. S. BERLIN.

The practice which prevails in the Bureau of Pensions of denying to claimants or their authorized attorneys the right to examine the evidence obtained by special examination, except that relating to criminal charges and investigations, is unjust to claimants and unwarranted by law; and all orders or instructions which have that effect are revoked.

Assistant Secretary Webster Davis to the Commissioner of Pensions, August 26, 1898.

On the 20th day of January, 1898, an appeal was filed by Mr. H. S. Berlin, a recognized attorney before the Department, from the practice which has obtained in the Bureau of Pensions refusing attorneys permission to examine the evidence taken by special examiners, in cases where they are the attorneys of record.

The appeal was forwarded to you January 24, 1898, with the request that the contentions of the appeal be given due consideration and a report rendered thereon.

Your report dated March 21, 1898, is as follows:

MARCH 21, 1898.

The honorable the SECRETARY OF THE INTERIOR.

SIR: In compliance with your request for a report on the appeal of H. S. Berlin, of this city, from the refusal of this Bureau to permit attorneys to examine evidence obtained by special examiners in pension claims wherein they are the recognized attorneys, I have the honor to submit that this refusal is based upon a well established practice sustained by a long line of decisions of the War and Interior Departments. These precedents are very fully set forth in the decision of the Secretary of the Interior of March 21, 1892, in re E. W. Whitaker (6 P. D., 179). A brief summary of these citations is herewith submitted.

In 1833, while the Bureau of Pensions was under the control of the War Department, Hon. Lewis Cass, then Secretary of War, addressed to Hon. J. L. Edwards, then Commissioner of Pensions, a letter of instructions relative to the preference given to agents at the seat of Government. The letter is dated September 4, 1833. Mr. Cass said:

"In the future examination of pension cases they will be taken up in the order of presentation, nor will any preference be shown to cases which are urged by agents attending at the seat of Government for that purpose. I consider the attention of such agents useless in itself subjecting the applicants to unnecessary expense."

Hon. J. R. Poinsett, Secretary of War, under date of May 7, 1838, addressed a letter of instructions to the Commissioner of Pensions laying down a set of rules to govern the practice. Rules 2 and 3 were as follows:

"2. No agent will be permitted to examine books or papers in the Pension Office in any case whatever without first making a written application to the Commissioner of Pensions for that purpose, stating fully the object for which he wishes to make such examination and what particular facts he expects to obtain. The Commissioner will then determine whether the request can be complied with.

"3. To prevent the examining clerks from being interrupted in the discharge of their duties, no person acting on behalf of claimants or pensioners will be allowed to hold any conversation with such clerks in relation to claims presented by them, and no examination of papers deposited by agents or pensioners shall be made in the presence of persons who deposit the same, or who may have any interest in the claim or claims presented."

These rules were adopted April 9, 1850, by the Hon. Thomas Ewing, the first Secretary of the Interior, to which Department the Bureau of Pensions had been transferred from the War Department.

Hon. C. Delano, Secretary of the Interior, under date of September 19, 1874, also affirmed the above rules in a letter addressed to the Commissioner of Pensions, in which he said:

"It is an established rule of your office that upon due application therefor by claimant or attorney wishing to appeal an abstract of all the evidence in a claim excepting record evidence and medical or other evidence of a confidential nature is furnished to the applicant. This rule was sanctioned by my predecessors and is believed to be an eminently proper one. I find nothing in the appeal to induce me to direct any modification in the rule, and therefore I approve the action of your office in the claim."

Under date of March 6, 1876, the Hon. Z. Chandler, in a letter addressed to E. W. Whitaker, on an appeal taken by the latter from the action of the Commissioner of Pensions in refusing to permit him, as attorney for M. N. Snell, to examine the evidence in his claim for increase of pension, said:

"The rule which has obtained with regard to furnishing evidence to claimants or attorneys is that, upon due application to the Commissioner of Pensions, that officer shall furnish the party applying therefor with an abstract of such evidence in the claim as, under the rules of the Department, is permitted to be given out. Under the rules just referred to, record evidence, or evidence obtained by a special agent of the Pension Office, is invariably excluded from the abstract thus furnished.

"The action of the Commissioner, from which you appeal, was in strict conformity with the rule of the Department, and I am not at liberty therefore to disturb it."

In a decision dated December 19, 1891, in re S. E. Adler, attorney (5 P. D., 229), the Department approved and reaffirmed the rule of practice which forbids attorneys, pending the adjudication of pension claims, to examine transcripts from the records of the War Department, certificates of examining surgeons, confidential communications, and reports of special examiners. In this decision the Secretary said, with reference to special examiners' reports, that "the purpose of a special examiner is never to defeat a claim, but to get at the facts essential to a just decision upon its merits." If the claimant desires to satisfy himself that the investigation is fairly conducted he may be present in person or represented by an attorney during the examination of witnesses. He may also cross-examine witnesses in regard to any statements made by them before the special examiner. The claim that he could not do this intelligently unless he is permitted to inspect all the papers in the case is believed to be without any foundation. The Secretary said:

"After careful consideration the Department does not perceive how any benefit could possibly accrue to an honest claimant by the concession of the privilege demanded in this case, but can readily perceive how such a privilege might be used by either dishonest claimants or unscrupulous attorneys for the futherance of their nefarious schemes and the defeat of justice. It is doubtful whether any good purpose is subserved by permitting attorneys to inspect the papers in pension claims under any circumstances."

Under date of January 4, 1892, Order No. 174 was issued as follows:

"In accordance with the decision of the Secretary of the Interior December 19, 1891, S. E. Adler, attorney, it is hereby ordered that no examination of papers relating to claims for pension or bounty land by attorneys, counsel, or agents, shall extend to reports from the War Department, confidential communications, certificates of examining surgeons, or reports of special examiners relating to criminal charges and investigations. The papers herein designated shall be taken out by the file clerk and placed in an envelope, properly briefed, and retained until the return of the papers."

The Secretary of the Interior, in a decision dated February 1, 1892, in re M. B. Stevens & Co. (5 P. D., 254), after fully discussing the subject, said:

"It is not practicable to furnish copies of the reports to claimants and attorneys living at a distance. The ultimate effect of the rule which has prevailed within the last few years (until the issuance of your order) must therefore be to throw the business of prosecuting claims for increase entirely into the hands of attorneys residing in this city; that is to say, into the hands of those who have the least acquaintance with the claimants whom they represent, and therefore the least personal knowledge of the facts upon which their claims are based. It does not appear to the Department that the interests either of claimants or the Government would be best served by such a consummation.

"In conclusion, the Department would say that Order No. 174 might have circumscribed the privilege of personal examination by attorneys of papers on file in your Bureau to narrower limits than it does without conflicting with the views expressed in the departmental decision of December 19, 1891, and that after careful consideration those views have not been modified in the least, but are hereby reaffirmed."

After referring to the precedents, the Secretary, in the decision of March 21, 1892, in re E. W. Whitaker, above referred to (6 P. D., 179), says:

"It is borne in mind that there are about sixty thousand attorneys practicing before the Bureau of Pensions, and it is readily perceived that, but for the rule now under consideration, they or their representatives would crowd the Bureau for the purpose of making an unrestricted investigation of papers, thereby requiring the extra service of a large clerical force, not only to find the cases, but to exercise a surveillance over them while, for the ends of such an examination, the cases remained out of the files. Otherwise the attorney or his representative would have unrestrained control over all the papers in such cases—a privilege that can not be safely accorded nor prudently sanctioned in any office of the Government."

In view of the above precedents and citations, I do not consider that I have any discretion in the premises, but respectfully submit that, in my opinion, Order No. 174 is eminently proper, and recommend that no change or modification be made unless it be to still further restrict the privilege of personal examination by attorneys of papers in pension claims.

Very respectfully,

J. L. DAVENPORT,
Acting Commissioner.

On April 27, 1898, it was deemed proper to return the foregoing report with suggestions as follows:

WASHINGTON, *April 27, 1898.*

The COMMISSIONER OF PENSIONS.

SIR: In the interests of claimants and the Government alike, and also in consonance with our respective official duties, I am constrained to return the accompanying appeal of H. S. Berlin & Co., with additional correspondence, for a further report upon the question at issue.

Your letters of March 21, 1898, and of April 25, 1898, are not fully responsive to the request made or the contention of appellant.

I infer from your communications that Order No. 174, issued January 4, 1892, is still in force in your Bureau; at least you make reference to no other. It is fair to presume that the portion of the order relating to "Certificates of examining surgeons" has been eliminated in accordance with the last proviso of the act of July 18, 1894, although I have no official notice that an order of record has been issued to that effect. Order 174 provides that in accordance with the decision of the Secretary of the Interior of December 19, 1891 (S. E. Adler, attorney), that no examination by attorneys of papers relating to claims for pension, etc., shall extend to "reports from the War Department, confidential communications, certificates of examining surgeons, or reports of special examiners relating to criminal charges and investigations."

Eliminating "certificates of examining surgeons," in accordance with subsequent legislation, I see no objection to the order.

In the absence of any additional order, it is not clear upon what ground or authority recognized attorneys are denied the privilege of examining the evidence obtained by special examiners, upon which claims are often rejected, and which do not relate to "criminal charges and investigations."

"Reports of special examiners," consisting of their individual impressions as to the merits of a claim, credibility of witnesses, etc., may reasonably be considered "confidential communications," and may be withheld, but it is questionable whether the evidence thus obtained, which in many cases determines the rights of claimants, should be so considered.

Without entering into a discussion of the question at this time, it is respectfully requested that you give the matter careful consideration, with the view of determining whether, in the interest of harmony and good practice, the apparent construction of Order No. 174 may not be so modified as to permit recognized attorneys to examine the evidence obtained by special examiners, except in criminal cases.

I am convinced from an examination of the appeal files that in many cases, if attorneys were fully cognizant of the nature of such evidence upon which adverse action has been taken by your Bureau, they would refrain from filing an appeal, and thus relieve your Bureau and the Department of additional and increasing labor.

An early reply is respectfully requested, with the return of the accompanying papers, in order to dispose of this and other pending appeals.

Very respectfully,

WEBSTER DAVIS,
Assistant Secretary.

As a final report had not been received, you were again requested to forward the same on August 12, 1898, to which you responded, August 13, 1898, as follows:

AUGUST 13, 1898.

The honorable the SECRETARY OF THE INTERIOR.

SIR: I have the honor to return herewith the appeal of H. S. Berlin, attorney, appealing from the practice of this Bureau in withholding from the attorney the evidence taken and reports by special examiners, together with the subsequent correspondence.

I have given much attention and consideration to this matter of special examinations. The Government is expending annually for special examiners and expenses in that branch of the service $900,000, or near that amount. It is the only check or protection the Government has. All other cases are passed upon ex parte evidence.

When a case is sent to a special examiner in the field the claimant and his attorney have the privilege of being present and cross-questioning the witnesses and of having the evidence taken read.

During last year there were about 95,000 cases allowed; there were about 85,000 rejected. Of this number about 14,800 cases were specially examined. The remainder were adjudicated strictly on the ex parte cases presented by claimants through their attorneys. About 6,000 of the cases of those that were specially examined were rejected on the reports of the special examiners. And, as you know, although they were rejected, they are still pending, and these reports of special examiners we believed were the property of the Department—confidential papers.

The trouble comes right here. Where that evidence has been taken the credibility of the same and the credibility of the witness is unquestioned, and the case returned here. The Washington expert, who knows every word, term, phrase, or sentence necessary to controvert or impeach the evidence secured, is called in and affidavits are prepared and sent out to be sworn to and returned to the Bureau, frequently impeaching the testimony of reliable witnesses. The Government seems to have absolutely no rights in these matters. If the case is an absolute fraud, and the examiner shows it to be, then time is an element. The examiner must be gotten out of that territory or wait until another set of officials come in; then the case is tried again. A claim once filed is always pending under the established practice until it is allowed. I will say frankly that some of the attorneys practicing before this Bureau are getting so bold and so bad I am disposed to think of sending every one of their cases for special examination, but to do this might work hardship upon the legitimate claimants, and calls for delay in getting their claims adjudicated.

With reference to the present practice of this Bureau as to exhibiting certificates of examining surgeons, I am doing exactly what the law requires, and what I am sworn to do, "open to the inspection of the claimant or his attorney," and I prohibit their clerks and others coming here and copying these returns. The attorneys secured the passage of this law and I am simply making them live up to it.

Very respectfully, your most obedient servant,

H. CLAY EVANS,
Commissioner.

Referring to your report of March 21, 1898, it will be observed that the rules in force in 1833, 1838, 1850, 1874, and 1876, as indicated, were established under different conditions. There was then no special examination of pension cases as now. Investigations then were wholly ex parte, by designated agents, and often the evidence obtained was of a confidential character. But even then claimants or their agents were not absolutely prohibited from examining the evidence thus obtained. Also, as late as 1874 the Secretary of the Interior, Mr. Delano, sanctioned and approved the practice which had obtained of furnishing a claimant or his attorney wishing to appeal an abstract of all the evidence in his claim excepting "record evidence and medical or other evidence of a confidential nature." He said "this rule was sanctioned by my predecessors and is believed to be an eminently proper one."

This rule of practice, having reference to record and medical evidence and evidence obtained on an ex parte examination, was also approved by Secretary Chandler in March, 1876.

The case to which you refer, on appeal by S. E. Adler, attorney, raised substantially the same question, and in the departmental decision rendered December 19, 1891, it was held that where permission was granted to claimants or attorneys to examine the evidence, "there are obvious reasons why it should not extend to transcripts from the records of the War Department, certificates of examining surgeons, confidential communications, and reports of special examiners relating to criminal charges and investigations."

This departmental decision was made the basis of Order No. 174, issued by your predecessor, Gen. Green B. Raum, on January 4, 1892, as follows:

In accordance with the decision of the Secretary of the Interior December, 19, 1891, S. E. Adler, attorney, it is hereby ordered that no examination of papers relating to claims for pension or bounty land by attorneys, counsel, or agents shall extend to reports from the War Department, confidential communications, certificates of examining surgeons, or reports of special examiners relating to criminal charges and investigations. The papers herein designated shall be taken out by the file clerk and placed in an envelope, properly briefed, and retained until the return of the papers.

It will be observed that this order points out definitely what evidence shall be withheld, viz:

Reports from the War Department, confidential communications, certificates of examining surgeons, or reports of special examiners relating to criminal charges and investigations.

The last proviso of the act of Congress approved July 18, 1894, eliminated one of these, as follows:

Provided, That the report of such examining surgeons, when filed in the Pension Office, shall be open to the examination and inspection of the claimant or his attorney, under such reasonable rules and regulations as the Secretary of the Interior may provide.

Presumably this statutory provision has been complied with, although no order of record modifying Order No. 174 has been filed with the Department, and it is observed that in your report of March 21, 1898, you make no reference to it, but, on the contrary, you state, in the concluding paragraph, as follows:

In my opinion, Order No. 174 is eminently proper, and recommend that no change or modification be made unless it be still further to restrict the privilege of personal examination of papers in pension claims.

A proper construction of Order No. 174 has continuously received the recognition and support of your predecessors, and, together with the exception contained in the provision of the act of Congress of July 18, 1894, referred to, it has repeatedly received the sanction and approval of the Department.

I am led to infer from your report and the prevailing practice in the Bureau of Pensions that you construe said order in a different light, and apply it to all reports of special examiners, and deny the right of claimants or their attorneys to inspect the evidence obtained by special examiners in all cases. I have no hesitancy in saying that this construction of Order No. 174 is disapproved, and if, under verbal instructions, the Bureau of Pensions refuses to allow claimants or their attorneys the right to read the evidence obtained by special examiners, excepting "reports of special examiners relating to criminal charges and investigations," such instructions can not receive the approval of the Department.

As you are aware, the prime object of special examination is, through an open, full, and impartial investigation, to obtain the material facts for or against the parties at interest, without bias or prejudice. The special examiner is not in any sense the attorney of the claimant or the Government. His mission is to give the claimant every opportunity to supply the evidence necessary to complete his claim. It is not an ex parte examination, conducted after the manner which prevailed many years ago; hence the claimant is entitled to be present, or to be represented by an attorney throughout the examination, and to cross-examine witnesses if he desires. In other words, it is his right to hear or know every word of testimony in his case, whether favorable or unfavorable. No court in the land would deny him this privilege. It is a constitutional right, which can not be abridged.

It is true, if the claimant were present or was represented by an attorney throughout the special investigation, and was then made fully cognizant of the nature of all the testimony, there could be no just cause for complaint. But the records of the Bureau of Pensions will show that such instances are exceedingly rare, and although the privilege is granted to claimant to be present, it is in most instances impossible for him to do so. As a rule, his statement is taken and he is compelled by force of circumstances to waive his right to be present, as the special examination proceeds from place to place, often in different States; nor is he able to employ attorneys to follow the investigation in the field.

The result is, in a very large proportion of the cases, the special examination is conducted in his absence, with no attorney to represent his interests, and the rejection of the claim follows by reason of the testimony thus obtained.

Practically it has been an ex parte examination, and under the present practice in your Bureau the claimant has no knowledge of the adverse testimony upon which his claim has been rejected.

It would be impracticable to furnish him with a copy of the evidence, as was the practice formerly, but his request to see the evidence, or a like request by his authorized attorney, can not lawfully and justly be denied.

As indicated in my communication of April 12, 1898, I am convinced that the number of appeals has been largely augmented by reason of this practice.

I think you will agree with me that due respect for the rights of claimants or their authorized attorneys will be in harmony with the letter and spirit of the pension laws, and at the same time the rights of the Government will be preserved.

I am led to the conclusion that the practice which prevails in your Bureau of denying to claimants or their authorized attorneys the right to examine the evidence obtained by special examination, except that contained in " reports of special examiners relating to criminal charges and investigations," is unjust to claimants and unwarranted by law. It is therefore directed that all orders or instructions which have that effect shall be revoked.

Approved:

C. N. BLISS, *Secretary.*

ATTORNEYS—REPRESENTATIVES OF ATTORNEYS.
CHARLES AND WILLIAM B. KING.

1. Under the authority conferred by the act of July 18, 1894, it is suggested the instructions of the bureau be modified to the extent that representatives of recognized attorneys who have written authority from their employers be granted the same privilege of examining the certificates of examining surgeons as is provided by law for the attorneys in person.
2. Hereafter, under section 471 of the Revised Statutes, all orders or circulars affecting the rights of claimants, or their properly accredited attorneys, shall be submitted to the Secretary of the Interior for his information and approval prior to their promulgation.

Assistant Secretary Webster Davis to the Commissioner of Pensions, August 27, 1898.

Messrs. Charles and William B. King, attorneys of record before the Department, entered an appeal from the practice of the Bureau of Pensions, by your authority, in refusing their representative to examine the reports of examining surgeons in cases where they are the recognized attorneys.

I have your report of March 21, 1898, relating thereto, and also your letter of August 13, 1898, which reads as follows:

AUGUST 13, 1898.

The honorable the SECRETARY OF THE INTERIOR.

SIR: Replying to your inquiry about appeal of Charles and William B. King, attorneys, from the practice of this bureau in refusing permission of others than the registered attorneys in a case to see the reports of medical examinations:

The practice of this bureau is exactly in accordance with the law. The attorneys of this city secured a rider on an appropriation bill providing that "the attorney or claimant should be privileged to examine the reports submitted by medical examiners." This I am doing, and I am limiting them to the law. In other words, I do not permit any but the attorney of record in the case or the claimant to see these papers. The act was secured over the protest of the Secretary of the Interior and the Commissioner of Pensions. The privilege had been much abused, by sending clerks here copying these reports and sending them back, to the annoyance of the best medical examiners. It was used as a system to intimidate the medical examiners, to compel them to give high ratings. There is a history to all this. I am complying with the law literally.

Very respectfully, your obedient servant,

H. CLAY EVANS, *Commissioner.*

In your report of March 21, 1898, you state that the present practice is based upon the proviso contained in the appropriation act of July 18, 1894, as follows:

That the report of such examining surgeons when filed in the Pension Office shall be open to the examination and inspection of the claimant or his attorney, under such reasonable rules and regulations as the Secretary of the Interior may provide.

It appears that in pursuance of the foregoing the following order (No. 268) was issued ten days later:

The proviso contained in the pension appropriation act of Congress of July 18, 1894, as follows: "That the report of such examining surgeons when filed in the

Pension Office shall be open to the examination and inspection of the claimant or his attorney, under such reasonable rules and regulations as the Secretary of the Interior may provide," should be complied with in such manner as will afford all proper information to claimants and their attorneys in all pending claims, and at the same time interfere as little as may be with the work of the bureau.

Any indiscriminate exhibition of surgeons' reports, especially in cases disposed of by admission or rejection, can only be productive of evil, by occupying the time and attention of clerks, and giving opportunity for making public the physical injuries and ailments of pensioners and claimants. The object of the proviso is only to aid claimants and their accredited attorneys in preparing their evidence and arguments for submission of pending cases; therefore—

1. No one but the claimant in person and his recognized attorney in the claim shall be permitted to examine the reports of the examining surgeons filed in the claim; and such examination shall be made subject to the rules of the Pension Bureau in respect to the calling up and examination of cases by attorneys.

2. No examination of reports of examining surgeons shall be permitted in admitted cases wherein there is no claim pending.

3. No examination of such reports shall be permitted in rejected cases, after the lapse of six months from the date of rejection, until the claim has been regularly reopened, according to the practice of the bureau, or unless an appeal from the decision is pending.

4. Where such a report of examining surgeons has been submitted to the inspection of the claimant or his attorney the fact and date shall be noted on the jacket, and the same shall not again be so submitted within the period of six months thereafter.

WM. LOCHREN, Commissioner.

Approved:
  HOKE SMITH, Secretary.

It will be observed that this order was issued by your predecessor, with the concurrence and approval of the Secretary of the Interior, the latter being required under the specific provisions of the act quoted.

This order (No. 268) was the rule of practice until, according to your report, October 5, 1897, when you issued the following instructions, viz:

Hereafter no attorney shall be permitted to examine the reports of examining surgeons in any pension claim except upon the personal order of the Commissioner or one of the deputy commissioners of this bureau.

This was supplemented on October 20, 1897, by the following:

The certificates of examining surgeons may be examined or inspected by the claimant or his recognized attorney in person only after final adverse action is taken thereon and within three months after date of notice of such action.

It will be observed that these instructions, issued without the authority of the Department, modify to some extent order No. 268, which received the approval of the Secretary of the Interior. But this is immaterial to the question at issue in this appeal.

As already indicated, the act of July 18, 1894, provides that the certificates of examining surgeons shall be open to the examination and inspection of the claimant or his attorney "under such reasonable rules and regulations as the Secretary of the Interior may provide."

It was the evident intention of the lawmaking power that the claimant or his accredited attorney should have personal knowedge of the findings of the boards of examining surgeons. The act also conferred upon the Secretary of the Interior power to prescribe such reasonable rules and regulations as will best convey to the claimant or his attorney the right conferred.

While it may be true, as indicated in your letter of the 13th instant, by granting the claimant or his attorney this privilege you comply with the letter of the law, yet is it not true that often, by refusing to the properly accredited representative of the attorney this privilege, you fail to comply with the spirit of the law, and by so doing an injustice to the claimant is done?

It is well known that many recognized attorneys have confidential clerks in their employ, who are charged with the supervision of their pension business. If such employees appear with proper authority from their employers, would not the spirit of the law be complied with by granting to them the same privileges which the law gives to their superiors?

You say the privilege is sometimes abused, and refer to a single instance of that character.

If that be so, the remedy is in your hands; there is ample authority for requiring an attorney or his accredited agent to comply fully with the law and established rules and regulations.

While I do not deem it proper to issue an imperative order relating to this practice, I feel free to suggest, under the authority conferred by the act of July 18, 1894, that your instructions be modified to the extent that representatives of recognized attorneys, who have written authority from their employers, be granted the same privilege of examining the certificates of examining surgeons as is provided by law for the attorneys in person.

It is believed that this change in the rules of practice will be in harmony with the spirit of the law and will result in no hindrance to the dispatch of public business, and the rights of the claimant will be duly observed.

In this connection I desire to invite your attention to the following departmental instructions:

DEPARTMENT OF THE INTERIOR,
Washington, June 5, 1884.

Chiefs of bureaus and offices are requested to submit to the Secretary for his information, and prior to their promulgation, any orders or circulars prepared in their respective offices.

H. M. TELLER, *Secretary.*

The foregoing is evidently based upon the provisions of section 471, Revised Statutes, which provide as follows:

The Commissioner of Pensions shall perform, under the direction of the Secretary of the Interior, such duties in the execution of the various pension and bounty-land laws as may be prescribed by the President.

This order is still in force and meets with the approval of the Department.

It is therefore directed that all orders or instructions affecting the rights of claimants, or their properly accredited attorneys, shall be submitted to the Secretary of the Interior for his information and approval prior to their promulgation.

Approved:

C. N. BLISS, *Secretary.*

———

AID AND ATTENDANCE—RATE.

MARTIN B. FITCH.

It appears from the evidence in this case that the disability of this appellant resulting from the pensioned rheumatism was practically the same at the date his pension was reduced from $72 to $30 per month, and has so remained since that date, as it was when he was given his present rating of $50 per month under the provisions of the act of July 14, 1892, and is and has been such as to incapacitate the appellant for the performance of any manual labor, and necessitate the frequent and periodical, but not the regular and constant aid and attendance of another person:

Held, That he is entitled to the rating of $50 per month from the date his pension was reduced to $30 per month, but is not entitled to restoration to the rate of $72 per month.

Assistant Secretary Webster Davis to the Commissioner of Pensions, August 27, 1898.

Martin B. Fitch, late private Company H, Eighteenth Iowa Volunteer Infantry, is, and has been since date of discharge from the service, a pensioner under the provisions of sections 4692 and 4693, Revised Statutes, for rheumatism at the rates of $6 per month from February 4, 1863; $30 per month from June 16, 1886; $50 per month from November 7, 1888, and $72 per month from March 4, 1890.

In February, 1895, his rating was, after due and legal notice, reduced to $30 per month from January 4, 1895.

An appeal was taken from this action on August 26, 1897, which was considered by this Department on March 31, 1898, when said action was reversed, and the case remanded with instructions that it be reopened by your Bureau and investigated by special examination, a test medical examination of the pensioner made, and it be readjudicated in the light of the facts thus developed.

The instructions of the Department having been complied with, the case was again adjudicated by your Bureau on June 14, 1898, when restoration of the former rating of $72 per month was refused, but increase was granted at the rate of $50 per month from June 1, 1898, and on June 21, 1898, pensioner's certificate was reissued to allow him that rate from said date.

From this action the present appeal was taken on July 16, 1898.

It is the contention of the present appeal not only that the reduction of appellant's rate of pension to $30 per month was unjust and erroneous, but that his pensionable disability has been the same in degree and severity from the date of said reduction in January, 1895, to the present time, and that during said period it had rendered him so totally and permanently helpless as to require the regular and constant aid and attendance of another person, and entitled him to receive the "first-grade" rating of $72 per month provided by the act of March 4, 1890.

The "first-grade" rate of $72 per month formerly received by this appellant is provided by the act of March 4, 1890, for a disability producing permanent and total helplessness requiring the constant and regular personal aid and attendance of another person. The rate of $50 per month, which he is now receiving, is provided by the act of July 14, 1892, for a disability which incapacitates for the performance of any manual labor, and also necessitates the frequent and periodical, though not regular and constant personal aid and attendance of another person, and this rating must be made to commence from the date of a certificate of medical examination by an examining surgeon or board of surgeons, showing the existence of such degree of pensionable disability, and made after the passage of said act.

The test medical examination of this appellant, pursuant to the departmental instructions above referred to, was made by the board of surgeons at McGregor, Iowa, on June 1, 1898, who certify and describe his physical condition and existing disability as found by them on said date as follows:

Pulse rate, 90; respiration, 20; temperature, 98.6; height, 5 feet 10½ inches; weight, 210 pounds; age, 57 years. He can raise his right arm to a right angle with his body. Any effort to raise it above this point or while in this position to carry it forward or rotate it causes pain. The forearm can be flexed to an angle of about 20 degrees and extended to an angle of 45 degrees, and an attempt to rotate it while either flexed or extended causes pain. Motion in wrist joint is impaired to the extent that he can not fully extend the hand or straighten it, and it can be flexed to an angle of about 20 degrees only. This joint is slightly enlarged; measures one-third of an inch in circumference more than the left. All the joints and fingers are anchylosed in a semiflexed position, and he has not the power to either grasp or hold an object. There is partial anchylosis of joints of thumb, and mobility is impaired to the extent that he is unable to grasp or hold an object between the thumb and index finger.

A description of right arm and hand describes the left with the following difference: Forearm can be flexed to an angle of 20 degrees and extended to about 55 degrees. There is about 30 degrees motion in wrist joint and the joint measures one-third less in circumference than the right.

The right leg immediately below the gluteal fold measures 1 inch more in circumference than the left and from anterior superior spinous process of ilium to lower border of patella measures 1 inch more than the left. There is marked flattening posterior to trochanter major, as the result of shrinking of the gluteal muscles. The leg can not be fully extended and can be flexed to an angle of about 25 degrees only.

There is partial anchylosis of knee joint and leg can be extended to an angle of 25 degrees and flexed about 30 degrees from that point; the same is true of the ankle joint.

The left leg can be flexed at hip joint to a right angle and nearly fully extended.

The knee joint is slightly impaired; it can be almost fully extended and flexed to a right angle. There is partial anchylosis of ankle joint; the toes can be moved through an arc of about 20 degrees.

In the region of inner condyle of right femur there is a cicatrix 1½ inches in length and 1 inch wide, depressed and adherent and sensitive, the result of an abscess.

In right groin, over Poupart's ligament, there is a cicatrix, extending in line of ligament, 3 inches long, presenting a marked depression, adhesions, and sensitiveness. About an inch below this cicatrix there are smaller cicatrices. All these, claimant states, are the results of a very large abscess. We believe his statement to be true.

Contour of back appears to be normal, but there is marked tenderness in region of spinous processes of all vertebræ from last cervical to sacrum.

The action of the heart is somewhat rapid and irregular, and although a slight murmur may exist we are not fully convinced that such is the case. The extremely thick walls of the chest and irregular action of the heart preclude the possibility of a positive diagnosis. Claimant is unable to perform any manual labor. His gait is slow and somewhat uncertain, hence walks with difficulty. He can neither dress nor undress himself, and can with difficulty grasp and carry food to his mouth. He is, in our opinion, so totally and permanently helpless as the result of rheumatism that he requires the regular personal aid of another person. No evidence of vicious habits. Rating, first grade.

The conditions found and described on the foregoing medical examination, as well as the facts developed, relative to the need of aid required by the appellant, by the testimony taken on the special examination of this case, directed by the Department, attributable to and resulting from the pensioned causes, were carefully reviewed and considered by the medical referee on July 14, 1898, who held that the same justified the conclusion that the pensionable disability of appellant was such as to necessitate and require the frequent and periodical personal aid and attendance of another person, and entitled him to the rating of $50 per month provided by the act of July 14, 1892, but that a condition of total and permanent helplessness, necessitating the regular and constant personal aid and attendance of another person, which would entitle him to the rating of $72 per month as provided by the act of March 4, 1890, was not shown to exist, and consequently he should not be restored to that rating.

I have carefully examined and considered the evidence bearing upon this point, and I agree with the foregoing conclusion of the medical referee. The statements of the appellant himself, the testimony of witnesses, and the findings of the boards of examining surgeons, fail utterly to establish the existence of such a condition of disability as is required by the provisions of the act of March 4, 1890, to warrant a rating of $72 per month, and therefore the refusal of your Bureau to restore appellant to said rating was correct and is hereby affirmed.

The remaining question to be considered is whether the reduction of appellant's pension to $30 per month from January 4, 1895, was justified by the facts in his case. Your Bureau has accepted the conditions of pensionable disability found upon the foregoing test medical examination, and shown by the recent special examination of this case, as sufficient to warrant the rating of $50 per month under the act of July 14, 1892, from the date of said examination. The previous medical examinations of appellant and the testimony would seem to indicate very clearly, however, that this condition of disability existed substantially in the same degree, so far as the need of aid required by the appellant as a result of the pensioned rheumatism is concerned, at the time said reduction was made, and has since continued in the same degree.

The principal source of the appellant's helplessness consists in the condition of his hands, which are described in the testimony and the certificates of medical examination as being drawn up in a half-closed condition, stiffened and partially paralyzed, without power to open or close the fingers, or to grasp anything, except a very slight ability to hold light objects between the thumb and the side of the first finger. In short, his hands are described and shown to be practically useless for all ordinary purposes. It clearly appears from the evidence that he is unable to dress or undress himself, attend the calls of nature, or perform any of the ordinary duties and functions of daily life, where the hands are required to be used, without assistance to a greater or less extent, and that he has been in this condition without material change for the better since sometime previous to the date at which his pension was reduced to $30 per month.

The appellant was medically examined by the board of surgeons at Cresco, Iowa, on May 9, 1894, who certify and describe his condition on that date from rheumatism and results, and state that there was partial paralysis of both hands and partial anchylosis of metacarpophalangeal articulations—unable to open or shut either hand. They state that he was totally disabled for manual labor by reason of the disability in both hands; that they did not think he required the constant aid and attendance of another person, but that he did need periodical aid.

The medical examination upon which the reduction of appellant's pension appears to have been principally based was made by the board at Decorah, Iowa, on October 3 and November 21, 1894, the appellant having apparently been called twice before the board. The appellant contends (and it would seem from the evidence not without reason) that the certificate of this examination was not a true reflex of his physical condition at that time, and that great injustice was done him by the report made and filed in your Bureau of said examination and the manner in which it was conducted. The certificate of said examination is undoubtedly exceedingly imperfect, unsatisfactory, and meager in its details for an examination upon which to base action reducing pension from a "first-grade" rating. It contains no description whatever of the appellant's general physical condition, makes no mention of any other results of rheumatism than disability existing in hands and right knee joint, and as to these results gives no specific description by which the extent of pensionable disability resulting therefrom could be definitely ascertained, and scarcely does more than to mention the fact of their existence. Said certificate is as follows:

Shortening of flexor muscles of left hand, but he can extend fingers full length by manipulation, as pressing the hand on a flat surface. Slight contraction and wasting of fingers, slight anchylosis of joint of right knee; but he came upstairs to office without use of hand rail or cane. No enlargement of joint; partial atrophy of muscles. Left leg measures 11¾ inches; right, 14½ inches. Biceps and dorsal muscles contract under Faradism.

The examining surgeon, who signed the foregoing certificate as president of said board, testified positively and directly, on the special examination of this case made pursuant to the aforesaid departmental directions, that it did not truly set forth the facts found by the board on said examination, and did not correspond with the description of the appellant's disability and the recommendations of said board as agreed on by them at the time of said examination. When questioned as to how his signature happened to be appended to said certificate if it was not a correct statement of the facts and findings of said board, he stated that the members of the board sometimes signed the certificates in blank, leaving the description of the disability and the body of the certificate to be afterwards filled up and written out, by the member of the board who acted as secretary, from memoranda made out and agreed on by the members of the board at the time of the examination, and he supposed this was an instance of that kind. The member of said board in whose handwriting said certificate is made out declined and refused, on said special examination, to answer any questions relative thereto, and when the special examiner insisted on cross-examining him with regard to said certificate left the examination, refused to sign his deposition, or to afterwards be interviewed or give further testimony.

This gives decided color to the charges of the appellant that said medical examination was improperly conducted and that said certificate was fraudulent and unjust to him. It undoubtedly shows that there was something wrong and out of the usual course with said certificate of examination; that it was not above suspicion of bad faith, and was not such a document as the action of your Bureau reducing this appellant's pension should have been based upon.

Under the decisions and rulings of this Department it has been the uniform practice to rarely disturb the adjustment of former ratings made by your Bureau except where fraud, mistake, or palpable injustice was made clearly apparent by the evidence. In view, however, of the suspicions of bad faith attaching to the certificate of medical examination upon which appellant's pension was reduced that have been herein pointed out, and the fact that, in my opinion, it has been clearly proved that the appellant's disability and resulting need of aid from the pensioned rheumatism was fully as great at the date when his pension was reduced to $30 per month, and has so remained since, as it was shown to be when his present rating of $50 per month was granted by your Bureau, I believe this to be an instance where the ends of justice would be best subserved by directing a readjustment of his rating from the date of said reduction.

I am of the opinion that the conditions found and described by the board of surgeons at Cresco, Iowa, on May 9, 1894, justified and warranted the allowance of the $50 rating provided by the act of July 14, 1892, and that the certificate of said examination fulfilled the conditions of said act and entitled him to receive the rating therein provided from and after the date of said certificate, and that the reduction of his rate of pension from $72 per month to $30 per month from January 4, 1895, was error.

Therefore the action of your Bureau reducing this appellant's pension from $72 per month to $30 per month from January 4, 1895, is hereby set aside and reversed, and you are requested to cause a reissue of his certificate to be made to allow and pay him the rate of $50 per month from and after said date, deducting all subsequent payments.

RATE—ACT JUNE 27, 1890.

JAMES CALDWELL.

The maximum rate of pension under the act of June 27, 1890, corresponds with total disability and the minimum and intervening rates correspond, proportionately, with all partial degrees of inability to earn a support by manual labor.

Assistant Secretary Webster Davis to the Commissioner of Pensions, August 31, 1898.

James Caldwell, the appellant, enlisted on July 29, 1863, in Company A, First Kentucky Cavalry, from which time he was in the military service of the United States until May 25, 1865, when he was discharged.

On March 17, 1897, he filed a declaration for pension (No. 1054961) under the act of June 27, 1890, alleging general debility. He filed another declaration under said act on August 12, 1897, alleging catarrh, rheumatism, piles, and injury to chest.

The claim was adjudicated on March 21, 1898, and rejected on the medical ground that no ratable disability was shown to exist.

From said action appeal was taken on April 21, 1898, resting upon the following assignment of error:

The claimant was examined on November 27, 1897, to determine his right to a pension, and the board reported him to be entitled to a rating of six-eighteenths for catarrh, six-eighteenths for disease of heart, and four-eighteenths for rheumatism.

It appears from this examination that this soldier is entitled to at least the minimum rating under the act of June 27, 1890, and I therefore request that the action of the Commissioner of Pensions be reversed and a pension be allowed this soldier.

The objective conditions described in a certificate of medical examination executed on November 27, 1897, are as follows:

Pulse rate, 86; respiration, 17; temperature, 98; height, 5 feet 6½ inches; weight, 149 pounds; age, 51 years. There is engorgement and congestion of entire post-nasal region, half arches, tonsils, uvulas, pharynx, and up into the nasal passages. Mucous membrane is bathed in a stringy mucus; eustachian tubes are open. Hearing is slightly impaired, but can hear with either ear at 6 feet. Rate disability from naso-pharyngeal catarrh at six-eighteenths.

The area of heart dullness is increased about one-third above normal; no murmur, apex beat, 2¼ inches to right and 1 inch below nipple; sounds and rhythm normal; action easily disturbed; 86 sitting; 110 on exercise; rate at six-eighteenths.

There is some crepitus in each shoulder joint when motion is made, with tender-ness and very considerable impairment of motion, being unable to put hands above head or across back; rate at four-eighteenths.

The anal vessels are very slightly congested, but no piles or other rectal disease; general physical condition good; muscles well developed and firm. Find no disease of chest on either percussion or auscultation; respiration full and regular; no rating.

In support of the application are the affidavits of George W. Denni-son, Joseph E. Hines, Theodore Oliver, and William L. Eckman to the effect that witnesses have known the soldier intimately for several years, during which time he has constantly complained and shown symptoms of catarrh of head and throat, irritable heart, and rheuma-tism; that they believe said disabilities to be permanent and not due to vicious habits; and in their opinion he is wholly unable to earn a support by the performance of manual labor.

Appellant contends that under a fair and reasonable construction of the act of June 27, 1890, he is legally entitled, at least, to the minimum rating therein provided.

Under the provisions of the second section of the said act claimants are required to produce evidence disclosing a disability—

which incapacitates them from the performance of manual labor in such a degree as to render them unable to earn a support.

When such proof is adduced, in accordance with the rules and regu-lations provided by the Secretary of the Interior, the statute declares that the applicant shall—

be entitled to receive a pension not exceeding twelve dollars per month, and not less than six dollars per mouth, proportioned to the degree of inability to earn a support.

This language indicates the obvious purpose and intention of Con-gress to fix the maximum rate therein mentioned to correspond with a total disability, and the minimum and intervening rates to correspond, proportionately, with all partial degrees of inability to earn a support by manual labor.

The material question then arises, Does the evidence and medical data in this case show with moral and reasonable certainty that appel-lant is partially disabled within the meaning of the act; in other words, is he disabled in such a degree as to be unable, by the performance of manual labor, to earn an entire support for himself? If so, he is entitled, at least, to the minimum rating under the statute.

The certificate of medical examination describes a very malignant type of naso-pharyngeal catarrh, and a rheumatic affection which so impairs his power of motion that he is unable to put his hands above his head or across his back. Besides, his heart is described as being irritable and the action thereof "easily disturbed."

The testimony of the lay witnesses is to the effect that soldier is wholly unable to earn a support by manual labor; and, allowing for any exaggeration incident to ex parte evidence, I am induced to believe that appellant is so much disabled as to be entitled to the minimum rating under the act of June 27, 1890.

The action of your office is therefore reversed, with directions that the case be readjudicated in accordance with this opinion.

DESERTION—VOIDABLE ENLISTMENT.

JASPER M. STINE.

A contract of enlistment made by a minor under 16 years of age is either void or voidable, and if he repudiate the same by deserting he can not be held to the performance of further service thereunder (though he may be punished for the offense of desertion) and his reenlistment, within the term covered by his former contract of enlistment, is not thereby invalidated.

Assistant Secretary Webster Davis to the Commissioner of Pensions, September 6, 1898.

The claim of Jasper M. Stine for pension on account of disabilities alleged to have been incurred in 1864 while serving as a soldier in Company M, Sixteenth Illinois Cavalry, was rejected by your Bureau in January, 1897. The ground of rejection is stated upon the brief as follows:

No title, claimant having deserted October 12, 1861, from Company E, Eighth Missouri Volunteer Infantry, as shown by the records of the War Department. A discharge from all services which a soldier engaged to perform during the war of the rebellion is necessary to give him a pensionable status under the general law.

An appeal from that action was filed April 24, 1897, the contention of which is that the law in regard to the effect of a record of desertion from a term of enlistment prior to that in which the disability was incurred was correctly stated by Assistant Secretary Bussey in the case of Dewitt C. Falkenburg (3 P. D., 336), and that this claim should be allowed in accordance with the decision in that case.

The records show that the claimant enlisted as a private in Company E, Eighth Missouri Volunteer Infantry, on June 25, 1861, to serve three years, and deserted October 12, 1861.

He again enlisted in Company F, Sixty-eighth Illinois Infantry, on June 5, 1862, to serve three months, and was mustered out with the company September 26, 1862.

He enlisted once more on the 18th of May, 1863, in Company M, Sixteenth Illinois Cavalry, to serve three years, and was mustered out July 14, 1865. During this term of service he was a prisoner of war for ten months and a half, having been captured in action at the battle of Jonesboro, Va., January 3, 1864. He claims that during his confinement in rebel prisons he contracted the disabilities for which he seeks pension.

The Adjutant-General United States Army, on April 27, 1889, reported that the soldier's enlistment in the Sixty-eighth Illinois Infantry was in violation of the fiftieth (formerly twenty-second) article of war, and that his office could not recognize the legality of such enlistment, or any claim for service rendered thereunder, the law viewing him as in a continuous state of desertion during the whole period of said enlistment. A similar report was made in regard to his enlistment in the Sixteenth Illinois Cavalry. It was further stated that there was no law under which the charge of desertion in his case could be removed.

The Falkenburg decision, upon which the appeal is based, held, in effect, that where a soldier, after desertion, reenlisted in another organization and served faithfully therein and received a formal discharge, the record of desertion from his former service was no bar to pension on account of any disability incurred in the latter (completed) term of service.

That decision was overruled by Assistant Secretary Reynolds in the case of Joseph O. Williams (7 P. D., 218), in which it was held that no right to pension could grow out of a service which the War Department refused to recognize as legal.

The position of the War Department with respect to the legality of a service entered upon by a soldier while in desertion from a prior service having been materially changed by an opinion of the Judge-Advocate-General in the case of John Turner, First Iowa Infantry, the subject of desertion with relation to pensions was again considered by Assistant Secretary Reynolds in connection with the case of George Lessor (8 P. D., 114) and the following ruling enunciated:

A claimant against whom there stands a charge of desertion under an enlistment for service in the war of the rebellion which the War Department declines to remove has no title to pension under any existing law on account of disability incurred in said war or service performed therein.

The rejection of the claim now under consideration was in conformity with the above ruling. Said ruling has, however, been recently modified by the decision in the case of John Norton (9 P. D., 382), which now stands as the latest exposition of the law relative to desertion as affecting title to pension.

It was held in the Norton case, among other things, that—

If the disability was incurred in the service under a subsequent enlistment while the claimant was a deserter from a prior enlistment which had not terminated prior to such reenlistment, the claim should be rejected on the ground that the disability was not incurred in the line of duty, but while claimant was absent from his proper command in violation of his former contract of enlistment.

As the appellant, Stine, enlisted in June, 1861, to serve three years, and, having deserted, reenlisted prior to the expiration of that time, he is, under the rule above stated, not pensionable for disability contracted during his last term of service.

This disposes of the appeal so far as the specific issue therein raised is concerned, but there is another feature of the case which seems to me to merit consideration. The appellant states that he was born on the 5th of January, 1846, and was, therefore, only a few months over 15 years of age at the time of his first enlistment. He pleads his extreme youth as an extenuating circumstance of his desertion, and alleges that he was led off by the influence of an older man. The question suggests itself whether his enlistment at that age was valid.

Enlistment is, essentially, a contract (Winthrop on Military Law, Vol. 1, p. 773), and the general rule is that a minor is not bound by his contract unless the same is manifestly beneficial to him. But, like marriage, enlistment is a contract sui generis, the rules which apply to contracts in general being, with respect to it, modified by considerations of expediency or public policy. It is necessary for the general good that the Government should be able to command the services of all its citizens, of whatever age, whenever the exigencies of the country require it, and this necessity overrides the usual rights of individuals. Hence it is held that Congress may constitutionally authorize the enlistment into the military service of the United States of any minors, either with or without the consent of their parents or guardians. (Story, J., in U. S. v. Bainbridge, 1 Mason, 81; In the matter of Riley, 1 Benedict, 410; In the matter of Beswick, 25 How. Pr., 151.)

And Congress has, by appropriate legislation, exercised its constitutional rights in this regard. (See acts of April 30, 1790; March 3, 1795; March 16, 1802; January 11, 1812; January 20, 1813; January 29, 1813; December 10, 1814; February 13, 1862; and July 4, 1864.) In all these statutes, except the last, the minimum age for enlistment is fixed at 18 years; in the last, enlistments (with the consent of parents or guardians) of persons as young as 16 are legalized. No act has ever been passed authorizing the enlistment in the army of persons under the age of 16 years. By section 1118 of the Revised Statutes the enlistment of such persons is expressly prohibited.

That Congress considered some legislation necessary in order to render contracts of enlistment binding on infants is plainly evinced by the language of the act of December 10, 1814, which is as follows

That from and after the passing of this act each and every commissioned officer who shall be employed in the recruiting service shall be, and he hereby is, authorized to enlist into the Army of the United States any free, effective, able-bodied man between the ages of eighteen and fifty years; which enlistment shall be binding upon all persons under the age of twenty-one years, as well as upon persons of full age, such recruiting officer having complied with all the requisitions of the laws regulating the recruiting service.

By section 5 of the act of September 28, 1850, which was in force at the time this appellant enlisted, it was made the duty of the Secretary of War to order the discharge of any soldier of the Army who, at the time of his enlistment, was under the age of 21 years, upon evidence being produced that such enlistment was without the consent of parent or guardian. So that the contract of enlistment of a minor was then voidable even though he had reached the military age at the time of making such contract.

Congress having legislated on the subject and declared what minors may make binding contracts of enlistment, it is a legitimate inference that such contracts on the part of other minors are not necessarily binding, but are subject to the rules which govern contracts in general. One of these rules is that the contract of a minor is void or voidable unless manifestly for his interest.

In re Davison (21 Fed. Rep., 618) the court, after citing the provisions of sections 1116, 1117, and 1118 of the Revised Statutes, said:

The reasonable conclusion warranted by these sections would seem to be that the contract of enlistment of a minor under 16 years of age is void.

And as to the effect of a void enlistment, it said:

If the relator was not duly enlisted in the service of the United States he is not amenable to the jurisdiction of courts-martial. Not only is this the plain deduction from the statutory provisions which confer jurisdiction upon these tribunals, but such would be also the result from general principles. If his contract of enlistment was void the Government acquired no right to his services; he never became a soldier and could not be a deserter.

In a case in which the proof showed that an infant, aged 20 years and 8 months, enlisted in the Army without the consent of his father, who was living and entitled to his custody and control, and that two months after his enlistment he deserted and was arrested after he became 21, it was held by the United States circuit court that he was entitled to a writ of habeas corpus and to his discharge on the ground that his enlistment was void, and that, therefore, he was not a deserter. (Re Chapman, 2 Law Rep. Ann'd., 352; 37 Fed. Rep., 327.)

But in the case of Cosenow (37 Fed. Rep., 668) it was held that a minor's contract of enlistment is not void but voidable; that if he be over 16 years the enlistment is valid and binding as to him and no one but his parents or guardian can claim his discharge; but that if under 16 the enlistment is voidable at the election of the minor himself. This distinction was based on the wording of sections 1117 and 1118 of the Revised Statutes.

It has also been held in a number of cases that pending the final disposition of a trial by court-martial for desertion the deserter is not entitled to a discharge on habeas corpus on the ground of his minority but must await the result of his trial. (In re Cosenow, 37 Fed. Rep., 668; Com. v. Gamble, 11 Serg. & R., 93; McConologue's Case, 107, Mass. 170; ex parte Anderson, 16 Iowa, 595.)

An examination of these cases shows that the decision in each case turned not on the question as to whether the minor's contract of enlistment was valid or invalid, but on the question as to whether he could commit the crime of desertion.

But the two questions are entirely distinct as was well stated by the court of errors of New York in the case of Grace v. Wilber (12

Johns, 68). In that case it was held by the supreme court of the State of New York that if an infant, not liable to be enrolled in the militia, afterwards deserted the service he could not be compelled to return, and an action of trespass would lie against a person who apprehended and detained him as a deserter. The court of error, in reversing the decision (10 Johns, 453), said:

> The question is not whether the contract is valid or void, nor is it whether the soldier is entitled to be discharged from the service or not. The contract may be void, and he may be entitled to his discharge, but it does not follow that he is to be his own judge, and to discharge himself by desertion.

Desertion may be viewed in two different aspects—as the repudiation of a contract and as a crime. It is in the former aspect only that this Department and the civil courts are concerned with it. As a crime it is cognizable only by military courts. If a minor repudiates his voidable contract in such a way as to involve the commission of a crime he may be held to answer for the crime, but he is no longer bound by his contract.

The appellant having made a void, or at most voidable, contract of enlistment in 1861 to serve three years, and having by desertion shown his intention to repudiate it was no longer bound to serve by virtue of that contract. Hence his reenlistment in 1863 was not in violation of his former contract, and he was not during his service under such reenlistment absent from his proper command and out of the line of duty. The action of your Bureau is reversed and the case is remanded for further adjudication.

DEATH CAUSE.

MARGARET MORAN (WIDOW).

Soldier, who was suffering from varicose veins of left leg, of service origin, for which he was pensioned third-grade rate, was thrown from a wagon in which he was riding, striking on the back part of his head, resulting in his death two days later.

Held, That soldier's varicose veins were not the immediate or proximate cause of the injury which resulted in his death, and that his death had no relation, immediate or proximate, with his pensioned cause or his army service.

Assistant Secretary Webster Davis to the Commissioner of Pensions, September 6, 1898.

Margaret, widow of Michael A. Moran, sergeant, Company K, Seventeenth United States Infantry, by her attorneys, appealed September 13, 1897, from the Bureau action of November 28, 1882, rejecting her widow's claim, No. 296257, filed September 1, 1882, on the ground that soldier's death resulted from an accidental injury occurring after his discharge, not dependent on or a result of disease contracted during service.

It is contended that the fatal accident was directly due to the pensioned cause and that the claim should have been admitted in accordance with the rule announced in the case of Mary A. Cox (3 P. D., 313); that as a doubt exists as to cause of death, claimant should be afforded the benefit of the doubt.

Soldier enlisted March 28, 1861, and was discharged January 22, 1864, on account of reenlistment, at which date he reenlisted and was assigned to company H, Fourth United States Infantry, from which service he was discharged January 22, 1867. He again reenlisted February 7, 1868, for three years, and was discharged February 7, 1871, by reason of expiration of service. He again reenlisted the same day he was last discharged for five years, and was discharged February 7, 1876, when he again reenlisted, for five years, and was discharged April 2, 1878, on surgeon's certificate of disability, by reason of varicose veins of left leg and general debility, resulting from old age, he being then 62 years of age.

He was pensioned July 29, 1878, at $8 per month on account of varicose veins of left leg, which pension was increased to $12 per month from February 19, 1879; to $14 from June 6, 1881; $16 from July 16, 1880, and $18 from June 6, 1881, which pension he was receiving at date of his death. He died July 25, 1882, as a result of injuries sustained by being thrown from a wagon and striking on his head.

The circumstances of the accident which resulted in his death, as appears from the testimony of claimant and soldier's physician, are as follows:

Claimant, in an affidavit filed September 1, 1882, testified:

That on the 23d day of July, 1882, her said husband, Michael A. Moran, with herself and her four children, the eldest 13 years of age, started from their home in Yorkton for a short wagon ride. That at the time her husband was so crippled with rheumatism and varicose veins on his left leg that he was hardly able to walk, and required help to get into the wagon. That he seated himself in a chair in the wagon, holding in his arms the youngest child, the oldest boy, aged 13 years, driving. That after proceeding about 100 feet from the house the wheels struck a deep place in the road, and as the hind wheels dropped from this projection the jolt threw Mr. Moran and the child suddenly from the wagon. That in trying to save the child and himself he was thrown upon his head, sustaining injuries which resulted in his death on the 25th of July, 1882. That had it not been for his crippled condition, occasioned by disabilities contracted while in the military service of the United States, she positively believes he could have saved himself. That at the time his left leg was almost useless on account of said rheumatism and varicose veins. That she married said Michael A. Moran fifteen years ago, and that their four children were born while he was in the United States military service. That altogether her said husband had served about thirty years in the military service of the United States. That he was 74 years of age at the time of his death. That he has left her in a destitute condition, with four children to support. That he was almost entirely dependent upon his pension during his lifetime. That she makes this application that she may obtain a continuance of the pension drawn by her said husband, Michael A. Moran, because she believes his death was indirectly caused by his disabilities for which he was pensioned.

Dr. Frank Etter testified, in an affidavit filed at the same date as claimant's:

That he was the family physician of deceased, and that on the 21st day of June, 1882, he was sent for to prescribe for said Michael A. Moran, who at that time was suffering intense pain and loss of power in the entire portion of left leg and lower part of spinal column, the resultant effects of the varicose veins; and the said Michael A. Moran remained and was under affiant's professional care on the day of the reception of the injury which eventuated in his death several days thereafter.

Affiant further says that the said Michael A. Moran, on the 23d day of July, 1882, in company with his wife and children, started from his home to take a wagon ride, and in consequence of his crippled and helpless condition he occupied a chair in the back part of the wagon box, and carried the infant child in his arms. After proceeding, and when but a short distance from the house, the front wheels of the wagon dropped into a ditch which crossed the road at right angles, and the chair which the deceased occupied was perforce tilted forward and the deceased, by losing his balance, fell from the wagon, and in falling upon the ground struck upon the back part of his head, in the region of the atlas and axis vertebræ, and thereby sustained injuries which speedily proved fatal.

Affiant further says that the crippled and helpless condition of the deceased at the time of the accident was the indirect and primary cause of his death; for if he had not been disabled in the lumbar region and inferior extremities he would, in all probability, not have fallen from the wagon, or if he had, it would have been possible for him to have saved himself from falling on his head and receiving fatal injuries.

Affiant further says that, owing to the enfeebled, helpless, and crippled condition of deceased at the time of the accident, the fatal injuries which he sustained could not be averted, but might have been, and in all probability would, had he been in ordinary possession of physical ability.

From the foregoing testimony it would appear that soldier's death was due to his fall from the wagon, and the cause assigned for the fall, varicose veins of left leg, is too remote to be accepted as the immediate or proximate cause of death.

In law the immediate, not the remote, cause of any event is regarded.

The immediate or proximate cause of any event is that which in a natural and unbroken continuous sequence produces the event and without which that event would not have occurred. As stated by Justice Miller in the case of Insurance Company *v.* Tweed (7 Wall., 52):

If a new force or power has intervened, of itself sufficient to stand as the cause of the misfortune, the other must be considered too remote.

Also by Justice Strong in the case of Milwaukee Railway Company *v.* Kellogg (94 U. S., 474):

The primary cause may be the proximate cause of a disaster, though it may operate through successive instruments, as an article at the end of a chain may be moved by a force applied to the other end, that force being the proximate cause of the movement. * * * The question always is, Was there an unbroken connection between the wrongful act and the injury—a continuous operation? Did the facts constitute a continuous succession of events, so linked together as to make a natural whole, or was there some new and independent cause intervening?

In the case of Hayes *v.* Michigan Central Railroad (111 U. S., 241), it was said:

It must be the cause which if it had not existed the injury would not have taken place.

As stated by Broom, in his Legal Maxims, page 220:

If, in the ordinary course of events, a certain result usually follows from a given cause, the immediate relation of the one to the other may be considered to be established.

Following the well-known rule that the immediate or proximate and not the remote cause is considered, it was held by Assistant Secretary Bussey, in the case of Harriet S. Bishop (4 P. D., 354), that death from erysipelas of the head and face could not be attributed to the wound of foot received in service, the cause being remote and not immediate.

In the case of Sarah A., mother of John G. Stack (2 P. D., 153), her claim was rejected on the ground that soldier's death from an overdose of laudanum was not the direct or the proximate result of diarrhea.

It was held by Secretary Schurz, in the case of the widow of James Hoy (2 P. D., o. s., 210), that the death cause alleged, diarrhea, was too remote to justify the conclusion that it was the immediate cause of death. (See Pension Digest (1897), p. 122.)

In the case of Ruth L. Miller (2 P. D., 214), soldier was killed by the fall of a building. It was contended that deafness of service origin was the real cause of his death, and the Department, applying the maxim that "in law the immediate and not the remote cause is regarded," rejected the cause alleged, deafness, as too remote.

In the case of Mary E., widow of George W. Lewis (2 P. D., 334), soldier, who was subject to epilepsy of service origin, was a fireman on a tugboat, and while so employed he fell overboard and was drowned. When last seen he was sitting in a position where a slight movement would have caused him to lose his balance. There was no evidence that his fall was the result of an epileptic attack. It was held that the accident resulting in his death had too remote and uncertain connection with the service, as a consequence, to justify the conclusion that death resulted from his service disability.

The case of Henrietta Petersdorf (4 P. D., 96) was somewhat similar to the case under present consideration. In that case the soldier, who was pensioned for the loss of the left arm above the elbow, while returning home in a wagon, his horses became frightened, ran away, and he was thrown from the wagon to the ground, fracturing his skull, and he died the next day of his said injury.

It was urged in that case that but for the loss of his left arm he would have been able to control his horses, and that his death was thus indirectly attributable to his disability incurred in service, but Assistant Secretary Bussey, in deciding the case, said:

It may have been that he would have been enabled to better control his frightened horses, and perhaps extricate himself in safety, or without serious injury, had it not been for the loss of his arm, but it is equally as probable that he would not. Such accidents are continually occurring to those in the full possession of all their members and faculties and with like results, and in the absence of any evidence showing that the disability incurred in the service either contributed directly to bring about the accident or prevented the soldier from escaping with his life, his death could not reasonably be attributed thereto upon the bare presumption that said disability might have had that effect. The cause of death is too remote from the soldier's military service and is not sufficiently connected therewith as a result to afford a basis for pension to his widow.

See also the cases of Elizabeth Edgell (5 P. D., 96); Emma E. Johnson (7 P. D., 415); Frederick W. Kerner (7 P. D., 305); Diana B. Groff (8 P. D., 93).

The case of Rebecca Maness (7 P. D., 110) is illustrative of the immediate or proximate cause. There the soldier's fall, resulting in death, was caused by his weak and disabled leg, the result of a gunshot wound received in service, for which he was pensioned, and his pensioned cause of disability was held by Assistant Secretary Reynolds to be the immediate cause of the fatal accident.

In the case under consideration the varicose veins of left leg in no manner contributed to soldier's fall and injury which resulted in his death.

A new and independent or immediate and proximate cause intervened; the ditch across the road caused the wagon to tip, and this, not his varicose veins, or his condition resulting from the varicose veins, was the cause of his being thrown from the wagon.

The theory that because of his varicose veins he was seated in a chair, and that by reason of his being seated in a chair he was thrown from the wagon, is mere theory and conjecture, which is not supported or justified by the evidence. People frequently ride seated in chairs in a wagon who do not have varicose veins, and people are thrown from their wagons and carriages when seated on the wagon and carriage seats instead of in chairs and are killed, and the question of whether they did or did not have varicose veins is not considered an important factor.

It would be quite as reasonable to assume that claimant's age, 74 years, was the cause of his inability to save himself as to attribute his inability to save himself from his fall to his varicose veins. Both are too remote. They were not the immediate or proximate cause of death, and the law regards the immediate, not the remote, cause.

In the Mary A. Cox case (3 P. D., 313), relied upon by claimant's attorneys, the evidence showed soldier's hernia of service origin, on account of which he was pensioned, was complicated with cerebrospinal meningitis, causing death. Dr. Gerstenberg, the resident physician at the infirmary where soldier died, and who was soldier's attending physician, testified that the cause of the soldier's death was "hernia, complicated with cerebro-spinal meningitis," and the preponderance of the evidence, medical and lay, sustained him, as was held by Assistant Secretary Bussey in that case.

The Cox case was followed by me in the case of Napoleon B. Trask (9 P. D., 113), and the word "complicated" as used in both the Cox and the Trask case was defined in the case of Nanna J. Smith (9 P. D., 359) as being used in the sense of—

being involved or interwoven or connected with the disease which was the immediate cause of death, and that to entitle a widow to a pension under section 4702,

Revised Statutes, she is required to show that the disease for which soldier was pensioned, or which originated in the service and in line of duty, had some probable connection with and was a contributing and presumptive predominating factor in death cause.

In the case under consideration no reasonable doubt is raised as to the cause of soldier's death. His death is shown to be the result of injuries received in his fall from the wagon, and the mere opinion of the physician that the fatal injuries which he sustained could not be arrested, but

might have been, and in all probability would, had he been in the ordinary possession of physical ability,

is at best but mere speculation. Soldier's death is shown to be the result of an accident merely.

An accident is defined as an event happening without the concurrence of the will of the person by whose agency it was caused; an event which takes place without one's foresight or expectation.

I am therefore of the opinion that soldier's varicose veins were not the immediate or proximate cause of the injury which resulted in his death, and that his death had no relation, immediate or proximate, with his pensioned cause or army service. The widow is, therefore, not entitled to a pension under section 4702, Revised Statutes, and no application appears to have been filed under the act of June 27, 1890.

The action appealed from is affirmed and the papers in the case are herewith returned.

MARRIAGE AND DIVORCE—IMPEDIMENT.

LOUISA S. HOEPFNER (WIDOW).

Claimant was married to soldier May 23, 1896, at which time she had a former husband living from whom she was not divorced, but who died August 13, 1896. Soldier died August 19, 1896. From August 13 to August 19, 1896, claimant lived with soldier as his wife in the same unchanged relation as prior to August 13, 1896.

Held, That under the laws of the State of Pennsylvania, in which the parties resided at the time of her first and second husband's death, a valid marriage is not shown, and claimant is therefore not the widow of the soldier and has no title to a widow's pension under any law.

Assistant Secretary Webster Davis to the Commissioner of Pensions, September 6, 1898.

Louisa S., alleged widow of Otto Hoepfner, late first lieutenant Company K, Third Pennsylvania Heavy Artillery, by her attorneys, appealed February 18, 1898, from the bureau action of December 11, 1897, rejecting her old and new law widow's claim No. 651591, filed April 9, 1897, on the ground that she was not the legal widow of soldier.

It is contended that under the authority most frequently recognized by the Pension Bureau in question of marriage and legal widowhood,

Bishop, that upon the death of claimant's first husband, whom she believed to be dead when she married soldier, her marriage to soldier became valid.

Soldier enlisted October 14, 1862; was honorably discharged March 4, 1863, and died August 19, 1896.

Claimant was married to soldier May 23, 1896, at which time she had a former husband living, from whom she had not been divorced, but who died August 13, 1896, six days prior to the death of soldier. From the date of her first husband's death until soldier's death, she lived and cohabited with him as his wife, in the State of Pennsylvania, in which State soldier died. While claimant's ceremonial marriage, May 23, 1896, took place in New Jersey, as that marriage was void, the marrige laws of that State are immaterial in this case.

The validity of her marriage to soldier is to be tested by the laws of the State of Pennsylvania, pursuant to section 2 of the act of August 7, 1882, and not according to the doctrine of Mr. Bishop, or any other elemental law writer, or the laws of other States.

This section provides:

That marriages, except such as are mentioned in section forty-seven hundred and five of the Revised Statutes shall be proven in pension cases to be legal marriages according to the law of the place where the parties resided at the time of marriage or at the time when the right to pension accrued.

Under the laws of Pennsylvania, and every other State and Territory of the United States, where either of the parties to the marriage has a husband or wife living from whom they have not been divorced, such marriage is void, not voidable merely, and in the State of Pennsylvania, cohabitation after the removal of the impediment to a legal marriage, without evidence of a new marriage contract, is not sufficient to raise the presumption of a marriage after the removal of such impediment.

See case of Sarah C. Hayden (8 P. D., 364), citing Hantz v. Sealy (6 Binn., 405); Hunt's Appeal (86 Pa., 294, 296), and Thomas v. Thomas (124 Pa., 646). In the latter case it was held that—

If at the time of the woman's second marriage her first and undivorced husband was in fact in full life, whatever the time of his absence, and her belief as to his death, she was incapable of contracting a second marriage, and it was therefore void.

I am forced to the conclusion that under the laws of the State of Pennsylvania a valid marriage between claimant and soldier is not established. There is no evidence of new consent or of any change in the relation of the parties subsequent to August 13, 1896.

The doctrine announced by Mr. Bishop in his work on Marriage, Divorce, and Separation, paragraph 970, that—

If the parties desire marriage, and do what they can to render their union matrimonial, yet one of them is under a disability, as, where there is a prior marriage undissolved, their cohabitation, thus matrimonially meant, will in matter of law make them husband and wife from the moment when the disability is removed; and it is immaterial whether they knew of its existence, or its removal, or not; nor is this a question of evidence—

does not appear to be adopted as the law in the State of Pennsylvania, as appears from the very case cited by Mr. Bishop in note 8, i. e., Hunt's Appeal (86 Pa., 294).

The doctrine appears to have been followed by the Department in the cases of Amy P. Sheets (3 P. D., 293), Margaret J. Anderson (4 P. D., 67), and Nancy J. Dorlas (5 P. D., 230), but in all these cases the provisions of section 2 of the pension laws of August 7, 1882, as well as the departmental decisions in the cases of Eliza W. Carter (5 P. D., 148), Fanny Curtis (2 P. D., 159), Elizabeth Schmidlin (5 P. D., 200), and Thankful Morse (1 P. D., 56), appear to have been overlooked, or at least not considered.

In the case of Ann E. Server (7 P. D., 468), the cases of Nancy J. Dorlas (5 P. D., 230), Amy P. Sheets (3 P. D., 293), and all other cases in conflict with the decision in said case, were in express terms overruled, and the cases of Mary B. McCullum (6 P. D., 931) and Elizabeth Schmidlin (5 P. D., 200) were approved.

In the case of Ellen A. Palmer (7 P. D., 363) it was held that—

Where one of the parties to a marriage has a legal husband or wife living at the time of such marriage from whom he or she is undivorced, such second marriage is not merely voidable, but void, and this status continues until the removal of the legal impediment to such second marriage. To establish a valid marriage in such a case subsequent consent must be shown after the removal of the impediment and the consent must be shown after the knowledge of the facts which rendered the marriage void is brought to the attention of the innocent party. In this case no such new consent is shown. The same relations appear to have continued after the death of the first husband as had existed prior to his death. As the second husband had no knowledge of the legal impediment to his marriage nor of its removal, the fact of their continued cohabitation as husband and wife can not be construed as a consent upon his part. Had the second husband known of the impediment to his marriage he could have repudiated and refused to recognize his marriage to claimant even after the death of said first husband. A relation which he could have elected to dissolve, had the facts been brought to his knowledge, he could not be said to have consented to when the knowledge of the fact was concealed from him. It does not appear that opportunity for consent was afforded after the removal of the impediment. So far as he was concerned, the impediment was never removed prior to his death. Consent is an essential part of all marriage contracts, and the law marries no one against his or her consent. (Am. and Eng. Ency. of Law, vol. 14, p. 508, par. 6.)

In fact, the law never marries any one, strictly speaking. The intent and acts of the parties under the law and in conformity with the law are necessary to constitute marriage. Marriage is a social domestic status, based upon contract, and consummated and controlled by law. The word contract implies a valid legal contract, and this implies that the parties to the contract must both be capable of contracting, and as the basis of the contract is a promise—i. e., consent—the parties to the contract must be legally competent to promise or consent.

* * * * *

The question of a common-law marriage, therefore, does not arise in this case, as the claimant had notice of the legal impediment to a legal marriage, but concealed that fact from her second husband and entered into a bigamous marriage. The relations resulting therefrom were void and illegal in their inception, and must remain so unless changed by some specific act which amounts to consent, after the removal of the legal impediment, and as no such act is shown claimant has no title to recognition as the legal widow of her second husband.

A different conclusion was reached, however, in the Indiana case of Louisa J. Doan (8 P. D., 377), following the decisions of the supreme court of that State.

See also the case of Margaret L. Thompson (9 P. D., 139), distinguished from the Palmer case on the ground that the claimant was the innocent party, who had no knowledge of the fact that her husband, the soldier, had a former wife living at the date of her marriage to him, but which former wife had procured a divorce from soldier some eighteen years prior to his death, and that the evidence in that case showed new consent, after the removal of the impediment, under the laws of Michigan as interpreted by the supreme court of that State.

The laws of Pennsylvania, as interpreted by the supreme court of that State in the cases heretofore cited, clearly indicate that evidence of new consent, after the removal of the impediment to a legal marriage, is not shown by the mere fact of cohabitation or an unchanged matrimonial relation or status, but that stronger evidence of new consent must be shown.

It may be stated that even if claimant's marriage to soldier in 1896 was valid, she would still not be entitled to a pension under the act of June 27, 1890, as that law does not grant pensions to those widows who married the soldiers subsequent to the passage of the act.

As a valid marriage of the claimant to soldier under the laws of Pennsylvania is not established, she is not entitled to a widow's pension under any act of Congress.

The action appealed from is accordingly affirmed, and the papers in the case are herewith returned.

EVIDENCE—PRESUMPTION OF DEATH.

HELEN L. PEPPER (WIDOW).

1. The death of the husband can not be presumed from the fact that he deserted his wife, howsoever long said desertion may continue.
2. The act of March 3, 1896, relates only to presumption of death of the enlisted man or officer on account of whose service and death pension is claimed.

Assistant Secretary Webster Davis to the Commissioner of Pensions, September 6, 1898.

Helen L. Pepper, of Wilkesbarre, Pa., October 22, 1897, appealed from the action of the Bureau in her claim for a pension under the general law as the widow of Eason Pepper.

The soldier served in Company E, Fifty-second Pennsylvania Volunteer Infantry, from September 18, 1861, to July 12, 1865. He married the appellant March 11, 1885, and died February 16, 1893. Her claim for a widow's pension under the general law was filed February 24,

1893, and was rejected June 28 following, upon the ground that she was not the widow of the soldier. It is from this action that appeal is entered.

The appellant was married to William A. Smith August 13, 1867, at Waverly, N. Y. She testified, as have nearly all the witnesses, that Smith deserted her on or about June 26, 1867; that he was a drunkard and a gambler by profession, and she believes he died in 1873 "in the West;" that none of his relatives have ever been able to inform her of his whereabouts.

The contention of the appellant is that the facts sworn to as above set forth bring the case within the act approved March 13, 1896, which reads as follows:

> That in considering claims filed under the pension laws the death of an enlisted man or officer shall be considered as sufficiently proved if satisfactory evidence is produced establishing the fact of the continued and unexplained absence of such enlisted man or officer from his home and family for a period of seven years, during which period no intelligence of his existence shall have been received.

Were any change worked in the common-law rule applicable to the question presented it could not apply to this case, as by its very terms said act is limited in its scope to the deaths of officers and enlisted men, and, as I take it, the officer or enlisted man on account of whose service and death pension is claimed by another in the particular case. In this case it does not appear that William A. Smith, the claimant's first husband, was in the military service of the United States; and certain it is that the appellant's claim for pension is not based on such service, if ever rendered.

However, in the act is contained a fair statement of the rule relative to the facts which must be shown that the death of any person may be presumed. Under the test of said rule the evidence in this case falls far short of proving such facts. The appellant positively swears that her first husband deserted her. The fact of desertion alone is not sufficient for the purpose; on the contrary, it fully explains the absence of her former husband, and howsoever long the desertion continues, no ground will be thereby afforded upon which to presume his death. Not only is his absence accounted for, but it fully explains why she never has heard from him. The evidence of the appellant—and all the witnesses substantially agree with her—has fully accounted for her husband's continued absence and thereby precluded any possibility of a presumption of his death, based upon the fact of such absence.

The evidence also is totally insufficient for proving the fact of her first husband's death. Appellant swears that she believes he died in 1873. She does not state upon what information she bases her belief. So far as the evidence now shows, her husband was last seen by a relative in 1869. This is the only relative of the husband sworn in the case. She testifies as to what said relative told her, or, rather the purport thereof. This is all the evidence tending to prove said husband's death.

If this claim were allowed and pension paid to the appellant as the widow of the soldier the Government may not be compelled to pay pension to some other person as the widow or minor child or dependent relative of the soldier. Presumably there is no person other than the claimant who may have title to pension on account of the services and death of the soldier. However, even in such cases evidence is required which at least makes out a prima facie case. The fact that a soldier considered that a claimant was his wife, and treated her as such up to the time of his death, fully warrants a careful consideration of her claim for a widow's pension. But in this case, if the evidence proves anything it proves that the appellant is not the widow of the soldier. Therefore the action of the Bureau is affirmed.

DEPENDENCE—WIDOW—ACT JUNE 27, 1890.

LUCINDA ELSTON (WIDOW).

The act of June 27, 1890, offers $8 per month as a supplement to the daily labor of such widows as do not possess the means therewith provided. As claimant is already in the enjoyment of the very means which the statute would bestow on one less fortunate, she is not pensionable.

Assistant Secretary Webster Davis to the Commissioner of Pensions, September 12, 1898.

Isaac Elston, enlisted on May 2, 1864, in Company G, One hundred and fifty-second Ohio National Guards, was discharged on September 2, 1864, and died on January 25, 1885.

His widow, Lucinda Elston, filed a declaration for widow's pension (No. 472,472), on September 8, 1890, under the provisions of the act of June 27, 1890, which was rejected on December 12, 1896, on the ground that she is not without other means of support than her daily labor within the meaning of said act.

Assigning said action as error, appeal was taken on May 13, 1897, presenting the following assignment:

The claimant appealed for reconsideration of her claim on the ground that her income was not sufficient to pay for her board and clothes, she only having the sum of $1,600 on interest of 8 per cent per annum, which is $128 per year; that her age is such that she is totally unable to perform any manual labor whatever, and that she believes herself entitled to a pension of $8 per month as a widow of a soldier under the law of 1890.

There is no evidence whatever to show what were the assets or means of support at the time of filing her declaration. Her own affidavit was filed on October 20, 1891, in which she stated that the probable value of all her property both real and personal was $2,400, and that after paying taxes her income would not exceed $100. Of like import is an affidavit of Levi Elston, filed on January 4, 1893, fixing her income not to exceed $100 per annum. On July 28, 1892, claimant filed an affidavit of John N. Trook, in which he deposes to the effect that claimant's income was limited to the rents of 60 acres of land owned by her, which did not exceed $150 per annum, and that after the payment of taxes and repairs her income would not exceed $100.

The rule which controls a case of this character is laid down in the case of Katherine Klein (7 P. D., 278), in which it is held that—

When a widow is shown to have an income considerably in excess of the pension provided by the third section of said act from sources independent of her daily labor she does not occupy a pensionable status thereunder.

The claimant is, according to the showing made by the evidence and the contention presented by the appeal, in the enjoyment of a yearly income quite commensurate with the pension provided by the act in question. The provision embodied in the third section of said act was intended, as therein declared, for the benefit of widows without other means of support than their daily labor. In construing this section and in administering the law thereunder the Department has not imposed upon claimants the rigid and inflexible requirement of showing absolute destitution as a basis of pension, as might be done by a strictly literal application of the statute. It would, however, be clearly inconsistent with the obvious purpose and intention of Congress to bestow a pension upon a claimant who is already in possession of the very means of support which the statute provides for such as have no resource except their daily labor. The statute offers $8 per month as a supplement to the daily labor of such widows as do not possess the means therein provided. The claimant is already in the enjoyment of the very means which the statute would bestow upon a less fortunate applicant who had nothing upon which to rely for subsistence except her daily labor, and for that reason she does not occupy a pensionable status under the act of June 27, 1890.

Under the evidence in the case the action of your office was without error and is hereby affirmed.

COMMENCEMENT—INCREASE—ACT JULY 14, 1892.

JOHN M. JOHNSON.

There is no authority of law for commencing the $50 rate prior to the date of the certificate of the examining surgeon, or board of examining surgeons, showing the requisite degree of disability, made subsequent to the passage of the act of July 14, 1892.

Assistant Secretary Webster Davis to the Commissioner of Pensions, September 12, 1898.

The appellant's husband, John M. Johnson, formerly a soldier in Company F, Sixty-fourth Illinois Infantry, was a pensioner at the rate of $30 per month when he, on May 20, 1893, filed a claim for increase to $50 per month under the provisions of the act of July 14, 1892. He was called on for evidence showing his need of aid and attendance, and on October 10, 1894, was informed that the evidence filed did not warrant a medical examination. Additional evidence was filed in March, 1897, and a medical examination was ordered September 3, 1897, which was made September 20, 1897. A certificate was issued December 9, 1897, allowing the $50 rate from the date of said examination, September 20, 1897. The pensioner died December 8, 1897. His widow filed an appeal December 27, 1897, contending that the increase should have been allowed to commence from an earlier date, either from the date on which the Bureau of Pensions refused to order a medical examination, in October, 1894, or from the date of filing the medical evidence on which an examination was finally ordered in September, 1897. She asserts also that the examination was made on September 13 instead of September 20.

The act of July 14, 1892, declares that the rate of $50 per month therein provided, when allowed, shall commence " from and after the date of the certificate of the examining surgeons or board of examining surgeons " showing the requisite degree of disability, "made subsequent to the passage of the act." There is no authority of law for commencing the increase in this case from either of the dates suggested by the appellant or from any date anterior to the date of the certificate of the medical examination made September 20, 1897, which was the first examination made subsequent to the passage of the act of July 14, 1892. The appellant is mistaken in regard to the date of the examination. The action appealed from was correct and is affirmed.

———

LIMITATION—DEPENDENT BROTHERS AND SISTERS.

DEPENDENT SISTER OF WILLIAM A. BAKER.

The evidence shows that claimant was over 16 years of age at the time of filing her declaration, as well as at the date of dependent mother's death, and she is not entitled to pension as dependent sister of the soldier, as the exception to the limitation contained in the act of March 3, 1879, does not apply to claims of dependent brothers and sisters of the soldier.

Assistant Secretary Webster Davis to the Commissioner of Pensions, September 12, 1898.

William A. Baker enlisted on December 17, 1862, in Company I, Third Tennessee Cavalry, and died in the service on April 27, 1865. It appears that soldier's father had previously died, and that he left neither widow nor children. The mother of the soldier subsequently died on May 30, 1888, pending an application for dependent mother's pension.

On April 23, 1897, Caleb H. Baker, John M. Baker, and Elizabeth B. Baker, now Norman, brothers and sister of the soldier, who were minors under the age of 16 years at the time of his death, filed an application for dependent brothers' and sister's pension (No. 652582).

The claim was rejected on July 26, 1897, on the ground that the claimants were over 16 years of age at the date of filing application and also at the time of the mother's death.

From this action Elizabeth B. Norman, the sister, appealed on October 23, 1897, contending that the act granting pensions to dependent brothers and sisters does not prescribe any limitation as to the time when an application shall be filed.

One of the provisions of section 4707, Revised Statutes, under which appellant claims title, reads as follows:

Provided, That if in any case said person shall have left father and mother who are dependent upon him, then, on the death of the mother, the father shall become entitled to the pension, commencing from and after the death of the mother; and upon the death of the mother and father, or upon the death of the father and the remarriage of the mother, the dependent brothers and sisters under sixteen years of age shall jointly become entitled to such pension until they attain the age of sixteen years, respectively, commencing from the death or remarriage of the party who had the prior right to the pension.

The proviso above mentioned disposes of the case at bar, whatever may be the law relating to the contention that there is no limitation as to the time when application shall be made. Under the law the mother had the sole title to such dependent pension during her lifetime, but when the mother died the claimant had passed the age of 16 years. She has, therefore, never, at any time, occupied a pensionable status as the dependent sister of soldier. There is no relevancy whatever in the contention that the limitation act of March 3, 1879, has no application in this case for the reason that during the whole period of dependency while claimant was under the age of 16 years, she had no title and could not, by herself or guardian, have prosecuted any claim to pension.

The act of March 3, 1879, simply declares the time at which certain pensions shall begin, and as to all claims filed since July 1, 1880, provides that they shall commence from the date of filing the application. This act only regulates the granting of pensions to certain applicants who are conceded to have, at some time at least, occupied a pensionable status, and can have no reference whatever to persons who have never sustained that relation to the pension laws.

The fact that the claimant was over 16 years of age at the date of application, as appears from the evidence, brings her claim within the rule announced in the case of Minor sisters of Alexander Sutton (8 P. D., 137), wherein it is held:

In claims of orphan brothers and sisters under the age of 16 years, filed under section 4709 of the Revised Statutes subsequent to June 30, 1880, pensions can not commence prior to the filing of the declaration, and such claims are barred when so filed after claimants arrive at the age of 16 years, there being no pensionable periods in such cases.

Under the evidence presented the action appealed from was without error and is hereby affirmed.

MARRIAGE AND DIVORCE—EVIDENCE.

MARY J. STOCKER (WIDOW).

It having been admitted by appellant that both she and the soldier on account of
whose service and death she claims pension, had been married previous to their
marriage to each other, it is incumbent upon her to establish the dissolution of
said prior marriage by either death or divorce before she can be regarded as the
lawful widow of said deceased soldier.

*Assistant Secretary Webster Davis to the Commissioner of Pensions,
September 12, 1898.*

Mary J. Stocker filed in your Bureau on December 2, 1897, an application for pension under the provisions of section 3, act of June 27, 1890, as widow of George A. Stocker (deceased), late private, Company I, Fifty-ninth New York Volunteer Infantry, alleging the death of said soldier on November 23, 1897, leaving her without other means of support than her daily labor, which was rejected on August 6, 1898, upon the ground that a lawful marriage between said Mary and the deceased soldier was not established. From said action appeal was taken on August 23, 1898.

It appears from a duly certified transcript of the public record of their marriage that the appellant was married to the deceased soldier at Rockville, Md., by a minister of the gospel on December 22, 1891. It furthermore appears, however, that both this appellant and the deceased soldier had been previously married, and there is no evidence on file showing that said former marriages had been dissolved by either death or divorce at the time of the marriage of the appellant to the soldier, and the appellant declares her inability to furnish any proof whatever of that fact.

It having been admitted by the appellant under oath that both she and the deceased soldier had been previously married, it was incumbent upon her to establish the dissolution of said prior marriages by either death or divorce in order to establish the fact that she was the lawful widow of the soldier and entitled to pension as such under the provisions of the act of June 27, 1890.

This was preliminary and material evidence which it was necessary for her to produce to make out her case.

It is contended in this appeal that the fact that the deceased soldier was a widower and the appellant a widow at the time of their marriage is shown by the records of the circuit court of Montgomery County, Md., but I find no evidence of this in the papers further than the certified copy of the record of marriage license and the return of marriage thereon, in which the soldier is described as a widower and this appellant as a widow. It is true that said license was issued by the clerk of said court and is recorded in his office, but this was a mere ministerial act on the part of said clerk; there was no judicial determination of the facts stated in said license, and the recitals therein relative to the competency of the parties to contract marriage are neither binding nor could they be received as evidence of that fact where the competency of the parties is afterwards called in question.

This case presents simply an instance of failure of proof necessary and material to the establishment of the appellant's claim for pension, and without which it can not be admitted under the provisions of the pension laws, and, therefore, the rejection of said claim upon the ground stated was not error, and is affirmed accordingly.

SERVICE—MEXICAN WAR.

THERESA BONNAVEAU (WIDOW).

It is shown by the official military records of the War Department that the military service of the deceased soldier terminated prior to the commencement of the Mexican war.

Assistant Secretary Webster Davis to the Commissioner of Pensions, September 17, 1898.

Theresa Bonnaveau is a pensioner under a special act of Congress, approved July 7, 1898, at the rate of $8 per month, as widow of John B. Bonnaveau (deceased), late private, Captain Bercier's battery, Louisiana Legion of Militia, Mexican war.

She filed in your Bureau on October 12, 1889, an application for pension under the provisions of the act of January 29, 1887, as widow of said deceased soldier, which was rejected on April 17, 1890, upon the ground that his military service had been rendered prior to the commencement of the Mexican war.

From said action an appeal was taken in October, 1897.

The facts relative to the military service of the deceased soldier, as well as the duration and character of the military service rendered by the organization to which he belonged, as shown by the official military records of the War Department, are set forth in the following communication from the Chief of the Record and Pension Office of the War Department to the chairman of the Committee on Pensions of the House of Representatives, on file with the papers in this case:

RECORD AND PENSION OFFICE, WAR DEPARTMENT,
Washington City, May 5, 1896.

SIR: Referring to your letter of the 2d instant, received yesterday, in which you request for the use of your committee in connection with H. R. 2336 a statement showing the military service of T. B. Bonnaveau, who enlisted August 21, 1845, in the First Battalion, Louisiana Light Artillery, for service in the Mexican war, and also showing where he was employed during his service, and for what purpose the organization was enlisted, and in which letter you also asked to be advised whether it is held by this Department that an actual state of warfare existed between this country and Mexico during the period of the soldier's service, I am directed by the Secretary of War to inform you that the official records show as follows:

T. B. Bonnaveau was enrolled and mustered into service August 21, 1845, as a private in Captain Bercier's battery, Louisiana Legion of Militia, which organization was also known as Captain Bercier's battery, Gally's battalion, Louisiana Militia Light Artillery, to serve three months. He was mustered out of service with that organization November 10, 1845. This organization was called into service by General Gaines, owing to the presence of a large force, of Mexicans on the Rio Grande apparently with hostile intent. It embarked for the army of occupation at Corpus Christi, Tex., on August 21, 1845, and in a letter dated August 23, 1845, from this Department, Gen. Z. Taylor was directed to accept into service the volunteers raised in Louisiana by order of General Gaines. It remained with the army of occupation at Corpus Christi, Tex., until November 2, 1845, when it was directed to embark for New Orleans to be mustered out of service.

It is held by this Department that the Mexican war commenced April 24, 1846.

Very respectfully,

F. C. AINSWORTH,
Colonel, United States Army, Chief Record and Pension Office.

Hon. HENRY C. LOUDENSLAGER,
Chairman Committee on Pensions, House of Representatives.

It has been uniformly held by this Department from its foundation that the Mexican war commenced on April 24, 1846, and that military service rendered prior to that date could not be considered as service in or during the Mexican war. (Opinion of Ewing, Secretary, Mayo and Moulton, 527; Thomas Daly, 2 P. D., 220.)

The act of January 29, 1887, provides pension only for the widows of those soldiers who served for sixty days, under the conditions therein named, in or during the Mexican war. Hence it is obvious that its provisions could have no application to the case of this appellant.

The rejection of this claim upon the ground stated was manifestly without error, and is affirmed accordingly.

INDEX TO DECISIONS.

ACT OF JUNE 27, 1890.

ACT OF JULY 14, 1892.

ACT OF JULY 27, 1892.

ACT OF JANUARY 5, 1893.

ACT OF DECEMBER 21, 1893.

ACT OF MARCH 2, 1895.

ACT OF MARCH 13, 1896.

AGGRAVATION AND RECURRENCE OF OLD DISABILITY.

ADJUDICATION.

ADULTEROUS COHABITATION.

Generally.

The evidence shows that from 1887 to about 1893 the appellant and one Daniel Boston lived together in a small tenement consisting of two rooms; that a part of the time they lived there alone and the remainder of the time a small boy lived with them; that it was the general opinion among their immediate neighbors that they were living as man and wife; that on several occasions the appellant stated that Boston was her husband; and that they, in fact, were not legally married.

Held, That the facts are sufficient to justify the action of dropping her name from the pension roll under the act of August 7, 1882.

Under Act June 27, 1890.

The adulterous cohabitation of a widow subsequent to the passage of the act of August 7, 1882, works a forfeiture of her pension, or right to a pension under the act of June 27, 1890.

The open and notorious adulterous cohabitation of a widow bars her right to pension under the act of June 27, 1890, on account of her husband's death.

The provisions of section 2 of the act of August 7, 1882, are applicable to widows' claims under section 3 of the act of June 27, 1890.

Adulterous cohabitation of a soldier's widow, on or subsequent to August 7, 1882, terminates her pensionable status as effectually as her remarriage.

Section 2 of said act of August 7, 1882, is in no sense a penal statute, nor is it to be construed according to the rules of construction of penal statutes, but is remedial and is liberally construed.

Widow not Entitled on Account of Minors.

As it is accepted that the widow has no title to individual pension under act of June 27, 1890, by reason of open and notorious adulterous cohabitation, she has no title to the $2 per month additional allowed the widow under said act for each minor until arriving at the age of 16 years.

AID AND ATTENDANCE.

Frequent and Periodical.

1. When it is established, beyond any reasonable doubt, that, on account of pensioned cause or causes, or any pathological sequelæ thereof, the pensioner is not only "totally incapacitated for performing manual labor," but can neither dress nor undress himself without the aid and attendance of another person, as is shown by the evidence and certificate of medical examination in this case, the Department will construe the said aid and attendance as such "frequent and periodical personal aid and attendance of another person" as is contemplated by the provisions of the act of July 14, 1892, and as warranting the allowance of the rate prescribed in the said act.

2. The soldier is now pensioned at $45 per month for loss of right arm at the shoulder joint.

   It is both claimed and shown that the wound which caused the loss of the right arm also caused destruction of the tissues about the shoulder joint to such an extent that it is necessary for the claimant to wear a pad or some other means of protection, in the adjustment of which the services of another person are required.

   Held, That inasmuch as the services of another person are required at least twice daily in the adjustment of the pad which the pensioner is compelled to wear over his right shoulder for its protection, the said services are considered as such "frequent and periodical personal aid and attendance of another person" as is contemplated by the act of July 14, 1892, and warrants allowance of the rate prescribed by the said act.

3. Inasmuch as the preponderance of the evidence on file in this case warrants the presumption that the pensioner is so disabled by reason of his military service as to require the frequent and periodical, but not regular and constant, personal aid and attendance of another person, the action of reduction from the $72 rate to second grade, instead of to the rate prescribed by the act of July 14, 1892, was error, and is, in so far as the amount of the reduction is concerned, reversed; the decision of October 24, 1896, affirming the said action and departmental letter of July 23, 1897, overruling a motion for reconsideration of the said decision, are rescinded and set aside, and the papers in the case are remanded for readjudication and allowance of a rate commensurate with the degree of disability shown to exist and believed to be of service origin.

4. It appears from the evidence in this case that the disability of this appellant resulting from the pensioned rheumatism was practically the same at the date his pension was reduced from $72 to $30 per month, and has so remained since that date, as it was when he was given his present rating of $50 per month under the provisions of the act of July 14, 1892, and is and has been such as

to incapacitate the appellant for the performance of any manual labor, and necessitate the frequent and periodical, but not the regular and constant, aid and attendance of another person.

Held, That he is entitled to the rating of $50 per month from the date his pension was reduced to $30 per month, but is not entitled to restoration to the rate of $72 per month.

Martin B. Fitch 481

AMENDMENTS.

(*See* DECLARATIONS, 1; RECORD.)

AMPUTATION.

The nearness of an amputation to the shoulder joint or hip joint is the only condition to be considered in determining the right to the increase of pension to $45 per month provided by the act of August 4, 1886. It is held that if more than one-half of the humerus or femur is left the stump is of sufficient length to permit the use of an artificial limb.

Samuel Scott 70

ANTEREBELLION SERVICE.

(*See also* WIDOW'S PENSION.)

Limitation.

Evidence alone that a claimant was treated in the service for the disease causing the disability for which pension is claimed is not sufficient to establish a claim; the continuance of the disease and the extent to which it disabled for the performance of manual labor must be shown.

As it appears that the disease causing the disability on account of which pension was claimed was contracted prior to March 4, 1861, claimant in this case is not pensionable, for the reason that his application was not filed within three years from the date of his discharge and was not completed prior to his death, as required by section 4713 of the Revised Statutes.

Matteo Bianchi (deceased) 220

APPEAL.

(*See also* LIMITATION; PRACTICE, 1, 6.)

Practice.

1. More than ninety days having elapsed since the attorney who filed this appeal was notified that he was not entitled to recognition, and he has filed no appeal in his own behalf, the appeal will be dismissed under rule 1, Rules of Practice, upon the ground that said attorney has not filed a power of attorney authorizing him to enter the appeal.

   James E. Oram 132

2. A letter from the Commissioner of Pensions, in response to a communication, reciting former action of the Bureau from which claimant had previously appealed, and which action had been affirmed on appeal, and reaffirmed on motion for reconsideration, is not such final action of the Pension Bureau as will furnish a basis for another appeal.

   Minors of William Hockey 164

ARMY NURSES.

Claimant admits, and the evidence shows, her work while in the hospital at Washington, D. C., during the war, was cleaning said hospital; gathering, washing, and putting away for use the bandages and bedclothing used therein; carrying out slops, and such general work as directed; the personal attendance upon and care for and administering of medicines to the inmates being by white nurses only. Claimant is colored.

Held, Claimant's services were not "nurse" services as contemplated by the act of August 5, 1892.

Millie, alias Minnie, Howard (now Payne) 188

ATTESTATION.

(*See* ATTORNEYS, 8.)

ATTORNEYS.

(*See also* APPEAL, 1; FEE, 6, 8.)

Examination of Record by.

1. The practice which prevails in the Bureau of Pensions of denying to claimants or their authorized attorneys the right to examine the evidence obtained by special examination, except that relating to criminal charges and investigations, is unjust to claimants and unwarranted by law; and all orders or instructions which have that effect are revoked.

H. S. Berlin 471

Fee.

2. As the appellants have, under rule 12, forfeited the attorneyship by neglecting the case for more than one year, they are not entitled to further recognition.

Eliza Jacob 213

3. When in a claim for straight increase, an order for medical examination has not been obeyed, and the attorney of record has been so notified and takes no further action in the case, and makes no satisfactory explanation of such failure within ninety days from the date of such notification, he is held to be in neglect and his attorneyship forfeited; and where subsequently another attorney files a new application for increase, secures an order for medical examination, with which the claimant complies, upon the allowance of the claim from date of such examination the latter attorney should be paid the fee.

William Boate. 375

Material Service.

4. As the appellant acquired the attorneyship, rendered material service, and was not in neglect when the claim was allowed, he is entitled to a fee.

The filing of a declaration in response to a call therefor by the Bureau, if filed at a time when deemed necessary and material, though subsequently deemed immaterial, is such service as may entitle an attorney to a fee.

Daniel B. Ford 137

Power of Attorney.

5. A power of attorney to prosecute a pension claim executed by a claimant after having been judicially declared insane, or while confined in an asylum for the insane, will not be recognized, and the attorney filing the same should be so notified. (Case of Joel Ames, 8 P. D., 171.)

Evidence filed by a duly authorized attorney when not entitled to recognition is actual service, and it inures to his benefit if he becomes entitled to recognition at any time before the claim is prima facie complete, and may entitle him to a fee.

Elishup P. Allen, insane (claimant) 19

6. A valid power of attorney filed in the Bureau at a time when no claim is pending in behalf of the person granting the same, and to which it may be applicable, does not entitle an attorney therein named to recognition as against another who subsequently is duly authorized by the same person to prosecute a claim for pension and has filed one in his behalf, to which both powers of attorney are applicable.

James M. Mulhollan (claimant) 38

7. As the appellant never filed any instrument which conferred upon him any rights
in the case, action denying him a fee was proper.

Anna L. McBride... 338

8. A power of attorney to which the signature of the claimant is not attested by two
witnesses confers no authority upon an agent or attorney to appear in a pension
claim, and without such authority a person can not have title to a fee.

Rebecca C. Vining.. 362

Practice.

9. Where two or more claims for pension are pending in behalf of the same person,
instruments of evidence filed by an attorney will not inure to his benefit as
material service rendered in more than one claim unless he indorses upon said
instruments, or sets forth in their contents, the several claims to which they
are intended to apply.

Thomas J. Edwards 340

Representatives of.

10. Under the authority conferred by the act of July 18, 1894, it is suggested the
instructions of the Bureau be modified to the extent that representatives of
recognized attorneys who have written authority from their employers be
granted the same privilege of examining the certificates of examining surgeons as is provided by law for the attorneys in person.

Hereafter, under section 471 of the Revised Statutes, all orders or circulars affecting the rights of claimants, or their properly accredited attorneys shall be
submitted to the Secretary of the Interior for his information and approval
prior to their promulgation.

Charles and William B. King... 478

CERTIFICATE OF MEDICAL EXAMINATION.

In the absence of medical examination describing a disabling cause it can not be
presumed, under the act of March 2, 1895, that it was the opinion of the board
of examining surgeons that no pensionable disability existed.

William H. Farmer 7

CIVIL DEATH.

(*See* MARRIAGE AND DIVORCE, 5.)

CIVILIAN EMPLOYEES.

(*See* SERVICE, 15, 16, 17, 18, 19, 20.)

COMBINATION OF CAUSES.

(*See* DEATH CAUSE, 4.)

COMMENCEMENT.

Under Act of June 27, 1890.

1. The evidence in this case fairly shows that a pensionable degree of disability
entitling claimant to $12 per month under the act of June 27, 1890, and on
account of which he was pensioned at such rate from September 23, 1886,
existed at the time of filing his first application July 9, 1890, and his pension
should have dated from said first application, deducting payments made.

Galen Peters............................... 102

2. Pension to minors under section 3, act of June 27, 1890, must commence from date
of application therefor.

Where one or more minors is insane, idiotic, or otherwise permanently helpless
he shall not be deprived of his share of the joint pension upon arriving at
the age of 16 years while there are other children under that age, but shall
continue to receive the same as if he were still under 16. But this rule
shall apply only to future payments.

Minors of David S. Sharer (deceased)...................................... 189

3. Pension under the second section of the act of June 27, 1890, must commence from the date of filing of the declaration, provided a pensionable degree of disability is shown to have existed on that date; but where such pensionable degree of disability did not exist at date of filing the declaration, but it appears that subsequent to the filing of such declaration and before a medical examination was had an applicant became pensionably disabled, another declaration must be filed.

4. Pension to an insane, idiotic, or otherwise permanently helpless minor under section 3 of the act of June 27, 1890, can not be made to commence prior to the date of filing the declaration therefor after the passage of said act.

Under Act of July 14, 1892.

5. There is no authority of law for commencing the $50 rate prior to the date of the certificate of the examining surgeon, or board of examining surgeons, showing the requisite degree of disability, made subsequent to the passage of the act of July 14, 1892.

Under Act of January 5, 1893.

6. The date of commencement in Mexican war claims for increase under said act is in each claim the day on which the case is legally approved by the Board of Review.

As this rule was followed in the action upon this claim, the same was proper, and is affirmed.

Under Section 4698½ of the Revised Statutes.

7. Appellant pensioned for rheumatism and resulting disease of heart filed a claim for increase September 12, 1895, which was allowed at third grade ($24 per month) from November 27, 1895, date of the certificate of the medical examination made under the pending claim. He contends the increased rate should commence from October 24, 1891, as the evidence of two physicians showed that on that date his disability was equivalent to the loss of a hand or a foot. It is held, that as claimant's disability is not permanent and specific his increase of pension was properly made to commence from the date of the certificate of medical examination made under the pending claim, showing the increased disability as provided by section 4698½ of the Revised Statutes.

Of Increase for New Disability.

8. Where a pensioner under the law of July 14, 1892, files an application for additional pension, based on a newly alleged cause of disability, not specific, such claim, if allowed, dates from the time of filing such application, and not from the date of the examining surgeon's certificate establishing a pensionable degree of disability from said newly alleged cause.

In such cases the date of commencement is governed by the proviso in section 2 of the act of March 3, 1879, and not by section 4698½, Revised Statutes.

CONTRIBUTORY NEGLIGENCE.

Death Cause.

9. A person disabled by deafness who adopts a railroad track as a highway of travel is required to exercise that care and caution which ordinary prudence would dictate to a person in his condition in order to avoid harm or peril, and a failure to do so is contributory negligence; and where a soldier is killed by a passing train while pursuing such course his widow is not pensionable under the general law.

DEAFNESS.

(*See* RATING, 3.)

DEATH CAUSE.

(*See also* CONTRIBUTORY NEGLIGENCE.)

Accident.

1. Soldier, who was suffering from varicose veins of left leg, of service origin, for which he was pensioned third-grade rate, was thrown from a wagon in which he was riding, striking on the back part of his head, resulting in his death two days later.

   Held, That soldier's varicose veins were not the immediate or proximate cause of the injury which resulted in his death, and that his death had no relation, immediate or proximate, with his pensioned cause or his army service.

   Margaret Moran (*widow*).. 492

Combination of Causes.

2. The rule laid down in decision in the case of Mary A. Cox (3 P. D., 313), that "where the evidence, lay and medical, goes to show that the cause for which pension was granted to soldier was complicated with a disease which was the immediate cause of his death, the Department will sustain the widow's claim," has not been amended, qualified, recalled, or annulled, and the same is reaffirmed.

   Napoleon B. Trask... 113

3. Soldier was pensioned for disease of heart and died of abscess of bowels, as shown by the records of death of the city of Lowell, Mass., and claimant's declaration filed about a week after soldier's death.

   The affidavit of one physician stating that disease of bowels would not have terminated fatally had it not been for the disease of heart amounts to no more than mere conjecture, and is not accepted as showing that death resulted from the pensioned cause.

   Angeline Emmons (*widow*)... 129

4. The sailor was pensioned for disease of heart. The attending physician certified that death was caused by "pneumonia, exhaustion, and purulent infiltration," after an illness of three months' duration. The widow's claim was rejected on the ground that the alleged cause of death was not due to the disability for which the sailor was pensioned.

   Held, That inasmuch as the principal desideratum in a case of lobar pneumonia is the maintenance of the proper action of the heart, to which the treatment is mainly directed; and in view of the fact that the sailor was pensioned for disease of that most important viscus, and that the evidence in the case shows that said disease, as well as pneumonia, was an important factor in the death cause, the question as to the relation of the acute disease of lungs to the pre-existing chronic disease of heart is one of complication, not of pathology, the claim is reopened and submitted for readjudication and allowance.

   Sarah J. Smith (*widow*) 266

5. The word "complicated," as used in the case of Napoleon B. Trask (9 P. D., 113), means involved, interwoven, or connected with, and to entitle a widow to a pension under section 4702, Revised Statutes, she is required to show that the disease, wound, or injury of soldier of service origin, in line of duty, had some probable connection with or relation to death cause, and was a contributing and presumptive predominating factor in producing death.

   Nanna J. Smith (*widow*)... 359

Line of duty.

6. Soldier, who had been home on a ten days' furlough for the purpose of voting at an election, while waiting at the wharf for passage on a steamer on which he

was to return to his command got into an altercation with some persons, one of whom struck him on the head with a stone, killing him instantly.

Held: He was not in line of duty, and therefore his death was not due to the service, and his widow is not pensionable under the general pension laws.

7. Soldier's death from an overdose of opium, which he was in the habit of taking as a remedy for diarrhea contracted in the service, but which was probably accidental and not intentional, could not be considered to have been in any way a result of the disease or otherwise connected with his military service.

DEATH IN SERVICE.

(*See* DISCHARGE, 3.)

DECLARATIONS.

(*See also* PRACTICE, 2.)

Amendments to.

1. A declaration containing all of the necessary allegations for minor's pension under the act of June 27, 1890, except it fails to state that it was filed under said act, an amendatory affidavit having been filed in which it is stated that the claim was intended to be filed under said act, is a valid declaration.

Act of June 27, 1890.

2. A declaration for widow's pension under the act of June 27, 1890, alleging all the essential elements of title except the date of her husband's discharge (or duration of his service), and that his discharge was honorable, but stating that he was a pensioner, and giving the number of his pension certificate, is a good and sufficient application under said act.

3. It being shown that the deceased soldier was, at the date of filing his application for pension and up to the date of his death, incapacitated for earning a support by manual labor in a pensionable degree, under the provisions of section 2, act of June 27, 1890, by disabling causes not alleged by him in his application, but shown not to be due to vicious habits, his claim should be admitted under instructions of this Department of July 28, 1897. (P. D., 93.)

4. As declaration is substantially in the terms of the law, and the claimant in his statement to the examining board alleged the disabilities he claimed for, said claim is held to be valid.

5. Every application for pension under the second section of the act of June 27, 1890, should state that the same is made under said act, the dates of enlistment and discharge, the name or nature of the diseases, wounds, or injuries by which the claimant is disabled, and that they are not due to vicious habits: *Provided, however,* That the omission of any of these averments shall not invalidate the application (the intent to claim pension being manifest and the declaration being executed in accordance with law), but such application shall be subject to amendment by means of a supplemental affidavit, in the particulars wherein it is defective; said supplemental affidavit or affidavits to be read in connection with and as a part of the application itself: *And provided further,* That a declaration *in the terms of the act* shall be sufficient.

Should the paper filed fail to show upon its face, with certainty, that it is intended as a claim for the benefits of the act of June 27, 1890, the claimant may make it certain, by means of a supplemental affidavit, which shall be read in connection with and as a part of the original application.

Should the medical examination disclose the existence of any disease, wound, or injury not alleged in the original or amendatory application, which is a factor in the applicant's inability to earn a support by manual labor, the claimant shall be called upon to state, under oath, the time, place, and circumstances when, where, and under which such wound or injury was received or disease contracted, and whether it was in any manner caused by vicious habits.

Should the wound, injury, or disease not specified in the original or amendatory declaration, but discovered on medical examination, be shown to have existed at the time when the original declaration was filed, and it is found not to be due to vicious habits, it shall be taken into account, the same as if formally specified in the original application, in estimating the degree of the permanent mental or physical disability to which it contributes.

Should it be found, however, not to have existed at the time when the original application was filed, but from a subsequent date prior to medical examination, the degrees of the disability of the applicant being below the maximum rating, pension may be increased accordingly from the date when such wound or injury was incurred or disease contracted, provided the degree of disability from all contributory causes is thereby enhanced to a sufficient extent to justify a higher rating.

Should it be found impossible to fix the exact date when such wound or injury was received or disease contracted, the higher rating shall commence from the date of the certificate of medical examination showing its existence.

Vicious habits.—A liberal and reasonable rule in regard to the proof as to "vicious habits" was laid down by the Department in the case of John Martin (7 P. D., 578), and the same is hereby affirmed: *Provided, however*, That where the nature of the disease, wound, or injury is such as to show that it is not due to vicious habits, the Commissioner of Pensions may, in his discretion, accept the sworn statement of the applicant as sufficient.

Original pension having been allowed, any subsequent *increase* of pension must be based on the fact that there is increased incapacitation for earning a support by manual labor, and must be adjudicated, so far as commencement of the increased rate is concerned, under section 4698½, Revised Statutes of the United States.

All former rules and decisions in conflict herewith are hereby set aside.

Act of July 4, 1864 (Sec. 4714, R. S.).

6. An unsworn application for pension filed subsequent to July 4, 1864, is fatally defective and does not authorize the commencement of pension subsequently allowed, on a sufficient declaration subsequently filed, to date from the filing of such defective declaration.

DEPENDENCE.

Widows, Act June 27, 1890.

1. In considering a widow's claim under the act of June 27, 1890, it is her condition, dependent or nondependent, that governs, and it matters not whether the property or income that keeps her from dependence is derived from her husband's estate. It is the widow's pecuniary condition, as a fact, that is the criterion under said act.

(Overruled; see page 320.)

2. The soldier died December 9, 1892, leaving a widow and seven minor children under 16 years of age. He owned a farm valued at $800, also some personal property.

Held, That when the income, as in this case, is derived mainly from the widow's manual labor, or the labor of her children, it is held that the widow is without other means of support, under the provisions of the act of June 27, 1890, and therefore occupies a pensionable status.

3. When it is proved that a widow, by reason of age, or permanent physical or mental infirmities, is incapable of exerting a reasonable effort to add to the income of which she is possessed, or the property of which she is possessed, reduced to an income, is not sufficient to provide her with the necessaries of life, such widow is dependent within the terms of the act of June 27, 1890.

4. The soldier, prior to his death, deeded certain real estate owned by him in Chicago, and valued at $8,000, to his brother-in-law, without consideration, who deeded it to the soldier's eldest daughter, without consideration, the purpose of these transfers being to save the property from his creditors. After his death the widow applied $2,500 of her own money to the cancellation of a mortgage upon the aforesaid property. She and her three children (all grown) live together and use the rents and profits of the property for their common support. They have a home and net income of $270 per year, independent of their earnings.

Held, That claimant is not without other means of support than her daily labor within the meaning of the law.

5. A widow who owns the house in which she lives, which is assessed at $930, and valued, according to her statement, at $1,600, and has $1,800 loaned out at 6 per cent interest, is not "without other means of support than her daily labor" within the meaning of section 3 of the act of June 27, 1890.

6. Claimant owns lots in Detroit, Mich., worth $1,000, and has $3,605.63 in bank drawing 4 per cent interest. She earns enough by keeping boarders to support her comfortably. *Held,* That she is not without other means of support than her daily labor within the meaning of the law. Accumulated savings of a widow's labor can not be excluded in estimating her means of support.

7. The evidence shows that claimant was, at the time of filing her declaration, in possession of ample means of support other than her daily labor, having been allowed $300 from her husband's estate for support for one year, and she is not pensionable under the act of June 27, 1890, under the declaration filed, though she may now be dependent.

8. As the evidence in this case fails to show the value of claimant's means of support, the motion is sustained, and departmental decision of March 13, 1897, reversed, and a special examination ordered.

9. The act of June 27, 1890, offers $8 per month as a supplement to the daily labor of such widows as do not possess the means therewith provided. As claimant is already in the enjoyment of the very means which the statute would bestow on one less fortunate, she is not pensionable.

DEPENDENT BROTHERS AND SISTERS.

(*See* LIMITATION, 2.)

DESERTION.

Generally.

1. In claims for pension under the acts of January 29, 1887, June 27, 1890, and July 27, 1892, an honorable discharge from all enlistments for service in the particular war to which these acts refer is a prerequisite to pension.

In claims for pension under sections 4692 and 4693, Revised Statutes, on account of disability incurred in the line of duty during a term of enlistment from which the claimant deserted, the claim should be rejected, for the reason that there is no period from which the pension could commence, as claimant had never been discharged from such term of service; and for the further reason that claimant having violated and repudiated his said contract of enlistment he thus forfeited all right to any benefits that were incident to such enlistment.

If the claim for invalid pension under sections 4692 and 4693, Revised Statutes, is based upon disability incurred in the line of duty during a term of enlistment from which the claimant was legally discharged, a desertion from a subsequent enlistment, of itself, is not a bar to pension. If the claim was filed prior to July 1, 1880, the pension would commence from the date of discharge from the term of enlistment during which the disability was incurred, but such pension will cease upon reenlistment and can not be restored while claimant is in the service, nor while in desertion from such subsequent enlistment. (Case of Henry Davinney, 7 P. D., 234.)

If the disability was incurred in the service under a subsequent enlistment, while the claimant was a deserter from a prior enlistment which had not terminated prior to such reenlistment, the claim should be rejected on the ground that the disability was not incurred in the line of duty, but while claimant was absent from his proper command in violation of his former contract of enlistment.

The decision in the case of George Lessor (8 P. D., 114), in so far as the same conflicts with the rules laid down here, is overruled.

2. This appellant was pensioned for disability incurred during his first term of service, from which he was honorably discharged May 24, 1862, from that date. He was subsequently drafted and served until April 8, 1864, when he deserted.

Held, That he is entitled to restoration of his pension, deducting pension for the whole period during which he could have been legally held to service under the draft. (John Norton, 9 P. D., 382.)

3. Claimant having enlisted for service in the war of the rebellion August, 22, 1864, and deserted said service November 14, 1865, he can not be held to have been honorably discharged from his service in the war of the rebellion.

The fact that he served after July 1, 1865, does not warrant a holding that he was honorably discharged on said date, as he was never either actually or constructively discharged.

Act of June 27, 1890.

4. As this soldier deserted from his first contract of enlistment during the war of the rebellion, which charge of desertion the War Department declines to remove, this claimant has no pensionable status.

Sections 4692, 4693, and 4694, R. S.

5. Desertion from the general service during the late war of the rebellion is no bar to pension on account of disability contracted in the United States service while serving under a contract of enlistment entered into since the close of said war, from which late service sailor was honorably discharged.

DISABILITY.

(*See also* AID AND ATTENDANCE, 1, 3; ANTEREBELLION SERVICE; DECLARATIONS, 3; PRACTICE, 1; RATE, 3, 5; TITLE.)

DISCHARGE.

(*See also* DESERTION, 3, 5, 6; SERVICE, 1, 22, 23.)

Dishonorable.

1. The soldier having been dishonorably discharged from his first term of enlistment during the war of the rebellion, and having subsequently reenlisted and served for more than ninety days during said war and received an honorable discharge, his widow is not entitled to pension under section 3 of the act of June 27, 1890, said act requiring an honorable discharge from all service contracted to be performed during the war. (Citing Stephen H. Carey, 6 P. D., 42; James Cullen, 6 P. D., 72; Franklin S. Cowen, 7 P. D., 374, and George Vansickle, 8 P. D., 336.)

Honorable.

2. Soldier was dishonorably discharged from the Regular Army March 19, 1861, having been in arrest for more than a year prior to that date. He enlisted March 22, 1862, and served in the Fourth California Volunteers until March 31, 1866, when he was mustered out. It is held that he was honorably discharged within the meaning and intent of the act of June 27, 1890.

3. When soldier has served a term of ninety days or more in the military or naval service of the United States during the late war of the rebellion and has been honorably discharged therefrom, reenlists, and dies during his subsequent term of service, his death not being the result of a violation of any law, rule, or regulation of the military or naval service, the requirements of the act of June 27, 1890, as to length of service and honorable discharge are fulfilled, and his widow is entitled to pension on compliance with the other conditions of the act.

DISLOYALTY.

As Affecting Claims under Act of June 27, 1890.

1. It appearing from the official military record in the War Department that this appellant had served in the Confederate army during the war of the rebellion, and there being no evidence to rebut the presumption that said Confederate service was voluntary, it not even being claimed or asserted by appellant that it was involuntary, payment of pension to him under the provisions of section 2, act of June 27, 1890, is expressly prohibited by the provisions of section 4716, Revised Statutes. See White's appeal (7 P. D., 312), Ozborn's appeal (Ibid., 317), and Longee's appeal (Ibid., 586).

2. Claimant was in the army of the Confederate States from May, 1861, to September, 1863, and was afterwards in the Army of the United States from October, 1864, to July, 1865. Having voluntarily engaged in and aided and abetted the rebellion against the authority of the United States, he is not entitled to pension under said act of June 27, 1890, his title being barred by the provisions of section 4716, Revised Statutes.

Said section 4716, Revised Statutes, has application to the act of June 27, 1890, as well as to that of July 14, 1862, or any other law, except as its operation is suspended by the act of March 3, 1877, in the case of those disabled in a service subsequent to the disloyal service, or as exemption from its operation is specifically provided for in other laws granting pensions for service in prior wars. No repeal of said section 4716, Revised Statutes, or exemption from its operation is provided in the act of June 27, 1890, and it is construed in *pari materia* with other laws to be subject to the inhibition of said section.

3. It clearly appearing from the official military record in the War Department of this appellant's army service during the war of the rebellion that he had voluntarily served in the Confederate army during said war, and the adverse presumption created by said record being unrebutted by any sufficient or satisfactory evidence that said Confederate service was involuntary, payment of pension to him under the provisions of section 2, act of June 27, 1890, is expressly and positively prohibited by the provisions of section 4716, Revised Statutes, United States.

(Job White, 7 P. D., 312; Sarah H. Ozborn, *ibid.*, 317; Augustus H. Longee, *ibid.*, 586; Emma H. Seymour, 8 P. D., 325; Anastatio Capella, *ibid.*, 308; William C. Couch, *ibid.*, 39; Aaron T. Bush, *ibid.*, 254.)

It being shown by the record and the testimony that the incapacity to earn a support by manual labor, for which this appellant was formerly pensioned under the act of June 27, 1890, is a direct result of disability contracted while confined as a Confederate prisoner of war at Camp Douglas, Illinois, the effect of restoring him to the rolls under said act would be to grant him a pension for disability contracted while serving in the ranks of the Confederate army, in open rebellion against and hostility to the authority of the United States.

4. Claimant at the age of 19 years voluntarily left his home in Tennessee and spent two months in a Confederate camp in the State of Alabama.

Held: That he voluntarily aided and abetted the late rebellion against the authority of the United States within the meaning of section 4716, Revised Statutes, and is not entitled to pension under the act of June 27, 1890.

DOUBLE PENSION.

Special Act.

This appellant is now in receipt of a pension of $20 per month, granted to her personally by a special act of Congress in recognition of services rendered by her individually to the Government during the war of the rebellion. She seeks, in addition thereto, a pension as widow of the deceased soldier under the general provisions of section 4702, Revised Statutes. The granting or payment of such pension to her is expressly and positively prohibited by the provisions of section 5 of the act of July 25, 1882, so long as she is in receipt of pension under said special act.

DRAFTED MEN AND SUBSTITUTE.

(*See* SERVICE, 16, 21, 22, 23, 24.)

DROPPING FROM THE ROLLS.

(*See* NOTICE, 1; SERVICE, 32.)

ELLET'S RAM FLEET.

(*See* EVIDENCE, 4.)

ENLISTMENT.

(*See* SERVICE, 24.)

EVIDENCE.

See also ATTORNEYS, 9; DECLARATIONS, 3; DISABILITY, 2; MARRIAGE AND DIVORCE,
1, 3; VICIOUS HABITS.

Burden of Proof.

1. The burden of proof against the validity of the ceremonial marriage does not
rest upon the widow, but upon the parties who attack the validity of such
ceremonial marriage, and the presumption of law favors innocence of the
latter marriage, until the contrary be proved.

    Jennette Burton (widow) 31

Disability.

2. Inasmuch as the evidence on file, including the last two certificates of medical
examination, is unsatisfactory as to the degree of disability existing at the
date of said examinations, on account of pensioned causes alone, a special
examination is deemed advisable, for which purpose the papers in the case
are remanded.

    Robert W. Matthews 333

Disloyalty.

3. This claim, having been adjudicated and rejected upon insufficient evidence, is
remanded for reopening and readjudication under instructions.

    John N. McCollum 150

Incurrence.

4. Appellant claims pension for disability from being scalded with hot water and
steam while serving on the ram *Lancaster* in an engagement with the Confederate ram *Arkansas*. There is no record of incurrence of said disabling cause
of service on the *Lancaster*, nor of the *Lancaster* herself; but it is an accepted
historical fact that said ram was disabled in July, 1862, by the ram *Arkansas*
and that many of her men were scalded; and it is shown that appellant served
on said ram, and was injured in line of duty as alleged; but the evidence of
the existence and continuance since his discharge of any permanent disabling
effects of said injury not being satisfactorily shown, the case is returned for a
special examination.

    Noah Perry 237

5. Appellant's allegation that he incurred sunstroke, or heat prostration, in August,
1862, while on a forced march with his command between Tullahoma and Manchester, Tenn., is fully sustained by the affidavits of three reputable comrades,
who are shown by the record to have been present with their command and
the claimant at the time and place alleged, and who, in correspondence with
the Bureau, fully adhere to and sustain the statements made in their affidavits.

    Held, That no reason appearing for discrediting their testimony, it is deemed
sufficient to show incurrence of the disability alleged in the service and line
of duty.

    George W. Warren 393

Identity.

6. One witness, in the absence of a record, whose statement is inconsistent with
claimant's allegations, is insufficient to establish the incurrence of an injury
on board of the *Naumkeag*, as alleged. Furthermore, the record shows that
the Christopher Columbus who served on said vessel was at date of enlistment,
December 12, 1864, 19 years old, 5 feet 5¼ inches tall, and by occupation a soldier; while claimant is shown to be 6 feet 3 inches tall, swears that he never
was a soldier, and that in 1896 he was 40 years old.

    Christopher Columbus Yancey 185

New Disability.

7. Whenever, in a claim for increase under the general law, an applicant, after
long and unexplained silence, alleges a new disability, of which there is

neither record nor medical evidence, the adverse presumption arising from
the absence of such evidence may be rebutted, but can be overcome only by
direct and positive proof of incurrence and existence, or by satisfactory evidence as to facts and circumstances from which such incurrence and existence
may be naturally, fairly, and reasonably inferred. (See case of Thomas H.
Strange, 7 P. D., 36.)

Presumptions.

8. Where the record shows that the statutory notice was duly issued and mailed to
claimant's address, and is not returned to your Bureau, the presumption is
that the notice was duly received by claimant, and this presumption is not
outweighed by the affidavit of claimant first made in his appeal; but in such
a case the Department will, on its own motion, examine into the merits of
the claim to ascertain if any injustice has been done claimant in the action
complained of.

9. The evidence in this case satisfactorily establishes the continued and unexplained absence of the above-named soldier from his home and family since
November, 1877, since which date no intelligence of his existence has been
received, and, therefore, his death should be considered "as sufficiently
proved," in accordance with the provisions of the act of March 13, 1896.

10. Claimant's first husband left her in Missouri, in 1873, to go to Chicago, Ill., for
medical treatment, and a few months later she received a letter from his sister
informing her that he was dead. Relying on the truth of this statement, she
married one Holmes in December, 1877, who procured a divorce from her on
the ground of desertion in 1882. In April, 1883, claimant married the soldier,
who died in July, 1890. Her first husband has never been heard of in that
community since 1873.

Held, That these facts are sufficient to raise the presumption that claimant's
first husband had died prior to her marriage to Holmes, and her marriage to
the soldier was legal, and she is his widow.

11. The continued unexplained absence of the soldier for more than twenty years,
though sufficient to raise the presumption of death, does not entitle his mother
to pension, as it must be further shown that such soldier died of a wound or
injury received or disease contracted in the United States service and in line
of duty.

12. Soldier was seen in Denver, Colo., about four years after he abandoned his home
and family in Ohio, by an acquaintance, whom he told that he had a wife in
Ohio with whom he had some difficulty and that he wanted to keep away from
her.

Held, That his absence from his home and family for more than seven years is
not unexplained, so that his death may be presumed under the act of March
13, 1896.

13. The act of March 13, 1896, relates only to presumption of death of the enlisted
man or officer on account of whose service and death pension is claimed.

14. The death of the husband can not be presumed from the fact that he deserted his
wife, howsoever long said desertion may continue. *Ibid.*

Specialist.

15. The evidence of a specialist, he being an agent of the Government and being required by law (section 4744, R. S.) to make his examination thorough and searching, will, when such evidence is made the basis of a holding by the medical referee, be ordinarily accepted as against the evidence of claimant's physicians.

William Harris 73

EXAMINATION OF RECORD.
(*See* ATTORNEYS, 1.)

EXAMINING SURGEONS.
(*See* MEDICAL EXAMINATION.)

FEE.
(*See also* ATTORNEYSHIP, 2, 3, 5.)

In Claims for Restoration and Increase.

1. Where a pensioner's name has been dropped from the roll solely because he has been allowed and has accepted pension under some other law, and upon application for restoration and increase of pension under the law under which he was pensioned when his name was dropped, his name is restored to the roll under said law at an increased rate, the sole object in filing such claims being to secure a higher rate of pension, and not involving question of title, the attorney prosecuting the same is entitled to a fee of $2 only, the claim being in no sense a claim for restoration, but for increase.

Jacob Young 147

In Cases of Motions for Reconsideration.

2. Under rule 9, Rules of Practice before the Secretary of the Interior, a second motion for reconsideration of a decision adverse to a fee or for recognition will not be considered, and the decisions in this case having been adhered to on a former motion to reconsider, this motion is dismissed.

Henry C. Williams (claimant) 39

In Case of Rule to Show Cause.

3. A fee not greater than $10 may be allowed to an attorney for services rendered in preparing and filing evidence under a rule to show cause why pensioner's name should not be dropped from the roll in cases under the act of June 27, 1890, but the attorney may not collect the same directly from the claimant or pensioner.

Commissioner of Pensions 136

No Fund, No Fee.

4. As the only fee provided by law is to be deducted from the pension, it follows that when the payment of accrued pension is expressly limited to the defrayal of the expenses of a pensioner's last illness and burial there is no fund from which the payment of a fee can be made. (Case of Lawrence H. Davis, dec., 8 P. D., 406.)

Dorcas Duggins 402

One Claim, One Fee.

5. Where a declaration filed in a widow's original claim for pension sets forth that the claimant is entitled to increase on account of helpless condition of a minor child of the soldier, the attorney who is authorized to prosecute said claims by a power of attorney contained in said declaration is not entitled to an additional fee for securing such increase upon the child attaining its sixteenth year.

Elizabeth M. Williams (widow) 117

6. As but one fee can be certified on each issue to allow pension in a claim, where an attorney refuses to refund a fee which was erroneously paid him, action refusing another fee to the attorney entitled to the one so paid is proper.

Material Service Must Be Rendered.

7. Where a claim for original pension stands rejected and a duplicate declaration is filed resulting in the reopening of the claim, the filing thereof is deemed material service.

Refundment of.

8. As there is no proper evidence on file of appellant's authority to secure the payment of accrued pension in the soldier's claim, he is not entitled to a fee.

The Bureau of Pensions has authority to demand the refundment of a fee or of any compensation purported to have been paid by a claimant to an attorney for services or expenses in a pension claim where the record shows a fee has been allowed by the Bureau and paid him when not entitled thereto, or where the receipt of compensation directly or indirectly from the claimant for such services or expenses is admitted by the attorney.

Fee Agreements in Claims for Restoration.

9. Where the Bureau, upon evidence procured by special examination, has approved action for dropping a pensioner's name from the roll upon the ground that his disability was not incurred in line of duty, and notice has been given him to show cause why his name should not be dropped, he may properly file a claim for restoration of pension, whether or not his name has been actually dropped from the pension roll. Such a claim is one in which the law directs that valid fee agreements be recognized if filed.

FINAL ACTION.

(*See* APPEAL, 2.)

PORFEITURE.

(*See* ADULTEROUS COHABITATION, 2; ATTORNEYSHIP, 2.)

FRAUD AND MISTAKE.

Reimbursement.

1. The soldier was pensioned for rheumatism and resulting disease of the heart. The widow stated in her application that he died of disease contracted in the service and filed a copy of a public record giving the cause of death as "paralysis of the heart," whereupon her claim was allowed. It was subsequently ascertained that the cause of death was inquired into by a coroner's jury and found to be the intemperate use of intoxicants and drugs, and her pension was, therefore, terminated.

Held, That the concealment by claimant of the fact that a coroner's inquest was had amounted to fraud and justified recovery of the amount paid under the old law from the pension subsequently allowed under the act of June 27, 1890.

2. It appearing that the disability of this appellant from disease of eyes can not be attributed to the results of sunstroke in service, and said disease of eyes not being shown by the evidence to have been otherwise due to his military service, the action terminating the pension granted him on account thereof and rejecting his claim for restoration of the same was proper and is affirmed, although the ground stated for said action was erroneous.

It being shown that the nervous affection of the face, from which this appellant suffered prior to his enlistment, was not a factor in the disability from disease of eyes for which he was first erroneously pensioned, and had no connection therewith, pathologically or otherwise, all basis for a charge of fraud in obtaining said pension is eliminated from this case, the same having been granted, not through fraud on his part, or a mistake of fact on the part of the Pension Bureau, but merely as the result of an erroneous judgment on the evidence, and no legal grounds exist for withholding payment of his present pension to reimburse the Government for former payments made to him under his original pension certificate as a result of such erroneous judgment. (Christian May, 8 P. D., 71.)

GILPIN'S BATTALION

(*See* SERVICE, 8.)

GRADE RATES.

(*See* RATING, 1; COMMENCEMENT, 7.)

GUARDIAN.

(*See also* PAYMENT OF PENSION, 2.)

Payment to.

The words appearing in the act of August 8, 1882, "But the payment to persons laboring under legal disabilities may be made to the guardians of such persons," are not mandatory, but permissive.

The pension system now in force, and the whole thereof, in substance and in form of procedure, is without the plane of State control and exclusively within the jurisdiction of the United States.

Payment of pension to the guardian of a pensioner under legal disability is not obligatory, and if the Commissioner of Pensions shall become satisfied that the pensioner's interests would be better subserved by payment to the pensioner himself he may so direct; but until there is evidence warranting the belief that the pensioner is deprived of his rights under the pension laws by the guardian, and the appointing court will not administer relief, the Commissioner of Pensions will not be warranted in refusing payment to such guardian.

HELPLESS MINOR.

Generally.

1. A claimant for pension under the first proviso of section 3, act of June 27, 1890, as a helpless minor, who was over the age of 16 years at the date of the soldier's death, has no pensionable status.

2. A child who is an incurable epileptic, having a falling fit once a week on an average and nervous attacks much oftener, who is vigorous in body but dull mentally, who is able to attend to his personal wants except when suffering from an epileptic seizure, and can perform some remunerative labor but not nearly sufficient to afford him a support, is "permanently helpless" in the contemplation of the law, and the pension on his account should be continued.

3. Claimant is 24 years old, has been since 1885 an inmate of an asylum for feeble-minded persons, does not know her age, is unable to comprehend numbers above 5, is capable of receiving only the most elementary instruction, and, in the opinion of the surgeon detailed to examine her, is permanently incapacitated for earning a living and requires the care and attendance of another person daily.

Held, That she is entitled to continuance of pension as claimed.

Widow's Increase on Account of.

4. Evidence shows that the child claimed for (for whom pension was received till she was 16 years of age) is afflicted with incurable epilepsy, rendering her liable to frequent spasms and spells of unconsciousness, and which has made her weak and of low vitality, so that she can perform only the lightest household duties and no remunerative labor, besides causing her to be the subject of constant watchfulness and of some aid and attendance.

Held, That she is permanently helpless in the contemplation of the law, and the pension on her account should be continued.

HOME GUARDS.

(*See* SERVICE, 25.)

IDENTITY.

(*See* EVIDENCE, 6.)

IMPEDIMENT.

(*See* MARRIAGE AND DIVORCE, 7, 8, 9.)

INCREASE.

(*See also* COMMENCEMENT, 3, 5, 6; EVIDENCE, 4, 5; FEE, 5; PRACTICE, 4, 5, 9; SPECIFIC DISABILITY.)

Specific Disability.

1. Increase of pension under the act of March 3, 1885, relating to pension on account of loss of arm at the shoulder joint can not commence prior to that date (Nichols's appeal, 4 P. D., 213).

2. The first provision of the act of August 4, 1886, does not increase pensions for disability from other causes than the loss of a hand or foot or total disability in the same. It does not increase pensions for disabilities equivalent to the loss of a hand or foot.

INDIAN WARS.

(*See* SERVICE, 3, 4, 5.)

INSANE PERSON.

(*See* ATTORNEYS, 5.)

INSTRUCTIONS.

(*See* RATING, 1.)

JURISDICTION.

(*See also* GUARDIANS; RECORD; SERVICE, 2.)

State and United States.

The pension system now in force, and the whole thereof, in substance and in form of procedure, is without the plane of State control and exclusively within the jurisdiction of the United States.

LEGITIMACY.

(*See also* MARRIAGE AND DIVORCE, 6.)

Minors.

It appearing that the marriage of the parents of this minor was "absolutely void" under the laws of the State of New York, where all the parties resided both before and after said marriage, she was not a legitimate child of said deceased sailor, and has no title to pension as a minor under the provisions of the pension laws.

LENGTH.

(*See* SERVICE, 13.)

LIMITATION

Claims of Dependent Brothers and Sisters.

1. The limitation as to the date of commencement of pension because of the date of filing the claim therefor, contained in the second section of the act of March 3, 1879, applies to claims in behalf of orphan brothers and sisters.

2. The evidence shows that claimant was over 16 years of age at the time of filing her declaration, as well as at the date of dependent mother's death, and she is not entitled to pension as dependent sister of the soldier, as the exception to the limitation contained in the act of March 3, 1879, does not apply to claims of dependent brothers and sisters of the soldier

Secretary's Power.

3. The power conferred upon the Secretary of the Interior to establish rules and regulations for the examination and adjudication of claims for pension does not authorize the enactment of a rule or statute of limitations, and the decisions in the cases of Jacob Wolhart (8 P. D., 226), Henry Groppe (id., 293), and Briggs Soper (id., 394), in so far as they limit the time of filing an appeal by a widow from the rejection of her husband's pension claim, are overruled and set aside.

LINE OF DUTY.

(*See also* DEATH CAUSE, 6.)

Accidental Injury.

1. Soldier was wounded by the accidental discharge of a gun while hunting for his own pleasure, and was not in the line of duty.

2. Soldier, while riding over the battlefield of Pea Ridge, Ark., after that battle, for his own amusement, on a horse he had borrowed from his captain, was thrown and sustained an injury upon which he based a claim for pension. It is held that said injury was not incurred in line of duty (Reaffirming action in same case, 2 P. D., 385, and 3 P. D., 111.)

3. Soldier, by permission of his superior officer, was engaged in hunting with a gun for his own pleasure and amusement, and while so engaged received the injury alleged as a basis for pension, by the careless and negligent handling of his gun. *Held*, That he was not in line of duty.

Impediment—Prior marriage.

4. Claimant at date of her marriage to soldier had a former husband living, from whom she had not been divorced, but who had been convicted of a felony and imprisoned.

Held, The doctrine of civil death is not recognized by the law or courts of the State of Virginia, and imprisonment for felony, while affording just grounds for a divorce, does not per se operate as a divorce.

Under the statutes of Indiana, where claimant married the soldier, all marriages where either party thereto has a former wife or husband living, if solemnized in that State, are declared to be absolutely void without any legal proceedings.

5. Claimant and soldier were divorced, a viniculo, on claimant's petition, May 6, 1887. The decree of divorce was disregarded by both parties, they continuing to cohabit together the same as if no decree had been granted. They were remarried by ceremony on February 27, 1891.

Held, The relation existing between soldier and claimant, from May 6, 1887, and February 27, 1891, was illicit, and claimant was not the legal wife of soldier on June 27, 1890.

6. There being evidence in the case showing that soldier had a wife living in Germany, whom he deserted prior to his marriage to claimant, it is incumbent upon her to show the death of said first wife, or that the parties were divorced, before she can be regarded the legal widow of said soldier; and in the absence of such proof the minor child of soldier by said claimant can not be regarded as legitimate.

7. Claimant was married to the soldier by a ceremony in 1875, and lived with him in Michigan until his death in 1895; at the time of said marriage soldier had a wife living who procured a divorce from him in 1877, all of which facts were unknown to claimant during the lifetime of the soldier.

Held, That as claimant was the innocent party, and was kept in ignorance of the fact that a legal impediment to her marriage to soldier existed at the time of such marriage, and that during all the time from the removal of the impediment in 1877 to soldier's death in 1895 the parties cohabited together as husband and wife, uniting in conveyances, and joining in church membership, and deporting themselves generally in accordance with good morals, and being universally recognized by their neighbors, friends, and acquaintances as husband and wife, a valid marriage subsequent to the removal of the impediment will be presumed, distinguishing this case from that of Ellen, widow of William A. Palmer (7 P. D., 363).

8. Claimant was married to soldier May 23, 1896, at which time she had a former husband living from whom she was not divorced, but who died August 13, 1896. Soldier died August 19, 1896. From August 13 to August 19, 1896, claimant lived with soldier as his wife in the same unchanged relation as prior to August 13, 1896.

Held, That under the laws of the State of Pennsylvania, in which the parties resided at the time of her first and second husband's death, a valid marriage is not shown, and claimant is therefore not the widow of the soldier and has no title to a widow's pension under any law.

Impediment of Blood.

9. Evidence secured by special examination shows that soldier was a white man and claimant is a negro. The intermarriage of the races being prohibited by the laws of Mississippi, in which State the parties resided, their cohabitation could not be regarded as a legal marriage, but was mere concubinage, and

MATERIAL SERVICE.

(*See* ATTORNEYS, 4; FEE, 7.)

MEDICAL EXAMINATION.

(*See also* PRACTICE, 3.)

By Civil Surgeon.

A certificate of a medical examination, not sworn to, made by a person who had ceased to be an examining surgeon or a member of a board of examining surgeons, can not be considered the certificate of a civil surgeon, but is without authority of law and null and void; and a claimant, having submitted to such examination under protest, should have the benefit of an examination by a duly authorized examining surgeon or a board of examining surgeons.

MEXICAN WAR.

(*See* POWELL'S BATTALION; SERVICE, 6, 7, 8, 9, 29, 34.)

MILITIA.

(*See* SERVICE, 26, 27, 28.)

MINORS.

(*See also* ACCRUED PENSION, 3; COMMENCEMENT, 2; LIMITATION, 1, 2.)

When Widow is Nonpensionable.

The rule promulgated in the case of the minors of Lafayette Howard (8 P. D., 230), that "the minor children of a deceased soldier have no title to pension in their own right under the act of June 27, 1890, while the widow of such soldier is living and not remarried, unless such widow has forfeited her right to pension under the act of August 7, 1882, or section 4706, Revised Statutes, notwithstanding such widow married such soldier subsequent to the passage of said act," is approved and adhered to.

MOTIONS FOR RECONSIDERATION.

(*See* FEE, 2.)

NEGLECT.

(*See* ATTORNEYS, 4.)

NEW DISABILITY.

(*See* COMMENCEMENT, 8; EVIDENCE, 7.)

NONRESIDENTS.

Claims by.

The lawmaking power has made no distinction between applicants for pension by reason of their place of residence since the war, and there should be none in the execution of the law; and all orders or instructions which, in effect, suspend or prevent a prompt and impartial adjudication of claims filed by nonresidents are revoked, and there shall be no distinction between claims filed by those who reside in this country and those who reside in foreign countries.

Henry McFadger 437

NOTICE.

(*See also* REDUCTION, 1, 3.)

Dropping from the Rolls.

1. As the evidence tends to show that claimant failed to receive notice of the proposed dropping from the rolls and to appear for a medical examination, the action dropping his name from the rolls is reversed and the case remanded for further adjudication, that claimant may have an opportunity to file rebutting evidence and to be examined.

Spencer Payne.. 50

2. Where the question involved on appeal is whether claimant had due notice of the proposed action as required by section 3 of the act of June 21, 1879, or the act of December 21, 1893, the report from the Commissioner of Pensions in response to the appeal should fully and clearly state whether notice was served on the claimant, and if so, the form of the notice or its substance, and the date and manner of service should be stated.

The notice specified in the act of June 21, 1879, and the thirty days' notice specified in the act of December 21, 1893, are essential prerequisites without which the reduction or suspension of a pension is not authorized. Due statutory notice is necessary to confer jurisdiction to reduce or suspend pensions once issued.

Where the record shows that the statutory notice was duly issued and mailed to claimant's address, and is not returned to your Bureau, the presumption is that the notice was duly received by claimant, and this presumption is not outweighed by the affidavit of claimant first made in his appeal, but in such a case the Department will, on its own motion, examine into the merits of the claim to ascertain if any injustice has been done claimant in the action complained of.

The evidence in this case shows that claimant was improperly pensioned at the rate of $12 per month under the act of June 27, 1890, and that his disability did not entitle him to a rate in excess of the minimum rate under said act.

Alva H. Hall.. 165

ONE CLAIM, ONE FEE.

(*See* FEE, 5.)

ORDER 352.

(*See* PRACTICE, 4, 5.)

ORIGIN.

(*See* ANTEREBELLION SERVICE. DISABILITY, 1.)

ORPHAN BROTHERS AND SISTERS.

(*See* LIMITATION, 1.)

PASS TO HUNT.

(*See* LINE OF DUTY, 5.)

PATHOLOGICAL SEQUENCE.

(*See also* GUARDIANS.)

Practice.

The soldier is now pensioned at $16 per month for "rheumatism and resulting disease of heart, and total deafness of left ear."

He claimed increase on the ground that the rheumatism had affected his spinal column.

On examination he was shown to be suffering from locomotor ataxia. The claim for increase was rejected on the ground that disease of the spinal cord could not result from rheumatism.

From this action the claimant appeals, contending—

First. That he has established by competent evidence that the locomotor ataxia did result from the rheumatism for which he is pensioned.

Second. That the symptoms upon which the claim for rheumatism were both based and established were but the earlier manifestations of the cord lesion, and that the name of the pensioned disability should be changed by substituting locomotor ataxia for rheumatism.

Third. That he is suffering from both rheumatism and locomotor ataxia; that both disabilities are of service origin, and that the evidence upon which his claim on account of the former disability was established should be accepted as also showing the service origin of the latter.

Held, first. That although it is almost universally conceded by the medical profession that rheumatism and locomotor ataxia have one or more etiological factors in common, and also, in the preataxic stage of the latter disease, certain similar subjective symptoms, they are, nevertheless, universally considered by all recognized medical authorities as entirely separate and distinct diseases, with no similarity whatever in their pathological anatomy, and are not regarded by the most modern observers as having any casual relation to each other, either pathological or otherwise.

Second. That inasmuch as both rheumatism and tabes dorsalis are shown to exist, the contention that the latter was mistaken for the former is untenable.

Third. That in view of the fact that the Department does not take primary action in any claim for pension, the contention that the evidence on file also establishes the service origin of locomotor ataxia can not be considered until the merits of the claim shall first have been passed upon by the Bureau of Pensions.

Thaddeus P. Reig 444

PAYMENT OF PENSION.

To Guardian of Insane Person.

1. Payment of pension to the guardian of a pensioner under legal disability is not obligatory, and if the Commissioner of Pensions shall become satisfied that the pensioner's interests would be better subserved by payment to the pensioner himself he may so direct; but until there is evidence warranting the belief that the pensioner is deprived of his rights under the pension laws, by the guardian, and the appointing court will not administer relief, the Commissioner of Pensions will not be warranted in refusing payment to such guardian.

Edward W. Moore 55

To Guardian of Minor Child.

2. Appellant filed an application in behalf of herself and minor children, and at the same time procured a next friend to file application as guardian for said

minors. Her application was denied and that of the guardian allowed. After
the youngest child arrived at the age of 16 years, her case was reopened and
allowed to begin from the time said youngest child became 16 years old.
Claimant now asserts title to that which was paid to the guardian.

Held, Her contention is untenable because she procured the filing of the application by the guardian, received the money paid thereunder, and disbursed
the same.

   Josephine Burns (widow). 197

PENDING CLAIM.

(*See also* LIMITATION.)

Accrued Pension.

Where soldier's application was not filed with the Commissioner of Pensions until
after his death he can not be said to have had an application pending, and his
widow is not authorized under any existing law to prosecute soldier's claim for
pension.

   Samuel Fitzpatrick (deceased) 171

PERSONAL ALTERCATION.

(*See* LINE OF DUTY, 6.)

PILOT.

(*See* SERVICE, 17, 20, 33.)

POISONING.

(*See* DEATH CAUSE, 7.)

POWELL'S BATTALION.

Mexican War.

The provisions of the act of Congress of January 5, 1893, providing an increase of
the rate of pension granted on account of services in the Mexican war to survivors of said war, are applicable to survivors of Powell's Battalion Missouri
Mounted Volunteers, Mexican war, who are pensioned under the provisions of
the act of March 3, 1891, for service during the war with Mexico, and such surviving members of said organization are entitled to receive the increased rate
of pension provided by said act of January 5, 1893, under the same conditions,
limitations, and regulations as other Mexican-war survivors who are pensioned
under the provisions of the act of January 29, 1887. Departmental decision
of June 16, 1896, on Brookman's appeal (7 P. D., 260) overruled, and ruling
No. 237 of the Commissioner of Pensions modified.

   Zachariah Winkler 173

POWER OF ATTORNEY.

(*See* ATTORNEYSHIP, 5, 6, 7, 8.)

PRACTICE.

(*See also* APPEALS, 1, 2; ATTORNEYS, 7, 9; DISABILITY, 6; EVIDENCE, 3; FEE, 2; PATHOLOGICAL SEQUENCE; RATING, 2, 3; REDUCTION, 1.)

Appeals.

1. Rule 6 of Rules of Practice in appeals applies only to cases where clerical errors
are made in rating, and not to cases where the question is one of judgment on
the evidence (Charles Yokel, 8 P. D., 431).

This claimant's capacity for earning a support is not impaired in a degree entitling under said act to any higher rate than $6 per month, the rate of pension he is now receiving.

William Rogers.. 399

Declarations.

2. This widow's declaration for pension under section 3 of the act of June 27, 1890, executed in 1897, can not be held to be a duplicate of a declaration filed in 1893 under the same act and rejected, but should be treated as a new original declaration. The mere statement by the Commissioner in a communication to claimant that her claim had been previously rejected is not a rejection of the new claim nor such final action as furnishes a basis for a new appeal.

Mary Haffner (widow) 169

Medical Examinations.

3. A medical examination should not be held to show the extent of alleged disabilities under a declaration filed under the act of June 27, 1890, until claimant has shown at least a prima facie title under said act.

Charles A. Armstrong... 71

Order 352.

4. Order No. 352, issued by the Commissioner of Pensions December 24, 1897, which prohibits the consideration of increase claims within one year of date of last adjudication in the case, is revoked and set aside, and the rule contained on page 52 of Walker's Treatise on the Practice in the Pension Bureau, holding that such claims would not be adjudicated until six months after the allowance of the original claim, though when declarations therefor were filed claimants should be ordered for examination as soon as practicable, reestablished.

John W. Granless... 285

5. As order No. 352, from the enforcement of which this appeal was filed, has been revoked and set aside, the contentions of appellant are no longer tenable. The appeal is therefore dismissed.

George Buck, jr.. 290

Readjudication.

6. Under departmental decision in the case of James Quigg (8 P. D., 248), claimant should first make application to the Pension Bureau for readjudication in accordance with the provisions of the act of March 6, 1896. As such application has not been made, the motion for reconsideration is overruled.

Leroy F. Wood... 64

Reopening.

7. As a matter of practice a claimant is entitled to file at any time new evidence and request action thereon by the Commissioner of Pensions. If said new evidence, either considered separately or in connection with previously filed evidence, establishes a prima facie case, the Commissioner of Pensions will order a new medical examination as a matter of course, and after the report of said examination has been received will take action on all of the evidence. If a request is made to the Commissioner of Pensions for a new medical examination without the filing of new evidence, such rejection goes to the sound discretion of that official, who will, nevertheless, take action upon such request. In such cases an appeal will lie to the Secretary only from the action taken by the Commissioner of Pensions.

Luther Case 72

Restoration.

8. Pensioner was receiving $12 per month on account of loss of sight of left eye, and was dropped from the rolls in 1895. He filed claims for renewal, and was restored to the rolls from October 20, 1896, at $6 per month, for the same disability. The medical referee expresses the opinion that he should not have

been dropped, but his rating only reduced. Refusal to restore him from date of dropping at reduced rating is based on the fact that he has only filed claim for renewal and not for restoration. It is held that this action is chiefly technical, that the words "renewal" and "restoration" in applications are generally interchangeable, and that this claimant, having applied for renewal and admitted to be entitled to restoration, should be restored from the date of dropping without other application.

9. A claim for restoration can not be regarded as a claim for increase. (Thomas Mallon, 8 P. D., 208.)

PRESUMPTIONS.

(*See* EVIDENCE, 1, 7, 8, 9, 10, 11, 12, 13, 14; MARRIAGE AND DIVORCE, 2; SERVICE, 1.)

PRESUMPTION OF DEATH.

(*See* EVIDENCE, 10, 12, 13.)

RANK.

Rating under Act June 27, 1890.

Rank in the service is not to be considered in any application under the act of June 27, 1890.

RATE.

(*See* AID AND ATTENDANCE, 1, 2, 4; DISABILITY, 3, 5; NOTICE, 2; REDUCTION, 4; RESTORATION.

Act March 19, 1886.

1. As claimant was married to soldier after his discharge from the service, and after the passage of the act of March 19, 1886, which increased the pensions of widows and dependent relatives of deceased soldiers from $8 to $12 per month, her pension was properly allowed at the rate of $8 per month only, as said act contained a proviso limiting its application to widows who were married to soldiers prior to the passage of the act, or during the service of such soldier.

Act of June 27, 1890.

2. The rates of pension under the general law are much higher than those under the act of June 27, 1890, the highest rate under the latter act being $12 per month, which is allowable for about the same degree of disability for which the general pension law provides the rate of $30 per month.

3. Disabilities which are pensionable under the second section of the act of June 27, 1890, must cause incapacity for performance of manual labor in such degree as to produce inability to earn a support, and the rate must, within the limits fixed, be proportioned to the degree of inability to earn a support.

The right to increase and the right to reduce rest upon the same basis; the only question to be considered is whether the increase or reduction was warranted by the law and the facts.

4. The maximum rate of pension under the act of June 27, 1890, corresponds with total disability, and the minimum and intervening rates correspond proportionately with all partial degrees of inability to earn a support by manual labor.

RECONSIDERATION.

(*See* RES JUDICATA.)

(REDUCTION.)

(*See also* COMMENCEMENT, 1; RATE, 3.)

Practice.

1. An unsworn statement by a claimant that he never received notice to appear before a board of surgeons in a reduction case is not sufficient to warrant a reversal of the action of the Commissioner of Pensions reducing the rate of his pension; but good practice demands that a record of such notices be kept in the future, and when a pensioner claims that he was not notified, he should be advised at once to file a sworn statement of the fact, and corroborative proof, when the issue thus raised will be passed upon.

John S. Hubley 48

Rate.

2. Where the allowance of a certain rate of pension was directed by a decision of the Department, and subsequently the Commissioner of Pensions ordered a medical examination of the pensioner by a specialist and upon the report of such examination proceeded to reduce the rate of pension, it is

Held, That such action was not ultra vires, but was within the scope of the authority given him by the proviso to section 3, act of June 21, 1879.

The rate allowed under departmental decision of June 13, 1894, not being manifestly erroneous, but the question as to its correctness being one of judgment merely, it will not be disturbed. (Citing decision of Secretary Teller in case of James S. Coleman, Digest of 1885, p. 422.)

Gottlieb Spitzer, alias Gottfried Brunner 83

3. Pensioner's rating having been reduced from $12 to $8 per month under the act of June 27, 1890, after due notice in accordance with the provisions of the act of December 21, 1893, he appealed, and such action was set aside for the purpose of according him another medical examination, it having been three years since his last examination. Such examination having been made, and it appearing therefrom that such reduction was justly and properly made, pensioner is not entitled to a new notice to reduce nor additional payment at a higher rate for the period from date of original reduction and the date of the action had on the last medical examination.

William Hulse 121

4. Soldier was pensioned at $12 per month in August, 1890, which rating was reduced to $6 per month in March, 1895. The contention is that his original rating was fixed in harmony with regulations which obtained at that time, and can not legally be affected by regulations formulated subsequent thereto.

Held, That it is the statute, not the regulations, which determines his rights.

Thomas Mallon 344

REFUNDMENT.

(*See* FEE, 8.)

REIMBURSEMENT.

(*See* FRAUD AND MISTAKE, 1, 2.)

REMARRIAGE.

(*See* MARRIAGE AND DIVORCE, 3.)

RENEWAL.

(*See* PRACTICE, 8.)

REOPENING.

(*See* PRACTICE, 7.)

REPRESENTATIVES OF ATTORNEYS.

(*See* ATTORNEYS, 10.)

RERATING.

(*See also* REDUCTION, 2.)

Grounds of.

The fact that the pensioner did not receive as high a rate of pension for slight deafness of both ears as others have received for the same disability during the same period (the schedule of rates for partial deafness having been modified prior to the adjudication of his claim) is not good ground for rerating, the inequality complained of resulting, not from any violation of law, but from a difference of judgment between two administrative officers, each of whom acted within the scope of his legal authority.

Henry Crittenden 66

RES JUDICATA.

Not Applicable to Pension Claims.

Neither the doctrine of res judicata nor stare decisis is strictly applicable to claims for pensions, and when adopted by the Department simply becomes a rule which each administration prescribes for itself as a matter of policy or convenience, and may be waived, suspended, or ignored, as justice, policy, or convenience requires. (Case of Mary E. Eastridge, 8 P. D., 5.)

James Duval 218

RESTORATION.

(*See also* DESERTION, 4; DISLOYALTY, 3; FEE, 1, 9; PRACTICE, 8, 9.)

Rate.

Where the degree of disability shown at time of original allowance did not warrant the rate of pension named in the original certificate, and pensioner's name was dropped from the rolls by reason of his failure to claim the same for three years, upon application for restoration pension may be restored at a less rate than that originally allowed.

Joseph C. King 430

REVENUE CUTTER.

(*See* SERVICE, 29, 30, 31.)

REVISED STATUTES.

(*See* DISLOYALTY, 1, 2, 4.)

RULE TO SHOW CAUSE.

(*See* FEE, 3.)

SECTIONS 4692, 4693, and 4694, R. S.

(*See* DESERTION, 5.)

SECTION 4698½, R. S.

(*See* COMMENCEMENT, 7.)

SECTION 4702, R. S.

(*See* ACCRUED PENSION, 2.)

SECTION 4711.

(*See* DECLARATIONS, 6.)

SECTION 4716.

(*See* DISLOYALTY, 1, 2, 3, 4.)

SERVICE.

(*See also* ARMY NURSES; DISCHARGE, 1.)

Presumption as to.

1. Where the record of the War Department shows soldier's enlistment in a three months' service in 1861, and said Department reports that it is unable from any evidence before it to determine soldier's final record; and the records of said Department show a subsequent honorable service and discharge of said soldier from a three years' service, it is

Held, That as no charge of desertion, absence without leave, or other counter presumption is involved, the legal presumption of innocence should prevail, and soldier be presumed to have been discharged from said first service at the expiration of his first term of enlistment.

Minors of Daniel Halloway 18

Record of.

2. The amended record of the War Department shows claimant accepted into service on December 20, 1864; paid as private up to and discharged on April 13, 1865. He was furloughed on January 14, 1865; availed himself of said furlough on February 2, 1865; held himself under military orders, and obeyed the order of the military authorities requiring him to report at Indianapolis. His discharge was delivered on May 29, 1865. He had no knowledge, neither did he receive any intimation of any kind, previous to April 13, 1865, that he had been or was to be discharged.

Held, 1. On the record, corroborated by reliable evidence, soldier was in the service of the United States during the war of the rebellion for more than ninety days. (Poland's Appeal, 8 P. D., 266, followed.)

This Department is bound to accept as true the unimpeached record of the War Department, but it alone has power to determine what effect such record shall have on a claimant's pensionable rights.

David H. Dyer 87

In Indian Wars.

3. The Florida war closed August 14, 1842. Soldier's service at Newport, Ky., from November 9, 1839, to October 31, 1842, when forwarded to his regiment, which he joined November 29, 1842, was not service "for thirty days in the Black Hawk war, the Creek war, the Cherokee disturbances, or the Florida war with the Seminole Indians, embracing a period from 1832 to 1842, inclusive," and his widow is not pensionable under the act of July 27, 1892.

Wilhelmina Roth (*widow*) 143

4. As the report from the War Department shows that the military organization in which this soldier served from August 26, 1832, to September 30, 1832, cooperated with the main body of troops in the suppression of the Indian hostilities during the Black Hawk war, his service is held to be sufficient to comply with the requirements of the act of July 27, 1892.

Susan C. Peniston (*widow*) 178

5. The official records show that the soldier did not serve the required time in the Florida war to entitle his widow to pension under the act of July 27, 1892.

Catharine Waters (*widow*) 206

In Mexican War.

6. Soldier enlisted March 20, 1848; was mustered in April 30, 1848, to serve during the war with Mexico, was forwarded May 5, and joined his company near

Civilian Employees.

Drafted Men and Substitutes.

Held, That soldier did not serve ninety days in the war of the rebellion, or in the Army of the United States, within the meaning of sections 2 and 3 of the act of June 27, 1890. (See case of Albert K. Ransom, 5 P. D., 183.)

23. The official military record of this appellant's service during the war of the rebellion shows that he did not render any pensionable service whatever in the Army of the United States during said war.

24. It appearing from the evidence that the deceased husband of this appellant served in the above-named organization as a substitute for and under the name of one Thomas F. Jessup, who had been drafted into the service, and by a private arrangement with Jessup took his place in the ranks and answered to his name, but was not sworn in, nor mustered into the military service, he was not in the military service of the United States, his service was not a pensionable service, and would not entitle his widow to pension under any existing law. (Christian, alias Ernest Ulrich, 4 P. D., 411.)

In Home Guards.

25. Hall's company, West Virginia Home Guards, to which this appellant belonged, and in which he alleges his military service was rendered during the war of the rebellion, was a State militia organization that was never in the military service of the United States, and the officers and enlisted men thereof are not pensionable under any existing law.

In the Militia.

26. Pennsylvania Emergency Militia, while serving in the Army of the United States, under command of United States officers, in response to the call of the President, were a part of that Army while so serving, and are, for that time and as regards the character of the service, brought within the scope of the first subdivision of section 4693, Revised Statutes, and the act of June 27, 1890, for pensionable purposes, other conditions of those laws having been met.

The peculiar conditions under which said militia were recognized as a part of the Army, the manner in which received into and released from the service of the United States, obviated the necessity of enlistment and discharge in the usual manner, the records of the State in that respect being taken as a substitute for the records of the War Department, and the period of actual service being counted as if rendered under enlistment by United States officers.

Two terms of service, each less than ninety days, may be added together to make the required period under said act of June 27, 1890.

27. A State militiaman, whose organization was not called into the United States service by the President, is pensionable only under subdivision 3 of section 4693, Revised Statutes, where his claim was prosecuted to a successful issue prior to July 4, 1874, notwithstanding he performed duty under the commander of the Department of Kansas.

28. The fact that the organization to which the claimant belonged was not regularly mustered into the service of the United States does not debar him from pension for disability incurred in the line of duty, it appearing that said organization was called into service by the authority of the President, turned over to the United States officers, and by them ordered outside the State for duty, and that the members were paid by the General Government at the time of muster out.

On Revenue Cutters.

29. Under the act of March 2, 1799 (section 2757, Revised Statutes), the revenue cutter *Forward* was embraced within and constituted a part of the naval establishment of the United States for more than sixty days in the war with Mexico, and claimant, being an officer on said revenue cutter and serving with the Navy of the United States in Mexico or on the coasts thereof during the war with that nation for more than sixty days and having engaged in battle in said war, he has title to pension under act of January 29, 1887

  William F. Rogers 96

30. A service of ninety days or more during the war of the rebellion in actual cooperation with the Navy under the orders of the President, and an honorable discharge from such service, is sufficient to give the officers and seamen of the United States Revenue-Marine Service a pensionable status under the provisions of section 2, act of June 27, 1890 (Roger's appeal, 9 P. D., 96).

 The departmental ruling in Oliver's appeal (7 P. D., 597) overruled and set aside, and the decision in Schaffer's appeal (6 P. D , 137) reaffirmed.

  William B. Watson 182

31. It appearing from the official records and from the testimony that the United States revenue cutter *Tiger*, upon which this appellant served, was, during the time of his service thereon, under orders by the President to cooperate with the Navy, and was stationed on Chesapeake Bay, and waters tributary thereto, in actual and active cooperation with the naval forces of the United States, guarding the approaches to the National Capital, and "arresting rebel depredations on American commerce and transportation" in those waters, his service on said cutter under such circumstances for ninety days or more, and an honorable discharge from such service, are sufficient to meet the requirements of section 2, act of June 27, 1890, and give him a pensionable status thereunder if other pensionable conditions required by said section are shown to exist.

  William B. Watson 395

Unassigned Recruit.

32. Soldier was enrolled as a substitute November 1, 1864; received at Indiana rendezvous November 3, 1864; examined by a board of inspectors and rejected by reason of extreme youth on November 7, 1864, and was furloughed to await discharge on the same day. The order for discharge was finally approved by the general commanding the department November 30, 1864, but the certificate for discharge was dated March 9, 1865.

 Held, That he was not in the service of the United States exceeding thirty days, and his name was properly dropped from the rolls under the act of June 27, 1890.

  James T. Veley 15

As Pilot.

33. Service as a pilot does not entitle to pension under section 2 of the act of June 27, 1890. (Citing Susannah, widow of Francis Mackey, 8 P. D., 535, and William P. Gordon, unpublished.)

  Henry N. Haynie 304

Not Service in War.

34. It is shown by the official military records of the War Department that the military service of the deceased soldier terminated prior to the commencement of the Mexican war.

  Theresa Bonnareau (widow) 507

SPECIAL ACT.

(*See* DOUBLE PENSION; SERVICE.)

SPECIALIST.

(*See* EVIDENCE, 15.)

SPECIFIC DISABILITY.

(*See* INCREASE, 1.)

Act of August 4, 1886.

Soldier is pensioned at the rate of $30 per month on account of the loss of a forearm. Upon an application for increase the evidence shows that soldier's arm was amputated at the elbow, and he is entitled to increase under the act of August 4, 1886.

Gibhart Kurtz.. 204

STARE DECISIS.

(*See* RES JUDICATA.)

SUBSTITUTE.

(*See* SERVICE, 305.)

TITLE.

Act January 29, 1887.

In order to be allowed pension under the act of January 29, 1887, an officer or enlisted man is not required to show that he is subject to a disability equivalent to some cause recognized by the pension laws as sufficient reason to allow pension under those laws at the rate of $8 per month; said officer or enlisted man may be entitled to the benefits of said act if it appear that he is subject to such disability as would be recognized by those laws as sufficient reason for the allowance of pension for any rate less than $8 per month.

Charles W. Johannes.. 341

TRAVEL PAY.

(*See* SERVICE, 24.)

VICIOUS HABITS.

There being nothing in the case to arouse a suspicion that the disability was in any way due to vicious habits, or that the claimant has ever been addicted to vicious habits, or that his statement as to the circumstances under which the disability was incurred is untrue, rejection was not warranted. (Citing John Martin, 7 P. D., 578.)

Morris Hess.. 252

VOIDABLE ENLISTMENT.

(*See* DESERTION, 7.)

WAR OF THE REBELLION.

(*See* SERVICE, 10, 11.)

WIDOWS.

(*See also* ADULTEROUS COHABITATION, 5; DEPENDENCE, 5, 9; HELPLESS MINOR, 4; PAYMENT OF PENSION, 2.)

On Account of Anterebellion Service.

It appearing that the alleged death cause of the soldier was contracted prior to March 4, 1861, in time of peace, and not in service during any war, there is no provision of law granting pension to his widow. (See Digest 1897, p. 500, 2 (a), and decisions there cited.)

Elizabeth Fritz (widow) 193

Lightning Source UK Ltd.
Milton Keynes UK
UKHW021324100219
336936UK00006B/556/P